COMPREHENSIVE HANDBOOK
OF
PSYCHOLOGICAL ASSESSMENT

COMPREHENSIVE HANDBOOK
OF
PSYCHOLOGICAL ASSESSMENT

VOLUME 1
INTELLECTUAL AND NEUROPSYCHOLOGICAL ASSESSMENT

Gerald Goldstein

Sue R. Beers

Volume Editors

Michel Hersen

Editor-in-Chief

WILEY

John Wiley & Sons, Inc.

Library of Congress Cataloging-in-Publication Data:

Comprehensive handbook of psychological assessment / editor-in-chief, Michel Hersen.
    p. cm.
    Includes bibliographical references and index.
    Contents: v. 1 Intellectual and neuropsychological assessment / editors, Gerald Goldstein
and Sue R. Beers — v. 2. Personality assessment / editors, Mark J. Hilsenroth and Daniel L.
Segal — v. 3. Behavioral assessment / editors, Stephen N. Haynes and Elaine M. Heiby — v. 4.
Industrial and organizational assessment / editor, Jay C. Thomas.
    ISBN 0-471-41610-X (set : hardcover : alk. paper) — ISBN 0-471-41611-8 (v. 1 :
hardcover : alk. paper) — ISBN 0-471-41612-6 (v. 2 : hardcover : alk. paper) — ISBN
0-471-41613-4 (v. 3 : hardcover : alk. paper) — ISBN 0-471-41614-2 (v. 4 : hardcover :
alk. paper)
    1. Psychological tests. I. Hersen, Michel.
BF176 .C654 2003
150′.28′7—dc21

                                                                2002193381

Printed in the United States of America.

10 9 8 7 6 5 4 3 2 1

Contents

Part Two: Neuropsychological Assessment of Cognitive Domains

Part Three: Professional Issues

Handbook Preface

Over the last century the scope of activity of clinical psychologists has increased exponentially. In earlier times psychologists had a much more restricted range of responsibilities. Today psychologists not only provide assessments but treat a wide variety of disorders in an equally wide variety of settings, consult, teach, conduct research, help to establish ethical policies, deal with human engineering factors, have a strong media presence, work with law enforcement in profiling criminals, and have had increasing influence in the business world and in the realm of advertising, to identify just a few of the major activities in which they are engaged. Nonetheless, the hallmark of psychologists has always been assessment and it continues to be a mainstay of their practices in the twenty-first century. Indeed, in each of the activities just described, psychologists and their assistants are performing assessments of some sort.

In the nineteenth century our predecessors in Germany began to study individual differences and abilities in what then was the most scientific way. In the more than 120 years that have elapsed since these early efforts were carried out, the field of psychological assessment has seen many developments and permutations, ranging from educational needs to identify individuals with subnormal intelligence to attempts to measure unconscious dynamics with unstructured stimuli, wide-range governmental efforts to measure intelligence and other capabilities to screen out undesirable military recruits during wartime, development of evaluative tools to ensure successful personnel selection, the advent of behavioral and physiological assessments, the increased reliance on computerized assessments, and, most recently, the spectacular innovation of virtual reality assessments using the latest electronic technologies.

Thousands of specific assessment strategies and tests that are carried out on both an individual and group basis have been devised for almost every conceivable type of human endeavor. Many of these strategies have been carefully developed, tested, and refined, with norms available for many populations and excellent reliability and validity data reported. To keep abreast of all new developments in the field of assessment is a near impossibility, although scores of journals, books, and yearly publications are available that catalog such developments.

In considering how the field of psychological assessment has evolved over the last century with the resulting explosion of new technologies and new assessment devices, it seemed to us imperative to create a resource (*Comprehensive Handbook of Psychological Assessment:* CHOPA) that distilled this vast reservoir of data in a more manageable format for researchers, clinicians, educators, and students alike. Therefore, Tracey Belmont, our editor at John Wiley & Sons, the volume editors (Gerald Goldstein, Sue R. Beers, Mark J. Hilsenroth, Daniel L. Segal, Stephen N. Haynes, Elaine M. Heiby, and Jay C. Thomas), and I as editor-in-chief developed this four-volume format. This decision was both conceptual, in order to best capture the scope of the field, and pragmatic, so that individuals wishing to purchase a single volume (as a consequence of their unique interest) would be able to do so.

CHOPA includes four volumes with a total of 121 chapters written by renowned experts in their respective areas of expertise. In order the volumes are: 1, Intellectual and Neuropsychological Assessment; 2, Personality Assessment; 3, Behavioral Assessment; and 4, Industrial and Organizational Assessment. Each volume has an introductory chapter by the editor. In the case of Volume 2, there is an introductory chapter for objective tests and an introductory chapter for projective tests. In general, introductory chapters are concerned with a historical review, range of tests, theoretical considerations, psychometric concerns, range of populations for which the tests are appropriate, cross-cultural factors, accommodation for persons with disabilities, legal and ethical issues, computerization, and future perspectives. Chapters on individual tests or approaches cover many of the same areas but in much more specific detail, in addition, of course, to the test description and development. Other chapters are more conceptual and theoretical in nature and articulate an approach to evaluation, such as the chapters on clinical interviewing and program evaluation in Volume 3.

In developing the CHOPA concept and selecting chapters and contributors, our objective has been to be comprehensive in a global sense but not encyclopedic (i.e., detailing every conceivable and extant assessment strategy or test). However, we believe that we are sufficiently comprehensive so that the interested reader can move to greater specificity, if needed, on the basis of the very current list of references for each chapter.

An endeavor as complicated as CHOPA has required the efforts of many people, and here we would like to acknowledge their various contributions. First, I personally would like to thank Tracey Belmont and her superb staff at John Wiley & Sons for recognizing the value of this project and for helping to bring the pieces together. Second, I thank the volume editors for their Herculean efforts in monitoring, reviewing, and reworking the contributions of their colleagues. Next, we owe a debt of gratitude to our eminent contributors, who so graciously have shared their high levels of expertise with us. And finally, I would like to thank all of our staff here at Pacific University who contributed technical assistance to bringing this four-volume set to publication: Carole Londeree, Kay Waldron, Angelina Marchand, and Alex Duncan.

Michel Hersen
Forest Grove, Oregon

Contributors

Wayne V. Adams, PhD
Brigham Young University
Provo, UT

Anna V. Agranovich, MS
The University of North Carolina at Wilmington
Wilmington, NC

Glen P. Aylward, PhD
Division of Developmental and Behavioral Pediatrics
Southern Illinois University School of Medicine
Springfield, IL

Sue R. Beers, PhD
University of Pittsburgh School of Medicine
Western Psychiatric Institute and Clinic
Pittsburgh, PA

Erin D. Bigler, PhD
Brigham Young University
Provo, UT

Nancy D. Chiaravalloti, PhD
Kessler Medical Rehabilitation Research and Education
  Corporation
West Orange, NJ *and*
University of Medicine and Dentistry of New Jersey
New Jersey Medical School
Newark, NJ

Diane Coalson, PhD
The Psychological Corporation
San Antonio, TX

J.P. Das, PhD
J.P. Das Developmental Disabilities Centre
University of Alberta
Edmonton, Canada

John DeLuca, PhD
Kessler Medical Rehabilitation Research and Education
  Corporation
West Orange, NJ *and*
University of Medicine and Dentistry of New Jersey
New Jersey Medical School
Newark, NJ

Connie C. Duncan, PhD
Clinical Psychophysiology and Nonpharmacology
  Laboratory
Department of Psychiatry
Uniformed Services University of the Health Sciences
Bethesda, Maryland *and*
Section on Clinical and Experimental Neuropsychology
National Institute of Health
Bethesda, MD

Deborah Fein, PhD
University of Connecticut
Storrs, CT

Patricia M. Fitzpatrick, PhD
Department of Veterans Affairs Medical Center
Boston, MA

Guila Glosser, PhD
University of Pennsylvania Medical Center
Philadelphia, PA

Charles J. Golden, PhD
Center for Psychological Studies
Nova Southeastern University
Fort Lauderdale, FL

Gerald Goldstein, PhD
VA Pittsburgh Healthcare System
Pittsburgh, PA

Jim Hom, PhD
The Neuropsychology Center
Dallas, TX

Garland Jones, BA
University of Connecticut
Storrs, CT

R.W. Kamphaus, PhD
The University of Georgia
Athens, GA

Elizabeth Kelley, MA
University of Connecticut
Storrs, CT

Marit Korkman, PhD
Abo Akademi University
Abo, Finland

Anna P. Kroncke, MEd
The University of Georgia
Athens, GA

Robert A. Leark, PhD
Pacific Christian College at Hope International University
Fullerton, CA

Michael J. Miller, BA
Brigham Young University
Provo, UT

Allan F. Mirsky, PhD
Section on Clinical and Experimental Neuropsychology
National Institute of Health
Bethesda, MD

Victor Nell, PhD
University of South Africa Institute for Social and Health Sciences
Johannesburg, South Africa

Janice Nici, PhD
The Neuropsychology Center
Dallas, TX

Jo Ann Petrie, BS
Brigham Young University
Provo, UT

Aurelio Prifitera, PhD
The Psychological Corporation
San Antonio, TX

Antonio E. Puente, PhD
The University of North Carolina at Wilmington
Wilmington, NC

Michael C. Ramsay, PhD
Texas A & M University
College Station, TX

Ralph M. Reitan, PhD
Tucson, AZ

Cecil R. Reynolds, PhD
Texas A & M University
Bastrop, TX

Richard D. Sanders, MD
Department of Veterans Affairs Mental Health Clinic
Dayton, OH

Lawrence G. Weiss, PhD
The Psychological Corporation
San Antonio, TX

Deborah Wolfson, PhD
Tucson, AZ

Jianjun Zhu, PhD
The Psychological Corporation
San Antonio, TX

INTELLECTUAL ABILITY

CHAPTER 1

Introduction to Section One

GERALD GOLDSTEIN AND SUE R. BEERS

REFERENCES   4

This volume of the *Comprehensive Handbook of Psychological Assessment* is devoted to intellectual and neuropsychological assessment. The combination of these two areas is an apt one because both of them are concerned with adaptive function and cognitive ability. In practice, neuropsychologists often use intelligence tests, and clinical and counseling psychologists may use some tests that now would be described as neuropsychological tests in their practice. However, intelligence testing is done for a broad range of the general population, whereas neuropsychological testing is typically done in cases where there is known or suspected impairment of brain function. Therefore, Part One of this volume deals largely with assessment in populations of normal individuals. Part Two is more clinically oriented, stressing assessment of individuals whose brain function is known to be or suspected of being impaired.

The first two chapters of this section are theoretical in nature. Chapter 2 by Dr. Das is a broad-ranging review of theories of intelligence. The formulation of theories of intelligence goes back to ancient times, with beginnings in ancient Eastern and Greek philosophy. It remains an area of controversy to the present time, with several viable theories having contemporary acceptance. Lending support to the unity of this volume as a whole, this chapter makes it clear that some of the more recent theories of intelligence are neuropsychological in nature in the sense that an effort is made to associate intellectual function with specific brain functions and areas. Although there was an underlying assumption for many centuries that intelligence was controlled by the brain, there is now an attempt to be more specific with regard to identifying relationships between specific brain systems and different intellectual abilities. As a simple example, it is now thought that portions of the left hemisphere of the brain mediate much of verbal intelligence.

Chapter 3 by Dr. Ramsay and Dr. Reynolds deals with the relationship between intelligence and achievement. Put in more general terms, it takes up the issue of how well general intelligence or IQ predicts performance of activities in a natural environment. In children, these activities usually relate to educational matters, such as learning to read or perform mathematics. In adults, the relationship is mainly with vocational considerations, stressing the ability to do a particular job. This matter is important because if intelligence tests do not successfully predict behavior in the environment, their usefulness is questionable. Indeed, critics of intelligence testing have pointed to instances of poor prediction. Critics suggest that some individuals obtain high scores on these tests but do not do well in school or at work; whereas other individuals with lower intellectual levels may do quite well. Ramsay and Reynolds review numerous studies in which intelligence tests are correlated with academic achievement tests. They indicate that many methodological problems remain in this research, but report that a reasonable degree of correspondence exists between the two kinds of measures.

Intelligence is a developmental phenomenon, and assessment methods that are appropriate for the different stages of life must be constructed. As described in Chapter 6, Dr. Aylward's chapter, it is possible to evaluate ability levels in infancy and early childhood. Tests have been developed for children in their preschool years and for older children. Intelligence tests have most commonly been used in educational planning for school-aged children. A more recent development, resulting from the mandate for early educational intervention, is the need to assess the abilities of young children in the their preschool years. Some tests, such as the various Wechsler adult intelligence scales, are suitable for a wide range of ages and may be used from early to late adulthood. Intelligence testing as we know it began with testing of

3

school children by Binet, and the idea of testing adults for intelligence developed later. By studying changes in intelligence in childhood through adulthood, we have learned a great deal about the development of intelligence into old age. Longitudinal intelligence testing or the administration of intelligence tests to people in cross-sectional studies of different age groups has led to an extensive literature that is not without controversy, particularly with regard to the nature of intellectual decline with aging. Thus, intelligence testing is now accomplished across the life-span, and we have included chapters describing tests for infants, children, and adults.

Chapters 4 and 5 of this section are devoted to the most widely used standardized intelligence tests: The Wechsler intelligence scales in their child and adult versions and the Stanford-Binet. David Wechsler was probably the major influence in the introduction of intelligence testing for adults, and in the development of psychometric procedures and test contents that were appropriate for adults. Both the adult and children's scales have received several restandardizations and revisions to keep them psychometrically sound and contemporary in content. The various Wechsler intelligence scales are commonly used in educational, industrial, and clinical settings. John McFie (1975) said, "It is perhaps a matter of luck that many of the Wechsler subtests are neurologically relevant (p. 14)." This remark, made some years ago, presaged the extensive use during recent times of the Wechsler scales in neuropsychological assessment.

The history of the Stanford-Binet tests goes back to the early years of the twentieth century, and the test has gone through five revisions. The fifth edition has just been made available. The phrase "Back to the Future" used in the title of the Kamphaus and Kroncke chapter characterizes this new edition because it resembles the original Binet-Simon scales more than it does the presently available fourth edition. The Stanford-Binet continues to be used mainly with children, although it may be given to adults. It is probably more widely used in educational applications than in clinical or industrial assessment. Its theoretical basis and format have changed over the various editions, but it continues to be based, at least in part, on a "g" or general intelligence factor model.

The assessment of infants and young children is a specialized skill that requires the use of instruments specifically designed for that purpose, and particularly extensive training of examiners. Such instruments as the Gesell Developmental Schedules, the Cattell Infant Intelligence Test, and the Bayley Scales of Infant Development have been used for many years to assess development in infants. The major emphases are on assessing development and possible maturational delay. In infants, prior to acquisition of language, assessment is done by observation, such as looking for visual tracking and reaching for objects, or seeking an object placed out of sight. Later in development, there is an interest in whether language and memory are normal for the child's age. Such areas as perceptual-motor coordination, number concepts, and imitative abilities are generally evaluated. The current trend is toward performing these assessments during the pre-school period, at increasingly earlier ages.

The chapters of Part One describe instruments for assessing intelligence from shortly after birth to old age. These evaluations are performed across the life-span and require different instruments and examiner skills. The different assessment instruments used vary not only in content but also in the underlying theory upon which they are based. Issues, such as the matter of whether intelligence is a unitary general ability ("g") or a combination of a number of intelligences, as proposed by Gardner (1999), are still debated. Currently, the conceptualization of intelligence within a neuropsychological framework is a matter of great interest. The relative roles of heredity and environment remain a hotly debated issue. The relationship between intelligence and achievement in natural environments has been intensively studied. Elsewhere in this book are discussions about the cultural fairness of cognitive tests. The considerations raised in these discussions have crucial implications for the use and interpretation of intelligence tests.

REFERENCES

Gardner, H. (1999). *Intelligence reframed: Multiple intelligence in the 21st Century*. New York: Basic Books.

McFie, J. (1975). *Assessment of organic intellectual impairment*. London: Academic Press.

CHAPTER 2

Theories of Intelligence: Issues and Applications

J.P. DAS

GENERAL INTRODUCTION

This chapter begins with a consensual definition of intelligence. Intelligence is cognition comprising sensory, perceptual, associative, and relational knowledge. It is the sum total of all cognitive processes including coding of information, planning, and attention and arousal. Of these, the cognitive processes required for planning have a higher status in intelligence. It is assumed that all the different mental abilities cannot be put on one scale of merit (Das, 1992).

This chapter includes a brief history of intelligence in European and a non-European philosophy. Then, I present a summary of selected contemporary theories of intelligence. Next, I highlight the traditional approach to intelligence as a general *ability* and as its counterpoint, three recent theories based on the framework of information *processing*. I discuss the revival of general intelligence or *g* as reaction time (speed) and consider arguments about why speed is not a good index of intelligence. Next, I discuss two issues related to two questions: What features should intelligence tests have? How far have the theories advanced in bridging the gap between mainstream psychology and intelligence testing? In the final parts of the chapter, I raise and discuss two big issues that are critical for a conceptualization of intelligence. These issues

pertain to modularity and gene-environment interactions that are bidirectional. At the end, in summary and concluding observations, I make a plea for expanding the context of re-conceptualization. The context should include global conditions that will foster a benign development of intelligence among the world's children and in consequence, will lead to an equitable distribution of intelligence.

Historical Background

The Western concept of intelligence originates with the Greeks. Plato described the three aspects of the soul as intellectual, emotional, and moral; later these were referred to as cognition, affection, and conation. He compared cognition to a charioteer and affection and conation to the charioteer's horses. The charioteer holds the reins, guiding the soul, while the horses supply the energy and pull the chariot. Aristotle combined the horses, the emotional and moral aspects, into one source of power, separate from the cognitive aspect. It is Cicero who seems to have first used the word *intelligentsia*. Much later, St. Augustine recognized intelligence as quickness of understanding and acuteness of discernment; St. Thomas Aquinas considered it to be success in acquiring perfect knowledge (see Sternberg, 1990 for a review).

In relatively recent times, work on intelligence in the Euro-American tradition began with Binet (1895), a leading experimental psychologist in France. He was interested in studying the way individuals differ from each other and suggested that when testing for differences in their intelligence, the tests should be appropriate to their background and occupation; therefore some items in the test should be stressed for one kind of background and other items for a different kind. This was suggested before Binet constructed the first intelligence test in 1904 for testing children with mental retardation, who might benefit from special education. In France, it was necessary to provide special education because of the government's requirement that all children receive school education. By 1918, all states in the United States had also passed laws for compulsory education, which led to a demand for intelligence testing in Europe and the United States. Before Binet, intelligence was a philosophical concept and could not be estimated. Binet gathered a set of tasks related to school achievement and arranged them in order of difficulty. His aim was to determine qualitatively the mental level at which a child functioned, rather than to give the child a number, such as mental age. Thus he would have thought the use of his tasks to determine a strictly quantitative score, such as IQ, a betrayal of the tests' objective:

> . . . it was a great pity that this total shift from qualitative to quantitative thinking in the decade that followed Binet occurred (Tyler, 1976).

In contrast to Binet, Charles Spearman was entirely quantitative and proposed intelligence to be a general ability. In his book (1927), he suggested a general factor of ability and some specific abilities as well. The concept of a general ability can be traced back to Galton, to the year 1869 when his book was published. General ability was widely accepted in Britain and became part of the definition of intelligence and IQ tests. Cyril Burt (1937) advanced this idea further and applied it to mental retardation, which was then called mental subnormality in Britain. According to this definition, individuals with mental deficiency were lagging behind in an innate general cognitive ability; their deficiency was mainly due to heredity (innate), and they were deficient in all aspects of mental ability. Recent conceptualizations of intelligence find faults with each of the terms in Burt's definition. First, it is not innate, because social-cultural learning can mold it. Certainly, it is not fixed, as Anderson (1989) remarked, because it grows, albeit with constraints. Second, it is not general, according to several new researchers who have evidence for multiple intelligences (Das, Kirby, & Jarman 1975; Gardner, 1983; Sternberg, 1985a, 1985b). Third, IQ as measured by standardized tests does not have a clear relationship with research on cognition. Finally, intelligence is now regarded as a cluster of cognitive processes, not as one ability. Intelligence is related to information processing comprising among other things, attention, plans, and strategies (see Sparrow & Davis, 2000, for a review).

A Non-European View of Intelligence

Two views of the nature of intellect are present in Western philosophy, which mainly followed Greek thought: contemplation of the nature of being and the deduction of implicates from premises true or imaginary. Views about intelligence in Indian philosophy are similar. Indian views of intelligence (Das, 1994), or *buddhi* (in Sanskrit), involve concepts, such as wisdom, prudence, emotion, societal values, and relations. The internal structure of wisdom comprises a unique blend of cognitive, interpersonal, social, and personality attributes. The cognitive view regards wisdom as a form of postformal and dialectic thought, a kind of integrative thought process that embraces paradox and transformation, awareness about the limits of one's personal knowledge, knowledge that effectively integrates emotional and cognitive components, such as expert knowledge regarding the fundamental pragmatics about life (Srivastava, Tripathy, & Misra, 1995).

The major components of intelligence or *buddhi* in Indian philosophy (Baral & Das, in press; Das, 1994) are introduced with the declaration that referential knowledge, a knowledge consisting of taxonomies, is not the essence of intelligence. Rather, the ability for discriminating thinking is the hallmark of intelligence. The concepts that jointly make up intelligence describe a hierarchy (Radhakrishnan, 1953):

> We know the name, but then we use speech and language
>   to articulate exactly what we know,
> We can then put our mind to obtain what is known
> We *will* to achieve, following what is in our mind.
> But only upon thinking and reflection.

Thus it is worthwhile to conclude the present section on the ancient concepts of intelligence in India by paraphrasing relevant parts of Bhagavad-Gita (Radhakrishnan, 1948):

1. *Buddhi* is above the mind, which is above the senses.
2. *Buddhi* can know things as they truly are, but is subject to confusion, error, and distortion especially if it depends on the senses. Desire and lust, as well as anger, obscure knowledge.
3. *Buddhi* is something that some people have, while others do not (including wisdom and good judgment).

4. *Buddhi* is a cognitive entity, hence a mode of thought.

5. *Buddhi* is also affective and purposive. Reason, will, emotion, cognition, judgment, decision—all share in some parts the meaning of buddhi.

SUMMARIZING CONTEMPORARY THEORIES OF INTELLIGENCE: REVIVAL OF SPEARMAN'S *g* OR GENERAL ABILITY

Jensen (1982) is singled out as the chief advocate of *g* for many years and continues with it in current literature. His evidence goes beyond factor analysis, although it maintains its roots in that statistical method (Jensen, 1998). Unlike Carroll who used hierarchical factor analysis (see discussion in the next section), Jensen derives *g* from the first unrotated factor. More recently confirmatory factor analysis has been pressed into the service of proving the existence of *g*. Two serious questions have been raised (Das, 1992) regarding the reality of *g*: Is *g* a reified statistical phenomenon, a creature of the particular method of statistics that gives a general factor? Are the factors essentially dependent on the tests that are put in, correlated, and subsequently analyzed?

A few of the following excerpts contain words of caution regarding the origin of *g*, a general factor of intelligence: Darlington (1962), who wrote the preface to Galton's book nearly 100 years after it was first published, wrote:

> Experts today may still want to follow a one-dimensional scale of merit or intelligence. The measurement of merit, the quantitative as opposed to qualitative method of study leads to simple assessment of superiority and inferiority. Hence, it justifies simple policies of opposition, of exclusion and oppression. These are all more dangerous in ignorant hands, for they contain an element of truth (p. 18).

Tyler (1986), reviewing a collection of papers on general ability concluded that:

> . . . the greatest weakness . . . is its reliance on correlational research exclusively. We must take in consideration research in special education, rehabilitation, mental retardation, and other specialized areas that has demonstrated that individuals at many *g* levels can do productive work (p. 449).

The old controversies generated by the science and politics of intelligence need not be rehashed here. However some authors, especially test makers, still support Spearman's theory of general intelligence. In elaboration of the theory, Jensen (1980) writes ". . . the *g* factor can be measured by an almost unlimited variety of test items and is therefore conceptually independent of the particular form or content of the items, which are merely vehicles for the behavioral manifestations of *g*" (p. 326). Jensen further claims that *g* is largely inherited, and the IQ tests are not biased. These claims have become so controversial that Jensen's contribution to intelligence has not received the attention it may deserve. If you are interested in debunking factor analysis as the major source of support of general intellectual ability, read Gould's (1981) book. If you wish to question the innate characteristic of *g* or general ability, read Kamin (1974).

Carroll's Three-Stratum Abilities and Limits of Factor Analysis

Factor analysis spawned *g,* which drives Carroll's three-stratum theory of human cognitive abilities. A quick review of Carroll's book is provided by Sternberg (1994). The theory is a result of reasonable solutions for four hundred and sixty-one data sets in Carroll's files. The three stratums comprise Stratum I (narrow abilities); Stratum II (broad abilities); and Stratum III (one general ability). Stratum II contains Catell's fluid and crystallized, learning and memory and many other abilities that Carroll regards as ill defined. None of these contributions appear to be new. In fact the second- and third-level abilities have been included in other theories based on factor analysis. In the same book review, Nathan Brody (1994) comments that the data sets were based on North American participants who were administered familiar North American tests. Many in the psychological community are not surprised that the result of Carroll's hierarchical factor analysis used on the data sets was predictable. Therefore Brody questions the usefulness of the results within a diverse cultural context. I think in this contemporary world, which is indeed a global village, any concept of intellectual abilities must acknowledge the nature of intellectual expression in a diversity of contexts. The three-stratum arrangement of test scores on a variety of tests using factor analysis is perhaps the last of the atheoretical uses of factor analysis that searches for a theory as an afterthought. However, it is consistent with Spearman's general factor: ". . . the *g* factor can be measured by an almost unlimited variety of test items and is therefore conceptually independent of the particular form or content of the items" (Jensen, 1980, p. 326).

Away from *g*: Multiple Intelligence, PASS Theory and Triarchic Theory

The three information-processing theories are discussed in this section. Gardner's multiple intelligence theory as revised in 1999 was reviewed by Earl Hunt (2001). Here I first provide a review that gives the background of his theory, as it was first proposed in 1983, and then Hunt's comment.

In the nineteenth century, faculty psychology took hold of the conceptualization of mental functions. The most notable name was that of Gall (1825, cited in Sternberg, 1990). His theory has often been caricatured because it resulted in examining bumps in the skull that represent separate faculties. However ridiculous such an idea may be, it appears to have a core of truth. Thurstone (1938) is perhaps the most well-known psychometrician in the first half of this century. He proposed separate primary abilities, such as verbal, spatial, fluency, and so on. These primary abilities were in opposition to the belief in one general ability or the g factor. The idea of separate abilities that resemble distinct faculties found a contemporary supporter in the work of Fodor (1983). Fodor suggested that the various measures of intellectual functions are modular in nature and relatively independent of each other. Language is the best example of a separate module, independent of general ability. Theories in linguistics and neuropsychology frequently support the modularity theory of linguistic functions. Thus, the module for language is relatively independent and works in parallel with another module, which could be a numerical ability. This concept of modularity has an appeal in that often a so-called intelligent person is extremely good with numbers but not so with language. Howard Gardner posited a theory of intelligence (1983) that includes seven separate modules. These multiple intelligences comprise linguistic, logical-mathematical, spatial, musical, bodily-kinesthetic, interpersonal, and intrapersonal: Sometimes the last two are combined. I describe each of these very briefly.

Linguistic intelligence, as the name suggests, relates to verbal ability. It is a person's ability to deal with grammar and speech. Logical-mathematical intelligence has to do with numerical ability, solving logical puzzles and mathematical problems. Thus, in general, it supports the notion that good logicians are also good at manipulating symbols. Examples abound, as instantiated by Whitehead and Bertrand Russell. Spatial intelligence is distinguished from logical-mathematical in that it is concerned with orientation in space-map reading, visual arts, and even playing chess. Musical intelligence is the next one singled out by Gardner. Certainly the existence of musical prodigies adds to the assumption that it might be an extremely specialized ability in people of all cultures. The next two or three modules are more controversial than the ones just mentioned. Bodily movements are essentially related to athletic ability, dancing, and, according to Gardner, surgery. These things are localized essentially in the motor cortex. However, there are skills and then there are intelligences. Those who agree with such a distinction question the appropriateness of designating athletics, such as moun-

tain climbing, as a sign of intelligence. However, that is exactly what Gardner wanted to impress on the readers and the academics, and indeed those of us who have kept logical-mathematical intelligence, or spatial intelligence, on a high pedestal. He believed it was necessary to climb down and realize the legitimacy of bodily-kinesthetic intelligence. The last two are intrapersonal and interpersonal intelligence. Interpersonal intelligence has to do with understanding the behavior of other people and their temperaments, and intentions. These skills are especially useful in politics, sales, and even in teaching. Intrapersonal intelligence deals with an understanding of oneself rather than understanding others. Generally speaking, some people cannot get along in this world, because they cannot put themselves in another person's shoes or may not realize that they are not able to put themselves in another person's shoes.

The different intelligences contained in Gardner's system of multiple intelligences are in line with investigations of distinct talents and skills found among individuals. We psychologists study the nature of musical ability, strategies involved in playing chess, the thought processes of logicians and mathematicians, as well as at the nonintellectual level, the early signs of being a hockey or cricket player or a smooth and persuasive sales person. It is not important to enumerate the reasons for the conceptualization of six or seven kinds of intelligences. Some may ask, why stop at seven? Why not include several dozen intelligences? For Gardner (1999) has already added two more: ecological, and spiritual.

Gardner's response would be that these seven, or nine, are supported by anthropological, historical, and psychological literature including current knowledge of neurological structures and functions. Neuropsychologists continuously discover new functions or dysfunctions associated with particular areas of the brain. For instance, if a certain area of a person's brain is injured, the individual may not be able to recognize small manipulable objects but may have no difficulty recognizing large objects (McCarthy & Warrington, 1990). The concept of multiple intelligences can be quite useful in investigating specialized functions or clinical cases of mental dysfunctions. The major objection to the concept, however, is that an excessive importance is placed on the independence of these intelligences from one another and divides human beings on the basis of a new typology. In fact, the brain and indeed the human being act as a whole, and no one mental activity can be truly independent of another.

Gardner's theory has also been criticized from a different angle. In reviewing Gardner's latest reframing of intelligence, Hunt (2001) asks "why have many psychologists and especially psychometricians, ignored the Theory of Multiple Intelligence (TMI)." The answer, which is arguable, is, "TMI cannot even be evaluated by the canons of science until it is made specific enough to generate measurement models" (p. 7).

The PASS Theory of Intelligence

The Planning, Attention-Arousal, Simultaneous and Successive (PASS) cognitive processing model is described as a modern theory of ability within the information-processing framework (Das, Naglieri, & Kirby, 1994). It is based on Luria's analyses of brain structures (1966; 1970; 1973; 1974; 1980). Luria described human cognitive processes within the framework of three functional units. The function of the first unit is cortical arousal and attention; the second unit codes information using simultaneous and successive processes; and the third unit provides for planning, self-monitoring, and structuring of cognitive activities. Luria's work on the functional aspects of brain structures formed the basis of the PASS model and was used as a blueprint for defining the important components of human intellectual competence. Because thorough reviews of the PASS model and related research are presented elsewhere (Das, Kirby, & Jarman, 1979; Das, Naglieri, & Kirby, 1994; Das & Naglieri, 2001), I provide only a brief summary here.

The cognitive processes that occur within the three functional units are responsible for and involved in all cognitive activity. The first functional unit, Attention-Arousal, is located in the brain stem and reticular activating system (Luria, 1973). This unit provides the brain with the appropriate level of arousal or cortical tone and "directive and selective attention" (p. 273).

Attentional processes are engaged when a multidimensional stimulus array is presented to the subject, and the task requires selective attention to one dimension, and the inhibition of response to other, often more salient stimuli. Luria stated that only under optimal conditions of arousal can the more complex forms of attention involving "selective recognition of a particular stimulus and inhibition of responses to irrelevant stimuli" occur (Luria, 1973, p. 271). Moreover, only when sufficiently aroused and when attention is adequately focused can an individual utilize processes within the second and third functional units.

Luria's description of the second functional unit follows the work of Sechenov. Luria described "two basic forms of integrative activity of the cerebral cortex" (Luria, 1966, p. 74). The processes of the second functional unit are responsible for "receiving, analyzing, and storing information" (Luria, 1973, p. 67) through the use of simultaneous and successive processing. Simultaneous processing is associated with the occipital-parietal areas of the brain (Luria, 1966). The essential aspect of simultaneous processing is surveyability; that

is, each element is related to every other element. For example, to produce a diagram correctly when given the instruction, "draw a triangle above a square that is to the left of a circle under a cross," the relationships among the shapes must be correctly comprehended. Successive processing is associated with the fronto-temporal areas of the brain and involves the integration of stimuli into a specific serial order where each component is related to the next. That is, in successive synthesis, "each link integrated into a series can evoke only a particular chain of successive links following each other in serial order" (Luria, 1966, p. 77). For example, in language processing, successive processes are involved with decoding and producing syntax, and articulating speech.

The third functional unit is located in the prefrontal divisions of the frontal lobes of the brain (Luria, 1980). Luria stated that "the frontal lobes synthesize the information about the outside worlds . . . and are the means whereby the behavior of the organism is regulated in conformity with the effect produced by its actions" (p. 263). Planning processes provide for the programming, regulation and verification of behavior and are responsible for behaviors, such as asking questions, problem solving, and the capacity for self-monitoring (Luria, 1973). Other activities of the third functional unit include regulation of voluntary activity, impulse control, and various linguistic skills, such as spontaneous conversation. The third functional unit provides for the most complex aspects of human behavior including personality and consciousness (c).

> The frontal lobes of the brain are the last acquisition of the evolutionary process and occupy nearly one-third of the human hemispheres. . . . They are intimately related to the reticular formation of the brain stem, being densely supplied with ascending and descending fibers. . . . They have intimate connections with the motor cortex and with the structures of the second block . . . their structures become mature only during the fourth to fifth year of life, and their development makes a rapid leap during the period which is of decisive significance for the first forms of conscious control of behavior. (Luria cited in Sapir & Nitzburg, 1973, p. 118).

The PASS theory, shown in Figure 2.1, provides a model to conceptualize human intellectual competence that is a blend of neuropsychological, cognitive, and psychometric approaches. Operational definitions of the four processes and the rationale for test construction are derived from the theory (Naglieri & Das, 1997), such that, consequently, the identification of good measures of each PASS process becomes possible.

Planning processes are required when a test demands that the individual make some decisions about how to solve a problem; execute an approach; activate attentional, simulta-

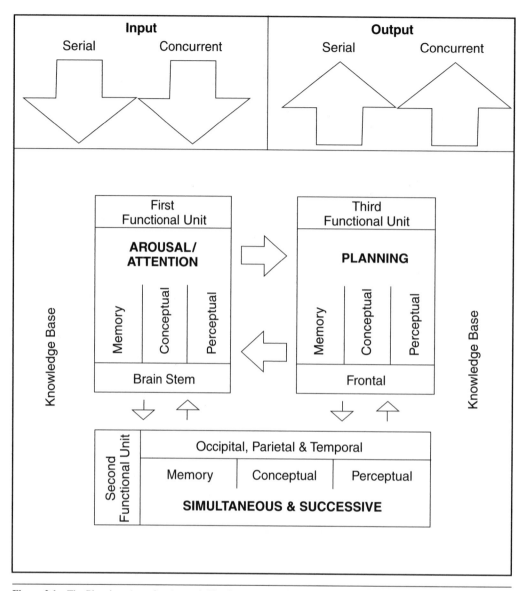

Figure 2.1   The Planning, Attention-Arousal, Simultaneous, and Successive processing model with knowledge-base.

neous, and successive processes; monitor the effectiveness of the approach; and modify it as needed. Planning processes are involved when a person is asked to decide how to perform a test and is inhibited by the imposition of strict rules about how to perform. For example, writing a composition involves generation of a plan, organization of the ideas, control over what is presented when, examination of the product, and revisions to make the final result consistent with the intended goal.

Knowledge base is an integral component of the PASS model and therefore all processes are embedded within this dimension. The base of knowledge included in the PASS figure is intended to represent all information obtained from the cultural and social background of the individual, because this

determines the form of mental activity. Children's use of language to analyze, generalize, and encode experience is a critical determinant of the base of knowledge, because mental processes cannot develop apart from the appropriate forms of social life. The importance of social interactions is perhaps most clearly presented by Luria (1976) when he states, "the significance of schooling lies not just in the acquisition of new knowledge, but the creation of new motives and formal modes of discursive verbal and logical thinking divorced from immediate practical experience" (p. 133). This statement emphasizes the role of knowledge, as well as planning processes (e.g., the creation of motives), in all forms of cognitive activity. Recognizing the importance of the base of knowledge obtained from all sources (formal as well as informal, practical as well as theoretical, etc.), I have incorporated this component within the PASS model.

Planning is clearly associated with the frontal lobes, especially the prefrontal cortex. It has connections with the rest of the brain as described before, including the parietal, temporal, and occipital lobes that are responsible for information coding (simultaneous and successive processing), as well as with subcortical areas that determine the level of arousal and affective reactions to different conditions on the basis of past experiences. If you have to locate a connection for personality in the PASS model, most probably its association will be the closest to the frontal lobes and the limbic system. The frontal lobes mature late, beginning at ages four and five, and their functions are more open to sociocultural influences and the individual's experience (Baker-Sennett et al., 1993). Thus, it is reasonable to assume that planning provides an important link between motivation and personality on the one hand, and cognitive activities on the other.

The PASS model views planning as a functional system that is similar to the concept of activity (Leont'ev, 1981). There are many paths to realizing a plan; these are actions. Actions can be substituted by other actions that are consistent with the plan. This dynamic occurs during problem solving. Planning, like activity, is goal directed; thus, plans change as goals change. Planning, as an activity, is directed by local goals, as in performing an action, but also by the overarching motivation of the individual. To create plans and execute them, people are guided by processed information as they attend to the relevant features of a problem or a situation. Thus, planning depends on the three other components of the PASS theory (see Das, Kar, & Parrila, 1996 for a book-length discussion).

Although the PASS theory has been updated to a certain extent (Das 2002), it needs further work. Four directions are suggested for future research: (1) the relation between successive processing and reading; (2) the role of language in planning—is language, for example, essential for planning? (3) the place of motivation and emotion in planning and decision making in the PASS theory; and (4) how the theory might accommodate the neuropsychological assumptions of Luria in the light of spectacular advances made in cognitive neuropsychology.

The Three Faces of Intelligence: Sternberg's Triarchic Theory

The first part of the theory relates to the internal world of the individual that specifies the cognitive mechanisms that result, more or less, in intelligent behavior. Its components are concerned with information processing. Learning how to

do things and actually doing them is the essential characteristic of the second face of Sternberg's theory of intelligence. This part is also concerned with the way humans deal with novel tasks and how they develop automatic routine responses for well-practiced tasks. The third face of the theory is concerned with intelligence that has to do with the external world. By this, Sternberg means how people adapt to their environment, how they select their environment, and how they shape their environment. These are the behaviors that are important in a practical world.

Explaining the first part then, Sternberg defines a component as a mental process that may translate a sensory input into a mental representation, translate one mental representation into another mental representation, or translate a mental representation into motor output. What it simply means is that when humans experience something, they have to represent it in their own minds, that is, form impressions of it themselves. Everyone has his or her own private representational mechanism, the symbols he or she uses, such as what is sometimes called *inner speech* (Luria, 1973). These representations provide the raw material for reasoning and inference and the impetus for motor activity. Sternberg proposes three components: the metacomponents that are used in planning, adopting strategies, evaluating how one did in performing a task; secondly, performance components that include cognitive processes used in performing the task; and, lastly, knowledge acquisition components that are concerned with how humans learn the meanings of words, a different language, or whatever is taught through formal instruction or is acquired spontaneously through experience.

In terms of the PASS model, metacomponents are a part of planning, including decision-making, judgment, and evaluation, to deal with the use of strategies for different kinds of problem solving. The performance components, on the other hand, are concerned with inductive reasoning or other kinds of mental activities, such as in problem solving, and in information processing tasks, such as choice reaction time. The knowledge acquisition component allows scientists to understand the process of learning. Such processes are different for people who are experts in their field, such as literature, mathematics, or chess, and those who are novices in the field, who are just beginning to learn about the various aspects of comprehension and writing, and solving mathematical problems. All three components refer to tasks that are executed more or less in the artificial environment of a laboratory or classroom. However, considering all aspects of intelligence, Sternberg takes into account experience as important. Here he is drawing upon Vygotsky's ideas of zones of proximal development (Vygotsky, 1962), that is, a child's ability to gain from instruction or experience in solving a problem. He divides the experiential aspect of intelligence into the ability to deal with novelty, and the development of automatic mechanisms for processing information. To quote:

"I propose that intelligence involves not merely the ability to learn and reason with new concepts but the ability to learn and reason with new kinds of concepts. Intelligence is not so much the ability to learn or think within familiar conceptual systems as it is the ability to learn and think with new conceptual systems, which can then be brought to bear upon already existing knowledge" (Sternberg, 1986, p. 30).

Within the ability to deal with novelty, Sternberg mentions such tasks as new games and puzzles that he describes as insightful learning. A common example is the following problem. Suppose that the lotus flowers in a pond double every night. It took 30 days for the lotus flowers to fill half of the pond. How many days will it take for them to fill the entire pond? Sternberg thinks that "fluid intelligence" measured by Cattell in Progressive Matrices (Cattell, 1971) is a good example of such tasks. It can be classified as requiring the ability to deal with novelty. The ability to automatize information processing, on the other hand, is exemplified by Cattell's tasks of "crystallized intelligence." These tasks essentially refer to things that people have overlearned in school, such as remembering multiplication tables or a series of unconnected words.

Finally, the third part of the theory deals with the external world of the individual. It fits in well with Sternberg's general definition of intelligence as mental activity involved in purposive adaptation, to the shaping of and selection of real-world environments relevant to one's life. Adaptation to one's environment is often believed by ordinary people to be a mark of intelligence. However, people not only adapt to a situation, they select an appropriate environment for their behavior. If humans are merely adapting to their environment, there would be no creative thinkers or imaginative social reformers. So, these people do select and shape their environment. People must capitalize on their strengths and compensate for their weaknesses if they are to survive as intelligent individuals in society.

Sternberg updated his theory of intelligence and advanced the idea of *successful intelligence,* which is defined as the ability to adapt to, shape, and select environments to accomplish one's goals and those of one's society and culture (Sternberg & Kaufman, 1998; p. 494). Even a cursory view of this new notion reveals a continuation of the main ideas in Triarchic theory that included metacomponents, novelty, experiential knowledge, and the relevance of intelligence for shaping and selecting of real-world environments. The cluster of cognitive abilities (note, not processes) for successful

intelligence is made up of analytical, creative, and practical abilities. That practical intelligence can be separated from IQ is emphasized. All three abilities appear to be related and can be viewed together as planning. I have discussed elsewhere (Das & Misra, 1995) that emotional and motivational predispositions of the person feature prominently in making practical decisions. The role of predisposition was recognized sometime ago by Simon (1967, 1987), who advocated the use of intuition and creativity in making complex decisions. Thus the ability to think analytically does not guarantee that irrational decisions will not be made. Sternberg and Kaufman (1998) refer to the work of Doerner (1990) to support their argument that IQ does not predict a person's ability to use strategies in problem solving. But I think Doerner's work is relevant for another important aspect of problem solving in practical situations by managers and executives. He analyzed the failure of logic and the logic of failure in decision-making. The reasons for failure consist of the indetermination of the antecedents and consequence of managerial problems, for instance, and the inability of the human mind to hold together the many components interacting with each other in a complex manner (Das & Misra, 1995). Therefore, I think practical intelligence is worthy of further theoretical conceptualization of the processes in decision-making.

In retrospect, Gardner and Sternberg propose theories of intelligence that are different from those of Galton, Spearman, or Cyril Burt. Both theories respond to the contemporary movement in psychology, which is to acknowledge the existence of mental functions and to direct research towards understanding cognitive processes. The major difficulty in these theories is in translating them to psychometric instruments for the measurement of cognitive abilities; this is not the case with PASS theory. Sternberg is attempting to transform parts of his theory into tests for measurement of intelligence; whereas Gardner prefers to validate his theory by direct observation of the way children learn and manifest their different talents.

Reaction Time and Intelligence

The idea that there is a general mental energy driving all mental functions, as Spearman (1927) conceptualized intelligence to be, has been obsolete for some time. However, in its place has arisen a new movement towards discovering a single culture-free index of intelligence. This new movement is best represented by the work of Jensen (1982) on reaction time, and Eysenck (1982) on *biological* measures including reaction time and electron encartography (ECG) measures (1986), but they still believe that Burt was essentially correct in that intelligence is a general factor derived from psychometric tests.

Jensen (1982) considered speed of processing as the basic component of intelligence. The speed of processing, however, is measured by several cognitive tasks. I emphasize *cognitive* because a review of the reaction time tests that Jensen considered to be measuring elementary cognitive processes reveals that these are really measures of cognitive processes that are contained in the PASS model. For example, besides tests of simple and choice reaction time, the elementary cognitive tests that Jensen uses require complex cognitive processing. In the odd-man-out paradigm, adopted as one of the elementary tasks, the individual is asked to turn off one of three lights that has a longer distance from the adjacent light than the two others. How quickly an individual can respond to this becomes a measure of processing speed. Obviously, the task requires strategies and judgments that are common to many higher order cognitive processes. In terms of the PASS model, the task involves simultaneous processing of the distance between all three lights and then deciding to press one that is farther than the other two. Visual Search is another example of the task that Jensen uses where a target digit, such as 3, is first exposed and is followed immediately by a row of seven digits, one of which may contain the target digit 3. The individual is asked to press a yes button or a no button depending on whether the target digit is present. This test requires attention and one of two strategies. Most subjects adopt a planned serial searching strategy: If the target digit occurs towards the last part of the series, the search time is longer than it is if it occurs towards the earlier part. However, if an individual is engaged in an exhaustive search, waiting to respond until he or she has looked at the entire series, the location of the target digit in the series does not influence reaction time.

The next task that I would like to choose from Jensen in order to illustrate complex cognitive strategies and not merely reaction time is called the Posner paradigm. As described in the PASS model and its battery of tests, this is a task in which pairs of letters (AA, BB, CC, DD, NN) are presented to the individual with the instruction that when the letter pairs are identical, a button should be pressed. In a second version of the task, the letter pairs that have the same name (Aa, Bb, Mm) should be detected. The time taken for the second condition of the task, that is, matching the name of the letters, is usually longer than the first one, which requires matching identical letters that are visually the same. A variation of the task has been used in the Das-Naglieri Cognitive Assessment System (CAS; Naglieri & Das, 1997) as a measure of selective attention. Jensen uses these tasks in establishing a

mental chronometry, an idea borrowed from Posner (Posner & Mitchell, 1967; Posner, 1978).

Speed Is Not a Good Measure of IQ Unless Researchers Understand 'Speed'

It is difficult to accept speed as an explanatory construct for intelligence; clever people know when to speed up and when to slow down before a response (Das, Naglieri, & Kirby, 1994). The nature of speed itself needs to be understood before using it as an explanation of intelligence.

Speed has at least two different connotations that lead to different explanations as related to cognitive performance: *speediness* and *speed* (Nettlebeck, 1994). Speediness is conceived as quickness in test performance when the test is undemanding and overlearned. This is an operational definition without hidden theoretical connotations. Speed, on the other hand, is more popularly accepted as the speed of information processing as measured by reaction time. Jensen and some others have claimed that speed is the measure of central nervous system efficiency; however, this is questionable. Although it may be attractive to believe that speed is a reflection of biological and culture-free intelligence (Vernon, 1987), even a slight delving into the biological domain (from cells to central nervous system) appears to make this concept untenable. The critical question relates to speed of information processing, which is a new name for *g*. Is it essentially derived from synaptic activity as Reed and Jensen (1992) suggest? If so, does this in turn mean the speed of release of appropriate neurotransmitters? How, then, does one consider speed of inhibition through the conduction of inhibitory nerves that slows down, and even eliminates, a neural response? Reed and Jensen (1993) in a later article found that reaction time and nerve-conduction measures do not show a correlation, casting doubt on their earlier assumption of a general speed of nervous conduction that can be captured in reaction time.

In conclusion, it is best to conceptualize speed specifically in terms of distinct cognitive processes, such as speed in planning and executing a specific response that varies with the kind of strategies used, speed of allocating attention, or speed of articulation when a subject is asked to read words and name colors quickly. Individual differences in response time are explained in terms of the specific cognitive operation(s) that are required by the tasks. So, for example, in Posner's task, if an individual is faster in matching letters that are physically identical (AA) and slower matching letters that have the same name (aA) this could be explained in terms of mechanisms determining lexical access.

THE BIG PICTURE: WHAT SHOULD THE THEORIES DO?

Even if we psychologists cannot spend our scientific careers trying to unify the diverse concepts and theories of intelligence, we can compare them on the basis of three major categories.

Does the theory give rise to measures for assessment of intelligence? Does it delineate the cognitive processes that can be measured? Lastly, can it prescribe instructions or remedial programs to reduce the deficits in cognitive processing that are observed or assessed? These are schematically presented in the following figure, as a cube (Figure 2.2). This cube will be a framework for the big picture. I will also discuss two issues that are hugely important for all theories of intelligence:

1. Is intelligence, or for that matter the human mind, full of modules, relatively independent of general cognitive activities in the mind? I shall discuss this in the context of PASS and Luria's functional organization.
2. Do we need to understand anew the role of heredity and environment as these influence intelligence (cognitive abilities)?

Judging by the three aspects of the cube, how does science evaluate the three theories discussed previously: Gardner's Multiple Intelligence (MI), Sternberg's Triarchic theory, and PASS? Multiple Intelligence does not measure competence in an objective and psychometrically reliable manner, as Hunt (2001) mentioned in his review quoted earlier in this chapter. But processes are discussed and the evidence, though not empirically verified using designs of studies in psychology, does refer to information processing capacities identified as six to eight kinds of intelligences. The theory is also prominently used for instruction in selected schools, but that may make it vulnerable to further criticism as the results of MI-guided instruction are not yet validated. In any case, the value of a theory need not be based mainly on the efficacy of prescription. Except that in this case, the theory of multiple intelligence allows itself to be judged as such.

Sternberg's Triarchic theory has not yet made itself specific enough to generate measurement models to borrow from Hunt's (2001) criticism of Multiple Intelligence. Parts of the theory, especially those referring to tacit knowledge, have been operationalized, and reliable measures have been available for some time. But a comprehensive group of tests arising out of the theory has not emerged. The theory's strongest aspect is its delineation of components or processes. The prescriptive aspect of the theory is scattered throughout Stern-

A Comprehensive Approach to Cognitive Assessment

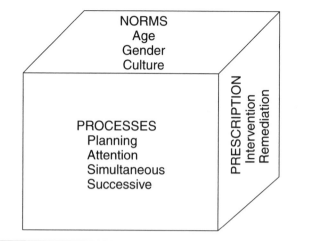

Figure 2.2   A comprehensive view of the aims of an ideal test of cognitive functions.

berg's prodigious publications, and you must judge whether serious attempts have been made at the training and remediation of deficient components found upon diagnosis based on observations (as tests, strictly speaking, are not used).

The PASS theory may fare better at evaluation. The theory has guided the construction of a psychometrically acceptable assessment system, the Cognitive Assessment System, and a cognitive enhancement program, the PREP (see Das & Naglieri, 2001, for a practical chapter). These are described briefly.

Das-Naglieri Cognitive Assessment System

Because information about Cognitive Assessment System (CAS) is given in a subsequent chapter of this edited volume, and its theoretical base, PASS theory, has been discussed earlier in this chapter, a bare minimum of its structure and the prescriptive sequel to CAS assessment are presented here (Naglieri et al., 1997).

There are four scales in CAS, one corresponding to each process. The examples of subtests from each scale given in the following sections are adapted from CAS (Naglieri, 1999).

Planning

Planning is a mental process by which the person determines, selects, and uses efficient solutions to problems. The basic elements of planning are:

• Problem solving.
• Forming mental representations.

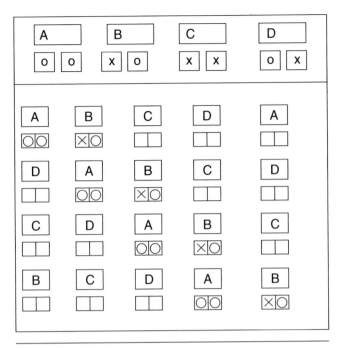

Figure 2.3 Planned codes: A planning test.

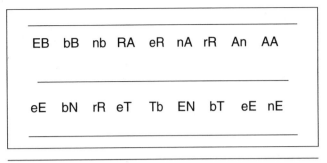

Figure 2.4 Example of receptive attention task.

- Impulse control.
- Control of processing.
- Retrieval of knowledge.
- Imaging students demonstrate selective prefrontal cortex activation during planning tasks.

The three planning subtests require the child to develop a plan of action, evaluate the value of the method, monitor its effectiveness, revise or reject a previous plan as the task demands change, and control the impulse to act without careful consideration. Planning is central to all activities in which there are both intentionality and a need for some method to solve a problem. This process includes self-monitoring and impulse control as well as plan generation.

The Planned Codes test, for example, (see Figure 2.3) requires the child to write a code (e.g. OO or XO) under the corresponding letter (e.g. A or B). A child can use different strategies to complete the test efficiently within a limited time.

Attention/Arousal

Attention is a mental process by which the person selectively attends to some stimuli and ignores others. The basic elements for arousal are:

- Focused cognitive activity.
- Selective attention.
- Resistance to distraction.
- Orienting response.
- Vigilance.
- Reticular formation as substrate.
- Under/over arousal implicated in ADHD.

One of the three tasks given to find out about children's processing in attention/arousal is a task called Receptive Attention, given in Figure 2.4 as an example. Each item in the task consists of a pair of letters; the child is asked to underline the pair that has the same letter in capital and small case. Some pairs have different letters; these are the distracters that the child must avoid and they should not be underlined.

Simultaneous Processing

Simultaneous processing is a mental activity by which the person integrates stimuli into groups. The basic elements of simultaneous processing are:

- Stimuli are seen as a whole or gestalt.
- Each piece must be related to the others.
- Simultaneous processing is not necessarily nonverbal.
- Associated with the integrity of the parieto-occipital temporal regions.

Simultaneous processing is measured by three tests; one of these is Verbal Spatial Relations (see Figure 2.5). This test requires the child to understand logical and grammatical relations such as a triangle within a circle that is within a square. The examiner reads each question at the bottom of the pictures, for example, "Which picture shows a square to the left of a circle that is under a triangle?" The child is asked to point to the correct picture as quickly as possible.

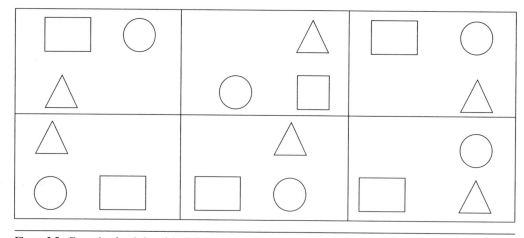

Figure 2.5   Example of verbal spatial relations: A simultaneous processing task.

Successive Processing

Successive processing is a mental activity by which the person integrates stimuli in a specific order. The basic elements of successive processing are:

- Stimuli form a chain-like progression.
- Successive processing is not necessarily verbal.
- Associated with the fronto-temporal regions.

A test that involves successive processing must demand that the child attend to and work with the linear order of events. This is most easily evaluated by three subtests. A complex successive subtest is Sentence Questions. The subtest, illustrated in Figure 2.6, requires the child to answer a question about a statement made by the examiner. For example, the examiner says, "The red greened the blue with a yellow. Who used the yellow?" and the child should say, "The

red." This item requires that the child comprehend the sequence of the words to arrive at the correct solution, making it an excellent measure of successive planning.

PASS Reading Enhancement Program (PREP; Das, 1999) is based on the PASS theory. Is it an advantage that a remedial program be heavily grounded in a reasonable theory? The answer is yes. The program is understood in the framework given by the PASS theory. Hence it provides a rationally prescribed program for improving reading.

The training tasks in PREP are recommended for those with learning difficulties, including dyslexia, to promote the same processes that are basic to reading/spelling/comprehension. So the pathway starts with cognitive and learning difficulties that lead to reading disabilities; with the application of PREP, the cognitive difficulties and learning problems are reduced and, consequently, reading is improved. Understanding the program's underlying theory is an important aspect of its use. The PASS profiles of dyslexics and generally poor readers are different; therefore, remediation can be focused according to the cognitive difficulties as revealed by CAS.

The PREP program consists of eight to ten tasks that vary considerably in content and the requirements of the student. Each task involves a global training component and a curriculum-related bridging component. The global component includes structured, nonreading tasks that require the application of simultaneous or successive strategies. These tasks also provide children with the opportunity to internalize strategies in their own way, thus facilitating transfer (Das, Mishra, & Pool, 1995). The bridging component involves the same cognitive demands as its global component and provides training in simultaneous and successive processing strategies, which have been closely linked to reading and spelling (Das, Naglieri, & Kirby, 1994).

---

1. The blue is yellow. Who is yellow?

2. The red greened the blue with a yellow. Who used the yellow?

3. The red blues a yellow green of pinks, that are brown in the purple, and then greys the tan. What does the red do first?

Figure 2.6   Example of sentence questions: A successive task.

The Gap Between Psychometrics of Intelligence Testing and Psychology: Is It Filled Yet?

In the wake of the widely cited charge that there is a gap between the psychometric measures of intelligence and psychology (Cronbach, 1957), psychologists began studying individual differences to bridge the gap. First, psychologists studying reaction time and other measures of information processing paid attention to individual differences. But have psychometric tests of abilities responded to the challenge? Have they become process oriented? How many of the routinely used IQ tests have changed to accommodate studying mental processes? The Wechsler Intelligence Scale for Children (WISC) and the Binet and their subsequent revisions are largely unchanged. An IQ divided into performance and verbal scores is still the norm, and even when factors, such as freedom from distractibility, are scored, the items that make up the score, such as Arithmetic and Digit Span tests, are not instances of attention tasks that are found in cognitive psychology. Consider verbal ability, a staple. No progress in measuring the psychological processes associated with verbal ability has been made, in spite of the fact that in 1975 concrete tests were suggested in the now classic paper by Hunt, Lunneborg, and Lewis (1975). The paper recommended that the truly verbal tests should not be dependent on old knowledge (e.g., Similarities, Vocabulary), but on current information processing ability. Examples are tests that require lexical access or ordering and sequencing (both types are included in CAS).

The revised Stanford-Binet test (SB-IV) attempts to include some cognitive abilities, such as verbal reasoning, quantitative reasoning, abstract-visual reasoning, and short-term memory; however, these abilities do not fit into a neat theoretical framework. Kaufman remarks that the revised tests represent bits and pieces of *g*, primary abilities, and Cattell's gf-gc. Furthermore, the categories of abilities are not supported as distinct factors (Kaufman, 2000).

Similarly, have the Bayley scales of mental abilities, another standard test for measuring cognitive development of infants and young children, kept up with advances in cognitive developmental psychology? You can judge this; for example, has it taken into consideration issues, such as modularity, domain-general and domain-specific abilities, and the effect of cultural context?

Among the theory-driven test batteries riding on the coattails of the information processing movement discussed in the present chapter are the Das-Naglieri Cognitive Assessment System (Naglieri et al., 1997), derived to a large extent from Luria (1966), and what has been called the Das-Luria model (Daniel, 2000). Kaufman and Kaufman (1993) pub-

lished an intelligence test for adolescents and adults based on Cattell and Horn's fluid and crystallized (gf-gc) notion of intelligence. I do think, like many in the field, that neither gf-gc nor the Kaufmans' test focuses on cognitive *processes* and that both are concerned with *abilities* instead.

If you want a quick and comprehensive idea of the topics, you can consult two recent reviews on intelligence tests: Kaufman (2000) and Daniel (2000).

The major disadvantage of an atheoretical assessment is encountered when the clinician is interpreting the results and pointing out to teachers and parents how test results explain referral problems: How does the child's performance on the IQ test explain the child's problems, such as learning and reading difficulties, mathematics failure, attentional deficits, and difficulties in planning and time management?

In the final part of the present chapter, I discuss two issues that are critical for conceptualization of intelligence: Is the mind full of modules? What is new in heredity-environment interactions in determining intelligence?

MODULES AND FUNCTIONAL BLOCKS

Are there cognitive processing modules (Fodor, 1983)? Does the brain function as a whole and, by inference, do the different processes of the brain lack regions dedicated to them? How has modularity been conceptualized in recent literature, especially relating to neuropsychology?

Modules in Neuropsychology

Why neuropsychology? One reason is that segmentation of cognitive functions has long been pursued in neuropsychology, first relating brain impairment locations to cognitive and behavioral changes and then in recent years by the use of brain imaging techniques that have led to deeper understanding of the intact as well as the damaged brain. If modularity is to be supported, not only its existence but also its borders have to be discovered. Experimental designs and the required statistics predated brain imaging. Now together, all three offer a unique opportunity for the researcher to define the modules that may be innate or acquired, and the extent to which a modular function is domain-specific.

In defining a module from neuropsychology, Gazzaniga (1988) refers to functional units that can produce behavior and trigger emotional responses as modules. In this sense his conception differs from that of Fodor's (1983), whose main concern is with cognitive functions, such as language. Gazzaniga suggests that his view of modularity is different from one that concerns specific brain structures and areas, which are identified as carrying out specific functional activities.

Some critics argue that Gazzaniga does not really make a distinction between his and Luria's views of modularity. Luria's view that brain structures carry out specific functional activities and Gazzaniga's view that modularity refers to functional units that can produce behaviors and trigger emotional responses are not so different. However, Luria (1966) did not explicitly include emotional responses as a part of the three blocks of the brain. Emotion or affect is implicitly inferred while discussing the close connection between the arousal system (brain-stem) and the planning functions (frontal lobes). Nevertheless, it is easier to agree with Gazzaniga's view, which is, by the way, weaker than the original view of Fodor, concerning the relationship between specific modules of intellectual function, on the one hand, and general cognitive function, on the other. In Gazzaniga's view, the two need not be completely separated. In a recent book, Goldberg (2001) had a softer view of modularization, similar to Gazzaniga.

Modules are automatic in their processing, that is, they operate without consciousness. Although according to Fodor (1983) modules are innate and are present from birth, one can argue about it, as shown in the following sections. The functional modules are quite consistent with Luria's functional organization of the brain, and hence relevant to PASS theory. The notion of two functional modules for simultaneous and successive information processing can be traced to Sechenov, a pioneer in physiology in the nineteenth century (Sechenov, 1956). Luria followed this notion to a certain extent. Sechenov would probably have agreed with a modular view of intellectual functions, for he clearly mentions simultaneous and successive processing as segregated functional units that are present from infancy. In that sense, he would not agree that the brain at birth is a clean slate. Sensations do not enter the empty brain; the brain already has designated regions to receive and process specific categories of information.

But how far do these regions remain impervious to cognitive activities in other parts of the brain? Are the simultaneous and successive processes (1) automatically activated and, at the same time, (2) innate? These being the two essential characteristics of modular functions, the matter is open to question. Luria's characterization of functional blocks as interdependent, not independent, does not prevent them from being designated as modular. If a less restrictive view of modularity is adopted as promoted by Karmiloff-Smith (1992), modularization allows for development, a gradual unfolding of the modular function through maturation and learning.

Modularization, Nativism, and Empiricism: Implications for Intelligence

For further clarification of the concept of modules, I recommend reading the characteristics of modules as succinctly summarized by a leading developmental psychologist, Karmiloff-Smith (1992), and the discussion that follows. Modules are hard-wired (not assembled from simple elementary processes); they are fixed neural architectures; they are domain-specific; they are fast; they are autonomous; they are mandatory; they are automatic; and they are stimulus driven. Karmiloff-Smith makes a distinction between her own system, which she calls "process of modularization," and Fodor's modules. For example, Fodor assumes that modules innately exist for spoken language and visual perception. By contrast, Karmiloff-Smith draws a distinction between the notion of modules that are specified from before and a process of modularization that occurs repeatedly as a product of development. So in this sense, she differs from and is not as strict a nativist as Fodor is. Her modularization concept admits that the mind becomes modularized as development proceeds. Her notion accepts that the human brain is plastic and that early development in infants occurs due to a recurring process. The process of modularization also assumes that the activation of different brain regions occurs generally in the beginning, and only with time are specific circuits formed and activated in response to domain-specific inputs.

Karmiloff-Smith argues that domain specificity of cognitive systems is suggested by developmental neuropsychology. In cases of brain damage, certain abilities are spared; whereas others are impaired. For example, in William's Syndrome spatial recognition is impaired, while language/phrase recognition is not. So also, the presence of idiot-savants among the population of individuals with mental retardation supports the development of domain-specific cognitive systems.

I do not think that these examples of domain-specific cognitive abilities, which may or may not be impaired due to genetic or traumatic causes, prove in any way the modularity of mind, with all its assumptions of being automatic, mandatory, and innate. It is consistent with a broader view of cognitive organization of functions in the brain, as Luria, for example, proposed. While in Luria's theory and in the PASS system the four processes are distinguished from input, knowledge base, and output, there is no assumption that the regions of the brain that are associated with the four processes work as strictly as modules do. Instead, the development of all four processes will support a process of modularization that occurs repeatedly as a product of development. This process applies to planning as well as to the basic processes of attention (orienting response) and the two ways of information coding (simultaneous and successive).

Because planning is higher order processing that is associated with frontal lobes, researchers may consider how its development in the brain can be documented as a process of modularization. The frontal lobes play a crucial part in the pruning process of excess synapses that are produced at different stages of development of the brain starting from the prenatal stage to as late as age 16. More importantly, the plasticity of the brain consists of genetically programmed overproduction of synapses and the environmentally determined maintenance and pruning of synaptic connections (Thatcher, 1992). The implication of Thatcher's finding for neuropsychology and practice is that impairment of frontal lobes during the developmental period has severe behavioral consequences, as its pruning and guiding hand in the development of the brain is not likely to be taken over by the other parts of the brain.

I think the readers will agree with the major point of view of Karmiloff-Smith: Development of cognition can be domain specific. A standard of general cognitive performance, as given by IQ, is not an accurate description, because processing abilities develop differently and sometimes are strictly preprogrammed to preserve the energy of the growing organism, such that perceptual systems and language systems (to take two important aspects of cognition) may develop uninterrupted and without being interfered with by development in other parts of the brain.

It is hard to deny that many characteristics that humans possess are innately predisposed, in consistency with lower animals. It is also well known in genetics that what appears in phenotypic behavior is not determined by genes themselves, there being thousands of them, but on the set of genes that have been expressed. The expression of genes depends, demonstrably, as in the case of frontal lobes, on the environmental conditions of the organism. These points are discussed in the next section.

In conclusion of the preceding discussion on modules and intelligence, which I admit is selective, it is easy to agree with the following statement of Frith that reflects contemporary thinking on functional segregation: "The brain consists of a great many modules that process information more or less independently of each other. It seems likely that it will be easier to discover how one of those modules works than to explain the functioning of the brain as a whole" (Frith, 1997, p. 5).

The controversy that has not been resolved concerns domain-specific and domain-general abilities (Frensch & Buchner, 1999). Should scientists regard multiple cognitive functions including PASS, multiple intelligences, and the components in Triarchic theory as innate and domain specific (mostly like the abilities at the sensory level, such as percep-tion, and also the broader abilities, such as speech) in opposition to being innate and domain general, such as IQ?

HEREDITY-ENVIRONMENT INTERACTIONS REVISITED

What is genetic expression and how does it highlight the role of environment? A prominent researcher in this area is Gottlieb. In a review article, he writes: "The theoretical crux of this article is that the internal and external environments supply the necessary signals to the genes that instigate the eventual production of the requisite proteins under normal as well as unusual conditions of development. There is no genetic master plan or blueprint that is self-actualized during the course of development" (Gottlieb, 1998, p. 799).

Genetic expression and probabilistic epigenesis suggest that the interaction of genes and environment is bidirectional. In contrast, less sophisticated theories found in some textbooks are as follows: unidirectionally, intelligence A is genotypically determined; intelligence B is a combination of genetic and environmental factors, which are additive; and intelligence C is the most impure of all, containing the artifacts of tests and testing conditions. This was the commonplace version of intelligence as found for example in Vernon (1969).

Vernon hoped that some day by using physiological methods, such as EEG, researchers might be able to discover direct evidence for intelligence A. That hope is ill founded if a genetic master plan does not exist and also based on the suggestion that environment during brain development influences gene expression (Sokolowski & Wahlsten, 2001). Wahlsten brought an interesting study by vom Saal (1981) to my notice; the study describes the effect of the embryo's position in the litter in relation to its siblings inside the uterus. The position is a randomly distributed genetic effect that, nevertheless, exerts a nonrandom environmental effect on the fetus—a male mouse among two females develops female behavior after birth and maturity (for example, raises its hindquarters for sexual encounters) and vice versa.

Search for a specific gene for intelligence has not been successful. A recent claim to the contrary, by Chorney et al. (1998), which includes among the authors Plomin, a respected researcher in heritability of intelligence, has been dampened by subsequent criticisms of the study (see chapter by Wahlsten, 2002). In the same book, Naglieri and Das (2002) question the usefulness of *g* and further demonstrate how deficits in a high-level cognitive function that affects arithmetic performance (planning) can be changed by self-verbalization techniques. In all fairness, Vernon, by 1969, had become a strong advocate of environmental factors, such as malnutrition and cultural contexts, as pervasive factors that influence intelligence B. Furthermore, he held the opinion that IQ, intelligence C, is not intelligence. Perhaps, like the observant cross-cultural English psychologist he was in England, he saw many a common clerk toiling in His Majesty's office despite having a brilliant academic degree from the prestigious Oxbridge universities, similar to some of their batch-mates who were brilliant scientists! So much for the invulnerable genes behind intelligence A.

The simple truth about the heredity-environment debate of bygone days (see Grigerenko, 1999 for a comprehensive traditional review) is that not only has behavior genetics changed the parameters of measuring heritability, but also in a broader perspective, the world events have forced researchers to look at the sociopolitical problems of IQ testing. Consider the two important cultural factors that affect intelligence: the absence of a literacy environment; and inadequate provision of health care, even in some affluent nations. Add to these the experience of millions of children traumatized by wars waged with the help of arms sales by the rich nations of the world to poor nations in combat. Can researchers still discuss fairness in intelligence testing, or assume a direct relation of heredity to intelligence that translates to socioeconomic status? Or hunt for the elusive true score in intelligence tests?

SUMMARY AND CONCLUSIONS

Following from the preceding arguments, look at intelligence and its testing from the sociohistorical synthesis founded on Vygotsky. Continuing with the sentiments just expressed, fairness of intelligence testing must factor in learning and culture. To the old question of whether intellectual deficiencies accumulate, Humphreys (1988), a psychometrician of prestige and authority, writes about the context within which learning deficiencies accumulate among poor black American students, contributing to their inadequate learning syndrome.

A summary of the main points in this chapter that will be of interest to both theorists and practitioners in the field of intelligence follows:

1. Intelligence is discernment and judgment, not merely quickness in thinking. The Western and the Eastern philosophers agree on this.

2. The total shift from qualitative to a quantitative estimate of intelligence is regretted. Intelligence includes not only reasoning, but also will and emotion, which may require qualitative analysis (Das, 1994).

3. Recent theories of intelligence comprise a mixture of the old factor-analytically derived constructs and those derived from information processing models. Among the latter are the theory of Multiple Intelligence, the PASS theory and the Triarchic theory; each one may make IQ obsolete. A revival of g as speed, specially, measured by reaction-time, straddles the border between the old and the new. However, its interpretation as a phenotypic measure, aspiring as it does to measure synaptic speed (correlation between IQ and nerve conduction speed is around $r = 0.05$), see Wahlsten (in press), is questionable. When reaction time and IQ correlate, RT is a surrogate for complex information processing.

4. Any theory of intelligence should specify how to measure intelligence, what processes underlie test performance and how to prescribe instructional and remedial procedures.

5. Does intelligence contain some cognitive modules? Probably not in a strict sense if modules are characterized as innate, fast, and autonomous of general cognitive activities. But the mind becomes modularized as development proceeds (Karmiloff-Smith, 1992). By assuming that the four PASS processes, for example, develop as such, it will be useful to discover how any one of them works rather than drowning their activities in general intelligence.

6. Lastly, a paradigm shift of sorts seems to have emerged in regarding the attribution of intelligence to heredity and environment. Genetic expression that occurs in the brain is distinctly led by environmental influences; the heredity-environment interactions are bidirectional. Added to this new knowledge is the accepted interaction between genes and the cultural context in which intelligence operates for an individual across the lifespan. Inadequate learning accumulates to cause intellectual deficiency. The world has changed since Galton suggested a general intelligence based on inheritance, as people now know that the vast majority of the world's children lack schooling and health care and have disrupted childhood due to wars and other disasters, much of which can be prevented by privileged nations. Should science still look for the true score in intelligence testing or promote the human values of compassion and a lack of greed for an equitable distribution of intelligence?

REFERENCES

Anderson, M. (1989). New ideas in intelligence. *The Psychologist, 3,* 92–94.

Anderson, M. (Ed.). (1999). *The development of intelligence.* Hove, England: Psychology Press.

Baker-Sennett, J., Matusov, E., & Rogoff, B. (1993). Planning as developmental process. In H.W. Reese (Ed.); *Advances in child development and behavior* (Vol. 24, pp. 253–281). San Diego, CA: Academic Press.

Baral, B.D. & Das, J.P. (in press). Intelligence: What is indigenous to India and what is shared? In R.J. Sternberg (Ed.); *International Handbook of Intelligence.*

Binet, A. & Henri, V. (1895). On the psychology of individual differences. *L'Annee Psychologique, 2,* 411–465.

Brody, N. (1994). Cognitive abilities. *Psychological Science, 5,* 63–68.

Burt, C. (1937). *The backward child.* London: London University Press.

Carroll, J.B. (1993). *Human cognitive abilities: Their survey of factor-analytic studies.* Cambridge, England: Cambridge University Press.

Cattell, R.B. (1971). *Abilities: Their structure, growth and action.* Boston, MA: Houghton-Mifflin.

Chorney, M.J., Chorney, K., Seese, N., Owen, M.J., Daniels, J., McGuffin, P., Thompson, L.A., Detterman, D.K., Benvow, C., Lubinski, D., Eley, T. & Plomin, R. (1998). A quantitative trait locus associated with cognitive ability in children. *Psychological Science, 9,* 159–166.

Cooper, C. (1999). *Intelligence and abilities.* New York, NY: Routledge.

Cronbach, L.J. (1957). The two disciplines of scientific psychology. *The American Psychologist, 12,* 671–684.

Daniel, M.H. (2000). Interpretation of intelligence test scores. In R.J. Sternberg (Ed.), *Handbook of intelligence* (pp. 477–491). Cambridge: Cambridge University Press.

Darlington, C.D. (1962). Introduction. In F. Galton (Ed.), *Hereditary genius: An inquiry into its laws and consequences.* Cleveland, OH: World Publishing.

Das, J.P. (1992). Beyond a unidimensional scale of merit. *Intelligence, 16,* 137–149.

Das, J.P. (1994). Eastern views on intelligence. In R.J. Sternberg (Ed.); *Encyclopedia of intelligence,* (pp. 387–391). New York, NY: Macmillan.

Das, J.P. (1999). *PASS reading enhancement program.* Deal, NJ: Sarka Educational Resources.

Das, J.P. (2002). A better look at intelligence. *Current Directions in Psychological Science, 11,* 28–32.

Das, J.P., Kar, B.C., & Parrila, R.K. (1996). *Cognitive planning: The psychological basis of intelligent behavior.* London: Sage Publications.

Das, J.P., Kirby, J.R., & Jarman, R. (1979). *Simultaneous and successive cognitive processes.* New York, NY: Academic.

Das, J.P., Mishra, R.K., & Pool, J.E. (1995). An experiment on cognitive remediation of word-reading difficulty. *Journal of Learning Disabilities, 28 (2),* 66–79.

Das, J.P., & Misra, S. (1995). Aspects of cognitive competence and managerial behavior. *The Journal of Entrepreneurship, 4,* 145–163.

Das, J.P., & Naglieri, J.A. (2001). The Das-Naglieri cognitive assessment system in theory and practice. In J.J.W. Andrews, D.H. Sakolfske, and H.L. Janzen (Eds.), *Handbook of psychoeducational assessment: Ability, achievement, and behavior in children* (pp. 34–64).

Das, J.P., Naglieri, J.A., & Kirby, J.R. (1994). *Assessment of cognitive processes.* Boston, MA: Allyn & Bacon.

Doerner, D. (1985). Thinking and organization of action. In J. Kuhl and J. Beckman (Eds.), *Action control: From cognition to behaviour.* Berlin: Springer Verlag.

Doerner, D. (1990). The logic of failure. *Philosophical Transactions of Royal Society of London, CCCXXVII.*

Eysenck, H.J. (1982). *A model for intelligence.* New York: Springer.

Eysenck, H.J. (1986). In R.J. Sternberg (Ed.), *Advance in human intelligence Vol. III.* Hillsdale, NJ: Lawrence Erlbaum Associates Inc.

Fodor, J.A. (1983). *The modularity of mind.* Cambridge, MA: MIT Press.

Frensch, P.A., & Buchner, A. (1999). Domain-generality versus domain-specificity in cognition. In R.J. Sternberg (Ed.), *The nature of cognition* (pp. 137–172). Cambridge, MA: MIT Press.

Frith, C.D. (1997). Linking brain and behavior. In R.S.J. Frackowiak, K.J. Friston, R.J. Dolan, & J.C. Mazziotta (Eds.), *Human brain function* (pp. 3–23). San Diego: Academic Press.

Gall, F. (1825). *Sur les functions du cerveau et sur cells de ses parties* (six volumes). Paris: Bailhere.

Galton, F. (1869). *Hereditary genius: An inquiry into its laws and consequence.* London: D. Appleton.

Gardner, H. (1983). *Frames of mind: The theory of multiple intelligences.* New York, NY: Basic Books.

Gardner, H. (1999). *Intelligence reframed: Multiple intelligence in the 21st century.* New York, NY: Basic Books.

Gazzaniga, M.S. (1988). Brain modularity: Towards a philosophy of conscious experience. In *Consciousness and Contemporary Science.* Marcel, A.J. & Bisiach, E. (Eds.) Oxford: Clarendon Press.

Geary, D.C. (2001). How much (or how many) does he have, and where did he get it? *Contemporary Psychology, 46,* 23–25.

Goldberg, E. (2001). *The executive brain: frontal lobes and the civilized mind.* Oxford: Oxford University Press.

Gottlieb, G. (1998). Normally occurring environmental and behavioral influences on gene activity: From central dogma to probabilistic epigenesis. *Psychological Review, 105,* 792–802.

Gould, S. (1981). *The mismeasure of man.* New York, NY: Norton.

Grigerenko, E.L. (1999). Heredity versus environment as the basis of cognitive ability. In R.J. Sternberg (Ed.), *The nature of cognition,* (pp. 665–696). Cambridge, MA: MIT Press.

Howe, M.J.A. (2001). Understanding abilities. *Contemporary Psychology, 46,* 31.

Humphreys, L. (1988). Trends in levels of academic achievement of blacks and other minorities. *Intelligence, 12,* (231–260).

Hunt, E. (2001). Multiple view of multiple intelligence. *Contemporary Psychology, 46,* (5–7).

Hunt, E., Lunneborg, C., & Lewis, J. (1975). What does it mean to be high verbal? *Cognitive Psychology, 7*, (pp. 194–227).

Jensen, A. (1981). *Straight talk about mental tests.* New York: The Free Press.

Jensen, A. (1982). Reaction time and psychometric g. In H.J. Eysenck (Ed.), *A model for intelligence.* Berlin: Springer.

Jensen, A. (1998). *The g factor: The science of mental ability.* New York: Praeger.

Jensen, A.R. (1980). Précis of bias in mental testing. *The Behavioral and Brain Sciences 3*, 325–371.

Kamin, L. (1974). *The science and politics of IQ.* New York, NY: Penguin Books.

Karmiloff-Smith, A. (1992). *Beyond modularity.* Cambridge, MA: MIT Press.

Kaufman, A.S. (2000). Tests of intelligence. In R.J. Sternberg (Ed.), *Handbook of intelligence,* (pp. 445–476). Cambridge: Cambridge University Press.

Kaufman, A.S., & Kaufman, N. (1983). *K-ABC interpretive manual.* Circle Pines, MN: American Guidance Services.

Kaufman, A.S., & Kaufman, N. (1993). Manual for Kaufman adolescent and adult intelligence test (KAIT). Circle Pines, MN: American Guidance Services.

Leont'ev, A.N. (1981). The problem of activity in psychology. In J.W. Werntsch (Ed.), *The concept of activity in Soviet psychology,* (pp. 37–71). Armok, NY: Sharpe.

Luria, A.R. (1966). *Human brain and psychological processes.* New York, NY: Harper & Row.

Luria, A.R. (1970). *Traumatic aphasia.* The Hague: Mouton.

Luria, A.R. (1973). *The working brain.* Harmondsworth, England: Penguin.

Luria, A.R. (1974). Language and brain: Towards the basic problems of neurolinguistics. *Brain and Language, 1*, 1–14.

Luria, A.R. (1976). *Cognitive development: Its cultural and social foundations.* Cambridge, MA: Harvard University Press.

Luria, A.R. (1980). *Higher cortical functions in man* (2nd ed.). New York, NY: Basic Books.

McCarthy, R.A. & Warrington, E.K. (1990). *Cognitive neuropsychology.* London: Academic Press.

Naglieri, J.A. (1999). *Essentials of CASAssessment.* New York: Wiley.

Naglieri, J.A. & Das, J.P. (1997). *Das-Naglieri Cognitive Assessment System.* Itasca, IL: Riverside Publishing Company.

Naglieri, J.A., & Das, J.P. (2002). Practical implications of general intelligence and PASS cognitive processes. In R.J. Sternberg & E. Grigorenko (Eds.), *The general factor of intelligence: How general is it?* (pp. 55–84). Mahwah, NJ: Lawrence Erlbaum Associates.

Nettlebeck, T. (1994). Speediness. In Sternberg, R.J. (Ed.), *Encyclopedia of human intelligence,* (pp. 1014–1019). New York, NY: MacMillan.

Posner, M. (1978). *Chronometric explorations of mind.* Hillsdale, NJ: Lawrence Erlbaum Associates, Inc.

Posner, M. & Mitchell, R.F. (1967). Chronometric analysis of classification. *Psychological Review, 74*, 392–409.

Rabbitt, P. (1988). Human intelligence. *The Quarterly Journal of Experimental Psychology, 40*, 167–185.

Radhakrishnan, S. (1948). *Bhagavad Gita.* London: George Allen & Unwin.

Radhakrishnan, S. (1953). *The Principal Upanishads.* (Chandogya Upanishad, Chapter 7, pp. 468–474). London: George Allen & Unwin.

Reed, T.E., & Jensen, A.R. (1992). Conduction velocity in a brain nerve pathway of normal adults correlates with intelligence level. *Intelligence, 16*, 259–272.

Reed, T.E., & Jensen, A.R (1993). Choice reaction time and visual pathway nerve conduction velocity both correlate with intelligence but appear not to correlate with each other: Implications for information processing. *Intelligence, 17*, pp. 191–203.

Sapir, S. & Nitzburg, A. (1973). *Children with learning problems* (p. 118). New York, NY: Brunner/Mazel.

Sechenov, I. (1956). *Selected physiological and psychological works* (Translated from Russian by S. Belsky). Moscow: Foreign Languages Publishing House.

Simon, H.A. (1967). Motivational and emotional controls of cognition. *Psychological Review, 74*, 29–39.

Simon, H.A. (1987). Making management decisions: The role of intuition and emotion. *The Academy of Management Executive, I-1*, 10–15.

Simon, H.A. (1992). What is an explanation of behaviour? *Psychological Science, 3*, 150–161.

Sokolowski, M.B., & Wahlsten, D. (2001). Gene-environment interaction and complex behavior. In H.R. Cin & S.O. Moldin, *Methods in genomic neuroscience.* Boca Ratan, FL.: CRC Press, (pp. 3–27).

Sparrow, S.S., & Davis, S.M. (2000). Recent advances in the assessment of intelligence and cognition. *Journal of Child Psychology and Psychiatry, 41*, 117–131.

Spearman, C. (1927). *Abilities of man.* London: Macmillan.

Srivastava, A.K., Tripathi, A.M., & Misra, G. (1995). Western and Indian perspectives on intelligence: Some reflections. *Indian Educational Review, 30*, 30–45.

Sternberg, R.J. (Ed.). (1985a). *Human abilities: An information processing approach.* New York, NY: W.H. Freeman.

Sternberg, R.J. (1985b). *Beyond I.Q.: A triarchic theory of human intelligence.* Cambridge: Cambridge University Press.

Sternberg, R.J. (1986). *Intelligence applied: Understanding and increasing your intellectual skills* (pp. 30). San Diego: Harcourt, Brace, Jovanovich.

Sternberg, R.J. (1990). *Metaphors of mind: Conceptions of the nature of intelligence.* New York, NY: Cambridge University Press.

Sternberg, R.J. (1994). Factor analytic data sets: What they tell us and don't tell us about human intelligence. *Psychological Science, 5*, 63.

Sternberg, R.J., & E. Grigorenko (Eds.) (2002). *The general factor of intelligence: How general is it?* Mahwah, NJ: Lawrence Erlbaum Associates.

Sternberg, R.J., & Kaufman, J.C. (1998). Human abilities. *Annual Review of Psychology 49,* 479–502.

Thatcher, R.W. (1992). Cyclic cortical reorganization during early childhood. *Brain and Cognition, 20,* 24–50.

Thurstone, L.L. (1938). Primary mental abilities. *Psychometric Monographs* (No. 1). Pp. 1–121.

Tyler, L. (1976). In L. Resnick (Ed.), *The nature of intelligence,* (p. 16). Hillsdale: Lawrence Erlbaum.

Tyler. L. (1976). The intelligence we test—an evolving concept. In Resnick, L. (Ed.), *The nature of intelligence.* (pp. 13–26). Hillsdale: Lawrence Erlbaum.

Tyler, L. (1986). Back to Spearman? *Journal of Vocational Behavior, 29,* 445–450.

Vernon, P.E. (1969). *Intelligence and cultural environment.* London: Methuen.

Vernon, P.J. (Ed.) (1987). *Speed of information-processing and intelligence.* Norwood, NJ: Ablex Publishing Corporation.

vom Saal, F.S. (1981). Variation in phenotype due to random intra-uterine positioning of male and female fetuses in rodents. *Journal of Reproduction and Fertility, 62,* 633–650.

Vygotsky, L.S. (1962). *Thought and language.* Cambridge, MA: MIT Press.

Wahlsten, D. (2002). The theory of biological intelligence: History and a critical appraisal. In R.J. Sternberg & E. Grigorenko (Eds.), *The general factor of intelligence: How general is it?* (pp. 245–247). Mahwah, NJ: Lawrence Erlbaum Associates.

CHAPTER 3

Relations Between Intelligence and Achievement Tests

MICHAEL C. RAMSAY AND CECIL R. REYNOLDS

Relationships between measures of intelligence and achievement are fundamental to the theory and practice of standardized psychological assessment. Practitioners use intelligence test results to predict achievement results. A discrepancy between the two may indicate the presence of a learning disability, thereby warranting intervention and special services for a student or other examinee. An intelligence test's ability to predict achievement results of any sort—test scores, school grades, or employee evaluations, for example—is cited as criterion-based evidence for the test's *validity,* defined later in this chapter. In addition, major issues such as test bias and racial and gender equity require, in part, an understanding of how intelligence test scores predict achievement for various groups of people (Reynolds & Ramsay, in press).

The practical importance, then, of the relationship between measured intelligence and achievement makes an understanding of it necessary for contemporary practitioners. Like all practical ramifications of science, this one rests on a theoretical position that intelligence and achievement are interrelated in the world at large. With respect to test results, this interrelatedness now has copious support from research (e.g., Roid, Prifitera, & Weiss, 1993; Weiss, Prifitera, & Roid, 1993), the indispensable link between theory and practice. Finally, an understanding of the relationships between intelligence and achievement measures is a major contributor—albeit a multifaceted and controversial one—to an understanding of the relationships of the constructs thought to underlie those measures.

INTELLIGENCE AND ACHIEVEMENT: THEIR NATURE AND INTERRELATIONS

Scientists frequently define intelligence, wholly or partly, as the ability to adapt to one's environment (Sattler, 1992). Ramsay (1997, 1998) has suggested that an added component is needed for specificity. A person's physical strength and attractiveness also increase adaptation but are distinct from intelligence. Thus, Ramsay defined intelligence as the ability to select responses that provide for adaptation to one's environment. This definition, drawn from an overarching selection model, appropriately makes intelligence an intellectual activity. The definition also allows additional, nonintellective characteristics to have a part in adaptation without creating a need to define them unrealistically as intelligence.

Intelligence is sometimes called *intellectual ability* or simply *ability.* Theorists have proposed, and researchers have reported, that intelligence is a set of relatively stable abilities, which change only slowly over time. Although intelligence can be seen as a potential, it does not appear to be an inherently fixed or unalterable characteristic. Rather, it varies around a central point. It can change in response to effective instruction, an appropriate intervention, or an educationally enriched home environment. In addition, intelligence is not a purely genetic capacity or, for that matter, a purely environmental one. Rather, contemporary psychologists and other scientists hold that intelligence results from a complex interaction of environmental and genetic influences. Despite more than one hundred years of research, this interaction remains poorly understood and detailed. Finally, intelligence is neither purely biological nor purely social in its origins.

Some authors have suggested that intelligence is whatever intelligence tests measure. This somewhat fatalistic observation stems from a misunderstanding of a key aspect of the scientific method, the principle of operational definition. According to this principle, researchers define the variables that they study by specifying the activities used to measure or otherwise obtain these variables (Gall, Borg, & Gall, 1996). Such definitions facilitate communication with other researchers and with research consumers (Christensen, 1988). Other researchers can then use the same definition, facilitating agreement as to what is being measured (Ramsay & Pashiardis, 2001). The primary operational definition of intelligence is a score from an accepted test or related measure of intelligence. Thus, a researcher might operationally define intelligence as participants' mean overall scores on the Kaufman Assessment Battery for Children (K-ABC; Kaufman & Kaufman, 1983a, 1983b). Misunderstanding develops when people take such operational definitions to be definitions in the conventional sense, leading to the truism that intelligence is what intelligence tests measure.

Intelligence tests should, of course, be measuring intelligence, but a scientific perspective requires that test developers define intelligence a priori, in such a way that researchers can gather evidence of various sorts and use it to evaluate the definition and the test derived from it. Does the definition accurately reflect an existing ability? How well does a particular test, as used with a particular population and purpose, conform to the definition? This two-part investigation provides evidence for *validity,* explained under "Validity and Relations Between Intelligence and Achievement Tests." The a priori definition of intelligence used by a test developer is much more complex and elaborate than an operational definition.

Test developers define intelligence, in part, as correlating with other variables—other aspects of life that are recognized as reflecting intelligence. Intelligence tests, then, are made up of tasks known to correlate with these variables, and the tests produce estimates of overall intelligence from performance on these tasks. Academic achievement is one of the most widely accepted of these aspects of life. Because achievement is expected to accompany intelligence, a test that corre-

lates with achievement has some evidence that it is measuring intelligence.

The number of abilities that collectively may be called intelligence is a current and growing source of controversy (see Chapter 1). The classical model consists of *g,* an overarching general ability, along with numerous *s*s, or highly specific abilities. The construct *g* has a central role in human activity and a sweeping influence over most or all intellectual processing. By contrast, *s*s are much more circumscribed, coming into play when specific tasks are undertaken. Increasingly, researchers have reported evidence for a number of intermediate abilities, such as verbal intelligence, perceptual organization, and processing speed. From the work of neuropsychologist Aleksandr Luria (1962–1980) have come simultaneous and sequential processing, now measured by two major intelligence tests, the K-ABC and the Cognitive Assessment System (CAS; Naglieri & Das, 1997). Such intermediate abilities have far-reaching roles in ability but have less sweeping influence than *g,* and they lack its central role. An alternative view that should be considered is that the generality of intellectual abilities, as evidenced by repeated demonstrations of its quantifiability, falls on a continuum. More general abilities are less numerous, and more specific ones, more numerous. Such an asymmetric pattern is called a *skewed distribution,* in this example, a positively skewed one.

A recent paradigm, and a major source of current controversy, posits that widely diverse abilities, such as musical and artistic abilities, are forms of intelligence. This paradigm, called *multiple intelligences*, challenges the generally accepted view. The paradigm has received a rocky reception among many scientists in the intelligence field, who have criticized it as lacking both empirical evidence and practical utility. By contrast, scientists and clinicians now take for granted the existence of intermediate abilities. Such abilities are now even built into commonly used intelligence tests, such as the various Wechsler and Kaufman scales. Most of the intermediate abilities mentioned previously, however, are general to many diverse activities and may best be characterized as a set of relatively general abilities.

In comparison with intelligence, achievement changes more rapidly; thus, it should be more responsive to interventions designed expressly to change it. Achievement acts as an interface between intelligence and the environment. As a flow of diverse environmental demands impinges upon a person, his or her intelligence responds by producing the skills needed to meet these demands. The schools require reading and mathematics activities; students respond with reading and mathematics achievement. Thus, the changeable character of achievement reflects the changing character of the environment. Although intelligence is hardly immutable, achievement changes the more readily of the two.

Correspondingly, researchers and clinicians can expect to see a difference between the two sets of characteristics when effective interventions are brought to bear on them: Achievement should change more, reducing the similarity and, therefore, the correlation between the two constructs. Furthermore, a relatively low correlation results, on the whole, in relatively low predictability. Thus, an intelligence test should predict achievement test results, but less well, in general, than it predicts results from other intelligence tests.

The desirability of this state of affairs depends upon the tester's goals. If a practitioner seeks to increase a client's achievement and intelligence, the latter should be the more difficult to change. The practitioner's target, however, is more often achievement alone. The relatively malleable nature of this construct means that a client's measurable intelligence is not a ceiling that prevents achievement from improving. By increasing achievement, a practitioner, client, and parent or teacher have beaten the prediction suggested by the intelligence test (Kaufman, 1979; Reynolds & Kaufman, 1990). This success would be impossible if intelligence, as stable as it is, were too good a predictor of achievement.

Whatever their goals, teachers and practitioners alike must avoid the problem of interventions targeted to the tests themselves. This practice is akin to buying a girl a snow cone, then taking her temperature and announcing that her fever has broken. The targeted test scores may increase, leaving the underlying characteristics largely unchanged. The increased scores then misleadingly suggest that the intervention has been successful, but the client continues to experience problems. Practitioners can no longer use the test to gauge accurately the effectiveness of the intervention.

VALIDITY AND RELATIONS BETWEEN INTELLIGENCE AND ACHIEVEMENT TESTS

An examination of relations between the types of tests examined here requires a basic understanding of *validity.* This term refers to the accuracy of interpretations made from test performance, with performance typically taking the form of scores. Theory and research findings should support these interpretations. For discussions of validity, see the most recent testing standards released by the American Educational Research Association, the American Psychological Association, and the National Council on Measurement in Education (AERA, APA, and NCME, 1999). See also Anastasi (1988); Ramsay and Reynolds (2000); and Ramsay, Reynolds, and Kamphaus (2002).

Many authors divide validity into types, with the three most widely recognized types being content, construct, and criterion validity. In this chapter, we take an approach similar to that of AERA, APA, and NCME (1999), which treat validity as a single, unitary concept. This concept is identical to the traditional idea of *construct validity,* defined by Anastasi (1988) as the extent to which a test's results measure a theoretical construct, such as an ability or a personality trait. Authors such as Anastasi have long held that this type of validity subsumes all the others. Evidence for the soundness of a test's construct definition is said to support construct validity, as is evidence that a test conforms to this definition.

We acknowledge classes of evidence for validity, rather than types of validity. *Evidence based on content* can include results that suggest that a test's items, item types, difficulty levels, and instructions cover an adequate sample of the behavior to be measured (Anastasi, 1988). Content-based evidence is important for all psychological and educational tests but is particularly central in researching achievement tests. A test interpreted as a measure of reading achievement should do more than measure reading. It should adequately sample the various aspects of reading achievement, such as decoding and comprehension (Anastasi, 1988).

Examinations of the relationships between intelligence tests and achievement tests generally focus on criterion-based evidence for validity and, particularly, on predictive evidence. *Evidence based on a criterion* supports the accuracy of assignments or predictions regarding an examinee's results on another measure, either of the same characteristic as the test being studied, or of a different characteristic. Scores on this outside measure are called a *criterion variable* or simply a criterion.

Test developers and users can subdivide criterion-based evidence into concurrent and predictive evidence. In studies of *concurrent evidence,* the criterion is available at the same time as the test results being assessed. A researcher may study a new version of a test by comparing it with older versions to investigate whether the results are fairly similar. Here, the researcher is likely to administer both versions at the same time, because a delay would be unnecessary and would even cloud the issue. In studies of *predictive evidence,* the criterion is available later. A clinician may examine students at a particular school to see if their intelligence results predict their achievement results. The clinician can administer the achievement test several years after the intelligence test to obtain evidence that the intelligence test is predictive over time. Here, a delay is useful. For further discussion of validity, see AERA, APA, and NCME (1999). For discussion of the three traditionally recognized types of validity, see Aiken (2000) and Groth-Marnat (1997).

Studies of criterion-based and other evidence of validity usually identify associations rather than causal relationships. When one variable is associated with another, it can also be used to predict it, although additional research is necessary to determine the degree of predictiveness. Researchers and practitioners can use ability test scores to predict achievement test scores, even in the unlikely event that the ability being measured has no effect on the type of achievement being measured. The question of causation is paramount in the sciences, but it is difficult to address, and evaluations of measuring instruments can proceed even if it is unanswered.

ASSOCIATIONS BETWEEN INTELLIGENCE AND ACHIEVEMENT TEST RESULTS

In this section we address empirical results for major intelligence and achievement measures, along with relevant results for lesser-known instruments. We focus primarily on standardized tests. Studies of nontest achievement measures, such as grade point average (GPA), are also available (e.g., concise reviews by Sattler, 2001). The review presented here is selective rather than exhaustive. Studies are included on the basis of relevance, methodological soundness, and a sample size of at least 30. In addition, recent studies are emphasized.

The Wechsler Intelligence Scale for Children– Third Edition

Sattler (2001) concisely reviewed 42 studies of the Wechsler Intelligence Scale for Children–Third Edition (WISC-III; Wechsler, 1991), analyzed with several intelligence and achievement tests and with school grades. Table 3.1 shows results with major achievement tests. Sattler found, in part, a mean correlation of $r = .54$ with measures of reading achievement and of $r = .64$ with measures of arithmetic achievement.

Lavin (1996) investigated the associations between scores from the WISC-III and the Kaufman Test of Educational Achievement (K-TEA; Kaufman & Kaufman, 1985), noting that both tests are commonly used to identify children for special education services. Participants were 72 children classified by their district special-education committees as emotionally handicapped and referred for placement in special schools. Most of these children had diagnoses of conduct disorder or oppositional defiant disorder. A smaller number had diagnoses of dissociative disorders. All participants resided in greater New York City. Most were male (49 vs. 23); 30 were White, 30 Black, and 12 Hispanic. Ages ranged from

TABLE 3.1   Correlations Between WISC-III IQs and Scores from Major Achievement Tests

WISC-III IQ Achievement Scale	Full Scale	Verbal	Performance
K-TEA			
Mathematics	.65	.57	.42
Reading	.53	.60	.19
WIAT			
Total Composite	.60	.62	.50
Reading Composite	.65	.50	.42
Mathematics Composite	.73	.69	.70
Language Composite	.57	.48	.15
Writing Composite	.56	.58	.45
WJ-R			
Broad Mathematics	.46	.54	.36
Broad Reading	.37	.47	.13
Broad Written Language	.47		
WRAT-III			
Arithmetic	.74	.72	.60
Spelling	.63	.58	.55
Reading	.65	.65	.55
WRAT-R			
Arithmetic	.32	.41	.34
Spelling	.15	.13	.12
Reading	.30	.25	.27

Note. For citations of individual studies, see Sattler (2001). WISC-III = Wechsler Intelligence Scale for Children–Third Edition, K-TEA = Kaufman Test of Educational Achievement, WIAT = Wechsler Individual Achievement Test, WJ-R = Woodcock-Johnson Revised, WRAT-III = Wide Range Achievement Test–Third Edition, WRAT-R = Wide Range Achievement Test–Revised. From Sattler (2001).

7 years to 16 years, with a mean of 13 years. The mean WISC-III Full Scale IQ was 88.9, SD = 13.9. K-TEA scores ranged from 85.4 for the Mathematics Composite to 89.9 for Reading Decoding.

Two statistically significant differences were found between achievement and ability scores. The K-TEA Mathematics Composite was lower than the WISC-III Full Scale and Verbal IQs, $t = 2.34$, $p < .05$ and $t = 2.91$, $p < .01$, respectively. These differences did not correspond to low correlations. Instead, K-TEA Spelling and the K-TEA reading scores showed low correlations with WISC-III Performance IQ. K-TEA Mathematics also showed low correlations with WISC-III Performance IQ. Table 3.2 presents these results.

The WISC-III Full Scale IQ was substantially associated with all K-TEA scores presented except Spelling when .40 was used as a cut-off score. Verbal IQ was substantially associated with all K-TEA scores, but Performance IQ, with the Mathematics Composite alone.

Clinicians may most usefully view these results (Lavin, 1996) as descriptive of the two tests when administered to emotionally handicapped students, rather than as suggesting diagnostic uses for the test. The statistically significant *t* val-

TABLE 3.2   Pearson Correlations Between WISC-III IQs and K-TEA Standard Scores

K-TEA Score	WISC-III IQ		
	Full Scale	Verbal	Performance
Subtest			
Math Applications	.66**	.64**	.37**
Math Computation	.54**	.52**	.27**
Spelling	.38**	.55**	.05
Reading Decoding	.51**	.63**	.13
Reading Comprehension	.53**	.67**	.10
Composite			
Mathematics	.65**	.57**	.42**
Reading	.53**	.60**	.19

Note. From Lavin (1996).
*$p < .05$. **$p < .01$.

ues found are too small to be useful in diagnosing emotional handicaps. They do, however, suggest further investigation, because they differ from the Pearson coefficients reported. For comparison, corresponding results with students not classified as having emotional handicaps or other learning disabilities would be informative.

Slate (1994) analyzed the relationship between WISC-III Full Scale, Verbal, and Performance IQs and subtest scores from the Wechsler Individual Achievement Test (WIAT; Wechsler, 1992). The 476 participants consisted of 202 students with specific learning disabilities (SLD), 115 with mental retardation (MR), and 159 who did not meet requirements for special services. All participants were White students in northeastern Arkansas school districts. All were referred and evaluated for special services.

Of the SLD students, 130 were male, 41 were female, and 31 were of unidentified gender. The mean age was 11 years 4 months, SD = 2–8. The mean Full Scale IQ was 84.6, SD = 9.0. Of the MR students, 53 were male, 41 were female, and 21 were unidentified. The mean age was 11 years 5 months, SD = 2–7. The mean Full Scale IQ was 60.0,

SD = 8.9. Of the remaining students, 83 were male, 57 were female, and 19 were unidentified. The mean age was 9 years 8 months, SD = 2–11, and the mean Full Scale IQ was 79.9, SD = 9.7. Thus, the Full Scale IQs of all three groups showed reduced variability.

WISC-III Full Scale IQ produced its highest correlations with WIAT Reading Comprehension, Mathematics Reasoning, Numerical Operations, and Listening Comprehension, with the exception of Reading Comprehension for the MR students. WISC-III Verbal IQ also showed this pattern, adding high correlations with Basic Reading for the SLD and MR students and with Written Expression for the MR students. WISC-III Performance IQ produced the lowest correlations, but relatively higher ones with Numerical Operations for SLD students; Mathematics Reasoning, Numerical Operations, and Listening Comprehension for MR students; and Mathematics Reasoning and Numerical Operations for the remaining students. Performance IQ showed negligible correlations with Basic Reading both for SLD students and for remaining students. The correlation representing Full Scale or Verbal IQ, and nearly always both, consistently showed an advantage over the corresponding correlation with Performance IQ. These results appear in Table 3.3.

Two richly reported studies using nationally representative samples addressed the relationships between WISC-III results and achievement scores. Among the results reported by Roid et al. (1993) were correlations between factor indices from the WISC-III and standard scores from WIAT subtests. Participants were 1,118 children used in the standardization of the WIAT. This stratified, nationally representative sample included approximately 100 children at each full year of age from 6 to 16. In this sample, 51.0% of participants were male and 49.0% were female. In addition, 75.6% were White; 12.4% were Black; 9.9% were Hispanic; and 2.0% were other. For additional demographic data, see Roid et al.

The Verbal Comprehension factor produced the highest correlations with WIAT subtest standard scores; the Freedom

TABLE 3.3   Corrected Correlations Between WISC-III IQs and WIAT Subtests

WIAT Subtest	Full Scale IQ			Verbal IQ			Performance IQ		
	SLD	MR	NSE	SLD	MR	NSE	SLD	MR	NSE
Basic Reading	.55	.60	.24	.70	.71	.36	.04	.41	−.06
Reading Comprehension	.76	.62	.78	.74	.61	.73	.46	.34	.48
Mathematics Reasoning	.79	.89	.85	.78	.90	.76	.58	.63	.64
Numerical Operations	.76	.83	.73	.63	.87	.55	.58	.63	.64
Spelling	.58	.57	.63	.64	.65	.59	.16	.36	.40
Listening Comprehension	.67	.72	.76	.66	.70	.66	.42	.66	.38
Oral Expression	.60	.62	.52	.65	.63	.53	.31	.33	.19
Written Expression	.62	.61	.37	.57	.77	.41	.36	.42	.06
Mean	.67	.68	.61	.59	.73	.57	.35	.48	.36

Note. From Slate (1994).

TABLE 3.4   Correlations Between WISC-III Factor Indexes and WIAT Subtest Standard Scores

	WISC-III Factor Index			
WIAT Composite	Verbal Comprehension	Perceptual Organization	Freedom from Distractibility	Processing Speed
Reading	.72	.49	.65	.43
Mathematics	.69	.54	.71	.47
Language	.61	.44	.49	.35
Writing	.57	.33	.58	.46

Note. WISC-III = Wechsler Intelligence Scale for Children–Third Edition, WIAT = Wechsler Individual Achievement Test. From Roid, Prifitera, and Weiss (1993).
All $p < .001$.

from Distractibility factor also produced substantial correlations. Results for Perceptual Organization and Processing Speed were lower. The highest correlations were those of WISC-III Verbal Comprehension and Freedom from Distractibility with WIAT Reading and Mathematics Composites. Table 3.4 shows these results.

These correlations were similar in rank order to those between the WISC-III and group achievement tests for the WISC-III norming sample (Wechsler, 1991, Table 6.18). Here, Full Scale IQ and Verbal IQ produced the highest correlations, as did reading achievement compared to mathematics, written language, and total achievement. In the four-factor solution, the Verbal Comprehension Index produced the highest correlations, followed by the Freedom from Distractibility and Perceptual Organization Indexes, respectively. For this analysis, the sample consisted of 358 children aged 6–16 years, Mdn = 11 years. The sample was 46% male and 54% female, as well as 76% White, 10% Black, 12% Hispanic, and 2% other.

In addition, Weiss et al. (1993) investigated slope and intercept bias in WISC-III FSIQ prediction of reading, mathematics and writing achievement scores, along with school grades in reading, mathematics, and English. The achievement scores used were normal curve equivalents (NCEs) from the Comprehensive Test of Basic Skills, Form U (CTBS; CTB/McGraw-Hill, 1987; $n = 177$), the Iowa Test of Basic Skills, Form G (ITBS; Hieronymus & Hoover, 1986; $n = 233$), the California Achievement Test, Form E (CAT; CTB/McGraw-Hill, 1988; $n = 121$), the Metropolitan Achievement Test, Sixth Edition, Form L (MAT; Prescott, Balow, Hogan, & Farr, 1986; $n = 61$), and the Stanford Achievement Test, Edition 7 Plus, Form E (SAT; Gardner et al., 1987; $n = 108$). Pothoff's Formula 1 permitted the researchers to investigate slopes and intercepts simultaneously. Participants for this portion of the study were 700 children aged 6 to 16 years, Mdn = 11 years, selected to be nationally representative by ethnicity, gender, and parental education level. The sample comprised 74.7% Whites, 14.7% Blacks, and

10.6% Hispanics, with each ethnic group evenly divided by gender.

F values were small for comparisons between White and Black children, between White and Hispanic children, and between boys and girls. Reading and writing NCEs in the White-Hispanic and male-female comparisons were somewhat larger than the others. All F values were statistically nonsignificant, $p < .01$. See Table 3.5 for these results.

Weiss et al. (1993) also obtained correlations between WISC-III IQ and NCE scores for Whites, Blacks, and Hispanics and for males and females. Correlations were highest for reading NCEs, followed by mathematics and writing NCEs, respectively. This pattern held for all groups except Hispanics, whose correlation for reading NCEs was lower than those of the other groups investigated; see Table 3.6. Correlations between WISC-III IQ and school grades in reading, mathematics, and English showed less consistency than the results with NCEs; Hispanics had lower correlations than the other groups. For these results, see Weiss et al. In addition, see Reynolds and Ramsay (in press) for a well-written treatment of ethnic bias in ability tests, including issues and findings.

Results obtained by Teeter and Smith (1993) included correlations between WISC-III factor scores and Woodcock-

TABLE 3.5   Simultaneous Comparison of Slopes and Intercepts for Paired Ethnic and Gender Groups in the Prediction of Group Achievement Scores from WISC-III Full Scale IQ

	Pairing					
	White-Black		White-Hispanic		Male-Female	
NCE Score	F	df	F	df	F	df
Reading	.49	2,602	4.30	2,575	3.97	2,667
Writing	2.40	2,282	.29	2,289	.74	2,333
Mathematics	2.76	2,592	1.28	2,563	.18	2,665

Note. WISC-III = Wechsler Intelligence Scale for Children–Third Edition, NCE = normal curve equivalent. From Weiss, Prifitera, and Roid (1993). All $p < .001$. F values from Pothoff's Formula 1.

TABLE 3.6   Correlations Between WISC-III Full Scale IQ and Achievement Test NCEs by Ethnic and Gender Group

| | Group | | | | | | | | | |
| | White | | Black | | Hispanic | | Male | | Female | |
NCE Score	r	n	r	n	r	n	r	n	r	n
Reading	.658[a]	505	.707[a]	101	.520[a]	74	.692[a]	323	.670[a]	348
Writing	.474[a]	242	.499[b]	44	.469[c]	51	.493[a]	163	.526[a]	174
Mathematics	.601[a]	494	.575[a]	102	.566[a]	73	.610[a]	328	.624[a]	341

Note. WISC-III = Wechsler Intelligence Scale for Children–Third Edition, NCE = normal curve equivalent. From Weiss, Prifitera, and Roid (1993).
[a]$p = .0001$. [b]$p = .0006$. [c]$p = .0005$.

Johnson–Revised (WJ-R; Woodcock & Johnson, 1989) Fluid Reasoning scores. Although Fluid Reasoning is part of the WJ-R Tests of Cognitive Abilities, some authors (e.g., Shinn, Algozzine, Marston, & Ysseldyke, 1982; Thompson & Brassard, 1984; as cited in Teeter et al., 1983) have characterized these cognitive tests as achievement oriented (an interpretation with which we agree). Participants were 30 students with severe emotional disturbance (ED) and 30 controls. All participants were male, aged 11 to 16 years, and in Grades 6 to 10. Mean ages were 171.73 months for the ED group and 166.80 for controls. Mean grade levels were 7.47 for the ED group and 8.17 for controls. Finally, ED participants included 11 Whites, 18 Blacks, and 1 Hispanic; control participants included 12 Whites and 18 Blacks. ED diagnoses were conduct disorders, $n = 12$; comorbid conduct disorders and attention deficit hyperactivity disorders, $n = 8$; oppositional and sexual acting out disorders, $n = 7$; and comorbid attention deficit hyperactivity disorders and depression, $n = 3$.

The WISC-III factor score correlating highest with WJ-R Fluid Reasoning was Perceptual Organization for the ED group but Verbal Comprehension for the control group. Correlations for the ED group were $r = .57$, Verbal Comprehension; $r = .71$, Perceptual Organization; $r = .42$, Freedom From Distractibility; and $r = .56$, Processing Speed. The corresponding correlations for the control group were $r = .70$, $r = .66$, $r = .63$, and $r = .51$.

Earlier Versions of the Wechsler Intelligence Scale for Children

A study by Figueroa and Sassenrath (1989) produced moderate correlations between IQs on the Wechsler Intelligence Scale for Children–Revised (WISC-R; Wechsler, 1974) and achievement results obtained ten years later. The participants were the 2,100 public school students in California, aged 5–11 years, who made up the standardization sample of the System of Multicultural Pluralistic Assessment (SOMPA; Mercer, 1979). The sample at retest consisted of 1,184 par-

ticipants, aged 13–19 years, including 439 Anglos, 384 Hispanics, 361 Blacks, and nearly equal numbers of males and females. Missing data made the sample size fluctuate slightly across analyses. The scores used were the WISC-R Full Scale, Verbal, and Performance IQs, and the Reading Comprehension and Mathematics subtests of the Stanford Test of Academic Skills (TASK; Gardner, Callis, Merwin, & Madden, 1972).

The researchers (Figueroa et al., 1989) also obtained results for the SOMPA Physical Dexterity tasks but did not report them because they were extremely low (all $r < .10$). For the SOMPA, Adaptive Behavior Inventory for Children, and the Bender Gestalt Test, the report noted statistical significance levels but not effect sizes. Therefore, this chapter addresses only the WISC-R results. The Estimated Learning Potential, a SOMPA correction of WISC-R results, is mentioned briefly. For correlations between the three WISC-R IQs and five GPA measures, see Figueroa et al.

As shown in Table 3.7, correlations were consistently higher for Full Scale and Verbal IQ than for Performance IQ. In addition, the WISC-R correlations with Stanford Reading

TABLE 3.7   Correlations Between 1972 WISC-R IQs and 1982 Stanford TASK Achievement Results for Three Ethnic Groups and the Total Sample

| | | WISC-R IQ | | |
Achievement Score	Group	Full Scale	Verbal	Performance
Reading	Anglo	.55	.55	.43
	Black	.49	.50	.36
	Hispanic	.60	.58	.49
	Total	.64	.62	.53
Mathematics	Anglo	.54	.51	.44
	Black	.53	.50	.46
	Hispanic	.52	.49	.44
	Total	.61	.58	.53

Note. WISC-R = Wechsler Intelligence Scale for Children–Revised, TASK = Test of Academic Skills. From Figueroa and Sassenrath (1989). All $p < .05$.

scores were higher for Hispanics than for Whites and somewhat lower for Blacks than for Whites. WISC-R correlations with Stanford Mathematics scores, however, were consistent for the three ethnic groups. The most notable results were the consistency and moderate size of the correlations, despite the 10-year interval between test and retest. Finally, as Figueroa et al. (1989) mentioned, the Verbal IQ Estimated Learning Potential of the SOMPA correlated more highly than uncorrected Verbal IQs ($r = .60$ & $.58$ vs. $r = .53$ & $.52$) with Stanford Reading and Mathematics scores, respectively, for Black students in the lowest quartile of the SOMPA Sociocultural scales. The corrected Verbal IQ also produced higher correlations with the GPA measures reported.

Brock (1982) conducted a joint factor analysis of standard scores from the WISC-R, the Peabody Individual Achievement Test (PIAT; Dunn & Markwardt, 1970), and the Wide Range Achievement Test (WRAT; Jastak & Jastak, 1965). The 183 participants were males identified as learning disabled. All were students enrolled in Grades 3–6 in rural Louisiana. Brock reported that the students ranged in age from 8 to 12 years and were predominantly White. Their average WISC-R Full Scale IQ was 89.38, SD = 9.12. The extraction procedure used was principal factors, and the rotation procedures were varimax and oblimin. We have presented the varimax results here because all factors appeared strong in this solution. A conceptually important factor, the third, was weak in the oblimin solution. Both solutions, however, led to the same interpretations.

We interpreted the results as follows, largely in agreement with Brock (1982). Factor 1 was a distinct achievement factor, reflecting linguistic abilities, and Factor 2, a distinct Perceptual Organization or Simultaneous Processing ability factor. The third factor appeared to be Verbal Comprehension or Semantic Processing, an ability factor, consistent with our interpretation of Keith and Novak's (1987) results, addressed under, "Multiple Intelligence Tests." A PIAT achievement subtest, General Information, also correlated highly with this factor. Finally, the fourth factor did not clearly reflect achievement or ability, because WISC-R Arithmetic, PIAT Mathematics, and WRAT Arithmetic correlated highly with it. The WRAT did not produce a separate achievement factor as it did in Keith et al. The reason may be that WRAT Reading Recognition could not be included in the analysis. Thus, the analysis produced only partial and equivocal evidence for a distinction between ability and achievement. Table 3.8 shows these results.

Simpson (1982) obtained correlations between Full Scale IQs from the Wechsler Intelligence Scale for Children–Revised (WISC-R) and the General Information subtest of the PIAT. The 144 participants ranged in age from 12 years 2

TABLE 3.8   Results of a Principal Factor Analysis[a] of WISC-R, PIAT, and WRAT Scores

Variable	Factor			
	1	2	3	4
Spelling (PIAT)	.88			
Reading Recognition (PIAT)	.87			
Reading Comprehension (PIAT)	.82			
Spelling (WRAT)	.81			
Picture Arrangement (WISC-R)		.75		
Picture Completion (WISC-R)		.71		
Block Design (WISC-R)		.54		
General Information (PIAT)			.74	
Information (WISC-R)			.73	
Comprehension (WISC-R)			.71	
Vocabulary (WISC-R)			.64	
Similarities (WISC-R)			.57	
Coding (WISC-R)			.42	
Arithmetic (WISC-R)				.79
Mathematics (PIAT)				.64
Arithmetic (WRAT)				.61

Note. Correlations of .40 and above are shown. WISC-R = Wechsler Intelligence Scale for Children–Revised, PIAT = Peabody Individual Achievement Test, WRAT = Wide Range Achievement Test. From Brock (1982).
[a]Varimax rotation.

months to 11 years 11 months. They were divided into two groups, mentally retarded (Full Scale IQ ≤ 75, $n = 95$) and non-retarded (Full Scale IQ > 75, $n = 49$).

The two groups differed markedly, with a correlation of $r = .60$ for the nonretarded group but $r = .05$ for the mentally retarded group. In addition, correlations were relatively consistent for nonretarded subgroups but inconsistent for retarded subgroups. Among the latter, only the correlation for Whites, $r = .43$, was substantial. These results suggested two possible interpretations. If the inconsistency was due to small sample sizes, the PIAT may be inappropriate for examinees with mental retardation. If not, the PIAT may be appropriate for Whites, but not Blacks, with mental retardation. Table 3.9 shows the results.

Wikoff (1978) conducted an exploratory factor analysis of the WISC-R with the PIAT, also examining the PIAT alone. Participants were 180 children, 123 male and 57 female, referred because of learning problems. Nearly all were described in terms suggestive of hyperactivity or distractibility. Participants' ages ranged from 6 years to 17 years, Mdn = 9.87, M = 10.1. No participants were minority children, and most were middle class.

Results for the PIAT alone suggested two factors. Reading Recognition, Reading Comprehension, and Spelling correlated with a factor that Wikoff (1978) labeled Word Recognition. Structure coefficients were .91, .73, and .70, respectively. General Information and Mathematics correlated with a fac-

TABLE 3.9   Correlations Between WISC-R Full Scale IQ and PIAT General Information for Retarded and Non-Retarded Groups

Subgroup	n	r
Nonretarded Group		
Males	59	.63*
Females	36	.54*
Whites	79	.56*
Blacks	16	.57*
Total	95	.60*
Retarded Group		
Males	31	.10
Females	18	−.04
Whites	22	.43
Blacks	27	−.17
Total	49	.05

Note. WISC-R = Wechsler Intelligence Scale for Children–Revised, PIAT = Peabody Individual Achievement Test. From Simpson (1982).
*$p < .01$.

tor that Wikoff labeled School-Related Knowledge. Structure coefficients were .71 and .66, respectively. Reading Comprehension and Spelling also correlated with this factor at .50 and .40.

Results for the WISC-R and the PIAT together included Wikoff's (1978) Word Recognition factor alongside the three factors typically found for the WISC-R and labeled Verbal Comprehension, Perceptual Organization, and Freedom from Distractibility. General Information correlated with the Verbal Comprehension factor, however, and Mathematics correlated with Freedom from Distractibility together with the WISC-R Arithmetic subtest. Because the Verbal Comprehension factor tends to subsume Freedom from Distractibility in two-factor solutions, additional research is needed to interpret these results with confidence. The PIAT may be measuring its own Word Recognition factor, as suggested by Wikoff, and a Verbal Comprehension factor shared with the WISC-R. If so, perhaps only the three PIAT Word Recognition subtests need to be administered when the WISC-R is also being administered. Researchers and clinicians might also explore possible discrepancies between a School-Related Knowledge composite and the Wechsler Verbal IQ.

In addition, the Freedom from Distractibility factor may be a numerical (Wikoff, 1978) or symbolic factor. Arithmetic, Digit Span, and Coding correlate with this factor. Stedman, Lawlis, Cortner, and Achterberg (1978), for example, reported that Coding correlated highest at .94, followed by Digit Span at .42, Arithmetic at .40, and Object Assembly at .36. In Stedman et al., it should be noted, 90% of the participants had Spanish surnames.

Ollendick and Ollendick (1976) investigated, in part, the association between Wechsler Intelligence Scale for Children (WISC; Wechsler, 1949) scores and PIAT scores. The report

described the 45 participants as "male delinquents" (p. 1112) of low to lower-middle socioeconomic status. The mean age was 14.57 years, and the mean WISC Full Scale IQ was 91.75. WISC Full Scale IQs correlated highly at $r = .70$, $p < .01$, with total PIAT scores.

The report by Stedman et al. (1978) presented, in part, correlations between scores from the WISC-R and the WRAT. The sample consisted of 106 students referred for evaluation because of learning or classroom behavioral problems. Of these students, 76 were male and 30 were female. Their ages ranged from 6 to 13 years, M = 9.5, and their grade levels were 1 to 8. Their IQs—probably WISC-R IQs—were 60 to 118, M = 88.1, SD = 13.1. As noted previously, 90% of the participants had Spanish surnames; 8% were Anglo; 2% were Black. The students attended parochial schools administered by the Archdiocese of San Antonio.

A principal components analysis with varimax rotation produced factor scores; the authors (Stedman et al., 1978) then obtained Pearson correlations between these scores and WRAT standard scores. Not surprisingly, WISC-R Verbal Comprehension factor scores correlated most highly with WRAT Reading and Spelling results. Similarly, WISC-R Freedom from Distractibility factor scores correlated most highly with WRAT Arithmetic results. Perceptual Organization factor scores produced low correlations. Only the correlation representing Verbal Comprehension and Reading reached or exceeded a cut-score of .40. Table 3.10 shows these correlations.

Wechsler Tests of Adult Intelligence

The Technical Manual of the Wechsler Adult Intelligence Scale–Third Edition and Wechsler Memory Scale–Third Edition (WAIS-III and WMS-III; Psychological Corporation, 1997) presents correlations between WAIS-III and WIAT composite scores. Correlations are highest for WAIS-III and Verbal Full Scale IQs, and generally for the WAIS-III Verbal Comprehension and Working Memory Indexes. Among WIAT

TABLE 3.10   Correlations Between WISC-R Factor Scores and WRAT Standard Scores

	WRAT Score		
WAIS-R Factor	Reading	Spelling	Arithmetic
Verbal Comprehension	.44**	.38**	.20*
Perceptual Organization	.19**	.17*	.10
Freedom from Distractibility	.04	.14	.37**

Note. WISC-R = Wechsler Intelligence Scale for Children–Revised, WRAT = Wide Range Achievement Test. From Stedman, Lawlis, Cortner, and Achterberg (1978).
*$p < .05$. **$p < .005$.

TABLE 3.11 Correlations Between WAIS-III and WIAT Composite Scores

WIAT Composite	WAIS-III IQ			WAIS-III Index Score			
	Verbal	Performance	Full Scale	VC	PO	WM	PS
Reading	.79	.61	.76	.77	.55	.72	.54
Mathematics	.81	.69	.81	.70	.65	.75	.56
Language	.70	.53	.68	.65	.45	.42	.48
Writing	.69	.55	.68	.65	.46	.69	.60

Note. N = 142. All correlations were corrected for the variability of the WAIS-III norming sample. WAIS-III = Wechsler Adult Intelligence Scale–Third Edition, WIAT = Wechsler Individual Achievement Test, VC = Verbal Comprehension, PO = Perceptual Organization, WM = Working Memory, PS = Processing Speed. From Psychological Corporation (1997).

scores, Mathematics produced the highest correlations, followed in turn by Reading, Writing, and Language. See Table 3.11 for these results. For correlations with WIAT subtests, see Psychological Corporation (1997).

Sattler (2001) reviewed these results, along with correlations between WAIS-III IQs and years of education with adults aged 25 years and older from the standardization sample (Tulsky and Ledbetter, 2000). WAIS-III Full Scale IQ correlated at .55 with years of education, as compared with .55 for Verbal IQ and .46 for Performance IQ.

A study by Spruill and Beck (1986) produced relatively high Pearson correlations between Full Scale, Verbal, and Performance IQs from the Wechsler Adult Intelligence Scale–Revised (WAIS-R; Wechsler, 1981) and standard scores from the Wide Range Achievement Test–Revised (WRAT-R; Jastak & Wilkinson, 1984), Level II. The 45 participants were clients referred for psychological evaluation to the Psychological Clinic at the University of Alabama. Participants' mean age was 24 years, SD = 7 years; 28 were female and 17 were male; 13 were White, and 32, Black. The mean WAIS-R Full Scale IQ was 76.60.

Table 3.12 shows the Pearson coefficients obtained. The results indicated that, for this sample, all WAIS-R IQs were substantially and about equally associated with WRAT-R standard scores. In addition, the association was strongest for WRAT-R Reading scores, followed by Arithmetic and Spelling scores, respectively.

Cooper and Fraboni (1988) reported Pearson correlations between scores on the same two instruments. The sample for this study was larger, consisting of 121 adults referred by insurance companies and rehabilitation agencies to a private practitioner for evaluation. Participants consisted of 80 males and 41 females. Their ages ranged from 19 to 58 years, M = 34.85, SD = 8.49. Their mean years of education were 10.26, SD = 1.68, and their mean WAIS-R Full Scale IQ was 93.09. Finally, their mean Verbal IQ of 91.95 was somewhat lower than their mean Performance IQ of 96.33.

The correlations found were lower than Spruill and Beck's (1986) for WRAT-R Reading and Arithmetic Composites but about the same for the WRAT-R Spelling Composite. Of note, the standard deviations of the three WAIS-R IQs were small, SD = 8.06, 8.70, and 8.70, respectively. This low variability may have reduced the observed correlations. Table 3.13 shows these results.

Cooper et al. (1988) also presented Pearson correlations between WAIS-R subtests and WRAT-R standard scores. In brief, these correlations were similar for WRAT-R Reading, with a range of .20–.54 and a median of .31, and WRAT-R Spelling, with a range of .16–.52 and a median of .34. Digit Span correlated the highest with both WRAT-R scores at $r = .54$ and $r = .52$, respectively. High correlations also accompanied Information at $r = .44$ and $r = .38$, Vocabulary at $r = .36$ and $r = .34$, and Similarities at $r = .34$ and $r = .38$. Digit Symbol, however, correlated notably lower with

TABLE 3.12 Pearson Correlations Between WAIS-R IQs and WRAT-R Scores as Reported by Spruill and Beck

WAIS-R IQ	WRAT-R Composite		
	Reading	Spelling	Arithmetic
Verbal	.70	.50	.60
Performance	.68	.47	.57
Full Scale	.71	.50	.60

Note. WAIS-R = Wechsler Adult Intelligence Scale–Revised, WRAT-R = Wide Range Achievement Test–Revised. From Spruill and Beck (1986). All $p < .01$ [sic].

TABLE 3.13 Pearson Correlations Between WAIS-R IQs and WRAT-R Scores as Reported by Cooper and Fraboni

WAIS-R IQ	WRAT-R Composite		
	Reading	Spelling	Arithmetic
Verbal	.53	.50	.46
Performance	.46	.45	.25
Full Scale	.56	.53	.43

Note. WAIS-R = Wechsler Adult Intelligence Scale–Revised, WRAT-R = Wide Range Achievement Test–Revised. From Cooper and Fraboni (1988). All $p < .01$ [sic].

Reading at $r = .20$ than with Spelling at $r = .36$. Correlations with WRAT-R Arithmetic were relatively low, ranging from $r = -.07$ for Object Assembly to $r = .39$ for WAIS-R Arithmetic. The median was .20. Information correlated at $r = .38$.

Finally, Cooper et al. (1988) presented multiple regression results obtained with the stepwise method of variable selection. WAIS-R Full Scale IQ served as the dependent variable and the three WRAT-R standard scores were the independent variables, reversing the usual direction of the analysis. R^2 was .43. Reading accounted for 32% of the variance among Full Scale IQs, Arithmetic for 8%, and Spelling for 3%. Caution is warranted in interpreting these results, because the stepwise method can lead to distortion or exaggeration.

The Kaufman Assessment Battery for Children

The Interpretive Manual of the Kaufman Assessment Battery for Children (K-ABC; Kaufman et al., 1983b) presented concurrent and predictive evidence for validity with achievement measures. In a study with 592 normal children, K-ABC Achievement standard scores produced notably higher correlations than K-ABC Sequential, Simultaneous, Mental Processing, and Nonverbal standard scores with Passage Comprehension results from the Woodcock Reading Mastery Tests (WRMT; Woodcock, 1987). In another study with 544 normal children, a similar difference emerged when these K-ABC scores were analyzed with the KeyMath Diagnostic Arithmetic Test (KMDAT; Connolly, Nachtman, & Pritchett, 1976). Correlations were generally lower in the second study, perhaps as a consequence of reduced standard deviations (SD = 9.0–10.3) or lower reliability or validity associated with the criterion.

Reports of both studies included a breakdown by ethnic group. K-ABC scores correlated more highly with WRMT scores for White examinees than for Black examinees. Sequential scores produced their lowest correlations with Hispanic examinees, who showed higher correlations on the remaining K-ABC scores, their highest. K-ABC scores correlated more highly with KMDAT scores for Black examinees than White, except that K-ABC Achievement produced equal correlations. Coefficients varied for Hispanics, but were highest for K-ABC Sequential and Achievement standard scores and lowest or intermediate for Simultaneous, Mental Processing, and Nonverbal standard scores. Table 3.14 shows these results.

The Interpretive Manual (Kaufman et al., 1983b) also reviewed correlations between K-ABC scores and achievement test results obtained 6 to 12 months later. Studies with sample sizes of at least 30 included one with culturally different

TABLE 3.14 Correlations of K-ABC Global Scale Standard Scores with WRMT Passage Comprehension and KMDAT Written Computation Achievement Scores by Ethnic Group

K-ABC Scale	White	Black	Hispanic	Total
WRMT Passage Comprehension				
Sequential Processing	.52	.48	.45	.53
Simultaneous Processing	.52	.50	.61	.56
Mental Processing	.60	.56	.70	.63
Achievement	.80	.78	.89	.82
Nonverbal	.56	.51	.61	.58
KMDAT Written Computation				
Sequential Processing	.28	.30	.43	.34
Simultaneous Processing	.39	.45	.38	.44
Mental Processing	.41	.47	.45	.47
Achievement	.54	.54	.62	.59
Nonverbal	.39	.48	.43	.46

Note. K-ABC = Kaufman Assessment Battery for Children, WRMT = Woodcock Reading Mastery Tests, KMDAT = KeyMath Diagnostic Arithmetic Test. From Kaufman and Kaufman (1983b).

Navajos, $n = 30$, and two with participants identified as normal, $n = 31$ and $n = 45$. With all three samples, K-ABC Achievement scores produced higher correlations than the remaining K-ABC composites. For culturally different Navajos, Sequential Processing correlated highest with PIAT Reading Recognition, Reading Comprehension, Mathematics, and Total scores. Simultaneous Processing and Nonverbal scores correlated highest with PIAT Mathematics.

For normal participants in one group, $n = 45$, Sequential Processing scores produced their highest correlations with CAT Total Reading scores, as did Simultaneous Processing and Nonverbal scores. For normal participants in the other group, $n = 31$, Sequential Processing produced its highest correlations with the WJ-R Preschool Cluster, and the remaining K-ABC scores, with the WJ-R Knowledge Cluster (Kaufman et al., 1983b). Table 3.15 shows results of these three studies.

In a well-designed and generally well-reported study, Hooper (1987) investigated the relationship between results from the K-ABC and the Stanford Achievement Test (SAT; Madden, Gardner, Rudman, Karlsen, & Merwin, 1973), with 87 reading disabled children. These participants ranged in age from 8 years, 4 months through 12 years, 5 months, M = 10–6, SD = 1–4. They were enrolled in Grades 2–6, M = 4.9, SD = 1.3. The children included 48 boys and 39 girls, of whom 82 were White and 5 were Black.

The children were selected from a group of 183 participants in a reading disability program. Hooper's (1987) selection criteria were intellectual ability in the average range (85–115) on the Short Form Test of Academic Aptitude (SFTAA; Sullivan, Clark, & Tiegs, 1970) and reading recognition at

TABLE 3.15 Correlations Between K-ABC Global Scale Standard Scores and Achievement Test Scores Obtained Later

Achievement Scale	K-ABC Global Scale				
	Sequential Processing	Simultaneous Processing	Mental Processing	Achievement	Nonverbal
Study 1 (N = 30,[a] interval = 10 months)					
PIAT					
Mathematics	.35	.62	.60	.67	.48
Reading Recognition	.49	.41	.51	.75	.39
Reading Comprehension	.42	.36	.43	.70	.35
Spelling	.52	.34	.46	.77	.33
General Information	.20	.38	.37	.61	.24
Total	.47	.48	.55	.82	.41
Study 2 (N = 31,[b] interval = 11 months)					
W-J					
Preschool Cluster	.51	.46	.61	.73	.33
Knowledge Cluster	.42	.61	.63	.84	.35
Study 3 (N = 45,[b] interval = 12 months)					
CAT					
Total Language	.49	.59	.62	.69	.58
Total Mathematics	.36	.55	.54	.64	.52
Total Reading	.58	.65	.70	.84	.65
Total Battery	.53	.61	.65	.77	.62

Note. The K-ABC Interpretive Manual (Kaufman & Kaufman, 1983b) identifies Studies 1, 2, and 3 as Studies 30, 22, and 9, respectively. K-ABC = Kaufman Assessment Battery for Children, PIAT = Peabody Individual Achievement Test, W-J = Woodcock-Johnson Psycho-Educational Battery, CAT = California Achievement Test. From Kaufman and Kaufman, 1983b.
[a]Culturally different Navajos. [b]Participants identified as normal.

least two grade levels below placement as measured by the Boder Test (Boder & Jarrico, 1982). The selected children had a mean SFTAA score of 91.4, SD = 3.6, and a mean Boder score 2.6 years below placement, SD = 1.5. The children's K-ABC and SAT scores all fell within the average to low-average range. Hooper (1987) noted that this uniformity was surprising, because all participants had low Boder reading recognition levels and were selected for their reading difficulties. An examination of the Boder may be in order. The SAT scores used for this study were Spelling, Language, and total scores for Reading, Math, and Auditory Processing.

Hooper (1987) reported Pearson coefficients comparing the K-ABC subtests with the SAT subtests. Among K-ABC measures, the Cognitive subtests produced markedly low coefficients, ranging from $r = -.23$ to $r = .31$ with 12 of 40 coefficients being negative. By contrast, the Achievement subtests produced coefficients ranging from $r = -.17$ to $r = .55$, and 5 were negative. Similarly, the Global scores produced coefficients of $r = -.07$ to $r = .51$, and 3 were negative.

Several K-ABC Achievement scores correlated at or above a cut-off of .40 with SAT scores. Notably, Reading Understanding correlated with SAT Vocabulary, Total Math, and Total Reading at $r = .41$, $r = .42$, and $r = .51$, respectively.

Reading Decoding correlated with Total Reading at $r = .42$. Faces and Places correlated with Vocabulary at $r = .46$, and Riddles correlated with Vocabulary at $r = .55$. Of the K-ABC Global scores, Achievement correlated with Total Reading at .45 and with Vocabulary at .51. All of these correlations were statistically significant at $p < .001$. Notably, no K-ABC score correlated with SAT Spelling or Language at .40 or above.

Hooper (1987) soundly interpreted these results as supporting convergent validity for the K-ABC Achievement subtests and discriminant validity for the K-ABC Cognitive subtests. Juxtaposed with the contrast between K-ABC Achievement and ability results, however, are the relatively low levels of both sets of observed correlations. A possible explanation for the low correlations is the sample's restricted range of ability and reading recognition scores. Still, the sample included children in Grades 2–6.

Among the results reported by Childers, Durham, Bolen, and Taylor (1985) were correlations of K-ABC Simultaneous, Sequential, and Mental Processing Composite scores with CAT scores obtained six months later. Participants were 44 students enrolled in public schools in eastern North Carolina. The students consisted of 19 males and 25 females—28 White students and 16 Black students. Their mean age was

TABLE 3.16   Correlations Between CAT and K-ABC Results

CAT Score	K-ABC Global Score			
	Simultaneous Processing	Sequential Processing	Mental Processing Composite	Achievement
Reading	.65	.58	.70	.84
Language	.59	.49	.62	.69
Mathematics	.55	.36	.54	.64
Total	.61	.53	.65	.77

Note. CAT = California Achievement Tests, K-ABC = Kaufman Assessment Battery for Children. From Childers, Durham, Bolen, and Taylor (1985).

11 years, 0 months, range = 9–6 to 12–3, and they were enrolled in Grades 4–6, n = 17, 20, and 7, respectively. The mean K-ABC Mental Processing Composite was 95.82, SD = 16.37.

As shown in Table 3.16, K-ABC Simultaneous scores correlated more highly than K-ABC Sequential scores with CAT Reading, Language, Mathematics, and Total scores. K-ABC Achievement scores correlated still higher with all four CAT variables, showing differential evidence of validity for K-ABC Cognitive and Achievement Composites.

The Woodcock-Johnson

The Technical Manual of the Woodcock-Johnson III (WJ-III; McGrew & Woodcock, 2001) reported several studies providing criterion-based evidence for validity, although most often for selected composites or subtests. Correlations between WJ-III Cognitive Factors and selected WJ-III Achieve-

ment Clusters are summarized here as being the most useful and clearly represented. Of the Achievement Clusters, Oral Expression produced relatively low coefficients, which fell into a distinctive pattern. This cluster produced a low correlation with WJ-III Cognitive Efficiency, which correlated highly with the other Achievement Clusters examined, and a notably high correlation with WJ-III Verbal Comprehension, which correlated low with the other Achievement Clusters.

As to the Cognitive factors, Cognitive Efficiency produced higher correlations with the Achievement Clusters than did Thinking Ability, except with the Achievement Cluster Oral Expression. Of the remaining Cognitive Factors, Phonemic Awareness, Processing Speed, Working Memory, and Short-Term Memory produced the highest correlations with the Achievement Cluster, again excepting Oral Expression. Finally, Predicted Achievement, Brief Intellectual Ability, and General Intellectual Ability generated relatively high correlations with the Achievement Cluster, and their correlations with Oral Expression were only slightly lower. The rank order of these coefficients was Predicted Achievement, followed in turn by General Intellectual Ability and Brief Intellectual Ability. For Oral Expression, this order was reversed. Table 3.17 shows the results. For results of correlations with other tests, see McGrew and Woodcock (2001).

McGrew, Flanagan, Keith, and Vanderwood (1997) used structural equation modeling to evaluate a hierarchical model of the WJ-R. The g + Gf-Gc model posits that, in addition to g, several more specific abilities, called Gf-Gc abilities, also have predictive and clinical utility. This McGrew et al. model is consistent with Carrol's (1993) three-stratum model

TABLE 3.17   Correlations Between WJ-III Achievement and Cognitive Measures

WJ-III Cognitive Measure	WJ-III Achievement Cluster					
	Broad Reading	Basic Reading Skills	Basic Writing Skills	Oral Expression	Phoneme/ Grapheme Knowledge	Academic Fluency
Predicted Achievement	.66	.62	.63	.42	—	—
Brief Intellectual Ability	.55	.54	.60	.51	.54	.51
General Intellectual Ability	.56	.56	.62	.47	.63	.48
Cognitive Factors						
Thinking Ability	.38	.45	.45	.38	.52	.29
Cognitive Efficiency	.60	.53	.56	.16	.55	.55
Verbal Comprehension	.32	.34	.40	.82	.33	.27
Long-Term Retrieval	.27	.23	.31	.33	.27	.23
Visual-Spatial Thinking	.19	.18	.25	.29	.29	.16
Auditory Processing	.42	.49	.41	.23	.51	.35
Phonemic Awareness	.44	.52	.45	.26	.56	.35
Fluid Reasoning	.22	.30	.31	.32	.32	.18
Processing Speed	.55	.37	.49	.21	.36	.52
Cognitive Fluency	.39	.15	.27	.26	.12	.33
Short-Term Memory	.45	.44	.39	.16	.46	.37
Working Memory	.50	.46	.49	.23	.49	.45

Note. WJ-III = Woodcock-Johnson III. From McGrew and Woodcock (2001).

of intelligence cited as Gf-Gc abilities Fluid Reasoning (Gf), Crystallized Intelligence (Gc), Visual Processing (Gv), Auditory Processing (Ga), Processing Speed (Gs), Short-Term Memory (Gsm), Long-Term Retrieval (Glr), Quantitative Knowledge (Gq), and Correct Decision Speed (CDS). These labels differed slightly from those presented later by McGrew and Woodcock (2001). The five samples for this study ($n = 222–255$), selected from the nationally representative WJ-R norming sample, represented five grade categories covering Grades 1 through 12 (McGrew et al., 1997).

When the path from g to general reading achievement, β (beta) $= .63$, was controlled, Ga had additional relationships with Letter-Word Identification and Word Attack of $\beta = .33$ and $\beta = .49$, respectively. In addition, Gc had relationships with Passage Comprehension and Reading Vocabulary of $\beta = .47$ and $\beta = .56$. Thus, Passage Comprehension skill could increase by .56 standard deviation for every 1.00 standard deviation increase in Gc. For the five grade categories, the paths from g to general reading achievement ($\beta = .57–.88$) were fairly large; the paths from g to general mathematics achievement ($\beta = .23–.56$) were smaller. Ga and Gc showed more variable results. McGrew et al. (1997) presented a selection of them in graphic form. The paths from Gc to Passage Comprehension ($\beta \approx .47–.74$) were particularly large and consistent across grade levels.

García and Stafford (2000) replicated these findings with low-SES White and Hispanic children. Participants were 82 English-speaking children in an inner-city school district located in the southwestern United States. This sample consisted of 38 White students, 17 in Grade 1 and 21 in Grade 2, and 44 Hispanic students, 17 in Grade 1 and 27 in Grade 2. Low-SES classification was based on the students' receiving free or reduced school lunches. The measures used were four WJ-R cluster scores: Gc and Ga as predictors and Basic Reading Skills and Reading Comprehension as criteria. W scores, a transformation of the Rasch ability scale, were used to render scores comparable for Grades 1 and 2.

Correlations between WJ-R cognitive and achievement scores were typically high, both for White students, $r = .66–.76$, and for Hispanic students, $r = .56–.74$. For both groups, all $p < .01$. García et al. (2000) found no statistically significant differences between Whites and Hispanics and therefore combined the two samples for multiple regression analysis. With Basic Reading Skills as the criterion, $\beta = .52$ and .35 for Ga and Gc, respectively. With Reading Comprehension as the criterion, $\beta = .46$ and .49 for Ga and Gc, respectively. For all variables, $p < .01$. The researchers reported that, together, the two predictors explained about 57% of the variance in Basic Reading Skills and 68% of the variance in Reading Comprehension. In partial F tests, Ga and

Gc behaved similarly with both criteria, $F(1,79) = 1.12$ and 0.00 for Basic Reading Skills and Reading Comprehension respectively, both $p \geq .05$.

McGrew and Knopik (1993) examined the relationship between the WJ-R cognitive clusters and the WJ-R achievement clusters Basic Writing Skills and Written Expression. The samples consisted of 5,386 examinees for Written Expression and 5,398 examinees for Basic Writing Skills. Fifteen samples represented ages 5–19 years, whereas six samples spanned 10-year adult age ranges covering 20–79 years.

All R^2s were moderate to large, ranging from .54 to .93 for Written Expression and from .61 to .89 for Basic Writing Skills. Standardized regression coefficients indicated that Gc and Gs, or Processing Speed, were the strongest predictors. Gc became increasingly predictive with age through the 20–29 year category. Gs followed the same pattern as a predictor of Written Expression. With Basic Writing Skills, however, Gs was most predictive from ages 5 to about 15 years. See McGrew and Knopik for a table of all standardized regression coefficients.

In a similar study, McGrew and Hessler (1995) examined the relationships between the WJ-R cognitive clusters and the WJ-R Basic Mathematics Skills and Mathematics Reasoning clusters. The sample specifications were the same as for McGrew and Knopik (1993), $n = 5,386$ for Basic Mathematics Skills, $n = 5,398$ for Mathematics Reasoning. Multiple R^2 again tended to be large at .66–.82 for Mathematics Reasoning and .69–.88 for Basic Mathematics Skills. The standardized regression coefficients indicated that Gc was most predictive, followed by Gf and Gs. Gc tended to become more predictive with age through 30–39 year and 40–49 year category, respectively. By contrast, Gs was somewhat more predictive at younger ages. Gf tended to be most predictive of the mathematics criteria used between the ages of 13 and 20–29.

The Cognitive Assessment System

Despite a recent controversy over what factors the CAS measures (Keith, Kranzler, & Flanagan, 2001; Kranzler & Keith, 1999; Naglieri, 1999), its scores have produced relatively high Pearson correlations with WJ-R Achievement scores. The *Interpretive Handbook* (Naglieri & Das, 1997) for the CAS presented results with 1,600 children, aged 5–17 years, included in the CAS standardization and WJ-R Achievement sample. All correlations were moderate to high.

As shown in Table 3.18, the CAS Full Scale produced the highest correlations. The Simultaneous and Successive composites followed and differed little between themselves, except that Successive scores showed relatively low correlations with

TABLE 3.18   Pearson Correlations Between the CAS PASS Scale and Full Scale Standard Scores and the WJ-R Tests of Achievement

WJ-R Score	CAS Standard Battery				
	Full Scale	Planning	Attention	Simultaneous	Successive
Broad Reading	.71	.50	.42	.59	.59
Basic Reading Skills	.68	.52	.42	.58	.58
Reading Comprehension	.72	.49	.40	.63	.56
Broad Mathematics	.72	.57	.50	.62	.49
Basic Mathematics Skills	.69	.55	.48	.62	.49
Mathematics Reasoning	.67	.49	.48	.62	.49
Basic Writing Skills	.66	.51	.48	.58	.55
Skills	.73	.57	.50	.67	.60

Note. CAS = Cognitive Assessment System, PASS = Planning, Attention, Simultaneous, Successive, WJ-R = Woodcock-Johnson–Revised. From Das and Naglieri (1997).

the three WJ-R mathematics subtests. Planning was next, and lastly, Attention. Results were about the same for the CAS Basic Battery. Among WJ-R scores, the Skills cluster produced the highest correlations, and results for mathematics exceeded those for reading, except with the Successive composite. Results again were similar for the Basic Battery. The Skills cluster consists of one subtest each from reading, mathematics, and writing: Letter-Word Identification, Applied Problems, and Dictation, respectively.

The *Interpretive Handbook* (Naglieri & Das, 1997) also presented Pearson coefficients broken down by age range. Naglieri (1999) compared these results with those for a sample of 3,055 children, also aged 5–17 years, from McGrew and Hessler (1995, as cited in Naglieri, 1999). The CAS Planning composite correlated with WJ-R Basic Mathematics at $r = .51$ to $r = .56$, Mdn = .56, for four age groups. The CAS Attention composite correlated with this same WJ-R subtest at $r = .42$ to $r = .47$, Mdn = .47. By comparison, WJ-R Perceptual Speed correlated with this subtest at $r = .20$ to $r = .37$, Mdn = .27. CAS Planning correlated with WJ-R Mathematics Reasoning at $r = .44$ to $r = .61$, Mdn = .52. For CAS Attention, coefficients ranged from $r = .41$ to $r = .49$, Mdn = .48. For WJ-R Perceptual Speed, coefficients were lower at $r = .18$ to $r = .28$, Mdn = .20.

The outcome was similar for scores on the CAS Simultaneous and Successive composites. Naglieri (1999) presented results with the 1,600 children noted previously (Naglieri & Das, 1997) alongside results with 888 children from the *WJ-R Technical Manual*, Table H-3 (McGrew, Werder, & Woodcock, 1991, as cited in Naglieri). In brief, the CAS Successive composite produced consistently higher correlations than WJ-R Memory Span with WJ-R Achievement composites and subtests (e.g., $r = .59$ and .49 vs. $r = .43$ & .34 for Broad Reading and Broad Mathematics, respectively). Similarly, the CAS Simultaneous composite produced

consistently higher correlations than WJ-R Broad Visualization ($r = .59$ and .62 vs. $r = .26$ and .26 for Broad Reading and Broad Mathematics) and WJ-R Fluid Intelligence ($r = .59$ and .62 vs. $r = .46$ and .58) with WJ-R Achievement composites and subtests.

Other Intelligence Tests

Two studies by Powers, Jones, and Barkan (1986) addressed the associations of the Standard Progressive Matrices (SPM; Raven, Court, & Raven, 1983) with the California Achievement Test (CAT). For the first study, the sample consisted of 212 sixth-grade students enrolled in four elementary high schools. Of these participants, 116 were male and 96 were female. In addition, 79 were White, non-Hispanic students; 112 were Hispanic; 4 were Black; and 17 were Native American. Mean SPM scores were 38.83 for boys, SD = 6.84, and 39.26 for girls, SD = 7.35. For the second study, the sample consisted of 214 seventh-grade students enrolled in one junior high school. Of these participants, 109 were male and 105 were female; 94 were White, non-Hispanic students; 99 were Hispanic; 5 were Black; 1 was Asian; and 15 were Native American. Mean SPM scores for this second sample were 39.48 for boys, SD = 8.06, and 38.88 for girls, SD = 8.21. All 426 participants were enrolled in one large, urban district in the Southwest.

As noted by Powers et al. (1986), correlations were higher for seventh-grade students than for sixth-grade students; for girls than for boys; and for CAT Math results, followed by Language and Reading results, respectively. These correlations differed from those reported for WAIS-R Performance IQs with WRAT-R standard scores (Cooper et al., 1988; Spruill et al., 1986) and for WISC-R Performance IQs with WRAT standard scores (Stedman et al., 1978), which were

TABLE 3.19   Correlations Between Scores on the Standard Progressive Matrices and the California Achievement Test

Group	n	Reading	Language	Math
Sixth Grade				
Boys	116	.34	.41	.39
Girls	96	.36	.50	.60
Total	212	.35	.45	.48
Seventh Grade				
Boys	109	.45	.49	.52
Girls	105	.54	.55	.57
Total	214	.49	.51	.54

Note. From Powers, Jones, and Barkan (1986).
All $p < .05$.

higher for WRAT Reading scores than for WRAT Arithmetic scores. Table 3.19 presents these results by Powers et al.

The search produced only two relevant studies of the Stanford-Binet Intelligence Scale (S-B; Thorndike, Hagen, & Sattler, 1986), and methodological or sample size limitations led to the exclusion of both. Follow-up searches, however, yielded two studies that included the S-B Fourth Edition (S-B 4; Thorndike et al.), both addressed in the "Multiple Intelligence Tests" section later in this chapter. In addition, the technical manual of the S-B 4 (Thorndike et al.) showed correlations with the K-ABC. Correlations were high, $r = .68–.87$, Mdn $= .77$, with the highest between S-B 4 Verbal Reasoning and K-ABC Achievement. S-B 4 Verbal Reasoning also tended to correlate highly with Full Scale and Verbal IQs on the WISC-R, WPPSI, and WAIS-R, so the K-ABC Achievement composite may simply be responding as the Wechsler Verbal Comprehension factor does (see Thorndike et al., Tables 6.7–6.10).

Vance, Kitson, and Singer (1985) reported Pearson correlations between PPVT-R total scores and WRAT Spelling, Arithmetic, and Reading scores. Participants were 37 children enrolled in a semirural school district in northeastern Ohio and referred for special education services. This sample consisted of 25 males and 12 females, of whom 17% were White and 20% were Black. Their mean age was 10 years, 10 months, SD $= 2–7$, range $= 5–11$ to $14–7$. Their grades ranged from 1 to 7, and their mean PPVT-R standard score was 85.08, SD $= 14.71$. PPVT-R standard scores correlated at $r = .07$, $r = .20$, and $r = .30$ with WRAT Arithmetic, Spelling, and Reading, respectively.

Valencia (1990) reviewed the psychometric properties of the McCarthy Scales of Children's Abilities (MSCA; McCarthy, 1972), paying particular attention to specific ethnic groups and children with special needs. Summarizing 29 predictive studies, Valencia made the following observations. Researchers had investigated a variety of standardized achievement

tests, including the PIAT, the WRAT, the CTBS, and the MAT. The studies spanned preschool through Grade 3. Correlations ranged from $r = .15$ for an LD sample to .79 for a normal sample. About two thirds of the observed rs, however, were in the .60s and .70s. Compared with the WISC-R, the WJ-R Tests of Cognitive Abilities, the WPPSI, and the S-B, the MSCA correlated higher than or as high as they did (i.e., results showed no statistically significant difference).

Sattler (2001) reviewed, in part, results with school-age children for the Differential Ability Scales (DAS; Elliot, 1990). Correlations with K-ABC Achievement and with K-TEA scores were generally moderate, except that DAS Spatial Ability scores produced variable and relatively low correlations. Table 3.20 presents these results.

Multiple Intelligence Tests

Studies in which several intelligence tests are administered to one sample, and their correlations with one or more achievement tests are compared, provide especially useful information regarding criterion-related validity. Results for the intelligence tests are then directly comparable; they would not be if they were derived from separate samples. In addition, this model lends itself to multiple regression analyses. Finally, the model is intuitively sensible, because in studies of criterion-related validity, an achievement test is commonly the measure of interest, the conceptual dependent variable.

Lassiter and Bardos (1995) obtained correlations for the Wechsler Preschool and Primary Scale of Intelligence–Revised (WPPSI-R; Wechsler, 1989), the Kaufman Brief Intelligence Test (K-BIT; Kaufman et al., 1990), and the Draw-A-Person: Quantitative Scoring System (DAP:QSS; Naglieri, 1988) with the K-ABC Achievement Scale. Participants were 50 kindergarten and first-grade students from three regular education classrooms in a northern Colorado school district. This group was actually a subsample; some

TABLE 3.20   Correlations of Scores from the Differential Ability Scales with K-TEA and K-ABC Achievement Scores

Achievement Score	Verbal Ability	Nonverbal Reasoning Ability	Spatial Ability	GCA
K-TEA				
Mathematics	.55	.59	.41	.69
Spelling	.38	.44	.25	.53
Reading	.56	.43	.32	.57
K-ABC				
Achievement	.64	.72	.39	.78

Note. K-TEA = Kaufman Test of Educational Achievement, K-ABC = Kaufman Assessment Battery for Children. From Sattler (2001).

TABLE 3.21   Pearson Coefficients Comparing Scores on Three Intelligence Tests with K-ABC Achievement Scores

| Intelligence Score | K-ABC Achievement Score | | | | |
	Global Achievement	Faces and Places	Arithmetic	Riddles	Reading Decoding
WPPSI-R IQ					
Verbal	.72**	.65	.58**	.70**	.48**
Performance	.46**	.25	.50**	.49**	.36**
Full Scale	.70**	.56**	.64**	.71**	.49**
K-BIT Score					
Vocabulary	.66**	.81**	.84**	.74**	.82**
Matrices	.33*	.18	.56*	.66**	.22
Composite	.62**	.56**	.51**	.66**	.36**
DAP:QSS Score					
Total	.44**	.39**	.49**	.07	.42**

Note. K-ABC = Kaufman Assessment Battery for Children, WPPSI-R = Wechsler Preschool and Primary Scales of Intelligence–Revised, K-BIT = Kaufman Brief Intelligence Test, DAP:QSS = Draw-A-Person: Quantitative Scoring System. From Lassiter and Bardos (1995).
*$p < .05$. **$p < .01$.

students did not have written parental permission to participate or did not complete the study. The original sample size was apparently $(50 + 7)/.71 = 80$.

Of the final participants, 44% were male and 56% were female; 58% were White, 30% Hispanic, 12% Black or other. Participants' ages ranged from 5 years 0 months to 7 years 3 months, $M = 5.8$ years, $SD = .57$ years. The average WPPSI-R Full Scale IQ was 95.2, $SD = 11.7$. Table 3.21 presents results for the three intelligence tests. For results with WPPSI-R subtests, see Lassiter et al. (1995).

In general, the overall composites and verbal composites of the WPPSI-R and the K-BIT showed the highest correlations with the K-ABC Achievement scores. The WPPSI-R Performance IQ and K-BIT Matrices produced lower and more variable results. WPPSI-R Verbal and Full Scale IQs produced particularly high correlations with K-ABC Faces and Places, Arithmetic, Riddles, and Reading Decoding. DAP:QSS correlated relatively low with all K-ABC scores, notably with K-ABC Riddles.

Next, Lassiter et al. (1995) tested several possible brief, screening measures using K-ABC Global Achievement as the criterion. With this sample, WPPSI-R Comprehension, Arithmetic, Picture Completion, and Block Design (Kaufman, 1972; Lobello, 1991) produced an R^2 of .47. For WPPSI-R Similarities, Information, Geometric Design, and Vocabulary, R^2 was .60. For the K-BIT Composite, the DAP:QSS Total, and the WPPSI-R Similarities and Block Design, R^2 was .63. Finally, WPPSI-R Similarities followed in turn by DAP:QSS Total, K-BIT Composite, and WPPSI-R Vocabulary produced an R^2 of .71. This last model made use of stepwise variable selection, however, so the results may be distorted, especially given the small sample size.

Keith and Novak (1987) conducted an exploratory factor analysis with the WISC-R and the K-ABC, which has intelligence and achievement components. Participants were 544 school-age children referred for psychoeducational evaluation. The children resided in California, Georgia, Illinois, Iowa, Ohio, New York, North Carolina, and Wisconsin. Their ages ranged from 6 years to 12.5 years, $M = 9.68$, $SD = 1.66$. Of these participants, 68% were male; 87% were White, and 9% were Black. In addition, 71% came from families in which the highest level of parental education was high school graduate or less. Most (77%) of the participants were referred because of problems with school achievement. The mean WISC-R Full Scale IQ was 89.32, $SD = 15.40$.

Sample sizes for individual subtests were at least 500 except those for Digit Span ($n = 463$) and Reading Understanding ($n = 493$). Principal factors analysis and varimax rotation were the procedures used. The results suggested a possible reinterpretation of K-ABC Achievement as measuring intelligence rather than achievement. See Table 3.22 for the results.

After rotation, the four-factor solution was strongest. Keith and Novak (1987) interpreted this solution to partially support the K-ABC model. The K-ABC Simultaneous Processing subtests correlated with the first factor, along with the WISC-R Performance subtests. The K-ABC Sequential Processing subtests correlated with the third factor, along with WISC-R Digit Span. These factors might be labeled Simultaneous and Sequential Processing, consistent with the K-ABC model. The K-ABC Achievement subtests, however, broke apart and loaded variously on three factors.

The third factor incorporated chiefly the WISC-R Verbal subtests, excluding Arithmetic. K-ABC Riddles and Faces

TABLE 3.22   One- and Four-Factor Solutions of K-ABC and WISC-R Subtests

Subtest	Unrotated First Factor	Rotated Factors			
		1	2	3	4
K-ABC					
Simultaneous Subtests					
Gestalt Closure	.509	.480	.387	−.016	−.003
Triangles	.642	.702	.240	.081	.117
Matrix Analogies	.599	.459	.258	.242	.198
Spatial Memory	.561	.633	.070	.221	.121
Photo Series	.709	.678	.277	.246	.094
Sequential Subtests					
Hand Movements	.536	.354	.132	.430	.190
Number Recall	.522	.093	.173	.769	.136
Word Order	.584	.220	.242	.657	.110
Achievement Subtests					
Faces and Places	.663	.212	.685	.160	.204
Arithmetic	.790	.481	.399	.349	.347
Riddles	.774	.324	.732	.206	.194
Reading Decoding	.646	.131	.322	.257	.781
Reading Understanding	.650	.106	.412	.174	.789
WISC-R					
Verbal Subtests					
Information	.758	.314	.608	.217	.358
Similarities	.748	.297	.592	.279	.312
Arithmetic	.708	.440	.269	.395	.348
Vocabulary	.773	.226	.746	.258	.276
Comprehension	.711	.327	.643	.237	.119
Digit Span	.548	.161	.190	.702	.143
Performance Subtests					
Picture Completion	.618	.536	.381	.160	.013
Picture Arrangement	.677	.578	.369	.225	.052
Block Design	.707	.759	.247	.121	.146
Object Assembly	.618	.700	.237	.089	.048
Coding	.408	.393	−.015	.195	.274

Note. Coefficients ≥ .400 are italicized. K-ABC = Kaufman Assessment Battery for Children, WISC-R = Wechsler Intelligence Scale for Children. From Keith and Novak (1987).

and Places also correlated with this factor. Subtests associated most highly with this factor call for the processing of semantic material, that is, meanings. These subtests require an examinee to think beyond the verbal presentation mode to the underlying meanings or referents. Only by accessing this underlying material can an individual respond correctly. The highest correlation, for example, represented Vocabulary, a subtest that repeatedly asks, "What does _____ mean?" Riddles may be seen as a reversal of traditional vocabulary subtests, providing aspects of a word's meaning and requiring examinees to provide the word (see also Kaufman & Kaufman, 1983b). This factor might be labeled Semantic Processing.

The traditional interpretation of this second factor as Verbal Comprehension does not account for the order of the correlations. The Vocabulary subtest appears to draw upon semantic material more heavily than Comprehension and Similarities do; whereas it does not clearly require more comprehension or verbal activity than they do. In addition, K-ABC

Faces and Places is a largely pictorial subtest, but it too has a high correlation with the second factor. A semantic interpretation also potentially explains why the Wechsler nonverbal subtests tend to correlate substantially with this factor. Finally, the fourth factor may be a Reading factor, dominated as it is by two K-ABC subtests: Reading Decoding and Reading Understanding.

The unrotated first factor was strong and general to all subtests. This factor closely resembled the Semantic Processing factor. The WISC-R and K-ABC subtests that correlated highest with factor two also correlated highest with this general factor. The resemblance suggested—with considerable intuitive credibility—that facility with meaning is general to many types of mental tasks, including those sampled by both tests examined by Keith and Novak (1987).

These results did not, in themselves, suggest a factor that could readily be labeled Achievement, with the possible exception of the Reading factor. Herein lay the main difficulty for the traditional interpretation of the K-ABC. The Achievement subtests correlated variously with Simultaneous Processing, Semantic Processing, and Reading. Possible interpretations are that no K-ABC subtests measure achievement; that only the K-ABC reading subtests measure achievement; and that the WISC-R Verbal IQ measures achievement rather than intelligence. The third interpretation seems improbable, given a long history of research addressing the Wechsler scales. As noted by Kamphaus (1993), however, both Anastasi (1988) and Kaufman (1979) have made similar arguments.

The Achievement subtests broke apart again in the five-factor solution, but not in the three-factor solution, which included no Reading factor. In the latter solution, these subtests all correlated with the second factor, here labeled Semantic Processing. As in the four- and five-factor solutions, the WISC-R Verbal subtests tended to correlate highly with this factor. Thus, despite the unity of the K-ABC Achievement subtests in this solution, the question of their distinctness from intelligence remained.

Keith and Novak (1987), then, sought to help answer the question of whether these subtests measured intelligence or whether, perhaps, the K-ABC Verbal subtests measured achievement. Thus, the researchers factor analyzed the K-ABC with the WISC-R and the WRAT. In the four-factor solution, the three WRAT components correlated with a separate factor along with the two K-ABC reading subtests. Keith and Novak labeled this factor Achievement. The remaining K-ABC Achievement subtests again broke apart, correlating with the Simultaneous Processing and Semantic Processing factors. The K-ABC reading subtests correlated with the Achievement factor. No reading factor emerged from this analysis. The results suggest that the K-ABC reading subtests measure achievement; whereas the remaining K-ABC Achievement subtests measure intelligence, an interpretation consistent with Keith and Novak's.

Prewett and McCaffery (1993) compared the K-BIT, the S-B 4, and the Vocabulary-Pattern Analysis (V-PA; Prewett, 1992) short form of the S-B 4. The researchers reported correlations between each of these tests and the K-TEA Brief Form (K-TEA BF; Kaufman & Kaufman, 1985). Participants were 75 students enrolled in a large, urban school district in the Midwest. Of the students, 49 were male, and 26, female; 35 were White, and 40, Black. All had been referred by their teachers for a psychoeducational evaluation because of academic difficulties. Their mean age was 9 years 7 months, range 6–0 to 15–9. Their mean S-B 4 Composite score was 81.6, SD = 13.3.

As shown in Table 3.23, K-BIT scores correlated highest with K-TEA BF Reading, followed in turn by K-TEA BF Mathematics and Spelling. The exception was that K-BIT Matrices correlated higher with Mathematics than with Reading. The S-B 4 Composite and the V-PA short form behaved

TABLE 3.23   Pearson Correlations of K-BIT and Stanford-Binet Scores with K-TEA Scores

K-TEA	K-BIT			Stanford-Binet	
	Vocabulary	Matrices	IQ Composite	V-PA	Composite
Mathematics	.52	.53	.57	.58	.66
Reading	.61	.45	.58	.55	.57
Spelling	.47	.39	.47	.48	.53

Note. K-BIT = Kaufman Brief Intelligence Test, K-TEA = Kaufman Test of Educational Achievement, V-PA = Vocabulary-Pattern Analysis short form. From Prewett and McCaffery (1993).

as K-BIT Matrices did, correlating highest with K-TEA BF Mathematics, followed in turn by K-TEA BF Reading and Spelling.

A report by Prewett and Farhney (1994) included correlations of the Matrix Analogies Test–Short Form (MAT-SF; Naglieri, 1985) and the S-B 4 with the K-TEA BF. Participants were 71 students in a large, urban school district; 44 were male, 27 female, 30 White, and 41 Black. The students were enrolled in Grades 1–8, with about half in Grade 3, $n = 20$, and Grade 4, $n = 15$. Most students qualified for the free or reduced lunch program. The participants' teachers had referred them for psychoeducational evaluation because of academic difficulties. The average S-B 4 Composite score was 81.2, SD = 12.8.

The students' MAT-SF scores correlated with K-TEA BF Mathematics, Reading, and Spelling at $r = .44$, $r = .44$, and $r = .38$, respectively. Their S-B 4 Composite scores correlated with these same measures at $r = .65$, $r = .65$, and $r = .59$, showing the same rank order as the MAT-SF scores but higher absolute values.

Prewett, Bardos, and Naglieri (1989) reported correlations of the MAT-SF and the DAP:QSS with K-TEA Reading and Mathematics Composites. Participants were 85 White students enrolled in a suburban, middle-class school district in central Ohio. This sample comprised a group drawn from five regular classrooms, $n = 46$, and a group drawn from four classes for developmentally handicapped students, $n = 39$.

The regular group consisted of 25 males and 21 females, of whom 14 were in Grade 4 and 32 were in Grade 5. Their mean age was 10 years, 6 months, SD = 0–8. Their mean MAT-SF score was 97.7, SD = 11.6. The developmentally handicapped group consisted of 20 males and 19 females, of whom 21 were in Grade 4 and 18 were in Grade 5. The mean age of this group was 10 years, 9 months, SD = 0–8. Their mean MAT-SF score was 75.8, SD = 8.6. Their handicaps were considered mild.

For the regular group, MAT-SF scores produced higher correlations with K-TEA Reading Composite scores, $r =$

.63, than with Mathematics Composite scores, $r = .37$. All DAP:QSS scores produced low correlations with both K-TEA Composites, $r = -.18$ to $r = .20$. These coefficients were corrected for restriction of range. For the developmentally handicapped group, however, MAT-SF scores produced higher correlations with K-TEA Mathematics Composite scores, $r = .57$ vs. $r = .35$. Moreover, DAP:QSS scores correlated substantially with the Mathematics Composite scores of this group, $r = .37–.50$. Correlations with Reading Composite scores were again low, $r = .03–.26$.

Cantwell (1966) investigated the correlations of the Standard Progressive Matrices (SPM) (Raven, 1963) and the D. 48 Test (Gough & Domino, 1963) with the SAT Verbal and Mathematics subtests. As Cantwell explains, the D. 48 Test presents 44 domino problems in various progressions from simple to relatively complex. The last domino in each series is blank, and the examinee completes it. All D. 48 problems are open-ended.

The participants in Cantwell's (1966) study were the 139 entering first-year students at a women's liberal arts college in the Midwest. Their mean SPM score was 50.88, SD = 4.59, and their mean SAT scores were 495.13 Verbal, SD = 82.55, and 486.46 Mathematics, SD = 86.99. As noted by Cantwell, the small standard deviations indicated that the sample was relatively homogeneous on these variables.

Although the D. 48 Test is little known, its results were comparable to the SPM results. Scores on both tests had low correlations with SAT Verbal scores, $r = .37$ and .36 for SPM and D. 48, respectively, but higher ones with SAT Mathematics scores, $r = .55$ and .57. This outcome is not surprising, given the nonverbal character of the SPM and D. 48.

Smith, Smith, and Dobbs (1991) examined the associations of the Peabody Picture Vocabulary Test–Revised (PPVT-R) and the WISC-R with the WRAT-R, permitting a comparison of the results of both intelligence tests. Participants were 181 children from rural areas of Arkansas, referred for evaluation by their teachers because of academic difficulties. The children included 124 males and 57 females, 129 Whites and 52 Blacks. The average age was 10 years, 6 months, SD = 2 years, 5 months. The average WISC-R IQs were 82.44, SD = 13.68 for Full Scale; 80.14, SD = 13.61 for Verbal; and 87.91, SD = 14.94 for Performance. The difference between Verbal and Performance IQs, with Verbal lower, suggested that some participants might have had learning disabilities.

Both the WISC-R Full Scale IQ and the PPVT-R correlated highest with WRAT-R Arithmetic at $r = .57$ and $r = .50$, respectively. WRAT-R Reading was next at $r = .41$ and $r = .42$, followed by WRAT-R Spelling at $r = .33$ for both Wechsler subtests. The two intelligence tests produced similar results, excepting the different correlations with WRAT-R Arithmetic.

BLIND AND LOW-VISION EXAMINEES

A report by Gutterman (1983) began with a review of the literature on measurement of intelligence of blind and low-vision examinees, including relations between intelligence and achievement measures. Among the results reviewed were those of Hecht and Newland (1973; as cited in Gutterman, 1983), whose results included correlations between WISC Mental Age and scores from the Braille version of the SAT (Hayes, 1941). Participants were 69 blind students enrolled in a residential school. The researchers subdivided this sample into three age groups: 9–11, 12–13, and 14–16 years. Correlations ranged widely, from .00 for SAT Spelling with the 9–11 year group to .87 for SAT Paragraph Meaning with the 12–13 year group.

Coveny (1973) reported regression results for the Perkins-Binet Tests of Intelligence for the Blind, Form U (P-B; Davis, 1980) and the WISC as predictors of SAT subtest scores. Both intelligence tests were predictive of SAT Word Recognition, Arithmetic Computation and Reasoning, and Social Studies scores. Gutterman (1983) also reviewed correlations with GPA, summarized briefly here. For 115 blind children, Rich and Anderson (1965) reported correlations of .51 for WISC Verbal scores, .36 for the Children's Tactual Progressive Matrices (CTPM; Rich & Anderson), and a multiple correlation of $r = .55$ for both instruments. Streitfeld and Avery (1968) administered the WAIS Verbal Scale and the Haptic Intelligence Scale for the Adult Blind (HIS; Shurrager, 1961; Shurrager & Shurrager, 1964) to 31 residential school students, 20 low vision and 11 blind. For the WAIS, the researchers were able to combine the two samples. Correlations with average grades were $r = .74–.81$.

Gutterman's (1983) own analysis compared the WISC-R Verbal Scale and the Perkins-Binet, as associated with WRAT scores. Participants were 52 low vision children enrolled in

TABLE 3.24 Correlations of Perkins-Binet[a] Scores and WISC-R Verbal Scores with WRAT Scores by Grade Level

WRAT Composite	Grade				
	3	5	7	9	All
Perkins-Binet					
Reading	.40	.33	.74**	.49	.43**
Spelling	.48	.27	.67*	.39	.37**
Arithmetic	.63*	.41	.52	.28	.38**
WISC-R Verbal Scale					
Reading	.35	.43	.87**	.82**	.53**
Spelling	.41	.18	.84**	.80**	.47**
Arithmetic	.57*	.49	.79**	.60**	.60**

Note. Correlations corrected for restriction of range are shown. WISC-R = Wechsler Intelligence Scale for Children, WRAT = Wide Range Achievement Test. From Gutterman (1983).
[a]Form U.
*p < .05. **p < .01.

Grades 3, 5, 7, and 9 in residential and public school programs in three Ohio public school systems and an Ohio school for the blind. This sample consisted of 24 males, 28 females; 30 Whites and 22 non-Whites; 14 students in Grade 3, 14 in Grade 5, 12 in Grade 7, and 12 in Grade 9. All participants used print as their primary reading mode.

The results suggested a trend toward higher correlations at Grades 3, 7, and 9. In addition, correlations were highest for WRAT Arithmetic at Grades 3 and 5, but for WRAT Reading at Grades 7 and 9. Finally, the WISC-R Verbal Scale produced higher correlations than the Perkins-Binet in Grades 7 and 9. Sample size considerations make these observations tentative. Table 3.24 presents correlations corrected for restriction of range.

DEAF AND LOW-HEARING EXAMINEES

In a well-designed and generally well-reported study with a review of literature, Blennerhassett, Strohmeier, and Hibbett (1994) first summarized correlations between intelligence and achievement measures for samples of deaf and low-hearing students. Most of the achievement measures sampled reading achievement; a few sampled language, writing, or spelling achievement. Results for the WISC, WISC-R, and WAIS-R Performance IQs with SAT and SAT-HI scores tended to be inconsistent, ranging from $r = .12$ to $r = .73$. Correlations with other achievement tests, such as the WRAT-R and the Reynell Developmental Language Scales, tended to be low but had too little representation for a judgment of consistency.

By contrast, K-ABC Nonverbal scores produced relatively consistent correlations with Metropolitan Achievement Test (MAT) Reading Comprehension, WRAT-R Reading and Spelling, and K-ABC Reading Decoding and Reading Understanding. These correlations ranged from .46 with MAT Reading Comprehension to .65 with K-ABC Reading Decoding (Brooks & Riggs, 1980; Kelly & Braden, 1990; Paal, Skinner, & Reddig, 1988; Phelps & Branyan, 1990; Porter & Kirby, 1986; Ulissi, Brice, & Gibbins, 1989; Watson, Goldgar, Kroese, & Lotz, 1986; Watson, Sullivan, Moeller, & Jensen, 1982; all as cited in Blennerhassett et al.). Sample sizes and other aspects of research design may be responsible for inconsistent results, such as those found with the Wechsler scales.

Blennerhassett et al. (1994) investigated, in part, SPM and SAT-HI scores with 107 students enrolled at two residential schools for the deaf. Participants' age range at test was 10 years, 10 months to 19 years, 3 months, M = 14–7, SD = 1–11. The researchers reported sample demographics in percentage form for comparison with a national sample of deaf residential students. In the study sample, 64.2% of the students were male, and 35.8%, female; 57.0% were White,

25.2% Black, 15.0% Hispanic, and 2.8% Asian American. According to audiological records, hearing loss was profound for 75.2% of the students, severe for 22.9%, and moderate for 1.9% (see Blennerhassett et al. for etiology of deafness and data from a national sample).

Among the results were correlations between SPM scores and SAT Reading Comprehension, Spelling, and Language. Correlations for these tests were relatively low, $r = .33$, $r = .38$, and $r = .44$, respectively. The results were consistent with, though somewhat lower than, the earlier results of Stedman et al. (1978) with normal participants, most of whom had Spanish surnames.

Kelley et al. (1990) explored the criterion-related validity of the WISC-R Performance IQ with scores from the Stanford Achievement Test, Special Edition for Hearing-Impaired Students (SAT-HI). Previous studies had produced low correlations but had employed small samples or grade-equivalent scores. Participants were 83 deaf students enrolled in a residential school. Their ages ranged from 7.5 years to 16.6 years, M = 12.6. All participants were prelingually deaf and had bilateral, severe to profound hearing loss.

The researchers reported rank-order correlations for SAT-HI subtests Reading Comprehension, Spelling, Concept of Number, Math Computation, and Math Applications. The correlation coefficients were relatively low ($r = .32$, .24, .46, .31, and .41, respectively) for scaled scores but higher ($r = .39$, .33, .57, .42, and .52) for percentile ranks. All coefficients except that for Spelling were statistically significant ($p < .05$; for Concept of Number, $p < .01$).

The earliest study found (Brown, 1930) utilized a sample of students attending a school for deaf children. This study addressed achievement tests and other correlates of nonlanguage mental tests. At the time, clinicians used nonlanguage tests routinely with all individuals who had "difficulty with the English language" (Brown, p. 371).

Of 390 total participants, 98 were above Grade 5. They were the population for whom correlations between mental and educational tests were obtained. The report provided little demographic information about these students. The mental tests administered included the Pintner Non-Language Mental Test and a point scale incorporating the Knox Cubes, three form boards, the Manikin and Feature Profile, the Mare and Foal, Healy Picture Completion I, and the Kohs Block Designs (Arthur, 1925). Many of these activities resembled modern Wechsler subtests. The education test correlates included the Stanford Achievement Arithmetic Tests and the Stanford Achievement Reading Tests.

The Pintner test correlated at $r = .45$ with total Arithmetic but $r = .00$ for total Reading. Similarly, the point scale correlated at $r = .37$ for total Arithmetic but $r = -.06$ for total Reading. Of note, more recent studies with deaf and low-hearing examinees (e.g., Blennerhassett et al., 1994; Kelley et al., 1990) have produced higher correlations with reading results, particularly when the K-ABC Nonverbal Composite is the intelligence score used.

CONCLUSIONS

The results addressed in this chapter suggest several possible generalizations. These generalizations must remain tentative, however, given the small numbers of studies addressing particular populations. In addition, many of the studies found had methodological limitations, as described later in this section. For the WISC-III and its predecessors, Full Scale and Verbal IQs may be more highly associated with achievement scores than are Performance IQs (Figueroa et al., 1989; Lavin, 1996). The distinction may not apply to low IQ ranges (Smith, Smith, & Dobbs, 1991). Higher results for verbal and overall composites may also characterize the WPPSI-R and the K-BIT, when K-ABC Achievement is used as the criterion (Lassiter et al., 1995; but see Keith & Novak, 1987). Again for the WISC-III and predecessors, Performance IQs may have stronger associations with mathematics achievement than with reading and other verbal forms of achievement. Other nonverbal composite scores, such as those of the SPM and D. 48 Test, may also correlate more highly with mathematics achievement than with other achievement results (Cantwell, 1966).

In four-factor solutions of the WISC-III, the Verbal Comprehension factor has produced higher associations than Freedom From Distractibility, Perceptual Organization, and Processing Speed (Roid et al., 1993; Teeter et al., 1993). This pattern may not hold in severe ED cases (Teeter et al., 1993). In addition, the WISC-III and its predecessors sometimes show lower associations with achievement for Hispanic examinees than with White or Black examinees (Weiss et al., 1993). Ethnic and gender differences, however, are inconsistent with Wechsler children's intelligence tests (e.g., Figueroa et al., 1989). For WISC-III results, correlations with reading achievement appear to be higher than with other forms of achievement (Weiss et al., 1993). This difference may also hold true for WAIS-R results (Spruill et al., 1986; but see Cooper et al., 1988).

Not surprisingly, the K-ABC Reading subtests correlated well with SAT Reading scores, and the Achievement Global score, with SAT Vocabulary scores (Hooper, 1987). A generalization from these results, however, is difficult to make with confidence. The K-ABC may have relatively high and consistent correlations when administered to deaf and hearing-impaired residential students (Blennerhassett et al., 1994). The K-ABC (Hooper, 1987), the CAS (Naglieri, 1999), and

the Wechsler scales (e.g., Roid et al., 1993; Teeter et al., 1993; Weiss et al., 1993) have produced reasonably high correlations with relevant achievement measures.

The studies found have a number of methodological limitations. A widespread limitation is that numerous studies present only Pearson correlation coefficients. The many available Pearson tables do have an advantage: They are directly comparable, because they are in the same metric. Correlations alone are not enough, however, to indicate that a test is predictive. A correlation coefficient indicates only that two measures are similar. Correlation is defined as *mathematical similarity,* with high degrees of one variable accompanied by high degrees of the other, or by low degrees if the correlation is negative. A correlation does not specify a direction: If variable A correlates with variable B at $r = .57$, for example, then variable B correlates with variable A at $r = .57$.

By contrast, prediction implies a particular direction. If variable A predicts variable B at $\beta = .53$, for example, then variable B may predict variable A at $\beta = .73$, at $\beta = .27$, or at any number of other levels. This is so because r is multiplied by a particular amount to make β. To greatly oversimplify, this amount differs depending on which variable is being used to predict which, because it is based on the standard deviations of the two variables.

Clearly, then, r and β themselves must differ, because r is multiplied to get β. As a result, scores on one test may correlate highly with scores on another test, but may not predict them satisfactorily, or vice-versa. The disjunction between correlation and prediction can occur whenever the two variables being analyzed have different standard deviations. Some studies reviewed in this chapter (Cooper et al., 1988; Kaufman & Kaufman, 1983b; Slate, 1994) reported reduced standard deviations for one or more variables, making such a disjunction possible.

Several researchers reported high correlations and concluded from them that scores on one test were good predictors of scores on another. This conclusion may seem natural but may overreach the evidence on which it is based. If standard deviations are unequal, additional analyses are necessary—and possible using correlational data. Any analysis that specifies a direction can help to support the predictiveness of a test. Multiple regression, exploratory factor analysis, and confirmatory factor analysis are examples. Even analysis of variance or the general linear model can serve this purpose, although interpretation and comparability may be troublesome.

A few studies utilized Cohen's (1988) definitions of a small, medium, and large effect size ($r = .10, .30,$ and $.50,$ respectively). This practice is questionable, at best, for assessments of standardized tests. An effect size has markedly different practical ramifications in these assessments, as compared with the studies considered by Cohen (personal communication, L. O'Dell, December 1997). A Pearson *r* of .50, for example, is frequently not large when it reflects the association between an intelligence test and an achievement test.

As construct-based evidence for validity has accumulated, research on criterion-based evidence has lagged behind. Examinations of the CAS were relatively rare, as was methodologically sound research on the Stanford-Binet with achievement tests. In addition, many studies presented results for overall tests but not for subtests. Thus, subtest patterns and detailed descriptions of associations were often unavailable for interpretation and analysis. Subtest patterns, frequently used to describe ability, may also help practitioners and researchers understand the complex associations between intelligence and achievement scores. Exploratory and confirmatory factor analyses (e.g., Keith & Novak, 1987; Lassiter et al., 1995) can produce detailed, informative results.

Some reports did not identify the correlation coefficient obtained: Pearson's *r* or Kendall's tau, for example. Different coefficients have slightly different metrics and therefore must be compared with caution. Moreover, unidentified coefficients leave a reader with no way of judging whether the coefficient used is appropriate to the data.

Results with nonreferred samples, and with individuals whose overall intelligence scores are average, are sparse outside the tests' technical manuals. In particular, the *DSM-IV* criteria for learning disabilities include average intelligence. Thus, studies applicable to learning disability diagnosis should include participants with average intelligence results, as in Hooper (1987). These studies should report Wechsler Verbal and Performance IQs, if applicable, in addition to Full Scale IQs, because a Verbal-Performance discrepancy commonly comes into play in learning disability diagnosis. Studies comparing learning disabled and learning nondisabled examinees would also be of value.

Similarly, results broken down by ethnicity and gender were frequently unavailable, as were results for deaf and hearing-impaired samples from which participants with other disabilities had been excluded. Unfortunately, exclusion is sometimes necessary when a subsample has too little representation to produce a separate set of results, but may affect the overall results if retained in the overall sample. One option is to present two sets of results: the first for an entire sample and the second for a smaller sample from which the subgroup in question has been excluded.

This approach is also possible when ethnic or other groups are underrepresented in the sample. Researchers can analyze the entire sample, followed by a subsample from which the underrepresented groups have been excluded. Results with the subsample are the statistically sounder ones because of their greater accuracy, and they are scientifically sounder because they provide greater clarity in generalizing the results

to particular groups. Results with the larger sample may be seen as providing for face validity, though with respect to the study rather than to a test. That is, the study may be relatively more acceptable to readers because diverse groups of people have been included. The results still, however, are not generalizable to the underrepresented groups. The only way to generalize with confidence to a particular group is to include sufficient numbers from that group in the sample. Arguably, this strategy is also an excellent way to increase face validity.

An interesting result of the review was that results for conceptually related tests—two verbal measures, for example—sometimes varied widely, with Pearson correlations ranging from the .30s and .40s (e.g., Cooper et al., 1988) to the .70s (e.g., some results of Spruill et al., 1986). Unknown variables, such as sample demographics, are probably responsible for these differences, and researchers should seek to identify these variables.

In summary, results for the relationships between intelligence and achievement tests are incomplete and tend to emphasize a few overall scores. Results are sometimes inconsistent, but thus far, they indicate reasonable correspondence between measures. The WISC-III and its predecessors show particularly high associations for Full Scale and Verbal IQs. Similar results may pertain to the WPPSI-R and the K-BIT, with verbal and overall composites correlating highest, when K-ABC Achievement serves as the criterion.

For many tests, important future steps are to progress from correlation to prediction and to investigate varying results for conceptually related tests. In addition, research is needed with nonreferred samples, with individuals whose overall intelligence scores are average, and with blind, deaf, low-vision, and low-hearing samples from which participants with other disabilities have been excluded. Frequently, breakdowns by ethnicity and gender are needed. The results available thus far show promise, but they are only a start.

REFERENCES

Aiken, L.R. (2000). *Psychological testing and assessment* (10th ed.). Boston: Allyn and Bacon.

American Educational Research Association (AERA), American Psychological Association (APA), and National Council on Measurement in Education (NCME). (1999). *The standards for educational and psychological testing.* Washington, DC: American Psychological Association.

Anastasi, A. (1988). *Psychological testing* (6th ed.). New York: Macmillan.

Arthur, G. (1925). A new point performance scale. *Journal of Applied Psychology, 9,* 390–416.

Blennerhassett, L., Strohmeier, S.J., & Hibbett, C. (1994). Criterion-related validity of Raven's progressive matrices with deaf residential school students. *American Annals of the Deaf, 139,* 104–110.

Boder, E., & Jarrico, S. (1982). *The Boder test of reading-spelling problems.* New York: Grune and Stratton.

Brock, H. (1982). Factor structure of intellectual and achievement measures for learning disabled children. *Psychology in the Schools, 19,* 297–304.

Brooks, C.R., & Riggs, S.T. (1980). WISC-R, WISC, and reading achievement relationships among hearing-impaired children attending public schools. *The Volta Review, 82,* 96–102.

Brown, A.W. (1930). The correlations of non-language tests with each other, with school achievement, and with teachers' judgments of the intelligence of children in a school for the deaf. *Journal of Applied Psychology, 14,* 371–375.

Cantwell, Z.M. (1966). Relationships between scores on the standard progressive matrices (1938) and on the D. 48 test of nonverbal intelligence and three measures of academic achievement. *The Journal of Experimental Education, 34,* 28–31.

Carroll, J.B. (1993). *Human cognitive abilities: A survey of factor-analytic studies.* Cambridge, England: Cambridge University Press.

Childers, J.S., Durham, T.W., Bolen, L.M., & Taylor, L.H. (1985). A predictive validity study of the Kaufman Assessment Battery for children with the California Achievement Test. *Psychology in the Schools, 22,* 29–33.

Christensen, L.B. (1988). *Experimental methodology* (4th ed.). Boston: Allyn and Bacon.

Cohen, J. (1988). *Statistical power analysis for the behavioral sciences* (2nd ed.). Hillsdale, NJ: Lawrence Erlbaum Associates.

Cooper, D., & Fraboni, M. (1988). Relationship between the Wechsler adult intelligence scale–revised and the wide range achievement test–revised in a sample of normal adults. *Educational and Psychological Measurement, 48,* 799–803.

Coveny, T.E. (1973). The Perkins-Binet and verbal WISC as predictors of academic achievement for visually handicapped children. (Doctoral dissertation, Nashville, TN: George Peabody College, 1973).

CTB/McGraw-Hill. (1987). *Comprehensive test of basic skills, Form U.* Monterey, CA: Author.

CTB/McGraw-Hill. (1988). *California achievement tests, Form E.* Monterey, CA: Author.

Davis, C.J. (1980). *The Perkins-Binet tests of intelligence for the blind.* New York: American Foundation for the Blind.

Dunn, L.M., & Markwardt, F.C. (1970). *Peabody individual achievement test: manual.* Circle Pines, MN: American Guidance Services.

Elliot, C.D. (1990). Differential Abilities Scales (DAS) Administration and Scoring Manual. San Antonio, TX: The Psychological Corporation.

Figueroa, R.A., & Sassenrath, J.M. (1989). A longitudinal study of the predictive validity of the System of Multicultural Pluralistic Assessment (SOMPA). *Psychology in the Schools, 26,* 5–19.

Gall, M.D., Borg, W.R., & Gall, J.P. (1996). *Educational research: An introduction.* New York: Longman.

García, G.M., & Stafford, M.E. (2000). Prediction of reading by Ga and Gc specific cognitive abilities for low-SES White and Hispanic English-speaking children. *Psychology in the Schools, 37,* 227–235.

Gardner, E.F., Callis, R., Merwin, J.C., & Madden, R. (1972). *Stanford test of academic skills.* New York: Psychological Corporation.

Gardner, E.F., Madden, R., Rudman, H.C., Karlsen, B., Merwin, J.C., Callis, R., & Collins, C.S. (1987). *Stanford achievement test, seventh edition plus.* San Antonio, TX: The Psychological Corporation.

Gough, H.G., & Domino, G. (1963). The D. 48 as a measure of general ability among grade school children. *Journal of Consulting Psychology, 27,* 244–249.

Groth-Marnat, G. (1997). *Handbook of psychological assessment* (3rd ed.). New York: Wiley.

Gutterman, J.E. (1983). Correlations of the scores of low vision children on the Perkins-Binet tests of intelligence for the blind, Form U; the Wechsler intelligence scale for children–revised, verbal scale; and the wide range achievement test. (Doctoral Dissertation, Columbus: Ohio State University, 1983).

Hayes, S.P. (1941). Stanford Achievement Tests for the blind: New and old. *Teachers Forum for Instructors of Blind Children, 14,* 2–18.

Hieronymus, A.N., & Hoover, H.D. (1986). *Iowa tests of basic skills, Form G.* Chicago: Riverside.

Hooper, S.R. (1987). The relationship between the K-ABC and the Stanford achievement test with reading disabled children. *Journal of Psychoeducational Assessment, 4,* 401–410.

Jastak, J.F., & Jastak, S.R. (1965). *The wide range achievement test.* Wilmington, DE: Guidance Associates.

Jastak, J.F., & Wilkinson, G. (1984). *The wide range achievement test: Manual of instructions.* Wilmington, DE: Jastak Associates.

Kaplan, R.M., & Saccuzzo, D.P. (1997). *Psychological testing: Principles, applications, and issues* (4th ed.). Pacific Grove, CA: Brooks/Cole.

Kamphaus, R.W. (1993). *Clinical assessment of children's intelligence.* Boston: Allyn and Bacon.

Kaufman, A.S. (1972). A short form of the Wechsler preschool and primary scale of intelligence. *Journal of Consulting and Clinical Psychology, 39,* 361–369.

Kaufman, A.S. (1979). *Intelligent testing with the WISC-R.* New York: Wiley-Interscience.

Kaufman, A.S., & Kaufman, N.L. (1983a). *Kaufman assessment battery for children: administration and scoring manual.* Circle Pines, MN: American Guidance Service.

Kaufman, A.S., & Kaufman, N.L. (1983b). *Kaufman assessment battery for children: Interpretive manual.* Circle Pines, MN: American Guidance Service.

Kaufman, A.S., & Kaufman, N.L. (1985). *Kaufman test of educational achievement–comprehensive form.* Circle Pines, MN: American Guidance Service.

Kaufman, A.S., & Kaufman, N.L. (1990). *Kaufman brief intelligence test (K-BIT).* Circle Pines, MN: American Guidance Service.

Keith, T.Z., Kranzler, J.H., & Flanagan, D.P. (2001). What does the cognitive assessment system (CAS) measure? Joint confirmatory factor analysis of the CAS and the Woodcock-Johnson tests of cognitive ability (3rd Edition). *School Psychology Review, 30,* 89–119.

Keith, T.Z., & Novak, C.G. (1987). Joint factor structure of the WISC-R and K-ABC for referred school children. *Journal of Psychoeducational Assessment, 4,* 370–386.

Kelly, M.D., & Braden, J.P. (1990). Criterion-related validity of the WISC-R performance scale with the Stanford achievement test–hearing-impaired edition. *Journal of School Psychology, 28,* 147–151.

Kranzler, J.H., & Keith, T.Z. (1999). Independent confirmatory factor analysis of the cognitive assessment system (CAS): What does the CAS measure? *School Psychology Review, 28,* 117–144.

Lassiter, K.S., & Bardos, A.N. (1995). The relationship between young children's academic achievement and measures of intelligence. *Psychology in the Schools, 32,* 170–177.

Lavin, C. (1996). The relationship between the Wechsler intelligence scale for children–third edition and the Kaufman test of educational achievement. *Psychology in the Schools, 33,* 119–123.

Lobello, S.A. (1991). A short form of the Wechsler preschool and primary scale of intelligence–revised. *Journal of School Psychology, 2,* 229–236.

Luria, A.R. (1980). *Higher cortical functions in man* (B. Haigh, Trans., 2nd ed., rev., expanded). New York: Basic Books. (Original work published 1962)

Madden, R., Gardner, E.F., Rudman, H.C., Karlsen, B., & Merwin, J.C. (1973). *Stanford achievement test (SAT).* New York: Harcourt, Brace, Jovanovich.

McGrew, K.S., Flanagan, D.P., Keith, T.Z., & Vanderwood, M. (1997). Beyond *g:* The impact of Gf-Gc specific cognitive abilities research on the future use and interpretation of intelligence tests in the schools. *School Psychology Review, 26,* 189–210.

McGrew, K.S., & Hessler, G.L. (1995). The relationship between the WJ-R *Gf-Gc* cognitive clusters and mathematics achievement across the life-span. *Journal of Psychoeducational Assessment, 13,* 21–38.

McGrew, K.S., & Knopik, S.N. (1993). The relationship between the WJ-R *Gf-Gc* cognitive clusters and writing achievement across the life-span. *School Psychology Review, 22,* 687–695.

McGrew, K.S., & Woodcock, R.W. (2001). *Woodcock-Johnson III: Technical manual.* Itasca, IL: Riverside.

Mercer, J.R. (1979). *The System of multicultural pluralistic assessment (SOMPA): Conceptual and technical manual.* New York: Psychological Corporation.

Naglieri, J.A. (1988). *Draw-a-person: A quantitative scoring system.* San Antonio, TX: Psychological Corporation.

Naglieri, J.A. (1999). How valid is the PASS theory and CAS? *School Psychology Review, 28,* 145–162.

Naglieri, J.A., & Das, J.P. (1997). *The cognitive assessment system: Interpretive handbook.* Itasca, IL: Riverside.

Ollendick, D.G., & Ollendick, T.H. (1976). The interrelationship of measures of locus of control, intelligence, and achievement in juvenile delinquents. *Educational and Psychological Measurement, 36,* 1111–1113.

Paal, N., Skinner, S., & Reddig, C. (1988). The relationship of nonverbal intelligence measures to academic achievement among deaf adolescents. *Journal of Rehabilitation of the Deaf, 21,* 8–11.

Phelps, L., & Branyan, B.J. (1990). Academic achievement and nonverbal intelligence in public school hearing-impaired children. *Psychology in the Schools, 27*(3), 210–217.

Porter, L.J., & Kirby, E.A. (1986). Effects of two instructional sets on the validity of the Kaufman assessment battery for children–nonverbal scale with a group of severely hearing impaired children. *Psychology in the Schools, 23,* 37–43.

Powers, S., Jones, P.B., & Barkan, J.H. (1986). Validity of the standard progressive matrices as a predictor of achievement of sixth and seventh grade students. *Educational and Psychological Measurement, 46,* 719–722.

Prescott, G.A., Balow, I.H., Hogan, T.P., & Farr, R.C. (1986). *Metropolitan achievement test* (6th ed.). San Antonio, TX: Psychological Corporation.

Prewett, P.N., Bardos, A.N., & Naglieri, J.A. (1989). Assessment of mentally retarded children with the Matrix Analogies Test-Short Form, Draw A Person: Quantitative Scoring System, and the Kaufman Test of Educational Achievement. *Psychology in the Schools, 26,* 254–260.

Prewett, P.N., & Farhney, M.R. (1994). The concurrent validity of the Matrix Analogies Test-Short Form with the Stanford-Binet: Fourth Edition and KTEA-BF (academic achievement). *Psychology in the Schools, 31,* 20–25.

Prewett, P.N., & McCaffery, L.K. (1993). A comparison of the Kaufman Brief Intelligence Test (K-BIT) with the Stanford-Binet, a two-subtest short form, and the Kaufman Test of Educational Achievement (K-TEA) Brief Form. *Psychology in the Schools, 30,* 299–304.

Psychological Corporation. (1997). *Wechsler adult intelligence scale–third edition (WAIS-III) and Wechsler memory scale–third edition (WMS-III): Technical manual.* San Antonio, TX: Author.

Ramsay, M.C., & Pashiardis, G. (2001). *Recruitment and retention of Texas special educators: Sources, strategies, programs, and evidence for effectiveness.* College Station, TX: Institute for School-University Partnerships.

Ramsay, M.C. (1998, February). *The processing system in humans: A theory.* Paper presented at the annual meeting of the Education Research Exchange, Texas A&M University, College Station.

Ramsay, M.C. (1997, January). *A new theory of cognition and behavior, with applications to depression and other disorders.* Paper presented at the annual meeting of the Southwest Educational Research Association, Austin, TX.

Ramsay, M.C., & Reynolds, C.R. (2000). Development of a scientific test: A practical guide. In G. Goldstein & M. Hersen (Eds.), *Handbook of psychological assessment* (3rd ed.), pp. 21–42. New York: Elsevier.

Ramsay, M.C., Reynolds, C.R., & Kamphaus, R.W. (2002). *Essentials of behavioral assessment.* New York: Wiley.

Raven, J.C. (1963). *Guide to the standard progressive matrices.* London: H.K. Lewis.

Raven, J.C., Court, J.H., & Raven, J. (1983). *Manual for Raven's progressive matrices and vocabulary scales (Research Supplement 1)*. London: H.K. Lewis.

Reynolds, C.R., & Kaufman, A.S. (1990). Assessment of children's intelligence with the Wechsler intelligence scale for children–revised (WISC-R). In C.R. Reynolds & R.W. Kamphaus (Eds.), *Handbook of psychological and educational assessment of children: Intelligence and achievement* (pp. 127–165). New York: Guilford.

Reynolds, C.R., & Ramsay, M.C. (in press). Understanding, identifying, and avoiding cultural bias in ability tests: An empirical review with recommendations. In J. Graham and J. Naglieri, *Handbook of psychological assessment*. New York: Wiley and Sons.

Rich, C.C., & Anderson, R.P. (1965). A tactual form of the progressive matrices for use with blind children. *Personnel and Guidance Journal, 43*, 912–919.

Roid, G.H., Prifitera, A., & Weiss, L.G. (1993). Replication of the WISC-III factor structure in an independent sample. *Journal of Psychoeducational Assessment* [WISC-III Monograph].

Sattler, J.M. (1992). *Assessment of children* (2nd ed., rev. & updated). San Diego, CA: Jerome M. Sattler, Publisher, Inc.

Sattler, J.M. (2001). *Assessment of children: Cognitive applications* (4th ed.). La Mesa, CA: Jerome M. Sattler, Publisher, Inc.

Shinn, M., Algozzine, B., Marston, D., & Ysseldyke, J. (1982). A theoretical analysis of the performance of learning disabled children on the Woodcock-Johnson Psycho-Battery. *Journal of Learning Disabilities, 15*, 221–226.

Shurrager, H.C. (1961). *A Haptic intelligence scale for adult blind.* Chicago: Illinois Institute of Technology.

Shurrager, H.C., & Shurrager, P. (1964). *The haptic intelligence scale for the adult blind: manual.* Chicago: Psychology Research.

Simpson, R.G. (1982). Correlations between the general information subtest of the Peabody individual achievement test and the full scale intelligence quotient of the WISC-R. *Educational and Psychological Measurement, 42*, 695–699.

Slate, J.R. (1994). WISC-III correlations with the WIAT. *Psychology in the Schools, 31*, 278–285.

Smith, T.C., Smith, B.L., & Dobbs, K. (1991). Relationship between the Peabody picture vocabulary test–revised, wide range achievement test–revised, and Wechsler intelligence scale for children–revised. *Journal of School Psychology, 29*, 53–56.

Spruill, J., & Beck, B. (1986). Relationship between the WAIS-R and wide range achievement test–revised. *Educational and Psychological Measurement, 46*, 1037–1040.

Stedman, J.M., Lawlis, G.F., Cortner, R.H., & Achterberg, G. (1978). Relationships between WISC-R factors, wide-range achievement test scores, and visual-motor maturation in children referred for psychological evaluation. *Journal of Consulting and Clinical Psychology, 46*, 869–872.

Streitfeld, J., & Avery, C. (1968). The WAIS and HIS tests as predictors of academic achievement in a residential school for the blind. *The International Journal for the Education of the Blind, 18*, 73–77.

Sullivan, E.T., Clark, W.W., & Tiegs, E.W. (1970). *Short form test of academic aptitude (SFTAA).* New York: McGraw-Hill.

Teeter, P.A., & Smith, P.L. (1993). WISC-III and WJ-R: Predictive and discriminant validity for students with severe emotional disturbance. *Journal of Psychoeducational Assessment* [WISC-III Monograph].

Thorndike, R.L., Hagen, E.P., Sattler, J.M. (1986). The Stanford-Binet intelligence scale: fourth edition. Technical manual. Chicago: Riverside.

Tulsky, D.S., & Ledbetter, M.F. (2000). Updating to the WAIS-III and WMS-III: Considerations for research and clinical practice. *Psychological Assessment, 12*, 253–262.

Ulissi, S.M., Brice, P.J., & Gibbins, S. (1989). Use of the Kaufman assessment battery for children with the hearing impaired. *American Annals of the Deaf, 134*, 283–287.

Valencia, R.R. (1990). Clinical assessment of young children with the McCarthy Scales of Children's Abilities. In C.R. Reynolds & R.W. Kamphaus (Eds.), Handbook of psychological and educational assessment of children: Intelligence and achievement. New York: Guildford Press.

Vance, B., Kitson, D., & Singer, M.G. (1985). Relationship between the standard scores of Peabody Picture Vocabulary Test-Revised and Wide Range Achievement Test. *Journal of Child Psychology, 41*, 691–693.

Watson, B., Goldgar, D., Kroese, J., & Lotz, W. (1986). Nonverbal intelligence and academic achievement in the hearing-impaired. *The Volta Review, 88*, 151–158.

Watson, B.U., Sullivan, P.M., Moeller, M.P., & Jensen, J.K. (1982). Nonverbal intelligence and English language ability in deaf children. *Journal of Speech and Hearing Disorders, 47*, 199–204.

Wechsler, D. (1949). *Wechsler intelligence scale for children: Manual.* New York: Psychological Corporation.

Wechsler, D. (1974). *Wechsler intelligence scale for children–revised: Manual.* New York: Psychological Corporation.

Wechsler, D. (1981). *Wechsler adult intelligence scale–revised: Manual.* New York: Psychological Corporation.

Wechsler, D. (1989). *Wechsler preschool and primary scale of intelligence–revised.* San Antonio, TX: Psychological Corporation.

Wechsler, D. (1991). *Wechsler intelligence scale for children–third edition: Manual.* San Antonio, TX: Psychological Corporation.

Wechsler individual achievement test (WIAT). (1992). San Antonio: The Psychological Corporation.

Weiss, L.G., Prifitera, A., & Roid, G. (1993). The WISC-III and the fairness of predicting achievement across ethnic and gender groups. *Journal of Psychoeducational Assessment* [WISC-III Monograph].

Wikoff, R.L. (1978). Correlational and factor analysis of the Peabody individual intelligence test and the WISC-R. *Journal of Consulting and Clinical Psychology, 46*, 322–325.

Woodcock, R.W. (1987). Woodcock Reading Mastery Tests. Circle Pines, MN: American Guidance Service.

Woodcock, R.W., & Johnson, M.B. (1989). *Woodcock-Johnson psycho-educational battery–revised.* Allen, TX: DLM.

CHAPTER 4

The Wechsler Intelligence Scales for Children and Adults

JIANJUN ZHU, LAWRENCE G. WEISS, AURELIO PRIFITERA, AND DIANE COALSON

INTRODUCTION

Since their publication, the Wechsler intelligence scales have had a tremendous influence on the field of psychological assessment. They have been the most often used instruments for assessing the cognitive abilities of children, adolescents, and adults nationally and internationally (Sparrow & Davis, 2000; Stinnett, Havey, & Oehler-Stinnett, 1994). Harrison, Kaufman, Hickman, and Kaufman (1988) found that 97% of their respondents routinely use Wechsler intelligence tests. Watkins, Campbell, Nieberding, & Hallmark (1995) reported that 93% of surveyed psychologists administer the Wechsler intelligence tests at least occasionally. Other surveys have also found that the Wechsler scales are used on a frequent basis (Lubin, Larsen, & Matarazzo, 1984; Lubin, Larson, Matarazzo, & Seever, 1985; Piotrowski & Keller, 1989). Currently, the Wechsler intelligence scales continue to rank number one in intelligence test usage among clinical psychologists and school psychologists (Wasserman & Maccubbin, 2002).

The Wechsler intelligence tests are also the most researched instruments. An immense volume of literature related to their clinical utility and psychometric properties has been accumulated since the original publication of each instrument. Among this body of literature exists substantial evidence of dependable clinical utility and sound psychometric properties for the Wechsler Intelligence Scale for Children–Third Edition (WISC-III) and Wechsler Adult Intelligence Scale–Third Edition (WAIS-III; Kaufman & Lichtenberger, 1999; Prifitera & Saklofske, 1998; Sattler, 2001).

David Wechsler (1896–1981) obtained his master's degree in 1917 and his doctoral degree in 1925 from Columbia University. During his graduate training, he was mentored by James M. Cattell, Robert S. Woodworth, Edward L. Thorndike, and Charles E. Spearman. These historical giants of psychology deeply influenced Wechsler's later work. Prior to the development of his first intelligence scale, the Wechsler–Bellevue Intelligence Scale (Wechsler-Bellevue; Wechsler, 1939), Wechsler had accumulated considerable experience in the fields of clinical assessment and test devel-

TABLE 4.1   History of Wechsler Cognitive Assessment Instruments

WAIS-III (1997)	WISC-III (1991)	WPPSI-III (2002)	WMS-III (1997)
WAIS-R (1981)	WISC-R (1974)	WPPSI-R (1989)	WMS-R (1974)
WAIS (1955)	WISC (1949)	WPPSI[a] (1967)	WMS[b] (1945)
Wechsler-Bellevue I (1939)	Wechsler Bellevue-Form II (1946)		

[a]WPPSI = Wechsler Preschool and Primary Scale of Intelligence
[b]WMS = Wechsler Memory Scale.

opment. His master's thesis consisted of a comprehensive battery of memory that was assembled using frameworks and procedures developed by Thorndike, Woodworth, Whipple, and other experimental psychologists (Wasserman et al., 2002). During World War I, Wechsler was employed as a military psychologist. As part of his position, he conducted several hundred individual assessments of mental ability and scored thousands of Army Alpha protocols. After World War I, Wechsler served as a staff psychologist at Bellevue hospital and worked as a research associate at The Psychological Corporation. From 1925 to 1927, he evaluated the intelligence in a variety of professional groups and developed a test of competency of automobile drivers. This variety of clinical and empirical experience contributed to his later success in test development.

Wechsler's original intelligence test, the Wechsler–Bellevue, made an indelible contribution to the history of intelligence assessment. Although Wechsler borrowed many ideas from existing measures (Zachary, 1990), the Wechsler–Bellevue was a significant innovation in the history of intelligence testing. Based on his considerable clinical expertise, Wechsler united the finest aspects of other's work to create a battery of intelligence that was more comprehensive, clinically useful, and ecologically valid.

Wechsler was innovative in his incorporation of scores for verbal and performance scales in addition to an overall composite score. Wechsler (1944) wrote:

The most obviously useful feature of the Wechsler–Bellevue scales is their division into a Verbal and Performance part. . . . Its a priori value is that it makes a possible comparison between a subject's facility in using words and symbols and his ability to manipulate objects, and to perceive visual patterns. In practice this division is substantiated by differences between posited abilities and various occupational aptitudes. Clerical workers and teachers, in general, do much better on verbal tests, whereas manual workers and mechanics do better on performance. The correlations are sufficiently high to be of value in vocational guidance, particularly with adolescents of high school age.

Apart from their possible relation to vocational aptitudes, differences between verbal and performance test scores, particularly when large, have a special interest for the clinician because such discrepancies are frequently associated with certain types of mental pathology. (p. 146)

The Wechsler–Bellevue was also innovative because it was the first instrument to use deviation IQ scores. Prior to the publication of Wechsler–Bellevue, the mental level of an individual was expressed in terms of mental age (MA), a concept originally introduced by Binet in 1908. However, this concept was misleading in practice. On one hand, children at different ages can obtain the same MA. On the other hand, clinically speaking, it is not correct to assume their intellectual levels are identical. Besides, MA changes as an individual ages, because MA is sensitive to the change of the raw score mean and standard deviation. In addition, because the growth curves of MA and chronicle age (CA) are not the same, IQ scores derived from MA/CA ratio do not form an interval scale. Furthermore, sometimes it is hard to determine what age should be considered as the MA of adults. These limitations caused significant problems on the interpretation of the test results. By using the deviation IQ scores that were based on standard scores computed with the same distributional characteristics at all ages, Wechsler successfully solved the problems posed by the concept of MA. The deviation IQ score makes the comparison among peers more meaningful and the interpretation more straightforward.

In addition to being an experienced clinician, Wechsler was a prolific test developer and researcher who authored four major instruments of cognitive assessment and a long list of publications related to the clinical assessment of intelligence. Table 4.1 provides a history of cognitive assessment instruments authored and published under the Wechsler name.

THEORETICAL FOUNDATION OF THE WECHSLER INTELLIGENCE TESTS

The evolution of the Wechsler intelligence scales began with the original Wechsler–Bellevue. Wechsler based this test on the premise that intelligence is a *global* entity because it characterizes the individual's behavior as a whole, and it is also *specific* because it is composed of elements or abilities that are distinct from each other. Based on his clinical expertise, Wechsler selected and developed subtests that highlighted the cognitive aspects of intelligence he thought were important to measure: abstract reasoning, perceptual organization, verbal comprehension, quantitative reasoning, memory, and processing speed. All of these areas have been confirmed as important aspects of cognitive ability in more contemporary theories and measures of intelligence (Carroll, 1993a, 1997; Horn, 1991). More than 60 years of research support the practical and clinical utility of the Wechsler scales across a wide range of settings and purposes. Consistently, the scales have demonstrated their clinical utility for such purposes as the identification of mental retardation and learning disabilities, placement in specialized programs, clinical intervention, and neuropsychological evaluation (Beres, Kaufman, & Perlman, 2000). With such overwhelming evidence of clinical utility, it is hard to accept, as some have asserted, that "it is a matter of luck that many of the Wechsler subtests are neurologically relevant" (McFie, 1975, p. 14), or that Wechsler did not have remarkable insight into the nature of intelligence when selecting and developing the subtests for his scales.

Intelligence Is a Global Entity Aggregated from Specific Narrow Abilities

Wechsler viewed the construct of intelligence not only as a global entity but also as an aggregate of specific abilities that are qualitatively different. Intelligence is global because it characterizes the individual's behavior as a whole. It is also specific because it is made up of elements or abilities that are qualitatively different. Therefore, he believed that intelligence could best be measured by a wide array of tests. Several decades of factor-analytic studies of intelligence measures indicate that intelligence is composed of specific narrow abilities that appear to cluster into higher order ability domains (Keith, 1990; Carroll, 1993). Wechsler (1974) wrote:

> Intelligence can manifest itself in many forms, and an intelligence scale, to be effective as well as fair, must utilize as many different languages (tests) as possible. (p. 5)

Some researchers presumed that because Wechsler split subtests into verbal and performance tasks, he assumed a two-factor structure of intelligence. However, Wechsler (1958) clarified the practical purpose of the split by noting

> [The grouping of subtests into Verbal and Performance areas] . . . does not imply that these are the only abilities involved in the tests. . . . The subtests are different measures of intelligence, not measures of different kinds of intelligence, and the dichotomy of Verbal and Performance areas is only one of several ways in which the tests could be grouped. (p. 64)

Although there are advantages to the assessment and division of more narrow domains of cognitive functioning,

several issues deserve note. First, cognitive functions are interrelated and interact with each other, which makes it difficult to measure a pure domain of cognitive functioning. Even traditional measures of narrow domains, such as processing speed, involve the ability of an individual to discriminate between visual stimuli, process the information, and indicate a response by performing a motoric function. Although the results of factor-analytic studies may be interpreted as reflecting the presence or absence of a measured domain, the results may not accurately reflect the variety of cognitive abilities required to complete a subtest task. Subtest loadings differ based on the composition and combination of subtests, so claims about what a subtest measures also vary based on the mix of subtests included in the analysis.

Second, it is ecologically valid to include subtests that require the use of multiple cognitive abilities. Cognitive tasks are rarely, if ever, performed in isolation. As Wechsler (1975) noted:

> . . . the attributes and factors of intelligence, like the elementary particles in physics, have at once collective and individual properties, that is, they appear to behave differently when alone from what they do when operating in concert. (p. 138)

The ecological validity of general intelligence is supported by the evidence of its ability to predict such things as job performance and overall psychological well-being. Measures of more discrete domains of cognitive and personality functioning do not show the same degree of predictive ability (Gottfredson, 1998). Measuring psychometrically pure factors of discrete domains may be useful diagnostically, but such measurements do not necessarily result in information that is clinically rich or practical in real-world applications (Zachary, 1990).

Third, it would be unreasonable to expect any single measure of intelligence to adequately test all domains in a meaningful and practical way (Carroll, 1997). Wechsler was successful in selecting measures that sampled a wide variety of domains (e.g., verbal comprehension, perceptual organization, memory), which have since proven to be important aspects of cognitive functioning. He also realized the possibility of obtaining invalid test results when examiners or examinees became fatigued. He selected a sufficient number of subtests to provide clinically meaningful information regarding an individual's cognitive functioning in a reasonable time period. Wechsler believed that other related factors, such as academic achievement, executive functioning, and motor skills, may influence performance on intelligence tests, but they are best measured by instruments designed specifically to assess these domains. His sensitivity to the practical aspects of intelligence testing is evidenced in his development of a separate memory scale (Wechsler, 1945a, 1945b).

Nonintellective Aspects of Intelligent Behavior

Finally, performance on measures of cognitive ability reflects only a portion of what comprises intelligence. Wechsler (1944) defined intelligence as the "capacity of the individual to act purposefully, to think rationally, and to deal effectively with his environment" (p. 3). He avoided defining intelligence in purely cognitive terms, because he believed that these factors only comprised a portion of intelligence. Wechsler was keenly aware that the results of factor-analytic studies accounted for only a percentage of the overall variance in intelligence, and he believed that another group of attributes contributed to this unexplained variance. These attributes included planning and goal awareness, enthusiasm, field dependence and independence, impulsiveness, anxiety, and persistence. Such attributes are not directly tapped by standardized measures of intellectual ability, yet they influence a child's performance on these measures and his or her effectiveness in daily living and meeting the world and its challenges (Wechsler, 1975).

Because scores on intelligence scales summarize performance on a particular sample of discrete tasks, the scores and their meanings are tied to specific test content. Although tests of intellectual ability provide a considerable amount of information about an individual's cognitive ability in a relatively short amount of time, the clinician should view each individual as unique and take into account attributes other than intelligence when interpreting test results (Matarazzo, 1972, 1990). It is widely recognized that children with similar test scores may not cope equally well with similar environmental challenges for reasons unrelated to their cognitive abilities. Conversely, because factors unrelated to intelligence influence test performance, children with different underlying levels of intellectual ability could achieve similar scores. The task of assessing a child's intelligence necessarily involves more than simply obtaining his or her scores on measures of intelligence. As Wechsler (1975) noted,

> What we measure with tests is not what tests measure—not information, not spatial perception, not reasoning ability. These are only a means to an end. What intelligence tests measure is something much more important: the capacity of an individual to understand the world about him and his resourcefulness to cope with its challenges. (p. 139)

In summary, although the Wechsler scales have been criticized for the lack of a strong theoretical basis, examination of the scales in historical perspective indicates their origins in prevailing intelligence theories of their time, strong evidence of clinical utility, and their revision to reflect changes

and advances in more contemporary intelligence theories. Wechsler tests tap most of the important aspects of cognitive ability in contemporary theories and measures of intelligence (Carroll, 1993, 1997; Horn, 1991). Additional support of a theoretical basis in the Wechsler scales is evident in the appearance of the same or similar subtests in other measures of intelligence (e.g., Differential Abilities Scale, [Elliott, 1990]; Kaufman Assessment Battery for Children, [KABC; Kaufman & Kaufman, 1983], Woodcock-Johnson–Third Edition, Test of Cognitive Ability [WJ-III; Woodcock, McGrew, & Mather, 2001]), and the high correlation of Wechsler intelligence scales with other measures of cognitive ability. Despite criticisms aimed at the basis of his test selection, many of the subtests that Wechsler selected, such as Block Design, and Vocabulary, continue to appear in modified form on most recent measures of intellectual ability with claims of strong foundations in intelligence theory. Similarly, evidence of the scale's validity is supported by its correlations with other, more recent measures of cognitive ability (e.g., DAS, K-ABC).

Revisions of Wechsler intelligence scales continue. Each new edition involves much more than a mere update of normative data. Each revision includes new tasks and indices carefully designed to reflect advances in theoretical and practical foundations of cognitive and neuropsychological assessment. At the time of this writing, the development of the *Wechsler Intelligence Scale for Children–Fourth Edition* (WISC-IV; Wechsler, in press) is nearing completion. The WISC-IV has incorporated new subtests to tap such constructs as fluid reasoning, working memory, and processing speed. The Matrix Reasoning and Picture Concepts subtests have been developed to provide measures of fluid reasoning ability. The Freedom From Distractibility index will be renamed as Working Memory Quotient, and the Letter-Number Sequencing subtest of the WAIS-III has been adapted for use with younger children to enhance this factor. In addition, the Cancellation subtest has been developed to strengthen the processing speed factor.

CONSTRUCT REPRESENTATION IN THE WISC-III AND WAIS-III

The WISC-III includes a total of 13 subtests, including 10 core subtests and 3 supplemental and optional subtests. The WAIS-III is composed of 14 subtests, including 11 core subtests and 3 supplemental and optional subtests. Both instruments provide three IQ scores: the Verbal IQ (VIQ), Performance IQ (PIQ), and Full Scale IQ (FSIQ). In addition, the scales provide four index scores, the Verbal Comprehension Index (VCI), Perceptual Organization Index (POI), Working Memory Index (WMI),[1] and Processing Speed In-

TABLE 4.2   Subtest Contribution to IQ and Index Scales of the WISC-III and WAIS-III

WISC-III Subtest	Contribution to IQ and Factor Index Scales						
	VIQ	PIQ	FSIQ	VCI	POI	FDI	PSI
Vocabulary	✓		✓	✓			
Similarities	✓		✓	✓			
Information	✓		✓	✓			
Comprehension	✓		✓	✓			
Arithmetic	✓		✓			✓	
Digit Span	(✓)		(✓)			✓	
Block Design		✓	✓		✓		
Object Assembly		✓	✓		✓		
Picture Completion		✓	✓		✓		
Picture Arrangement		✓	✓		✓		
Coding		✓	✓				✓
Symbol Search		(✓)	(✓)				✓
Mazes (Optional)		(✓)	(✓)				

WAIS-III Subtest	Contribution to IQ and Factor Index Scales						
	VIQ	PIQ	FSIQ	VCI	POI	WMI	PSI
Vocabulary	✓		✓	✓			
Similarities	✓		✓	✓			
Information	✓		✓	✓			
Comprehension	✓		✓	(✓)			
Arithmetic	✓		✓			✓	
Digit Span	(✓)		(✓)			✓	
Letter Number Sequencing						✓	
Block Design		✓	✓		✓		
Matrix Reasoning		✓	✓		✓		
Picture Completion		✓	✓		✓		
Picture Arrangement		✓	✓		(✓)		
Digit Symbol-Coding		✓	✓				✓
Symbol Search		(✓)	(✓)				✓
Object Assembly (Optional)		(✓)	(✓)				

dex (PSI). Approximately 75–80 minutes are required to obtain the three IQ scores, 70–75 minutes to obtain the four index scores, and about 80–85 minutes to obtain IQ and index scores.

Table 4.2 lists the subtests of the two instruments, and the IQ and index scales to which each subtest contributes. Those subtests noted with a check mark enclosed in parentheses are supplemental and can substitute for core subtests that contribute to the same scale. The Mazes subtest of the WISC-III and the Object Assembly subtest of the WAIS-III are optional subtests. They may be used to substitute a spoiled subtest that contributes to IQ or index scale.

IMPROVEMENTS TO THE WISC-III AND WAIS-III

Introducing Factor-Based Index Scores

Both the WISC-III and WAIS-III provide factor-based index scores that measure major cognitive domains identified in contemporary theories of intelligence. The primary advantage of the factor index scores is that they measure relatively purer cognitive domains than the traditional IQ scores mea-

sure. For example, the traditional Verbal IQ (VIQ) score summarizes an individual's performance on subtests that are designed to measure verbal comprehension and working memory. The traditional PIQ score summarizes an individual's performance on subtests that assess perceptual organization and processing speed. An individual can obtain an average VIQ score because he or she performs at an average level on both subdomains or at an above-average level on one domain and at a below-average level on the other domain. Because the factor indexes represent an individual's functioning in more narrowly defined domains, the clinician can more clearly evaluate specific aspects of cognitive functioning. An expanded discussion of the clinical utility of factor-based index scores is provided later in this chapter in the section where the validity evidence of the factor index scores is discussed.

Additional Normative Information

The WAIS-III provides normative data for ages 16–89 years, a wider age range compared to the WAIS-R. The WISC-III and WAIS-III provide additional normative information for clinical evaluation, such as profile analysis (e.g., determining strengths and weaknesses, scatter, IQ, and factor-index score discrepancies), memory-ability discrepancy, and achievement-ability discrepancy. To facilitate interpretation of assessment results, critical values and base rates are available in the test manual to determine the statistical significance of a given discrepancy and the frequency of occurrence in the normative sample, respectively. This information allows the clinician to determine whether a given score discrepancy is clinically meaningful. Previously, this type of normative data was available only in journal articles and related literature that appeared well after the test was published.

Enhanced Measure of Fluid Ability

In the WAIS-III, Matrix Reasoning replaces Object Assembly as a core subtest and contributes to PIQ, FSIQ, and Perceptual Organization Index (POI) scores. Currently, the research edition of the WISC-IV also incorporates new subtests such as Matrix Reasoning and Picture Concepts, to tap fluid reasoning ability. It has long been recognized that matrix analogy tasks are good measures of fluid intelligence (Sternberg, 1995) and reliable estimates of general cognitive/intellectual ability (g) (Brody, 1992; Raven, Raven, & Court, 1991). Studies have shown that scores on matrix analogy tests are highly correlated with the IQ scores of the Wechsler scales (Desai, 1955; Hall, 1957; Levine & Iscoe, 1954; Watson & Klett, 1974).

In addition, matrix-reasoning tasks are considered to be relatively culture-fair and language-free; they require no hand manipulation, and have no time limits. These features make these tasks an appealing measure of PIQ, particularly with older adults and minorities. Such measures also allow for contrast with other nonverbal reasoning tasks, such as Block Design. When performance on Block Design is low, for example, the hypothesis that an individual's score may have been affected by slow response times or due to motor problem can be evaluated by comparison with his or her performance on Matrix Reasoning, a subtest with greatly reduced time constraints. Such contrasts allow for more meaningful interpretation of test scores and performance.

Reliability coefficients of the WAIS-III Matrix Reasoning subtest across the different age groups range from .84 to .94, with an average coefficient of .90. The Matrix Reasoning subtest correlates highest with Block Design (.60) and loads on the Perceptual Organization factor. Results of two validity studies using samples of 26 nonclinical adults and 22 adults with schizophrenia found that the WAIS-III Matrix Reasoning subtest correlates with Raven's Progressive Matrices .81 and .79, respectively.

Conorming and Linkage to Other Measures

The WAIS-III was conormed with the Wechsler Memory Scale–Third Edition (WMS-III; Wechsler, 1997). Similarly, the WISC-III was linked to Children's Memory Scale (CMS; Cohen, 1997). This linkage allows clinicians to examine IQ/memory discrepancy scores and assist them in the interpretation of additional domains of cognitive functioning that include intelligence and memory assessment. The *WAIS-III/ WMS-III Technical Manual* and the CMS manual provide tables of critical values and base rates that allow clinicians to determine whether a given memory-IQ score discrepancy is statistically significant and how frequently it is observed in the normative sample. Discrepancies between intelligence and memory are sometimes used to evaluate memory impairment. With this approach, learning and memory are assumed to be underlying components of general intellectual ability and, as such, to be significantly related to the individual's performance on tests of intellectual functioning. In fact, IQ scores are often used as an estimate of the individual's actual memory ability. Several researchers have advanced the theory that when a memory score is significantly lower than an IQ score, the discrepancy is suggestive of a focal memory impairment (Milner, 1975; Prigatano, 1974; Quadfasel & Pruyser, 1955). This is especially true when the discrepancy is rarely observed in the normative sample.

In addition, both the WISC-III and WAIS-III are linked to the Wechsler Individual Achievement Test–Second Edition (WIAT-II; The Psychological Corporation, 2001). Such linkage provides a means of comparing an individual's general intellectual ability level to his or her level of academic achievement. Comparisons between intellectual ability and academic achievement have served as a primary criterion in determining eligibility for special educational services since the enactment of the Individuals with Disabilities Education Act (IDEA, 1997).

Two methods for comparing intellectual ability and academic achievement are presented in the *WIAT-II Examiner's Manual* (The Psychological Corporation, 2001): the simple-difference method and the predicted-difference method. The manual provides details related to the rationale for choosing these methods and the statistical procedures involved for this comparison. Although both methods are presented, the predicted-difference method is generally preferred because the formula for this method takes into account the reliabilities and the correlations between the two measures.

In general, the Full Scale IQ (FSIQ) score should be used as the best estimate of intellectual ability unless there is some compelling reason to use the VIQ or PIQ (e.g., visual or motor problems that may interfere with the validity of some subtests). The WIAT-II manual provides tables for ability-achievement discrepancy analysis using the FSIQ, VIQ, and PIQ scores of the WISC-III and WAIS-III and the WIAT-II subtest and composite scores. The base rate of ability-achievement discrepancy is based on only the cases whose achievement scores are lower than IQ scores.

WISC-III and WAIS-III are also linked to the Wechsler Abbreviated Scales of Intelligence (WASI; The Psychological Corporation, 1999). WASI was developed to meet the demands for a short and reliable measure of intelligence in clinical, psychoeducational, and research settings. It is individually administered and is designed for use with individuals aged from 6 to 89 years. WASI highly correlated to the WISC-III and WAIS-III ($r = .87$ and $.92$, respectively), and it provides consistent measurement results as the WISC-III and WAIS-III.

Psychologists, clinicians, and researchers often need a fast and reliable measure of intelligence when screening for mental retardation, giftedness, or for vocational or rehabilitation planning. They may need to retest individuals who received a comprehensive evaluation at an earlier time or obtain IQ estimates for individuals who are referred for psychiatric evaluations. Frequently, IQ estimates are needed for research purposes, such as preexperimental matching for cognitive ability. In these situations, administration of a full battery may not be feasible or necessary. Additionally, the expansion of mental health services and the effects of managed health care on these services have placed time and financial constraints on the practice of assessment. A valid and effective but also brief measure of intelligence is often needed to aid in treatment, intervention, and training decisions (Moon & Gorsuch, 1988).

Historically, psychologists, clinicians, and researchers have turned to the Wechsler intelligence scales to meet their need for a short form. Most agree that a short form of a Wechsler intelligence scale is the best alternative when time limits are the primary concern or when the purpose of administration is a quick estimate of intellectual functioning (Kaufman, 1990; Kaufman, Ishikuma, & Kaufman–Packer, 1991; Reynolds, Willson, & Clark, 1983; Silverstein, 1982). Short forms of well-established intelligence scales are clearly superior to many existing brief intelligence measures in terms of psychometric properties and normative data (Kaufman, 1990; Reynolds et al., 1983). On the other hand, short forms may have some limitations because they do not have independent norms, there are too many short forms to choose, and the samples used to derive the short forms may not be representative.

The WASI was developed and normed as an independent scale. It consists of four subtests: Vocabulary, Block Design, Similarities, and Matrix Reasoning. Administration of all four subtests is a means of quickly estimating an individual's verbal, nonverbal, and general cognitive functioning in approximately 30 minutes. When time is a major constraint, only two subtests of the WASI, namely, Vocabulary and Matrix Reasoning, are needed for estimating general cognitive functioning in 15 minutes or less.

The four subtests of WASI consist of items that differ from, but parallel those in the Wechsler scale. Such a design reduces practice effects when WASI is used in conjunction with the WISC-III and WAIS-III. WASI can screen for the need of comprehensive evaluation of intellectual functioning. After WASI administration, if it is necessary, the comprehensive measure of intellectual functioning may be obtained in two ways: administer the full battery of WISC-III or WAIS-III, or administer only the WISC-III or WAIS-III subtests that are not included in the WASI, then use WASI subtest scores to substitute the related WISC-III or WAIS-III subtest scores. Research demonstrated that both methods produce reliable, valid, and consistent measurement results (Zhu, Coalson, & Rolfhus, 2001; Zhu & Tulsky, 1999). The second method, however, is recommended because it is less time consuming and the additional measurement errors resulting from substitution are small.

In the near future, in addition to the linkage to measures of memory and achievement, the WISC-IV will be linked with measures of emotion, adaptive functioning, and language. It is expected that the additional linking studies will provide a more thorough evaluation of an individual's psychological functioning in a wider ecological context.

Optional Procedures for Process Analysis

The WAIS-III incorporated several optional procedures, including an evaluation of incidental learning after the Digit Symbol–Coding administration (see Hart, Kwentus, Wade, & Hamer, 1987; Kaplan, Fein, Morris, & Delis, 1991). Optional procedures for a process evaluation are also available in the WISC-III, including a companion instrument designed for this purpose, the WISC-III as a Processing Instrument (WISC-III PI; Kaplan et al., 1999). The WISC-III PI provides normative data for many optional procedures based upon the *process approach* to interpretation that was advocated by Kaplan and others (Kaplan, 1988). These procedures and normative data provide a method for evaluating the nature of errors that were made on the WISC-III. For details of the process approach and the optional procedures, refer to the WISC-III PI manual.

Extended Floors and Ceilings

Significant effort was made to enhance the measurement of the WISC-III and WAIS-III in individuals with very low or impaired intellectual functioning (e.g., people with mental retardation, and people with neuropsychological impairment). With the WAIS-R, a 70–74 year old who is unable to correctly answer one item can still obtain a VIQ score of 60 and a PIQ score of 61 points. This is likely due to the restricted floor of some subtests in the scale, the under representation of individuals in the normative sample with low true scores, and the failure of some subtest scaled scores to extend more than three standard deviations below the mean. The floors of the WISC-III and WAIS-III extend lower than their predecessors. To ensure that accurate scores were being obtained for individuals with low intellectual functioning, the samples included individuals with mild and moderate levels of mental retardation. The original diagnosis of mental retardation for included individuals was based on *DSM-IV* criteria, which included appropriate scores on an intelligence test (other than the WAIS-III) and impairment in adaptive functioning. Approximately 83% of WAIS-III FSIQ scores in the mild group were between 53 and 70, and 82% of FSIQ scores for individuals with moderate mental retardation were between 45 and 52 (Tulsky & Zhu, 1997). Similarly, the ceilings of the WISC-III and WAIS-III were significantly improved over their predecessors. Extension of the ceilings improves the ability of the clinician to differentiate between individuals with cognitive giftedness. The obtainable IQ score ranges of the two instruments are reported in Table 4.3.

Minimized Item Bias

During the research and development of the WISC-III and WAIS-III, considerable effort was made to minimize the potential test bias against race/ethnicity, sex, region, age, and social economic status. First, to ensure the representativeness of the U.S. population, the normative samples of the WISC-III and WAIS-III were stratified closely according to the most updated U.S. census data on five key demographic variables:

TABLE 4.3   Minimum and Maximum Obtainable IQ and Index Scores

IQ/Index Score	WISC-III	WAIS-III
VIQ	46–155	48–155
PIQ	46–155	47–155
FSIQ	40–160	45–155
VCI	50–150	50–150
POI	50–150	50–150
FDI/WMI	50–150	50–150
PSI	50–150	54–150

race/ethnicity, sex, region, age, and self or parent education of the participants.

Second, contemporary methodologies for testing item bias were used for the item selection. Problematic items were identified and deleted on the basis of formal expert reviews of the items and empirical data from statistical and bias analyses. The formal reviews were conducted by experts in cross-cultural research and intelligence testing at three key stages during the development of the test, with approximately 20–25 reviews obtained at each stage. Internal and external experts performed reviews of all subtests and items at each stage for potential bias, datedness, content relevance, and clinical utility. Along with these reviews, empirical data were used to test hypotheses and to assist in the decision process. Results from traditional Mantel–Haenszel bias analysis (Holland & Thayer, 1988) and item response theory (IRT) bias analyses (Hambleton, 1993) provided additional data on potentially problematic items. During the standardization phase, the procedures were repeated. Item bias analyses using the standardization data were performed for each subtest to determine the item sets for the final version. On the basis of these empirical analyses and the content reviews, items that did not meet acceptable criteria were removed.

Finally, extensive scoring studies were conducted to ensure that the scoring rules for all verbal items are fair for participants of different racial/ethnic, sexual, regional, age, and educational backgrounds. During the national tryout and standardization phase, the verbal responses of 450 to 500 participants were entered into a computer. These responses were then sorted, reviewed, and rank-ordered according to the type and quality of the response. The research team then assigned a unique code to each unique type of response. Using this preliminary coding system, two scorers independently coded each response. A third scorer identified the discrepancies between the code assignments from the first two scorers and resolved the differences so that each response had only one code. As appropriate, new codes were added and redundant codes removed. After the codes were assigned, the team evaluated the quality of responses and assigned a score value (0, 1, or 2) to each code on the basis of the accuracy of the response. The overall subtest performance and item-total correlations were then calculated. For this purpose, items that had low item-total correlations, poor IRT fit statistics, or other indicators of poor psychometric suitability (e.g., bias) were not included in the total subtest score. The remainder of the scoring study was an iterative process. The scoring criteria for all items were continuously reviewed, with particular focus on those items that had lower item-total correlations. Special efforts were made to ensure that localized or regional responses were scored according to the "true meaning" of the responses. When the final iteration was completed, three experts with extensive knowledge of Verbal sub-test scoring rules reviewed the final scoring rules, made minor modifications to eliminate any remaining areas of confusion, and deleted or modified inappropriate and redundant sample responses.

To the present, most studies designed to evaluate the ethnic bias of the Wechsler scales revealed no evidence of test bias (Prifitera, Weiss, & Saklofske, 1998; Reynold & Brown, 1984). Meanwhile, the Wechsler scales predicted achievement scores equally well for all ethnic groups.

Despite the efforts, described previously, to minimize potential test bias and the fact that expert reviewers and extensive statistical analysis revealed no biased items in the tests, the mean IQ scores of Hispanic and African Americans are about 9–10 points and 14–15 points lower, respectively than the mean scores of Whites. However, the lower mean scores of minorities on the Wechsler intelligence tests do not imply the test is biased against minorities. As pointed out by Wechsler (1971) and Prifitera, Weiss, and Saklofske (1998), the lower mean IQ scores of the minorities reflect not test bias but the unfairness of our society in socioeconomic, political, and medical opportunities. Although the normative samples were stratified according to most updated U.S. census data, larger percentages of Hispanic and African Americans in the normative samples have low socioeconomic status (SES). Because individuals with lower SES tend to score lower on IQ tests (Wechsler, 1971), the mean IQ scores of minorities were pulled lower than the average. On the other hand, because the individuals with higher SES tend to scorer higher on IQ tests and that larger percentage of the Whites in the normative sample have higher SES, the mean IQ scores of Whites were pushed higher than the average. Prifitera, Weiss, and Saklofske demonstrated that after matching minorities with Whites on five key demographic variables, the mean score differences between minorities and Whites are significantly reduced. Further analysis by Prifitera, Weiss, and Saklofske revealed that the mean IQ score differences between minorities and Whites increase as children grow older, which might be the evidence of interaction between cognitive development and social opportunities, such as SES.

Although further research is necessary to evaluate how SES, cultural, linguistic, home environment, medical, and other variables affect the opportunities to learn and cognitive development, the study by Prifitera, Weiss, and Saklofske clearly demonstrated the importance of assessing intelligence in an ecological context.

VALIDITY EVIDENCE OF FACTOR INDEX SCORES

Performance on the subtests of Wechsler intelligence scales can be summarized in several clinically meaningful ways that have long been recognized and well accepted by researchers and practitioners. For example, factor-analytic research by Cohen (1952a, 1952b, 1957a, 1957b) and Kaufman (1975, 1979) demonstrated that the subtests of Wechsler intelligence scales measure three different factors: Verbal Comprehension (VC), Perceptual Organization (PO), and Freedom from Distractibility (FD). Bannatyne (1974) proposed a set of subtest groupings that have become known as the Bannatyne composites. In his influential book, *Intelligent Testing with the WISC-R,* Kaufman (1979) discussed additional composites that can be derived from meaningful groupings of the WISC-R subtests.

During the research and development that preceded the release of the WISC-III, the Symbol Search subtest was developed to strengthen the Freedom From Distractibility factor. Unexpectedly, the introduction of Symbol Search caused the third factor to split into two factors, resulting in the now widely known four-factor structure of WISC-III. Arithmetic and Digit Span loaded together and this factor retained the name Freedom From Distractibility to maintain continuity with previous research. Coding loaded with Symbol Search and the resulting factor was labeled Processing Speed (PS; Wechsler, 1991).

Considerable evidence from several nonclinical samples has been reported supporting the validity of the WISC-III factor structure. Using exploratory and confirmatory factor analyses on data obtained from a nationally representative sample of 1,118 cases, Roid, Prifitera, and Weiss (1993) successfully replicated the four-factor structure. In separate confirmatory factor analyses of the WISC-III standardization sample, Kamphaus, Benson, Hutchinson, and Platt (1994) also found the fit of the four-factor to be superior to alternative models for all age groups and major ethnic groups. Further confirmation of the four-factor model has also been obtained in studies with such clinical populations as psychiatric inpatients (Tupa, Write, & Fristad, 1997) and children with traumatic brain injuries (Donders & Warschausky, 1997). Subsequent adaptations of the WISC-III and publication of the WAIS-III have provided additional evidence supporting the four-factor model of intelligence. For example, the four-factor solution has been independently replicated in Canada (Wechsler, 1995), Australia (Wechsler, 1995), Taiwan (Wechsler, 1997a), and Japan (Wechsler, 1998). In a factor analysis of WISC-III data from 15 nations ($n = 15,999$), Georgas, Van de Vijver, Weiss, and Saklofske (in press) replicated the four-factor structure, although in some countries, Arithmetic loaded primarily on the Verbal scale producing a three-factor structure. Factor-analytic investigations of the WAIS-III also confirmed the four-factor model using a representative sample of 2,450 adults ages 16 to 89. Taken together, results from these studies indicate that the latent traits measured by the WISC-III appear consistently across different ages, ethnicity, cultures, and specific clinical populations.

Other studies have been aimed at evaluating the clinical utility of factor index scores. Cluster analysis demonstrated that the factor-based index scores provide additional information to that provided by the traditional IQ scores (Donders, 1996; Donders, Zhu, & Tulsky, 2001). Results from these investigations indicate that there are five stable cluster types in the WISC-III and WAIS-III standardization samples. Two of the identified cluster types are defined by significantly higher or lower scores on the Processing Speed Index (PSI) relative to other factor index scores. In a separate study, Donders (1997) evaluated the performance of a sample of 88 children with traumatic head injury and found that this group tended to have lower POI and PSI scores than children without history of traumatic brain injury. In a study of 45 children with attention-deficit hyperactivity disorder (ADHD), Schwean, Saklofske, Yackulic, and Quinn (1993) found that children with ADHD scored significantly lower than a nonclinical sample of children on the PSI, Freedom from Distractibility Index (FDI), and VIQ and achieved significantly higher scores on POI. This finding is similar to results reported in other studies (Brown, 1996; Prifitera and Dersh, 1993; Wechsler, 1991).

Some investigations noted an inconsistency of factor loadings across different age groups or samples (Gregoire, 2003; Reynolds & Ford, 1994; Sattler, 1992; Thorndike, 1992; Witta & Keith, 1997). The lack of factor stability may be attributed to having an inadequate number of subtests to form a well-defined factor (Carroll, 1993; Woodcock, 1990). Factor analysis usually requires at least three variables to define each potential factor. For practical reasons, the WISC-III has only two subtests that contribute to the FDI and PSI factors, which increases the chance of underestimating the number of factors represented in the scale. Supporting evidence of this argument is found in results of the WAIS-III factor analysis. The addition of a third subtest (Letter-Number Sequencing) to better define the FDI factor appears to make this index more robust.

The meaning and labeling of the third factor have been topics of extended debate (Gussin & Javorsky, 1995; Riccio, Cohen, Hall, & Ross, 1997). Such debate is likely the result of the use of a confusing label and misconceptions regarding interpretation of the third factor. To maintain consistent terminology, the WISC-III labeled the third factor as the Freedom From Distractibility Index (FDI). However, the WISC-III FDI is different from the index originally proposed by Cohen (1957, 1959) and Kaufman (1975, 1979). The original FDI contains three subtests: Arithmetic, Digit Span, and Coding. Although this triad was repeatedly identified through factor

analysis, there was little agreement about why the subtests clustered together and what the FDI measured. Some have proposed that it measures attention and concentration or executive functioning (Kaufman, 1979), short-term and auditory memory (Cohen 1957a, 1957b), sequencing ability (Bannatyne, 1974), or numerical or quantitative ability (Osborne & Lindsey; 1967). Others believe that there is no common factor underlying these three subtests (Woodcock, 1990). In the WISC-III, the FDI contains only two subtests: Arithmetic and Digit Span. Following the addition of the Symbol Search subtest, a fourth PS factor appeared with highest loadings for the Symbol Search and Coding subtests. This left the Arithmetic and Digit Span subtests on the FDI factor. Based on advances in cognitive research (e.g., Kyllonen & Christal, 1990), most researchers now agree that the FDI term is a misnomer and more likely measures working memory (Kranzler, 1997; Sternberg, 1993; Wechsler, 1997b). For example, Riccio et al. (1997) demonstrated that the FDI did not correlate significantly with measures of attention. Instead, it had its most robust correlations with measures of immediate/working memory. The inclusion of the Letter-Number Sequencing subtest, a measure of working memory, on the WAIS-III more clearly defined the FDI that was subsequently renamed as the Working Memory Index (WMI).

Clinical Utility of the Verbal Comprehension Index

The Verbal Comprehension index (VCI) of the Wechsler intelligence scales is a measure of verbal reasoning and comprehension, acquired knowledge, and attention to verbal stimuli. Although this index highly correlates with the VIQ ($r = .95, .98$, for WAIS-III and WISC-III, respectively), it measures a narrower domain of cognitive function than the traditional VIQ score and is less confounded with other cognitive functions (working memory). The VCI is considered to be a purer measure of verbal reasoning than the VIQ. In particular, it may be a more appropriate indicator of verbal reasoning ability for an individual with depressed memory function or in situations where there is a large amount of scatter among the subtests that contribute to VIQ (Kaufman, 1994).

Clinical Utility of the Perceptual Organization Index

The Perceptual Organization index (POI) is a measure of fluid reasoning, spatial processing, attentiveness to detail, and visual-motor integration. Although this index correlates highly with the PIQ in the normative sample ($r = .94, .96$, for WAIS-III and WISC-III, respectively), it is less confounded with processing speed. This index may better reflect the true nonverbal reasoning ability of an individual with depressed processing-speed ability. Therefore, it is recommended that the discrepancy between POI and PSI be evaluated prior to interpretation of the PIQ.

Clinical Utility of the Working Memory Index

Working memory can be defined as the portion of memory that is in a highly active/accessible state as information is being processed. This includes the aspect of memory involved when an individual is simply attending to information (Kyllonen & Christal, 1987). Traditional short-term memory is believed to be a passive storage area for information that becomes encoded into long term memory or is forgotten. Working memory is where incoming information is temporarily stored and where calculations and transformation processing occurs. Furthermore, as Baddeley et al. (1974) noted, this component of memory also holds the products/output of these calculations and transformations (as well as the original information).

The model of working memory proposed by Baddeley (1986, 1992) is a generally accepted framework. Baddeley proposed an architecture for working memory consisting of two storage devices, one for verbal material and one for spatial material, and a central executive that regulates the operation of the storage devices. Neuroimaging studies of working memory have generally supported this model.

Digit Span backward is an excellent example of a task designed to tap working memory (The Psychological Corporation, 2002). Because the Digit Span forward task taps mostly short-term memory, separate norms are provided for the backward tasks in the updated WAIS-III/WMS-III technical manual (The Psychological Corporation, 2002). The Arithmetic subtest is an ecologically valid measure of working memory, because people are frequently called upon to mentally calculate arithmetic problems in real-life situations (Hitch, 1978; Sternberg, 1993). However, working memory interpretations of the Arithmetic subtest are too often confounded with the examinee's numerical ability. During development of the WAIS-III, the Arithmetic subtest was redesigned. The difficulty of arithmetic calculation was reduced while the load on working memory was increased. In addition, a new subtest, Letter-Number Sequencing, was included in the WAIS-III and joined Arithmetic and Digit Span on the more appropriately labeled Working Memory factor.

Recent literature has suggested that working memory is a key component to learning (Kyllonen, 1987; Kyllonen et al., 1989; Kyllonen et al., 1990; Swanson, 1999; Woltz, 1988). Individuals with greater working memory capacity are capable of processing and encoding more material than individuals with a smaller working memory capacity, thus accounting for individual differences in attention and learning capacities. Some cognitive psychologists have come to believe that working memory is an important predictor of individual differences in learning, ability, and fluid reasoning (Fry & Hale; 1996; Kyllonen et al., 1989; Sternberg, 1993). Clinical studies demonstrated that schizophrenia patients have impaired performance on the working memory tasks (Gold, Carpenter, Randolph, Goldberg, & Weinberger, 1997; The Psychological Corporation, 1997). Perhaps most interesting for school psychologists, researchers found that the WISC-III FDI contributed the second largest amount of variance, after the Verbal Comprehension index (VCI), to the prediction of reading, writing, and mathematics scores on the WIAT and other measures of achievement (Carpenter & Just, 1989; Daneman & Carpenter, 1980; de Jonge & de Jong, 1996; Hale, Fiorello, Kavanagh, Hoeppner, & Gaither, 2001; Konold, 1999).

Clinical Utility of the Processing Speed Index

Performance on the Processing Speed index (PSI) is an indication of the rapidity with which an individual can process simple or routine information without making errors. Cognitive research indicated that the speed of information processing correlates significantly with g (Jensen, 1982, 1987; Kranzler & Jensen, 1989; Neisser et al., 1996; Neubauer & Knorr, 1998). Because learning often involves a combination of routine information processing, such as reading, and complex information processing, such as reasoning, a weakness in the speed of processing routine information may make the task of comprehending novel information more time-consuming and difficult. A weakness in simple visual scanning and tracking may leave an individual less time and mental energy for the complex task of understanding new material. This is the way in which these lower-order processing abilities relate to higher-order cognitive functioning.

On the surface, the Coding and Symbol Search subtests are simple visual scanning and tracking tasks. Yet, there is consistent evidence that inspection time (hypothesized by some to be a measure of the rate that information is processed) correlates about .40 with intelligence test scores (see Deary, 2001; Deary & Stough, 1996). The speed of nerve conduction is moderately correlated with IQ, and specific qualities of brain waves correlate strongly with IQ (Berthier, DeBlois, Poirier, Novak, & Clifton, 2000; Cepeda, Kramer, & Gonzalez de Sather, 2001). Several investigations found that measures of processing speed for infants predict future scores on measures of intelligence (e.g., Dougherty & Haith, 1997;

Kail, 2000; Schatz, Kramer, Ablin, & Matthay, 2000). These findings led some to posit that differences in g result from differences in the speed and efficiency of neural processing.

Clinically speaking, the Processing Speed index of the Wechsler intelligence tests has been shown to be sensitive to such clinical conditions as ADHD, learning disability, epilepsy, Alzheimer's disease, Huntington's disease, Parkinson's disease, traumatic brain injury, chronic alcohol abuse, Korsakoff's syndrome, and schizophrenia (e.g., Brown, 1996; Donders & Warschausky, 1997; Prifitera & Dersh, 1992; Prifitera et al., 1998; Schwean, Saklofske, Yackulic, & Quinn, 1993; Wechsler, 1991; The Psychological Corporation, 1997).

Processing speed may be especially important in assessing young children, due to its relationship to neurological development, other cognitive abilities, and learning. Improvements in children's performance on measures of processing speed are mirrored by age-related changes in the number of transient connections to the central nervous system and increases in myelinization. Clinical research in developmental cognitive neuropsychology suggests a dynamic interplay between working memory, processing speed, and reasoning (e.g., Carpenter, Just, & Shell, 1990; Fry & Hale, 1996; Kail & Salthouse, 1994). More rapid processing of information enhances the effectiveness of working memory, which, in turn, enhances reasoning ability. Thus, children with deficits in processing speed may have more difficulty with tasks that require working memory and reasoning ability, both of which are important for the acquisition of new information.

Clinical Utility of the General Ability Index

The General Ability index (GAI) was developed for the WISC-III (Prifitera et al., 1998) and for the WAIS-III (Tulsky et al., 2001). The GAI is composed of subtests (eight subtests for the WISC-III and six subtests for the WAIS-III) that contribute to the VCI, and POI is highly correlated to the FSIQ for the normative samples ($r = .97, .98$, for WAIS-III and WISC-III, respectively). Although the FSIQ score is a reliable and valid measure of the general intellectual ability of individuals with balanced or near balanced development across major cognitive domains, FSIQ will be lower than GAI for individuals with relative weaknesses in working memory function or processing speed. If the VCI and POI are purer measures of verbal and nonverbal reasoning than the traditional VIQ or PIQ, the FSIQ may not be the best indicator of general intellectual ability in all circumstances. On the other hand, GAI may obscure the impact of working memory or processing speed deficits on the expression of intellectual behavior. In general, GAI may be appropriately

used to better understand cognitive functioning when significant discrepancy exists among its core components. In particular, GAI may add to the understanding of working memory deficits on school achievement for some learning-disabled children, or in understanding the impact of processing speed on the cognitive ability of individuals with traumatic brain injury.

SPECIAL GROUP STUDIES

Compared to the previous versions, both WISC-III and WAIS-III included more special group studies conducted using samples of various special populations. Table 4.4 provides a list of these studies by the instruments. The data of these studies were collected by independent researchers from a variety of clinical settings. The results of these studies are reported in the WISC-III and WAIS-III manual. Since the publication, independent researchers have provided much more evidence related to the reliability and validity of these instruments. Similar to many previous clinical studies with its predecessors, these clinical studies provided evidence of reliability and validity of the two Wechsler scales. However, it is important to note the following limitations of these studies: First, the samples were not randomly selected but were selected by convenience. Therefore, these samples may not be statistically representative. Second, because data of each sample were collected in a variety of clinical settings, the diagnosis of different cases might be made on the basis of different criteria and procedures. Third, the sample sizes for some studies are relatively small. And finally, only group performance is reported. For these reasons, the performance data from these samples are presented as examples and are not intended to be definitive representations of these diag-

TABLE 4.4 Special Group Studies of the WISC-III and WAIS-III

Special Group Studies	WISC-III	WAIS-III
Mental Retardation	✓	✓
Cognitively Gifted	✓	
Attention-Deficit Disorder	✓	✓
Learning Disability	✓	✓
Deaf and Hearing Impairment	✓	✓
Traumatic Brain Injury	✓	✓
Epilepsy	✓	✓
Conduct Disorder	✓	
Speech/Language Delays	✓	
Parkinson's Disease		✓
Alzheimer's Disease		✓
Temporal Lobe Epilepsy		✓
Chronic Alcohol Abuse		✓
Korsakoff Syndrome		✓
Schizophrenia		✓

TABLE 4.5   WISC-III Internal Consistency Reliability (Split-Half) for Special Groups

Subtest	Mental Retarded (n = 43)		Attention-Deficit (n = 79)		Learning Disabled	
	SD	r	SD	r	SD	r
Information	2.58	0.89	3.23	0.90	3.07	0.92
Similarities	3.06	0.88	3.24	0.86	3.04	0.90
Comprehension	3.95	0.77	3.20	0.86	3.33	0.91
Vocabulary	2.97	0.80	3.17	0.90	2.73	0.88
Arithmetic	2.40	0.93	3.30	0.88	2.56	0.89
Digit Span	3.08	0.94	2.94	0.87	2.60	0.86
Block Design	3.09	0.88	3.55	0.90	3.21	0.90
Picture Completion	3.72	0.90	2.86	0.74	2.93	0.84
Picture Arrangement	3.89	0.94	3.17	0.86	3.28	0.83
Object Assembly	3.74	0.86	3.09	0.75	3.02	0.61
Mazes	2.76	0.65	3.43	0.77	2.98	0.69

Subtest	Emotion (n = 51)		Speech (n = 46)		Hearing (n = 30)	
	SD	r	SD	r	SD	r
Information	2.32	0.91	3.05	0.92	3.54	0.89
Similarities	2.86	0.91	2.86	0.86	3.99	0.93
Comprehension	2.80	0.93	3.12	0.92	3.67	0.88
Vocabulary	2.40	0.91	2.29	0.88	3.67	0.97
Arithmetic	2.31	0.89	3.37	0.94	4.12	0.94
Digit Span	2.30	0.83	2.58	0.81	3.64	0.94
Block Design	3.49	0.94	3.64	0.94	4.78	0.96
Picture Completion	3.56	0.92	3.53	0.93	3.45	0.82
Picture Arrangement	3.97	0.90	3.32	0.93	3.54	0.70
Object Assembly	3.83	0.87	3.79	0.87	4.36	0.80
Mazes	3.27	0.83	4.17	0.95	2.77	0.59

nostic groups. The purpose of these special group studies is to demonstrate that the Wechsler can provide a reliable and valid measurement of intellectual functioning for individuals in these special groups.

In addition to the clinical studies reported in the manuals of the Wechsler intelligence scales, many independent studies have been conducted to evaluate the reliability and validity of the WISC-III and WAIS-III using samples with various clinical diagnosis. For instance, Zhu et al. (1999), and Zhu, Tulsky, Price, and Chen (2001) evaluated the WISC-III and WAIS-III internal consistency reliability for special groups. They reported that although the reliability coefficients may vary for different clinical groups and by subtest, the WISC-III and WAIS-III internal consistency reliabilities coefficients of the clinical groups were comparable to those reported for normative samples. The internal consistency reliability data of the WISC-III and WAIS-III for various clinical groups are presented in Table 4.5 and 4.6, respectively.

Further, a few independent studies have demonstrated that WISC-III has good long-term test-retest stability coefficients in groups of children outside of the normal range population (Canivez & Watkins, 1998; Slate, Jones, & Saarnio, 1997;

Stavrou & Flanagan, 1996; Zhu, Woodell, & Kreiman, 1997). Table 4.7 summarizes the stability results that were obtained from two independent studies.

Tulsky and Zhu (1997) evaluated the sensitivity and specificity of the WAIS-III in assessing adolescents and adults diagnosed with mental retardation. A sample of 108 adolescents and adults diagnosed with mental retardation (62 mild and 46 moderate) using *DSM-IV* and American Association on Mental Retardation (AAMR) criteria were tested using the WAIS-III. The results showed that the participants exhibited relatively flat-score profiles and that 99 percent of the sample obtained IQ scores 2 to 3 SDs below the mean. Further analysis showed that roughly 83 percent of the participants in the mild group had IQ scores between 53 and 70, and that 82 percent of the examinees in the moderate group had IQ scores between 45 and 52 (Tulsky et al., 1997). These results are consistent with previous findings by Atkinson (1992), Spruill (1991), and Wechsler (1991) for children.

In another study, the WISC-III was administered to a sample of 30 adolescents and adults diagnosed with attention-deficit hyperactivity disorder (ADHD) according to DSM-IV diagnostic criteria and the Brown Attention-Deficit Disorder

TABLE 4.6   WAIS-III Internal Consistency Reliability (Split-Half) for Special Groups

Subtest	Alzheimer (Mild)		Huntington and Parkinson		Traumatic Brain Injury	
	SD	r	SD	r	SD	r
Information	2.35	0.92	2.03	0.85	2.89	0.96
Similarities	2.73	0.88	2.33	0.84	3.03	0.93
Comprehension	2.86	0.78	2.48	0.79	2.57	0.82
Vocabulary	2.57	0.92	1.84	0.87	2.47	0.90
Arithmetic	3.38	0.91	2.51	0.91	3.03	0.93
Digit Span	2.67	0.85	1.93	0.78	2.22	0.85
Block Design	2.91	0.94	3.01	0.92	2.75	0.92
Matrix Reasoning	2.36	0.87	2.10	0.90	2.66	0.81
Picture Completion	2.80	0.83	1.68	0.70	3.76	0.92
Picture Arrangement	2.41	0.75	2.74	0.87	2.84	0.79
Object Assembly	2.65	0.64	2.56	0.79	2.85	0.91

Subtest	Temporal Lobe Epilepsy		Schizophrenia		Alcohol-Related	
	SD	r	SD	r	SD	r
Information	2.52	0.93	3.34	0.93	2.85	0.93
Similarities	2.30	0.81	2.92	0.73	2.19	0.84
Comprehension	3.10	0.85	3.19	0.85	2.62	0.88
Vocabulary	1.95	0.83	3.29	0.96	2.77	0.93
Arithmetic	4.50	0.89	2.72	0.90	2.48	0.80
Digit Span	2.69	0.92	2.51	0.86	2.87	0.94
Block Design	2.93	0.93	2.93	0.90	2.76	0.88
Matrix Reasoning	2.85	0.95	2.74	0.89	2.84	0.91
Picture Completion	3.32	0.90	2.64	0.85	2.65	0.79
Picture Arrangement	4.11	0.96	2.58	0.75	3.14	0.71
Object Assembly	4.08	0.88	2.58	0.81	2.38	0.78

Subtest	Mental Retarded		ADHD/ADD		Learning Disabled		Hearing Impaired	
	SD	r	SD	r	SD	r	SD	r
Information	1.47	0.74	2.57	0.90	2.53	0.90	2.69	0.83
Similarities	1.74	0.91	2.35	0.72	2.85	0.72	3.45	0.94
Comprehension	0.85	0.75	2.99	0.83	2.34	0.85	3.37	0.95
Vocabulary	1.00	0.70	2.50	0.94	2.59	0.90	3.00	0.97
Arithmetic	1.34	0.82	2.77	0.86	2.57	0.78	3.26	0.88
Digit Span	1.80	0.90	2.38	0.75	2.25	0.82	3.10	0.91
Block Design	1.62	0.91	3.49	0.95	2.64	0.81	2.76	0.77
Matrix Reasoning	1.27	0.67	2.66	0.89	2.33	0.71	2.68	0.91
Picture Completion	1.66	0.86	2.19	0.55	2.50	0.54	2.44	0.72
Picture Arrangement	1.95	0.79	3.31	0.74	2.75	0.55	2.64	0.78
Object Assembly	1.90	0.75	2.97	0.58	2.94	0.49	2.96	0.82

Scales (Brown, 1996). The results indicated that the mean FSIQ score of the sample was at the average range and there was no significant difference between mean VIQ and PIQ scores. Marked results were found in the index score profile. The mean Working Memory Index (WMI) score of the sample is about 8.3 points lower than the mean VCI score, and the mean PSI score of the sample is about 7.5 points lower than the mean POI score. About 30% of the sample had WMI scores at least 1 SD lower than their VCI scores, whereas

13% of the WAIS-III standardization sample obtained such discrepancies. About 26% of the sample had PSI scores at least 1 SD lower than their POI scores, whereas 14% of the WAIS-III standardization sample had such discrepancies. For differences between the higher of the VCI or POI score and the lower of the WMI or PSI score, 61.3% of the sample obtained differences of 1 SD, and 16.1% obtained differences of 2 SDs or more; only 30.5% and 3.5% of the WAIS-III standardization sample had such differences. These results

TABLE 4.7   Stability of the WISC-III

Subtest	Zhu et al. (1997) LD, $n = 60$ r (2.99 year)	Canivez and Watkins (1998) Mixed, $n = 667$ r (2.87 year)	Wechsler (1991) Nonclinical, $n = 353$ r (23 days)
Picture Completion	0.69	0.66	0.81
Information	0.73	0.73	0.85
Coding	0.70	0.63	0.77
Similarities	0.82	0.68	0.81
Picture Arrangement	0.61	0.68	0.64
Arithmetic	0.73	0.67	0.74
Block Design	0.65	0.78	0.77
Vocabulary	0.84	0.75	0.89
Object Assembly	0.64	0.68	0.66
Comprehension	0.65	0.68	0.73
Symbol Search	—	0.55	0.74
Digit Span	0.71	0.65	0.73
IQ/Index			
Verbal IQ	0.90	0.87	0.94
Performance IQ	0.83	0.87	0.87
Full Scale IQ	0.93	0.91	0.94
VCI	0.91	0.85	0.93
POI	0.82	0.87	0.87
FDI	0.76	0.75	0.82
PSI	—	0.62	0.84

are comparable to the findings by Brown (1996) using a larger adolescent and adult ADHD sample, and on the WISC-III and WAIS-R. They are also consistent with the findings by Wechsler (1991), Prifitera et al. (1992), and the research group lead by Biederman et al. (1993).

The studies using samples of children and adults diagnosed with traumatic brain injury further demonstrated the clinical utility of the WISC-III and WAIS-III. In a study by Donders et al. (2001), 100 adults diagnosed with traumatic brain injury were administered the WAIS-III. The results revealed that although the mean IQ and index scores of the sample were in average range, the mean PSI scores of the sample were significantly lower than the mean POI scores. The study also suggested that the new Letter-Number Sequencing subtest seems to have satisfactory criterion validity. These results are consistent with those reported in the WAIS-III/WMS-III Technical Manual (The Psychological Corporation, 1997). Using a sample of children diagnosed with traumatic brain injury, Donders (1997) revealed a similar index score profile on the WISC-III.

Interpretative Considerations

Because the WISC-III and WAIS-III continue the tradition of the Wechsler intelligence scales, many interpretation strategies, methods, and procedures that were developed and refined by experienced clinicians and researchers for its predecessors

continue to be valid and useful (see Kaufman, 1990, 1994; Prifitera et al., 1998; and Sattler, 1992, 2001, for detailed guidelines on interpretation of Wechsler intelligence scales). Although a detailed discussion of interpretation strategies, methods, and procedures is beyond the scope of this chapter, we would like to suggest a few basic interpretative considerations that may help readers understand the nature of clinical interpretation. However, the suggestions for interpretative considerations should not be used as a *cookbook* or comprehensive guideline for interpretation. Clinical interpretation is a complicated hypothesis-testing process that varies from situation to situation. Therefore, no single approach will work for all scenarios.

First, the interpretation of test results is a systematic hypotheses generation and hypotheses-testing process (Kamphaus, 1993; Prifitera et al., 1998). Results from the Wechsler intelligence scales provide important information regarding an individual's cognitive functioning, but they should never be interpreted in isolation. Four broad sources of information are typically available to the clinician conducting a psychological evaluation: psychiatric, medical, educational, and psychosocial history; direct behavioral observations; quantitative test scores; and qualitative aspects of test performance, such as motivation and test session compliance. The scores and item responses on the Wechsler intelligence scales provide quantitative and qualitative information that is best interpreted in conjunction with a thorough history and careful clinical observations of the individual. Results should always be evaluated within the context of the reasons for referral and all known collateral information.

Second, testing is different from assessment (Matarazzo, 1990; Prifitera et al., 1998; Robertson & Woody, 1997). Psychological testing is a data collection process in which an individual's behaviors are sampled and observed systematically in a standardized environment. Psychological assessment is a complicated problem-solving process that usually begins with psychological testing. Therefore, obtaining test scores is just the beginning of assessment, not the end.

Third, interpretation is an attempt to explain test results that often includes a complicated, multilevel, hypothesis-testing process, including profile, strength and weakness, scatter, and discrepancy analysis. Interpretation converts data collected through testing, such as a discrepancy score, and behavior observation notes, into meaningful information, which may be used as evidence supporting certain conclusions. Each segment of information is like a puzzle piece. Clinicians must first gather all the puzzle pieces and then assemble them in a meaningful way to draw appropriate conclusions. With this analogy in mind, it is clear that the identification of one puzzle piece is usually not sufficient to solve the whole puzzle, but it is a necessary and important step. It is similar to the physician who measures a patient's body temperature and blood pressure as the initial steps in forming a diagnosis. Temperature and blood pressure are universally performed procedures; however, in isolation, neither of them are conclusive for a final diagnosis. Similarly, scores on intelligence tests must be combined with scores on other measures, the examinee's demographic information (e.g., socioeconomic status, life history, educational background), and other extra-test information before any clinical decision can be made.

BASIC INTERPRETATION OF WECHSLER INTELLIGENCE SCALES

Types of Wechsler Scores

The Wechsler intelligence scales utilize two types of standard scores: scaled scores and composite scores (e.g., IQ and index scores). The conversion of raw scores into standard scores allows clinicians to interpret scores within the Wechsler intelligence scales and between the Wechsler intelligence scales and other related measures. The scaled scores and composite scores are age-corrected standard scores that allow the test user to compare each individual's cognitive functioning with other individuals in the same age group.

Scaled scores are derived from the total raw scores on each subtest. They are scaled to a metric with a mean of 10 and a standard deviation (SD) of 3. A subtest scaled score of 10 reflects the average performance of a given age group. Scores of 7 and 13 correspond to 1 SD below and above the mean, respectively, and scaled scores of 4 and 16 deviate 2 SDs from the mean.

Composite scores (e.g., VIQ and PIQ) are standard scores based on combinations of subtest scaled scores. They are scaled to a metric with a mean of 100 and a standard deviation of 15. A score of 100 on any of the composites defines the average performance of individuals of similar ages. Scores of 85 and 115 correspond to 1 SD below and above the mean, respectively, and scores of 70 and 130 deviate 2 SDs from the mean. About 68% of all examinees obtain scores between 85 and 115, about 98% score in the 70–130 range, and nearly all examinees (about 99.9%) obtain scores between 55 and 145 (3 SDs on either side of the mean).

In general, standard scores provide the most accurate description of test data. However, for individuals unfamiliar with test interpretation, standard scores are often difficult to understand. Other methods, such as percentile ranks and test-age equivalents, are often used in conjunction with standard scores to describe an examinee's performance. Scores on the Wechsler intelligence scales should be reported in terms of confidence intervals so that the actual score is evaluated in light of the score's reliability. Confidence intervals assist the examiner in test interpretation by delineating a range of scores in which the examinee's true score most likely falls and remind the examiner that the observed score contains measurement error.

Level of Performance

The IQ, index, and scaled scores can be characterized as falling within a certain level of performance (e.g., superior, high average, average, and low average). The level of performance refers to the rank obtained by an individual on a given test compared to the performance of an appropriate normative group. The descriptive classifications corresponding to scores on the Wechsler intelligence scales are presented in Table 4.8.

Test results on Wechsler intelligence scales can be described in a manner similar to the following example:

Relative to individuals of comparable age, this individual is currently functioning within the [descriptive classification] range of intelligence on a standardized measure of intellectual ability.

Clinically speaking, the level of performance is important for estimating the presence and severity of any relative strength or weakness in an individual's performance. Clinical deci-

TABLE 4.8   Qualitative Descriptions of IQ and Index Scores

Score	Classification	Percent Included in Theoretical Normal Curve
130 and Above	Very Superior	2.2
120–129	Superior	6.7
110–119	High Average	16.1
90–109	Average	50.0
80–89	Low Average	16.1
70–79	Borderline	6.7
69 and Below	Extremely Low	2.2

sions can then be made if the level of performance of the individual is significantly lower than the normative group. Alternatively to this normative approach, clinical decisions can also be made if a specific score is significantly lower than the individual's other scores (i.e., an intraindividual weakness).

In nonclinical settings (e.g., industrial and occupational settings), the emphasis on level of performance shifts slightly, and more weight is placed on competency and the patterns of a person's strengths and weaknesses without necessarily implying any type of impairment.

Interpreting IQ Versus Index Scores

IQ and index scores are estimates of overall functioning in their respective areas and should always be evaluated within the context of the subtests that contribute to them (Kaufman et al., 1999). The IQ and index scores are much more reliable measures than the subtest scaled scores, and, in general, they are the first scores the practitioner examines. Sometimes, VIQ or PIQ scores and various index scores are discrepant from one another, indicating that the individual performs better in some areas of cognitive functioning than others. When the discrepancy between the VCI and WMI or between the POI and PSI is statistically significant, the practitioner may need to shift the focus of interpretation from IQ scores to index scores. The VCI or POI scores should be utilized when there is a large amount of scatter among the subtests that contribute to the VIQ or PIQ scores, respectively. Consequently, when the interpretation is focused on VCI and POI scores, the GAI may be considered as a better indicator of general intellectual functioning than the FSIQ.

Profile Analysis and Cluster Interpretation

Sometimes the subtest scaled scores that contribute to the IQ and index scores are significantly different from one another. It is important to realize that when two component subtest scores are substantially different from one another, with one

unusually high and the other unusually low, the index score is likely be close to the average range. Such an average score reflects a dramatically different pattern of abilities than does an average index score obtained from two subtest scores that are both in the average range. In clinical practice, practitioners often compare the examinee's performance on the Wechsler subtests to see whether any patterns emerge from which they can make inferences about an examinee. This technique is called profile analysis.

Glutting, McDermott, and Konold (1997) reported that there are over 75 different patterns of subtest variation. Some have suggested various ipsative analyses to examine the subtests against the individual's own anchor point to determine relative strengths or weaknesses (see Kaufman, 1994; Sattler, 2001). Others have stressed using a normative approach to analyze the pattern of scores (McDermott, Fantuzzo, & Glutting, 1990; McDermott, Fantuzzo, Glutting, Watkins, & Baggaley, 1992). Some researchers have even used cluster-analytic techniques to develop subtest taxonomies as an alternative to profile analysis (McDermott, Glutting, Jones, & Nooman, 1989; McDermott, Glutting, Jones, Watkins, & Kush, 1989).

Unfortunately, by taking a strictly normative approach, the practitioner may miss some information about an individual's relative strengths and weaknesses. In fact, it is common for an individual to function at different ability levels in different cognitive areas. By examining deviations from the individual's average level of functioning (e.g., significant and unusual difference between subtests and the average of all subtests), the practitioner can use the base-rate data provided in the manuals to decide how rare the obtained difference is in the normative sample.

IQ-Score and Index-Score Discrepancies

As mentioned previously, it is good practice to evaluate the discrepancies among IQ and index scores, because such an evaluation allows practitioners to decide whether IQ or index scores should be used as appropriate indicators of verbal, nonverbal, or general abilities. In addition, discrepancy analysis may produce valuable information for clinical interpretation. Many clinical studies demonstrate that, compared with the normative sample, individuals diagnosed with certain clinical conditions, such as ADHD, learning disability, epilepsy, and traumatic brain injury, are more likely to show certain patterns of discrepancies among IQ or index scores (e.g., Brown, 1996; Donders et al., 1997; Prifitera et al., 1992; Prifitera et al., 1998; Schwean et al., 1993; Wechsler, 1991).

The first step of the discrepancy analysis is to determine the statistical significance of the difference between the IQ or index scores. A statistically significant difference between scores, for example, between the VIQ and the PIQ scores, refers to the likelihood that obtaining such a difference by chance is low (e.g., $p < .05$) if the true difference between the scores is zero (Matarazzo & Herman, 1985). The level of significance reflects the level of confidence the clinician can have that the difference between the scores, called the *difference score,* is a true difference.

Often the difference between an individual's VIQ and PIQ scores is significant in the statistical sense but is not at all rare among individuals in the general population. The statistical significance of discrepancies between scores and the rarity of the difference are two separate issues and have different implications for test interpretation. For a detailed discussion of the distinction between statistically significant and clinically meaningful differences between scores, see Payne and Jones, (1957); Matarazzo et al., (1985); Sattler, (2001); and Silverstein, (1981).

The Wechsler intelligence scales provide critical values and base-rate data in the manuals for evaluating whether a given discrepancy is statistically significant and how frequently such a discrepancy occurred in the normative sample. Because the discrepancies among IQ or index scores are related to ability level, the WAIS-III also provides the base-rate data by five ability levels. Note that the base-rate data provided in the WISC-III and WAIS-III manuals are based on the absolute value of the discrepancy. Subsequent research has demonstrated that the frequencies of score differences vary with the direction of the difference (Sattler, 2001). Thus, the percentage of the normative sample with VIQ scores greater than their PIQ scores is not the same percentage of the normative sample with PIQ scores greater than their VIQ scores. Clinically speaking, the direction of VIQ-PIQ discrepancy is related to different patterns of cognitive strengths and weaknesses (Rourke, 1998). For instance, Prifitera et al. (1998) reported that about 69 percent of the Hispanic children from the WISC-III normative sample obtained higher PIQ than VIQ scores. On the other hand, only 46.4% of White children obtained higher PIQ than VIQ scores. Therefore, social cultural factors should be considered when interpreting the discrepancies among IQ or index score. Base rate data by the direction of the difference for the WISC-III and WAIS-III are now available in Sattler's (2001) book, *Assessment of Children: Cognitive Applications–Fourth Edition.*

To meet the demand of practitioners, demographically adjusted norms of the WAIS-III are included in the updated WAIS-III/WMS-III scoring assistant. Also, separate norms for the forward and backward tasks of the Digit Span subtest are also available for the WAIS-III in the updated WAIS-III/

WMS-III technical manual (The Psychological Corporation, 2001).

Interpretation in a Neuropsychological Setting

Neuropsychology is a highly specialized approach to the understanding of individual differences (Hynd & Semrud-Clikeman, 1989). Often, the Wechsler intelligence scales are used to gauge the individual's current overall ability and play an important part in helping the neuropsychologist detect gross intellectual deterioration. The IQ scores generated by the Wechsler scales are typically sensitive to generalized intellectual impairment. However, these same IQ scores are also relatively insensitive to focalized lesions of the brain (Chelune, Ferguson, & Moehle, 1986; Hynd et al., 1989; Matarazzo, 1972). Therefore, other tests that measure more distinct cognitive functions are frequently used to supplement Wechsler scales to detect specific deficits.

Because the emphasis of the evaluation typically focuses on specific abilities, the clinician may place more weight on the measurement of a person's ability in various functional areas than on an overall IQ score. Various researchers have identified between five and seven major functional areas, including intelligence, language, spatial or perceptual ability, sensor motor functioning, attention, memory, emotional or adaptive functioning, psychomotor speed, and learning (see Larrabee & Curtiss, 1995; Lezak, 1995; Smith et al., 1992 for a comprehensive review). The new factor index scores of the Wechsler scales should be more informative than the traditional IQ scores to the neuropsychologist, because they measure more refined domains of cognitive functioning. For instance, the PSI index is sensitive to certain types of neuropsychological disorders, such as Alzheimer's disease, Parkinson's disease, and traumatic brain injury (Hawkins, 1998; Martin, Donders, & Thompson, 2000). Therefore, clinicians should administer a Symbol Search subtest routinely so that PSI can be derived and evaluated. Moreover, the subtest-level interpretation may also be appropriate for assessing specific abilities.

Predict Premorbid Functioning

Because the neuropsychologist is attempting to detect some of the cognitive consequences of brain damage, he or she must compare an individual's current score to his or her estimated (or known) premorbid level of functioning or use demographically corrected scores, or both, to factor in the effects attributable to various demographic variables. A difficult task faced by any psychologist is determining whether an individual's current test scores reflect a drop in performance from the same individual's previous ability before an accident occurred or illness began (Franzen, Burgess, & Smith-Seemiller, 1997). This process can help the neuropsychologist determine whether the individual has sustained loss in functioning from the accident or illness as compared with his or her previous ability. Wechsler was the first person to propose that there was a "deterioration index" that could be derived by comparing the performance on a so-called *hold subtest* of the Wechsler scales (e.g., those subtests' scores that were found not to decline with the age of the examinee) to the *don't hold subtest* (e.g., those subtests' scores in which performance was not expected to remain stable over time and would ultimately deteriorate with the age of the examinee). However, some research has demonstrated that basing the assessment of premorbid function on hold tests can underestimate premorbid IQ by as much as a full standard deviation (Larrabee, Largen, & Levin, 1985).

Alternative techniques include using scores that are obtained on vocabulary or reading tests because the skills they reflect were believed to be relatively independent of general loss of functioning and could therefore be used as an index of premorbid functioning. Yates (1956) was the first person to hypothesize that, using the WAIS Vocabulary score, testers could estimate premorbid functioning, because it is relatively independent of age-related decline in performance. Follow-up research by Russell (1972) and Swiercinsky and Warnock (1977) showed that individuals with brain damage perform worse than the general population does on the Vocabulary subtest, a finding that contradicted Yates' hypothesis.

The more recent focus has been on using reading tests as an indicator of premorbid functioning (Nelson, 1982; Nelson & McKenna, 1975; Nelson & O'Connell, 1978). Nelson et al. (1978) introduced the National Adult Reading Test, subsequently named the New Adult Reading Test (NART), which was a reading test using irregularly pronounced words. They developed a regression-based formula for estimating WAIS IQ scores from the scores on NART and concluded that the predictions based on NART scores are fairly accurate.

Alternative methods of determining premorbid functioning utilize the relationship between Wechsler IQ scores and demographic variables, such as age, education, sex, race, and occupation. For a detailed discussion about the relationship between demographic variables and IQ scores, see reviews by Heaton, Ryan, Grant, and Matthews (1996), and Kaufman, McLean, and Reynolds (1988). In general, two methods have prevailed. One method uses the correlation between the demographic variables and the IQ scores to develop prediction equations (e.g., Barona, Reynolds, & Chastain, 1984; Wilson,

et al., 1978). The other method is to develop demographically adjusted norms. During the standardization of the WAIS-III and WMS-III, additional effort was made to ensure that at least 30 individuals were sampled for each of the age-by-education levels. In addition, a new word reading test—Wechsler Test of Adult Reading (WTAR; The Psychological Corporation, 2001) was developed and conormed with the WAIS-III and WMS-III. The test uses words that are phonetically difficult to decode and would probably require previous learning. Regression analyses demonstrate that this reading test adds more incremental validity in predicting IQ and memory scores than do equations that just include demographic variables. Moreover, by being conormed directly with the Wechsler scales, the WTAR should provide invaluable information to the clinician who is trying to determine premorbid IQ.

SUMMARY

The Wechsler intelligence scales have a glorious and demonstrated history of success in the field of intelligence assessment. They will continue to play the leading role in intellectual assessment in the years to come. Like most inventions, the Wechsler intelligence scales are not perfect. Revisions to the Wechsler intelligence scales will continue to reflect advances in the theoretical and practical foundations of intelligence assessment. We hope the new features, the demonstrated clinical utilities, and the accumulated clinical knowledge discussed in this chapter will assist clinicians in their practice.

However excellent the Wechsler intelligence scales are, they are of course tools that clinicians use to gather data. It is the clinician, not the instrument that assesses the examinee in a complex social environment. The assessment and evaluation of intellectual functioning must be conducted within a wider ecological context, taking consideration of psychiatric, medical, educational, and psychosocial history, direct behavioral observations, quantitative test scores, and qualitative aspects of test performance, such as motivation and test session compliance.

NOTE

1. The third factor of the WISC-III was named the Freedom from Distractibility Index (FDI). This factor was named the Working Memory Index in the WAIS-III. Detailed rationale for this is discussed later.

REFERENCES

American Association of Mental Retardation. (1992). *Mental retardation: Definitions, classifications, and systems of support (9th ed.)*. Washington, DC: Author.

American Psychiatric Association. (1994). *Diagnostic and statistical manual of mental disorders (4th ed.)*. Washington, DC: Author.

Atkinson, L. (1992). Mental retardation and WAIS-R scatter analysis. *Journal of Intellectual Disability Research, 36*, 443–448.

Baddeley, A.D. (1986). *Working memory*. Oxford: Oxford University Press.

Baddeley, A.D. (1992). Working memory. *Science, 255*, 556–559.

Baddeley, A.D. & Hitch, G. (1974). Working memory. In G.H. Bower (Ed.), *The psychology of learning and motivation: Advances in research and theory* (Vol. 8, pp. 47–90). San Diego, CA: Academic Press.

Bannatyne, A. (1974). Diagnosis: A note on recategorization of the WISC scaled scores. *Journal of Learning Disabilities, 7*, 272–274.

Barona, A., Reynolds, C.R., & Chastain, R. (1984). A demographically based index of premorbid intelligence for the WAIS-R. *Journal of Consulting and Clinical Psychology, 52*, 885–887.

Beres, K.A., Kaufman, A.S., & Perlman, M.D. (2000). Assessment of child intelligence. In G. Goldstein & M. Hersen (Eds.), *Handbook of psychological assessment 3rd ed.* (pp. 65–96). Kidlington, Oxford, United Kingdom: Elsevier Science Ltd.

Berthier, N.E., DeBlois, S., Poirier, C.R., Novak, M.A., & Clifton, R.K. (2000). Where's the ball? Two and three-year-olds reason about unseen events. *Developmental Psychology, 36*(3), 394–401.

Biederman, J., Faraone, S.V., Spencer, T., Wilens, T., Norman, D., Lapey, K.A., Mick, E., Lehman, B.K., & Doyle, A. (1993). Patterns of psychiatric comorbidity, cognition, and psychosocial functioning in adults with attention deficit hyperactivity disorder. *American Journal of Psychiatry, 150*(12), 1792–1798.

Brody, N. (1992). *Intelligence.* (2nd Ed.). San Diego, CA: Academic Press.

Brown, T.E. (1996). *Brown attention-deficit disorder scales.* San Antonio, TX: The Psychological Corporation.

Canivez, G.L., & Watkins, M.W. (1998). Long-term stability of the Wechsler intelligence scale for children–third edition. *Psychological Assessment, 10*, 285–291.

Carpenter, P.A. & Just, M.A. (1989). The role of working memory in language comprehension. In D. Klahr & K. Kotovsky (Eds.), Complex information processing: The impact of Herbert A. Simon (pp. 31–64). New Jersey: Lawrence Erlbaum Associate.

Carpenter, P.A., Just, M.A., & Shell, P. (1990). What one intelligence test measures: A theoretical account of the processing in the Raven progressive matrice test. *Psychological Review, 97*(3), 404–431.

Carroll, J.B. (1993a). *Human cognitive abilities: A survey of factor-analytic studies.* New York: Cambridge University Press.

Carroll, J.B. (1993b). What abilities are measured by the WISC-III? *Journal of Psychoeducational Assessment Monograph Series.*

Advances in Psychological Assessment: Wechsler Intelligence Scale for Children-Third Edition, 134–143.

Carroll, J.B. (1997). The three-stratum theory of cognitive abilities. In D.P. Flanagan, J.L. Genshaft, & P.L. Harrison (Eds.), *Contemporary intellectual assessment: Theories, tests, and issues* (pp. 122–130). New York: Guilford Press.

Cepeda, N.J., Kramer, A.F., & Gonzalez de Sather, J.C.M. (2001). Changes in executive control across the life span: Examination of task-switching performance. *Developmental Psychology, 37*(5), 715–730.

Chelune, G.J., Ferguson, W., & Moehle, K. (1986). The role of standard cognitive and personality tests in neuropsychological assessment. In T. Incagnoli, G. Goldstein, & C.J. Golden (Eds.), *Clinical application of neuropsychological test batteries.* New York: Plenum Press.

Cohen, J. (1952a). A factor-analytically based rationale for the Wechsler–Bellevue. *Journal of Consulting Psychology, 16*, 272–277.

Cohen, J. (1952b). Factors underlying Wechsler-Bellevue performance of three neuropsychiatric groups. *Journal of Abnormal and School Psychology, 47*, 359–364.

Cohen, J. (1957a). The factorial structure of the WAIS between early adulthood and old age. *Journal of Consulting Psychology, 21*, 283–290.

Cohen, J. (1957b). A factor-analytically based rationale for the Wechsler adult intelligence scale. *Journal of Consulting Psychology, 6*, 451–457.

Cohen, J. (1959). The factorial structure of the WISC at ages 7–6, 10–6, and 13–6. *Journal of Consulting Psychology, 23*, 285–299.

Cohen, M. (1997). *Children's memory scale.* San Antonio, TX: The Psychological Corporation.

Daneman, M. & Carpenter, P.A. (1980). Individual differences in working memory and reading. *Journal of Verbal Learning and Verbal Behavior, 19*, 450–466.

de Jonge, P. & de Jong, P.F. (1996). Working memory, intelligence and reading ability in children. *Personality and Individual Differences, 21*, 1007–1020.

Deary, I.J. (2001). *Intelligence: A very short introduction.* Oxford: Oxford University Press.

Deary, I.J., & Stough, C. (1996). Intelligence and inspection time: Achievements, prospects, and problems. *American Psychologist, 51*, 599–608.

Desai, M.M. (1955). The relationship of the Wechsler-Bellevue verbal scale and the progressive matrices test. *Journal of Consulting Psychology, 19*, 60.

Donders, J. (1996). Cluster subtypes in the WISC-III standardization sample: Analysis of factor index scores. *Psychological Assessment, 8*, 312–318.

Donders, J. (1997). Sensitivity of the WISC-III to injury severity in children with traumatic head injury. *Assessment, 4*(1), 107–109.

Donders, J. & Warschausky, S. (1997). WISC-III factor index score patterns after traumatic head injury in children. *Child Neuropsychology, 3,* 71–78.

Donders, J., Zhu, J., & Tulsky, D.S. (2001). Factor index score patterns in the WAIS-III standardization sample. *Assessment. 8,* 193–203.

Dougherty, T.M., & Haith, M.M. (1997). Infant expectations and reaction times as predictors of childhood speed of processing and IQ. *Developmental Psychology, 33(1), Jan 1997,* 146–155.

Elliott, C.D. (1990). *DAS introductory and technical handbook.* San Antonio, TX: The Psychological Corporation.

Franzen, M.D., Burgess, E.J., & Smith-Seemiller, L. (1997). Methods of estimating premorbid functioning. *Archives of Clinical Neuropsychology, 12*(8), 711–738.

Fry, A.F. & Hale, S. (1996). Processing speed, working memory, and fluid intelligence: Evidence for a developmental cascade. *Psychological Science, 7,* 237–241.

Georgas, J., Van de Vijver, F., Weiss, L., & Saklofske, D. (2002). A cross-cultural analysis of the WISC-III. In J. Georgas, L. Weiss, F. Van de Vijver, & D. Saklofske (Eds.), *Cross-cultural analysis of the WISC-III: Cultural considerations in assessing intelligence.* Academic Press: New York.

Glutting, J.J., McDermott, P.A., & Konald, T.R. (1997). Ontology, structure, and diagnostic benefits of a normative subtest taxonomy from the WISC-III standardization sample. In D.P. Flanagan, J.L. Genshaft, & P.L. Harrison (Eds.), *Contemporary intellectual assessment: Theories, tests, and issues* (pp. 349–372). New York: Guilford.

Gold, J.M., Carpenter, C., Randolph, C., Goldberg, T.E., & Weinberger, D.R. (1997). Auditory working memory and Wisconsin card sorting test performance in schizophrenia. *Archives of General Psychiatry, 54,* 159–165.

Gottfredson, L.S. (1998). The general intelligence factor. *Scientific American, November,* 1–10.

Gregoire, J. (2003). France and French-speaking Belgium. In J. Georgas, L.G. Weiss, F. van de Vijver, & D.H. Saklofske (Eds.), *Culture and children's intelligence: Cross-cultural analysis of the WISC-III* (pp. 89–108). San Diego, CA: Academic Press.

Gussin, B. & Javorsky, J. (1995, Fall). The utility of the WISC-III freedom from distractibility in the diagnosis of youth with attention deficit hyperactivity disorder in a psychiatric sample. *Diagnostique, 21*(1), 29–42.

Hale, J.B., Fiorello, C.A., Kavanagh, J.A., Hoeppner, T.S., & Gaither, J.B. (2001). WISC-III predictors of academic achievement for children with learning disabilities: Are global and factor scores comparable? *School Psychology Quarterly Special Issue, 16*(1), *Spring 2001,* 31—55.

Hall, J.C. (1957). Correlation of a modified form of Raven's progressive matrices (1938) with Wechsler adult intelligence scale. *Journal of Consulting Psychology, 21,* 23–26.

Hambleton, R.K. (1993). Principles and selected applications of item response theory. In R.L. Linn (Ed.), *Educational measurement* (3rd ed., pp. 147–200). Phoenix, AZ: Oryx Press.

Harrison, P.L., Kaufman, A.S., Hickman, J.A., & Kaufman, N.L. (1988). A survey of tests used for adult assessment. *Journal of Psychoeducational Assessment, 6,* 188–198.

Hart, R.P., Kwentus, J.A., Wade, J.B., & Hamer, R.M. (1987). Digit symbol performance in mild dementia and depression. *Journal of Consulting and Clinical Psychology, 55* (2), 236–238.

Hawkins, K.A. (1998). Indicators of brain dysfunction derived from graphic representations of the WAIS-III/WMS-III technical manual samples: A preliminary approach to clinical utility. *The Clinical Neuropsychologist, 12,* 535–551.

Heaton, R.K., Ryan, L., Grant, I., & Matthews, C.G. (1996). Demographic influences on neuropsychological test performance. In I. Grant & K.M. Adams (Eds.), *Neuropsychological assessment of neuropsychiatric disorders* (pp. 141–163). New York: Oxford University Press.

Hitch, G. (1978). The role of short-term working memory in mental arithmetic. *Cognitive Psychology, 10,* 302–323.

Holland, P.W., & Thayer, D.T. (1988). Differential item performance and the Mantel-Haenszel procedure. In H. Wainer & H.I. Braun (Eds.), *Test validity* (pp. 129–145). Hillsdale, NJ: Erlbaum.

Horn, J.L. (1991). Measurement of intellectual capabilities: A review of theory. In K.S. McGrew, J.K. Werder, & R.W. Woodcock, *Woodcock-Johnson technical manual* (pp. 197–232). Chicago: Riverside.

Hynd, G.W., & Semrud-Clikeman, M. (1989). Dyslexia and brain morphology. *Psychological Bulletin, 106*(3), 447–482.

Individuals with Disabilities Education Act Amendments of 1997, 20 U.S.C. 1431 et seq. (Fed. Reg. 34, 1997).

Jensen, A.R. (1982). Reaction time and psychometric g. In H.J. Eysenck (Ed.), *A model for intelligence* (pp. 93–132). Berlin: Springer.

Jensen, A.R. (1987). Process differences and individual difference in some cognitive tasks. *Intelligence, 11,* 107–136.

Kail, R. (2000). Speed of information processing: Developmental change and links to intelligence. *Journal of School Psychology, 38*(1), 51–61.

Kail, R., & Salthouse, T.A. (1994). Processing speed as a mental capacity. *Acta Psychologica, 86,* 199–225.

Kamphaus, R.W. (1993*). Clinical assessment of children's intelligence.* Needham Heights, MA: Allyn and Bacon.

Kamphaus, R.W., Benson, J., Hutchinson, S., & Platt, L.O. (1994, Spring). Identification of factor models for the WISC-III. *Educational and Psychological Measurement, 54*(1), 174–186.

Kaplan, E. (1988). A process approach to neuropsychological assessment. In T.J. Boll & B.K. Bryant (Eds.), *Clinical neuropsychology and brain function: Research, measurement, and practice* (pp. 129–167). Washington, DC: American Psychological Association.

Kaplan, E., Fein, D., Kramer, J., Morris, R., Delis, D.C., & Morris, R. (1999). *WISC-III PI Manual.* San Antonio, TX: The Psychological Corporation.

Kaplan, E., Fein, D., Kramer, J., Morris, R., & Delis, D.C. (2000). *Manual for WISC-III as a neuropsychological instrument.* San Antonio, TX: The Psychological Corporation.

Kaplan, E., Fein, D., Morris, R., & Delis, D.C. (1991). WAIS-R as a *Neuropsychological instrument manual.* San Antonio, TX: The Psychological Corporation.

Kaufman, A.S. (1975). Factor analysis of the WISC-R at 11 age levels between 6½ and 16½ years. *Journal of Consulting and Clinical Psychology, 43,* 135–147.

Kaufman, A.S (1979). *Intelligent testing with the WISC-R.* New York: Wiley.

Kaufman, A.S. (1990). *Assessing adolescent and adult intelligence.* Boston: Allyn & Bacon.

Kaufman, A.S. (1991). King WISC the third assumes the throne. *Journal of School Psychology, 11,* 345–354.

Kaufman, A.S. (1994). *Intelligent testing with the WISC-III.* New York: Wiley.

Kaufman, A.S., Ishikuma, T., & Kaufman-Packer, J.L. (1991). Amazingly short forms of the WAIS-R. *Journal of Psychoeducational Assessment, 9,* 4–15.

Kaufman, A.S., & Kaufman, N.L. (1983). *Kaufman assessment battery for children.* Circle Pines, MN: American Guidance Service.

Kaufman, A.S. & Lichtenberger, E.O. (1999). *Essentials of WAIS-III assessment.* New York: Wiley.

Kaufman, A.S., McLean, J.E., & Reynolds, C.R. (1988). Sex, race, residence, region, and education differences on the 11 WAIS-R subtests. *Journal of Clinical Psychology, 44*(2), 231–248.

Keith, T.Z. (1990). Confirmatory and hierarchical confirmatory analysis of the differential ability scales. *Journal of Psychoeducational Assessment, 8,* 391–405.

Konold, T.R. (1999). Evaluating discrepancy analysis with the WISC-III and WIAT. *Journal of Psychoeducational Assessment, 17,* 24–35.

Kranzler, J.H. (1997). What does the WISC-III measure?: Comments on the relationship between intelligence, working memory capacity, and information processing speed and efficiency. *School Psychology Quarterly, 12* (2), 110–116.

Kranzler, J., & Jensen, A.R. (1989). Inspection time and intelligence: A meta-analysis. *Intelligence, 13,* 329–347.

Kyllonen, P.C. (1987). Theory-based cognitive assessment. In J. Zeidner (Ed.), *Human productivity enhancement: Organizations, personnel, and decision making.* Vol. 2, pp. 338–381. New York: Praeger.

Kyllonen, P.C., & Christal, R.E. (1987). Cognitive modeling of learning disabilities: A status report of LAMP. In R. Dillon & J.W. Pellegrino (Eds.), *Testing: Theoretical and applied issues.* New York: Freeman.

Kyllonen, P.C. & Christal, R.E. (1989). Cognitive modeling of learning abilities: A status report of LAMP. In R. Dillon & J.W. Pellegrino (Eds.), *Testing: Theoretical and applied issues.* New York: Freeman.

Kyllonen, P.C. & Christal, R.E. (1990). Reasoning ability is (a little more than) working-memory capacity?! *Intelligence, 14,* 389–433.

Larrabee, G.J., & Curtiss, G. (1995). Construct validity of various verbal and visual memory tests. *Journal of Clinical and Experimental Neuropsychology, 17,* 536–547.

Larrabee, G.J., Largen, J.W., & Levin, H.S. (1985). Sensitivity of age-decline resistant ("hold") WAIS subtests to Alzheimer's disease. *Journal of Clinical and Experimental Neuropsychology, 7,* 497–504.

Levine, B., & Iscoe, I. (1954). A comparison of Raven's progressive matrices (1938) with a short form of the Wechsler–Bellevue. *Journal of Consulting Psychology, 18,* 10.

Lezak, M.D. (1988). IQ: R.I.P. *Journal of clinical and experimental neuropsychology, 10,* 351–361.

Lezak, M.D. (1995). *Neuropsychological assessment* (3rd ed.). New York: Oxford University Press.

Lubin, B., Larson, R.M., Matarazzo, J.D., & Seever, M.F. (1985). Psychological test usage patterns in five professional settings. *American Psychologist, 40,* 857–861.

Lubin, B., Larson, R.M. & Matarazzo, J.D. (1984). Patterns of psychological test usage in the United States: 1935–1982. *American Psychologist, 39,* 451–454.

Martin, T.A., Donders, J., & Thompson, E. (2000). Potential of and problems with new measures of psychometric intelligence after traumatic brain injury. *Rehabilitation Psychology, 45,* 402–408.

Matarazzo, J.D. (1972). *Wechsler's measurement and appraisal of adult intelligence* (5th ed.). Baltimore: Williams & Wilkins.

Matarazzo, J.D. (1990). Psychological assessment versus psychological testing: Validation from Binet to the school, clinic, and courtroom. *American Psychologist, 45,* 999–1017.

Matarazzo, J.D. & Herman, D.O. (1985). Clinical uses of the WAIS-R: Base rates of differences between VIQ and PIQ in the WAIS-R standardization sample. In B.B. Wolman (Ed.), *Handbook of intelligence: Theories, measurements, and applications* (pp. 899–932). New York: Wiley.

McDermott, P.A., Fantuzzo, J.W., & Glutting, J.J. (1990). Just say no to subtest analysis: A critique on Wechsler theory and practice. *Journal of Psychoeducational Assessment, 8,* 290–302.

McDermott, P.A., Fantuzzo, J.W., Glutting, J.J., Watkins, M.W., & Baggaley, A.R. (1992). Illusions of meaning in the ipsative assessment of children's ability. *The Journal of Special Education, 25*(4), 504–526.

McDermott, P.A., Glutting, J.J., Jones, J.N., & Nooman, J.V. (1989). Typology and prevailing composition of core profiles in the WAIS-R standardization sample. *Psychological Assessment, 1,* 118–125.

McDermott, P.A., Glutting, J.J., Jones, J.N., Watkins, M.W., & Kush, J. (1989). Core profile types in the WISC-R national sample: Structure, membership, and applications. *Psychological Assessment, 1,* 292–299.

McFie, J. (1975). *Assessment of organic intellectual impairment.* Oxford, England: Academic Press.

Milner, B. (1975). Psychological aspects of focal epilepsy and its neurosurgical management. *Advances in Neurology, 8,* 299–321.

Moon, G.W., & Gorsuch, R.L. (1988). Information inventory: The quicker quick test of intelligence. *Journal of Clinical Psychology, 44*(2) 248–251.

Neisser, U., Boodoo, G., Bouchard, T.J., Boykin, A.W., Brody, N., Ceci, S.J., Halpern, D.F., Loehlin, J.C., Perloff, R., Sternberg, R.J., & Urbina, S. (1996). Intelligence: Knowns and unknowns. *American Psychologist, 51*(2) 77–101.

Nelson, H.E. (1982). *National adult reading test (NART) manual.* Windsor, UK: NFER-Nelson.

Nelson, H.E., & McKenna, P. (1975). The use of current reading ability in the assessment of dementia. *British Journal of Social and Clinical Psychology, 14,* 259–267.

Nelson, H.E., & O'Connell, A. (1978). Dementia: The estimation of premorbid intelligence levels using the new adult reading test. *Cortex, 14,* 234–244.

Neubauer, A.C., & Knorr, E. (1998). Three paper-and-pencil tests for speed of information processing: Psychometric properties and correlations with intelligence. *Intelligence, 26*(2), 123–151.

Osborne, R.T., & Lindsey, J.M. (1967). A longitudinal investigation of change in the factorial composition of intelligence with age in young school children. *Journal of Genetic Psychology, 110,* 49–58.

Payne, R.W., & Jones, H.G. (1957). Statistics for the investigation of individual cases. *Journal of Clinical Psychology, 13,* 115–121.

Piotrowski, C. & Keller, J.W. (1989). Psychological testing in outpatient mental health facilities in 1975. *Professional Psychology: Research and Practice, 20* (6), 423–425.

Prifitera, A. & Dersh, J. (1992). Base rates of the WISC-III diagnostic subtest patterns among normal, learning-disabled, and ADHD samples. *Journal of Psychoeducational Assessment Monograph Series. Advances in Psychological Assessment: Wechsler Intelligence Scale for Children-Third Edition,* 43–55.

Prifitera, A. & Saklofske, D.H. (1998). *WISC-III clinical use and interpretation: Scientist–practitioner perspectives.* San Diego, CA: Academic Press.

Prifitera, A., Weiss, L.G., & Saklofske, D.H. (1998). The WISC-III in context. In A. Prifitera & D.H. Saklofske (Eds.), *WISC-III clinical use and interpretation: Scientist-practitioner perspectives* (pp. 1–38). San Diego, CA: Academic Press.

Prigatano, G.P. (1974, May). *Memory deficit in head injured patients.* Paper presented at the meeting of the Southwestern Psychological Association, El Paso, TX.

Quadfasel, A.F., & Pruyser, P.W. (1955). Cognitive deficit in patients with psychomotor epilepsy. *Epilepsia, 4,* 80–90.

Raven, J., Raven, J.C., & Court, J.H. (1991). *Manual for Raven's progressive matrices and vocabulary scales.* Oxford, England: Oxford Psychologists Press.

Reynolds, C.R. & Brown, R.T. (Eds.). (1984). *Perspectives on bias in mental testing.* New York: Plenum Press.

Reynolds, C.R. & Ford, L. (1994). Comparative three-factor solutions of the WISC-III and WISC-R at 11 age levels between 6½ and 16½ years. *Archives of Clinical Neuropsychology, 9,* 553–570.

Reynolds, C.R., Willson, V.L., & Clark, P.L. (1983). A four-test short form of the WAIS-R for clinical screening. *Clinical Neuropsychology, 5*(3), 111–116.

Riccio, C.Y., Cohen, M.J., Hall, J., & Ross, C.M. (1997). The third and fourth factors of the WISC-III: What they don't measure. *Journal of Psychoeducational Assessment, 15,* 27–39.

Robertson, M.H., & Woody, R.H. (1997). *Theories and methods for practice of clinical psychology.* Madison, CT: International Universities Press.

Roid, G.H., Prifitera, A., & Weiss, L.G. (1993). Replication of the WISC-III factor structure in an independent sample. *Journal of Psychoeducational Assessment Monograph Series. Advances in Psychological Assessment: Wechsler Intelligence Scale for Children-Third Edition,* 6–21.

Rourke, B.P. (1998). Significance of verbal-performance discrepancies for subtypes of children with learning disabilities: Opportunities for the WISC-III. In A. Prifitera & D. Saklofske (Eds.), *WISC-III clinical use and interpretation: Scientist-practitioner perspectives* (pp. 139–156). San Diego, CA: Academic Press.

Russell, E. (1972). WAIS factor analysis with brain-damaged subjects using criterion measures. *Journal of Consulting and Clinical Psychology, 39,* 133–139.

Sattler, J.M. (1992). *Assessment of children: WISC-III and WPPSI-R supplement.* San Diego, CA: Author.

Sattler, J.M. (1992). *Assessment of children (revised and updated 3rd ed.).* San Diego, CA: Author.

Sattler, J.M. (2001). *Assessment of children: Cognitive applications (4th ed.).* San Diego, CA: Author.

Schatz, J., Kramer, J.H., Ablin, A., & Matthay, K.K. (2000). Processing speed, working memory and IQ: A developmental model of cognitive deficits following cranial radiation therapy. *Neuropsychology, 14*(2), 189–200.

Schwean, V.L., Saklofske, D.H., Yackulic, R.A., & Quinn, D. (1993). WISC-III performance of ADHD children. *Journal of Psychoeducational Assessment Monograph Series. Advances in Psychological Assessment: Wechsler Intelligence Scale for Children-Third Edition,* 56–70.

Silverstein, A.B. (1981). Reliability and abnormality of test score differences. *Journal of Clinical Psychology, 37*(2), 392–394.

Silverstein, A.B. (1982). Two- and four-subtest short forms of the Wechsler adult intelligence scale-revised. *Journal of Consulting and Clinical Psychology, 50*(3), 415–418.

Slate, J.R., Jones, C.H., & Saarnio, D.A. (1997). WISC-III scores and special education diagnosis. *Journal of Psychology, 131,* 119–120.

Smith, G.E., Ivnik, R.J., Malec, J.F., Kokmen, E., Tangalos, E.G., & Kurland, L.T. (1992). Mayo's older Americans normative studies (MOANS): Factor structure of a core battery. *Psychological Assessment, 4*(3), 382–390.

Sparrow, S.S., & Davis, S.M. (2000). Recent advances in the assessment of intelligence and cognition. *Journal of Child Psychology and Psychiatry, 41,* 117–131.

Spruill, J. (1991). A comparison of the Wechsler adult intelligence scale-revised with the Stanford-Binet intelligence scale (4th edition) for mentally retarded adults. *Psychological Assessment: A Journal of Consulting and Clinical Psychology 3*(1), 1–3.

Stavrou, E. & Flanagan, R. (1996, March). *The stability of WISC-III scores in learning disabled children.* Paper presented at the Annual Convention of the National Association of School Psychologists, Atlanta, GA.

Sternberg, R.J. (1993). Rocky's back again: A review of the WISC-III. *Journal of Psychoeducational Assessment Monograph Series. Advances in Psychological Assessment: Wechsler Intelligence Scale for Children-Third Edition* 161–164.

Sternberg, R.J. (1995). *In search of the human mind.* Orlando, FL: Harcourt Brace & Company.

Stinnett, T.A., Havey, J.M., & Oehler-Stinnett, J. (1994). Current test usage by practicing school psychologists: A national survey. *Journal of Psychoeducational Assessment, 12,* 331–350.

Swanson, H.L. (1999). What develops in working memory? A life span perspective. *Developmental Psychology, 35,* 986–1000.

Swiercinsky, D.P., & Warnock, J.K. (1977). Comparison of the neuropsychological key and discriminate analysis approaches in predicting cerebral damage and localization. *Journal of Consulting and Clinical Psychology, 45,* 808–814.

The Psychological Corporation. (1997). *WAIS-III–WMS-III technical manual.* San Antonio, TX: Author.

The Psychological Corporation. (1999). *WASI manual.* San Antonio, TX: Author.

The Psychological Corporation. (2001). *WIAT-II examiner's manual.* San Antonio, TX: Author.

The Psychological Corporation. (2001). *Wechsler test of adult reading.* San Antonio, TX: Author.

The Psychological Corporation. (2002). *WAIS-III–WMS-III technical manual–updated.* San Antonio, TX: Author.

Thorndike, R.L. (1992, March). *Intelligence tests: What we have and what we should have.* Papers presented at the meeting of the National Association of School Psychologists, Nashville, TN.

Tulsky, D.S., Saklofske, D.H., Wilkins, C., & Weiss, L.G. (2001). Development of a general ability index for the Wechsler adult intelligence scale-third edition. *Psychological Assessment, 13*(4), 566–571.

Tulsky, D. & Zhu, J. (1997, August). Lowering the floor of the WAIS-III. In D. Tulsky & J. Zhu (Co-Chairs), *Methodological considerations and innovations in the development of the WAIS-III.* Symposium conducted at the 105th annual American Psychological Association convention, Chicago, Illinois.

Tupa, D.J., Write, M.O., & Fristad, M.A. (1997). Confirmatory factor analysis of the WISC-III with child psychiatric inpatients. *Psychological Assessment, 9*(3), 302–306.

Wasserman, J.D., & Maccubbin, E.M. (2002). *Wechsler at the psychological corporation: Chorus girls and taxi drivers.* Paper presented at the 110th Annual Convention of the American Psychological Association, Chicago, IL.

Watkins, C.E., Campbell, V.L., Nieberding, R., & Hallmark, R. (1995). Contemporary practice of psychological assessment by clinical psychologists. *Professional Psychology: Research and Practice, 26*(1), 54–60.

Watkins, M.W., & Kush, J.C. (1994). Wechsler subtest analysis: The right way, the wrong way, or no way? *School Psychology Review, 23,* 640–651.

Watson, C.G. & Klett, W.G. (1974). Are nonverbal IQ tests adequate substitutes for WAIS? *Journal of Clinical Psychology, 30,* 55–57.

Wechsler, D. (1939). *Wechsler-Bellevue intelligence scale.* New York: The Psychological Corporation.

Wechsler, D. (1944). *The measurement of adult intelligence (3rd ed.).* Baltimore: Williams & Wilkins.

Wechsler, D. (1945a). A standardized memory scale for clinical use. *The Journal of Psychology, 19,* 87–95.

Wechsler, D. (1945b). *Wechsler memory scale.* New York: The Psychological Corporation.

Wechsler, D. (1946). *Wechsler-Bellevue intelligence scale–form ii.* New York: The Psychological Corporation.

Wechsler, D. (1949). *Wechsler intelligence scale for children.* New York: The Psychological Corporation.

Wechsler, D. (1950). Cognitive, conative, and non-intellective intelligence. *American Psychologist, 5,* 78–83.

Wechsler, D. (1955). *Wechsler adult intelligence scale.* New York: The Psychological Corporation.

Wechsler, D. (1958). *The measurement and appraisal of adult intelligence (4th ed.).* Baltimore: Williams and Wilkins.

Wechsler, D. (1967). *Wechsler preschool and primary scale of intelligence.* New York: The Psychological Corporation.

Wechsler, D. (1971). Intelligence: Definition, theory, and the IQ. In R. Cancro (Ed.), Intelligence: Genetic and environmental influences (pp. 50–55). New York: Gruene and Stratton.

Wechsler, D. (1974). *Wechsler intelligence scale for children–revised edition.* San Antonio, TX: The Psychological Corporation.

Wechsler, D. (1975). Intelligence defined and undefined: A relativistic appraisal. *American Psychologist, 30,* 135–139.

Wechsler, D. (1981). *Wechsler adult intelligence scale–revised.* San Antonio, TX: The Psychological Corporation.

Wechsler, D. (1987). *Wechsler memory scale–revised.* San Antonio, TX: The Psychological Corporation.

Wechsler, D. (1989). *Wechsler preschool and primary scale of intelligence–revised.* San Antonio, TX: The Psychological Corporation.

Wechsler, D. (1991). *Wechsler intelligence scale for children–third edition.* San Antonio, TX: The Psychological Corporation.

Wechsler, D. (1995). *Manual for the Wechsler intelligence scale for children–third edition. Australia edition.* Marrickville, Australia: The Psychological Corporation.

Wechsler, D. (1995). *Manual for the Wechsler intelligence scale for children–third edition. Canadian edition.* Toronto, Canada: The Psychological Corporation.

Wechsler, D. (1997a*). Manual for the Wechsler intelligence scale for children–third edition. Taiwan edition.* Taipei, Taiwan: The Chinese Behavior Science Corporation.

Wechsler, D. (1997b). *Wechsler adult intelligence scale–third edition.* San Antonio, TX: The Psychological Corporation.

Wechsler, D. (1997c). *Wechsler memory scale–third edition.* San Antonio, TX: The Psychological Corporation.

Wechsler, D. (1998). *Manual for the Wechsler Intelligence scale for children–third edition. Japanese edition.* Tokyo, Japan: The Psychological Corporation.

Wechsler, D. (1999). WASI: Wechsler Abbreviated Scale of Intelligence. San Antonio, TX: The Psychological Corporation.

Wechsler, D. (2002). *Wechsler preschool and primary scale of intelligence–third edition.* San Antonio, TX: The Psychological Corporation.

Wilson, R.S., Rosenbaum, G., Brown, G., Rourke, D., Whitman, D., & Grissell, J. (1978). An index of premorbid intelligence. *Journal of Consulting and Clinical Psychology, 46,* 1554–1555.

Witta, E.L., Keith, T.Z. (1997, Summer). Hierarchical and cross-age confirmatory factor analysis of the WISC-III: What does it measure? *School Psychology Quarterly, 12*(2), 89–107.

Woltz, D.J. (1988). An investigation of the role of working memory in procedural skill acquisition. *Journal of Experimental Psychology: General. 117,* 319–331.

Woodcock, R.W. (1990). Theoretical foundation of the WJ-R measures of cognitive ability. *Journal of Psychoeducational Assessment, 8,* 231–258.

Woodcock, R.W., McGrew, K.S., & Mather, N. (2001). *The Woodcock-Johnson III.* Itasca, IL: Riverside.

Yates, A. (1956). The use of vocabulary in the measurement of intellectual deterioration—A review. *Journal of Mental Science, 102,* 409–440.

Zachary, R.A. (1990). Wechsler's intelligence scales: Theoretical and practical considerations. *Journal of Psychoeducational Assessment, 8,* 276–289.

Zhu, J., Coalson, D., & Rolfhus, E. (2001, October). *Using WASI in conjunction with the WISC-III.* Paper Presented at the annual convention of the Texas Psychological Association, Austin, TX.

Zhu, J. & Tulsky, D.S. (1999, November). *Using WASI in conjunction with the WAIS-III.* Paper presented at the annual convention of the National Academy of Neuropsychology, San Antonio, TX.

Zhu, J., Tulsky, D.S., Price, L., & Chen, H. (2001). WAIS-III reliability data for clinical groups. *Journal of International Neuropsychological Society, 7,* 862–866.

Zhu, J., Woodell, N.M., & Kreiman, C.L. (1997, August). *Three-year reevaluation stability of the WISC-III.* Paper presented at the 105th annual convention of American Psychological Association, Chicago, IL.

CHAPTER 5

"Back to the Future" of the Stanford-Binet Intelligence Scales

R.W. KAMPHAUS AND ANNA P. KRONCKE

INTRODUCTION

A century ago, the Binet-Simon intelligence scales were about to emerge as a scientific breakthrough (Kamphaus, 2001) as the first scales to solve the previously intractable problem of inadequate predictive validity[1]. The other inventors who attempted to create the first practical test of intelligence struggled to obtain predictive validity coefficients as mediocre as .20. James McKeen Cattell's battery of tests that were administered to entering freshman at Columbia College (now Columbia University) struggled to obtain predictive validity coefficients as high as .23 (Wissler, 1901). His measure of "fatigue" correlated .23 and "grip strength" − .08 with class standing. Of course, Binet and Simon used different intelligence tasks, involving more academic activities, but different from formal measures of academic achievement, that far exceeded these dismal findings.

The Binet-Simon scale, adapted for the United States by Lewis Terman, still faced challenges from other measures including the Goddard-Binet, Yerkes-Binet, and many other imitators after World War I. The Stanford-Binet (named after Terman's academic home of Stanford University) reached as-

cendancy among the others, and remained the gold standard for measurement of the intelligence construct until challenged by David Wechsler in 1939 with the Wechsler-Bellevue I. By the early 1950s, the combination of the Wechsler adult and child scales, which offered subtest scores in contrast to the Stanford-Binet, which offered only a total score, proved a formidable challenge.

The Stanford-Binet developers took a great risk in 1986 when they changed the format of the scales, for the first time in 81 years, to be more like that of the Wechsler series. Specifically, longer subtests were created to mimic the interpretive flexibility of the Wechsler, but this attempt proved futile. In fact, few of us in this field encounter psychological reports that utilize the Stanford-Binet. The Stanford-Binet was soon heading toward the fate of name brands that have lost out to the competition.

It is not clear whether the newest edition of the Stanford-Binet can stem the tide of disuse. The Stanford-Binet Fifth Edition (S-B 5), as described later in this chapter, attempts to capture the spirit of the original scales by utilizing sets of short subtests, named *testlets*, to recapture its unique place in intelligence testing history and practice. Regardless of the outcome, the serious student of intelligence testing should become familiar with the historical ebb and flow of the Binet-Simon scales, as no doubt there will be other attempts to resurrect the hallowed history of the scales in one way or another.

We gratefully acknowledge the contributions of Ying Lu, Laneé Rivers, Cheryl Nemeth Hendry, Lauren Jones, and Dr. Leslie Munson to this chapter.

This chapter begins with an overview of the current Stanford-Binet Fourth Edition, which still enjoys usage in some quarters. A brief overview of the Fifth Edition will then be presented.

STANFORD-BINET FOURTH EDITION

The Stanford-Binet Fourth Edition (S-B 4) adopted a theoretical model that places *g,* or general intelligence, at the apex of a hierarchical model of intellectual abilities (Kamphaus, 2001). The S-B 4 authors observed: "Still, the general ability factor, *g,* refuses to die. Like a phoenix, it keeps rising from its ashes and will no doubt continue to be an enduring part of our psychometric practice" (Thorndike, Hagen, & Sattler, 1986, p. 6).

The second level of the Binet hierarchy is based on the work of Cattell and his fluid and crystallized dimensions of intelligence (Kamphaus, 2001). The crystallized abilities are measured by subtests from the Verbal Reasoning and Quantitative Reasoning areas. The fluid analytical abilities at the second level of the hierarchy consist of primarily abstract/ visual reasoning tasks. In addition, a short-term memory composite is available.

The third level in the Binet theoretical hierarchy consists of finer discriminations of the fluid and crystallized abilities. The crystallized abilities are subdivided into the Verbal Reasoning and Quantitative Reasoning areas. The Abstract/ Visual Reasoning subtests represent the assessment of fluid analytical abilities. This third level of interpretation—Verbal Reasoning, Quantitative Reasoning, and Abstract/Visual Reasoning—was designed to receive less emphasis in interpretation than the two higher levels (Thorndike et al., 1986). At its most basic level, the S-B 4 consists of 15 subtests, 4 subtests each for the Verbal Reasoning and Short-Term Memory, and 3 subtests for Quantitative Reasoning.

The S-B 4 theoretical model, however, is now easily subsumed under the comprehensive three-stratum theory of intelligence offered by Carroll (1993). The S-B 4 subtests, along with a proposal for their membership in the three-stratum theory, are provided in Table 5.1.

Administration and Scoring

Only certain portions of the S-B 4 are administered to each age group. Although S-B 4 subtests and items were devised in accordance with its theoretical model, an attempt was also made to include as many item types as possible from previous editions of the Binet scales (Anastasi, 1988). To some extent, however, this decision complicated the administration of some

of the individual subtests. On some subtests of the S-B 4, two earlier versions of the Binet were, in a sense, collapsed to form one subtest with different item types used at different age levels. This situation created problems from an administration standpoint, because the examiner may have become familiar with two distinct sets of procedures for an individual subtest. One example is the Copying subtest, on which items for preschoolers require the examiner to become familiar with the administration of items using single-color blocks. The item type then switches at older ages, requiring the child to use pencil and paper skills.

The S-B 4 uses an adaptive testing design. This design was one of the unique features of previous editions of the Binet. Adaptive procedures are included, primarily to make testing efficient and brief (Thorndike et al., 1986). The basic procedure is to administer the Vocabulary subtest first to all children. The Vocabulary subtest then serves as a routing subtest that is administered to locate the most appropriate starting point for each individual child and has traditionally led to obtaining an excellent measure of *g* (Kamphaus & Reynolds, 1987). The Vocabulary subtest is an extremely high correlate of all the other subtests in the S-B 4 battery, (Reynolds, Kamphaus, & Rosenthal, 1988). Therefore, it will most likely do a good job of routing the examiner to items of an appropriate difficulty level on subsequent subtests.

This approach is in contrast to others, such as those used on the Wechsler scales and the Kaufman Assessment Battery for Children (K-ABC) on which starting points for children are designated by the child's chronological age. The S-B 4 routing procedure may be an efficient procedure for a child whose mental age is different from his or her chronological age. If a child is precocious, beginning at a point appropriate for his or her chronological age is not a wise use of testing time. The S-B 4 adaptive testing strategy using the Vocabulary subtest is intended to counteract this problem by basing starting points for individual subtests on ability rather than on chronological age.

The efficiency of this adaptive testing strategy, however, is dependent on the correlation of the Vocabulary subtest with the other subtests of the S-B 4. Consequently, the Vocabulary subtest is a better routing test for some tests than for others. It is likely to be an excellent routing test for the Comprehension subtest, with which it shares a high intercorrelation (Thorndike et al., 1986). On the other hand, the Vocabulary subtest is likely to be an inefficient and perhaps inaccurate routing for a test such as Bead Memory, which has a considerably lower correlation with Vocabulary.

One of the complications of the S-B 4 for examiners is the use of a standard score metric that is not comparable with other modern tests of intelligence and, for that matter, with

TABLE 5.1   Binet IV Subtest Descriptions, Three-Stratum Theory Classifications, and Psychometric Properties

Subtest Name	Description of Test	Three-Stratum Theory Classification	Description of Classification	Psychometric Properties
Vocabulary	This subtest requires a child to point to a picture named by the examiner and, for more difficult items, to define words given by the examiner.	Crystallized Intelligence	The factor loadings for this subtest and its content indicate that it is a marker test of language ability or crystallized intelligence.	Ave. reliability = .87 g loading = .76 Loading on verbal factor = .86 Memory factor = .06 Quant. factor = −.00 Abstract/visual factor = .03 Subtest specificity = .25
Comprehension	This subtest requires a child to identify body parts on a card with a picture of a child and respond to questions about everyday problem situations, ranging from survival behavior to civic duty.	Crystallized Intelligence	The factor loadings for this subtest and its content indicate that it is a marker test of ability to define verbal concepts.	Ave. reliability = .89 g loading = .71 Loading on verbal factor = .70 Memory factor = .07 Quant. factor = −.00 Abstract/visual factor = .11 Subtest specificity = .47
Absurdities	This subtest requires a child to point to inaccurate pictures showing a situation contrary to common sense and describe absurdities that are depicted.	Crystallized Intelligence	The factor loadings for this subtest and its content indicate that it is a marker test of ability to define verbal concepts.	Ave. reliability = .87 g loading = .67 Loading on verbal factor = .40 Memory factor = .03 Quant. factor = −.14 Abstract/visual factor = .45 Subtest specificity = .57
Verbal Relations	This subtest requires a child to state how three words of a four-word set are similar.	Crystallized Intelligence	The factor loadings for this subtest and its content indicate that it is a marker of language ability and concept development or crystallized intelligence.	Ave. reliability = .91 g loading = .66 Loading on verbal factor = .74 Memory factor = −.07 Quant. factor = .18 Abstract/visual factor = −.01 Subtest specificity = .54
Quantitative	This subtest requires a child to solve applied mathematics problems and show knowledge of mathematics concepts.	Crystallized Intelligence	The factor loadings for this subtest and its content indicate that it is a marker test of acquired mathematics knowledge.	Ave. reliability = .88 g loading = .78 Loading on verbal factor = .25 Memory factor = .20 Quant. factor = .37 Abstract/visual factor = .21 Subtest specificity = .48
Number Series	This subtest requires a child to review a series of four or more numbers presented by an examiner, identify the principle underlying the series, and generate the next two numbers in the series consistent with the others.	Fluid Intelligence	The factor loadings for this subtest and its content indicate that it is a marker test of quantitative reasoning and fluid intelligence.	Ave. reliability = .90 g loading = .79 Loading on verbal factor = .05 Memory factor = .26 Quant. factor = .42 Abstract/visual factor = .33 Subtest specificity = .45
Equation Building	This subtest requires a child to take numerals and mathematical signs and resequence them to form an equation.	Fluid Intelligence	The factor loadings for this subtest and its content indicate that it is a marker test of quantitative skill and fluid ability.	Ave. reliability = .91 g loading = .65 Loading on verbal factor = .13 Memory factor = .11 Quant. factor = .71 Abstract/visual factor = .01 Subtest specificity = .49

(continued)

TABLE 5.1 *(Continued)*

Subtest Name	Description of Test	Three-Stratum Theory Classification	Description of Classification	Psychometric Properties
Pattern Analysis	This subtest requires a child to place puzzle pieces into a form board and reproduce patterns with blocks.	Broad Visual Perception	The factor loadings for this subtest and its content indicate that it is a marker for visualization, forming a mental image of a visual stimulus and then correctly arranging the response stimuli in space.	Ave. reliability = .92 g loading = .67 Loading on verbal factor = .00 Memory factor = .00 Quant. factor = .08 Abstract/visual factor = .74 Subtest specificity = .22
Copying	This subtest requires a child to produce models with single-color blocks and draw a variety of designs to match a model.	Broad Visual Perception	The factor loadings for this subtest and its content indicate that it is a marker for visualization, forming a mental image of a visual stimulus and then correctly arranging the response stimuli in space.	Ave. reliability = .87 g loading = .60 Loading on verbal factor = .09 Memory factor = .13 Quant. factor = −.08 Abstract/visual factor = .54 Subtest specificity = .69
Matrices	This subtest requires a child to identify the missing element from a figural matrix.	Fluid Intelligence	The factor loadings for this subtest and its content indicate that it is a marker for the ability to manipulate or transform the image of spatial patterns into other visual arrangements based on reasoned inferences.	Ave. reliability = .90 g loading = .75 Loading on verbal factor = .12 Memory factor = .16 Quant. factor = .27 Abstract/visual factor = .39 Subtest specificity = .57
Paper Folding and Cutting	This subtest requires a child to choose the correct picture of how a piece of paper might look if it were folded as shown in a drawing.	Broad Visual Perception	The factor loadings for this subtest and its content indicate that it is a marker for the ability to manipulate or transform the image of spatial patterns into other visual arrangements.	Ave. reliability = .94 g loading = .69 Loading on verbal factor = .09 Memory factor = .09 Quant. factor = .35 Abstract/visual factor = .55 Subtest specificity = .60
Bead Memory	This subtest requires a child to recall which of one or two beads was exposed briefly and place beads on a stick in the same sequence shown by an examiner.	General Memory and Learning/ Broad Visual Perception	The factor loadings for this subtest and its content indicate that it is a marker for the ability to give attention to a temporally ordered stimulus, register it in immediate memory, and reproduce it.	Ave. reliability = .87 g loading = .69 Loading on verbal factor = .04 Memory factor = .31 Quant. factor = .05 Abstract/visual factor = .44 Subtest specificity = .59
Memory for Sentences	This subtest requires a child to repeat a sentence exactly the way it was stated by the examiner.	General Memory and Learning	The factor loadings for this subtest and its content indicate that it is a marker for the ability to recall a series of words.	Ave. reliability = .89 g loading = .67 Loading on verbal factor = .44 Memory factor = .52 Quant. factor = −.06 Abstract/visual factor = −.07 Subtest specificity = .53
Memory for Digits	This subtest requires a child to repeat digits exactly as they were stated by the examiner and sometimes in reverse order.	General Memory and Learning	The factor loadings for this subtest and its content indicate that it is a marker for the ability to recall the identity of numbers in serial order.	Ave. reliability = .83 g loading = .58 Loading on verbal factor = .01 Memory factor = .70 Quant. factor = .13 Abstract/visual factor = −.02 Subtest specificity = .49
Memory for Objects	This subtest requires a child to look at objects on a page and then identify objects in the correct order from a larger array.	General Memory and Learning	The factor loadings for this subtest and its content indicate that it is a marker for the ability to use verbal skills to encode stimuli.	Ave. reliability = .73 g loading = .51 Loading on verbal factor = .00 Memory factor = .50 Quant. factor = .00 Abstract/visual factor = .18 Subtest specificity = .50

tests of academic achievement. Although virtually all the tests discussed in this volume use standard score metrics with a mean of 100 and standard deviation of 15, the S-B 4 defies this trend. The S-B 4, resurrects an older metric in which the mean of the standard score distribution is set at 100 and the standard deviation is set at 16. This scaling procedure used for the S-B 4 test composite score and four area scores can be an annoyance. For example, the standard score-to-percentile rank conversion table for all tests that use normalized standard scores with the mean of 100 and the standard deviation of 15 is universal.

Perhaps the most confusing of the different metrics used by the S-B 4 is that used for the subtest scores. These are normalized standard scores with a mean of 50 and a standard deviation of 8. This metric seems to be wholly idiosyncratic and is not used by any other popular tests. It is reminiscent of the T-score method used heavily in personality assessment, for which the mean is 50 and the standard deviation is 10. However, the subtest score metric on the S-B 4 differs enough from the T-score metric to make for little transfer of training. As a result, examiners have to think differently when interpreting S-B 4 composite, area, and subtest standard scores, because these scores have different percentile rank conversions than those of other popular tests.

A scoring procedure that is unique to the S-B 4 is the use of common area score norm tables regardless of the subtest used to assess the child. For example, the manual includes only one norm table for converting the sum of the Short-Term Memory subtest score to an area composite score, and yet, anywhere from one to four of the Short-Term Memory subtests may be used to enter the table and derive a composite. A clinician may use Bead Memory, Memory for Digits, and Memory for Objects to enter the norm table and obtain a composite score. Without separate tables for the specific tests used, the tester basically assumes that all subtests intercorrelate equally, an untenable assumption.

Standardization

The Stanford-Binet Fourth Edition was normed on 5,013 children between the ages of 2 and 23 years. Cases were drawn from 47 states in the United States, including Alaska and Hawaii, so as to be representative of the 1980 U.S. census. A stratified random sampling procedure was employed, with stratification variables that included geographic region, community size, gender, ethnicity, and socioeconomic status. Parental occupation and education were used as the measures of socioeconomic status (SES; Thorndike et al., 1986). The sample was weighted during the norm development process to counteract the effect of including too many children from

higher socioeconomic status families than would be indicated by the appropriate census statistics.

Reliability

The internal consistency of the S-B 4 composite score is extraordinarily high over its 2- to 23-year age span. Internal consistency reliabilities for the composite score ranged from .95 to .99. The internal consistency reliabilities of the S-B 4 subtests are also strong.

Test/retest reliabilities for the S-B 4 are typically acceptable as well. An exception is the test-retest reliability of the Quantitative subtest that, in a study of 55 elementary-grade children (Thorndike et al., 1986), yielded a reliability coefficient of only .28. In the same investigation, reliability coefficients for the four area scores ranged from a .51 for the Quantitative Reasoning scale to an .87 for the Verbal Reasoning scale. The composite score reliability for this investigation was .90. These results caution practitioners to have less faith in the stability of the Quantitative subtest and area score.

Validity

The S-B 4 is supported by considerable validity evidence, although relatively few validity investigations have been published within the last decade. Some of the earliest studies of concurrent validity are reported in the *Technical Manual* and summarized by Kamphaus (2001). These studies show a strong correlational relationship between the S-B 4 and its predecessors, suggesting that the S-B 4 is much like other well-respected intelligence measures in terms of its ability to measure general intelligence. The focus of these studies, however, is on the composite score of the S-B 4. The area scores of the test are not the subject of significant research efforts, by comparison.

Exceptional Children

The relationship of the S-B 4 to other tests for samples of children with disabilities has also not been well studied (Kamphaus, 2001). The findings of the Thorndike et al. (1986) study of gifted children are particularly striking. This study involved 82 children who were administered the S-B 4 and the S-B LM. The resulting means differed greatly, with the S-B 4 mean being 13 points lower than the S-B LM mean. This finding did not occur in the other Thorndike et al. (1986) study of gifted children that used the Wechsler Intelligence Scale for Children-Revised (WISC-R). In this study, the S-B 4 mean was only one point lower than that of the WISC-R.

A first hypothesis to consider for the difference between the two Binet scales is simple regression toward the mean. You may then ask why no regression was apparent in the WISC-R study. It could also be that the old and new Binet measure different constructs, and this difference becomes apparent in only some investigations. This hypothesis is plausible given that the item content of the scales is different, with the old Binet being more verbally loaded and the S-B 4 giving more weight to spatial, memory, and quantitative skills in addition to verbal skills. This hypothesis of content differences is supported by some of the concurrent validity studies.

Furthermore, in the Thorndike et al. (1986) study of 82 gifted children, the correlation between the S-B 4 Verbal Reasoning scale and S-B LM composite (.40) was higher than that between the two test composites (.27). This result also occurred for the study of 19 children in which the correlation between the S-B 4 and WISC-R verbal scores was .71 and the correlation between the two composites was lower at .62. These results suggest that the older Binet may be more influenced by verbal skills than the S-B 4, and when the two tests differ, the verbal ability of the sample (or child for that matter) may produce considerable score differences. The content of the S-B 5 is destined to change again, thus raising the possibility that score differences are simply due to content differences. Given the likelihood of change, the S-B 5 will have to be validated for specific purposes yet again, because little of the current validity data will be generalizable.

Test content differences may also influence score differences for children with developmental challenges or disabilities. A study by Prewett and Matavich (1994) showed, for example, that at-risk children of low socioeconomic status scored about eight points lower on the WISC-III than the S-B 4.

Factor Analysis

Keith, Cool, Novak, White, and Pottebaum (1988) used confirmatory factor-analytic procedures to conclude that there was general support for the four area scores; whereas Kline (1989) used these same procedures to conclude that Sattler's (1988) two- and three-factor models were a better fit to the data. Upon closer inspection there is considerable agreement among these studies.

A general intelligence (g) loading is typically defined as the loading of each test on an unrotated first factor (Kamphaus, 2001). Analyses of the S-B 4 suggest that tests, such as Vocabulary, Quantitative, Number Series, Comprehension, and Matrices, are likely to produce scores that are consistent with one another, meaning that they have high g loadings

(Reynolds et al., 1988; Sattler, 1988; Thorndike et al., 1986). On the other hand, Memory for Digits, Memory for Objects, and Copying are likely to produce discrepant scores from the remainder of the test battery, meaning that they have low g loadings (Reynolds et al., 1988; Sattler, 1988; Thorndike et al., 1986).

Although all factor-analytic researchers have concluded that the S-B 4 test composite is a good measure of g (Glutting & Kaplan, 1990), there is not unanimity regarding the factorial validity of the four area scores: Verbal Reasoning, Abstract/Visual Reasoning, Quantitative Reasoning, and Short-Term Memory. Several researchers have used confirmatory factor-analytic methods to support the validity of the area scores (Keith et al., 1988; Owenby & Carmin, 1988; Thorndike et al., 1986), and yet, several studies using both confirmatory and exploratory methods have concluded that some of the four area scores lack factor-analytic support (Kline, 1989; Reynolds et al., 1988; Sattler, 1988). Again, despite the obvious differences, consistency can be found across many of the studies by looking closely at the results.

There is agreement that the Verbal Reasoning and Abstract/Visual Reasoning areas show strong evidence of factorial support (Keith et al., 1988; Kline, 1989; Owenby & Carmin, 1988; Reynolds et al., 1988; Sattler, 1988; Thorndike et al., 1986). This finding is sensible given the well-documented evidence of the existence of verbal and spatial abilities across instruments and samples (Kamphaus, 2001).

There is also considerable agreement that the Quantitative scale lacks clear evidence of a corresponding factor (Kline, 1989; Reynolds et al., 1988; Sattler, 1988). This observation is true even when researchers inspect the results of supportive studies. The analysis of Thorndike et al. (1986) that generally supports the area scores shows some problems with the Quantitative Reasoning scale. In this analysis, the Quantitative and Number Series subtests have paltry loadings of .21 and .26, respectively on the quantitative factor. The Quantitative Reasoning area score is also suspect because it is most appropriate for older children. The typical procedure many clinicians use is to administer only one or two subtests from this domain. If a clinician uses the general-purpose six-subtest battery, he or she uses only one subtest (Quantitative) from this area. Finally, some critics argue that the Quantitative Reasoning area, although certainly measuring aspects of intelligence, is so similar to mathematics tests that it is difficult to establish its content validity as an intelligence measure (Kaufman & Kaufman, 1983b).

Some researchers have found support for the Short-Term Memory area score (Keith et al., 1988; Owenby et al., 1988; Thorndike et al., 1986), others have not (Reynolds et al., 1988), and still others have found support for it in elementary-

and secondary-school age groups but not for preschoolers (Kline, 1989; Sattler, 1988). Two subtests seem to contribute to the disagreement regarding this area score: Memory for Sentences and Bead Memory.

Memory for Sentences loads as highly, and in some cases higher, on the Verbal Reasoning factor as on the Memory factor. Sattler (1988), for example, found Memory for Sentences to have an average loading of .57 on the Memory factor and .58 on the Verbal factor. Keith et al. (1988), although generally supportive of the S-B 4 structure, found that in their "relaxed" confirmatory model, Memory for Sentences loaded .43 on the memory factor and .40 on the verbal factor.

Sattler (1988) found the average loading for Bead Memory on the Memory factor to be .36, and on the Abstract/Visual factor its loading was higher at .51. Again, in the Keith et al., (1988) relaxed model, Bead Memory loaded higher on the abstract/visual factor (.49) than on the memory factor (.27).

These results all bring into question the routine interpretation of the Quantitative Reasoning and Short-Term Memory area scores as homogeneous scales. These results suggest that the Verbal and Abstract/Visual area scores are interpretable with greater confidence.

Interpretation

The S-B 4 authors (Thorndike et al., 1986) clearly emphasize the importance of the composite score and relegate the area and subtest scores to a lesser status. Factor-analytic findings generally support this approach, with one exception: the equal treatment of the area scores. The Verbal Reasoning and Abstract/Visual area scores are factorially more viable than the Quantitative and Short-Term Memory scores. Given the lack of validity evidence for these latter two scales, they are more similar to shared hypotheses than composite score hypotheses.

Tables for determining significant composite score differences and the rarity of differences can be found in Delaney and Hopkins (1987), Spruill (1988), and Rosenthal and Kamphaus (1988). The average differences between the A/V and V/R area scores for the norming samples are shown in Table 5.2.

BACK TO THE FUTURE WITH THE FIFTH EDITION

The S-B 5 is currently being standardized at the time of this writing. Production schedules are difficult to predict, but the new version may be available at the time of release of this chapter. Regardless of its timing, the S-B 5 differs substan-

TABLE 5.2   Clinical Rarity of Differences Between Abstract/Visual and Verbal Reasoning Area Scores for Two Age Groups

A/V vs. V/R Difference in Points	Ages 2–10	Ages 11–23
10	48	39
15	29	20
20	16	8
25	8	3
30	3	1
35	1	1

Percentage of Norm Sample obtaining a difference this size or larger. Table values were computed based on data provided by Rosenthal and Kamphaus (1988).

tially from the S-B 4 in that it more closely resembles the Binet-Simon and other early versions of the Binet scales.

Gone are the arduously long, Wechsler-like subtests of the S-B 4 in favor of shorter items subsets designed for specific chronological or mental ages. Those baby boomers who remember the 1972 edition of the Binet form L-M will find themselves comfortable with the new format. Similar to the older versions, the S-B 5 is more child-friendly, with a larger array of toys designed to better hold the attention of young children.

The S-B 5 uses five key sub-measures, of verbal and non-verbal varieties, to measure *g* or general intelligence. The five measures or constructs are Reasoning, Knowledge, Visual-Spatial Processing, Quantitative Reasoning, and Working Memory. Matrices, Verbal Absurdities, and Analogies items measure Reasoning. Vocabulary and Picture Absurdities items measure the Knowledge construct. The Form Board, Exercises in Position and Direction, and Form Patterns items assess Visual-Spatial Processing. And, Quantitative Reasoning is defined as the ability to work with numbers and applied problem solving. Finally, Working Memory is assessed by Transforming and Sorting, Short-Term Memory, Memory for Sentences, Block Span, and the Last Word. The submeasures are assessed in 11 blocks of questions, a portion of which are administered to each examinee. In each block, four short sections, called *testlets*, test the examinee in four of the five submeasures. This new test can be used with individuals aged 2 through 90.

Administration and Scoring

Administration and scoring for the S-B 5 differ greatly from that of the S-B 4. To simplify administration and keep administration time around 90 minutes, the new edition uses a different routing test to place examinees into a starting block. The idea is to place an examinee into 1 of 11 blocks that represents the individual's ability level. The examiner then establishes a basal level and continues through the blocks until a ceiling is established. To establish a basal level, the examinee must answer a certain number of questions correctly in each of four testlets in one block. If the examinee is unable to do this, the examiner drops back a block and administers those questions until a basal level is established. To establish a ceiling, the examinee must miss a certain number of questions in each testlet of a block. When a ceiling is established, the examiner should discontinue testing.

Scoring on the S-B 5 is quite simple with one or two points being awarded for each correct response.

Routing Section

The Routing section of the S-B 5 consists of an Object Series and Matrices section and a Verbal Knowledge section. For each section, the examiner picks a starting point based on the age of the examinee and continues until the examinee obtains a score of zero on five consecutive questions. The Object Series and Matrices section uses patterns, matrices, and picture identification questions; whereas the Verbal Knowledge section asks examinees to identify pictures and define words. The tester tallies the score for these two sections to determine a starting block for administering the remainder of the test.

Measures of *g*

Measures of *g* or general intelligence include reasoning, knowledge, visual-spatial processing, quantitative reasoning, and working memory.

Reasoning

The reasoning section is made up of three testlets:

- *Early Reasoning:* This testlet appears in blocks 3 and 5. The examinee is asked to describe a picture in block 3 and to sort chips with pictures and explain how they are alike in block 5. In block 3, children can score from zero to two on each item, and in block 5, they receive one point for each correct sort.
- *Verbal Absurdities:* This testlet appears in blocks 7 and 9. In blocks 7 and 9, the examinee is asked to tell what is absurd about a statement. Zero to two points are awarded based on the answer given.
- *Verbal Analogies:* This testlet appears in blocks 9 and 11. The examinee is asked to complete the analogy, and the response is awarded zero, one, or two points.

Knowledge

The knowledge section is made up of two testlets:

- *Procedural Knowledge:* This testlet appears in blocks 2 and 4. In block 2, the examinee is asked to identify body parts on a picture and understand directions like "clap your hands." The examinee scores one point for a correct response. In block 4, the child responds to the question, "show me what you do with this?" in response to a ball, bowl of cereal, whistle, and so on. The examinee scores one point for each correct response.
- *Picture Absurdities:* This testlet appears in blocks 6, 8, and 10. In each block, the examinee is asked to tell the examiner what is wrong in a picture. These questions get progressively more difficult with each block. One point is awarded for a correct response.

Visual-Spatial Processing

The visual-spatial processing contains the following testlets:

- *Form Board:* This testlet appears in blocks 1 and 3. It simply requires an examinee to place shapes on a board in a certain place. These shapes get more complex in block 3. One point is awarded for a correct response.
- *Position and Direction:* This testlet appears in blocks 2, 4, 6, 8, and 10. Blocks 2, 4, and 6 require an examinee to place a block on a picture after being given a direction or a command. Block 8 requires an examinee to give verbal directions about a picture, and block 10 requires solving word problems involving directions. One point is scored for each correct response.
- *Form Patterns:* This testlet appears in blocks 5, 7, 9, and 11. In block 5 an examinee is asked to use blocks to make designs, by laying the blocks on a picture. One point is scored for each correct response. In blocks 7, 9, and 11, the examinee is asked to make a pattern or design on his or her own using blocks. In these blocks, zero to two points can be scored.

Quantitative Reasoning

This area is still made up of two subtests:

- *Nonverbal Quantitative Reasoning:* This testlet appears in blocks 2, 4, 6, 8, and 10. In block 2, a child uses chips to identify "more" or "bigger" and to count using small numbers like 1, 2, and 3. One point is awarded for a correct answer. In block 4, an examinee is asked to identify numbers, show with blocks which is more, and answer "how many?" In block 6, the examinee is asked to count and compare with blocks, order numbers, and figure out patterns. The examiner awards 1 point for each correct answer. In block 8, the examinee is asked to use fractions, numbers, and patterns, and 1 point is given for a correct answer. Finally in block 10, scales and equalities are used as well as pictures and patterns. The patterns become more complex over the different blocks. One point is scored for a correct answer.

- *Verbal Quantitative Reasoning:* This testlet appears in blocks 3, 5, 7, 9, and 11. Early blocks include counting, simple addition, adding pictures, and verbal word problems. Later blocks include toy blocks that make a figure and more complex word problems. One point is scored for each correct response.

Working Memory

The working memory section is made up of four testlets:

- *Delayed Response:* This testlet is used in block 1. A child is asked to watch the examiner hide a toy under a cup in front of the child. The child is then asked to find the hidden toy. One point is scored for a correct response.

- *Memory for Sentences:* This testlet appears in blocks 2 and 4, and requires the child to repeat short sentences after the examiner reads them. One point is scored for each correct response.

- *Block Span:* This testlet appears in blocks 3, 5, 7, 9, and 11. The subject is asked to watch the examiner as he or she taps blocks in two rows. The examinee is then asked to tap the blocks that have just been tapped, first in order and then by colored rows, red before yellow. This task gets more complex as the blocks get advanced. One point is scored for a correct response.

- *Last Word:* This testlet appears in blocks 6, 8, and 10. The examinee is asked to answer a question and then tell the examiner the last word in the question. As increasingly more questions are asked at a time, the examinee is asked to recall the last words in order. In blocks 8 and 11, the examiner asks more questions. One point is awarded for a correct response.

CONCLUSIONS

It is remarkable to observe how little intelligence testing has changed over the course of the last 100 years. A specific example of the lack of change is the fact that Alfred Binet's

and Theophilius Simon's original predictive validity breakthrough is yet to be superceded by a newer technology. The utility of the Binet scales is somewhat analogous to that of the internal combustion engine. Both variations of Binet and Simon's original work, and of the internal combustion engine, are likely to be useful for some time. Given that the S-B 5 should be similar to its legacy, it, too, will likely be of interest to practicing psychologists as has its progenitors.

NOTE

1. Portions of this chapter are adapted from our prior work, especially that of Kamphaus (2001).

REFERENCES

Anastasi, A. (1988). *Psychological testing* (6th ed.). New York: MacMillan.

Carroll, J.B. (1993). *Human cognitive abilities: A survey of factor analytic studies.* New York: Cambridge University Press.

Delaney, E., & Hopkins, T. (1987). Examiner's handbook: An expanded guide for Fourth Edition users. Chicago: Riverside.

Glutting, J.J. & Kaplan, D. (1990). Stanford-Binet intelligence scale: (4th ed.). Making the case for reasonable interpretations. In C.R. Reynolds & R.W. Kamphaus (Eds.), *Handbook of psychological and educational assessment of children* (pp. 277–295). New York: Guilford.

Kamphaus, R.W. (2001). *Clinical assessment of children's intelligence (2nd ed.).* Needham Heights, MA: Allyn & Bacon.

Kamphaus, R.W., & Reynolds, C.R. (1987). *Clinical and research applications of the K-ABC.* Circle Pines, MN: American Guidance Service.

Kaufman, A.S., & Kaufman, N.L. (1983b). *Interpretive manual for the Kaufman assessment battery for children.* Circle Pines, MN: American Guidance Service.

Keith, T.Z., Cool, V.A., Novak, C.G., White, L., & Pottebaum, S.M. (1988). Confirmatory factor analysis of the Stanford-Binet Fourth Edition: Testing the theory-test match. *Journal of School Psychology, 26,* 253–274.

Kline, R.B. (1989). Is the fourth edition Stanford-Binet a four-factor test? Confirmatory analysis of alternative models for ages 2 through 23. *Journal of Psychoeducational Assessment, 7,* 4–13.

Owenby, R.L., & Carmin, C.N. (1988). Confirmatory factor analysis of the Stanford-Binet intelligence scale, fourth edition. *Journal of Psychoeducational Assessment, 6,* 331–340.

Prewet, P.N., & Matavich, M.A. (1994). A comparison of referred students' performance on the WISC-III and Stanford-Binet intelligence scale: Fourth edition. *Journal of Psychoeducational Assessment, 12*(1), 42–48.

Reynolds, C.R., Kamphaus, R.W., & Rosenthal, B. (1988). Factor analysis of the Stanford-Binet fourth edition for ages 2 through 23. *Measurement and Evaluation in Counseling and Development,* 21, 52–63.

Roid, G. (2001). *Technical manual for the Stanford-Binet intelligence scales (5th ed.).* Chicago: Riverside Publishing.

Rosenthal, B.L., & Kamphaus, R.W. (1988). Interpretive tables for test scatter on the Stanford-Binet Intelligence scale: Fourth edition. *Journal of Psychoeducational Assessment,* 6, 359–370.

Sattler, J.M. (1988). *Assessment of Children* (3rd ed.). San Diego, CA: J.M. Sattler.

Spruill, J. (1988). Two types of tables for use with the Stanford-Binet intelligence scale: Fourth edition. *Journal of Psychoeducational Assessment,* 6, 78–86.

Thorndike, R.L., Hagen, E.P., & Sattler, J.M. (1986). *Technical manual for the Stanford-Binet Intelligence scales (4th ed.).* Chicago: Riverside Publishing.

Wissler, C. (1901). The correlation of mental and physical tests. *Psychological Review Monograph Supplement,* 3(6), pp. 1–62.

CHAPTER 6

Measures of Infant and Early Childhood Development

GLEN P. AYLWARD

Over the last several decades, there has been increased interest in the developmental evaluation of infants and preschoolers (Aylward, 1994; 1997a). This fact is due in part to federal legislation mandating the provision of early intervention (EI) services for those in the 0–3 age range, and early childhood education (ECE) programs for children ages 3 through 5 years. Developmental evaluation is necessary to determine whether children qualify for such intervention services. Improved survival rates of biologically at-risk infants who have a higher probability of subsequent problems have also heightened interest in developmental testing (Aylward, 2002). However, pressure to quantify development has caused professionals working with infants and young children to attribute a degree of preciseness to developmental screening and assessment that is neither realistic nor attainable (e.g., estimating a 40% delay). Additional problems include test administration by examiners who are not adequately trained, and the use of instruments that have varying degrees of psychometric rigor, thereby raising questions regarding reliability and validity. Nonetheless, developmental evaluation is critical, as timely identification of children with developmental problems affords the opportunity for early intervention, which enhances self-righting or prevents additional deterioration. A broad range of professionals, other than psychologists, including early interventionists, pediatricians, child neurologists, educators, and child psychiatrists employ developmental tests.

Choice of the type of developmental assessment that is administered is driven by the purposes of the evaluation. These purposes include determination of eligibility for EI or ECE services, documentation of developmental change after provision of intervention, evaluation of children who are at risk for developmental problems because of established biomedical or environmental issues, documentation of recovery of function, research protocols involving innovative medical procedures, and prediction of later outcome (particularly in biologically at-risk infants born prematurely or at low birth weight).

There are different levels of developmental evaluation. *Screening tests* are administered to whole populations of children, the purpose being early identification of those with unsuspected deviations from normal. Screening is brief, indicative, and flags children needing further assessment. In actuality, *focused screening*, whereby the screening test is administered to an infant or young child who is highly suspect with regard to developmental status, is more typical. *Prescreening* is the process by which a caretaker report or a short, structured interview is used to identify infants who will need further hands-on screening, thereby reducing time and cost by eliminating those who do not appear to have problems on the caretaker-completed questionnaire (Glascoe, 1997; Squires, Nickel, & Eisert, 1996). An *assessment* is more definitive and conclusive and involves the use of a more detailed and lengthy instrument, usually in conjunction with evaluations made by other professionals (Aylward, 1997b). Assessment typically produces a diagnosis. It is estimated that approximately 25% of children will fail a developmental screening (the percentage depending on the nature of the population being screened and the type of screening instrument used). Additional, more detailed assessment will confirm problems in approximately 10% of these children (again depending on the population and test used). Various underlying reasons for positive test findings exist. These include mental retardation, an emerging learning disability, language dysfunction, environmental deprivation, testing problems, or some combination of these etiologies. Maturational delay, recovery from biomedical problems, neural dysfunction, motor deficits, or variables specific to the infant (e.g., state or temperament) can also influence test results (Aylward, 1994).

PRAGMATIC ISSUES

There are several pragmatic issues that must be considered in developmental screening and assessment of infants and young children. The first involves psychometric qualities, while the second addresses test content.

Sensitivity/Specificity

The terms *sensitivity* and *specificity* are particularly relevant for purposes of concurrent and predictive validity. Sensitivity, the true positive rate of a screening or assessment instrument, measures the proportion of children with a developmental problem who are also identified by the test. It is computed as (the number of children with delays who were identified) / (those identified + children with delays who were not identified by the screening test). Children with developmental problems who are not identified are considered false negatives. In actuality, sensitivity should be termed *copositivity* because of the lack of a true gold standard in developmental assessment. Instead, a criterion measure is more accurately viewed as being a reference standard. Specificity, the true negative rate of the test, measures the proportion of children who have no developmental problems who also are identified as normal by the test; the tests identify such children as normal. Specificity is computed as (the number of normal infants, also scored normal on the test) / (normal children + normal children identified by a test as having delays). Normal

children incorrectly identified as being delayed are considered false positives. Specificity should be termed *conegativity*, because the gold standard is again merely a reference standard. There often is a trade-off in specificity if the sensitivity of a measure is high (when the normal/abnormal threshold is set at a level designed to maximally identify infants with problems). Conversely, if the threshold for abnormality is restricted, the specificity will be inflated at the expense of the sensitivity (Aylward, 1994; 1997b). Sensitivity (copositivity) values of 70% and specificity (conegativity) values of 70%–80% are realistic in developmental screening and assessment.

Related to this is the concept of positive and negative predictive values. The predictive value of a positive test is the proportion of children with a positive test result who actually are delayed; the predictive value of a negative test is the proportion of children with a negative test result who do not have developmental problems. The lower the prevalence of a disorder, however, the lower the positive and negative predictive values will be. In developmental screening and assessment, a positive predictive value of 50% is acceptable (Glascoe, 1997).

Areas/Streams of Development

Development can be conceptualized as falling into four areas or streams:

- Motor (gross, fine).
- Language (receptive, expressive, articulation).
- Cognitive (problem solving, object permanency, imitation, planning, understanding cause-effect relationships).
- Adaptive/personal-social (self-help skills, interactions).

Developmental tests typically measure these areas to varying degrees. Language and cognitive processes are the best predictors of later intelligence; whereas motor and adaptive/personal-social are least predictive. Patterns of congruence in developmental levels between different streams or areas of function are helpful in determining the underlying cause for poor test scores. Biological risk factors have an impact on motor function; whereas environmental variables influence cognitive and language development (Aylward, 1997b).

CONCEPTUAL ISSUES

Related to the aforementioned pragmatic concerns are conceptual issues. These involve testing considerations that influence prediction and interpretation of results.

Continuity in Function

A major question in developmental testing involves whether there is continuity in developmental functions, and whether normal development at one age is predictive of later, normal development. Information processing is a continuous function, whereby attention, measured by novelty, preference, and recognition memory, might be an early indication of later cognitive abilities (Bornstein & Sigman, 1986). Mental representations, motivation, and self-regulation are other underlying continuous processes. Manifestations of these underlying processes might differ, depending on age. For example, cognitive processes in a 2- to 3-month old infant might be manifest in visual tracking or reaching for a suspended ring (Aylward, 1995); at 5 to 6 months, an indicator of cognitive processes might be demonstration or precursory object permanency, with the infant seeking an object dropped out of sight in conjunction with an auditory cue. By 12-months, problem solving, displayed by the infant removing a small pellet from a bottle, reflects the underlying function of cognitive processes. Therefore, every effort must be made to identify continuous functions, despite the fact that they might not be readily apparent.

Canalized Behaviors

The concept of canalization might also help to explain the appearance of discontinuity. Many early developmental acquisitions are canalized, meaning that a number of behaviors assessed early in life are species-specific, prewired, and self-righting (McCall, 1983). The infant is born with canalized, fixed behavior patterns such as smiling, babbling, or even reaching for an object. Canalized behaviors generally are not highly complex, in contrast to behaviors such as problem solving. The more strongly canalized the behavior is, the less it is affected by adverse circumstances, such as mild to moderate biological or environmental risks. Conversely, the less canalized the behavior, the weaker the self-righting and the greater the likelihood of disruption by adverse influences. Sensorimotor behaviors are strongly canalized and are heavily represented in early screening and assessment; more complex language and cognitive functions are less canalized and are more sparsely represented in early evaluations. Therefore, early screening and assessment might have limitations because of the types of items evaluated and the likelihood that these items are passed because of the resiliency of these early, canalized skills.

Integrated Functions

Neither the individual developmental function nor the ability per se is most critical in understanding development. Rather, the integration of abilities and the functional units of the brain that control them are critical and provide the best window through which to view and predict development. An individual function, such as visual perception (ability to see a pellet), is not complex nor is it predictive of later functioning. When the child attempts to reach for a pellet and bring it to his mouth or dump it from a container, or if an older child completes a form board, visual perception is combined with memory, intentionality, spatial reasoning, and learning. This involves the integration of various abilities and underlying neural units—in other words, a process (Aylward, 1995). Therefore, test items that reflect cognitive processes or language involve coordination of abilities and several functional units of the brain and are particularly useful in characterizing the child's true developmental potential. In fact, the ability to integrate functions seamlessly might be the ultimate continuous process discussed earlier (Aylward, 1997b).

Testing Concerns

The practice of developmental screening and assessment is unique, because it occurs against a backdrop of qualitative and quantitative developmental, behavioral, and structural changes, with the velocity of change being greater during infancy and early childhood than at any other time. The rapidly expanding behavioral repertoire of the infant and young child, and the corresponding divergence of cognitive, motor, and neurological functions, pose distinct evaluation challenges (Aylward, 1997b). Problems in one stream of development, such as motor, might preclude adequate evaluation of other areas, for example, cognitive processes (Aylward, Verhulst, Bell, & Gyurke, 1995). There is a gradual divergence of cognitive, motor, and neurological functions over time. It is extremely difficult to evaluate a young infant with neurological or motor dysfunction, because the available tests typically involve sensorimotor components. A similar situation is found with children with sensory impairments. Adequate early evaluation can occur only when test items can bypass the motor function or sensory limitation (e.g., measuring receptive vocabulary, looking at a selection versus pointing). Along these lines, abnormal findings may be termed deficits, delays, lags, or retardation, bringing up the question of whether such findings are indicative of pathology or immaturity. The terms *delays* and *lags* are noncategorical, and their use implies the possibility of catch-up where development will become normal over time after brain development has been completed. Prolonged use of these terms may foster unrealistic expectations in the child with true deficits.

Another significant testing concern involves refusals and uncooperative behavior that occur in 12%–18% of infants and toddlers. This rate is much higher than that found in older children and is a potentially problematic factor in developmental assessment. Debate continues regarding whether to score such refusals as failures or to prorate scores. It has been demonstrated, however, that children who are untestable at early ages have a greater risk of later visual-spatial skill problems, lower nonverbal intelligence scores, minor neurological dysfunction, behavioral problems, attention deficit hyperactivity disorders, and the need for school assistance (Langkamp & Brazy, 1999; Wocaldo & Rieger, 2000). It is possible that because of sensitization to weaknesses or areas of difficulty, these children find testing stressful and adopt a negative, avoidant coping style.

TRENDS

Before discussing specific testing instruments, a brief discussion of several evolving trends is warranted. A hybrid offshoot of developmental assessment is found in *early developmental neuropsychology* (Aylward, 1988, 1994), also termed *infant and early childhood neuropsychology* (Aylward, 1997a). This hybrid is defined as "the assessment of brain-behavior relationships in the context of developmental change and maturation" (Aylward, 1988, p. 226). This approach incorporates an interpretive orientation or mindset that involves quantification of qualitative information in a developmental/ neurodevelopmental approach. More specifically, in many instances the same developmental tests used in other disciplines may be employed, but interpretation of data and conceptual bases differ. The age range for infant and early childhood neuropsychology extends from the neonatal period through infancy and culminates at age 5 years. Emphasis on neurological, developmental, and intellectual functions and their relationships evolves, with the importance of each varying, depending on age. For example, in the neonatal period, neurological/neurobehavioral functioning typically is assessed. During infancy, developmental (cognitive and motor) as well as neurodevelopmental functions are tapped (e.g., the Bayley Infant Neurodevelopmental Screener; Aylward, 1995). From age 3 years onward, assessment of intelligence and other more circumscribed cognitive functions is possible.

The second trend involves a new vision of assessment (Greenspan & Meisels, 1996; Meisels, 1996) that eschews standardized, norm-referenced assessments (SNRAs; Gyurke & Aylward, 1992) such as the Bayley Scales of Infant Development-II (Bayley, 1993). SNRAs, administered on a single occasion, are designed to discriminate among children on a linear scale by comparing the child's performance to a reference group on which the test was normed. The end result

is a diagnosis. Critics of this approach emphasize that intervention strategies cannot be readily extrapolated from this procedure (Greenspan et al., 1996); instead, emphasis is placed on assessments that rely on *criterion-referenced* and *curriculum-based* approaches. These approaches provide an absolute criterion against which a child's performance can be evaluated (level of mastery, determined by achievement of a specified number of successes in a given stream of development). In criterion-referenced assessment, the score obtained reflects the proportion of skills the infant has mastered in a particular area; in curriculum-based evaluations, the emphasis is on specific objectives that are to be achieved. These procedures involve observation by a team on multiple occasions in homes, child-care locations, or other environments familiar to the infant or young child. Interestingly, in agreement with advocates of the new vision approach, many users of SNRAs would agree that no single, norm-referenced instrument can provide all the information needed for a comprehensive developmental assessment, but instead should be considered a component of the total evaluation (Gyurke et al., 1992).

DEVELOPMENTAL SCREENING INSTRUMENTS

Screening instruments fall into two categories: prescreening questionnaires and screening tests that are administered directly. The former typically are administered first in a screening protocol, followed by hands-on testing if the initial results are suggestive of developmental problems.

Prescreening Instruments

The concept of prescreening has received much support in primary care pediatrics (American Academy of Pediatrics, 2001). Unfortunately, this approach is somewhat obscure in psychological circles and, hence, underutilized by psychologists. Selected prescreening instruments are listed in Table 6.1. These instruments vary in length, areas screened, time required for scoring, and applicable age ranges. These techniques are most useful in the preliminary identification of children for early intervention services, or in Child Find programs where the goal is to then administer hands-on screening tests to identify children who qualify for early childhood education (Squires et al., 1996). The basic function of a prescreening approach is to sort infants and young children who should subsequently be given a hands-on screening test, from those whose development appears to be within the normal range.

TABLE 6.1   Selected Prescreening Instruments

Instrument	Age Range	Description
Ages and Stages Questionnaire (Bricker & Squires, 1999; formerly Infant Monitoring System)	4–48 months	Eleven questionnaires, 30 items at each age; fine motor, gross motor, communication, adaptive, personal-social.
Child Development Inventories (Ireton, 1992; formerly Minnesota Child Development Inventories)	Birth–72 months	Three separate instruments each with 60 items; infant, toddler, preschool levels; Scored yes/no; cutoff 1.5 SD below mean.
Parents' Evaluations of Developmental Status (PEDS; Glascoe, 1998)	Birth–8 years	Ten questions tap behavior, language, fine motor, social preschool skills; flags those needing further screening.
Prescreening Developmental Questionnaire (R-PDQ; Frankenburg, Fandal, & Thornton, 1987)	Birth–6 years	Based on Denver Developmental Screening Test; personal-social, gross motor, fine motor, language; "delay" is failed item completed by 90% of younger children.

Administered Screening Instruments

Psychologists generally are more familiar with these hands-on screening instruments. Selected tests are listed in Table 6.2. Such tests are considered to be the second stage in the developmental evaluation process. In that function, these instruments are helpful, gross measures of development. However, they generally do not provide a diagnosis, nor do they accurately portray a child's functional levels (i.e., provide age equivalents); unfortunately, they are often misused in that manner. Content areas vary from neurodevelopmental function (e.g., Bayley Infant Neurodevelopmental Screener; Aylward, 1995) to understanding of basic concepts (e.g., Bracken Basic Concepts Scale-Revised; Bracken, 1998), to broader sampling of the major areas or streams of development (e.g., Brigance Infant and Toddler Screen; Brigance & Glascoe, 2002). These tests can be individually or, in certain instances, team administered. (The latter arguably is least desirable, as this moves the screening from a clinical technique to a more assembly-line status, thereby obscuring potentially useful observations gleaned over time.)

DEVELOPMENTAL ASSESSMENT INSTRUMENTS

Developmental assessment instruments are employed to provide an actual diagnosis, with the end product being a clinical decision by the examiner as to what intervention would be appropriate to facilitate development. These are most familiar to psychologists and therefore will be discussed in more detail. An assessment instrument determines the existence of a delay or disability, and it typically is combined with data from other sources (i.e., parent interview, home observation).

Gesell Developmental Schedules/Cattell Infant Intelligence Test

The Gesell Developmental Schedules (Gesell, 1925) and the Cattell Infant Intelligence Test (Cattell, 1940) are the oldest developmental assessment instruments. The most recent version of the former is Knobloch, Stevens, and Malone's (1980) *Manual of Developmental Diagnosis* (1 week to 36 months). Gesell specified key ages (ages at which major developmental acquisitions occur): 4, 16, 28, and 40 weeks, and 12, 18, 36, and 48 months. Gross motor, fine motor, adaptive, language, and personal-social areas are assessed with 1 to 12 items at each age. Unfortunately, a developmental quotient (DQ) is computed for each area using the formula maturity age level/chronologic age x 100. The Cattell essentially is an upward extension of Gesell's instrument over the first 21 months and a downward extension of earlier versions of the Stanford-Binet from 22-months onward (age range of the Cattell is 2–36 months).

Griffiths Developmental Scale

The Griffiths Developmental Scale (Griffiths, 1970) was popular in Europe and Canada and assessed locomotor, hearing and speech, eye and hand coordination, performance, practical reasoning, and personal-social areas (first two years). It has limited use in this country.

Bayley Scales of Infant Development

Bayley, working on the Berkeley Growth Study, developed the California First Year Mental Scale (1934) followed by the California Infant Scale of Motor Development (1936). There

TABLE 6.2 Selected Screening Instruments

Instrument	Age Range	Description
Battelle Developmental Inventory Screening Test (Newborg et al., 1994).	0–96 months	Two items/age level in personal-social, adaptive, gross motor, fine motor, receptive and expressive language, cognitive; three-point scoring.
Bayley Infant Neurodevelopmental Screener (BINS; Aylward, 1995).	3–24 months	Six item sets grouped by age, each with 11–13 items scored optimal/nonoptimal; basic neurologic functions, expressive (motor, verbal), receptive (visual, auditory), cognitive processes. Low-, moderate-, high-risk summary scores.
Bracken Basic Concept Scale–Revised (Bracken, 1998).	2.5–8 years	School readiness composite (colors, letters, numbers/counting, sizes, comparisons, shapes); five supplementary tests; scale scores. Premise: concepts are fundamental agents of intelligence.
Brigance Infant and Toddler Screen/Brigance Early Preschool Screen (Brigance, 1990; Brigance & Glascoe, 2002).	0–23 months/ 2–4 years	Infant 0–11 months, toddler 12–23 months, early preschool 2–2½ years, preschool 3–4 years; fine motor, receptive and expressive language, gross motor, self-help, social-emotional; 8–15 items in each.
Clinical Adaptive Test/Clinical Linguistic Auditory Milestone Scale (CAT/CLAMS, Capute & Accardo, 1996a; 1996b).	Birth–36 months	Language, problem solving, visual-motor skills; 100 items; DQs calculated: developmental age/chronologic age $\times$ 100; total DQ is average of CAT and CLAMS DQs.
Developmental Indicators for The Assessment of Learning-Third Edition (DIAL-3; Mardell-Czudnowski & Goldenberg, 1998).	3.0–7 years	Five areas: motor, concepts, language, self-help, social development; first three direct evaluation; others based on parent observation; team screening.
Denver Developmental Screening Test-II (DDST-II; Frankenburg et al., 1990).	1 month–6 years	Personal-social, fine-motor adaptive, language, gross motor. Developmental chart/inventory; includes delays and cautions (fails item between 75th and 90th percentile). Parent report and administration.
Early Screening Profile (Harrison, 1990).	2.0–7 years	Cognitive/language (verbal concepts, visual discrimination, logical relations, gross motor, fine motor, basic school skills, articulation survey, home survey, behavior survey (questionnaires); Total Summary Index.
Early Language Milestone Scale-2 (ELMS-2; Coplan, 1993).	Birth–36 months	Auditory expressive, auditory receptive, visual (prelinguistic behaviors, gestures—up to 18 months); 41 items, formatted similar to DDST-II.
FirstSTEP (Screening Test for Evaluating Preschoolers; Miller, 1993).	2.9–6.2 years	Twelve subtests in five domains; composite based on Cognition, Communication, and Motor; three classifications.

was a fair degree of overlap with the Gesell and other tests. Subsequently, in the 1950s and 1960s precursors of the Bayley Scales of Infant Development (BSID; Bayley, 1969) were administered to infants enrolled in the National Collaborative Perinatal Project. The BSID was the reference standard (gold standard to some) in the assessment of infant development, being administered to infants 2–30 months of age. The BSID was a theoretically eclectic assessment that borrowed from different areas of research (Aylward, 1997a). It contains three parts: the Mental Developmental Index (MDI), the Psycho-

motor Developmental Index (PDI), and the Infant Behavior Record (IBR). The mean score is 100 ($SD = 16$) with 50 being the lowest MDI or PDI. The MDI assesses perceptual abilities, object permanence, memory, problem-solving skills, imitative abilities, and early symbolic thinking (Aylward, 1994). The PDI provides evaluation of gross and fine motor development; whereas the IBR includes a general assessment of social, behavioral, and emotional functioning.

The BSID was revised and is now the Bayley Scales of Infant Development-II (Bayley, 1993). It continues to be the premier developmental assessment instrument. The revision was due in part to the fact that there had been an upward drift of approximately 11 points on the MDI and 10 points on the PDI, this pattern being referred to as the Flynn effect (1999). As a result, scores on the BSID-II are 12 points lower on the MDI and 10 points lower on the PDI when compared to the original BSID (Bayley, 1993; Black & Matula, 2000). Therefore, if a child had been given the BSID and subsequently the BSID-II, scores would be lower, but this decline would not necessarily reflect a worsening of developmental function. The BSID-II maintains the same structure as the original Bayley; however, the Behavior Rating Scale replaced the IBR. Overall, approximately 30% of the original items were dropped, and roughly 50% of the items are new, designed to improve content coverage, although the theoretical foundation continues to be eclectic. Many new items represent higher order cognitive processes that involve reasoning, memory, and process integration (Aylward, 1997a; Black et al., 2000). On the MDI, there was an increase in language items, and addition of early number concepts, prewriting skills, visual perception, and perceptual-motor integration items. The PDI was also expanded to include muscle tone, dynamic and static balance, and perceptual motor development. The age range of the BSID-II is 1–42 months, and the SD was changed to 15.

The Behavior Rating Scale (BRS) enables assessment of the infant's state, orientation toward the environment, motivation, and engagement with people (Black et al., 2000). These aspects of testing are critical with regard to test performance, as indicated in the earlier discussion. The first two items represent the caregiver's interpretation of the infant's performance, namely, how typical the infant's behavior was and whether the test results accurately portrayed the infant's abilities (as per caretaker report). BRS items were factor analyzed with factor structures differing for the three age groups (1–5 months, 6–12 months, and 13–42 months). Examples of these factors are Attention/Arousal, Motor Quality, Orientation/Engagement, and Emotional Regulation. The enhanced psychometric properties of the BRS in comparison to the former IBR enable a broader evaluation of the infant's overall functioning.

The BSID-II has specified item sets (22) and changes in basal and ceiling rules that differ from the original BSID. Each item set includes scores that are roughly + 1 SD from the mean (78–122). However, there is controversy surrounding the BSID-II regarding whether to begin the item set corresponding to the child's corrected or chronological age (in the case of premature infants) or at lower item sets for children suspected of having developmental delays (Gauthier, Bauer, Messinger, & Closius, 1999; Matula, Gyurke, & Aylward,

1997; Ross & Lawson, 1997; Washington, Scott, Johnson, Wendel, & Hay, 1998). More specifically, if correction is used to determine the item set to begin administration or if an earlier item set is employed because of developmental problems, scores tend to be somewhat lower, because the child is not automatically given credit for passing the lower item set.

Although the BSID-II incorporates facet scores to identify strengths and weaknesses (cognitive, language, social, and motor), it would be helpful to provide area scores compatible with Individuals with Disabilities Education Act (IDEA), namely, cognitive, motor, communication, social, and adaptive (Black et al., 2000). Several other testing concerns are applicable to the BSID-II as well as other developmental assessment instruments: Standardized materials and standardized administration are critical for making comparisons to established norms; and deviation vitiates such a comparison. Similarly, it is critical to determine whether the infant's success on an item is purposeful/intentional rather than serendipitous (e.g., trial-and-error form-board approach versus looking at the form and placing it in the proper hole). The examiner's effort to obtain a response (too many attempts facilitates teaching to task), patterns of refusals, and use of testing of limits in the case of splinter skills is helpful. Similarly, differences between cognitive and motor scores should not be overlooked (sometimes called cognitive referencing), as these differences have diagnostic utility (Aylward et al., 1995).

Several other developmental assessment instruments deserve mention and are covered in the following sections.

Mullen Scales of Early Learning

The Mullen Scales of Early Learning (MSEL; Mullen, 1984) assess the learning abilities and patterns in multiple developmental domains in children 2- to 5½-years of age. The MSEL measures unevenness in the child's learning, with particular emphasis placed on differentiation of visual and auditory learning. The MSEL enables the clinician to differentiate receptive or expressive problems in the visual or auditory domain by using four scales: Visual Receptive Organization (VRO), Visual Expressive Organization (VEO), Language Receptive Organization (LRO), and Language Expressive Organization (LEO). At the receptive level, processing that involves one modality (visual or auditory) is defined as *intrasensory* reception, and processing that involves two modalities (auditory *and* visual) is termed *intersensory* reception. This design provides assessment of visual, auditory, and auditory/visual reception, and visual-motor and verbal expression. This assessment instrument fits nicely into the early developmental neuropsychology framework mentioned earlier, although basic neurological functions/intactness, gross motor expressive, and mental activity functions are not tapped (Aylward, 1997).

Differential Ability Scales

The Differential Ability Scales (DAS; Elliott, 1990) are applicable from 2½ to 17 years, 11 months, but are useful developmentally in the late toddler and early childhood range. The DAS was derived from the earlier (1979) British Ability Scales. Many consider the DAS an intelligence test, even though it yields a range of developed abilities and not an IQ score. However, DAS is rich in developmental information of a cognitive nature. On the DAS, a composite score, based on reasoning and conceptual abilities, is derived; namely, the General Conceptual Ability score (GCA; M = 100; SD = 15, range 45–165). Subtest ability scores have a mean of 50 (SD = 10, range 20–80). In addition, Verbal Ability and Nonverbal Ability Cluster scores are produced for upper preschool age children; Verbal Ability, Nonverbal Reasoning Ability, and Spatial Ability Cluster scores are produced for the school-age level. This allows for three levels of interpretation: the GCA, cluster scores, and subtest scores. From ages 2–6 to 3–5, four core tests constitute the GCA (Block Building, Picture Similarities, Naming Vocabulary, and Verbal Comprehension); there are also two supplementary diagnostic tests (Recall of Digits, Recognition of Pictures). From ages 3–6 to 5–11, six core tests are included in the GCA (Copying, Pattern Construction, Early Number Concepts are added to Verbal Comprehension, Picture Similarities, and Naming Vocabulary; Block Building is now optional) and five diagnostic tests (Block Building, Matching Letter-Like Forms, Recall of Digits, Recall of Objects, Recognition of Pictures). Cluster scores for verbal and nonverbal abilities are produced from 3½ years onward. The test is unique in that it incorporates a developmental and an educational perspective. It enables identification of a child's capabilities and contains a progressive refinement of abilities as the child's age advances. Each subtest is homogeneous and can be interpreted in terms of content. This interpretability facilitates the identification of the child's specific strengths and weaknesses, which is particularly helpful in the formulation of intervention strategies.

McCarthy Scales of Children's Abilities

The McCarthy Scales of Children's Abilities (MSCA; McCarthy, 1972) essentially bridges developmental and IQ tests (Aylward, 1994) and is most useful in the 3- to 5-year age range (age range is 2½–8½ years). Again, some clinicians may question viewing the MSCA as a developmental test per se; however, the term IQ was avoided initially, with the test considered to measure the child's ability to integrate accumulated knowledge and adapt it to the tasks of the scales. A total of 18 tests is divided into Verbal (five tests), Perceptual-Performance (seven tests), Quantitative (three tests), Motor (five tests), and Memory (four tests) categories. Several tests are found on two scales. The Verbal scale is considered a measurement of a child's ability to understand, process, and express verbal information. The Perceptual-Performance scale measures visual-motor coordination and nonverbal practical reasoning abilities. The Quantitative scale evaluates the child's understanding of numbers, number concepts, and counting. The Memory scale measures auditory and visual short-term memory. Gross and fine motor coordination are measured on the Motor scale.

The Verbal, Perceptual-Performance, and Quantitative scales are combined to yield a General Cognitive Index (GCI; M = 100, SD = 16). The MSCA is attractive to the clinician, because it enables production of a profile of functioning (with age equivalents). On the negative side, the test is almost 30 years old, and hence there is inflation of scores (perhaps by as much as 1 SD), vis-à-vis the aforementioned Flynn (1999) effect. Many subtests have weak test ceilings after age 4 or so, meaning that older children will quickly reach the maximum score. There are short forms of the test available, but these are not useful in the younger age ranges (Aylward, 1994).

Miller Assessment for Preschoolers

The Miller Assessment for Preschoolers (MAP, Miller, 1988) is designed to identify preschoolers who are at risk for developmental delay. MAP is applicable from ages 2.9–6 years. The test has definite neuropsychological underpinnings. Items are grouped into five performance areas: Neural Foundations, Coordination (sensory and motor functions), Verbal, Non-Verbal (cognitive functions), and Complex Tasks (combined abilities).

Assessed abilities fall into three main conceptual categories:

- *Sensory and motor:* This includes Neural Foundations and Coordination. The former consists of basic motor tasks and awareness of sensations (position, movement, and touch). Many of these items are included in the standard neurological examination (stereogenesis, finger localization, and hand-nose). The Coordination subtests measure gross, fine, and oral motor functions (tower building, tongue movements, articulation, walking on a line, and rapid alternating movements).

- *Cognitive:* Included in this category are Verbal and Non-verbal areas. The verbal items evaluate memory, sequencing, comprehension, association, and verbal expression (general information, following directions, and sentence and digit repetition). Nonverbal functions assessed include memory, sequencing, and visual performance (block tapping, object memory, and puzzles).
- *Combined abilities:* This area combines sensory, motor, and cognitive abilities that are required for interpretation of spatial-visual information (block designs, mazes, draw-a-person, and imitation of postures).

The MAP has three color-coded diagnostic areas, and children are placed: red (< 5th percentile), yellow (between 6th and 25th percentiles), and green (> 25th percentile). The test is useful in identifying mild and moderate preacademic problems.

Battelle Developmental Inventory

The Battelle Developmental Inventory (BDI; Newborg, Stock, Wnek, Guidubaldi, & Svinicki, 1984) evaluates the child's development in five areas from birth to 8 years: personal-social, adaptive, motor, communication, and cognitive. The full BDI contains 341 items (the Screening test contains 96). The inventory was developed utilizing a milestone approach from which a child's development could be characterized by the attainment of critical skills and/or behaviors in a particular sequence. Item sequences were determined based on the age level at which approximately 75% of the children received full credit for the item (as a result, the number of items at each level is not equal).

Test items are arranged in ten age categories, grouped in 6-month increments from birth to age 2 years and yearly thereafter. Information is gleaned through interviews with caregivers, observation in natural settings, or structured assessment. Items are scored on a three-point system: The child receives a 2 if the response met specified criteria, a 1 if the child attempted the task but was not totally successful (a so-called *emerging* response), or a 0 when the response was clearly incorrect or absent. Domain and subdomain scores have a mean of 10 (SD = 3), and the Developmental Quotient (DQ) based on a composite of the five separate domains has an M of 100 (SD = 15). The five domains are shown in the following list:

- *Personal-Social.* This contains six subdomains: adult interaction, expression of feelings/affect, self-concept, peer interaction, coping, and social role.
- *Adaptive.* This is organized into five subdomains: attention, eating, dressing, personal responsibility, and toileting.
- *Motor.* This domain contains five subdomains: muscle control, body coordination, locomotion, fine muscle, and perceptual motor.
- *Communication.* This is grouped into two subdomains: receptive communication and expressive communication.
- *Cognitive.* This is grouped into four areas: perceptual discrimination, memory, reasoning and academic skills, and conceptual development.

A major strength of the BDI is that standardized adaptations for testing handicapped children are provided. The 5 domains and 24 subdomains enable identification of the child's strengths and weaknesses and help to differentiate overall versus specific deficits. As a result, it is helpful for planning early intervention strategies.

CONCLUSIONS

Developmental evaluation, whether it involves prescreening, screening, or assessment, must be undertaken by professionals who are knowledgeable about normal development, neurodevelopmental issues, and brain-behavior relationships. Similarly, an appreciation of how medical/biologic and environmental factors influence developmental functioning (Aylward, 1997b), and how the testing encounter is more vulnerable to child-related and situation-related variables at this age, is necessary. The boundary between developmental and intelligence tests (and IQs and DQs) is blurred, particularly at these younger ages. Currently an eclectic approach is most prominent in the field, but at its core is the assessment of brain-behavior relationships in the context of developmental change and maturation. Whether this approach is termed infant and early childhood neuropsychology, early developmental neuropsychology (Aylward, 1988; 1997a), or simply developmental assessment, is open to question. As such, the range of measures of infant and early childhood development is broadly defined, and should also include tests from other disciplines, such as occupational and physical therapy, neurology, developmental/ behavioral pediatrics, and speech/language therapy.

REFERENCES

American Academy of Pediatrics, Committee on Children with Disabilities. (2001). Developmental surveillance and screening of infants and young children. *Pediatrics, 108,* 192–196.

Aylward, G.P. (1988). Infant and early childhood assessment. In M. Tramontana & S. Hooper (Eds.), *Assessment issues in child neuropsychology* (pp. 225–248). New York: Plenum.

Aylward, G.P. (1994). *Practitioner's guide to developmental and psychological testing.* New York: Plenum Medical Books.

Aylward, G.P. (1995). *The Bayley infant neurodevelopmental screener manual.* San Antonio, TX: The Psychological Corporation.

Aylward, G.P. (1997a). *Infant and early childhood neuropsychology.* New York: Plenum.

Aylward, G.P. (1997b). Conceptual issues in developmental screening and assessment. *Journal of Developmental and Behavioral Pediatrics, 18,* 340–349.

Aylward, G.P. (2002). Cognitive and neuropsychological outcome: More than IQ scores. *Mental Retardation and Developmental Disabilities Research and Reviews, 8,* (in press).

Aylward, G.P., Verhulst, S.J., Bell, S., & Gyurke, J.S. (1995). Cognitive and motor score differences in biologically at-risk infants. *Infant Behavior and Development, 18,* 43–52.

Bayley, N. (1933). *The California first-year mental scale.* Berkeley: University of California Press.

Bayley, N. (1936). *The California infant scale of motor development.* Berkeley: University of California Press.

Bayley, N. (1969). *Bayley scales of infant development.* San Antonio, TX: The Psychological Corporation.

Bayley, N. (1993). *Bayley scales of infant development. (2nd ed).* San Antonio, TX: The Psychological Corporation.

Black, M.M., & Matula, K. (2000). *Essentials of Bayley scales of infant development-II assessment.* New York: John Wiley & Sons.

Bornstein, M.H., & Sigman, M.D. (1986). Continuity in mental development from infancy. *Child Development, 57,* 251–274.

Bracken, B.A. (1998). *Bracken basic concept scale-revised.* San Antonio, TX: The Psychological Corporation.

Bricker, D., & Squires, J. (1999). *Ages and stages questionnaires: A parent-completed child monitoring system.* Baltimore, MD: Paul H. Brookes.

Brigance, A.H. (1990). *Early preschool screen.* North Billerica, MA: Curriculum Associates, Inc.

Brigance, A.H., & Glascoe, F.P. (2002). *Brigance infant and toddler screen.* North Billerica, MA: Curriculum Associates, Inc.

Capute, A.J., & Accardo, P.J. (1996a). The infant neurodevelopmental assessment: A clinical interpretive manual for CAT-CLAMS in the first two years of life. Part 1. *Current Problems in Pediatrics, 26,* 238–257.

Capute, A.J., & Accardo, P.J. (1996b). The infant neurodevelopmental assessment: A clinical interpretive manual for CAT-CLAMS in the first two years of life. Part 2. *Current Problems in Pediatrics, 26,* 279–306.

Cattell, P. (1940). *Cattell infant intelligence scale.* New York: The Psychological Corporation.

Coplan, J. (1993). *The early language milestone scale-2.* Austin, TX: PRO-ED, Inc.

Elliott, C.D. (1990). *Differential abilities scale administration manual.* San Antonio, TX: The Psychological Corporation.

Flynn, J.R. (1999). Searching for justice. The discovery of IQ gains over time. *American Psychologist, 54,* 5–20.

Frankenburg, W.K., Dodds, J.B., Archer, P., Shapiro, H., & Bresnick, B. (1990). *Denver II screening manual.* Denver, CO: Denver Developmental Materials.

Frankenburg, W.K., Fandall, A.W., & Thornton, S.M. (1987). Revision of Denver prescreening developmental questionnaire. *Journal of Pediatrics, 110,* 653–657.

Gauthier, S.M., Bauer, C.R., Messinger, D.S., & Closius, J.M. (1999). The Bayley scales of infant development II: Where to start? *Journal of Developmental and Behavioral Pediatrics, 20,* 75–79.

Gesell, A. (1925). *The mental growth of the preschool child.* New York: Macmillan.

Glascoe, F.P. (1997). Parents' concerns about children's development: Prescreening technique or screening test? *Pediatrics, 99,* 522–528.

Glascoe, F.P. (1998). *Collaborating with parents: Using parents' evaluation of developmental status to detect and address developmental and behavioral problems.* Nashville, TN: Ellsworth & Vandermeer Press.

Greenspan, S.I., & Meisels, S.J. (1996). Toward a new vision for the developmental assessment of infants and young children. In S.J. Meisels & E. Fenichel (Eds.), *New visions for the developmental assessment of infants and young children* (pp. 11–26). Washington, D.C.: Zero to Three: National Center for Infants, Toddlers & Families.

Griffiths, R. (1970). *The abilities of young children. A comprehensive system of mental measurement for the first eight years of life.* London: University of London Press.

Gyurke, J.S. & Aylward, G.P. (1992). Issues in the use of norm referenced assessments with at-risk infants. *The Child, Youth, and Family Services Quarterly, 15,* 6–9.

Harrison, P.L. (1990). *Early screening profiles manual.* Circle Pines, MN: American Guidance Service.

Ireton, H. (1992). *Child development inventories manual.* Minneapolis, MN: Minneapolis Behavioral Science Systems.

Knobloch, H., Stevens, F., & Malone, A.E. (1980). *Manual of developmental diagnosis.* New York: Harper & Row.

Langkamp, D.L., & Brazy, J.E. (1999). Risk for later school problems in preterm children who do not cooperate for preschool developmental testing. *Journal of Pediatrics, 135,* 756–760.

Mardell-Czudnowski, C., & Goldenberg, D.S. (1998). *Developmental indicators for the assessment of learning. 3rd ed.* Circle Pines, MN: American Guidance Service.

Matula, K, Gyurke, J.S., & Aylward, G.P. (1997). Response to commentary: Bayley scales II. *Journal of Developmental and Behavioral Pediatrics, 18,* 112–113.

McCall, R.B. (1983). A conceptual approach to early mental development. In M. Lewis (Ed.), *Origins of intelligence: Infancy and early childhood* (pp. 107–134). New York: Plenum.

McCarthy, D.A. (1972). *Manual of the McCarthy scales of children's abilities.* New York: The Psychological Corporation.

Meisels, S.J. (1996). Charting the continuum of assessment and intervention. In S.J. Meisels & E. Fenichel (Eds.), *New visions for the developmental assessment of infants and young children* (pp. 27–52). Washington, D.C.: Zero to Three: National Center for Infants, Toddlers and Families.

Miller, L.J. (1988). *Miller assessment for preschoolers.* San Antonio, TX: The Psychological Corporation.

Miller, L.J. (1993). *FirstSTEP: Screening test for evaluating preschoolers.* San Antonio, TX: The Psychological Corporation.

Mullen, E.M. (1984). *Mullen scales of early learning.* Circle Pines, MN: American Guidance Service.

Newborg, J., Stock, J.R., Wnek, L., Guidubaldi, J., & Svinicki, J. (1994). *The Battelle developmental inventory.* Itasca, IL: Riverside.

Ross, G., & Lawson, K. (1997). Using the Bayley-II: Unresolved issues in assessing the development of prematurely born children. *Journal of Developmental and Behavioral Pediatrics, 18,* 109–111.

Squires, J., Nickel, R.E., & Eisert, D. (1996). Early detection of developmental problems: Strategies for monitoring young children in the practice setting. *Journal of Developmental and Behavioral Pediatrics, 17,* 420–429.

Washington, K., Scott, D.T., Johnson, K.A., Wendel, S., & Hay, A.E. (1998). The Bayley Scales of Infant Development II and children with developmental delays: A clinical perspective. *Journal of Developmental and Behavioral Pediatrics, 19,* 346–349.

Wocaldo, C., & Reiger, I. (2000). Very preterm children who do not cooperate with assessments at three years of age: Skill differences at five years. *Journal of Developmental and Behavioral Pediatrics, 21,* 107–113.

SECTION TWO
NEUROPSYCHOLOGY

CHAPTER 7

Introduction to Section Two

GERALD GOLDSTEIN AND SUE R. BEERS

This section of Volume I of the *Comprehensive Handbook of Psychological Assessment* covers the area of clinical neuropsychological assessment. Clinical neuropsychological assessment is the evaluation of individuals for indicators of brain dysfunction. It makes use of specialized tests and tests of cognitive function used with both normal and patient populations, but it provides interpretations of these latter tests in a manner that is neurologically relevant. Ralph Reitan has provided perhaps the most cogent definition of a neuropsychological test as a test that is sensitive to the condition of the brain. Thus, neuropsychological assessment identifies brain-behavior relationships through the use of procedures that research has validated as indices of brain function or dysfunction. During its beginning, neuropsychological assessment was characterized as testing for brain damage, and was accomplished largely by clinical psychologists using traditional clinical psychological procedures, such as the Rorschach inkblot test, human figure drawings, or various intelligence tests, notably the Wechsler scales. However, during the 1930s and 40s, tests were developed that had specific neuropsychological implications, notably the Bender-Gestalt and Goldstein-Scheerer tests of abstract reasoning. Psychologists, and some neurologists and psychiatrists, used these tests while examining neurological patients. As the field grew, many more of these specialized tests were developed, some of which ultimately became parts of extensive, comprehensive neuropsychological assessment test batteries. At present, numerous specialized tests are either used individually or as part of a battery. In addition, these tests are appropriate for different age groups ranging from infants to elderly people. Clinical neuropsychology has become a separate specialty in psychology, and professional training that educates practitioners in this specialty area has become available. These individuals have the necessary training in neuroscience, psychometrics, and clinical psychology to provide clinical services to patients with known or suspected brain dysfunction.

Neuropsychological assessment differs from other forms of psychological assessment with respect to its basic scientific and theoretical foundations. Although there is no question that neuropsychological tests should be psychometrically sound, the development of these tests involves far more than psychometrics. A strong relationship exists between many branches of neuroscience and experimental psychology. Thus, each chapter in Section Two contains theoretical considerations and a review of pertinent neurobiological and experimental psychological literature. For example, neuropsychological tests of language have their theoretical foundations in the neurobiology of language and neurolinguistics, or the study of how the brain mediates language. Memory tests are associated with the extensive literature on the psychology of memory that goes back to the nineteenth century. There is also a strong interplay between animal model research and assessment of humans. For example, some current tests of reasoning are modifications of tests first used for the study of nonhuman primates. Most recently, there has been great interest in neuroimaging. The behavioral activation methods, such as functional magnetic resonance imaging (fMRI), have provided the opportunity to observe brain activity while the individual is performing some cognitive task, such as interpreting language.

Aside from the interest in experimental science, neuropsychological tests and test batteries are associated with conceptual models proposed by leading theoreticians. In several chapters in Section Two, the influence of Luria is clear. In others, the influences of major theoreticians, such as Kurt Goldstein, Ward Halstead, and Heinz Werner, are apparent. Concepts such as Luria's functional systems and executive function, Goldstein's abstract attitude theory, and Werner's process approach are still alive. More recently developed concepts, such as working memory, and Allan Mirsky's multidimensional attention model also have a substantial influence on the field. The extensive experimental work of the late Nelson Butters and Laird Cermak with patients with Korsakoff's syndrome and other forms of amnesia has profoundly influenced the field. An enormous amount of work has been done to try to relate different areas of the brain to different behaviors, with notable emphases on the frontal lobes and the functional differences between the two cerebral hemispheres. Thus, neuropsychological assessment is probably more model-based and theoretically oriented than other areas of psychological assessment.

A field of developmental neuropsychology that is well reflected in this volume now exists. The literature in this area not only contains studies of children and adults, but also of changes in neuropsychological function across the life span. The inclusion of separate chapters on children would probably not have been possible as recently as a decade ago. Although intelligence and achievement tests for children have been around for many years, specific neuropsychological tests for children are relatively new. The NEPSY, the children's version of the Luria-Nebraska battery, and the tests of memory for children described in the chapter by Miller and associates are recent developments. In addition to new tests, neuropsychological assessment now includes extensive literature on disorders that begin in childhood, such as learning disability, attention-deficit hyperactivity disorder, and autism. This expansion of the field appears to be based at least to some extent on a growing interest in development and a growing concern with neurodevelopmental disorders. Although mental retardation has been recognized for some time, it is becoming increasingly clear that many neuropsychological disorders may begin before birth. Thus, while the field of clinical neuropsychological assessment probably began with the study of brain damage, such as stroke or brain tumors acquired during adulthood, it now is strongly involved with disorders across the lifespan. This growing interest is associated with an interest in the study of brain development in animals and humans, and of the effects of various influences on brain development. The chapter on children by Mirsky and Duncan provides some excellent examples of this type of research. There is also a great interest in disorders, such as autism and schizophrenia, in which the brain develops in an abnormal way.

In practice, some neuropsychologists prefer to use the standard, comprehensive batteries described in the first part of this section; whereas others select tests individually from the various specific cognitive domain tests described in the second part of this section. This selection is based on initial information about the patient. There has been much discussion of fixed vs. flexible batteries that has not been particularly productive. Extraneous matters, such as testing time constraints, the nature of the population served, and insurance regulations, greatly complicate this matter, and theoretical preference is not the only issue. By including material on both approaches in this section, we wished to make the implication that the competent clinical neuropsychologist should

be prepared to do a comprehensive assessment of the major cognitive domains with such procedures as the Halstead-Reitan battery, or a specialized assessment of a particular domain if it is indicated. Sometimes, probably in rare instances, it may be necessary to acquire the services of a superspecialist who can do a detailed evaluation of patients who, for example, have a particularly difficult to diagnose aphasia or amnesic disorder. However, in most patients, if only language or memory is evaluated, albeit in a detailed and thorough way, deficits in other domains may go unevaluated. For this reason, the neuropsychologist should consider referrals for testing of memory or language, because apparent difficulties in those areas may actually reflect more basic and explanatory difficulties in such areas as executive and reasoning abilities or attention. On the other hand, if preliminary examination suggests a specific syndrome in one of the cognitive domains, the neuropsychologist should be prepared to do a detailed evaluation of that syndrome, or to refer the patient to a specialist. For example, in attempting to give a patient a comprehensive neuropsychological assessment, we discovered that she could not identify objects visually, but could do so by touch. It turned out that she had visual agnosia, a relatively rare disorder, which we went on to examine in detail. However, by working around her visual dysfunction, we found that she had a substantial abstract reasoning deficit, which would substantially compromise her adaptive functioning. Thus, her visual agnosia was studied in some detail, but the use of a comprehensive battery also revealed deficits in other areas relevant to making a full diagnosis and to rehabilitation/management planning.

Finally, the highly artificial testing constraints imposed by third-party payers deserve mention here. While the financial impact of these restraints on the field is widely appreciated, it is our experience that managed-care requirements that limit testing hours actually increase the theoretical demands on clinicians as they apply hypothesis-testing procedures using fewer instruments. This, in turn, requires more rigorous training and expertise, as more and more limitations are placed on our usual and customary testing procedures. We hope that Section Two of this book will prove to be a useful tool in assessment planning.

The first part of Section Two contains descriptions of standard, comprehensive neuropsychological test batteries. The Halstead-Reitan Battery is the most widely used of the three procedures covered here and has versions for young children, older children, and adults. It originated in Ward Halstead's University of Chicago laboratory and was established on the basis of the study of a much larger number of tests than is contained in the actual battery. It was the first factor-analyzed battery in neuropsychology and was originally conceptualized in terms of a theory of biological intelligence formulated by Halstead over many years of research with various clinical populations. Ralph Reitan, on the basis of hundreds of publications, was responsible for the establishment of the clinical validity of the battery and for its application to clinical practice. Over several decades, it remains the most accepted of the comprehensive batteries.

The Luria-Nebraska battery was devised by Charles Golden and was based on a manual containing a number of the tests used by the Russian neurologist and psychologist Aleksandr Luria. The manual was written by Anne-Lise Christensen after a period of study with Luria and then translated into English. Although the English-speaking professional public knew something of Luria's theoretical and experimental work, his actual test procedures were not readily available. Christensen's manual provided Luria's rationale for conducting neuropsychological examinations and many of the test items themselves, including a kit containing many of the materials he used. The items were organized into several sections, such as Receptive Language, Memory, and Intellectual Processes. Golden and his colleagues developed a scoring system for these items and did the necessary reliability and validity studies needed to establish, at least on a preliminary basis, the psychometric properties needed for a viable test battery. Numerous studies followed reporting on the application of the Luria-Nebraska battery to many different clinical populations, and to problems of lesion lateralization and localization. There are now adult and child versions of this battery available.

The NEPSY is a developmental battery designed for neurocognitive assessment of preschool and school-aged children, with particular emphasis on assessment of the subtle deficiencies that interfere with learning. It is also based on Luria's work, but in a different way from the Luria-Nebraska battery. It is not based on Luria's specific tests, but on his theories that provided rationales for the development of new tests. It provides a comprehensive evaluation of areas relevant to learning disability, such as oromotor sequencing and word recognition. It is a well-standardized, psychometrically satisfactory instrument.

The second part of Section Two provides reviews of the various cognitive domains typically included in neuropsychological assessment. The domains are separate aspects of cognitive function that may become selectively impaired depending upon type and location of brain dysfunction, or even in normal individuals, that reflect patterns of relative strengths and weaknesses. Here we review the domains of language, memory and learning, attention, abstraction, and sensory-perceptual and motor function. Where the domain

has substantial literature regarding children, separate chapters on children and adults are provided.

The areas of language, memory, abstract reasoning, attention, and perceptual and motor skills have all been intensively studied by scientists with particular expertise in each of these cognitive domains. Experimental research has provided the groundwork for the development of clinical tests that often have exceptionally powerful construct validity. Clinical neuropsychologists use these tests to good advantage, particularly with patients who have disorders of a single domain. The comprehensive batteries often do not provide sufficient detail to elicit the specific details needed to characterize such disorders as aphasia or amnesia. In the case of aphasia, it is generally necessary to conduct a detailed analysis of the language system to determine areas of impaired and preserved function. Some patients with aphasia may have severe difficulty with producing grammatical, comprehensible speech but may have reasonably good understanding of the speech of others; whereas other patients may have the opposite pattern. Without going into further detail, numerous types of aphasia reflect patterns of impairment and preservation in many aspects of language production and comprehension. Patients with amnesia may have specific deficits in the aspects of memory described in classical experimental psychology. Thus, the difficulty may be in the initial encoding, storage, or retrieval of information, or the memory deficit may be for words but not for objects, or the reverse. Complexities of this type have generated an extensive literature on various neuropsychological syndromes and on detailed analyses of disorders associated with the different cognitive domains. Crucial differences between children and adults regarding these disorders are reflected in separate chapters within Section Two for these age groups.

The third part of this section deals with two professional practice topics: cross-cultural and forensic neuropsychology. The cross-cultural matter is complex, ranging across the practical matter of the best way to evaluate a patient who does not speak the examiner's language to the vivid examples provided in the chapter by Mirsky and Duncan on how culture can influence neurobehavioral development in children. Several technical problems are associated with cross-cultural considerations, such as difficulties associated with translating tests written in one language into another language, or use of an interpreter. Clinical neuropsychology is a patient-care related area of psychology, and characterizing individuals as ill when in fact a language barrier or cultural differences produce abnormal appearing test results in individuals who are not, in fact, ill is obviously a serious matter and requires careful consideration. Thus, for example, Victor Nell's advice to perform the evaluation in the patient's native language if at all possible may lead to substantial reduction in diagnostic error in cases in which the examiner and patient do not share the same language. The contributions and advice of neuropsychologists who were brought up in or who lived in different cultures, as is the case here, are of great value to the field.

Forensic neuropsychology is an expanding field, with its own literature, journal, and recognized authorities. In the chapter by Hom and Nici, emphasis is placed upon provision of evidence-based testimony and the scientific validity of the testimony provided in court by neuropsychologists. The forensic neuropsychologist needs to have training in clinical neuropsychology and in the legal system. Aside from doing clinical evaluations of patients, these individuals often have to appear in court as expert witnesses and need to be informed about such matters as rules of evidence and admissibility of testimony. Increasingly, neuropsychologists are being recognized as competent expert witnesses in areas related to such matters as malpractice, residuals of head injuries associated with automobile or industrial accidents, and toxic exposure.

In summary, neuropsychological assessment utilizes comprehensive and specialized methods to evaluate brain function to identify areas of intact and impaired function. Beginning with the use of standard clinical psychological tests to identify presence or absence of brain damage, neuropsychology has evolved and now makes sophisticated inquiries regarding specific brain-behavior relations. The field has a close relationship with neuroscience and the experimental investigation of brain function. Although initially concerned with acquired brain damage in adults, neuropsychology now possesses a developmental framework that provides evaluation capabilities across the lifespan, with specialized tests available for young children and older adults. It makes use of both comprehensive test battery procedures and individual tests of specific cognitive domains, such as memory and abstract reasoning. This section is organized to reflect the contribution of these methods (fixed batteries and the specialized assessment of cognitive domains). as well as the recent concern with professional issues, particularly assessing people with differing cultural backgrounds and providing forensic evaluations. The field of clinical neuropsychology has grown and changed remarkably over the past twenty years. We hope these developments are represented here.

PART ONE

COMPREHENSIVE NEUROPSYCHOLOGICAL ASSESSMENT BATTERIES

CHAPTER 8

Theoretical, Methodological, and Validational Bases of the Halstead-Reitan Neuropsychological Test Battery

RALPH M. REITAN AND DEBORAH WOLFSON

BACKGROUND AND DEVELOPMENT OF THE HALSTEAD-REITAN BATTERY (HRB)

After earning his PhD in physiological and comparative psychology at Northwestern University in 1935, Ward Halstead moved to the University of Chicago, established a working relationship with two neurosurgeons, Percival Bailey and Paul Bucy, and started the first full-time laboratory for the ex-

amination and evaluation of brain-behavior relationships in human beings.

Halstead's first step in evaluating patients was to observe them in their everyday living situations and attempt to discern which aspects of their behavior were different from the behavior of normal individuals. Fortunately, Halstead was relatively unencumbered by knowledge of the routine approach that existed in this era for studying the effects of brain damage. In fact, at this time and for quite a number of years previously, the principal approach of psychologists was to develop a single test that would diagnose brain damage.

Halstead's observations of persons with cerebral lesions made it apparent at the beginning that brain-damaged individuals had a wide range of deficits and that a single test would not be able to adequately identify and evaluate the severity of their deficits. Some patients demonstrated motor and sensory-perceptual disorders, often involving one side of the body more than the other. Some patients had specific language deficits representing dysphasia. Other individuals were confused in a more general yet pervasive way, even though in casual contact they often appeared to be quite intact.

As Halstead studied brain-damaged persons in their everyday living situations, he observed that most of them seemed to have difficulties understanding the essential nature of complex problem situations, in analyzing the circumstances that they had observed, and in reaching meaningful conclusions about the situations they faced in everyday life.

The initial orientation and approach to research and evaluation may have long-term implications. For example, Binet and Simon (1916) began developing intelligence tests using academic competence as the criterion. IQ tests, although used to assess cerebral damage, are probably still best known for their relationship to school success. It was important and fortuitous that Halstead decided to observe the adaptive processes and difficulties that brain-damaged persons demonstrated in everyday life. If he had focused only upon academic achievement or classroom activities, it is probable that he would have developed tests that are different from the ones he did produce. The tests that are included in the Halstead-Reitan Battery (HRB) emanated from a general consideration of neuropsychological impairment, and as a result, have much more relevance than IQ measures to practical aspects of rehabilitation and adaptive abilities.

Halstead devised and experimented with numerous psychological testing procedures. The design of his instruments placed them more in the context of standardized experiments than of conventional psychometric tests. Many of the procedures developed by Halstead contrasted sharply with psychometric testing procedures, inasmuch as they required the subject not only to solve the problem but to observe the nature of the problem, analyze the essential elements, and after having defined the problem, proceed to solve it.

Halstead developed a series of 10 tests that ultimately formed the principal basis for his concept of biological intelligence. He described these tests and presented his theory in his book, *Brain and Intelligence: A Quantitative Study of the Frontal Lobes* (Halstead, 1947). Only seven of the original ten tests have withstood the rigors of clinical and experimental evaluation. These seven tests constitute a substantial component of the HRB and are the seven tests used to compute the Halstead Impairment Index.

It became apparent that Halstead's seven tests had to be supplemented with an extensive array of additional procedures for the battery to attain clinical usefulness. The General Neuropsychological Deficit Scale (GNDS), a measure that provides an overall characterization of an individual's neuropsychological abilities and has proved to be clinically useful as a method of comparing areas of deficit, is based upon a total of 42 variables derived from measures in the HRB, including the original seven tests developed by Halstead (Reitan, & Wolfson, 1988, 1993).

Another significant feature of the HRB is that it was developed and validated not only by formal research, but also by evaluating thousands of patients with brain lesions and control subjects. This procedure involved administering the tests, evaluating the results, preparing a written report about their significance for brain functions, and only then turning to the independent data produced by complete and independent evaluations performed by neurologists, neurological surgeons, and neuropathologists.

After the two sets of data had been collected, conferences were held to correlate the neuropsychological findings with the independently obtained history and neurological, neurosurgical, and neuropathological findings (data concerning location, type, and duration of the lesion). In this way, each subject served as an independent experiment. Using this procedure, Reitan studied over 8,000 patients. The HRB served as a focus for research in the area of human brain-behavior relationships long before the area of clinical neuropsychology emerged as a discipline, and in this sense, this battery has played a role in the development of the field of neuropsychology.

During the 1950s and early 1960s, published research in the field of neuropsychology stimulated much interest; however, it also generated a considerable degree of skepticism and criticism from psychologists, neurologists, and neurological surgeons. There was a general reluctance toward accepting findings that proposed that the higher-level aspects of brain functions, which had been elusive for so many years, could actually be measured, quantified, and even used as a basis for predicting blindly the location and type of a brain lesion (Reitan, 1964). The HRB was used with increasing frequency in many hospitals and clinics in the United States and other countries, and the apparent validity of the findings among researchers and clinicians gradually overcame this kind of skepticism.

Hartlage and DeFilippis (1983) reported the results of a survey conducted in 1980 of all neuropsychologists in the National Academy of Neuropsychologists and all members of the Division of Clinical Neuropsychology of the American Psychological Association. The results indicated that 89% of the respondents used the Wechsler scales in their neuropsychological assessments, 56% included portions of the HRB, 49% used the Bender-Gestalt Test, 38% used the entire HRB, 32% employed the Benton Visual Retention Test, and 31% used the Luria-Nebraska Battery. McCaffrey and Isaac (1984) reported that in 1982, 65% of their respondents used the HRB; the later survey by McCaffrey and Lynch (1996) found that this percentage had risen to 77%.

Dean (1985) reviewed the Halstead-Reitan Neuropsychological Test Battery in the *Ninth Mental Measurements Yearbook*. In his review, he indicated that "neuropsychological assessment in North America has focused on the development of test batteries that would predict the presence of brain damage while offering a comprehensive view of a patient's individual functions. Numerous batteries have been offered as wide-band measures of the integrity and functioning of the brain. However, the HRB remains the most researched and widely utilized measure in the United States."

Meier (1985) also reviewed the Halstead-Reitan Neuropsychological Test Battery and had the following introductory comment:

> This comprehensive neuropsychological test battery has a long and illustrious history of clinical research and application in American clinical neuropsychology. Following its inaugural presentation to the psychological community (Halstead, 1947), and the careful nurturance of concept and application by Reitan (1974), the battery has had perhaps the most widespread impact of any approach in clinical neuropsychology. It seems reasonable to state that in the first half of the period since World War II, during which neuropsychology expanded so remarkably, this approach was the primary force in stimulating clinical research and application in this country."

PRACTICAL CONSIDERATIONS IN THE DEVELOPMENT OF A NEUROPSYCHOLOGICAL TEST BATTERY

Relation to Specialized Neurological Diagnostic Procedures

The relationship between neuropsychological testing and the many excellent specialized medical diagnostic procedures, especially Computerized Tomography (CT) and Magnetic Resonance Imaging (MRI), is important in validating neuropsychological tests. In addition, it has been a cause of concern regarding the independent value of neuropsychological testing to those psychologists and physicians who consider the principal purpose of neuropsychological examination to be the diagnosis of brain damage rather than evaluation of brain-behavior relationships.

It is important to recognize that neuropsychological evaluation draws on a different domain of evidence, to a major extent, than the diagnostic methods used by neurologists and neurological surgeons. The HRB focuses on higher-level aspects of brain functions, and more specifically on central processing; whereas the neurological diagnostic procedures relate principally to lower-level aspects of brain functioning or nonbehavioral variables, such as electrophysiological manifestations or brain imaging procedures. Neuropsychological evaluation provides the only rigorous and objective method of assessing higher-level aspects of brain functions.

CT and MRI scans are highly accurate diagnostic techniques. Both procedures identify structural abnormalities in the brain, such as space-occupying lesions and the types of tissue abnormalities characteristic of diseases such as multiple sclerosis. However, in cases of closed head injury, in which small vascular lesions or shearing of neurons may occur on a widespread basis, CT and MRI scans are frequently within normal limits. Despite their sensitivity to structural lesions and disorders of brain functions, even functional MRI, positron emission tomography, and single photon emission spectroscopy are not able to identify deficits in higher-level aspects of brain functions. An important need, therefore, has arisen for detailed studies of the correlation between these imaging procedures and neuropsychological test results, because these imaging procedures cannot evaluate an individual's general intelligence or other adaptive abilities. (The usefulness of the clinical neurological examination and specialized neurological diagnostic procedures is discussed in detail in Reitan & Wolfson, 1992a).

The fact that results from the HRB have been shown to correlate closely with the findings of the overall neurological examination validates the neuropsychological data as indicators of the biological condition of the brain. However, it is important to recognize that these various procedures complement rather than compete with each other in providing information about the patient. If an individual's higher-level brain functions need to be evaluated, a neuropsychological examination must be performed to obtain the relevant information.

Fixed Versus Flexible Neuropsychological Testing Procedures

The comparative advantages of fixed, or standard, versus flexible, or composed to meet the immediate assessment needs, batteries have received a considerable amount of attention (Incagnoli, Goldstein, & Golden, 1986).

The terms *fixed battery* and *flexible battery* are misleading, insofar as fixed may be taken to mean inflexible and not able to be supplemented with other tests. Flexible, on the other hand, may imply that adaptations are possible to meet the requirements of the individual situation without a loss of validity in evaluation. In practice, fixed batteries could be equated with a standard set of instruments that has been validated through extensive research with thousands of patients, with resulting consensus among thousands of psychologists around the world.

In contrast, the psychologist evaluating the patient, usually according to the history and complaints of each patient, makes up flexible batteries. To the degree that they differ from standard batteries, these individualized series of tests have never been evaluated as a battery in research studies or assessed by consensus of other psychologists.

Flexible batteries tend to deny the concept of a battery of tests that has been designed to assess human brain functions. In this sense, fixed batteries might be better labeled as *validated* batteries, and flexible batteries as casually composed batteries that have never been rigorously validated or, in most instances, evaluated with regard to accuracy in diagnosing a single pathological condition, such as traumatic brain injury, cerebrovascular disease, and so on. To the extent that they are composed to assess specific referral complaints or the subjective complaints of the patient (Christensen, 1975), flexible batteries may be referred to as "symptom-oriented" batteries.

Supposed advantages of the flexible battery include the prerogative to select tests to evaluate specific areas of function that accord with the patient's complaints. Of course, such a procedure might be circular in nature if the end result were only to confirm through psychological testing the patient's own initial self-evaluation (self-diagnosis).

Further, if the patient's subjective complaints are not sufficiently comprehensive, or if the patient is not able to offer an adequate and complete self-diagnosis, the resulting test battery may fail to recognize and evaluate significant areas of cerebral dysfunction. In any case, the series of tests selected by the psychologist will demonstrate a range of scores. Consequently, using this approach, the tests with low scores are usually selected as indicators of cognitive impairment.

In contrast, the fixed battery approach uses a constant group of tests. In this sense, the HRB can be thought of as a comprehensive battery, validated on thousands of patients to ensure that all relevant areas of brain functions are included in the assessment, thereby providing a balanced representation of the various neuropsychological functions subserved by the brain.

Finally, each test in the HRB has been subjected to rigorous research validating it as a neuropsychological test. In addition, the tests in the HRB have been validated for their complementary significance and interpretation for assessment of the individual.

Results obtained on the HRB regularly demonstrate the advantage of using a standard and comprehensive battery of tests. As shown in formal studies (Reitan, 1964), it is often possible, using only the HRB test results, to determine that cerebral damage has been sustained, to identify the area or location of principal involvement, and to assess whether the injury is recent or the brain has had an opportunity to stabilize. Further, from the point of view of rehabilitation, it is imperative to have a balanced representation of the nature and degree of neuropsychological deficit.

Considering the importance of assessing all neuropsychological aspects of brain function in a balanced and comparative manner, and the advantages of determining the complementary nature of results on various tests, thus achieving a battery effect in which the sum is greater than the individual components, and considering the obvious facilitation of validational research, Halstead and Reitan decided at the beginning to develop a standardized battery rather than use a variable selection of individual tests.

Differing Approaches to Neuropsychological Interpretation

Neuropsychologists have developed differing attitudes toward neuropsychological testing and the use of supplemental information to obtain valid results. The problem appears to arise from an attempt to emulate the medical model, or more specifically, the procedures used in neurology. In the field of neurology, it is routinely recommended that the results of the EEG, CT, MRI, and other specialized diagnostic procedures be evaluated only in the context of the patient's clinical history. This approach represents a double-edged sword inasmuch as historical information may influence the interpretation of the diagnostic procedure or the diagnostic procedure may be used to controvert the historical information.

Some neuropsychologists contend that neuropsychological evaluation is of value only if the test results are interpreted with full knowledge of the patient and his/her usual behavior. In some instances, the neuropsychologist requires personal observation of the patient at considerable length and in various types of settings to obtain enough information to be able to interpret the test results. In other instances, the neuropsychologist requires the findings of other professionals, knowledge of the subject's demographic and personal behavior characteristics, detailed academic and occupational histories, and interaction with family members and other persons in the environment as a basis for interpreting the neuropsychological test results. Psychologists who adopt this approach obviously feel that neuropsychological test data does not constitute a significant source of independent information and needs to be interpreted in the framework of complementary sources of information to achieve validity.

Other neuropsychologists believe that neuropsychological testing is of value, but that a score or index cannot adequately reflect a subject's performances. This contention derives historically from the insistence by Goldstein (1942a, 1942b) that the procedures used by brain-damaged individuals to solve problems differ from the methods utilized by persons with normal brain functions, and that the principal value of the testing has been lost if the procedures used by the patient are not observed and recorded. Goldstein believed that a final score, representing the adequacy of the subject's performances, was entirely inadequate, and that the process by which the individual achieved the end result was of critical importance. This contention has been carried forward by a number of other investigators (most notably Edith Kaplan), who have differentiated performances on the same task in accordance with the types of errors made by the subject, and related such information to neuropsychological interpretations of brain functions.

A final approach to this problem, represented principally by Reitan and others, recommends that the neuropsychological examination evaluate brain functions generally for every subject, and that a "blind" interpretation of the test findings be prepared before referring to any history information, conclusions reached by other professionals, or the results of additional diagnostic procedures. If the psychologist administers the tests personally, it is inescapable that he/she will observe the subject's performances and will formulate opinions based on the process the subject used to perform a task rather than on the test scores alone. The important point in this procedure, however, is related to the sequence the neuropsychologist follows to evaluate the subject. We recommend the sequential steps described below.

First, the neuropsychological test data is evaluated, including notations about any deviations from standard testing procedures, and perhaps about the process the subject uses to reach a solution. This first step should be completed before referring to any additional information, such as the history, findings of other examinations, or conclusions of other professionals. This procedure allows the neuropsychologist to evaluate the relevance of the test data and determine the extent to which it can make an independent contribution to understanding the patient's brain functions and cognitive structure.

After blindly interpreting the neuropsychological test data, all additional information should be evaluated, including the complete history, the results of examinations by other professionals, the findings of neurological diagnostic procedures, the individual's behavior in everyday living situations, his/her interaction with family members and other significant persons in the environment, and the academic, employment, military, and professional records. Wolfson (1985) has systematized the history-gathering procedures by preparing a formal guide that explores an extensive range of relevant areas. You will notice that our method differs from the other approaches mentioned previously only in terms of the sequence in which information is reviewed. In our system, the final interpretation of the data depends, as it does in the other approaches, upon an integration and evaluation of the consistency of all available information relating to the patient.

We prefer to avoid the risk of prejudicing the interpretation of the neuropsychological test results with supplemental information. Therefore, we perform an initial blind interpretation of the test data and then relate these findings to any other available information. It is important to recognize that much of the history information and personal observations of the patient's behavior is obtained under inadequately standardized and uncontrolled conditions, which certainly impair interjudge reliability and the potential for unprejudiced interpretation of the test data.

A number of neuropsychologists have emphasized the importance of supplementing the information provided by the quantitative testing with observations of qualitative behavior. Such qualitative observations can be useful, but it must be recognized that some psychologists are more adept than others in reaching valid conclusions on the basis of their behavioral observations. In fact, if conclusions are based on impressions of qualitative aspects of behavioral manifestations, a considerable degree of interjudge unreliability is likely to result.

Many studies have shown that behavioral ratings among psychologists and/or psychiatrists tend to be variable, even when the judges are thoroughly experienced. However, these kinds of problems of reliability do not necessarily detract from the valid observations that some judges may make. In our own practice, we have observed many subjects experiencing the stress involved with neuropsychological testing. The Tactual Performance Test, for example, is often more stressful for brain-damaged persons than individuals with normal brain functions. Thus, the difficulty-level of the task and the subject's reactions during testing almost certainly contribute information over and beyond the quantitative score for the test.

Halstead and Reitan, having observed the various approaches to problem-solving utilized by normal and brain-damaged persons, were keenly aware of the potential implicit in assessing a subject's qualitative performances during neuropsychological testing. They were interested, nevertheless, in exploring the potential value of standardized procedures that produced quantitative scores as a basis for evaluating brain-behavior relationships. It is generally accepted that a standardized procedure that produces a quantitative score is more replicable and reproducible, and thus has greater reliability, than judgments about the qualitative aspects of behavior.

In discussing the strategy that they wished to employ in neuropsychological examination, Halstead and Reitan believed that it would be desirable to differentiate and separate the quantitative scores, which more closely meet the hallmark in science of replicability, from the observations of the patient's behavior. This decision was not intended to either deny the potential value of behavioral observations or to rule out the use of behavioral observations to supplement and complement the quantitative data produced by neuropsychological testing. However, if neuropsychology was to be established as a science rather than an art, it was critical to define the standardized testing procedures that would produce quantitative scores separate from the clinician's insightful observations of the subject's behavior.

It is not surprising that many investigators continue to emphasize the importance of qualitative observations. In fact, it appears that neuropsychologists who depend upon these procedures have a clinical orientation, and through their training have developed skills in understanding impaired brain functions through the subject's behavioral manifestations. Proponents of this approach may also include psychologists who have had a lesser degree of success in validating their conclusions based upon interpretation of quantitative scores.

The debate concerning the use of qualitative versus quantitative methods for assessment of the effects of cerebral damage has a long history. Qualitative observations and analyses of behavior necessarily precede translation of such observations into standardized and quantified neuropsychological tests, which is the precise procedure used by Halstead and Reitan in developing the tests included in the HRB. Goldstein (1942a, 1942b) argued that only qualitative evaluations were valid, and that quantitative assessments might only confuse the issue because a brain-impaired and a normal subject might earn the same quantitative score but use different approaches to do so. Goldstein claimed that brain damage inevitably produced a "concrete" approach to problem-solving, whereas the person with normal brain functions was able to adopt an "abstract" approach. According to Goldstein, it was imperative to observe the performances of brain-damaged subjects to determine whether the brain damage had imposed any limitations on the individual's cognitive functioning.

Luria (personal communication, 1967) had a similar orientation towards this question. In a letter to one of the authors (RMR), he stated explicitly that little, if anything, could be gained by translating neuropsychological deficits into quantitative values and believed that it was necessary to observe the performance style of the brain-damaged individual to understand that person's limitations.

As we have noted, the use of a standardized and replicable procedure in neuropsychological examination in no way obviates or even interferes with the use of clinical observation by those neuropsychologists who feel that they are skilled in this respect. At the same time, clinical observation, as contrasted with quantitative measurement of performances, should not be proposed—as Goldstein and Luria have done—as the only method that can validly identify the deficits of brain-injured persons.

The Development and Incorporation of Multiple and Complementary Methods of Inferring Cerebral Damage into a Single Battery

A critical incident that led to the development of the HRB as a battery that describes the uniqueness of brain impairment of individual subjects occurred in 1945. One of the authors (RMR) examined an extremely competent physician who had sustained a depressed skull fracture and complained of significant deficits following the injury. Despite his complaints, this physician consistently performed above average on the tests he had been given. Although the examination demonstrated that he had excellent abilities, his complaints seemed clinically valid. If this physician was indeed impaired as compared to his premorbid status, we needed to find a way to assess his deficits. Thus, the challenge was set. The problem required a methodology that described the impairment in the individual subject, regardless of whether the subject's premorbid level of functioning was high or low.

We realized that it was necessary to design the battery so that methods of inference other than level of performance would contribute to the clinical conclusions. Four approaches could be used to evaluate a subject's performances: (1) level of performance (how well the subject performed compared to others), (2) pathognomonic signs (specific deficits that rarely occur without cerebral damage), (3) patterns and relationships among test results (identification of score patterns that reflected localized or lateralized damage as well as relationships which compared premorbid abilities with evidence of acquired impairment), and (4) comparisons of a subject's performances on the same test on each side of the body. A great deal of formal research and clinical evaluation was necessary to develop tests that met the above requirements and were also valid measurements of the biological integrity of the brain. It was necessary that the tests complemented each other in interpretation, were as economical as possible in the time required for administration, were consistently sensitive to cerebral damage or dysfunction across a broad range of neurological conditions, and reflected an individual's deficits in a balanced and equivalent manner.

CONTENT OF THE HALSTEAD-REITAN BATTERY AND ITS CONCEPTUAL AND THEORETICAL BASES

Theory-building requires basic facts on which to develop constructs, and the short lives of many of the molar theories of brain-behavior relationships can be directly attributed to their inconsistency with the facts (see Reitan et al., 1988, 1993 for a review of theories in clinical neuropsychology). Our method of developing a theory differed from those customarily used. We tried, at first, to generate a fairly extensive body of facts, which in turn could lead us to a broader conceptualization or generalization about relationships between the brain and neuropsychological functions. Our approach was therefore "fact-driven" rather than "theory-driven." We tried initially to meet the methodological requirements noted previously and to compose a set of tests (the HRB) that was consistently valid, in research and clinical application, as a basis for describing the ways in which the brain relates to behavior. Our empirical approach, guided by validated research findings and clinical verification in the individual case, led to the development of the Reitan-Wolfson model of neuropsychological functioning. We believe that this procedure may have more objectivity than an approach that postulates a theory and then searches for facts to support it.

The brain-based functions an individual needs in order to be efficient in his/her everyday behavior fall into several categories. The Reitan-Wolfson model of neuropsychological functioning (Figure 8.1) provides a conceptual framework for organizing the behavioral correlates of brain functions and describing the tests that measure these functions.

A neuropsychological response cycle first requires input to the brain from the external environment via one or more of the sensory avenues. Primary sensory areas are located in each cerebral hemisphere, indicating that this level of central processing is widely represented in the cerebral cortex and involves the temporal, parietal, and occipital areas particularly (see Reitan et al., 1993 for a description of the anatom-

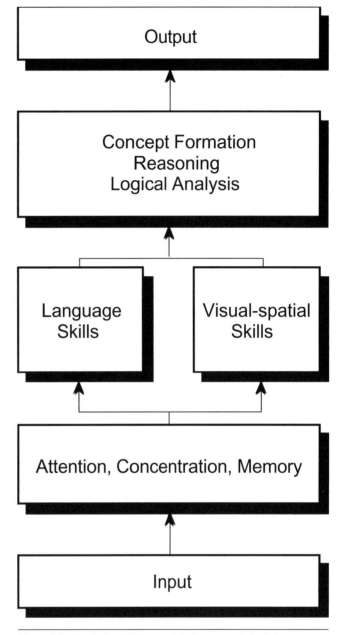

Figure 8.1   The Reitan-Wolfson model of neuropsychological functioning.

ical structures and systems for each of the elements of the Reitan-Wolfson model).

After sensory information reaches the brain, the first step in central processing is the "registration phase" that represents alertness, attention, continued concentration, and the ability to screen incoming information in relation to prior experiences (immediate, intermediate, and remote memory). When evaluating this level of functioning, the neuropsychologist is concerned with answering questions: How well can this individual pay attention to a specified task? Can the person utilize past experiences (memory) effectively and efficiently to reach a reasonable solution to a problem? Can the person understand and follow simple instructions?

If an individual's brain is not capable of registering incoming information, relating the new information to past experiences (memory), and establishing the relevance of the information, the subject is almost certainly seriously impaired in everyday behavior. A person who is not able to maintain alertness and a degree of concentration is likely to make very little progress as he or she attempts to solve a problem. Persons with such severe impairment have limited opportunity to effectively utilize any of the other higher-level abilities that the brain subserves, and they tend to perform quite poorly on almost any task presented to them.

Because alertness and concentration are necessary for all aspects of problem solving, a comprehensive neuropsychological test battery should include measures that evaluate the subject's attentiveness. Such tests should not be complicated and difficult, but should require the person to pay close attention over time to specific stimulus material. The HRB evaluates this first level of central processing primarily with two measures: the Speech-Sounds Perception Test (SSPT) and the Rhythm Test.

The SSPT consists of 60 spoken nonsense words that are variants of the "ee" sound. The stimuli are presented on a tape recording, and the subject responds to each stimulus by underlining one of four alternatives printed on an answer sheet.

The SSPT requires the subject to maintain attention through the 60 items, perceive the spoken stimulus through hearing, and relate the perception through vision to the correct configuration of letters on the test form.

The Rhythm Test requires the subject to differentiate between 30 pairs of rhythmic beats. The stimuli are presented by a standardized tape recording. After listening to a pair of stimuli, the subject writes "S" on the answer sheet if he or she thinks the two stimuli sounded the same, and writes "D" if they sounded different.

The Rhythm Test requires alertness to nonverbal auditory stimuli, sustained attention to the task, and the ability to perceive and compare different rhythmic sequences. Although many psychologists have presumed that the Rhythm Test is dependent upon the integrity of the right hemisphere (because the content is nonverbal), the test is actually an indicator of generalized cerebral functions and has no lateralizing significance (Reitan & Wolfson, 1989).

After an initial registration of incoming material, the brain customarily proceeds to process verbal information in the left cerebral hemisphere and visual-spatial information in the right cerebral hemisphere. At this point the specialized functions of the two hemispheres become operational.

The left cerebral hemisphere is particularly involved in speech and language functions, or the use of language symbols for communication purposes. It is important to remember that deficits may involve simple kinds of speech and language skills, or conversely, may involve sophisticated higher-level aspects of verbal communication. It also must be recognized that language functions may be impaired in terms of expressive capabilities, receptive functions, or both (Reitan, 1984). Thus, the neuropsychological examination must assess an individual's ability to express language as a response, to understand language through the auditory and visual avenues, and to complete the entire response cycle, which consists of perception of language information, central processing and understanding of its content, and the development of an effective response.

The HRB measures simple and complex verbal functions. The Reitan-Indiana Aphasia Screening Test (AST) is used to evaluate language functions, such as naming common objects, spelling simple words, reading, writing, enunciating, identifying individual numbers and letters, and performing simple arithmetic computations.

The AST is organized so that performances are evaluated in terms of the particular sensory modalities through which the stimuli are perceived. Additionally, the receptive and expressive components of the test allow the neuropsychologist to judge whether the limiting deficit for a subject is principally receptive or expressive in character. The verbal subtests of the Wechsler Adult Intelligence Scales (WAIS) are also used to obtain information about verbal intelligence.

Right cerebral hemisphere functions are involved with spatial abilities, mediated principally by vision but also by touch and auditory function, and spatial and manipulatory skills (Reitan, 1955a; Wheeler & Reitan, 1962). It is important to remember that an individual may be impaired in the expressive aspects or the receptive aspects of visual-spatial functioning, or both. It must also be kept in mind that we live in a world of time and space as well as in a world of verbal communication. Persons with impairment of visual-spatial abilities are often severely handicapped in terms of efficiency of functioning in a practical, everyday sense.

The HRB assesses visual-spatial functions with simple as well as complex tasks. Particularly important are the drawings of the square, cross, and triangle of the Aphasia Screening Test, the WAIS Performance subtests, and to an extent, Parts A and B of the Trail Making Test.

In evaluating the drawings on the AST, the criterion of brain damage relates to specific distortions of the spatial configurations rather than to artistic skill. The square and triangle are relatively simple figures and do not usually challenge an individual's appreciation and production of spatial configurations. The cross involves many turns and a number of directions and can provide significant information about a subject's understanding of visual-spatial form.

Comparisons of performances on the two sides of the body, using motor and sensory-perceptual tasks, provide information about the integrity of each cerebral hemisphere, and more specifically, about areas within each hemisphere. Finger tapping and grip strength yield information about the posterior frontal (motor) areas of each cerebral hemisphere.

The Tactual Performance Test (TPT) requires complex problem-solving skills and can provide information about the adequacy of each cerebral hemisphere. The subject is blindfolded before the test begins and is not permitted to see the formboard or blocks at any time. The first task is to fit the blocks into their proper spaces on the board using only the preferred hand. After completing this task (and without having been given prior warning), the subject is asked to perform the same task using only the nonpreferred hand. Finally, and again without prior warning, the task is repeated a third time using both hands. The amount of time required to perform each of the three trials provides a comparison of the efficiency of performance of the two hands. The Total Time score of the test reflects the amount of time needed to complete all three trials.

After the subject has completed the third trial, the board and blocks are taken out of the testing area and the subject's blindfold is removed. The subject is then asked to draw a diagram of the board with the blocks in their proper spaces. The Memory score is the number of shapes correctly remembered; the Localization score is the number of blocks correctly identified by both shape and position on the board.

An important aspect of the Tactual Performance Test relates to the neurological model. The test's design and procedure allow the functional efficiency of the two cerebral hemispheres to be compared and provide information about the general efficiency of brain functions. During the first trial, data are being transmitted from the preferred hand to the contralateral cerebral hemisphere (usually from the right hand to the left cerebral hemisphere). Under normal circumstances, positive practice-effect results in a reduction of time of about one-third from the first trial to the second trial. A similar reduction in time occurs between the second trial and the third trial.

The TPT is undoubtedly a complex task in terms of its motor and sensory requirements, and successful performance appears to be principally dependent on the middle part of the cerebral hemispheres. Ability to correctly place the variously shaped blocks on the board depends upon tactile form discrimination, kinesthesis, coordination of movement of the upper extremities, manual dexterity, and an appreciation of the relationship between the spatial configuration of the shapes and their location on the board. Obviously, the TPT is considerably more complex in its problem-solving requirements than either finger tapping or grip strength.

The tests for bilateral simultaneous sensory stimulation include tactile, auditory, and visual stimuli. Impaired perception of stimulation occurs on the side of the body contralateral to a damaged hemisphere.

The Tactile Form Recognition Test requires the subject to identify shapes through the sense of touch and yields information about the integrity of the contralateral parietal area.

Finger localization and fingertip number writing perception also provide information about the parietal area of the contralateral cerebral hemisphere. Fingertip number writing requires considerably more alertness and concentration, or perhaps even more general intelligence, than finger localization (Fitzhugh, Fitzhugh, & Reitan, 1962c).

In the Reitan-Wolfson theory of neuropsychological functioning, the highest level of central processing is represented by abstraction, reasoning, concept formation, and logical analysis skills. Research evidence indicates that these abilities have a general rather than specific representation throughout the cerebral cortex (Doehring & Reitan, 1962). The generality and importance of abstraction and reasoning skills may be suggested biologically by the fact that these skills are distributed throughout the cerebral cortex rather than being limited as a specialized function of one cerebral hemisphere or a particular area within a hemisphere. Generalized distribution of abstraction abilities throughout the cerebral cortex may also be significant in the interaction of abstraction with more specific abilities, such as language, that are represented more focally.

Impairment at the highest level of central processing has profound implications for the adequacy of neuropsychological functioning. Persons with deficits in abstraction and reasoning functions have lost a great deal of the ability to profit from their experiences in a meaningful, logical, and organized manner. However, because their deficits are general rather than specific in nature, such persons may appear to be relatively intact in casual contact. Because of the close relationship between organized behavior and memory, these subjects often complain of memory problems and are grossly inefficient in practical, everyday tasks. They are not able to organize their activities properly, and frequently direct a considerable amount of time and energy to elements of a situation that are not appropriate to the nature of the problem.

This inappropriate activity, together with an eventual withdrawal from attempting to deal with problem situations, constitutes a major component of what is frequently (and imprecisely) referred to as personality change. Upon clinical inquiry, such changes are often found to consist of erratic and poorly planned behavior, deterioration of personal hygiene, a lack of concern and understanding for others, and so on. Neuropsychologically, examination often reveals that these behaviors are largely caused by cognitive changes at the highest level of central processing rather than emotional deterioration per se.

Finally, in the solution of problems or expression of intelligent behavior, the sequential element from input to output frequently involves an interaction of the various aspects of central processing. Visual-spatial skills, for example, are closely dependent upon registration and continued attention to incoming material of a visual-spatial nature, but analysis and understanding of the problem also involves the highest element of central processing, represented by concept formation, reasoning, and logical analysis. Exactly the same kind of arrangement between areas of functioning in the Reitan-Wolfson model would relate to adequacy in using verbal and language skills. In fact, the speed and facility with which an individual carries out such interactions within the content categories of central processing probably represent a significant aspect of efficiency in brain functioning.

The HRB uses several measures to evaluate abstraction skills, including the Category Test, the Trail Making Test, and the overall efficiency of performance demonstrated on the Tactual Performance Test.

The Category Test has several characteristics that make it unique compared to many other tests. The Category Test is a relatively complex test of concept formation that requires the ability (1) to note recurring similarities and differences in stimulus material, (2) to postulate reasonable hypotheses about these similarities and differences, (3) to test these hypotheses by receiving positive or negative information (bell or buzzer), and (4) to adapt hypotheses based on the information received after each response.

The Category Test is not particularly difficult for most normal subjects. Because the subject is required to postulate solutions in a structured (rather than permissive) context, the Category Test appears to require particular competence in abstraction ability. The test, in effect, presents each subject with a learning experiment in concept formation. This is in contrast to the usual situation in psychological testing, which requires solution of an integral problem situation.

The primary purpose of the Category Test is to determine the subject's ability to use negative and positive experiences as a basis for altering and adapting performance (i.e., developing different hypotheses to determine the theme of each subtest). The precise pattern and sequence of positive and negative information (the bell or buzzer) in the Category Test is probably never exactly the same for any two subjects (or for the same subject upon repetition of the test). Because it can be presumed that every item in the test affects the subject's response to ensuing items, the usual approaches toward determination of reliability indices may be confounded. Nevertheless, the essential nature of the Category Test, as an experiment in concept formation, is clear.

The Category Test is probably the best measure in the HRB of abstraction, reasoning, and logical analysis abilities, which in turn are essential for organized planning. As noted previously, subjects who perform especially poorly on the Category Test often complain of having memory problems. In fact, the Category Test requires organized memory (as contrasted with the simple reproduction of stimulus material required of most short-term memory tests) and is probably a more meaningful indication of memory in practical, complex, everyday situations than most so-called "memory" tests, especially considering that memory, in a purposeful behavioral context, necessarily depends on relating the various aspects of a situation to each other (see Reitan et al., 1988, 1993, for a discussion of this concept).

The Trail Making Test is composed of two Parts, A and B. Part A consists of 25 circles printed on a sheet of paper. Each circle contains a number from 1 to 25. The subject's task is to connect the circles with a pencil line as quickly as possible, beginning with the number 1 and proceeding in numerical sequence. Part B consists of 25 circles numbered from 1 to 13 and lettered from A to L. The task in Part B is to connect the circles in sequence, alternating between numbers and letters. The scores represent the number of seconds required to complete each part.

The Trail Making Test requires immediate recognition of the symbolic significance of numbers and letters, ability to scan the page continuously to identify the next number or letter in sequence, flexibility in integrating the numerical and alphabetical series, and completion of these requirements under the pressure of time. It is likely that the ability to deal with the numerical and language symbols (numbers and letters) is sustained by the left cerebral hemisphere, the visual scanning task necessary to perceive the spatial distribution of the stimulus material is represented by the right cerebral hemisphere, and the speed and efficiency of performance may reflect the general adequacy of brain functions. It is therefore not surprising that the Trail Making Test, which requires simultaneous integration of these abilities, is one of the best measures of general brain functions (Reitan, 1955d, 1958).

VALIDATION OF THE HALSTEAD-REITAN NEUROPSYCHOLOGICAL TEST BATTERY

As noted previously, Dean (1985) cited the HRB as the most researched neuropsychological battery in the United States. Of even greater significance is the fact that the clinical usefulness of the HRB has been demonstrated in thousands of settings around the world, in laboratories ranging from clinical offices to major medical centers and universities.

Reitan's own research efforts began with general issues relating to brain-behavior relationships and proceeded to increasingly specific questions. Investigations were ordered in such a way that serially forthcoming information would arrive in a context of prior data.

First, the general effects of heterogeneous brain lesions were investigated; second, the differential effects of lateralized cerebral lesions without regard to type were studied; third, regional localization effects were identified; fourth, differences in effects of various pathologies and duration of lesion were researched; fifth, the neuropsychological correlates of brain lesions that were relatively chronic and static were compared with lesions that were acute and/or rapidly progressive; and sixth, the interaction among these variables and their relationship to the full range of cerebral damage, disease, and disorders was studied. Because our unit of value continually focused on the individual, the generality and specificity of application of the research results to individual subjects was routinely evaluated. No other test battery, or set of neuropsychological tests, has evolved or been studied in this organized and systematic manner.

General Neuropsychological Effects of Cerebral Damage

Reitan's first study on the HRB compared results obtained with Halstead's 10 tests in a group of 50 subjects with documented cerebral damage or dysfunction and a group of 50 control subjects who had no history of cerebral disease or dysfunction (Reitan, 1955c). A heterogeneous and diverse group of subjects with cerebral damage was included to ensure that an extensive range of conditions would be represented.

Persons with diverse medical conditions were deliberately included among the control subjects, and persons with brain damage were carefully excluded. Normally functioning individuals comprised 24% of the control group, and the remaining 76% was composed of patients hospitalized for a variety of difficulties not involving impaired brain functions. The control group included a substantial proportion of paraplegic and neurotic patients to minimize the probability that

any intergroup differences could be attributed to variables such as hospitalization, chronic illness, and affective disturbances.

The two groups were matched in pairs on the basis of race and gender, and as closely as possible for chronological age and years of formal education. The difference in mean age for the two groups was .06 years, and the difference in mean education was .02 years. The two groups were obviously closely matched for age and education, and the standard deviations for age and education in the two groups were nearly identical.

Although the two groups should have produced essentially comparable results on the basis of the controlled variables alone, the presence of brain damage in one group was responsible for a striking difference in the test results. Seven of the measures devised and described by Halstead showed differences between the mean scores for the two groups with relation to variability estimates, which achieved striking significance from a statistical point of view. In fact, according to the most detailed tables we had been able to find, the probability estimates not only exceeded the .01 or .001 levels, but exceeded .000000000001. However, even these tables were inadequate to express the appropriate statistical probability level.

As noted previously, statistical comparisons of the two groups reached extreme probability levels on seven of the ten measures contributing to the Halstead Impairment Index, and these seven tests have been retained in the battery. The most striking intergroup differences were shown by the Category Test and the Halstead Impairment Index, even though the Impairment Index included three of the ten measures that were not particularly sensitive to brain damage. Not one brain-damaged subject performed better than his matched control on the Impairment Index, although the Impairment Indices were equal in six of the 50 matched pairs.

The Category Test was the most sensitive of any single measure to the effects of cerebral damage. Three subjects with brain lesions performed better than their matched control, but in the remaining 47 pairs of subjects, the control performed better than the brain-damaged subject.

These results indicate that Halstead demonstrated remarkable insight in developing tests that reflected the nature of neuropsychological impairment due to brain damage. On 3 of his 10 tests, the results were not statistically impressive, but this may have been due to procedural problems in administration of these tests (Reitan et al., 1993). The remaining seven tests covered a broad range of adaptive abilities, involving such diverse performances as finger tapping speed, attentional capabilities to verbal and nonverbal stimuli, psychomotor problem-solving capability, memory for stimulus material to which the subject previously had been exposed, and abstraction, reasoning, and logical analysis skills.

These results, demonstrating highly significant differences between groups with and without cerebral damage, were produced at a time when most investigations had shown relatively minimal differences. Hebb (1939, 1941) had recently reported case studies of persons who had obtained IQ values in the superior range despite having had as much as one-third of their cerebral hemispheres surgically removed. A serious question existed, therefore, about why brain-damaged persons should perform so much more poorly than controls, especially considering the findings that had been reported by other researchers in earlier investigations.

At our current stage in the development of clinical neuropsychology, a retrospective review of this apparent conflict provides an explanation. Psychologists had been using measures devised to evaluate general intelligence, presuming that these tests would also be equivalently sensitive to impaired brain functions. However, as research has clearly demonstrated over the years since that time, tests developed to predict academic success are quite different from tests that are specifically sensitive to the biological condition of the brain. In fact, the IQ measures, which relate more closely to academic success, also appear to be heavily influenced by environmental and cultural advantages. On the other hand, tests developed specifically to evaluate impairment of brain functions seem to be less biased in terms of cultural and environmental experiences and advantages.

The basic reason for the striking differences in the results obtained using Halstead's tests and other measures appeared therefore to stem directly from the procedures used to develop the tests. As noted previously, general intelligence measures were initially designed to predict academic success. Halstead ignored factors of this type almost entirely and instead directly observed the daily living activities of persons with documented cerebral damage. It is not surprising that Halstead's measures appear to relate much more closely than general intelligence measures to the biological adequacy of brain functions as well as to practical aspects of everyday life.

We continued to conduct additional studies of all of the measures that have been included in the HRB, comparing groups of patients who had documented cerebral damage with groups of subjects who had no history of cerebral disease. In one study the results indicated that the Trail Making Test was extremely sensitive to the biological condition of the brain (Reitan, 1958). Part A showed significant results, and the results for Part B were even more striking.

Similar results were obtained with the Aphasia Screening Test (Wheeler et al., 1962). Most persons with cerebral dam-age do not show any significant evidence of dysphasia, and essentially no individuals without past or present evidence of brain damage demonstrate such signs. However, when evidence of impairment is demonstrated on the AST, it almost invariably is associated with independent (medical) evidence of brain disease or injury. Control subjects sometimes exhibit minor deficits, but any significant evidence of dysphasia is a valid sign of cerebral damage, particularly involving the left cerebral hemisphere (Reitan, 1984).

The HRB customarily includes the WAIS. Certain of the verbal subtests of the WAIS are usually within the normal range in persons with cerebral damage, provided that no evidence of aphasia has been elicited on the Aphasia Screening Test. In addition, control subjects usually show no evidence of frank dysphasic manifestations. Scores for the Wechsler subtests are usually somewhat lower for brain-damaged subjects than for controls, except for Digit Span, which is often poorly performed by controls as well as brain-damaged subjects (Reitan, 1959).

Lateralization Effects

The highly significant results obtained in comparing control subjects without brain damage and groups with heterogeneous cerebral damage laid the foundation for more detailed studies of human brain-behavior relationships using the HRB. One of these studies compared groups of subjects with left and right cerebral lesions to obtain information about the differential or specialized functions of the two cerebral hemispheres.

The initial investigation involved the Wechsler-Bellevue Intelligence Scale (Reitan, 1955a) and was one of the first studies to lay the groundwork for the left brain versus right brain differentiation. The findings indicated that the Verbal IQ (VIQ) was consistently depressed in persons with destructive lesions of the left cerebral hemisphere; whereas Performance IQ (PIQ) was lowered in persons with right cerebral damage.

These results were confirmed in an extensive series of studies that used various criteria for implicating the left or right cerebral hemisphere. These lateralized criteria included EEG disturbances (Kløve, 1959), homonymous visual field defects (Doehring, Reitan, & Kløve, 1961), and dysphasia versus constructional dyspraxia (Kløve & Reitan, 1958). Thus, a number of studies established the link between the differential impairment of VIQ and PIQ and damage to either the left or the right cerebral hemisphere respectively.

Throughout these investigations we continued to monitor the extent to which the generalizations applied to individual cases and found that certain subjects did not fit the expected pattern, even though they had lateralized cerebral lesions.

Other studies identified factors in addition to lateralization that influenced scores on neuropsychological tests. These factors included chronicity of the lesion, the developmental period during which the lesion occurred (childhood as compared with adulthood), the age of the adult subject when the lateralized brain damage was sustained, the education level, and the type of cerebral damage.

For example, subjects with extrinsic tumors, which usually do not involve the brain tissue in a direct structural sense, demonstrated no evidence of differential impairment of verbal and performance intelligence, regardless of the side of the brain involved, even though other lateralizing findings were present. Traumatic head injuries showed a statistically significant but rather mild effect, correlating with the diffuse or generalized involvement (as well as lateralized damage) from a blow to the head from the outside environment.

The set of conditions that demonstrated the most profound effect on verbal or performance intelligence as a result of lateralized cerebral damage included (1) normal prior development into adulthood of brain-behavior relationships, (2) a recent lateralized insult to a previously normal brain, and (3) a lesion that represented definite cerebral tissue damage and also structurally involved only one cerebral hemisphere. Interestingly, these conditions tend to describe persons who were normal before the lateralized cerebral damage was sustained (in contrast to a number of subjects included in split-brain studies and in evaluation of surgical excisions for epilepsy) and therefore have generalization value for normal brain functions, as contrasted with impairment of the brain sustained before neuropsychological maturation (Reitan et al., 1993).

In their review of the historical development of clinical neuropsychology, Reitan and Wolfson (1993) have identified two historical trends: one emanating from the areas of biopsychology and clinical psychology and the other developing from the medical field of neurology. Precedents in psychology have led largely to the development of tests and procedures rated on continuous distributions that generally follow the normal probability curve. Conversely, the rather simple procedures and tests derived from the field of behavioral neurology customarily produce dichotomous distributions, with results being classified as either normal or abnormal.

The HRB was deliberately composed to include procedures from each of these historical areas. The tradition of behavioral neurology is principally represented in the HRB by the Aphasia Screening Test and the Sensory-Perceptual Examination. Control subjects almost always earn normal scores on these simple tasks, and even persons with cerebral damage often do well. (See Reitan & Wolfson, 1986, 1988,

1993 for detailed discussions of the limitations of the "sign" approach.)

When abnormal performances are demonstrated on these relatively simple tasks, the results frequently have a fairly specific significance for implicating either the left or right hemisphere and often identify impaired regional areas within each cerebral hemisphere. Deficits elicited by the sign approach, derived from procedures in behavioral neurology, therefore have special significance. However, considering the relatively simple nature of the tasks, normal performances are expected from persons without brain damage as well as a substantial number of persons with cerebral damage.

Using these procedures, we have compared the performances of control subjects with groups having left, right, and generalized cerebral damage (Doehring & Reitan, 1961; Heimburger & Reitan, 1961; Wheeler et al., 1962). In each of these studies the subjects met independent neurological criteria for the groups to which they were assigned. Subjects selected for inclusion in the study had had the advantage of normal physical growth and development without being influenced by cerebral damage early in life. The subjects for these groups permitted inferences about the organization of neuropsychological functions subserved by normal development rather than deviant neuropsychological organization influenced by the effects of early cerebral damage.

The results indicated that manifestations of dysphasia were consistently associated with left cerebral damage; whereas the presence of constructional dyspraxia (deficits in ability to deal effectively with simple spatial relationships) characterized subjects with right cerebral damage. Many deficits were nearly exclusively manifested in association with damage to either the left or right hemisphere.

For example, dysnomia occurred in 53% of subjects with left cerebral lesions, but did not appear at all among subjects with right cerebral damage. This type of deficit occurred in 1% of the controls and 17% of the subjects with diffuse cerebral involvement.

Similar results were obtained on measures included in the Sensory-Perceptual Examination. For example, finger agnosia involving the right hand occurred in 36% of subjects with left cerebral damage, but in less than 2% of subjects with right cerebral damage. Impairment on a sensory-perceptual task on one side of the body had adverse implications for the contralateral cerebral hemisphere.

Wheeler et al. (1962) compared 104 control subjects: 47 subjects with left cerebral lesions, 45 subjects with right cerebral lesions, and 54 subjects with bilateral or diffuse damage. Four simple rules were developed to classify any subject to one of the four groups. Applying these rules gave the following conditional probabilities of correct classifications:

controls, 78%; left cerebral damage, 80%; right cerebral damage, 85%; and nonlateralized cerebral damage, 84%. These findings indicate that results from the HRB are not only accurate in identifying and differentiating subjects with and without cerebral damage, but also in identifying which hemisphere is involved.

Similar studies have been done using discriminant function analyses to produce a single weighted score for each subject and an optimum, least-squares type of separation. Wheeler, Burke, and Reitan (1963) used a total of 24 scores for each subject (11 from the WAIS and 13 from the HRB) and analyzed them using groups of 61 control subjects: 25 subjects with left cerebral damage, 31 subjects with right cerebral damage, and 23 subjects with diffuse or bilateral involvement.

The bases for classifying subjects to these groups were derived entirely from independent neurological, neurosurgical, and neuropathological findings. Analysis of the test results fell in the following categories of correct predictions: controls vs. all categories of cerebral damage, 90.7%; controls vs. left damage, 93.0%; controls vs. right damage, 92.4%; controls vs. diffuse damage, 98.8%; and right vs. left damage, 92.9%.

A number of studies compared persons with acute versus chronic brain lesions. Clinical observations suggested that specific deficits tend to resolve, at least partially, as the patient progresses from an acute to a chronic stage. In this context, Fitzhugh, Fitzhugh, and Reitan (1961, 1962a, 1962b, 1963) studied results from the HRB, the Wechsler Scale, and the Trail Making Test. The results generally indicated that persons who had chronic brain lesions (thus implying the possibility of some recovery of function over time) tended to perform somewhat better than subjects with recent, acutely destructive lesions.

Particularly striking were the results concerning the association between lateralized cerebral damage and differential impairment on the VIQ and PIQ. Persons with recent lateralized cerebral lesions showed consistent impairment of either VIQ or PIQ, depending upon the hemisphere involved. However, persons with chronic lateralized cerebral damage demonstrated less consistent relationships between differential VIQ and PIQ scores and the side of the brain that was injured. These results supported our later finding that neuropsychological recovery occurs in the area of initial deficit (Reitan et al., 1988).

The HRB has been extensively researched and studied in group comparisons and in application to individual persons, across essentially the full range of conditions that comprise the field of clinical neuropsychology. The characteristic results found with the HRB have been described for all major

categories of brain disease and damage, including neoplasms, cerebral vascular disease, traumatic brain injury, degenerative and demyelinating diseases, and infectious and inflammatory diseases (see Reitan & Wolfson, 1992b, 1993 for a summary of research and clinical findings in adults and children).

Traumatic brain injury has been an area of special emphasis in neuropsychology (Reitan & Wolfson, 1986, 1988, 2000a). In fact, Reitan's first publications were based on brain-impaired soldiers during World War II (Aita, Armitage, Reitan, & Rabinovitz, 1947; Aita, Reitan, & Ruth, 1947; Aita & Reitan, 1948). Reitan and Wolfson reviewed the neuropathological manifestations of head injury, the neurological and neuroradiological diagnostic methods, and the neuropsychological consequences (1986); the mechanisms of repair of traumatic brain damage, prognosis and outcome, methods of rehabilitation and retraining of neuropsychological deficits, and the natural history of traumatic head injury based on an 18-month follow-up of clinical and neuropsychological examinations (1988). They have also reviewed the pathology of mild head injury, the neuropsychological literature, and research studies that showed the sensitivity of the HRB to deficits in cases of mild head injury that met certain criteria as contrasted with the relatively routine recovery of most cases of mild head injury (2000).

Of course, many additional studies have been published in the area of head injury. Dikmen and Reitan (1976), based on the 18-month follow-up study of traumatic brain injury cases referred to previously, found that a combination of neuropsychological test results, obtained at about one month following injury, permitted a 91% accuracy rate in classifying subjects who would have significant deficits 18 months after the injury as contrasted with persons who recovered much better. Rojas and Bennett (1995) used the General Neuropsychological Deficit Scale (GNDS) (based on 42 measures from the HRB) and other measures to compare subjects with mild head injury with volunteer college students. They found that the Stroop Neuropsychological Screening Test did not differentiate the groups, but the GNDS correctly identified 92% of the subjects.

The HRB has also been extended to evaluate young adults with learning disabilities, especially considering the striking sensitivity of the HRB for Older Children in differentiating groups with brain damage, learning disabilities, and no evidence of brain damage (Reitan et al., 1992b).

Oestreicher and O'Donnell (1995) compared the GNDS scores of three groups: learning-disabled young adults (N = 60), traumatically brain-injured young adults (N = 30), and nondisabled volunteers (N = 30). The groups were equivalent in gender and Full-Scale IQ (FSIQ). The results indicated that the GNDS differentiated the three groups at highly significant levels. The nondisabled volunteers all had GNDS scores of less than 27, whereas 29 of the 30 traumatically brain-injured subjects had GNDS scores of 27 or higher. Among the learning-disabled subjects, 29 (49%) had GNDS scores of 27 or higher.

In addition to confirming the validity of the GNDS in differentiating between brain-damaged subjects and subjects without brain damage, as represented by a 98% hit rate, these researchers noted that the results confirmed prior studies (O'Donnell, 1991; O'Donnell, Kurtz, & Ramanaiah, 1983) in demonstrating that learning-disabled young adults show neurobehavioral impairment that, in some instances, is surprisingly severe.

Oestreicher and O'Donnell (1995) also compared the GNDS and the Halstead Impairment Index (HII). They concluded that "the Omega Squared statistic showed that the GNDS was 45% more efficient than the HII in discriminating neuropsychologically normal from neuropsychologically impaired individuals. Thus, a single measure, the GNDS, which summarizes all the data from a neuropsychological examination and incorporates multiple methods of neuropsychological inference, yields an index that is highly sensitive to brain impairment. Therefore, the present study justifies extending the GNDS to both research and clinical assessment with LD (learning-disabled) and HI (head-injured) persons" (p. 189).

Clinical Inferences Regarding Individual Subjects

Finally, we have been interested in applying these various research results to interpretation of test protocols for individual subjects. To test the validity and accuracy of the HRB, we conducted a complex study in which both location and type of cerebral damage were carefully controlled (Reitan, 1964).

The first step in the procedure was to identify subjects with criterion-quality frontal, nonfrontal, or diffuse cerebral lesions. To provide a rigorous test of the generality of any conclusions relating to these various groups, we designed the study so that each group had the same number of subjects with various types of lesions. Each regional localization group was therefore composed of equal numbers of subjects with intrinsic tumors, extrinsic tumors, cerebral vascular lesions, and focal traumatic lesions.

Through a review of thousands of neurological protocols, we were able to identify four individual subjects with each of these types of lesions in each of the left anterior, left posterior, right anterior, and right posterior cerebral locations. We therefore had a total of 64 subjects. When subdivided into groups of 16 subjects with different locations of damage,

each group contained equal representations of four different types of lesions. When subdivided into groups of 16 subjects according to type of lesion, each group had equal representations of the four different locations. Three additional groups were included in the study: 16 subjects with diffuse cerebral damage or dysfunction due to cerebrovascular disease, 16 subjects with closed head injuries, and 16 subjects with multiple sclerosis. The inclusion of these groups resulted in a total of 112 patients.

In the first study, a form was designed to record independent judgments based on the psychological test results for each subject. This form required three general decisions: First, a judgment was made from the neuropsychological test results alone about whether the lesion was focal or diffuse; second, a lesion category was selected; finally, more detailed judgments were made within certain lesion categories. For example, if the initial decision was that the lesion was focal rather than diffuse, the next judgment required selection of the right or left cerebral hemisphere, followed by selection of an anterior or posterior location within the hemisphere.

Next, a judgment was made about whether the lesion represented cerebral vascular disease, tumor, multiple sclerosis, or trauma. If the cerebral vascular disease category was selected, the lesion was further classified as a hemorrhage or vascular insufficiency. Additional forced judgments about the underlying basis for the evidence of cerebral vascular disease were made under each of these two categories.

If the tumor category was selected, the rater had to judge whether the lesion was intrinsic or extrinsic. If the intrinsic tumor category was selected, a further classification was made concerning whether the lesion was metastatic or a primary glioma.

Under the trauma category, the lesions were classified as an open or closed head injury. All of these ratings were based solely on the neuropsychological test results.

The rating form was sufficiently complete to permit classification of all subjects according to neurological criterion information. Because the classification of subjects to their respective groups had initially been based on neurological information, judgments made on the basis of neurological information represented the criterion. The purpose was to determine the degree of concurrence between neurological criterion information and ratings made on the basis of the psychological test results alone.

Each of the 112 subjects was assigned a number before the ratings were begun, and all information other than the psychological data was concealed to avoid any identifying clues when the ratings were made. There was no attempt to assign an appropriate number of subjects to any particular group. For example, no running record was kept to limit assignment of only 16 subjects to the multiple sclerosis group, and so on. Every effort was made to classify the test results for each subject independently, and ratings were completed without using any type of running tally.

Using the neurological ratings as the criterion, there were 64 subjects with focal cerebral lesions. Of these subjects, 57 were classified correctly on the basis of psychological testing, and 7 were judged to have diffuse damage. In the group of 48 subjects with diffuse cerebral damage, 46 were classified correctly and 2 were judged to have focal lesions.

As mentioned previously, there were 16 subjects in each regional localization group. The number of correct classifications on the basis of psychological test results for each of the locations was as follows: left anterior, 9; left posterior, 11; right anterior, 7; and right posterior, 15. Thus, 42 of the 64 patients were placed in their correct groups. Adding to this the correct classification of 46 of the 48 subjects with diffuse cerebral involvement, 88 of the 112 subjects were correctly classified.

With respect to the type of lesion, the 112 subjects fell in the following neurological diagnoses: intrinsic tumor, 16; extrinsic tumor, 16; cerebral vascular disease, 32 (16 focal, 16 diffuse); head injury, 32 (16 focal, 16 diffuse); and multiple sclerosis, 16.

The number of correct classifications on the basis of psychological inferences was as follows: intrinsic tumor, 13; extrinsic tumor, 8; cerebral vascular disease, 28; head injury, 30; and multiple sclerosis, 15. Thus, 94 of the 112 patients were correctly classified according to type of lesion.

Additionally, 13 of the 16 subjects with focal cerebral vascular disease were classified correctly, and 12 of these 13 were judged to have focal lesions. Of the 15 subjects with diffuse cerebral vascular disease who were correctly placed in this category, 14 were judged to have diffuse cerebral vascular disease. A total of 30 of the 32 head injury subjects had been placed in this category on the basis of their psychological test results, and 27 of these 30 had been correctly classified according to whether the lesion was focal or diffuse. It is particularly noteworthy that the HRB is differentially sensitive to traumatic brain injury, considering the frequency with which subjects in this category are involved in litigation. A review of the literature yields no evidence that any other neuropsychological tests or methods are able to differentiate traumatic brain injury from other conditions of brain damage.

The degree of concurrence between the neurological criteria and the neuropsychological ratings indicated in the preceding paragraphs could scarcely have happened by chance. The results confirmed that neuropsychological test results are differentially influenced by (1) focal and diffuse lesions, (2) which cerebral hemisphere sustained damage,

(3) frontal and nonfrontal lesions within the hemisphere involved, (4) type of lesion (intrinsic tumors, extrinsic tumors, cerebral vascular lesions, head injuries, and multiple sclerosis), (5) focal occlusion as compared with generalized insufficiency in cerebral vascular disease, and (6) focal as compared with diffuse damage from head injuries.

It is important to note that a study of this type serves a significant purpose in providing insight into the degree to which psychological test results may be determined by brain lesions. Furthermore, this study indicates the multifaceted nature of the concept of "brain damage," and demonstrates that many neurological variables, which occur in varying combinations for individual subjects, are relevant in determining psychological measurements.

The validational studies of the HRB leave no doubt that an individual's test results are closely dependent on his or her neurological status or diagnosis. The research findings reveal not only statistically significant intergroup differences, but also demonstrate the validity of the test results for specific neuropathological conditions that affect the individual.

THE HALSTEAD-REITAN BATTERY AND CURRENT PROBLEMS IN NEUROPSYCHOLOGY

A number of recent studies have used the HRB to investigate problems of current clinical significance in neuropsychology. While the human brain subserves a broad range of abilities ranging from sensory-perceptual functions, through complex aspects of central processing, to adaptive motor responses (see the Reitan-Wolfson model described previously), a need has existed both for clinical and research purposes for an overall indicator of general neuropsychological status. The Halstead Impairment Index (Halstead, 1947; Reitan, 1955c) and the Average Impairment Rating (Russell, Neuringer, & Goldstein, 1970) have been found to be valid and have served usefully, but these measures do not fully summarize the broad range of tests included in the HRB.

A Summary Index of Overall Performance on the HRB

Reitan and Wolfson (1988, 1993) addressed this deficiency by developing the General Neuropsychological Deficit Scale (GNDS), an instrument that produces a summary score based on 42 variables from the Halstead-Reitan Neuropsychological Test Battery for Adults. The field of clinical neuropsychology has identified major areas of neuropsychological functioning, and there is general recognition that a comprehensive evaluation requires assessment of these areas for clinical purposes as well as for planning a rehabilitation regimen.

The GNDS was developed for this purpose and was devised in such a manner that four methods of evaluating data are represented. Of the 42 variables that contribute to the GNDS score, 19 are based on the subject's level of performance and reflect how well the subject performed on a broad range of neuropsychological tests. Nine variables representing motor and sensory-perceptual performances evaluate differences between the preferred and the nonpreferred sides of the body. This approach reflects the fact that brain damage often affects one side of the body more than the other side. Using the differential-score approach, two variables evaluate relationships among tests that differentiate brain-damaged subjects from control subjects. Finally, 12 variables representing dysphasia and constructional dyspraxia constitute the pathognomonic sign approach.

The GNDS was not designed to replace competent clinical interpretation of the test results (which involves characterization of the individual's deficits), but only as an overall indication of the degree of neuropsychological impairment. To achieve this purpose, each of the 42 variables contributing to the GNDS score is represented by four score ranges: 0 (a perfectly normal performance), 1 (a normal performance that is mildly deviant but without clinical significance), 2 (a mildly to moderately impaired performance), and 3 (a severely impaired performance). These score ranges are useful when the clinician wants to assess a subject's degree of impairment on an individual test in the HRB, and the cutoff score between 2 and 3 differentiates normal from brain-damaged subjects. Thus, in a general sense, the classifications represent normative data.

The GNDS score represents the sum of the scores for the 42 variables on which it is based. This procedure produces low GNDS scores for normal controls and high GNDS scores for persons with cerebral dysfunction. The normal range extends from 0–25; mild impairment from 26–40; moderate impairment from 41–67; and severe impairment from 68 to the maximum possible score of 168 (Reitan et al., 1988, 1993). More detailed information about the GNDS as well as computerized scoring is published in Reitan et al. (1993).

Using control groups and brain-damaged groups, Reitan et al. (1988, 1993) presented the results of several validational studies indicating that the GNDS was adversely affected by (1) left, right, or generalized heterogeneous cerebral damage, (2) left, right, or generalized cerebral vascular damage, (3) left, right, or diffuse cerebral damage due to trauma, and (4) left or right cerebral damage when type of lesion was held comparable. All the non-brain-damaged control groups had lower (better) mean GNDS scores than any of the brain-damaged groups. The following control groups were used:

(1) a normal group with a mean Full Scale IQ of 129.26 (mean GNDS, 12.48), (2) a young group (mean GNDS, 15.90), (3) a heterogeneous group (mean GNDS, 17.20), and (4) an older group (mean GNDS, 24.82). (See Reitan et al., 1988 for additional details.) A group of subjects who had sustained a cerebral concussion but had not demonstrated any objective evidence of brain damage, examined at the time of discharge from the hospital, had a mean GNDS score of 25.36, a score that was significantly poorer than the score earned by a heterogeneous control group.

The groups with definite brain damage consistently had mean GNDS scores ranging from 43.73 to 64.33. Subjects with traumatic brain injuries tended to score better than other groups, and subjects with left cerebral strokes tended to do most poorly. No significant differences were found within studies among subjects with left, right, or generalized cerebral damage, suggesting that the GNDS score, as intended, was a valid overall summary indicator. Males and females showed no significant differences on the GNDS when other variables were held constant. In a study comparing a group of subjects who had cerebral concussion with a group of traumatic brain-injured subjects who had documented tissue damage, the group with concussion had a significantly better mean GNDS score. Studies comparing older and younger control subjects demonstrated that the older groups performed more poorly.

Sherer and Adams (1993) published a cross-validation study of the GNDS and indices reported by Reitan et al. (1988) to be differentially sensitive to damage of the left or right cerebral hemisphere and concluded that their findings provided "limited support for the validity of these new scales with patients commonly seen in clinical practice" (p. 429). These investigators compared 73 brain-damaged subjects with 41 "pseudoneurologic" subjects. The pseudoneurologic group was composed of subjects who reported "neurologic" symptoms but had no biomedical evidence of brain damage and included "30 subjects who had received psychiatric diagnoses" (p. 429).

The results of Sherer and Adams agreed essentially with the findings reported by Reitan et al. (1988) insofar as (1) the brain-damaged group was significantly more impaired on the GNDS than the pseudoneurologic group, (2) the subgroups with left, right, or generalized damage did not differ on the GNDS, (3) males and females showed no statistical difference, and (4) older subjects performed more poorly than younger subjects. The principal differences between results reported by Sherer et al. (1993) and Reitan et al. (1988) was that 53.6% of the pseudoneurologic group scored in the brain-damaged range as compared to only 10% of Reitan and Wolfson's controls. Sherer et al. (1993) state that "the poor classification of our pseudoneurologic subjects may be due to a limitation with the use of pseudoneurologic control groups" (p. 434).

Wolfson and Reitan (1995) designed an additional study to further investigate the validity of the GNDS in differentiating between groups of subjects with and without evidence of cerebral damage, comparing 50 brain-damaged subjects with 50 controls that were similar in age and education.

The mean GNDS score for the brain-damaged group (55.02) was very similar to the mean of 53.22 reported by Reitan et al. (1988) for 169 brain-damaged subjects. The mean GNDS score for the control subjects (19.66) was slightly higher than the mean of 17.20 found for 41 controls (Reitan et al., 1988). In each case, the brain-damaged subjects performed more poorly than the controls at a highly significant level.

In Reitan and Wolfson's 1988 study, the best cutoff score was 25/26, which resulted in a 9% rate of misclassification. The 1995 study identified 28/29 as the best cutoff score, which misclassified 12% of the subjects. An inspection of the two distributions indicated that individual cases of GNDS scores differing by one or two points were responsible for the differences in the two distributions. In the 1995 study, 80% of the controls and 96% of the brain-damaged subjects were classified correctly using the original cutoff score of 25/26, again yielding a 12% rate of misclassification. Obviously, the "best" cutoff score depends upon whether researchers want to avoid false negatives or false positives, but the best clinical conclusion would identify the gray area (where the groups overlap) as falling between 26 and 29 points.

Sherer et al. (1993) stated that the value of using pseudoneurologic controls was that such patients are frequently seen in clinical practice. However, their pseudoneurologic control group had a mean GNDS score of 26.56, a value considerably higher than the means reported by Reitan and Wolfson (17.20, Reitan et al., 1988; 19.66, Wolfson et al., 1995). In order to obtain completely "clean" comparisons, we believe that the initial validation studies should compare groups of subjects who fall unequivocally into either a brain-damaged or non-brain-damaged group.

Following such a determination, other comparison groups, composed according to clinically relevant criteria, may be evaluated, and a pseudoneurologic comparison group would certainly be clinically relevant. The group with cerebral concussion reported by Reitan et al. (1988) would be another such relevant group, and it might also qualify as a pseudoneurologic group because all members of the group had neurologic complaints but no biomedical evidence of brain damage. (See Reitan et al., 1988 for a review of the debate concerning whether the symptoms of concussion should be considered psychiatric or neurologic.) In Reitan and Wolfson's previous study, the group with cerebral concussion had a mean GNDS score of 25.36, a value similar to the mean of 26.56 reported by Sherer and Adams for their pseudoneurologic group (Reitan et al., 1988).

In summary, empirical research results have established that the GNDS score is a valid general indicator of the presence or absence of cerebral damage.

Practical and Legal Implications in the Use of the Halstead-Reitan Battery

The United States Supreme Court identified four considerations for trial judges to use in evaluating expert testimony or, in some cases, in deciding whether to admit expert testimony. This directive requires that neuropsychologists carefully consider their testing methodology in accordance with whether their procedures meet these four criteria. Briefly, these include the following:

1. Has the method been tested?
2. Has the method been subjected to peer review and publication?
3. What is the error rate in applying the method?
4. To what extent has the method received general acceptance in the relevant scientific community?

In our experience, trial judges and lawyers are gradually giving increased consideration to these guidelines and giving serious consideration to the admissibility of testimony based on whether these guidelines have been met. In the main, concerns have centered around (3) and (4) mentioned in the preceding list, namely, the error rate and the question of general acceptance.

It would seem perfectly legitimate, and even necessary, to know how accurate a method is in achieving its purpose. Acceptance in the scientific community, however, would carry with it a time factor, inasmuch as newer methods would need time to be incorporated into the knowledge, experience, and practical testing that might be required for acceptance. Neuropsychological tests and procedures, which have been subject to peer review and publication in acceptable outlets, however, might well be viewed as having appropriate acceptance by the scientific community.

Our recent experiences have mainly concerned (3) above—the error rate. The error rate is a different matter than the statistical probability of accepting the null hypothesis (or a chance effect), which some neuropsychologists have referred to in responding to this requirement. Even supplying a probability statement for multiple tests is hardly an answer, inasmuch as the independence of the tests is unknown and, in any case, this kind of information says nothing about the rate of errors in conclusions about the individual person. In legal matters concerning personal injury, data relating to the probability that groups of subjects are, or are not, drawn from the same population are essentially irrelevant, because the matter concerns the person rather than inferential statistics based on group comparisons.

In fact, the customary models of statistical analyses—the ones we all learned in school and are usually required to meet publication standards—have limited meaning when judgments, diagnoses, and conclusions must be made about the individual person. We often offer "more probable than not" statements with little or no hard evidence to support these conclusions. If knowledge of the error rate concerning the question of brain damage or impairment was actually required to permit one to testify as an expert, not many neuropsychologists would be allowed to testify. Few studies on individual neurological tests, or even conclusions based on batteries of tests, ever report the number of false positives and false negatives. Such data are published for other diagnostic methods that require conclusions about the individual person (such as computed tomography and magnetic resonance imaging), and questions of accuracy were among the first issues studied when these procedures were developed and became available. Why have psychologists failed to produce such data when it clearly is so necessary as a basis for giving neuropsychological methods a degree of credence? There are a number of possible answers to this question, a principal one being that a specified procedure or set of tests must be applied to each subject in a precise and standardized manner in order to evaluate accuracy, or concurrence with independent criterion information. In cases involving litigation, neuropsychologists appear to be shying away from such specified and standardized procedures in favor of so-called "flexible" batteries, instead choosing to give the tests they wish and to thereby gain the right to draw the conclusions they wish, or that may be requisite in terms of the role they have accepted and the conclusions they have committed themselves to support.

In a recent case a federal judge was asked, on the basis of the Daubert challenge, to dismiss the testimony of a prominent neuropsychologist who was testifying on behalf of a plaintiff who had sustained a head injury. In many prior instances, in his publications and sworn testimony, this neuropsychologist had supported the use of neuropsychological tests in evaluating individual persons. In this case, however, the results of the extensive set of tests that had been administered under his direct supervision fell essentially in the normal range. He admitted that the test findings were essentially normal, and, in fact, this conclusion was readily subject to documentation, inasmuch as the test findings were based on the HRB. However, he insisted that the plaintiff had sustained significant and serious impairment. There was strong evidence against this conclusion, such as the plaintiff's having earned a greater income the year after the injury than the year before the injury. However, this prominent neuropsychologist pointed out that he had interviewed the plaintiff, his relatives, and a few friends, all of whom cited a host of complaints and problems that they attributed to the injury. When asked about the disparity between his conclusions and the normal neuropsychological test results, the neuropsychologist replied that neuropsychological tests contributed no more than 10% to his conclusions and that his clinical impressions were the primary basis for his testimony. The opposing attorney then appealed to the judge to exclude the neuropsychologist's testimony on the grounds that his methodology had not been adequately tested, had not been subjected to peer review, the error rate was unknown, and the neuropsychological community would disagree that neuropsychological tests should count for 10% and clinical impressions for 90%. The defense attorney said that, in his opinion, the judge "came very close to excluding the neuropsychologist's testimony, but in the end felt that he did not have enough information about prevailing practices in neuropsychology to make such a decision." Another consideration may have been that the judge was reluctant to make a ruling that would have devastated the plaintiff's case since, aside from the neuropsychologist's opinion, there was little additional credible evidence of brain impairment.

It seems clear that the time has come to support clinical conclusions with hard evidence. Unfortunately, it is the legal processes that are forcing the field in this direction rather than clinically responsible standards of practice.

The problem of testing the accuracy of neuropsychological test data must receive much more critical consideration than it has up to this point. One approach might be to make predictive judgments using whatever test data was available for each subject, then checking the accuracy of these predictions against criterion information. The problem with this approach is that there would be no clear definition of the test data used for making the predictions, inasmuch as the tests administered would surely vary from one subject to another. Neuropsychologists who use so-called flexible batteries would face exactly this problem, because their test batteries, designed according to the supposed complaints or deficits of the client, necessarily vary from one client to another. In fact, a procedure that first discerns the client's area of possible deficit via history information, relatives' observations of the client, or interview information, and then seeks to confirm or refute such hypotheses through the selection of a range of tests judged to be appropriate, is circular and can only be considered to be relevant to the complaints initially deemed significant. Under these circumstances, there can be no assurance that the battery of tests selected for each client represents a comprehensive, balanced, and validated set of measures of brain function or dysfunction. Of course, if each of these many symptom-oriented batteries had been checked for accuracy in correlating with and identifying brain lesions of a diffuse and/or focal nature, in varying locations of the brain, representing the full range of types of brain disease, and injury in identifying chronic and stabilized brain lesions versus acute and progressive brain conditions and effectively differentiating this entire cadre of people with brain involvement from non-brain-damaged people, there would be no problem. The field of neuropsychology (the discipline based on establishing brain-behavior relationships) would be secure. It is obvious, however, that there is no likely prospect that multiple test batteries can be checked out in the detail necessary to establish their relationships to the broad range of conditions that, in total, represent brain damage. Yet, unless evidence is available that all the categories of brain damage are reflected by a particular neuropsychological battery, or that the battery validly differentiates between brain-damaged persons and non-brain-damaged persons regardless of all the variations that occur under the rubric of brain damage, researchers cannot presume that the battery validly reflects brain pathology. In the absence of evidence supporting this presumption, neuropsychologists lose the claim that identifies the essential nature of neuropsychology as the area of psychology that relates behavioral measurement to the biological status of the brain. Without a firm anchor to the brain, neuropsychologists become clinical psychologists, school psychologists, consulting psychologists, educational psychologists, or any type of psychologist appropriate to particular interests. Of course, neuropsychologists also find themselves failing to compare favorably to the experts in each of these areas.

It is apparent that neuropsychologists cannot have it both ways. Neuropsychologists either have to respect the brain as the basis for behavior and validate their measures in accordance with the many things that go wrong with the brain, or recognize that the neuro prefix of neuropsychology is added for respectability alone. If neuropsychologists are unable to document valid relationship to brain status, in terms of scientific methods and procedures, as responsible professionals they should at least admit that the Supreme Court was reasonable and correct in requiring that the error rate in neuropsychology be specified with respect to individual subjects. Such an admission, of course, would also verify their inadequacy to function as expert witnesses.

One way out of this dilemma would be to use competently a neuropsychological test battery for which published evidence is available that meets the four criteria identified by the Supreme Court as necessary for admission as an expert witness. The Halstead-Reitan Neuropsychological Test Battery meets these four criteria, but competent interpretation (which can be judged by the many published examples of test interpretation) is required over and beyond training in test administration. Fortunately, detailed information is available for administration and interpretation of these batteries of neuropsychological tests for adults, older children, and young children (Reitan et al., 1985, 1988, 1992, 1993).

RECENT RESEARCH WITH THE HALSTEAD-REITAN BATTERY

The manner in which the HRB has been developed and validated, and the broad range of brain-related conditions that have been studied with it, make it an invaluable tool to study other issues as they arise. Although it is of value to study brain-related impairment with other tests and procedures, and clinical evaluation often calls for supplementation with additional tests after the basic neuropsychological condition has been established, a balanced and comprehensive assessment of brain-behavior relationships that compares the individual's overall brain functions with a generalized concept of normal (or impaired) brain functions represents an invaluable foundation in neuropsychological assessment. The alternative, using a variable selection of tests that have not been validated as a battery, risks a focus on individual tests rather than on the individual person.

The extensive research bases of the HRB, together with its demonstrated validity in assessment of individual persons, help create a springboard in the investigation of additional neuropsychological problems. Findings suggest that emotional problems have little influence on neuropsychological test results—provided that the tests have established validity as brain-sensitive measures (Reitan & Wolfson, 2000). Space considerations prevent a full review of recent investigations, but a few areas can be mentioned.

With respect to the neuropsychological consequences of mild head injury, the prevailing view had been that recovery was routine and essentially complete in a matter of one to three months (Levin, Eisenberg, & Benton, 1989). Binder, Rohling, and Larrabee (1997) reviewed the literature and concluded, It can be argued that the average effect of MHT (mild head trauma) on neuropsychological performances is undetectable. Over the years, evaluation of such cases with the HRB indicated that this conclusion was hardly true for a number of individual cases. In fact, some persons, with apparently mild head injuries, showed evidence of significant neuropsychological impairment on the HRB. This observation was possible because the HRB produces data not only on tests but also provides a basis for evaluation of the individual. As a result of these observations of HRB findings, a formal study was designed that led to a paper entitled, "The Two Faces of Mild Head Injury" (Reitan & Wolfson, 1999), which showed that persons who returned weeks or months after a mild head injury, with significant complaints of the type that could be attributed to brain damage, actually performed much more poorly on the HRB than did similarly injured persons whose recovery was routine. Thus, the neuropsychology of a mild head injury cannot routinely be considered as relatively innocuous and subject to prompt recovery but in some cases constitutes a significant clinical problem.

Another study in the area of mild head injury, also arising from clinical evaluation of individuals using the HRB, concerned the nature of resulting neuropsychological deficits, even though presumed to be brief in duration (Reitan et al., 2000). The literature (Levin et al., 1989) had concluded that initial deficits (before recovery) might include impairment of attention and concentration, speed of information processing, and immediate memory (see Reitan et al., 2000 for a review of this literature). Clinical evaluation using the HRB indicated that most persons with mild head injuries performed better than persons with more serious structural damage of the brain. However, when considering a range of neuropsychological tests, the deficits did not appear to be restricted to the areas of attention and concentration, speed of information processing, and immediate memory. In fact, considering the deficits as a whole, they appeared to be generally distributed. Another formal study was then designed based on 19 tests from the HRB, using a group with mild head injuries for comparison with patients diagnosed with structural damage of the brain resulting from physical trauma (Reitan et al., 2000). Comparisons of these two groups showed a strikingly similar pattern of test scores across the 19 tests, with a rank-difference correlation of 0.87 between the two groups. In a study of correlations across an extensive set of tests, as included in the HRB, contrasted with prior studies that were largely limited to preselected areas of function, the findings showed that neuropsychological test findings were remarkably similar (rather than unique or distinct in mild head injury) for mild and more severe head injury. These findings were clearly a result of using a comprehensive, validated test battery in contrast to using individual, selected tests.

It is important to negate incorrect conclusions that have pervaded the field, and the HRB provides a vehicle for this purpose. As noted earlier in this chapter, the Seashore Rhythm Test was presumed by many neuropsychologists to reflect the status of the right temporal lobe, presumably because it was a nonverbal auditory test. Clinical use with the HRB indicated that many brain-damaged persons, without specific right temporal lesions, performed poorly on this test. A study was designed to explore the question formally, and the results showed that impairment was equivalently present with either left, right, or generalized brain lesions (Reitan et al., 1989). Apparently, the requirement for paying close attention to repeated stimuli for a period of time, which is dependent on cerebral functions generally, overrode any effects of the specific content of the Rhythm Test in determining the results.

Exactly the same type of study was done to test the oft-repeated hypothesis that the Speech-sounds Perception Test reflects the status of the left temporal lobe. Again, the results failed to support the hypothesis but showed the test to be generally sensitive to brain damage regardless of location (Reitan & Wolfson, 1990).

Perhaps an even more pervasive belief has been that both the Category Test and Part B of the Trail Making Test reflect frontal lobe functions. This question was tested empirically by comparing four groups of persons who had lesions in the following areas: left frontal, right frontal, left posterior, and right posterior. The results failed to show significant differences on either test among the four groups (Reitan & Wolfson, 1995a).

It is possible to achieve accuracy levels that far exceed chance, with respect to localization and type of brain lesions, using the complete HRB, as shown in an earlier part of this chapter. The complexity of brain functions, however, requires an extensive set of tests as investigators have learned, patient by patient, in the development of the HRB. These tests include both higher-level and lower-level brain-related tests designed to implement the various methods of inference described previously. Simplistic generalizations, based on single tests or concepts, whether stated as principles or applied in clinical evaluation, cannot be expected to do justice to the human brain.

The availability of a brain-sensitive general measure, such as the General Neuropsychological Deficit Scale (GNDS), has facilitated an economical and organized approach to the important question of the relation of attribute variables, such as age and education, to results obtained with neuropsychological testing. Among children, the influence of these variables is obvious during the developmental years. Older adults without clinical evidence of brain damage have demonstrated deterioration on neuropsychological tests (Reitan, 1955b, 1967), and better educated people would be presumed, on an overall basis, to have the brain-related abilities to achieve higher levels of education. Thus, it seems only reasonable that age and education must be considered and are variables for which test scores must be adjusted in clinical evaluation regarding possible brain damage.

In fact, studies have shown that age and education are variables of influence among persons without brain damage (Reitan & Wolfson, 1995b). Better educated people tend to perform better on brain-sensitive tests, and older people tend to show some deterioration. However, the clinically relevant question in most evaluations concerns subjects who have, or are suspected of having, some type of brain disease or damage. Do the effects of age and education have equivalent influence when brain damage has already affected the test results? If the tests are brain-sensitive, and thus reflect the clinical condition of the brain, does it not seem likely that brain damage has already determined the deficits shown by the test results and that the effects of age and education, as shown in normal subjects, have been disrupted, if not overruled? Is there anything about being young and having an advanced degree that immunizes one against the devastating impairment that can be caused by severe brain damage? In such cases, age and education are negatively correlated with neuropsychological test performance.

The influence of age and education on the HRB was put to an empirical test initially by Reitan et al. (1995b). Although significant correlations were found among the control subjects between age and education and the GNDS, the correlations were not significant for the brain-damaged subjects. Brain damage had apparently been a third factor that negated the usual influence of age and education. The same effect is often cited in statistics books regarding, for example, the correlation between crop yield and rainfall, a correlation that may be entirely negated by low rather than normal temperatures.

Recently, many neuropsychologists have been influenced to adjust raw scores for brain-damaged persons on the basis of age and education on HRB measures, as well as other tests, by using tables established on a normal rather than brain-damaged sample (Heaton, Grant, & Matthews, 1991). Obviously, if there is no relationship of age and education to test performances among brain-damaged people, the adjustment based on normal subjects can do nothing but change or alter the brain-sensitive results.

The effect of adjusting scores earned by brain-damaged subjects on brain-sensitive tests, using data derived solely from non-brain-damaged subjects, has yet to be determined empirically. As a first step in this direction, in the course of preparing this manuscript, the Heaton et al. (1991) tables were used to adjust the HRB scores for a sample of 26 patients with clinically established diffuse cerebral vascular disease whose HRB findings had been previously published

(Reitan, 1970). We deliberately selected a group with diffuse cerebral involvement rather than a group with focal lesions, because focal lesions more seriously disrupt specific functions (producing deficits such as dysphasia and greater deviations from scores of normal subjects). Nevertheless, when the age and education adjustments were made, 37% of the adjusted scores, based on overall results using nine brain-sensitive tests from the HRB, fell in the normal range. Although the impact of age and education needs more study, in this particular instance the adjustment of raw test scores earned by brain-damaged subjects tended to transpose evidence of neuropsychological impairment to that of a normal performance.

The studies reviewed in this chapter concerning adjustment of raw neuropsychological test scores stimulated additional investigations based on the Wechsler Adult Intelligence Scale (WAIS) (Reitan & Wolfson, 1996). As expected, educational level had significant correlations with Verbal, Performance, and Full Scale IQ values for the control group but were significantly lower in each instance for the brain-damaged group. Within the age range of the groups studied, the effects of age were less clear. In general, the findings of differences between the control and brain-damaged groups were not as clear as they were in studies with the GNDS, possibly reflecting a differential sensitivity to brain damage of the WAIS and GNDS. Investigation of age and education correlates of the WAIS subtest scores suggested a general trend toward lower correlations among the subtests that were dependent upon immediate problem-solving abilities and higher correlations for tests requiring stored information, which also reflected the pattern of results with subtests that are more sensitive to brain damage as compared with tests that are generally less sensitive (Reitan et al., 1996).

Finally, age and education correlations with the GNDS were determined in groups with mild head injuries (Reitan et al., 1999a). No significant correlations were found, as was also true for a group with definite traumatic tissue damage of the brain. The results indicated that the influence of age and education was diminished to the point of statistical insignificance in mild head injuries as well as in more severe head injuries or diversified groups of brain damage. These results serve as the foundation for the initial question regarding adjusting raw neuropsychological test scores for brain-damaged subjects, using the relationships based on the study of persons with normal brain conditions.

The HRB has served as a springboard for many additional studies that are beyond the scope of the review but that justify Meier's (1985) statement that during the period of remarkable expansion of neuropsychology, the HRB "was the primary force in stimulating clinical research and application in this country." According to McCaffrey et al. (1984), their initial survey showed that 65% of the respondents used the HRB. In the survey reported by McCaffrey and Lynch in 1996, the percentage had risen to 77%, a 12% increase.

REHABIT: A STRUCTURED PROGRAM FOR RETRAINING NEUROPSYCHOLOGICAL ABILITIES BASED ON THE HALSTEAD-REITAN BATTERY

Before retraining of the damaged brain can begin, the nature and severity of impairment must be identified. Target points for retraining must be established. The preceding parts of this chapter have been devoted to elucidation of the basic aspects of neuropsychological impairment and methods for valid measurement of these deficits. Considering the range of adaptive abilities represented by brain functions, unless the deficits are known for the individual person, attempts to devise a specifically appropriate retraining program are almost like shooting in the dark. Thus, the final step in the neuropsychological sequence involves remediation. The neuropsychologist must (1) identify neuropsychological deficits, (2) conclude validly that these deficits are due to brain damage rather than other possible causes, and (3) define and select training procedures that are pertinent to the needs of the individual. If a remediation program is to be of value, the behavioral deficits must be evaluated in terms of their comparative severity for the individual, and rehabilitation must be appropriate to the subject's ability level and needs. These requirements presume that the neuropsychological evaluation has assessed the full range of brain-related functions. Evidence indicates that results on the HRB provide this kind of information by identifying an individual's neuropsychological impairment in the framework of a comprehensive model of brain-behavior relationships. Thus, evaluation with the HRB provides a diagnosis that serves as the basis for developing a rehabilitation program capable of remediating an individual's particular deficits.

Training of children and adults is viewed within this same framework. Differences in neuropsychological evaluation of children and adults must be recognized, largely due to the fact that children are in a developmental phase of achieving brain-related abilities. However, children and adults who sustain impairment in a particular area may demonstrate many of the same types of neuropsychological deficits. The training program materials for children and adults are essentially similar, except that in many instances the training begins at a simpler level for the child.

As noted previously, verbal and language functions are customarily related to the integrity of the left cerebral hemisphere, and visual-spatial and manipulatory skills are dependent on the status of the right cerebral hemisphere. Recent investigations have emphasized the specialization of brain functions in association with the cerebral hemisphere involved; however, the nonspecialized types of abilities, which are dependent upon the brain generally, have been relatively neglected. Because the abilities that characterize generalized brain functions involve all cerebral tissue rather than represent specialized capabilities, it might be reasonable to postulate that these abilities are of special significance in a cognitive retraining program.

Our research has shown that the broad range of abstraction abilities represents cerebral cortical functioning generally and may be more fundamental to rehabilitation than the specialized skills. A cognitive retraining program that emphasizes abstraction and reasoning abilities would seem to provide the most appropriate basis for rehabilitation, especially considering the research and clinical findings that demonstrate the pervasive and limiting effects of impairment in this area.

Based on many years of prior work with individual patients, REHABIT (Reitan Evaluation of Hemispheric Abilities and Brain Improvement Training) was formalized by Reitan in 1979 to provide tasks that reflect the specific and generalized functions of the brain. The REHABIT training program does not use a shotgun approach to brain retraining; instead, it has specifically been organized to remediate an individual's neuropsychological deficits, as determined by an evaluation with the HRB.

Considering the importance of abstraction abilities and their central role in brain training, five tracks of training materials have been established in REHABIT:

1. Track A contains equipment and procedures specifically designed for developing expressive and receptive language and verbal skills and related academic abilities.

2. Track B also specializes in language and verbal materials, but it deliberately includes an element of abstraction reasoning, logical analysis, and organization.

3. Track C includes various tasks that do not depend upon particular content as much as reasoning, organization, planning, and abstraction skills.

4. Track D also emphasizes abstraction, but its content focuses on material that requires the subject to use visual-spatial, sequential, and manipulatory skills.

5. Track E specializes in tasks and materials that require the subject to exercise fundamental aspects of visual-spatial and manipulatory abilities.

Regardless of the content of the training materials used for the individual subject, every effort is made to emphasize the basic neuropsychological functions of attention, concentration, and memory.

With many children and adults it is necessary to provide training in each of the five tracks. In some instances, one area should be emphasized more than the other areas. The decision for prescribing training should be based upon the results of testing with the HRB. The REHABIT program, which includes over 600 items, provides extensive training in all areas of neuropsychological functioning.

Formal research regarding the effectiveness of REHABIT has been developing slowly, but this is to be expected, considering the difficulties inherent in evaluating a procedure that, for each individual subject, is extended over a substantial period of time. The first study was possible only through the occurrence of fortuitous circumstances that resulted in collaboration by Reitan and Sena (1983). Sena collected neuropsychological test results on subjects before and after 12 months' training with REHABIT. To study the effects of practice and spontaneous recovery, it was necessary to compose two control groups: (1) normal subjects who had been tested initially and retested 12 months later (to evaluate positive practice-effects) and (2) brain-injured subjects who had been tested initially and retested 12 months later but had not received any training with REHABIT or any other cognitive rehabilitation program (to study spontaneous recovery of neuropsychological functions). Fortunately, one of the authors (RMR) did have data on such groups, and a preliminary study was devised (Reitan et al., 1983).

The findings indicated that the subjects who had been trained with REHABIT demonstrated substantial improvement on neuropsychological tests compared with the other two groups. The results reached levels of statistical significance on a number of variables, even considering the small number of subjects. This investigation suggested that cognitive brain retraining using REHABIT was a definite advantage in terms of facilitating the recovery process.

Sena and his associates have continued investigating the efficacy of REHABIT. One study conducted by Sena (1985) evaluated a group of 12 subjects who had sustained brain injury an average of 18.4 months before the initial evaluation. Spontaneous recovery should have been largely completed before the subjects were enrolled in the study. In addition, retesting 12 months after the initial examination may well have represented a long enough interval to minimize positive practice-effects.

The retest results indicated that statistically significant improvement occurred on 31 of 39 measures, covering a broad range of neuropsychological functions. However, additional evaluation was necessary to make direct comparisons of persons who had undergone treatment with REHABIT as compared with those who had not received such treatment.

Sena and Sena (1986) retrained 13 subjects with two to three sessions of REHABIT per week for at least one year and compared their initial and retest results with a group of eight subjects who had similar brain injuries but had received no cognitive retraining. The initial testing indicated that the neuropsychological functions of the two groups were similar before training with REHABIT began. The subjects were also similar with respect to age, education, and gender distribution, and the only known difference between the groups related to cognitive training.

Neuropsychological retesting was done for both groups 12 months after the initial examination. The group that had received no treatment showed little change in their test results, earning scores similar to those obtained initially. However, the group receiving training with REHABIT demonstrated significant improvement on 18 of 30 measures.

These studies also included six subjects who had continued cognitive rehabilitation over a second year. Improvement in neuropsychological test scores from year one to year two continued on 42% of the measures, yielding evidence of statistically significant improvement on 90% of the tests in the battery used for assessment over the two-year period.

Sena, Sena, and Sunde (1986a) administered an extensive range of neuropsychological tests to family members of the brain-injured sample to assess changes at a 12-month interval. They found that the family members who had not sustained brain damage or disease showed minimal changes on the test results obtained 12 months later.

Another study by Sena, Sena, and Sunde (1986b) compared test results of brain-injured subjects and those of the family members and found that the brain-injured subjects who had received cognitive retraining showed substantially more improvement than their family members did.

Alfano and Meyerink (1986) and Meyerink, Pendleton, Hughes, and Thompson (1985) also reported a great degree of improvement of neuropsychological functions in brain-injured persons who received training oriented toward remediation of deficits as compared with a matched control group, most of whom had received only traditional rehabilitation therapies such as speech therapy, occupational therapy, or physical therapy. Excellent reviews of this subject have been published by Alfano and Finlayson (1987) and Finlayson, Alfano, and Sullivan (1987). In summary, this series of studies supports a conclusion that cognitive retraining is of value in facilitating the recovery process in persons with brain injury.

SUMMARY

We have presented a brief description of the Halstead-Reitan Neuropsychological Test Battery, including information that relates the test results to the biological condition of the brain and the implications and uses of the test results for retraining neuropsychological deficits.

This chapter reviewed the roots from which Halstead began his investigations, the significance of his original collaboration with neurological surgeons, and the long-term implications of his practical approach of observing the problems and limitations in everyday living experienced by brain-damaged patients. This practical approach resulted in the development of neuropsychological tests that represent standardized experiments in adaptive behavior as contrasted with more conventional psychometric instruments.

The HRB was gradually developed by adding tests, organized in accordance with complementary inferential procedures, until a battery was developed that covers the full range of neuropsychological dysfunction as determined by evaluation of thousands of patients with brain disease and damage. The sensitivity of the HRB to neuropsychological deficit has been demonstrated by the differential relationship of the test results to a broad range of neurological variables including location, type, and status of brain lesion.

Recent research has demonstrated the value of results of the HRB with relation to a number of current clinical problems, ranging from deficits in mild head injury, the relation of attribute variables to neuropsychological test results, the possibility of specific frontal lobe deficits, to the development of an index for dissimulation or possible malingering. This comprehensive development of a set of measures sensitive to cerebral damage laid the groundwork for a cognitive retraining program that incorporates neuropsychological evaluation (identification of the subject's neuropsychological needs) and cognitive retraining, using an approach that can be designed to restore the individual's functional ability structure (as contrasted with approaches oriented only toward a general, nonspecific notion of brain damage).

REFERENCES

Aita, J.A., Armitage, S.G., Reitan, R.M., & Rabinovitz, A. (1947). The use of certain psychological tests in the evaluation of brain injury. *Journal of General Psychology, 37*, 25–44.

Aita, J.A., & Reitan, R.M. (1948). Psychotic reactions in late recovery period following brain injury. *American Journal of Psychiatry, 105*, 161–169.

Aita, J.A., Reitan, R.M., & Ruth, J.M. (1947). Rorschach's Test as a diagnostic aid in brain injury. *American Journal of Psychiatry, 103*, 70–79.

Alfano, A.M., & Meyerink, L.H. (1986). Cognitive retraining with brain-injured adults. *VA Practitioner, 12*, 13.

Alfano, D.P., & Finlayson, M.A.J. (1987). Clinical neuropsychology in rehabilitation. *The Clinical Neuropsychologist, 1*, 105–123.

Binder, L.M., Rohling, M.L., & Larrabee, G.J. (1997). A review of mild head trauma. Part I. Meta-analytic review of neuropsychological studies. *Journal of Clinical and Experimental Neuropsychology, 19*, 421–431.

Binet, A., & Simon, T. (1916). *The development of intelligence in children.* Baltimore: Williams & Wilkins.

Christensen, A. (1975). *Luria's Neuropsychological Investigation.* New York: Spectrum.

Dean, R.S. (1985). Review of Halstead-Reitan Neuropsychological Test Battery. In J.V. Mitchell (Ed.), *The Ninth Mental Measurements Yearbook* (pp. 642–646). Highland Park, NJ: The Gryphon Press.

Dikmen, S., & Reitan, R.M. (1976). Psychological deficits and recovery of functions after head injury. *Transactions of the American Neurological Association, 101*, 72–77.

Doehring, D.G., & Reitan, R.M. (1961). Certain language and nonlanguage disorders in brain-damaged patients with homonymous visual field defects. *AMA Archives of Neurology and Psychiatry, 5*, 294–299.

Doehring, D.G., & Reitan, R.M. (1962). Concept attainment of human adults with lateralized cerebral lesions. *Perceptual and Motor Skills, 14*, 27–33.

Doehring, D.G., Reitan, R.M., & Kløve, H. (1961). Changes in patterns of intelligence test performances associated with homonymous visual field defects. *Journal of Nervous and Mental Disease, 132*, 227–233.

Finlayson, M.A.J., Alfano, D.P., & Sullivan, J.F. (1987). A neuropsychological approach to cognitive remediation: Microcomputer applications. *Canadian Psychology, 28*, 180–190.

Fitzhugh, K.B., Fitzhugh, L.C., & Reitan, R.M. (1961). Psychological deficits in relation to acuteness of brain dysfunction. *Journal of Consulting Psychology, 25*, 61–66.

Fitzhugh, K.B., Fitzhugh, L.C., & Reitan, R.M. (1962a). The relationship of acuteness of organic brain dysfunction to Trail Making Test performances. *Perceptual and Motor Skills, 15*, 399–403.

Fitzhugh, K.B., Fitzhugh, L.C., & Reitan, R.M. (1962b). Wechsler-Bellevue comparisons in groups with "chronic" and "current" lateralized and diffuse brain lesions. *Journal of Consulting Psychology, 26*, 306–310.

Fitzhugh, L.C., Fitzhugh, K.B., & Reitan, R.M. (1962c). Sensorimotor deficits of brain-damaged subjects in relation to intellectual level. *Perceptual and Motor Skills, 15*, 603–608.

Fitzhugh, K.B., Fitzhugh, L.C., & Reitan, R.M. (1963). Effects of "chronic" and "current" lateralized and non-lateralized cerebral lesions upon Trail Making Test performances. *Journal of Nervous and Mental Disease, 137*, 82–87.

Goldstein, K. (1942a). *Aftereffects of Brain Injuries in War.* New York: Grune & Stratton.

Goldstein, K. (1942b). The two ways of adjustment of the organism to cerebral defects. *Journal of Mt. Sinai Hospital, 9*, 504–513.

Halstead, W.C. (1947). *Brain and Intelligence: A Quantitative Study of the Frontal Lobes.* Chicago: University of Chicago Press.

Hartlage, L.C., & DeFilippis, N.A. (1983). History of neuropsychological assessment. In C.J. Golden & P.J. Vicente (Eds.), *Foundations of Clinical Neuropsychology* (pp. 1–23). New York: Plenum Press.

Heaton, R.K., Grant, I., & Matthews, C.G. (1991). *Comprehensive norms for an expanded Halstead-Reitan Battery.* Odessa, FL: Psychological Assessment Resources.

Hebb, D.O. (1939). Intelligence in man after large removals of cerebral tissue: Report of four left frontal lobe cases. *Journal of General Psychology, 21*, 73–87.

Hebb, D.O. (1941). Human intelligence after removal of cerebral tissue from the right frontal lobe. *Journal of General Psychology, 25*, 257–265.

Heimburger, R.F., & Reitan, R.M. (1961). Easily administered written test for lateralizing brain lesions. *Journal of Neurosurgery, 18*, 301–312.

Incagnoli, T., Goldstein, G., & Golden, C.J. (Eds.). (1986). *Clinical Application of Neuropsychological Test Batteries.* New York: Plenum Press.

Kløve, H. (1959). Relationship of differential electroencephalographic patterns of distribution of Wechsler-Bellevue scores. *Neurology, 9*, 871–876.

Kløve, H., & Reitan, R.M. (1958). The effect of dysphasia and spatial distortion on Wechsler-Bellevue results. *Archives of Neurology and Psychiatry, 80*, 708–713.

Levin, H.S., Eisenberg, H.M., & Benton, A.L. (Eds.). (1989). *Mild head injury.* New York: Oxford University Press.

McCaffrey, R.J., & Isaac, W. (1984). Survey of the educational backgrounds and specialty training of instructors of clinical neuropsychology in APA-Approved graduate training programs. *Professional Psychology: Research and Practice, 15,* 26–33.

McCaffrey, R.J., & Lynch, J.K. (1996). Survey of the educational backgrounds and specialty training of instructors of clinical neuropsychology in APA-Approved graduate training programs: A 10-year follow-up. *Archives of Clinical Neuropsychology, 11,* 11–19.

Meier, M.J. (1985). Review of Halstead-Reitan Neuropsychological Test Battery. In JV Mitchell (Ed.), *The Ninth Mental Measurements Yearbook* (pp. 646–649). Highland Park, NJ: The Gryphon Press.

Meyerink, L.H., Pendleton, M.G., Hughes, R.G., & Thompson, L.L. (1985). Effectiveness of cognitive retraining with brain-impaired adults. *Archives of Physical Medicine and Rehabilitation, 66,* 555.

O'Donnell, J.P. (1991). Neuropsychological assessment of learning-disabled adolescents and young adults. In J. Obrzut & G. Hynd (Eds.), *Neuropsychological foundations of learning disabilities* (pp. 331–353). New York: Academic Press.

O'Donnell, J.P., Kurtz, J., & Ramanaiah, N.V. (1983). Neuropsychological test findings for normal, learning-disabled, and brain-damaged young adults. *Journal of Consulting and Clinical Psychology, 51,* 726–729.

Oestreicher, J.M., & O'Donnell, J.P. (1995). Validation of the General Neuropsychological Deficit Scale with nondisabled, learning-disabled, and head-injured young adults. *Archives of Clinical Neuropsychology, 10,* 185–191.

Reitan, R.M. (1955a). Certain differential effects of left and right cerebral lesions in human adults. *Journal of Comparative and Physiological Psychology, 48,* 474–477.

Reitan, R.M. (1955b). The distribution according to age of a psychologic measure dependent upon organic brain functions. *Journal of Gerontology, 10,* 338–340.

Reitan, R.M. (1955c). An investigation of the validity of Halstead's measures of biological intelligence. *Archives of Neurology and Psychiatry, 73,* 28–35.

Reitan, R.M. (1955d). The relation of the Trail Making Test to organic brain damage. *Journal of Consulting Psychology, 19,* 393–394.

Reitan, R.M. (1958). The validity of the Trail Making Test as an indicator of organic brain damage. *Perceptual and Motor Skills, 8,* 271–276.

Reitan, R.M. (1959). The comparative effects of brain damage on the Halstead Impairment Index and the Wechsler-Bellevue Scale. *Journal of Clinical Psychology, 15,* 281–285.

Reitan, R.M. (1964). Psychological deficits resulting from cerebral lesions in man. In J.M. Warren & K.A. Akert (Eds.), *The Frontal Granular Cortex and Behavior.* New York: McGraw-Hill.

Reitan, R.M. (1967). Psychological changes associated with aging and cerebral damage. *Mayo Clinic Proceedings, 42,* 653–673.

Reitan, R.M. (1970). Objective behavioral assessment in diagnosis and prediction. In A.L. Benton (Ed.), *Behavioral change in cerebrovascular disease* (pp. 155–165). New York: Medical Department, Harper & Row.

Reitan, R.M. (1974). Methodological problems in clinical neuropsychology. In R.M. Reitan & L.A. Davison (Eds.), *Clinical neuropsychology: Current status and applications* (pp. 19–46). Washington, DC: Hemisphere Publishing Corporation.

Reitan, R.M. (1984). *Aphasia and sensory-perceptual deficits in adults.* Tucson, AZ: Neuropsychology Press.

Reitan, R.M, & Sena, D.A. (1983, August). *The efficacy of the REHABIT technique in remediation of brain-injured people.* Paper presented at the meeting of the American Psychological Association, Anaheim, CA.

Reitan, R.M., & Wolfson, D. (1985). The Halstead-Reitan neuropsychological test battery: Theory and Clinical Interpretation (1st ed.). Tucson, AZ: Neuropsychology Press.

Reitan, R.M., & Wolfson, D. (1986). *Traumatic brain injury. Vol. I. Pathophysiology and neuropsychological evaluation.* Tucson, AZ: Neuropsychology Press.

Reitan, R.M., & Wolfson, D. (1988). *Traumatic brain injury. Vol. II. Recovery and rehabilitation.* Tucson, AZ: Neuropsychology Press.

Reitan, R.M., & Wolfson, D. (1989). The Seashore Rhythm Test and brain functions. *The Clinical Neuropsychologist, 3,* 70–77.

Reitan, R.M., & Wolfson, D. (1990). The significance of the Speech-sounds Perception Test for cerebral functions. *Archives of Clinical Neuropsychology, 5,* 70–78.

Reitan, R.M., & Wolfson, D. (1992a). *Neuroanatomy and neuropathology: A clinical guide for neuropsychologists* (2nd ed.). Tucson, AZ: Neuropsychology Press.

Reitan, R.M., & Wolfson, D. (1992b). *Neuropsychological evaluation of older children.* Tucson, AZ: Neuropsychology Press.

Reitan, R.M., & Wolfson, D. (1993). *The Halstead-Reitan Neuropsychological Test Battery: Theory and clinical interpretation* (2nd ed). Tucson, AZ: Neuropsychology Press.

Reitan, R.M., & Wolfson, D. (1995a). The Category Test and Trail Making Test as measures of frontal lobe functions. *The Clinical Neuropsychologist, 9,* 50–56.

Reitan, R.M., & Wolfson, D. (1995b). The influence of age and education on neuropsychological test results. *The Clinical Neuropsychologist, 9,* 151–158.

Reitan, R.M., & Wolfson, D. (1996). Differential relationships of age and education to WAIS subtest scores among brain-damaged and control groups. *Archives of Clinical Neuropsychology, 11,* 303–313.

Reitan, R.M., & Wolfson, D. (1999a). The influence of age and education on neuropsychological performances of persons with mild traumatic brain injuries. In M.J. Raymond, T.L. Bennett, L.C. Hartlage, & C.M. Cullum (Eds.), *Mild traumatic brain injury* (pp. 49–76). Austin, TX: Pro-ed.

Reitan, R.M., & Wolfson, D. (1999b). The two faces of mild head injury. *Archives of Clinical Neuropsychology, 14,* 191–202.

Reitan, R.M., & Wolfson, D. (2000a). *Mild head injury: Intellectual, cognitive, and emotional consequences.* Tucson, AZ: Neuropsychology Press.

Reitan, R.M., & Wolfson, D. (2000b). The neuropsychological similarities of mild and more severe head injury. *Archives of Clinical Neuropsychology, 15,* 433–442.

Rojas, D.C., & Bennett, T.L. (1995). Single versus composite score discriminative validity with the Halstead-Reitan Battery and the Stroop Test in mild head injury. *Archives of Clinical Neuropsychology, 10,* 101–110.

Russell, E.W., Neuringer, C., & Goldstein, G. (1970). *Assessment of brain damage: A neuropsychological key approach.* New York: Wiley.

Sena, D.A. (1985). The effectiveness of cognitive retraining for brain-impaired individuals. *The International Journal of Clinical Neuropsychology, 7,* 62.

Sena, D.A., Sena, H.M., & Sunde, R.R. (1986a). Changes in cognitive functioning on non-impaired family members. *Archives of Clinical Neuropsychology, 1,* 263.

Sena, D.A., Sena, H.M., & Sunde, R.R. (1986b). Comparison of changes in cognitive functioning of non-impaired family members and brain-impaired patients. *Archives of Clinical Neuropsychology, 1,* 262.

Sena, H.M., & Sena, D.A. (1986). A quantitative validation of the effectiveness of cognitive retraining. *Archives of Clinical Neuropsychology, 1,* 74.

Sherer, M., & Adams, R.L. (1993). Cross-validation of Reitan and Wolfson's Neuropsychological Deficit Scales. *Archives of Clinical Neuropsychology, 8,* 429–435.

Wheeler, L., Burke, C.J., & Reitan, R.M. (1963). An application of discriminant functions to the problem of predicting brain damage using behavioral variables. *Perceptual and Motor Skills, [Monograph supplement], 16,* 417–440.

Wheeler, L., & Reitan, R.M. (1962). The presence and laterality of brain damage predicted from responses to a short Aphasia Screening Test. *Perceptual and Motor Skills, 15,* 783–799.

Wolfson, D. (1985). *The Neuropsychological history questionnaire.* Tucson, AZ: Neuropsychology Press.

Wolfson, D., & Reitan, R.M. (1995). Cross-Validation of the General Neuropsychological Deficit Scale (GNDS). *Archives of Clinical Neuropsychology, 10,* 125–131.

CHAPTER 9

The Adult Luria-Nebraska Neuropsychological Battery

CHARLES J. GOLDEN

The Luria-Nebraska Neuropsychological Battery (LNNB) is a method that integrates the qualitative information generated by the techniques of A.R. Luria with traditional American psychometric procedures. This hybrid approach takes elements from both significant traditions. The test has been found to have both a strong psychometric base and to provide the clinician with the opportunity to make valuable qualitative observations and discriminations, which cannot be easily made with traditional psychometric instruments, of highly specific problems in clients. The test battery provides a brief but comprehensive evaluation in less than three hours, which makes it practical to use in situations where time is limited and with impaired clients whose ability to be tested over long time periods is limited. It is also easily portable so that it can be used in nursing homes, hospital rooms, prisons, and other sites outside of the psychologist's office.

The LNNB consists of 12 scales derived from Luria's work, based on his descriptions in Luria (1980) and the excellent work of Christensen (1975). Each of these scales consists of items within a given theme area, such as receptive language, but each tests a different qualitative aspect of performance within the theme area. For example, a traditional test, such as the Wechsler Adult Intelligence Scale (WAIS)

Block Design, may consist of items that are similar except for difficulty level and complexity. In contrast, a scale such as the LNNB Receptive Speech scale consists of items requiring phonemic recognition, writing of phonemes, simple commands, vocabulary, complex commands, abstractions, grammatical inversions, and so on, with each item focusing on a different aspect of receptive speech. This variability allows the clinician to use differences in item presentation and content to survey quickly the wide range of problems possible in the area of receptive language. As used by Luria, this information could be used to skip or redesign items. In the quantitative version, the information can be used to compare to other similar but not identical items or to design "testing the limits" procedures.

A more traditional test would have a scale for each of these subareas, a common practice but one that is time consuming, so that in the end many additional specific areas are not evaluated. This more detailed and finer evaluation of skills (but with less depth and repetition) is consistent with Luria's emphasis on the specific details of the client's deficits rather than more generalized and less specific information generated from other tests. At the same time, this structure allows for the construction of a device that is time limited and still possesses psychometric reliability and validity. A traditional exam that evaluated all the areas contained in the LNNB would likely take two to four times longer to complete.

HISTORY AND DEVELOPMENT

The original goal of neuropsychological tests was the classification of individuals as brain damaged or normal. Extensive literature throughout the twentieth century attempted to validate individual tests or batteries of tests for the purpose of this basic identification. Although this classification remains a goal of neuropsychological testing, its importance has diminished with the introduction of Computerized Tomography (CT), Magnetic Resonance Imaging (MRI), and measures of brain metabolism, including Regional Cerebral Blood Flow (rCBF), Positron Emission Tomography (PET), and Single Photon Excitement Computed Tomography (SPECT). These neuroradiological techniques have increased the ability to diagnose the presence of brain injury, although certain disorders still manage to evade detection by these techniques. As neuroradiological techniques have improved, neuropsychological testing has increasingly focused on the sequelae of brain injuries rather than focusing on only the presence or location of a brain injury. Such description can range from localizing an injury to detailed descriptions of the client's strengths and weaknesses.

Luria's qualitative procedures were ideally suited for a detailed evaluation of the client's strengths and weaknesses. However, their application to clients was difficult, because the examination lacked consistently employed content, was devoid of a scoring system other than the examiner's impressions, and lacked a systematic interpretive strategy that could be evaluated for its accuracy and usefulness in different populations. Traditional neuropsychological techniques, alternatively, were psychometrically sound but lacked the ability to provide the rich clinical interpretive information that could be gained from Luria's qualitative work. Still, the lack of detail of Luria's procedures made attempts to standardize the approach nearly impossible.

The publication of Christensen's (1975) version of Luria's battery gave much more detail on the actual procedures employed than was available in Luria's seminal works (Luria, 1966; Luria, 1973). With this information, it appeared possible to adapt the information in Christensen (1975) so as to produce a quantitative and qualitative hybrid of her purely qualitative presentation.

Working with a group of dedicated graduate (and undergraduate) students at the University of South Dakota, Golden developed an initial adaptation of Christensen (1975) and

Luria (1966) that attempted to cover everything presented in both works. This led to a battery with nearly 2000 procedures, which took about 18 hours to administer to normal subjects. From this extremely comprehensive battery, items were statistically deleted based on their redundancy, failure to produce reliable scores, and failure to measure what was intended. Other items were eliminated clinically due to their length or because they did not return enough useful information. This allowed the battery to be cut down to slightly over three hours. Additional data were collected, and some items were eliminated because of lack of reliability or their inability to discriminate between normal and brain-injured clients.

The battery, labeled the Luria-South Dakota, was first presented in a symposium chaired by Golden at the 1977 APA convention in Montreal. The test was immediately popular despite the fact that there had been relatively little research at that time. Apparently this was because it seemed to tap a strong area of interest in Luria's work and the need for briefer more focused instruments. The test was initially copied and distributed to individuals interested in the battery, leading to more research and increased demand. The battery was revised one last time to produce the Luria-Nebraska Neuropsychological Battery (LNNB; Golden, Purisch, & Hammeke, 1980), which was published by Western Psychological Services. Initial publication of the LNNB data was published in the *Journal of Consulting and Clinical Psychology* (Golden, Hammeke, & Purisch, 1978; Purisch, Golden, & Hammeke, 1978) as well as the *International Journal of Neuroscience* (Hammeke, Golden, & Purisch, 1978), which exposed the battery to an even larger stage. The battery's popularity was helped by an ongoing debate within the literature on the appropriateness of a test that combined psychometric and qualitative traditions in what was then a unique manner.

After the introduction of the LNNB, work began immediately on an alternative form of the test to provide a parallel form and improve on the battery. The major changes on Form II were the addition of a Delayed Memory scale and a new set of stimulus items that were more "modern" and appropriate for some populations. This was also intended to make the battery more widely available, especially because the Christensen (1975) materials on which Form I were based were frequently unavailable due to printing issues. Form II of the test was published in 1985, along with a newly expanded and more extensive test manual for both forms of the test (Golden, Purisch, & Hammeke, 1985).

The LNNB provides a framework for Luria's evaluative style by adding an objective scoring system and standard administration procedures. This structure provides a foundation of items that can be given to all clients, scored in an objective and reliable manner, and evaluated for systematic effectiveness across different populations. At the same time, Luria's qualitative and flexible administration is retained around this framework, yielding an instrument that can be studied psychometrically while, at the same time, being used in a purely clinical and impressionistic manner if so desired. The ideal administration is one that combines elements of both approaches.

To reach these dual goals, it was necessary to carefully modify the administration of the test in a manner that was reproducible but that accounted for the client's individuality and allowed the clinician adequate flexibility to investigate qualitative behavior of the client. To achieve this adaptability, a number of techniques were adopted for the test administration. First, instructions for items were made flexible so that the clinician could be assured that the client understood the instructions. In the case of many standardized instructions, clients make errors because they do not understand the task requirements. Although this can be important in determining the presence of a cognitive disorder, it distorts the interpretation and meaning of the item that is given. The LNNB allows paraphrasing and repeating instructions, answering client questions, and offering examples to ensure that the client understands what is required. This procedure, however, is limited by the nature of the items. For example, the instructions for a memory item may be repeated but not the actual stimuli. Instructions and stimuli, however, may be repeated for an item measuring the ability to expressively repeat a word.

Not only does this procedure ensure more consistency, the interaction with the client generates important qualitative information that may illuminate the client's day-to-day interactions with the environment. For example, if the client learns only from examples, or rapidly forgets instructions and needs frequent repetition, information directly relevant to the client's condition and learning style is gained. Attention to this communicative process throughout the test can assist in making an accurate diagnosis and description of the client.

Second, testing-of-the-limit procedures are encouraged throughout the evaluation. Although some such procedures are built into the items, the test organization allows the clinician to add additional procedures without affecting the validity of the standard scores. An important aspect of this flexibility is the emphasis on scoring and the client's underlying performance mechanism. Any item on any test, regardless of the simplicity, can be missed for a variety of reasons. A full understanding of the client's condition can be achieved only with comprehension of the client's failure.

Furthermore, qualitative observations are encouraged throughout the test. These observations not only focus on the question of *why* an item was missed but also on behavior between items throughout the test. For example, a person with attentional problems, who is otherwise intact, may receive normal scores on the test if sufficiently redirected to the questions. The need and nature of such redirection, while not scored in any item, becomes a significant part of the evaluation. In traditional tests, client errors are often misinterpreted in terms of item content rather than the attentional process. Through clinician involvement in the testing process, the LNNB separates the content issues of the items from such conditions as arousal, attention, concentration, emotionality, frustration, motivation, and fatigue.

Finally, the emphasis of the LNNB is on obtaining optimal client performance. Many traditional tests encourage suboptimal performance in brain-injured clients through minimal feedback, excessive testing times, misunderstood instructions, and other similar features. Such procedures maximize differences between the brain-injured clients and normal subjects, increasing hit rates but decreasing individual differences among brain-injured clients. Many of these tests may end up maximizing the manifestations of client impairment.

The LNNB emphasizes having only clients with a deficit in an area missing a specific item. The aim is not subtests or items that identify all brain-injured clients, but rather items that only individuals with specific deficits will miss. We believe that optimal performance tells us more about how the brain functions, although the individual may not perform at such levels due to various potential psychiatric and environmental reasons. By understanding what arises from brain injury and what arises from other sources, the understanding of an individual can be maximized. For example, on motor speed items on any test, clients might become distracted, forget what they are doing, lose interest, or perform at an inappropriate rate, resulting in performance less than their capability. The LNNB accounts for this problem qualitatively and diagnostically. Any item may be readministered so that the final standard score is not affected by this extraneous factor. This method has the effect of making individual items and scales less sensitive to brain injury but more specific to the underlying cause of impaired performance.

The LNNB, Form II, consists of 279 items organized into 12 basic scales (Golden et al., 1985). Because many of the items have more than one subpart, the actual number of procedures in the test is about 1000. The LNNB scales are nontraditional, because the same procedure or question is not asked repeatedly at different levels of difficulty. The purpose of the LNNB is not to stratify individuals as average or superior but rather to address the basic functions that underlie all complex behavior. Each scale is organized to test different aspects of behavior within each area evaluated. Although the items differ from one another in a variety of ways, they all have a common theme such as memory functions or language functions.

The content of the LNNB scales differs within each scale, with items varying around a single theme. The following sections contain a more detailed description of the content of each scale. The content for the two forms of the test is identical, except for the addition of the Intermediate Memory Scale to Form II.

Motor (C1)

The 51-item motor scale begins with four items measuring motor speed of the left and right hand. Speed is measured on one simple item (opening and closing a hand) and one complex item (touching each finger in sequence with the thumb). This is followed by 4 items that examine the role of muscle feedback when performing simple motor behaviors, and 10 items examining the ability to perform simple bilateral motor movements by imitation. Two items examine the ability to perform simple items by command. Three items examine bilateral speeded coordination. Perseverative response tendencies and fine motor skills are examined in an item that requires copying a repetitive figure (alternating m's and n's).

The ability to perform complex motor movements by verbal instruction and without props is measured by four items, such as "Show me how you would open up a can with a can opener." This evaluation is followed by 9 items evaluating the ability to perform simple and speeded oral motor movements, and 13 items looking at the speed and quality of simple drawings by command and from copying. The final four items request contradictory behavior under verbal control, such as "If I tap once, you tap twice." These latter items examine the ability of the client to inhibit imitation and to control behavior through inner speech.

Rhythm (C2)

The 12-item Rhythm scale evaluates the ability to hear rhythmic patterns and musical tones, evaluate these stimuli, and reproduce them. Items range from identifying the similarity of patterns or tones to reproducing patterns, tones, and musical sequences.

Tactile (C3)

This 22-item scale uses a series of 11 measures on the right and left sides of the body independently. These tasks include indicating where the person is touched, whether a touch is hard or soft, whether a touch is sharp or dull, how many points are touching the person, the direction of movement of a touch, which letters or numbers are written on the wrist, copying gross motor movements by muscle feedback, and identifying simple objects placed in the hand.

Visual (C4)

The 14-item visual scale examines visual and visual-spatial skills that do not require motor movements. Although some of the items involve verbal feedback, clients do not need to name objects accurately but must indicate they recognize the object's purpose or use. The items include simple identification, identification when parts of the item are missing, and identification of overlapping items. Spatial items include completing visual patterns (similar to Raven's Matrices), telling time on an analog clock, identifying directions, imagining items in three dimensions, and rotating items into new configurations.

Receptive (C5)

The 33-item Receptive Language scale evaluates speech comprehension, including basic phonemes and complex sentences. Eight items examine phonemic comprehension. Six items examine word comprehension, and the remainder evaluate the comprehension of sentences at various levels of complexity. These may be verbal-spatial items, such as "Tell who is taller" "Is Brian shorter than Kim but taller than Barbara?" or items of logic, such as "If I told you that Brian hit Tim, who was the victim?"

Expressive Language (C6)

The 42-item Expressive Language scale evaluates speech utilizing simple sounds and complex sentences under a variety of conditions. The first ten items look at repetition of sounds and words; the next 11 involve reading similar sounds and words (with the diagnostic emphasis on the fluency of pronunciation rather than accuracy of reading). Three items involve the repetition of sentences. Three items examine naming skills, and five items evaluate automatic naming, such as counting or the days of the week. The remainder of the items concern complex and less structured speech, such as responding to a question, describing a picture, speaking about the weather, using specific words in a sentence, and reorganizing words into a sentence.

Writing (C7)

This 12-item scale scores for motor-writing errors (the motor performance of forming letters and words) and spelling. The items range from single letters to sentences. One composition sample is included as well. The scale measures basic writing and spelling skills up to a seventh-grade level.

Reading (C8)

The 13-item Reading scale involves the reading of items ranging from single letters to paragraphs. Two items look at the ability to hear letters and articulate them into sounds and words. Unlike the reading items on the Expressive Language scale, the items are scored for reading accuracy, not expressive fluency. As with the Writing scale, the test measures basic abilities up to a seventh-grade level.

Arithmetic (C9)

This 22-item scale evaluates the reading and writing of numbers and simple computational skills. Nine items examine number recognition and writing at various levels of complexity. Two items involve simple number comparison, and nine items look at basic computational skills up through a seventh-grade level. The final two items involve serial sevens and serial thirteens. Items are designed to examine the spatial nature of numbers as well as more basic number recognition.

Memory (C10)

The 13-item Memory scale evaluates verbal and nonverbal immediate memory with and without interference. The scale begins with the learning of a seven-item word list, followed by picture memory with and without delays. Immediate rhythmic and tactile/visual memory are assessed, as is verbal/visual memory. These appraisals are followed by simple list learning with interference and sentence learning with interference. One item involves recall of a paragraph, and the last item examines visually cued verbal memory using a seven-item paired list.

Intelligence (C11)

The 34-item Intelligence scale yields an estimate of general IQ, employing many types of items traditionally used in intelligence evaluations. Four items involve picture interpretations, and an additional two involve picture sequencing. Verbal items include interpretations of stories and proverbs, vocabulary, similarity items, difference items, the ability to generalize from the specific to the general, the ability to make deductions from general rules to specific instances, and categorization skills. The final 12 items involve simple mathematical word problems.

Delayed Memory (C12)

This scale tests delayed memory of items that initially required memory (from the Memory scale) and recognition and retention of material in the remainder of the test. This procedure usually involves delays ranging from 30 minutes to two hours. Verbal and nonverbal items are included.

Psychometric Properties

The psychometric properties of the test have been extensively studied. These studies have been broken down into those that reflect the reliability of the LNNB and those that investigated validity. This is not an exhaustive review but rather a sample of the literature.

Reliability

The reliability of the LNNB has been examined from a number of perspectives, including interrater agreement, internal consistency, and test-retest reliability. A study by Golden et al. (1978), examined 1,345 comparisons resulting from the battery administration to five separate clients by five independent pairs of examiners. A high level of interrater agreement was obtained, based on 95% of identical comparisons. This was further corroborated by a follow-up study by Bach, Harowski, Kirby, Peterson, and Schulein (1981).

The internal consistency estimates (alpha) ranged from .82 on C2 to .94 on C1, for the 14 clinical/summary scales on 146 brain damaged and 74 control subjects (Mikula, 1981). Another study examined this in a mixed sample of brain damaged and normal subjects (n = 559), along with separate brain impaired (n = 451), schizophrenic (n = 414), mixed psychiatric patients (n = 128), and a normative sample with 108 subjects (Maruish, Sawicki, Franzen, & Golden, 1984). The correlations for all the groups except the normative sample were high, ranging from .81 to .93.

The test-retest reliabilities of the clinical scales ranged from .78 on C3 to a high of .96 on C9 (Golden, Berg, & Graber, 1982). Another study by Plaisted and Golden (1982) analyzed the test-retest reliability for the 14 original scales, localization scales, and the factor scales. For the 14 original scales, the reliability ranged from .83 to .96. For the eight localization scales, the range was between .78 to .95. However, the widest range was for the original factor scales, where the reliability ranged from .01 to .96, with an overall mean of .81. Those scores with lower reliabilities were eliminated from the test to yield a sample of 30 scales.

Validity

A number of empirical studies have estimated the criterion-related, concurrent, and construct validity of the LNNB. One study by Golden et al. (1978) tested the diagnostic efficiency of items in discriminating between brain-damaged and normal subjects. They found the two groups differed significantly with regard to education, but not to age and gender (T (98) = 3.51 p < .01). Covariance was used to control for the effect of education. Significant differences were found between the performances of the two groups on all 14 original scales (P < .001). Hit rates for these scales ranged from 74% for C6 to 96% for C10 in the control group, and from 58% for C2 to 86% for C6 in the brain-damaged group. Discriminant analysis was able to classify correctly all 50 controls and 43 out of 50 brain-damaged subjects, for an overall hit rate of 93%. Cross-validation of this study was conducted by Moses and Golden (1979) comparing a neurological and control sample, using Form I of the LNNB. The neurological diagnoses included cerebral trauma, CVAs, epilepsy, neoplasms, and metabolic or toxic disorders. Here, the results obtained were almost identical to Golden et al. (1978).

Noting the paucity of research in assessing neuropsychological functioning in an elderly population, MacInnes et al. (1983) compared results of a "healthy" geriatric sample (mean age of 72 years), and a brain-damaged elderly sample (with a mean age of 68 years). Multivariate analysis of variance suggested significant differences (P < .001) between the two groups on 11 clinical scales, using age, sex, and education as covariates. The hit rates using the classification rules were 92% for the healthy group, 86% for the brain-damaged group, and 88% for the total sample.

Lewis et al. (1979) and Osmon, Golden, Purisch, Hammeke, and Blume (1979) completed the most ambitious studies, identifying the usefulness of the LNNB in localizing and lateralized brain injuries. These studies demonstrated that the Left and Right Hemisphere scales alone were able to lateralize more than 80% of cases with clear lateralized disorders, and the test as a whole showed a 74% accuracy in discriminating among eight groups of localized injuries (compared to an expected finding of 12.5% by chance).

ASSETS AND LIMITATIONS OF THE LNNB

The major assets of the LNNB lie in several areas. First, the test is relatively brief yet allows an investigation of many neuropsychological functions. In cases in which time is limited, this allows the clinician to gather efficiently a wide range of data that can be interpreted qualitatively and quantitatively. In cases in which more time is available, the LNNB can effectively identify areas where further investigation may reveal the most useful information. Second, the test offers an interface that allows for flexibility in administering the test to seriously impaired clients. This flexibility allows the user to tease out which deficits are basic and which are only secondary results of other deficits.

The ability to determine basic underlying deficits makes the LNNB more useful in a rehabilitation setting. Although rehabilitation can be more general, it is usually more efficient when focused on specific rather than general problems. Another advantage is the simple interface of the items, which makes them easier to translate across cultures and across languages. The simpler tests have a cleaner relationship to basic brain functions, which are less effected by culture and language and have a more understandable relationship to functions of specific systems of the brain. For examples of this, see Marwaha-Sonali and Barnes (1991), Xun, Gong, and Matthews (1987), and Kang (1992).

The limitations of the test are rooted in its strengths. Although the LNNB is useful for assessing the complex neuropsychological functions, the simple nature of the items preclude observation of complex functions that are a sum of these basic skills. In some cases of injury, especially in high-functioning people, the major deficits lie in the integration of these basic functions rather than the functions itself. It should be noted, however, that such deficits are not always the result of brain injury but may arise from emotional problems and environmental issues. In the experience of the author using the LNNB with other test batteries in a wide variety of medical and forensic settings, the LNNB is much more likely to underdiagnose brain injury compared to other tests and rarely overdiagnoses problems that turn out to be related to nonneurological factors. As with most other tests, relevant history, detailed clinical observations, and special medical diagnostic procedures should be used to supplement, corroborate, and investigate the test results.

Certain client characteristics are required for the administration of the LNNB. Hence, these tests are inappropriate for clients who are overtly hostile and uncommunicative or clients with extremely disorganized thinking processes. In addition, individuals with low verbal abilities have difficulty completing this test battery.

For individuals who wish to rely on quantitative information alone, the reliance of the LNNB on qualitative information generally causes some distress. In contrast, individuals who believe in only qualitative data may view the imposition of a standardized, quantitative framework as inappropriate. The goal of the exam was to integrate those two disparate approaches, a tendency seen in many newer tests as well.

Perhaps the largest limitation of this approach is the demands on the user. To be used in the most effective manner, this test requires an understanding of the theoretical underpinnings of the test and of neuropsychology. Although the test can be used based on basic rules (see the test manual and the interpretation section), this approach uses only a tiny part of the information generated by the test. As a result, mastering the test is a complex process that demands more of the user but also delivers more when done properly.

ADMINISTRATION AND SCORING

Scoring the LNNB occurs on several different levels, including scoring of specific items, scoring of the scales, and qualitative scoring.

Item Scoring

All items on the LNNB are scored as 0 (indicating normal performance), 1 (borderline performance), or 2 (impaired performance). For items that are only scorable as right or wrong, a 0 represents right and a 2 represents wrong. For those items, such as motor speed items, that involve counting responses, the raw score is translated into a 0, 1, or 2, using norms given on the test form. The use of this common scoring procedure allows for statistical and clinical interitem comparisons.

Scale Scoring

Each scale is scored by adding the 0, 1, and 2 scores from each of the items. A total raw score is generated and converted into a T-score using the table in the test form. The T-scores have a mean of 50 and a standard deviation of 10. High scores reflect poorer performance. Using a table in the test form, these scores are classified as normal or impaired by reference to a cutoff score, which is individually determined by the client's age and education. Scores above the cutoff are considered impaired. The average cutoff is 60, but may vary from 50 to over 70 depending on the age and education of the client.

In addition to these basic scales, the LNNB items may be rearranged into scales for specific purposes. Three of these scales are used frequently. The Left Hemisphere scale consists of all items related to the right side of the body; the Right Hemisphere scale consists of all items related to the left side of the body. The Pathognomonic scale consists of a series of items that are sensitive to the severity and acuity of the cognitive dysfunction. Additional scales also include the factor scales, which represent factors extracted from individual scales and the overall test. All of these additional scales are scored, just as the original scales are, by adding up the scale scores on each item. These scales represent subfactors, such as motor speed, drawing, basic language, spatial skills, repetition, verbal memory, verbal arithmetic, general intelligence, simple tactile, complex tactile, naming, verbal-spatial skills, phonemic skills, complex expressive language, basic reading, and so on. Other scales have been developed for specific uses. There is no limit to the range and type of scales that can be developed from the basic item data.

Qualitative Scoring

In addition to the item and scale scoring, the LNNB includes 60 qualitative scoring categories that can be scored at any time during the test, including in between items. It is not within the scope of this chapter to review all of these indices, but we discuss a sample to show their usefulness. In general, qualitative indices represent the recording of observations by the tester during the course of the examination. These reports generally fall into the following categories:

1. Problems related to inadequate client comprehension of procedures.
2. Observations that explain why the client is missing an item.
3. Unusual behaviors between items that impact the testing.
4. Problems that manifest during an item performance but are not related to the objective scoring of the test.

Problematic client comprehension generally involves confusion, insufficient vocabulary, attention deficits, arousal problems, fatigue, and motivation. Observations during the items that clarify errors differ depending on the scale but include paralysis, motor slowness, motor awkwardness, hearing difficulties, attentional problems, tactile sensation loss, visual difficulties, visual agnosia, inability to comprehend speech, naming problems, slowness in comprehension, inability to attend to the left side of stimuli, dysarthria, slowness of speech, word substitutions in speech, sound substitutions in speech, syllable substitution in words, the inability to progress from one sound to another, perseveration, concreteness, dyslexia, failure to recognize letters, failure to recognize sounds, failure to recognize number, visual-motor problems, memory problems, fatigue, and so on.

Unusual behaviors may include distractibility, inability to recall instructions, or the examiner may note, inappropriate emotional reactions, excessive fatigue, hyperactivity, lack of cooperation, poor arousal, seizures, and other related problems. The final category can include any problems seen when the person responds correctly but still shows a problem. For example, an individual may correctly describe an object but fail to name it correctly, thus demonstrating dysnomia. An individual may be literate, but only in a dysfluent manner, suggesting expressive speech problems such as dysarthria.

The qualitative indices are not limited to those discussed here and in the test manual, but rather reflect any behaviors that help further understanding of the client. The examiner should record any behaviors that do not make sense or seem unusual, even if the examiner does not know what they mean or their etiology.

INTERPRETATION

With the LNNB there are many levels of client classification, ranging from normal/abnormal to sophisticated analysis of the precise deficits and precise neurological causes of a given deficit. The first and most basic classification concerns quantifying profiles as normal or abnormal. The second classification involves a more detailed pattern analysis using the quantitative scores. The third classification involves a detailed item analysis yielding a description of what the client can and cannot do without any inferences about neurological causes. The fourth classification involves an analysis of the qualitative data and its integration with the quantitative data. The fifth classification examines the role of the client history in the analysis. The final classification involves the integration of psychometric, qualitative, historical, and medical findings to form a definitive picture of the client's problems, their causes, their interaction with the environment, the role of the client's personal and medical history, and the implications of this data for rehabilitation and prognosis in general.

Level I: Identifying Brain Damage

The LNNB provides several independent methods to identify the possible presence of a brain injury. The first involves a comparison of the 12 basic skills along with the Pathognomonic scale to the critical level (CL) discussed in the scoring section. The CL decision rules are as follows: More than three scores above the critical level indicates brain injury. The probability of this occurrence in a normal individual is less than 1 in 100. If one scale is elevated, the profile is considered to be normal; the same applies if no scales are elevated. If two scales are elevated, which is likely to happen in 1 of 25 normal subjects, the profile is a borderline case.

Because the CL is dependent on age and education, the accuracy of the CL decision rule depends on the accuracy of the information. Although age is rarely misstated in a significant fashion, education can be much more difficult to calculate. For example, the CL overestimates the premorbid abilities of a client who has simply attended school for 12 years but was impaired due to retardation or brain injury. In such a case, the choice of a specific level of education for the formula often depends on the question being asked. If a clinician wishes to know how the person is performing in relation to other people with 12 years of education, using 12 is appropriate. If a clinician wishes to know whether the person had a recent brain injury (since the end of school), using the client's actual achievement level may be more appropriate. In individuals with disorders arising from early childhood, the use of 12 years of education is appropriate if the clinician wishes to compare the person to expected normal development. In addition, the test manual includes a formula for calculating the critical level from premorbid IQ levels.

A second method for identifying brain injury is to note the difference between the lowest and highest T-score. Normal individuals typically show less than a 20-point spread between the lowest and highest scores, with a few normal subjects showing up to a 25-point difference, with the highest scores often being on Arithmetic or Writing (because of spelling) in such cases. Brain-injured clients typically show greater variability. Using this information, score differences exceeding 30 points are considered indicative of brain dysfunction. Ranges between the highest and lowest scores that are less than 30 but more than 20 are considered borderline; whereas ranges 20 and under are considered normal. It should be emphasized that the absence of a wide range does not itself make a profile normal.

Level II: Pattern Analysis Using the Quantitative Scores

The basic quantitative scales of the LNNB yield profiles much like those of the Minnesota Multiphasic Personality Inventory (MMPI) and other similar tests. These profiles suggest which scales represent the highest elevations and are most likely to show the general areas in which the client has the most difficulty. Two-point codes (the highest two scales) and three-point codes (the highest three scales) can be determined to generate statistical descriptions of the client's most likely problems. This information can be generated without reference to the full complexity of the profile, often yielding a valuable starting point for profile classification.

Most work has been done on the interpretation of the two-point profiles, with some work on three-point profiles. Before interpretation, a distinct profile classification must be determined. A clear-cut two-point profile is one in which the two highest scales are at least ten points higher than the third highest scale among the 12 basic scales plus the Pathognomonic, Right Hemisphere, and Left Hemisphere scales or one in which the two scales are the only scores elevated over the critical level. A clear-cut three-point profile is one in which all three of the three highest scales are at least ten points higher than the fourth highest scale, or when the three scales are the only scales higher than the critical level. Four-point and five-point code types may be defined in a similar manner. A scale is generally not included in a high-point profile if it does not exceed the critical level. Interpretive suggestions given in research or in the test manual are generally more accurate when the profile is clear-cut.

Although the test manual provides more extensive descriptions of the many possible high-point codes, several common two-point examples are given here to clarify the process. The following interpretations are abstracted from Golden et al. (1985).

Motor/Tactile

This combination often occurs in clients when lateralized impairment, often caused by a cerebral vascular accident of some kind, exists. In general, these occurrences are cortical strokes, whose side can be reliably determined by the comparison of the Left and Right Hemisphere scales. These strokes are generally accompanied by severe cognitive deficits, the nature of which depends on lateralization of injury. In general, the scales representing those cognitive areas (e.g., Expressive Language) show secondary elevations.

Motor/Visual

Elevations are most often associated with anterior right hemisphere injuries. The client shows intact basic visual skills but has trouble with more abstractive and visual reasoning tasks. Motor impairment is generally greatest on the left side of the body. Impairment elevations on the Rhythm scale may be seen as well, producing a Motor-Visual-Rhythm three-point code. When the two-point code is Motor/Rhythm, the lesion is generally more anterior than when the two-point code is Motor/Visual. The Motor/Rhythm combination is generally associated with attentional problems, difficulties in emotional control or emotional recognition, poor insight, poor social skills (especially if the lesion is long-standing), and difficulties in following the relationships between sequences of events. This profile may also be seen in many subcortical injuries, including mild to moderate head injuries.

Motor/Receptive Language

This combination is rare and occurs most often in anterior left hemisphere and subcortical left hemisphere injuries. Such individuals have problems with bilateral coordination and difficulty following complex verbal commands, especially those that require an action that is inconsistent with what the client is seeing, such as "When I tap once, you tap twice." However, the individual's basic verbal communications and understanding are usually intact.

Motor/Expressive

This combination occurs in anterior left hemisphere injuries, usually arising from a relatively serious problem, such as a stroke or a fast growing tumor. Such clients have dysfluent speech. They may slur their words, speak haltingly, repeat sounds, and substitute sounds, which makes them unintelligible. In extreme cases, they may be mute or unable to communicate verbally at any level, although nonverbal communication skills, such as reading and writing, may be intact. Naming problems are frequently present and may be consistent with expressive aphasia, also called Broca's aphasia.

Motor/Writing

This two-point occurs primarily in subjects with disorders in which the dominant hand is dysfunctional. This result can be seen in lateralized, subcortical disorders but can also be a peripheral disorder where the function of the arm is disrupted by spinal cord or nerve injuries, or fractures. When the disorder is in the brain, there are usually secondary attentional or arousal problems, which are noted in the testing process. When the injuries are peripheral, the deficits are generally limited to items that tap motor speed and coordination, and tactile sensitivity. Thus, drawing is often disrupted, along with writing and speeded items. Secondary elevations may be seen on the Tactile, Right Hemisphere, or Left Hemisphere scales.

Motor/Reading

The Motor/Reading combination is rarely present in a normal person who has had a brain injury, but does occur in people who have a learning disorder (dyslexia) prior to a brain injury. This situation is most often seen in teenagers and young adults who have had a head injury and who also have a history of school problems. The occasional exception to this tendency is seen in individuals with multiple strokes, who may develop acquired dyslexia from a small stroke along with more general motor problems. This condition is usually a precursor to a more fully developed multi-infarct dementia.

Motor/Arithmetic

The Motor/Arithmetic code occurs in individuals who have primarily subcortical lesions and who exhibit motor and attentional problems. It is also seen in many individuals with preexisting arithmetic disorders, which occur in up to 30% of normal controls on the LNNB. In cases in which an arithmetic difficulty is premorbid, it is best to ignore this scale and look for the two-point code without Arithmetic included. This discrimination usually provides a more accurate picture of the impact of a current lesion, although the premorbid Arithmetic elevation may reflect a learning disability and early brain injury in some cases.

Motor/Memory

The Motor/Memory combination nearly always occurs in cases of subcortical injuries. This deficit is common after mild to moderate head injuries. The clients have generally mild but pervasive motor problems and difficulty retaining information, especially with interference. They perform better with simple memorization tasks. They generally have little insight into their condition or the impact of their memory problems. Emotional lability and irritability are also common.

Motor/Intermediate Memory

This two-point code has a similar interpretation as for Motor/Memory, but the condition tends to be somewhat milder than when Motor/Memory is the two-point code, although both may have serious consequences for day-to-day functioning.

Motor/Intelligence

As in the case of Motor/Reading, the Motor/Intelligence code type rarely occurs. It may represent preexisting problems or reflect a multi-infarct or similar process, such as multiple tumors. It is important with this and similar codes to discriminate what was preexisting, particularly if the testing is administered to assess the effects of an injury. This concern is less important when the test is used simply to determine the degree of a client's deficit. If this finding represents a new disorder, such as a multi-infarct process, it generally represents a more advanced dementing process than does the Motor/ Reading code. However, these codes are rare and few clinicians are likely to encounter them.

Rhythm/Visual

This two-point code is associated with defects in nonverbal processing. In mild elevations, this profile is associated with subcortical injuries that may effect the processing of items demanding attention or detail; whereas in more severe forms, it is usually associated with lesions in the temporal/parietal areas of the right hemisphere where such processing is interrupted by the inability to analyze novel or less overlearned material.

Rhythm/Receptive

The Rhythm/Receptive code is associated with problems in auditory processing. This code can be caused by poor hearing abilities, so peripheral hearing loss must be ruled out as a possible cause. In the absence of a peripheral hearing loss, a bilateral, central hearing loss must also be investigated. In the presence of adequate hearing, the deficit is most often associated with damage to the left temporal area but can also occur in subjects with bilateral, temporal injuries. In severe forms, this code may represent a stroke or an open head trauma, but it can also occur in a variety of degenerative processes.

Rhythm/Memory

This code is generally associated with subcortical injuries to either hemisphere depending on the analysis of the exact deficits shown on the scales. This code rarely occurs in purely cortical injuries but often follows closed-head traumas and other diffuse processes.

Tactile/Reading

This combination often occurs in subjects with left parietal injuries. These injuries may be long standing (as seen in learning disabilities) or more recent injuries that are generally along the lines of a stroke, open head injury, abscess, hemorrhage, or other condition that destroys brain tissue. These latter injuries are usually associated with other substantial problems, although this may be seen as residual many years after an event.

Visual/Receptive, Visual/Arithmetic, and Visual/ Memory

These high-point codes are often associated with right hemisphere problems, usually in the posterior areas. Such deficits can reflect an inability to do spatial processing and visualize material, although the person may function well in terms of verbal skills, depending of course on the elevation of the entire profile. It is important when considering any Arithmetic deficit that the clinician establish that the deficit is not a preexisting condition, but is the result of some type of more recent cerebral event. This issue is highlighted in that arithmetic difficulties, along with poor spelling skills (on the Writing scale), even the simple ones measured on the LNNB, are the deficits most commonly seen in otherwise normal people in the United States.

Receptive/Expressive

A high point, comprised of Receptive and Expressive, may represent a breakdown of speech processes in general. This is most often seen in victims of strokes and other disorders that destroy brain tissue, with lesser elevations reflecting residual deficits. These deficits are often associated with high profiles, because these basic skills are necessary to understand the test instructions. Such a profile may also occur in subjects with severe dementing processes.

Receptive/Intelligence

This combination, with elevations on one or more of the achievement scales, reflects a more posterior injury than the Receptive/Expressive combination. This can occur as the result of an adult onset injury or may reflect longstanding learning disabilities or mental retardation. Such profiles are usually associated with substantial disabilities that effect day-to-day life.

In summary, the previous two-point combinations provide a wide range of possible interpretations. A full consideration of the power of this technique would involve all possible two-point codes, as well as the common three- and four-point codes. A similar process may be used with the major factor scales. Refer to the test manual for a more detailed consideration of these codes.

Level III: Item Analysis.

The next level of interpretation involves the pattern of errors. Each scale can be divided into groups of items that explore a specific aspect of the overall scale area. Item analysis involves focusing on these specific item groupings to evaluate contributions to the overall scale elevations. Consequently, more specific hypotheses of the underlying deficits are generated. This information can be used to modify the more statistically based interpretations generated from the high point codes and provide precise details about the specific problems.

The item analysis is conducted scale by scale and begins with the highest (most impaired) T-score. In general, as the scale elevations decrease, the contribution of these scales to

the item analysis also decreases. In many cases, the deficits seen on the more normal scales reflect the impact of the client's major deficits. For example, a client may miss some items on the Intelligence scale, not for a lack of intelligence but due to visual or visual-spatial problems. Thus, if the client performs poorly on the Visual scale and performs better on the Intelligence scale, except in this one area, such deficits are better explained on the basis of the deficits on the Visual scale.

By analyzing the more impaired scale first, clinicians can avoid over-diagnosing such secondary deficits, which may otherwise appear to be additional problem areas. In making an analysis, the attempt is always to identify the fewest number of problems that can account for the full range of the client's errors. This distillation yields a more parsimonious description of the client and leads to more accurate diagnoses and better targeted treatment suggestions.

The analysis of any case will differ considerably depending on the exact items missed, but the general analysis follows the item subtypes listed earlier. For example, if the Receptive Language scale is the most impaired, the client's ability to discriminate phonemes is examined in the first section of the test. Half of the items require writing the letter of the phoneme; whereas the other half require repeating the sound. If the client can do either half, phonemic hearing is likely to be intact and the problem can be attributed to pronunciation, writing, or sound-letter conversions. If the client is unable to solve both types of problems, there may be confusion as to the task or an inability to discriminate phonemes. A finer analysis can be made to see whether the client can understand phonemes when presented singly, or whether problems show up only when they are presented in groups, such as two or three sounds at a time. The ability to hear them singly may reflect a basic phonemic discrimination deficit; whereas an inability to hear them only in groups may suggest a milder discrimination problem.

These scenarios can be compared with the next set of items, which require the client to follow simple commands. A client who can complete these items but not the phonemes may be unable to discriminate sounds in isolation but able to do so in context or with well-learned words. In such cases, the client is likely to have problems with single phonemes and unfamiliar words. Such clients may appear to understand more than they do in reality, because they follow the simple or common elements of communication.

However, if the client can manage phonemes but not simple commands, this deficit would suggest an inability to comprehend the meaning of sentences and words. The items may be analyzed to evaluate the complexity level at which the client fails: single concrete words, abstract words, similar sounding words, simple sentences, or complex sentences. The higher the level the person can achieve, the milder the impact of the injury and differences in the probable location of the injury. A client who cannot perform any of these items may be experiencing confusion, dementia, or a severe receptive language deficit, which is seen most often in infarcts or bleeding aneurysms or some forms of open head injury.

The last group consists of the more complex verbal-visual items. If the client shows no problem up until this point, these errors often reflect injuries in the right hemisphere or anterior areas of the brain. Such deficits may reflect difficulty understanding the relationship or spatial nature of some words, or in following the sequential learning required by such items. Such individuals appear to have intact receptive speech, but they develop misunderstandings when sentences become multipart and require retention and analysis. This limitation may be due to memory or to a direct verbal-spatial problem. Errors in these items after failure to process simple commands, however, are most likely due to the client's inability to follow speech. When phonemes are impaired, and simple items are intact, but these verbal-spatial items are impaired, the client may have a language problem that spares well-practiced or automatic language but not other forms of receptive language.

By combining this analysis with a similar analysis on each of the other scales along with the scale patterns, a reasonably detailed description of which areas affect the client can be developed and etiologic hypotheses may be formed. The accuracy of the analysis depends on attentiveness to precise item patterns and recognition of the differential emphasis of each item.

Level IV: Qualitative Data

At this point, addition of the qualitative data enables the examiner to focus on the etiology of the client's deficits. These data are more descriptive and rely heavily on the observations and recognition of the examiner. Familiarity with the range of client behavior permits more insights relevant to the neuropsychological diagnosis. Developing these skills requires experience and appropriate supervisory instruction to avoid the oversight of subtle aspects. The LNNB, through its qualitative scales, expedites this process by alerting the user to the general categories and specific types of qualitative information that have been useful in understanding neuropsychological deficits. However, observations should not be limited to these categories, because more information may explain the client's behavior and enlighten the examiner.

The interpretation of the qualitative information can occur at two levels. The first is purely descriptive. Statements such

as "The client needed frequent redirection to attend to each item," or "motor behavior was marked by severe tremors that occurred only when the client's hands were at rest," help clarify a client's performance. The rule of thumb is that any deviant or extraordinary behavior or activity that necessitated a change in the testing procedures should be recorded and presented.

The second level is more complex and requires a working knowledge of how different brain injuries affect behavior. The goal at this level requires recognition of the neurological and neuropsychological implications of the observed behavior. To reach this level successfully, the user needs a wide range of knowledge in the areas of neurophysiology, neuroanatomy, neuropathology, and recognized neuropsychological syndromes. This experience cannot be accomplished through the simple administration of the test, but rather requires study within these distinct areas. This preparation is the essence of Luria's original evaluation approach. It is arguably the most difficult to master.

Level V: Integration of Psychometric, Qualitative, Historical, and Medical Findings

Although at one time neuropsychology emphasized "blind analysis" that transpired in the absence of any client information except age, education, gender, handedness, and test scores, it has become well recognized that client history is an integral part of any neuropsychological evaluation or testing. Thus, in addition to generating the data, researchers must also become familiar with the client and the client's past. This background helps characterize the symptoms as they relate to such variables as rate of onset, age of onset, duration, severity, complicating factors, potential etiologies, and so on. In addition, issues such as non-neurological psychiatric problems, which could alter the test results, must also be examined. However, the patient history is not received without scrutiny. For example, prior head injury does not necessarily explain the patient's current complaint or neuropsychological status. There must be integration with the test data to demonstrate that the history is reliable and related to the test results. In cases that involve forensic issues, multiple methods of ascertaining the accuracy of history are advocated when possible.

The final and most complex step is the integration of these data sources. In some cases, integration may be relatively simple; for example, if the lesion is localized, the data consistent, the history simple, and the quantitative and qualitative data concur. In many other cases, such as varying levels of motivation and arousal, the impact of their injuries, secondary emotional issues, preexisting problems, ethnic and cultural variations, variable learning and educational experiences, and different premorbid strengths and weaknesses, clients will be inconsistent. Although in research the differences among lesions may appear to be straight forward, such research eliminates subjects with many of the complicating problems that are faced in real practice.

As a result, this final process is highly dependent upon knowledge, experience, and a rigorous examination of all the data for patterns and inconsistencies that focus on the client as an individual rather than as a diagnosis, such as left hemisphere injury. This procedure is primarily a clinical process for which there are no consistent or unambiguous rules, yet it represents the apex of neuropsychological training. Ultimately this analysis/assessment reflects the capability of the clinician.

CONCLUSIONS

The LNNB is a useful diagnostic tool when used to its full capability by employing the full range of diagnostic levels. The test is most useful with lower performing clients who have widespread deficits and those who have good functioning overall but focal areas of specific deficits. Although the LNNB will identify these latter clients well, their overall performance may not be classified as brain damaged using the statistical rules, because their problems may be confined to one scale or one subscale. The LNNB is also less useful with high-functioning clients who have subtle disorders that are not primarily cognitive in nature. In such cases, the LNNB will identify the client's cognitive strengths.

REFERENCES

Bach, P.J., Harowski, K., Kirby, K., Peterson, P., & Schulein, M. (1981). The interrater reliability of the Luria-Nebraska neuropsychological battery. *Clinical Neuropsychology, 3 (3),* 19–21.

Christensen, A.L. (1975). *Luria's neuropsychological investigation.* New York: Spectrum.

Golden, C.J. (1976a). Identification of brain disorders by the Stroop color and word test. *Journal of Clinical Psychology, 32,* 654–658.

Golden, C.J. (1976b).The identification of brain damage by an abbreviated form of the Halstead-Reitan neuropsychological battery. *Journal of Clinical Psychology, 32,* 821–826.

Golden, C.J., & Anderson, S.M. (1977). Short form of the speech sounds perception test. *Perceptual and Motor Skills, 45,* 485–486.

Golden, C.J., Berg, R.A., & Graber, B. (1982). Test-retest reliability of the Luria-Nebraska neuropsychological battery in stable,

chronically impaired patients. *Journal of Consulting and Clinical Psychology, 50,* 452–454.

Golden, C.J., Hammeke, T.A., & Purisch, A.D. (1978). Diagnostic validity of a standardized neuropsychological battery derived from Luria's neuropsychological tests. *Journal of Consulting and Clinical Psychology, 46,* 1258–1265.

Golden, C.J., Purisch, A., & Hammeke, T. (1985). *Manual for the Luria-Nebraska neuropsychological battery.* Los Angeles: Western Psychological Services.

Golden, C.J., Zillmer, E., & Spiers, M. (1992). *Intervention and diagnosis in clinical neuropsychology.* Springfield, IL: Charles C. Thomas.

Hammeke, T.A., Golden, C.J., & Purisch, A.D. (1978). A standardized, short, and comprehensive neuropsychological test battery based on the Luria neurosychological evaluation. *International Journal of Neuroscience, 8,* 135–141.

Kang, Y. (1992). A preliminary study for a Korean version of the Luria-Nebraska neuropsychological battery–children's revision. *Korean Journal of Child Studies, 13,* 203–216.

Lewis, G., Golden, C.J., Moses, J.A., Jr., Osmon, D.C., Purisch, A.D., & Hammeke, T.A. (1979). Localization of cerebral dysfunction with a standardized version of Luria's neuropsychological battery. *Journal of Consulting and Clinical Psychology, 47,* 1001–1019.

Luria, A.R. (1966). Human brain and psychological processes. New York: Harper & Row.

Luria, A.R. (1973). *The working brain.* New York: Basic Books.

Luria, A.R. (1980). *Higher cortical functions in man.* New York: Plenum.

Luria, A.R. (1980). *Higher cortical functions in man.* (2nd Ed.) New York: Plenum.

MacInnes, W.D., Gillen, R.W., Golden, C.J., Graber, B., Cole, J.K., Uhl, H.S., & Greenhouse, A.H. (1983). Aging and performance on the Luria-Nebraska neuropsychological battery. *International Journal of Neuroscience, 19,* 179–190.

Maruish, M.E., Sawicki, R.F., Franzen, M.D., & Golden, C.J. (1984). Alpha coefficient reliabilities for the Luria-Nebraska neuropsychological battery summary and localization scales by diagnostic category. *The International Journal of Clinical Neuropsychology, 7,* 10–12.

Marwaha-Sonali, B., & Barnes, B.L. (1991). Application of the Luria-Nebraska neuropsychological battery (form I) to the Indian population. *Indian Journal of Clinical Psychology, 18* (1), 19–23.

Mikula, J.A. (1981). The development of a short form of the standardized version of Luria's neuropsychological assessment. *Dissertation Abstracts International, 41,* (UMI 3189B).

Moses, J.A., & Golden, C.J. (1979). Cross validation of the discriminative effectiveness of the standardized Luria neuropsychological battery. *International Journal of Neuroscience, 9,* 149–155.

Osmon, D.C., Golden, C.J., Purisch, A.D., Hammeke, T.A., & Blume, H.G. (1979). The use of a standardized battery of Luria's test in the diagnosis of lateralized cerebral dysfunction. *International Journal of Neuroscience, 9,* 1–9.

Plaisted, J.R., & Golden, C.J. (1982). Test-retest reliability of the clinical, factor, and localization scales of the Luria-Nebraska Neuropsychological battery. *Journal of Consulting and Clinical Psychology, 50,* 525–529.

Purisch, A.D., Golden, C.J., & Hammeke, T.A. (1978). Discrimination of schizophrenic and brain damaged patients by a standardized version of Luria's neuropsychological tests. *Journal of Consulting and Clinical Psychology, 34,* 661–663.

Reynolds, C.R. & Fletcher-Jantzen, E. (1997). *Handbook of clinical-child psychology.* New York: Plenum.

Xun, Y., Gong, Y.X., Matthews, J.R. (1987). The Luria—Nebraska neuropsychological battery revised for China. *International Journal of Neuropsychology, 9,* 97–101.

CHAPTER 10

The Luria-Nebraska Neuropsychological Battery–Children's Revision

ROBERT A. LEARK

HISTORY AND THEORETICAL FRAMEWORK OF THE LURIA-NEBRASKA NEUROPSYCHOLOGICAL BATTERY–CHILDREN'S REVISION

During the early to middle 1970s there was a surge of interest in the development of neuropsychological test batteries that could provide for a comprehensive assessment of neuropsychological functions. This approach varied from the prevailing model in that it encouraged a multimethod approach towards understanding brain functioning as compared to a single function design (i.e., copying tasks or memory) that were constructed to localize brain function. Along with this came a holistic model of understanding brain functions, that of Aleksandr Luria (1966, 1973). The Lurian model was premised on the theory that the neuropsychological functions are the result of molecular skills and that successful functioning is dependent upon cooperation between several brain areas to create a functional behavior link (Franzen, 1985). Luria used open-ended qualitative approaches towards his understanding of patient etiology. Building upon this model, Golden and his associates developed an instrument that combined the features of the Lurian model along with psychometric theory. The Luria-Nebraska Neuropsychological Battery (LNNB) (Golden, 1982) utilizes quantitative and qualitative analysis of selected behaviors from Lurian theory, and this is where the test battery parts from the Lurian method-

ology and Luria's neuropsychological investigation (Golden, this volume).[1]

The LNNB was formulated based upon the basic assumptions of Luria's theory of brain development. Accordingly, Golden outlined five stages of development (Golden, 1981, 1991). The first four of these stages (cortical arousal; primary and secondary motor areas; and, finally, the primary, secondary, and tertiary zones) are thought to be developed before a person reaches the age of eight, with the fifth stage (tertiary frontal zones) developing during adolescence (Golden, 1981). The Lurian items selected for inclusion into the LNNB rest heavily upon this interpretation of brain development. These items were then organized into functional neuropsychological aspects: motor activity, auditory processing, visual-spatial processing, expressive and receptive language functions (including reading, writing, and arithmetic), general intellectual processing, and memory (short-term, intermediate, and long-term). Golden and colleagues then conducted standardization of the items into the LNNB. The LNNB requires the use of a subset of the stimuli cards developed by Anne-Lise Christiansen (1975).

Concurrent with the development of the LNNB, Golden began the development of a downward extension of this battery for children, the Luria-Nebraska Neuropsychological Battery–Children's Revision (LNNB-CR). In consultation with Lawrence Majovski, who had worked with Luria and was fluent in Russian, Golden began to explore which items from the original LNNB would be suitable for use with younger children. In keeping with the understanding that the tertiary frontal zones do not develop or mature until adolescence, items that measured prefrontal lobe functions or skills were eliminated from the battery. To assist with this, the LNNB was actually administered to children aged from 5 to 12 years of above-average intelligence (Wilkening, Golden, MacInnes, Plaisted, & Hermann, 1981). After further consultation with Majovski, along with item analysis from the Wilkening et al. (1981) study, items from the LNNB were extracted from that battery. Modifications of the LNNB items continued in conjunction with pilot sampling using unimpaired children until a final version for children was established. This final version was called the LNNB-CR (Golden, 1991).

The LNNB-CR consists of 149 items; however, it is important to understand that in keeping with Lurian theory, approximately 497 discrete behaviors are sampled by the instrument (Gustavson, 1984). There is a three-point scoring system for each item. The scoring system was established by transforming z-scores into scaled scores. A scale score of 0 was given to items with z-scores greater than -1; a scale score of 1 was given to items with z-scores between -1 and 2; and a scale score of 2 was given to items with z-scores below -2. Scale scores of 0 reflect normal performance; scale scores of 2 reflect performances two standard deviations or more below the mean of the normative sample; and scales scores of 1 represent equivocal performance (Golden, 1991; Gustavson, 1982; Gustavson et al., 1982)).

The 149 items are clustered into clinical scale classifications consistent with the LNNB. In addition, three Summary Scales were developed (Sawicki, Leark, Golden, and Karras, 1984). Factor analytically derived scales have also been developed (Karras et al., 1987). There are two nonstandardized optional scored scales.

LNNB-CR Scales

The early versions of the LNNB-CR used scale names. Some confusion resulted from this, as it was seen as limiting the scale to a single function. Because the scales are not homogeneous, the current protocol of the LNNB-CR has switched from scale names to scale numbers. Given that these are deemed to measure clinical functions, the scales are numbered C1, C2, and so forth. It is important to note, however, that some scales measure only one primary function (for example, Motor Functions) and others may measure multiple functions. Following are the clinical scale numbers (along with former name) and a description of each. Also, Table 10.1

TABLE 10.1   Scales of the Luria-Nebraska Neuropsychological Battery–Children's Revision

Scale		Number of Items
Clinical Scales		
C1	Motor Functions	34
C2	Rhythm	08
C3	Tactile Functions	16
C4	Visual Functions	07
C5	Receptive Speech	18
C6	Expressive Speech	21
C7	Writing	07
C8	Reading	07
C9	Arithmetic	09
C10	Memory	08
C11	Intellectual Processes	14
Optional		
O1	Spelling	07
O2	Motor Writing	05
Summary		
S1	Pathognomonic	13
S2	Left Sensorimotor	09
S3	Right Sensorimotor	09
Factor		
F1	Academic Achievement	17
F2	Integrative Functions	06
F3	Spatial-Based Movement	06
F4	Motor Speed and Accuracy	06
F5	Drawing Quality	06
F6	Drawing Speed	06
F7	Rhythm Perception and Production	04
F8	Tactile Sensations	08
F9	Receptive Language	05
F10	Expressive Language	08
F11	Word and Phrase Repetition	04

Note. From *The Luria-Nebraska Neuropsychological Battery–Children's Revision Manual* (p. 2), by C.J. Golden, 1991, Los Angeles: Western Psychological Services. Reprinted with permission.

provides a summary of scale numbers, scale measures, and number of items within each scale.

C1 (Motor Functions)

This scale is the longest of the 11 scales and begins with items that are easy to perform, even for the youngest of children. Items 1 through 3 involve simple hand movements; items 4 through 7 involve kinesthetic movement; 8 through 14 optic-spatial movement; 15 through 18 represent Luria's idea of dynamic organization; 19 and 20 are oral-motor skills; items 21 through 32 are drawing items (quality and speed); and items 33 and 34 involve verbal control of simple motor behaviors (Golden, 1991). The scale primarily measures fine motor speed, coordination, imitation of movement, and visual-spatial construction (Gustavson et al., 1982). Some of these scale items require activity from one side of the body, others require coordinated activity (Franzen, 1985).

C2 (Rhythm)

The C2 scale requires the use of a standardized cassette audiotape and tape player. The scale primarily measures the child's ability to perform simple tonal discrimination, to maintain melodic pattern in singing, to count tones, and to reproduce simple rhythmic patterns (Gustavson et al., 1982; Golden, 1991).

C3 (Tactile)

The C3 items were selected to measure finger and arm localization, two-point discrimination, discrimination by pressure and pain (pinprick), movement detection, shape discrimination, and stereognostic skills (Gustavson et al., 1982). It is essential to highlight that this scale is designed to measure perceptual ability, not sensory ability (Golden, 1991).

C4 (Visual)

The C4 scale was constructed to measure visual skills independent of motor movements. Thus, the scale measures such tasks as simple visual recognition from real or actual objects and from pictures, spatial relationships (simple and overlapping), and perception of visual dimension (three-dimensional objects represented in two-dimensions) (Gustavson et al., 1982; Golden, 1991).

C5 (Receptive Speech)

The primary purpose of the C5 scale is to measure a child's understanding of spoken speech. Children with motor skill deficits are not penalized for inability to express themselves. These items cover such neuropsychological functions as the ability to decipher phonemes, follow simple commands, and understand simple and complex grammatical structures (Gustavson et al., 1982; Golden, 1991).

C6 (Expressive Speech)

On the C6 scale, the items measure the child's ability to correctly repeat phonemes, words, phrases, and sentences. These items are presented orally and visually. Automatized speech and spontaneous speech are both measured (Gustavson et al., 1982; Golden, 1991).

C7 (Writing)

These items assess the child's ability to analyze letter sequences, and to spell, copy, and write from dictation (Gustavson et al., 1982; Golden, 1991).

C8 (Reading)

The C8 scale items assess the child's ability to recognize letters, words, phrases, and read sentences and paragraphs (Gustavson et al., 1982; Golden, 1991).

C9 (Arithmetic)

Items for the C9 scale begin with simple number recognition and continue on to simple addition, subtraction, division, and multiplication. Additionally, the child must perform number comparisons (Gustavson et al., 1982; Golden, 1991).

C10 (Memory)

The items on the C10 scale tap into the child's ability to perform verbal and nonverbal memory tasks presented with or without interference, over short, intermediate, and long terms.

C11 (Intellectual Processes)

The C11 utilizes Lurian items that assess the integrity of general intellectual functioning, including complex reasoning and problem-solving skills (Golden, 1991).

S1 (Pathognomonic)

The intended purpose of the S1 scale was to discriminate globally between impaired and unimpaired performance (Sawicki et al., 1984). This scale was empirically derived by performing student t-tests on each of the 149 items with the analysis ranked by magnitude of the resulting t value. The top 40 items were submitted to a discriminant function analysis, which identified 18 items that separated impaired from unimpaired subjects. A final weighted linear combination of the items was summed until the criterion sum produced the maximized correct classification. This final analysis yielded 13 items that maximally discriminated brain-impaired subjects from subjects without brain impairment (Sawicki et al., 1984). The S1 scale is reported to have contributed the most variance to the discriminant function analysis identifying brain impaired from children without brain impairment (Golden, 1991).

S2 (Left Sensorimotor Scale)

The items for the S2 scale (and the corresponding Right Sensorimotor scale) were selected from those items on the C1 (Motor) and C3 (Tactile) scale that are laterally performed by the right hand (Sawicki et al., 1984).

S3 (Right Sensorimotor Scale)

The S3 items correspond to the S2 scale, only they are items performed by the child's left hand.

LNNB-CR Factor Scale

To confirm that the LNNB-CR is associated with Lurian theory, factor analysis was performed. Karras et al. (1987) submitted the 149 items and each of the 11 clinical scales into a series of principal components analyses using 719 subjects. The subjects consisted of unimpaired (240), brain impaired (253), learning disabled (39), leukemic (5), suspected brain impaired (32), and psychiatric (150) pooled together. Using both (screen test methods and summed unit weighting) for factor limitation and summed unit weighting, factor scores were created over 17 factors. Internal consistency coefficients were determined for each factor, and then each factor was correlated to each other factor. A final factor solution consisting of 11 different factors was derived (Karras et al., 1987; Golden, 1991).

Factor one (F1) is the factor containing the most items. It consists primarily of measures from the three achievement scales (C7, C8, and C9) and from C6. The factor items are those related to general academic achievement (Golden, 1991). Factor two (F2) is primarily spatial organization (left-right discrimination). Factor three (F3) is spatially based movement; whereas Factor four (F4) is motor speed. Factor five (F5) evaluates drawing quality, with Factor six (F6) evaluating drawing time. Factor seven (F7) assesses rhythm and pitch, but these items also require sustained attention. Factor eight (F8) is somatosensory functioning. Speech functions are contained in Factor nine (F9), receptive speech, and Factor 10 (F10), expressive speech. The last factor (F11) reflects abstractive reasoning (Karras et al., 1987, Golden, 1991).

Test Interpretation

The raw scores are summed over each scale (clinical, summary, and factor), and then each scale is converted to a standardized T-score (mean of 50, standard deviation of 10). For comparative purposes, higher scores reflect more impairment; lower scores reflect less impairment. To interpret an individual child's performance, a critical level formula is used. The critical level was derived by a stepwise regression equation with age and education used to predict average or baseline scores (Gustavson et al., 1984). Most studies (Gustavson et al., 1982, 1984; Plaisted, Gustavson, Wilkening, & Golden, 1983; Geary & Gilger, 1984; Gilger & Geary, 1985) have reported the use of a general rule of at least three scales elevated above the critical level as a means of determining placement into the brain-impaired category. Use of this critical level formula in combination with the three-scale rule has allowed for about 90% accuracy of hit-rate classifications (Golden, 1991).

Test interpretation follows the qualitative/quantitative approach recommended by the test author. A pattern analysis of the scales and items is preferred (Golden, 1991), and analysis based on a single scale elevation is ill-advised. As is true for neuropsychological tests in general, the classification of a child's test performance as brain-impaired is based upon probability theory. The LNNB-CR itself should not be used as the sole determination of brain functioning. The test, like the related LNNB, is a psychometrically sound version of an extended mental status examination. Thus, it represents a screening of functioning. The test author does stress that test performance can be affected by a variety of sources unrelated to the testing process (i.e., depression, anxiety, family problems, etc.). As with other neuropsychological tests, the interpretation of a child's performance on the LNNB-CR requires an understanding of brain development and brain processing, coupled with knowledge of child development. It is also imperative that the test user have an understanding of Lurian theory of brain development and brain functioning. Luria's approach rests heavily upon qualitative hypothesis testing of individual performance during the testing process. This requires that the test user have sufficient education, training, and experience prior to the onset of testing.

The interpretation strategies for LNNB-CR have been the subject of criticism. Hynd (1988) argues that there is little empirical support for Golden's assertion that the frontal lobes do not mature or develop until adolescence. He also disagrees with Golden's view that children are "merely less skilled adults" (Hynd, 1988, p. 74). Although holding that the LNNB-CR shows ability to discriminate between normal and brain-impaired groups of children, Hynd further cautions against reliance on the quantitative aspects of test interpretation. Hynd (1988) advises an item and qualitative error analysis approach that he asserts the LNNB-CR can provide. Hynd further argues that the support for the factor scales

TABLE 10.2   Alpha Coefficients for the Clinical and Summary Scales for Five Diagnostic Groups

Scale	Number of Items	Nonimpaired ($n = 240$)	Brain Damaged ($n = 253$)	Suspected Brain Damage ($n = 39$)	Learning Disabled ($n = 32$)	Psychiatric ($n = 150$)	Total ($n = 719$)
Clinical							
C1	34	.73	.92	.89	.72	.77	.88
C2	8	.54	.82	.67	.70	.69	.78
C3	16	.54	.90	.84	.60	.68	.87
C4	7	.19	.73	.72	−.13	.28	.67
C5	18	.43	.85	.56	.59	.64	.82
C6	21	.45	.90	.82	.67	.75	.86
C7	7	.44	.81	.67	.69	.64	.78
C8	7	.60	.86	.82	.78	.80	.83
C9	9	.64	.91	.84	.88	.83	.90
C10	8	.67	.79	.72	.56	.61	.75
C11	14	.45	.87	.79	.67	.62	.82
Summary							
S1	13	.58	.83	.83	.73	.78	.85
S2	9	.27	.85	.81	.33	.42	.79
S3	9	.32	.81	.74	.33	.37	.77

Note. From *The Luria-Nebraska Neuropsychological Battery–Children's Revision Manual* (p. 181), by C.J. Golden, 1991, Los Angeles: Western Psychological Services. Reprinted with permission.

(Karras et al., 1987) is weak, as 75 of the 149 test items actually load independently on the 11 factors.

PSYCHOMETRIC CHARACTERISTICS

Like the LNNB, this test has prompted some controversy. Some of this controversy may be due to theoretical aspects of the test development, namely, the quantification of a revered qualitative approach. Spiers (1981, 1982) provided much of the criticism of the LNNB by arguing that the battery violates the very nature of Luria's model. Luria relied heavily upon experiential interpretation of a patient's performance. The Lurian model places reliance upon the examiner's training and is thus qualitative in nature. Spiers argued that the LNNB approach rested too heavily upon a standardized, quantitative approach. This quantitative approach relies upon average scores. Spiers argued that this reliance upon average scores limited the understanding of individual differences (i.e., differences within the individual, a nomothetic approach). However, much of the criticism did not offer much in the way of empirical evidence for the criticism. This section of the chapter reviews the validity and reliability components of the test. Those authors providing empirical support in their criticism are included, the others are not.

Reliability

There are no temporal reliability studies reported in the literature or the manual. The reliability data that is available investigates the test's internal consistency. Internal consistency (Rothermel, Karras, & Golden, 1985) was assessed through the use of five clinical samples of varying sample size. These sample groups consisted of 240 nonimpaired, 253 brain-impaired, 32 learning disabled, 150 psychiatric, and 39 children suspected of having brain impairment. The authors performed correlation analyses over each sample (see Table 10.2) for each clinical scale and the three summary scales (Sawicki et al., 1984). Of interest is that the alpha reliability coefficients for the nonimpaired subjects were reported as the lowest of the samples. These ranged from a low of .19 (C4) to high of .73 (C1), an average coefficient of 0.49. The authors argue, as does Golden (1991), that the low coefficients do not represent a real loss of consistency. The argument that is offered is that for the normal subjects there is little item score variance, making the prediction process stable. Coefficients for the brain-impaired sample were noted as more robust, ranging from .73 (C4) to .92 (C1) for an average coefficient value of 0.85. There was marked variability of internal consistency for the learning-disabled subjects; the coefficient values ranged from a −0.13 (C4) to 0.88 (C9). Of interest is that the C4 scale had the lowest coefficient value over each of the five samples.

Hyman (1984) used a different approach to evaluating internal consistency for the battery. Rather than assessing the coefficients over each scale, all 149 items were pooled into one analysis using two different groups of equal size. The two groups, learning disabled and non-learning disabled, were each comprised of 30 children aged between 10 and 11 years. An alpha coefficient value of 0.92 was reported for combined sample. The nondisabled group value was 0.43; whereas the learning-disabled group value was reported at 0.83. Hyman suggests that the strikingly low alpha value for the nondisabled group was most likely due to a lowered ceiling effect.

The internal consistency of the factor scales was also explored, as reported by Karras et al. (1987), using the pooled sample of 719 subjects reported earlier. The alpha coefficient values ranged from 0.70 to 0.94. Not surprisingly, the measure of academic achievement was noted as having the highest ranking of consistency.

Given that neuropsychological tests are often repeatedly given to clinical patients, the absence of temporal stability estimates for the instrument is a concern. The test manual does provide standard error of measurement (S_{em}) values that the author suggests can be used to compare changes over time (Golden, 1991). However, these values are not anchored to temporal stability coefficients.

Validity

A primary purpose in creating the LNNB-CR was to develop an instrument that would assist neuropsychologists in the process of evaluating whether a child might be exhibiting behaviors consistent with brain impairment. In line with this, the initial studies of the LNNB-CR examined the test's ability to predict placement into brain-impaired groupings accurately. This approach brought some criticism (Hynd, 1988) that challenged the construct validity of the test.

Construct Validity

One procedure used to provide evidence that a test is measuring what it purports to measure is construct validity. Several methods are used to determine the construct validity of a test. These include internal consistency, contrasted groups (i.e., brain impaired and non-brain impaired), convergence, and factor analysis. Internal consistency was reported upon in the earlier section on reliability.

Gustavson et al. (1984) utilized a contrasting group method to provide support of the test's ability to measure impaired brain functioning. Using normative scale scoring developed within the study, these authors formulated a critical level as used in the LNNB. The critical level represented the derived score for which 90% of the normal controls obtained scores less than that particular score. The initial analysis revealed significant differences in group mean score of the brain-impaired group, with means elevated above one standard de-

viation. The second analysis yielded classification rates of 93% in normal subjects and 78% in the brain-impaired group.

Geary et al. (1984) reported the test to be sensitive to learning disability deficits not reflected in normal IQ testing. Their study examined LNNB-CR scale mean score differences between academically normal (n = 17) and reading disabled children (n = 17). The analysis yielded significant mean scores differences for expressive language (C6), writing (C7), reading (C8), and rhythm (C2) scales. Given that the subjects manifested only specific reading deficits, the authors concluded that those three language-based scales were sensitive to language-based dysfunction not measured by intellectual tests.

To further assess the test's sensitivity to language-based neuropsychological functioning, Gilger et al. (1985) examined differences between three distinct groupings. One group consisted of children with performance intelligence greater than 12 points of their verbal intelligence. A second group consisted of age-similar children whose performance intellectual scores were 12 points less than their verbal scores; the third group was comprised of children who did not have differences between verbal and performance functioning. Univariate ANOVA tests revealed significant differences among the groups on receptive speech (C5) and expressive language (C6) scales. The subjects with lower verbal functioning scores (i.e., performance greater than verbal) scored significantly poorer on the test than did the other two groups. The authors concluded that the LNNB-CR was sensitive to verbal and nonverbal deficits.

Pfeiffer, Naglieri, and Tingstrom (1987) used a sample of 32 learning-disabled children to cross-examine the findings reported by Gustavson et al. (1984) and Geary et al. (1984). Their study found that 84% of the subjects were correctly classified as impaired, confirming that the test is sensitive to neurological impairment.

Convergent validity for the test has also been reported. Synder, Leark, Golden, Grove, and Allison (1983) examined the relationship between the LNNB-CR and the Kaufman Assessment Battery for Children (KABC). The KABC was also formulated upon Lurian theory. A linear regression using the LNNB-CR as the predictor and KABC as criteria found robust correlations among the scale scores (Table 10.3). The findings support the commonalities, yet distinct differences, between the two tests.

Snow, Hartlage, Hynd, and Grant (1983) noted the lack of significant correlations between the LNNB-CR and the Minnesota Percepto-Diagnostic Test (MPD) in a learning-disabled sample of children. The authors state that although the LNNB-CR may be able to discriminate between learning disabled and non-learning disabled subjects, the test does not

TABLE 10.3   Multiple Correlations Between Subtest Standard Scores on the Luria-Nebraska Neuropsychological Battery–Children's Revision (Predictors) and the KABC Global Scale Standard Scores (Criteria)

KABC Scales	Luria-Nebraska Predictor	r
Sequential Processing	Intelligence	.58
	Rhythm	.66
	Receptive Speech	.68
	Motor	.69
	Tactile	.71
Simultaneous Processing	Intelligence	.52
	Visual	.64
	Motor	.69
Mental Processing Composite	Intelligence	.64
	Motor	.70
	Visual	.73
Achievement	Arithmetic	.58
	Receptive Speech	.62
	Writing	.66
	Memory	.68
Nonverbal	Intelligence	.50
	Visual	.61
	Motor	.67

Note. From "Correlations of the KABC, WISC-R and the Luria-Nebraska Neuropsychological Battery–Children's Revision for Exceptional Children," by T.J. Synder, R.A. Leark, C.J. Golden, T. Grove and R. Allison, 1983. Paper presented at the annual meeting of the National Association of School Psychologists, Detroit, MI, March 1983. Used with permission.

have sufficient strength in subjects with visual perceptual deficits.

To investigate the receptive language components of the instrument, Quattrocchi and Golden (1983) correlated the LNNB-CR and Peabody Picture Vocabulary Test (PPVT) results obtained from 59 normal children. They reported significant correlations between the PPVT and the receptive speech (C5) and intellectual performance (C11) items.

Tramontana, Sherrets, and Wolf (1983) studied the relationship between the LNNB-CR and the Halstead Reitan Neuropsychological Battery for Older Children (HRNB). At the time of this study, the HRNB was the established standard instrument for the evaluation of brain functions in children. The authors reported that results of the two batteries correlated from 0.44 to 0.92. The HRNB scores that were the most sensitive to detecting brain-impaired children from non-brain impaired children were ranked higher than those HRNB scores with less sensitivity. Furthermore, the authors reported a 0.86 classification agreement between the two instruments.

Sweet, Carr, Rossini, and Kaspar (1986) studied the relationship between the LNNB-CR and the Wechsler Intelligence Scale for Children–Revised (WISC-R) among three diagnostic groups (psychiatric, normal, and brain damaged). Using Verbal Comprehension (VC), Perceptual Organization

(PO), and Freedom From Distractibility (FD) indices from the WISC-R, they found significant correlations between the LNNB-CR and the indices within only the brain-damaged group. Sweet et al. (1986) asserted that the results support that the two tests are measuring distinct brain functions that converge when used with a brain-damaged sample. When the measurements are used with normal (i.e., non-brain damaged) subjects, they become divergent.

Discriminant evidence of the validity of the test are evident in a study of the relationship between the LNNB-CR and attention deficit disorders. Schaughency et al. (1989) administered the test to 54 children with attention-based disorders. Using a multimethod model, the authors report that they failed to find significant differences between normal controls and children with attentional disorders. This finding confirms that reported by Karras et al. (1987) who failed to find any factor cluster measuring components of attention. As symptoms found in attention-disordered subjects are akin to frontal lobe dysfunction, their findings add credence to Golden's assertion that frontal lobe functioning is not prominent until adolescence.

Factor confirmation of Lurian test constructs has been reported on by Karras et al. (1987). Their findings support the complexity of the test and the heterogeneity of the scales.

Concurrent Validity

Carr, Sweet, and Rossini (1986) used three groupings of children (neurological, psychiatric, and normal) to study the diagnostic validity of the test. Their results yielded large and significant differences between the performances of the three groups, with the neurologically impaired subjects showing the poorest performance. A discriminant analysis found that the LNNB-CR correctly classified 78% of the brain impaired and 84% of the psychiatric, with an overall 81% classification rate.

The test's ability to discriminate adequately between children with different patterns of learning disability was studied by Morgan, and Brown (1988). They failed to find significant LNNB-CR score differences between three distinct groups of learning-disabled children (auditory-linguistic, visual-spatial, and mixed). Although other studies (Geary et al., 1984; Gilger et al., 1985) have reported differences using learning-disabled children, it is important to note that each of those studies compared normal controls to learning-disabled children. These authors did not find differences among learning-disabled subject groupings. As a result, the authors called for caution when using the test to discern differences between learning-disabled subjects.

Case studies can also be used to confirm the test's ability to detect brain dysfunction. McKay et al. (1985) reported on their findings of a neuropsychological evaluation of an 11-year-old child with a craniopharyngioma. The neurosurgical procedures resulted in right frontal cortical damage. Pre- and post-LNNB–CR test scores confirmed the test's sensitivity to the existence of cognitive deficits. McKay et al. (1984) highlighted that the qualitative interpretation of item performance provided distinct information from the quantitative analysis. The item behavior analysis confirmed Luria's information processing approach. However, the findings conflict with those of Golden (1991) and Schaughency et al. (1989).

CROSS-CULTURAL CONSIDERATIONS

It is essential to note that the entire normative sample is described as White (Golden, 1991). No additional distinctively different ethnic norms are reported in the test manual or in the literature. Although it is also important to note that there are no known ethnic differences in the development of the brain, the influences of culture cannot be overlooked. This is especially true considering that the test is loaded heavily with academic achievement and verbal language tasks. This is a major shortcoming of this instrument. Given that warning, the use of the test with other populations merits caution.

Even though there are no distinct norm references for other ethnic backgrounds reported for the test, there are foreign language translations of the LNNB-CR available: a German translation (Neumaeker & Bzufka, 1989) and an Icelandic translation (Arnkelsson, 1993). The German translation is also known as the Berlin Luria-Neuropsychological Procedures (BLNP). Derivation of separate norms for these tests has not been reported.

ACCOMMODATIONS FOR PERSONS WITH DISABILITIES

The test author notes that administration of test items can and should be flexible, and use of the test with all children is not recommended. Children with language disorders will be particularly difficult because the test is loaded heavily with language-based items. Because the test is often used in the assessment of children with brain dysfunction, premorbid learning deficits do need to be taken into consideration, given the conflicting findings reported (Geary et al., 1984; Gilger et al., 1985; Morgan et al., 1988). The test has been found to be sensitive to brain dysfunction, and the test user needs to ascertain whether handicapping situations may be due to peripheral nervous system disorders.

LEGAL AND ETHICAL CONSIDERATION

No known legal cases were noted during a legal case review conducted at the time this chapter was written. It is also important to note that federal and state law determinations for learning disabilities do not include the LNNB-CR. Furthermore, the use of the LNNB-CR as the sole determinant of neuropsychological dysfunction is not recommended (Golden, 1991). Use of the test does require advanced training in neuropsychology and extensive training in LNNB-CR test administration. Golden (1991) implores users to maintain psychological and neuropsychological test standards. Test use needs to be consistent with user's scope of education, training, and experience.

COMPUTERIZATION

A computerized scoring service is available through the test publisher, Western Psychological Services (WPS), or with the use of a scoring program. The mail-in service requires the use of a special scannable answer sheet. The microcomputer-based scoring requires the purchase of a scoring program separate from the test materials kit. Both are available by contacting WPS. Neither of the computer-based services can be used for test administration. Use of the computerized scoring does not adequately address the qualitative analysis of the subject's performance.

CURRENT RESEARCH STATUS

The majority of the literature for this test was reported over a decade or two ago. In a book reflecting the twentieth anniversary of the LNNB, the most current peer review citation found in Berg's chapter on the LNNB-CR (1999) was from 1991. Golden (1997) noted changes in the generation of T-scores for the current protocol. The initial development generated distinct T-score conversions for each age (from 8 through age 12) based on age groupings. This was changed so that the T-scores are now generated based on the entire sample of 125 subjects.

One reason for this lack of scientific literature may be due to the current assessment approach that discourages using a sole test battery during the neuropsychological evaluation. Another reason may be due to the decision to develop a single test to be used over the developmental span. WPS, in conjunction with Golden, began development of the Luria-Nebraska Neuropsychological Battery-III (LNNB-III). The LNNB-III is being designed to allow for the use of one instrument covering ages seven through adulthood. The items for LNNB-III are derived from the LNNB and the LNNB-CR in addition to several additional items that measure behaviors not addressed in the current batteries (for example, covering intermediate memory). This version is presently in the standardization sample collection phase. Golden and his colleagues (Teichner, Golden, Bradley, & Crum, 1999; Teichner, Golden, Crum, Azrin, Donohue, & Van Hasselt, 2000) have begun to report test development findings. However, much of that literature reports only findings from adolescent and adult populations.

Although it may be that the test publisher and author have been investing toward standardization of a newer instrument, the lack of current research findings presents a major concern. The development of norms that are representative of the various ethnic populations within the United States must also be addressed.

NOTE

1. In G. Goldstein and S.R. Beers (Eds.), *The comprehensive handbook of psychological assessment, Volume I: Intellectual and neuropsychological assessment.* 2004. New York: Wiley.

REFERENCES

Arnkelsson, G.B. (1993). Reading-retarded Icelandic children: The discriminant validity of psychological tests. *Scandinavian Journal of Educational Research, 37,* 163–174.

Berg, R.A. (1999). The Luria-Nebraska neuropsychological battery-children's revision. In C.J. Golden, W.L. Warren & P. Espe-Pfeiffer (Eds.), *LNNB handbook 20th anniversary. A guide to clinical interpretation and use in special settings.* Los Angeles: Western Psychological Services.

Berg, R.A., Bolter, J.F., Ch'ien, L.T., Williams, S.J., Lancaster, W., & Cummins, J. (1984). Comparative diagnostic accuracy of the Halstead-Reitan and Luria-Nebraska neuropsychological adult and children's batteries. *The International Journal of Clinical Neuropsychology, 6*(3), 200–204.

Carr, M.A., Sweet, J.J., & Rossini, E. (1986). Diagnostic validity of the Luria-Nebraska neuropsychological battery-children's revision. *Journal of Consulting and Clinical Psychology, 54,* 354–358.

Christiansen, A.L. (1975). *Luria's neuropsychological investigation.* New York: Spectrum.

Franzen, M.D. (1985). Review of the Luria-Nebraska neuropsychological battery. In D.J. Deyser & R.C. Sweetlands (Eds.), *Test critiques,* Vol. III (pp. 402–414). Kansas City: Test Corporation of America.

Geary, D.C., & Gilger, J.W. (1984). The Luria-Nebraska neuropsychological battery-children's revision: Comparison of learning disabled and normal children matched on full scale IQ. *Perceptual and Motor Skills, 58,* 115–118.

Gilger, J.W., & Geary, D.C. (1985). Performance on the Luria-Nebraska neuropsychological test battery-children's revision: A comparison of children with and without significant WISC-R VIQ-PIQ discrepancies. *Journal of Clinical Psychology, 41,* 806–811.

Golden, C.J. (1981b). The Luria-Nebraska children's battery: Theory and formulation. In G.W. Hynd & J.E. Obrzut (Eds.), *Neuropsychological assessment and the school-aged child: Issues and procedures* (pp. 277–302). New York: Grune & Stratton.

Golden, C.J. (1991). *Luria-Nebraska neuropsychological battery: Children's revision manual.* Los Angeles: Western Psychological Services.

Golden, C.J. (1997). *The Luria-Nebraska neuropsychological battery-children's revision.* In C.R. Reynolds & E. Fletcher-Janzen (Eds.), *Handbook of clinical child neuropsychology* (2nd ed.) (pp. 237–251). New York: Plenum Press.

Golden, C.J., Purisch, A.D., & Hammeke, T.A. (1982). *The Luria Nebraska neuropsychological battery.* Los Angeles: Western Psychological Services.

Gustavson, J.L. (1984). The Luria-Nebraska Neuropsychological battery-children's revision: Use in school assessment. *Texas Psychologist, 36*(4), 3–7.

Gustavson, J.L., Golden, C.J., Leark, R.A., Wilkening, G.N., Hermann, B.P., & Plaisted, J.R. (1982). *The Luria-Nebraska Neuropsychological battery-children's revision: Current research findings.* Paper presented at the meeting of the American Psychological Association, Washington, D.C.

Gustavson, J.L, Golden, C.J., Wilkening, G.N., Hermann, B.P., Plaisted, J.R., MacInnes, W.D., & Leark, R.A. (1984). The Luria-Nebraska Neuropsychological battery-children's revision: Validation with brain-damaged and normal children. *Journal of Psychoeducational Assessment, 2,* 199–208.

Hyman, L.M. (1984). An investigation of the neuropsychological characteristics of learning disabled children as measured by the Luria-Nebraska (Children). *Dissertation Abstracts International, 44*(11), 7110A.

Hynd, G.W. (1988). *Neuropsychological assessment in clinical child psychology.* Beverly Hills, CA: Sage Publications.

Karras, D., Newlin, D.B., Franzen, M.D., Golden, C.J., Wilkening, G.N., Rothermel, R.D., & Tramontana, M.G. (1987). Development of factor scales for the Luria-Nebraska neuropsychological battery-children's revision. *Journal of Clinical Child Psychology, 16*(1), 19–28.

Luria, A.R. (1966). *The working brain.* New York: Basic Books.

Luria, A.R. (1973). *Higher cortical functions in man* (2nd Ed.). New York: Basic Books.

McKay, S.E., Stelling, M.W., Baumann, R.J., Carr, W.A., Jr., Walsh, J.W., & Gilmore, R.L. (1985). Assessment of frontal lobe dysfunction using the Luria-Nebraska neuropsychological battery–children's revision: A case study. *The International Journal of Clinical Neuropsychology, 7,* 107–111.

Morgan, S.B., & Brown, T.L. (1988). Luria-Nebraska neuropsychological battery-children's revision: Concurrent validity with three learning disability subtypes. *Journal of Consulting and Clinical Psychology, 56*(3), 463–466.

Neumaeker, K.J. & Bzufka, M.W. (1989). An evaluation of neuropsychological investigation methods for the mentally handicapped. *European Journal of Child and Adolescent Psychiatry: Acta Paedopsychiatrica, 52,* 307–316.

Pfeiffer, S.I., Naglieri, J.A., & Tingstrom, D.H. (1987). Comparison of the Luria-Nebraska neuropsychological battery-children's revision and the WISC-R with learning disabled children. *Perceptual and Motor Skills, 65,* 911–916.

Plaisted, J.R., Gustavson, J.L., Wilkening, G.N., & Golden, C.J. (1983). The Luria-Nebraska neuropsychological battery-children's revision: Theory and current research findings. *Journal of Clinical Child Psychology, 7,* 13–21.

Quattrocchi, M.M., & Golden, C.J. (1983b). Peabody picture vocabulary test-revised and Luria-Nebraska neuropsychological battery for children: Intercorrelations for normal youngsters. *Perceptual and Motor Skills, 56,* 632–634.

Rothermel, R.D., Jr., Karras, D., & Golden, C.J. (1985, April). *Reliability of the Luria-Nebraska neuropsychological battery-children's revision scales.* Paper presented at the meeting of the Southwestern Psychological Association, Austin, TX.

Sawicki, R.F., Leark, R., Golden, C.J., & Karras, D. (1984). The development of the pathognomonic, left sensorimotor, and right sensorimotor scales for the Luria-Nebraska neuropsychological battery-children's revision. *Journal of Clinical Child Psychology, 13*(2), 165–169.

Schaughency, E.A., Lahey, B.B., Hynd, G.W., Stone, P.A., Piacentini, J.C., & Frick, P.J. (1989). Neuropsychological test performance and the attention deficit disorders: Clinical utility of the Luria-Nebraska neuropsychological battery-children's revision. *Journal of Consulting and Clinical Psychology, 57*(1), 112–116.

Snow, J.H., Hartlage, L.C., Hynd, G.W., & Grant, D.H. (1983). The relationship between the Luria-Nebraska neuropsychological battery-children's revision and the Minnesota percepto-diagnostic test with learning disabled students. *Psychology in the Schools, 20,* 415–419.

Snow, J.H., & Hynd, G.W. (1985). A multivariate investigation of the Luria-Nebraska neuropsychological battery-children's revision with learning disabled children. *Journal of Psychoeducational Assessment, 3,* 101–109.

Snow, J.H., Hynd, G.W., & Hartlage, L.C. (1984). Differences between mildly and more severely learning-disabled children on the Luria-Nebraska neuropsychological battery-children's revision. *Journal of Psychoeducational Assessment, 2,* 23–28.

Snyder, T.J., Leark, R.A., Golden, C.J., Grove, T., & Allison, R. (1983). *Correlation of the K-ABC, WISC-R, and Luria-Nebraska children's battery for exceptional children.* Paper presented at the meeting of the National Academy Association of School Psychologists, Detroit, MI.

Spiers, P.A. (1981). Have they come to praise Luria or bury him? The Luria-Nebraska neuropsychological battery controversy. *Journal of Consulting and Clinical Psychology, 49,* 331–341.

Spiers, P.A. (1982). The Luria-Nebraska neuropsychological battery revisited: A theory in practice or just practicing? *Journal of Consulting and Clinical Psychology, 50,* 301–306.

Sweet, J.J., Carr, M.A., Rossini, E., & Kaspar, C. (1986). Relationship between the Luria-Nebraska neuropsychological battery-children's revision and the WISC-R: Further examination using Kaufman's factors. *The International Journal of Clinical Neuropsychology, 8,* 177–180.

Teichner, G., Golden, C.J., Bradley, J.D., & Crum, T. (1999). Internal consistency and discriminant validity of the Luria-Nebraska neuropsychological battery-III. *International Journal of Neuroscience, 98,* 141–152.

Teichner, G., Golden, C.J., Crum, T., Azrin, N.H., Donohue, B., & Van Hasselt, V.B. (2000). Identification of neuropsychological subtypes in a sample of delinquent adolescents. *Journal of Psychiatric Research, 32,* 129–132.

Tramontana, M.G., Klee, S.H., & Boyd, T.A. (1984). WISC-R interrelationships with the Halstead-Reitan and Children's Luria neuropsychological batteries. *The International Journal of Clinical Neuropsychology, 6,* 1–8.

Tramontana, M.G., Sherrets, S.D., & Wolf, B.A. (1983). Comparability of the Luria-Nebraska and Halstead-Reitan neuropsychological batteries for older children. *Clinical Neuropsychology, 4,* 186–190.

Wilkening, G.N., Golden, C.J., MacInnes, W.D., Plaisted, J.R., & Hermann, B. (1981). *The Luria-Nebraska neuropsychological battery-children's revision: A preliminary report.* Paper presented at the meeting of the American Psychological Association, Los Angeles.

CHAPTER 11

NEPSY—A Tool for Comprehensive Assessment of Neurocognitive Disorders in Children

MARIT KORKMAN

INTRODUCTION

Neurocognitive disorders and learning disabilities in children are often characterized by overlapping and multiple difficulties. For instance, many children with specific verbal learning disorders also exhibit attention deficits (Dykman & Ackerman, 1991; Gilger, Pennington & DeFries, 1992; Schuerholz et al. 1995; Stanford & Hynd, 1994), motor coordination problems (Denckla, 1985; Purvis & Tannock, 2000), and/or visuomotor problems evident in copying figures (Fletcher-Flinn, Elmes, & Strugnell, 1997; Gupta & Garg, 1996; Korkman & Pesonen, 1994, Masutto & Bravar, 1994). Similarly, children with neurological conditions and children who have been exposed to neurodevelopmental risks tend to have diffuse impairments. This is the case, for example, with children born with low birth weights (Herrgård, Luoma, Tuppurainen, Karjalainen, & Martikainen, 1993; Korkman, Liikanen, & Fellman, 1996; Robertson & Finer, 1993) and children with prenatal exposure to alcohol (Conry, 1990; Carmichael Olson, Sampson, Barr, Streissguth, & Bookstein, 1992; Don & Rourke, 1995; Korkman, Autti-Rämö, Koivulehto, & Granström, 1998).

For the purpose of outlining an individual intervention program, it is important to identify all neurocognitive im-

pairments that interfere with the child's learning and adaptation. Equally important is to identify the strengths on which to build new learning and compensatory strategies as well as self-esteem. Thus, one major aim of a neuropsychological assessment is to perform a comprehensive evaluation of the child's neurocognitive development. This evaluation should highlight the weaknesses and the strengths of the child. An assessment including only a test of intelligence, a memory test, and perhaps a figure-copying task does not serve this purpose.

To enable such a comprehensive analysis, the assessment should include a wide range of specific tests that cover all important aspects of neurocognitive development and functioning. A comprehensive set of tests can be achieved by using many separate tests from different sources. However, these tests may have been standardized on different groups of children at different times—if standardized at all. Therefore, a collection of separate tests may come to reflect not only the strengths and weaknesses of the child but also differences in test norms and standardization procedures. Furthermore, tests of all important types may not be available for all ages.

The ideal instrument for assessing children's neurocognitive profiles would therefore be a systematic and comprehensive set of tests that are standardized on the same normative sample. Such an instrument would ensure that the results of the tests are comparable and that they can be presented as test profiles based on the distribution of same-age children. The first important goal for the development of the NEPSY was, therefore, to construct a comprehensive series of neuro-psychological tests and to standardize them on the same group of children.

A second important aim of a neuropsychological assessment is to analyze significant impairments in depth to provide an understanding of the nature of the child's problems. Knowing the mechanisms behind a specific impairment is necessary when planning rehabilitation and school arrangements. It is also helps to make realistic expectations of the child's performance and development. Accordingly, the second main goal for developing the NEPSY was to provide a tool for detailed analyses of the main types of neurocognitive impairments in children.

Diagnostic assessments are but one step in the treatment of children with neurocognitive impairments. Diagnostic conclusions are useless if not implemented in practice. A neuropsychological assessment serves the purposes of providing a basis for the planning of intervention. Renewed assessments with the same methods are necessary to evaluate the effects of intervention. The NEPSY was normed for a wide age range—3 to 12 years—and may therefore be used for evaluation of treatment effects. It also provides possibilities for evaluating long-term effects of neurodevelopmental risk factors or acquired brain injury. Furthermore, it permits comparisons of children of different ages. In addition, normal development may be studied—an area that has been surprisingly neglected in neuropsychological research. Thus, the benefits of covering a wide age range were also recognized in the construction of the NEPSY.

THEORETICAL FRAMEWORK

The theoretical basis of the NEPSY is the theory developed by A.R. Luria. Working with adult patients with focal brain damage, Luria was interested in the way in which different parts of the brain contributed to cognitive processes. The analyses of the effects of focal brain damage in individual patients also led to a theory of the structure of cognitive functions—the first cognitive neuropsychological theory.

The central concept in Luria's theory is that of functional systems. Luria considered cognitive processes to be dynamic, functional systems characterized by a specific aim and carried out as complex patterns of participating subprocesses. A simple action, such as opening a door, includes several different components: the aim, a visual-spatial evaluation of the distance

to the door, the motor performance that, in itself, consists of a series of muscular contractions and sensory perceptions, and finally, a verification that the action was completed. In a similar way, Luria described the structures and subcomponents of more complex functions: language, memory, attention, motor performance, and thinking. Language processes, for example, include at least the following subcomponents:

- Inner speech, or the preverbal formulation of a message or a thought.
- Oromotor sequences required for producing speech.
- Sensations and feedback from the articulatory sequences.
- Auditory phonological analysis of speech.
- Short-term memory that permits whole linguistic sequences to be interpreted.
- Perception of the spatial relations of the words as expressed in morphology and syntactic structure.
- Recognition of the meaning of the word.
- Naming.

On the neural level, Luria viewed the brain as a functional mosaic. The different parts of the brain are responsible for different subprocesses. For example, the production of speech was already at Luria's time known to be associated with Broca's area, in the left precentral area of the brain; understanding speech was known to depend on Wernicke's area, in the left posterior temporal regions. The same brain processes participate in different constellations, in different functions, and in flexible and variable ways. Sometimes one specific deficit (e.g., poor short-term memory) may affect many complex functions, such as language comprehension, reading, and learning. Other times, the secondary effects may be more restricted, for example, effects of sensory impairments (Luria, 1973, 1980; Korkman, 1999).

Although working with adult patients, Luria also mentioned some developmental changes. Functions and skills change during development from the child's effortful execution of every component of activities, for example in reading or writing, to the adult's automatized and reduced schemes of action. Another developmental topic that interested Luria was the development of attention and executive functions. Luria called the latter *voluntary attention* or *verbal regulation* as the term *executive functions* was not yet established in the neuropsychology of his time. According to Luria (1961a; 1961b; 1973) attention and executive functions are closely related; but the balance between them changes during development. A young child automatically attends to novel and interesting stimuli and acts impulsively. Verbal rules and commands that are in conflict with direct impulses exert little influence on behavior. For example, it is difficult for a two-year-old to obey a command to take off the shoes that he/she just started to put on. The ability to control attention and activity develops in the child's interaction with the adult. At first, the adult controls the behavior of the child with signals, such as gestures and words. Gradually the child internalizes rules and motives, mainly through verbal codes.

Luria's clinical assessment is based on his theoretical view. Disordered complex functions are analyzed by separately assessing all subprocesses that normally participate in the function. The purpose is to specify the deficient link in the chain of subprocesses. Thus, analyzing a language disorder requires an assessment of at least oromotor production, auditory phonological analysis, short-term memory, comprehension of morphology and syntax, recognition of word meaning, and naming. However, almost all tasks involve more than one skill, which makes it difficult to assess purely one subprocess. Primary underlying deficits have to be inferred from the overall pattern of strengths and weaknesses. These inferences may be guided by Luria's descriptions of clinical syndromes, for example aphasias, apraxias, agnosias, and amnesias (Christensen, 1984; Luria, 1973; 1980).

Analyzing neurocognitive disorders was not the only aim of Luria's neuropsychological assessment. The clinical assessment started with an orienting assessment in which the patient was interviewed and preliminary tasks were administered. This preliminary assessment provided an overall status of brain functions. Stated problems were then analyzed in depth.

Modern child neuropsychology recognizes the complexity of cognitive functions. Attention and executive functions, language, reading, and so on are considered to be complex processes that involve many types of subprocesses. For example, the prevalent view of specific reading disorders is that an important underlying deficit is impaired phonological awareness and analysis, which makes it difficult to recognize the phonemes of words (Bradley & Bryant, 1985; Lovett, Steinbach, & Frijters, 2000; Torgesen, Wagner, & Rashotte, 1994; Schuerholz et al., 1995; Shaywitz, 1996). In addition, naming difficulties may underlie reading disorders by complicating the normal acquisition and use of a lexicon for written words (Denckla, 1985; Mauer & Kamhi, 1996; Lovett et al., 2000; Wolf & Obregon, 1992). Also poor phonological working memory is often prevalent in reading-disordered children and may hamper their verbal learning (DeJong, 1998; Gathercole & Baddeley, 1993; Korkman et al., 1994; Mauer et al., 1996).

Similarly, language disorder and disorders of attention and executive functions or visuomotor production may take various forms depending on different underlying primary defi-

cits. Some deficits may affect many types of performances, as is the case with attention deficits. Others, such as visuomotor problems, may not widely affect cognitive activities. On a general level, Luria's concept of functional systems and his clinical principle of analyzing cognitive disorders, therefore, seem to apply also to children.

DEVELOPMENT AND CONTENT OF THE NEPSY

In the development of the NEPSY, Luria's general diagnostic principles provided the starting point. These principles were modified and integrated with contemporary traditions in child neuropsychology and with psychometric conventions. The components of important cognitive functions were represented by 27 subtests, organized into 5 domains. The models for the subtests were derived from other child neuropsychological tests and from Luria's assessment.

Modifying Luria's Assessment for Children

The first version of the NEPSY, called the NEPS, was published already in 1980 (Korkman, 1980). At the time, there was a growing interest in neuropsychology, but diagnostic tools for assessing children neuropsychologically were sparse. The NEPS was a direct adaptation of Luria's assessment for five- and six-year-old children. In 1988, this method was expanded to cover the age range of four to nine years. Subtests were added and modified in accordance with emerging child neuropsychological traditions (Benton, Hamsher, Varney, & Spreen, 1983) Many test ideas were adopted and modified relatively freely; whereas other tests were relatively close to the original versions. (See references to these in the subtest section.) For a more detailed account of the origins of the test ideas, see Korkman (1995, 1999). Some unique subtests were also added. The subtests were psychometrically elaborated (Korkman, 1988a, 1988b, 1995).

Following the original Finnish versions of the NEPSY, a Swedish version of the test was published in 1990 (Korkman, 1990), and a Danish version in 1993 (Korkman, 1993). In 1988, the work on an expanded American and international version began simultaneously in Finland and the United States. This version was published in Finland in 1997 (Korkman, Kirk, & Kemp, 1997), in the United States in 1998 (Korkman, Kirk, & Kemp, 1998), and in Sweden in 2000 (Korkman, Kirk, & Kemp, 2000). The age range of the revised version was expanded to 3 to 12 years. The adjustments for expanding the age range were undertaken by adding easier and more difficult tasks to previous tests. In addition, some entirely new subtests were added, and some were dropped. The scor-

Attention / Executive Functions	Language	Sensori-motor Functions	Visuospatial Processing	Memory and Learning
Tower	**Body Part Naming**	**Fingertip Tapping**	**Design Copying**	**Memory for Faces**
Auditory Attention and Response Set	**Phonological Processing**	**Imitating Hand Positions**	**Arrows**	**Memory for Names**
Visual Attention	**Speeded Naming**	**Visuomotor Precision**	**Block Construction**	**Narrative Memory**
Statue	**Comprehens. of Instructions**	Manual Motor Sequences	Route Finding	**Sentence Repetition**
Design Fluency	Repetition of Nonsense Words			List Learning
Knock and Tap	Verbal Fluency	Finger Discrimination		
	Oromotor Sequences			

Figure 11.1 Domains and subtests of the NEPSY. Bolded subtests are recommended as core subtests to perform a comprehensive evaluation. Other subtests are recommended for expanded assessments of a problem or in a domain.

ing system was changed to using standard scores that correspond to those of the Wechsler scales of intelligence. Still, the basic structure of the new NEPSY remained the same as in the previous versions.

The present NEPSY (Korkman et al., 1997; 1998) consists of 27 subtests, which are organized in 5 domains: Attention and Executive Functions, Language, Sensorimotor Functions, Visuospatial Functions, and Learning and Memory. Each domain includes five to six subtests that represent different aspects of functioning within the domain (see Figure 11.1). The domains are therefore relatively heterogeneous. Most subtests depend mainly on some narrow, specific ability. Other subtests are more complex and could even belong to more than one domain. For example, the Verbal Fluency subtest puts demands on verbal capacities and executive functions and could belong to both domains. An overview of the subtests and the domains is given in Figure 11.1. Subtests that are recommended as a standard, core assessment to be administered to all children are bolded. The other subtests may be used for expanded assessments.

In the recent NEPSY version, the Lurian tradition is represented in the comprehensiveness of the assessment; whereas the specific subtests and their psychometric elaboration have their models in contemporary trends of child neuropsychology. One difficulty in achieving a comprehensive and up-to-date form and content is that there are important lacunae in the literature and test traditions for many aspects of neuropsychological functioning. Although attention, executive functions, language and memory, and their disorders have been extensively studied, sensorimotor and visual-spatial domains have been subjected to much less research. Furthermore, even processes that have been extensively studied, such as attention, may be defined in different ways by different authors. Existing child neurological tests that correspond to the processes represented in Luria's assessment have served as models for the subtests. Some complementary subtest ideas have been derived from Luria's assessment for adults, or constructed specifically for the NEPSY (see Korkman 1995; 1999 for details).

Subtests of Attention and Executive Functions

The subtests included in this domain are intended to assess the following subprocesses of complex functions: planning, attention to auditory stimuli and the ability to establish a mental set in doing so, selective visual attention, behavioral motor control, and nonverbal fluency.

Tower

This subtest requires the child to plan sequences of moves before performing the tasks. The child is asked to place three balls on pegs, by moving one ball at a time from one peg to another, in accordance with patterns shown in pictures. Only a certain number of moves in each are allowed, which makes it necessary to plan the sequence of moves. The test is an adaptation of the Tower of London test by Shallice (1982).

Auditory Attention and Response Set

This subtest is intended to assess the child's ability to selectively attend to certain auditory stimuli and to remember and apply a rule in doing so. In the first part of this subtest, a long and monotonous sequence of words is presented on tape to the child. Every time the word *red* is said the child should take a red token from a pile of tokens of different colors and place it into a box. In the second and more complex part of the subtest, the child should put a yellow token in the box every time the word *red* is presented and a red token every time the word *yellow* is presented. When the word *blue* is said, the child should put a blue token in the box.

Visual Attention

In this subtest, the child is given two sheets with figures and is asked to find and mark target figures as quickly as possible. The first sheet contains randomly placed figures (cats), and the second sheet contains figures placed in lines (faces). The target pictures are placed on the top of the sheet.

Statue

This subtest is intended to assess behavioral control and ability to inhibit impulsive reactions. The child is asked to stand still as a statue, with eyes closed, until the examiner says "Time's up." During the 75 seconds of the task, the examiner presents noise distracters, such as coughing and knocking on the table.

Design Fluency

In this paper-and-pencil subtest, the child is required to draw different designs by connecting dots contained in small squares. The score consists of the number of different figures

the child can come up with in one minute. The subtest is an adaptation of the 5-Point test by Regard, Strauss, and Knapp (1982).

Knock and Tap

This subtest is intended to assess the child's capability of inhibiting the impulse to repeat the examiner's action. The examiner performs a series of knocks (with knuckles and with side fist) and taps (with palm) on the table and the child is asked to perform the opposite action, for example, knocking when the examiner is tapping and vice versa. This subtest is adopted from Luria's assessment (Christensen, 1984).

Language Subtests

The following aspects of language are assessed: phonological processing, body part and speeded naming, comprehension of instructions, repetition and articulation of nonsense words, verbal fluency, and production of oral motor sequences.

Body Part Naming

The child is asked to name different body parts of a doll shown in a picture.

Phonological Processing

This subtest is intended to assess phonological awareness and analysis. It includes tasks of sound blending, word completion, word segment deletion, and changing word segments. In the easiest items, the child is asked to show which picture of three corresponds to the verbal stimulus, for example "Point to *kitchen*" when pictures of children, chicken, and kitchen are shown. In the more difficult items, the child is asked to omit or change one part of the word, for example, "Say *changing.* Now say it again, but change *-ange-* to *-omp.*"

Speeded Naming

The child is shown a sheet with 20 figures of different sizes, colors, and shapes and is asked to name them as quickly as possible, for example: *Big blue square, little yellow circle.*

Comprehension of Instructions

The examiner gives the child verbal instructions to show different figures on a sheet, for example, "Show me the figure that is above one cross and beside another cross."

Repetition of Nonsense Words

This test is constructed to be sensitive to problems with articulation and phonological analysis. The child is asked to repeat phonologically complex nonsense words, for example *incusement* or *pledgyfriskree*.

Verbal Fluency

In the first part of this subtest, the child is asked to name as many animals and, thereafter, as many things to eat or drink as he or she can come up with in one minute (semantic fluency). In the second part of the subtest, the child should name as many words beginning with F and S as possible in one minute (phonological fluency).

Oromotor Sequences

This subtest is intended to assess the child's oromotor control. The child is asked to repeat phonological sequences, such as *scoobelly doobelly, scoobelly doobelly*, or tongue twisters, such as *Sue said she should sell shoes*, five times.

Subtests of Sensorimotor Functions

The sensorimotor subtests in the NEPSY aim at assessing speed of finger movements, by imitating complex hand positions, using a pencil with speed and precision, learning manual motor sequences, and demonstrating tactile discrimination of fingers.

Fingertip Tapping

This subtest is intended to assess the speed and accuracy of repetitive and sequential series of finger movements. In the first part of the subtest, the child is asked to tap the tips of the index finger and the thumb together 32 times, as quickly as possible. In the second part, the child is asked to tap the tip of the thumb against the tips of other fingers in a sequence, eight times. The subtest is an adaptation of a procedure developed by Denckla (1973).

Imitating Hand Positions

This subtest is intended to assess manual motor control. The child is to imitate different positions of the hand, for example pointing outward with the thumb and the little finger while keeping the other fingers in a fist.

Visuomotor Precision

The child is asked to draw continuous lines on curvilinear routes on a sheet of paper. Crossing the edge of the route is counted as an error. Each child completes two routes of different complexity.

Manual Motor Sequences

This subtest is intended to assess manual motor learning. The child is given demonstrations of manual motor series (e.g., knocking the right-hand knuckles on the table, then the left-hand knuckles; then tapping the right palm, then the left palm). The child is then asked to repeat the series five times in a sequence. The task is based on Luria's assessment (Christensen, 1984).

Finger Discrimination

A cardboard shield is placed so that the child cannot see his or her hand. The examiner touches one or two of the child's fingers at a time, and the child is asked to indicate which two fingers were touched. The task is performed on each hand separately.

Subtests of Visual-Spatial Functions

The visual-spatial functions processes assessed in the NEPSY are copying two-dimensional geometric figures, perceiving line orientation, reconstructing three-dimensional block constructions from a model, and visual-spatially perceiving schematic routes.

Design Copying

The task is to copy increasingly difficult geometrical designs.

Arrows

The Arrows subtest is intended to assess judgment of line orientation. In each item, the child is asked to indicate which two arrows of several alternatives are pointing to the center of a target.

Block Construction

The child is asked to build block constructions from two- and three-dimensional models.

Route Finding

This subtest is intended to assess the perception of visual-spatial relations and directions. The child is asked to locate which house is the target house on a schematic map with roads and houses after viewing a schematic map of the route to the target house.

Subtests of Memory and Learning

The subtests of memory and learning assessed by the NEPSY represent the following processes: visual memory for faces, learning of names, memorizing and reproduction of a narration, repetition of sentences, and memorizing word lists. Three of the subtests assess immediate and delayed reproduction.

Memory for Faces

The child is presented 16 black-and-white photographs of children after which 16 pages are shown each with one target photograph and two distracters. The child is asked to indicate the photograph that was seen earlier. Half an hour later, the child is again presented 16 new pages and is asked to indicate the target photographs again among new distracters.

Memory for Names

The child is presented eight line drawings of children and is told the names of the children. Thereafter the child is asked to recall the names. The correct answers are provided if the child does not remember. The latter procedure is repeated twice. Half an hour later, the child is asked to tell the names again.

Narrative Memory

The child hears a story and is asked to tell the story again (free recall). Thereafter, the examiner presents questions about the details that were not mentioned by the child (cued recall).

Sentence Repetition

The child is asked to repeat sentences of increasing length.

List Learning

A list of 15 words is presented. The child is asked to repeat as many words as possible. The list is presented four more times and the child repeats them each time. Thereafter, a new list is introduced and taught once (interference). The child tries to recall the new list and thereafter the first list again.

Half an hour later, the child is asked to recall the words of the first list once more. This test is adopted from Luria's assessment (Christensen, 1984), but it is also similar to the California Verbal Learning Test (Delis, Kramer, Kaplan, & Ober, 1987).

PSYCHOMETRIC CHARACTERISTICS

The results of the NEPSY may be expressed as different types of scores of which the subtest scores, yielding a test profile, are the most important. Other, optional scores are those that reflect performance on a domain level, scores that reflect different parts of a subtest or different aspect of performance, and scores based on observing the child's behavior.

The scores of a standardized test compare the child's performance to those of a norm group of children the same age. The test norms of the NEPSY are based on the performance of 1,000 children in the pertinent age range from the United States. The psychometric elaboration of the data included extensive reliability analyses. In addition to the norm sample, 600 children, including clinical groups, were assessed for validational purposes. The different types of test scores and some data from the psychometric analyses and validity studies are presented in the following sections.

Types of Scores

The results of the subtests are expressed as scaled scores with a mean of 10 and a standard deviation of 3. In addition, domain scores may be computed. These scores are based on two or three specified subtests (core subtests) from each domain. The core domain scores have a mean of 100 and a standard deviation of 15. The primary aim of the NEPSY is to provide a comprehensive assessment; therefore the test profile consisting of the subtest scores is the main result. The core domain scores may be regarded as a way of summarizing the results.

In some subtests the distributions of the raw scores are skewed in the older age groups. In these subtests percentiles are more appropriate than standard scores. The raw scores in these subtests are converted to cumulative percentile ranks expressing that a score corresponds to a certain percentage of the scores of normal children (i.e.: >75%, 26–75%, 11–25%, 3–10%, or <3% obtain a score below this level).

Supplementary scores may be derived for many subtests. For example, if the subtest scaled score is based on performance time and the number of correct responses, as in the Visual Attention subtests, norm tables are separately presented for speed and the number of correct responses. The supple-

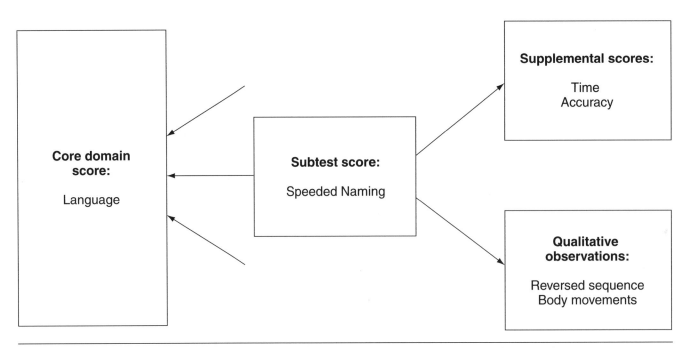

Figure 11.2 Examples of different types of scores: Core domain score, subtest score, supplemental scores, qualitative observations.

mentary scores may yield relevant information. They should always be considered for the Visual Attention subtest. In this subtest, a child with attention problems may decide to finish the task before all target figures are located. In such a case, a short performance time may counterbalance a low number of located targets. The poor attention may then be masked in a weighted score by the quick performance. In such instances, the number of correct responses alone is a more appropriate measure of the performance level.

Systematic qualitative observations may be made during the sessions or in scoring the test protocol. The test manual specifies which kinds of behaviors to observe, for example, off-task behaviors indicating attention problems, different types of errors, tremor or slow motor performance, or raising the voice or body movements as a sign of effort in some of the language subtests. Base rates for normal children at various age levels are given in the manual. The different types of test scores are illustrated in Figure 11.2.

Standardization and Reliability

The standardization of the 1998 NEPSY was performed on a sample of 1000 3- to 12-year-old children, one hundred per age level. The sample was geographically, ethnically, and socially representative of the population of the United States. An equal number of boys and girls were included in each age group. Because the norm sample is representative of the large social and ethnic variation within the United States, the normal variation is relatively large, and the norms are relatively permissive. The Finnish standardization was performed on 40 children per age group, and the Swedish on 50 children per age group.

Reliability was examined by calculating internal consistency, standard errors of measurement, confidence intervals, and stability coefficients for all subtests. Interrater reliability was calculated when relevant. Interrater reliability was also calculated for the qualitative observations.

The internal consistency reliabilities were calculated separately for the different age groups. The mean reliabilities across the age groups for most subtests were between .70 and .90 (one mean reliability was below and one above this range). The stability coefficients were calculated as correlations of two assessments 2 to 10 weeks apart. The mean coefficients of the different age groups varied between .53 and .81.

The interrater agreement for qualitative observations varied from .52 to .81. In general, the various reliability measures indicated adequate to good reliability for the different types of scores.

Validity

Traditionally, the validity of a test was regarded as a property of the test to be expressed in exact statistical figures. The concept of validity has, however, changed over the years and refers now more to a process of accumulating data concerning the usefulness of a test and the information it provides (Cronbach, 1988; Messik, 1988). Investigating the validity of a test can thus be performed in several ways: by reviewing experiences from the practical employment of the test, comparing the test results to those obtained with other measures constructed for the same purposes, conducting group studies on relevant groups of subjects, and performing statistical analyses to clarify the structure of the test.

Content and External Validity

Before the standardization process, panels of experts that included pediatric neuropsychologists and school psychologists reviewed the NEPSY twice for breadth and appropriateness of content. Validation studies of many types were performed alongside the standardization. A total of 600 children were assessed for validation purposes, in addition to those that were assessed for the standardization. In general, the findings confirmed that the NEPSY subtests scores correlated with those from other measures as expected, and that they discriminated between relevant clinical groups and normal children (Korkman et al., 1998). Some of these studies are reviewed in the following sections.

The external validity of the NEPSY was evaluated by looking at the correlations of the NEPSY subtests with other child neuropsychological tests. Examples are given in Table 11.1 and 11.2.

The tests by A.L. Benton (Benton & Hamsher, 1989; Benton et al., 1983) assess many types of neuropsychological functions, including language, motor, perception, and memory. Some of these tests and the NEPSY were administered to a mixed sample of 18 children with various diagnoses. The correlations of the Benton test scores with the scores from the corresponding tests in the NEPSY are presented in Table

TABLE 11.2   Intercorrelations Between NEPSY Subtests and CMS Subtests

NEPSY	CMS	Correlation Coefficient
Immediate Memory for Faces	Faces (Immediate Memory)	0.60
Delayed Memory for Faces	Faces (Delayed Memory)	0.45
Narrative Memory	Stories	0.36
List Learning	Word Lists (Learning)	0.56

Note. Adapted with permission from *NEPSY: A Developmental Neuropsychological Assessment* (Korkman et al., 1998). Copyright © 1988 by The Psychological Corporation.

11.1. The table shows strong correlations between most of Benton's verbal test scores with the corresponding measures from the NEPSY, as well as between the score from Benton's Judgment of Line Orientation test and the score from the NEPSY Arrows subtest. Intermediate correlations were found on two measures and insignificant correlations on three. The latter, negative findings may be related to the fact that Benton's tests were developed for adult patients and may differ from the NEPSY subtest in complexity and difficulty.

Children's Memory Scale (CMS; Cohen, 1997) is a new test of memory specifically developed for children. The correlations of the scores from this test with the NEPSY memory subtest scores were examined by assessing a mixed clinical sample of 27 children. The correlations are presented in Table 11.3. Table 11.3 shows that correlations between the NEPSY and the CMS subtest scores vary between .36 and .60, thus confirming the correspondence of the tests.

The Auditory Continuous Performance Test (Keith, 1994) provides scores for inattention and impulsivity errors. The inattention error score had a high correlation ($-.76$) with the Auditory Attention and Response Set subtest; whereas the impulsivity error score correlated with the Visual Attention subtest ($-.40$) and the Statue subtest ($-.59$). In contrast, the scores provided by Conner's Continuous Performance Scale (CCPT; Conners, 1994) did not, in general, correlate highly with the NEPSY subtests, possibly due to the two-dimensional scale of the CCPT scores.

Validation Studies with Clinical Groups

Several validation studies were conducted on different clinical groups. The control groups for these studies were selected from the standardization group to match clinical groups with respect to age, gender, race/ethnicity, and parent education. A summary of these studies is presented in Table 11.3. Means and standard deviations for three clinical groups are shown in the table. These groups were children with ADHD as the

TABLE 11.1   Intercorrelations Between NEPSY Subtests and Some Tests by Benton

NEPSY	Benton	Correlations
Statue	Motor Impersistence	0.28
Comprehension of Instructions	Token Test	0.48
Comprehension of Instructions	Aural Comprehension of Words and Phrases	0.76
Verbal Fluency	Controlled Oral Word Association	0.44
Visuomotor Precision	Rating of Praxis Features of Writing	0.52
Finger Discrimination	Finger Localization	-0.16
Design Copying	Visual Retention Test (Copy)	0.35
Arrows	Judgment of Line Orientation	0.77
Route Finding	Judgment of Line Orientation	0.69
Memory for Faces	Facial Recognition	-0.03
Sentence Repetition	Sentence Repetition	0.01

Note. Adapted with permission from *NEPSY: A Developmental Neuropsychological Assessment* (Korkman et al., 1998). Copyright © 1988 by The Psychological Corporation.

TABLE 11.3   Performance on NEPSY Subtests by Three Clinical Groups: Children with ADHD ($N = 51$); Children with Specific Reading Disorders ($N = 36$); and High-Functioning Autistic Children ($N = 23$)

	ADHD M (SD)	Reading Disorder M (SD)	Autistic M (SD)
Attention/Executive Functions			
Tower	9.5 (3.0)	10.4 (2.7)	6.8 (2.8)*
Auditory Attention and Response Set	9.1 (2.2)*	10.4 (1.9)*	10.6 (2.9)
Visual Attention	9.1 (2.5)	9.3 (2.1)	8.3 (3.5)
Statue	21.9 (8.5)*	28.3 (1.8)*	21.6 (7.9)
Design Fluency	9.7 (3.2)	9.4 (3.0)	5.5 (3.0)*
Knock and Tap	26.0 (5.1)*	28.4 (1.7)	25.3 (7.5)
Language Functions			
Phonological Processing	8.9 (2.9)*	6.3 (3.4)*	8.3 (3.3)
Speeded Naming	10.0 (2.8)	7.9 (2.0)*	9.6 (3.0)
Comprehension of Instructions	8.8 (3.5)*	8.3 (2.7)	8.8 (4.2)
Repetition of Nonsense Words	9.4 (2.4)*	8.2 (2.5)	10.0 (3.2)
Verbal Fluency	9.3 (2.6)*	8.0 (3.1)	7.4 (3.5)*
Oromotor Sequences	48.6 (11.6)*	44.6 (8.4)*	49.5 (13.2)
Sensorimotor Functions			
Fingertip Tapping	10.8 (2.7)	9.5 (3.9)	10.2 (2.7)
Imitating Hand Positions	8.3 (3.3)*	8.1 (3.1)	5.5 (3.2)*
Visuomotor Precision	8.7 (3.3)	9.6 (3.0)	6.9 (3.4)*
Manual Motor Sequences	43.3 (12.4)*	46.6 (0.1)	40.8 (13.9)
Finger Discrimination Dominant Hand	15.6 (1.9)*	16.2 (1.5)	15.2 (3.4)*
Finger Discrimination Nondominant Hand	15.5 (2.4)	15.9 (2.2)	14.4 (3.3)*
Visuospatial Processing			
Design Copying	9.2 (2.9)	8.3 (2.6)	11.2 (4.7)
Arrows	10.2 (3.5)	0.9 (9.1)	7.4 (3.9)*
Block Construction	9.1 (2.2)	9.5 (3.0)	7.0 (3.5)*
Route Finding	6.6 (3.0)	6.3 (2.9)*	4.4 (3.3)*
Memory and Learning			
Memory for Faces	9.0 (3.0)	9.9 (2.8)	6.6 (2.8)*
Memory for Names	9.3 (3.3)	7.3 (3.1)*	8.8 (4.2)
Narrative Memory	9.6 (2.6)	7.8 (2.8)*	8.2 (4.1)*
Sentence Repetition	9.5 (2.6)	7.3 (2.2)*	9.4 (3.6)
List Learning	8.6 (2.8)*	8.3 (2.8)	7.5 (3.8)*

Note. *subgroup differs significantly ($p < .01$) from its matched control group (see Korkman et al., 1998).

only diagnosis (N = 51), children with specific reading disorders but no other diagnosis (N = 36), and high-functioning autistic children (N = 28). The scores of the control groups that corresponded to each of the clinical groups are not shown (see instead Korkman et al., 1998), but subtests in which significant differences were obtained as compared to the respective control groups are noted in the table.

The test profiles demonstrate expected differences between the clinical groups. The children with ADHD had relatively widespread impairments, suggesting that attention may influence many types of performance. Another, even more important explanation is that these children may tend to have comorbid problems in other domains in spite of the fact that no children with diagnoses other than ADHD were included (Dykman et al., 1991; Gilger et al., 1992; Stanford et al., 1994; Korkman & Pesonen, 1994). Children with specific reading disorders had difficulties, especially on the Language

and the Verbal Memory subtests, as was expected on the basis of previous studies (e.g., Lovett et al., 2000; Mauer et al., 1996; Schuerholz et al., 1995; Torgesen et al., 1994). The children were significantly impaired also on the Route Finding subtest, suggesting either comorbid problems or that reading disorder may be associated with visual-spatial problems. A separate group, not shown in the table, with diagnosed, comorbid attention and learning disorders performed poorly on the attention subtests and second, on the language and verbal memory subtests.

The group of children with autism formed an interesting contrast to the other groups. This group was characterized by some impairments that were not seen in other groups, notably impairments on the Design Fluency, Verbal Fluency, Visuomotor Precision, and Memory for Faces subtests. Instead, the children differed to their advantage from the children with ADHD or reading disorder with respect to their results on the

Auditory Attention and Response Set, Statue, Phonological Processing, and Oromotor Sequences subtests. The good performance on these language tasks was probably related to the requirement that the included children should have average intelligence. Furthermore, poor performance on the Tower subtest together with the poor performance on the fluency subtests seems to suggest expected difficulties with executive functions. The results on proper attention subtests were less affected. To conclude, the differences in these test profiles between the clinical groups gives further evidence of the clinical validity and usefulness of the NEPSY.

Earlier Validation Studies

In addition to the validation studies performed for the publication of the 1998 NEPSY, many clinical studies using the earlier 1988 version (Korkman, 1988b) have been conducted. Korkman and Peltomaa (1991) demonstrated that poor performance on the subtests of inhibition and control, corresponding to the Statue and Knock and Tap subtests, predicted attention problems in school. Korkman and Pesonen (1994) reported that the NEPSY test profiles discriminated between children with attention problems and children with reading and spelling problems. The former children were impaired on the attention and executive functions subtests; whereas the latter were impaired on language and verbal memory subtests. Children with attention problems and reading and spelling problems were impaired on both types of measures. They also showed additional impairment on visuomotor subtests, indicating that these children also had the most widespread impairments.

In a large study on subtypes of language disorders by Korkman and Häkkinen-Rihu (1994), children with language problems ($N = 80$) were examined before school age. Four subgroups were identified on the basis of their test profiles: children with global language problems; children with only articulatory, dyspraxic impairments; children with receptive impairments and dysnomic problems; and a small group of children with specific dysnomic problems. At follow-up until school age, the children with global language problems and those with receptive problems were found to have significant learning problems. In contrast, few children with dyspraxic problems had academic learning problems. The subgroup of children with dysnomic problems only was too small for follow-up.

A second study on language-disordered children conducted by Korkman et al. (1993) evaluated the efficiency of a preventive treatment program of reading and spelling. A group of preschool children with language problems took part in a 45-minute training session once a week during one year

before starting school. The training was designed to reduce problems caused by impaired phonological awareness and dysnomia. A control group received more traditional forms of treatment (speech therapy and/or attending specific kindergartens for children with language problems). The children were assessed with the NEPSY before the intervention and one year after the intervention ended, at the end of the first school year. The children in the intervention group did significantly better than those in the control group on tests of reading and spelling. They also improved on the NEPSY attention and language subtests. In contrast, the control group had not improved on any neuropsychological measure. This study demonstrates an application of the NEPSY in the study of effects of intervention.

A number of studies were also performed on children with neurological risks or disorders. These studies were conducted to explore the comprehensive test profiles in different clinical groups. They may illustrate the utility of a comprehensive assessment. One of the studies was conducted on hemiplegic children to examine the effects of lateralized brain damage. The children with left- and right-sided brain damage performed similarly on the language subtests, which confirmed earlier findings of a resilience of language development in congenital left-sided brain damage (Satz, Strauss, Hunter, & Wada, 1994; Vargha-Khadem & Polkey, 1992). The children with right-sided damage tended to have visual-spatial impairment, but the difference was not significant (Korkman & von Wendt, 1995).

Children born with very low birth weights (VLBW) and children born at term with severe birth hypoxia were followed until school age and compared. Children with motor impairment and/or retardation were not included. The children from the VLBW group exhibited a diffuse pattern of mild impairments relative to the control group, but they still performed within the average range. Children who were born small for their gestational age were the most impaired group. Children born at term but who had suffered from birth hypoxia did not perform differently from the control group (Korkman et al., 1996). Herrgård et al. (1993) also found diffuse impairment on the NEPSY in children born at ≤ 32 weeks gestation.

Children prenatally exposed to alcohol were followed until school age. Children who had been exposed throughout pregnancy showed significant and diffuse impairment across most types of tasks. The most severe effects were seen on the Language and the Attention and Executive Functions subtests. Exposure during only early pregnancy did not have significant neurocognitive effects (Korkman et al., 1998a). The results were in agreement with previous findings (Carmichael Olson et al., 1992; Conry, 1990; Don et al., 1995).

CLINICAL APPLICATION

The NEPSY is a complex test that may produce an extensive pool of data, at most 27 subtest scores, 5 core domain scores, and many additional supplemental scores and qualitative observations. The assumption is that one or a few specific measures or quotients cannot reveal neurocognitive functions. The bottlenecks for development as well as the capacities and resources on which to build education need to be identified. At the same time, it is recognized that time restrictions often prevent a complete assessment of neurocognitive functions. The general design of the NEPSY is, therefore, more that of a repertoire of optional measures rather than that of a single test. In the clinical application of the NEPSY, the starting point is the questions to which clarifications are sought. Subtests may be selected and administered according to these questions and the aims of the assessment. It is not necessary to administer the whole test.

Neuropsychological assessment often aims at providing a comprehensive overview of the neurocognitive status in a child with risks for compromised brain functions or learning capacities. In such cases, all subtests may be administered. Alternatively, a selection of sensitive tests from all domains may be administered. Such a selection, the core assessment, is proposed in the manual (see Figure 11.1). In using the NEPSY, it is recommended that this relatively comprehensive assessment be administered to all children. The subtests not included in the core subtests are called expanded subtests. These subtests are proposed as complementary tests for more in-depth analysis of specific problems.

Another aim of the assessment may be to analyze and clarify some specific problems of the child. These may be specified already in the referral question, or stated in the course of the preliminary contacts with the child or in the core assessment. Problems to be analyzed may be a reading disorder, a language disorder, an attention problem, and so on. For this analysis, subtests that are considered relevant in relation to the problem may be administered. For example, a reading disorder should be analyzed by administering at least tests of phonological processing, speeded naming and name learning, and verbal memory. Because reading disordered children may have generalized language disorders, other language subtests may need to be administered as well. To verify that the child does not have generalized impairments across all domains, contrasting nonverbal subtests are useful. In practice, therefore, it is advisable to administer first the core assessment and thereafter continue with selective subtests. If, however, the examiner prefers to concentrate on some specific problem, such an assessment may be called a selective assessment.

To summarize, frequent types of assessments include full assessments (all subtests), core assessments (core subtests only), expanded assessments (selected subtests in addition to the core subtests), or selective assessments (selective subtests only for the purpose of clarifying a certain problem).

The interpretation is an essential part of the application of the NEPSY. In an exploration of the child's neurocognitive test profile, the interpretation is relatively straightforward: The patterns of strengths and weaknesses in the test profile are reviewed. Findings and conclusions regarding specific impairments need to be verified: At least two test findings should point in the same direction, or related findings should be obtained in other assessments or should be evident as problems in practice. Single, unsupported subtest findings should not be considered evidence for impairment.

When the task is to analyze disorders, the interpretation requires knowledge in the area of learning disorders and developmental neuropsychology. The interpretation of which specific deficits may be causally related to the overt disorder should rest on research findings and theoretical views supported by empirical research. For example, an experienced neuropsychologist would probably not regard poor visual memory as causally related to dyslexia, even if a dyslexic child presents such a deficit.

Interpreting the mechanisms of a disorder is further complicated in children by the tendency to present several overlapping disorders. When this is the case it may be difficult to determine which deficits are causally related to a problem and which are simultaneous. In these cases, relevant theories and research findings are even more important as a basis for the interpretation of mechanisms of the disorder. Case studies that illustrate clinical inferences are presented in Korkman, Kemp, and Kirk (2001), and Kemp, Kirk, and Korkman (2001).

Table 11.4 provides an overview of impairments or problems that may be analyzed with the NEPSY and possible primary deficits that may underlie the problems. Also relevant subtests and observations are proposed. The table is intended mainly to illustrate how the conceptual and the assessment levels, including qualitative observations, relate to each other.

APPLICABILITY AND LIMITATIONS

As was evident in the previous sections, the NEPSY was developed as an instrument for comprehensive evaluation and analysis of neurocognitive disorders of various kinds. It may be administered to most children with such disorders. However, some limitations need to be kept in mind. The NEPSY does not cover all important aspects of a child's behavior and

TABLE 11.4   Illustrative Overview of Relations Between Stated Problems, Possible Underlying Primary Deficits, Subtests in Which These May Be Observed, and Qualitative Observations That May Support These Inferences

Problems in Complex Functions	Possible Primary Deficits	Poor Results in the Following Subtests	Qualitative Observations
Attention problems	Inattentiveness	Audio Attention	Off-task behavior
		Visual Attention	Off-task behavior
	Problems with control and inhibition	Statue	Body movements, opening the eyes, vocalizing
		Knock and Tap	
	Hyperactivity	Statue	Body movements, opening the eyes, vocalizing
Problems with executive functions	Poor mental control	Auditory Response Set	
		Knock and Tap, Part 2	
		Visual Attention	
		List Learning	
	Problems of planning and strategies	Visual Attention: Cats	
		Tower	
		List Learning	Poor learning curve, intrusions, repetitions
	Poor fluency and inventiveness	Verbal Fluency	Signs of effort (increasing voice volume, body
		Design Fluency	movement), reversed sequences
Language problems	Poor expressive language	Body Part Naming	
		Verbal Fluency	
		Narrative Memory: Free Recall	
		Speeded Naming	
	Oromotor problems	Oromotor Sequences	Poor articulations
		Repetition of Nonsense Words	Poor articulations
	Problems with phonological perception and analysis	Phonological Processing	Asks for repetitions
		Repetition of Nonsense Words	
		Sentence Repetition	
	Problems with verbal comprehension	Comprehension of Instructions	
		Narraative Memory, Cued Recall	
	Naming problems	Body Part Naming	
		Speeded Naming	
		Memory for Names	
Problems of reading and spelling	Problems with phonological analysis	Phonological Processing	
		Repetition of Nonsense Words	
		Sentence Repetition	
	Naming problems	Body Part Naming	
		Speeded Naming	
		Memory for Names	
	General language problems	All language subtests	
Visuomotor problems	Fine motor problems	Imitating Hand Positions	Incorrect positions, other hand helps
		Finger Discrimination	
		Visuomotor Precision	
		Design Copying	Immature pencil grip
	Problems with learning motor sequences	Manual Motor Sequences	Rate changes
		Fingertip Tapping	Rate changes, visual guidance
	Psycho-motor slowness	Oromotor Sequences	Slowing, slow rate
		Fingertip Tapping	Slowing, slow rate
		Visuomotor Precision; Time	Neglect of visual half-field
		Visual Attention; Time	
	Difficulties with visio-spatial perception	Arrows	
		Route Finding	
	Visuo-constructive problems	Design Copying	Rotations
		Block Construction	
Problems with memory and learning	Problems with verbal learning (secondary to language problems)	Sentence Repetition	
		Repetition of Nonsense Words	
		Narrative Memory	
		Memory for Names	
		List Learning	
	Poor visual memory (secondary to visuo-spatial perception problems)	Memory for Faces	
	Problems with active memorising (secondary to attention/executive functions deficits)	Narrative Memory, Free Recall	
		Memory for Names	
		List Learning	

Note. The list of subtest results and qualitative observations supporting an inference of a specific primary deficit is not exhaustive.

functioning; other complementary evaluations are often motivated as well. Furthermore, although the NEPSY is relatively culture free, the possibility of cultural and linguistic bias needs to be considered when administering the test to persons from other cultures. When assessing children with disabilities, some modifications of the testing procedure may be required.

Range of Applications

As the validation studies demonstrated, the NEPSY may be used to assess clinically children with various types of learning and developmental problems, such as general or specific learning disorders, language disorders, attention problems, problems with executive functions, and visual-spatial or visuomotor problems. Furthermore, it is used to assess children at risk for neurocognitive disorders due to very low birth weight, prenatal alcohol exposure, medical treatment, and so on; children with known neurological conditions, such as brain trauma, epilepsy, hydrocephalus, cerebral palsy, and chromosome abnormalities; and children with neuropsychiatric syndromes, such as Asperger's syndrome and Tourette's syndrome.

Common to these groups of children is a possibility of compromised neurocognitive development. An assessment with the NEPSY clarifies the neurocognitive strengths and weaknesses of the children and sheds light the nature of stated impairments. In doing so, it provides a basis for the planning of intervention and special education.

The NEPSY is also useful as a means of long-term follow-up of children with some active neurological process, such as epilepsy, or who receive medical treatment. It has been used also for evaluating the effects of intervention. For example, the study by Korkman and Peltomaa (1993), mentioned previously, demonstrated that an intervention program for language-disordered children was efficient through strengthening linguistic capacities and attention.

As the validation studies demonstrated, the NEPSY is applicable in many types of research. In addition to clinical studies, it may also be a device for cross-cultural comparisons as well as studies on normal development. Examples of such studies will be provided in the following sections.

Some Limitations

The NEPSY is not sufficient for a complete neuropsychological assessment. A thorough assessment usually starts with an assessment of general cognitive capacity with some test of psychometric intelligence. Achievement measures are also needed to clarify the child's performance level in reading,

spelling, and arithmetic. Furthermore, the NEPSY was not developed with the aim of providing a tool for medical diagnosis, such as ADHD, specific reading disorders, or autistic disorders. To establish such diagnoses, clinical criteria that are commonly agreed upon are more useful. The NEPSY is the tool for a more thorough evaluation that needs to follow an initial diagnosis.

An unintended limitation of the test is a problem connected to the assessment of attention. This problem is common to most other corresponding tests as well. To assess attention psychometric tests are not always sufficient. A child may find the tests challenging and motivating, which may be sufficient for a good mobilization of attentional capacities and effort. Attention problems, therefore, do not always become evident on a test level. Parent and teacher evaluations and unstandardized interviews are necessary complements in this respect.

The Auditory Attention and Response Set subtest may be problematic to administer to young 5-year-olds. These children may have difficulties grasping the complex instruction in the Response Set part of the subtest. When this occurs, the less complex Auditory Attention subtest may be administered alone as separate norms are provided for both parts in the test manual.

Cross-Cultural Considerations

The recent version of the NEPSY has been published in the United States, Finland, and Sweden. National standardization is under way in some other European countries. Basically the same version of the NEPSY has been translated and adopted in all countries (with the exceptions of some differences in the Finnish version due to changes that were undertaken after this first version had appeared). Revisions to adjust for cultural differences have not been necessary.

The applicability of the NEPSY cross-culturally was confirmed by a study using the NEPSY with 9- and 11-year-old Zambian children (Mulenga, Ahonen, & Aro, 2001). In Zambia, English is the language of instruction in most schools. The results showed that the Zambian children mostly performed within the average range compared to the American norms. Mean scores that differed more than one standard deviation from the mean were obtained in only 4 of 20 core subtests. Poorer results were obtained on the Visual Attention, the Speeded Naming, and the Repetition of Nonsense Words subtests (only for the 11-year-olds). Better results were obtained on the Design Copying subtest. In addition, the Zambian children performed slightly poorer than the U.S. norms on most subtests in the Language and the Attention and Executive Functions domains. The poorer performance on the language subtests may be due to the fact that the children in the study, albeit attending school in English, were not native English speakers. Poorer scores on the Visual Attention and the Speeded Naming subtests seemed to be affected by the time factor. The Zambian children did not respond to the urge by the examiners to work as fast as possible, but tended to work slowly. The good result on Design Copying subtest might also be explained by cultural factors: In Zambian schools, most of the education is based on the children copying from the blackboard. The authors concluded that the NEPSY is relatively culturally insensitive, at least among literate, urban Zambian children.

Another study was undertaken in Great Britain to examine the applicability of the American NEPSY to English 3- and 4-year-olds (Dixon & Kelly, 2001). Core subtests were administered. The authors found that these subtests were appropriate for English children, but that the English children scored somewhat higher on the language and attention subtests. The authors explained the differences with the English children attending nursery school from a young age.

Both of the reviewed studies underlined the necessity to collect comparative data and take into consideration some cultural differences if the U.S. test norms are applied in non-U.S. countries. Certainly, national standardization is the best safeguard against cultural bias. Both studies as well as the existing national standardizations demonstrate that the NEPSY is sufficiently culture-free to be translated and standardized in different countries and cultures.

Assessing Persons with Disabilities

When administering the NEPSY some clinical groups of children may require specific arrangements. These groups include children who are blind, hearing impaired, language impaired, or have motor or attention deficits. Detailed instructions on how to administer the NEPSY with disabled children can be found in Kemp, Kirk, and Korkman (2001). Some advices are summarized later in this section.

When modifying the administration of a test, the examiner should note the modifications made and interpret the results with appropriate caution. If the examiner has to undertake major modifications of the administration of the tasks, the test norms might be invalidated. Even so, the experienced examiner will be able to make clinical observations regarding the child's abilities and adaptive strategies.

When assessing blind children, the NEPSY administration is limited to subtests that are or can be adapted to be presented verbally or can be demonstrated physically. The subtests that can be administered with blind children are Statue, Knock and Tap, Phonological Processing, Verbal Fluency, Oromotor

Sequences, Body Part Naming, Repetition of Nonsense Words, Fingertip Tapping, Finger Discrimination, List Learning, Narrative Memory, and Sentence Repetition. Some modifications of the administration may be needed. For example, in the subtest Knock and Tap, the examiner may let the child feel the hand positions of the examiner and train the auditory discrimination of the different sounds of the knock and the tap.

When assessing hearing-impaired children, all NEPSY subtests except the Phonological Processing and the Repetition of Nonsense words subtests may be administered. Means and standard deviations from a group of hearing impaired children are presented in the NEPSY manual. These results can be used as a frame of reference when undertaking the assessment. The administration of the NEPSY with hearing-impaired children should be conducted in collaboration with a certified interpreter, unless the examiner is fluent in sign language. Before starting the assessment, the child's proficiency level of sign language should be determined. For children who read well, the examiner may use written directions.

When assessing children with autistic disorders, it is important to prepare the assessment in advance. As autistic children tend to be sensitive to changes, they should be given the chance to familiarize themselves with the location of the assessment and the examiner. The examiner should interview the child's caretakers in advance to find out about the child's possible themes of perseveration as well as if the child is hypersensitive to certain objects or topics.

When assessing children with motor problems, time limits may need to be modified. The child may be allowed to finish a task after passing the time limit to see if he/she is capable of accomplishing the task given more time. Some of the subtests that require fine motor ability may be modified, so the motor problems of the child will not affect the child's performance more than necessary. For example, on the Auditory Attention and Response Set, the child may be allowed to touch the tokens instead of picking them up.

When assessing language-impaired children, the examiner needs to use as simple instructions as possible and give demonstrations when needed. It is more essential that the child comprehend the task than it is to follow administration rules verbatim. The nonverbal subtests are important to obtain a fair evaluation of the child's abilities.

When assessing children with attention problems, the assessment may be divided into many short sessions. The testing environment should be plain with few distracters. Children who are assessed to confirm a presumed diagnosis of attention problems should be tested when not under medication. Children who already have a diagnosis may be assessed when under medication to evaluate the effects of the treatment.

Legal and Ethical Considerations

The NEPSY is a complex assessment instrument and should therefore be used only by examiners with appropriate graduate-level training. Experience of administrating and interpreting standardized clinical tests is necessary. The NEPSY examiner should also have training in clinical child neuropsychology. User qualifications, issues concerning test security, and copyright restrictions are found in Standards for Educational and Psychological Testing (American Psychological Association, 1985). All examiners using the test should be familiar with these standards.

CURRENT DEVELOPMENTS AND FUTURE PROSPECTS

The internationally published version of the NEPSY is still a relatively recent instrument. Further elaborations or modifications of the test may be anticipated. One development that has already been undertaken is the publication of a computer-assisted scoring system. Other developments include the ongoing accumulation of research findings.

Computerization

To facilitate the calculation of scores a computer program, the NEPSY Scoring Assistant, was recently developed (Psychological Corporation, 2000). After entering the raw scores and the age of the child, this program computes the standard scores for the subtests and the core domain scores.

The NEPSY Scoring Assistant also designates which core domain scores represent statistical strengths (S) and which represent weaknesses (W) in the child's neurocognitive profile. Similarly, the program designates strengths and weaknesses of single tests when a full assessment has been undertaken. The NEPSY Scoring Assistant further computes which differences between core domain scores and subtest scores are statistically significant.

It should be underlined that the statistical differences are but data on which to base clinical interpretations. They do not tell which differences are meaningful from a clinical point of view. In a single child there may be various reasons for failing a test, which need to be inferred from the way the child performs the task or from the overall pattern.

Current Research Status

The NEPSY has provided research findings that have shed light on neurocognitive abilities and impairment in different developmental and neurological disorders. No doubt, this line

of research will continue. Korkman, Renvaktar, and Sjöström (2001) performed one recent study. This study investigated the pattern of impairments that were comorbid to reading disorders. Sixty-seven children who failed a screening test in reading but had average psychometric intelligence were assessed with a selection of subtests from the NEPSY and compared to a control group. The results showed that the children with reading disorders had comorbid impairments on tasks of auditory verbal attention, design copying, and visuomotor performance as well as the expected impairments within the language domain (on the Phonological Processing, Speeded Naming, Name Learning, and List Learning subtests). These results demonstrate that not only the functions related to the referral problem of the child, but that other domains might also be impaired. These impairments may also be important to know about when planning the individual intervention program of a child.

In recent studies, the NEPSY has also been used for comprehensive exploration of neurocognitive status in risk groups. These include children exposed to organic solvents prenatally (Till, Koren, & Rovet, 2001), children who have undergone renal transplantations (Qvist et al., 2002), and older children followed-up after prenatal alcohol exposure (Korkman, Kettunen, & Autti-Rämö, in press). Other groups of children are those with complicated clinical conditions, such as juvenile neuronal ceroid lipofuscinosis (Lamminranta et al., 2001), and brain lesion with epilepsy (Kolk, Beilman, Tomberg, Napa, & Talvik, 2001). A few studies have also been conducted on clinical groups to explore the correlations of MRI findings with neurocognitive impairment (Autti-Rämö et al., 2002; Olsén et al., 1998).

Some studies were also previously mentioned in which the NEPSY was useful in investigating cross-cultural differences in cognitive development. A third line of studies has more recently been emerging: that of studying normal cognitive development in children. Korkman, Kemp, and Kirk (2001b) analyzed the standardization data of the NEPSY to investigate developmental patterns in the normal neurocognitive development of children. The data from 800 5- to 12-year-old children from the United States were used. The results showed that the neurocognitive development in children is more accentuated in the age range from 5 to 8 years than in the age range from 9 years to 12 years. Similar trends have been observed in other normative studies (e.g. McKay, Halperin, Schwartz, & Sharma, 1994; Steese-Seda, Brown, & Caetano, 1995; Vakil, Blachstein, & Sheinman, 1998; Waber & Bernstein, 1995). Significant age-related improvement continued after the age of 10 years only in subtests of fluency and verbal memory (the Design Fluency, Verbal Fluency, Speeded Naming, and Sentence Repetition subtests). The authors explained the latter findings by the nature of the fluency tasks and, possibly, by continued development of executive functions. They proposed that, in general, neurocognitive functions may become established before adolescence and later improvements may come about as a result of new combinations of the established skills and increased efficiency and experience.

A second study by Klenberg, Korkman, and Lahti-Nuuttila (2001) examined the development of attention and executive functions. For this study, NEPSY scores of 400 Finnish 3- to 12-year-old children were analyzed. Results indicated that the development of attention and executive functions followed a sequential pattern. The 12-year-level was reached earliest in the Statue and the Knock and Tap subtests measuring the capability of the child to inhibit impulsive reactions. Maturity in these subtests was reached at the age of 6 years, followed by relative maturity of selective visual and auditory attention at 10 years; whereas fluency continued to develop into adolescence. The stages were confirmed by obtaining separate factors in a factor analysis. These results are in line with theoretical views proposed by Barkley (1997), suggesting that inhibitory functions serve as a basis for the development of more complex forms of attention and executive functions.

Future Developments

One of the developments that may be expected in the future is that standardized versions of the NEPSY will probably appear in other countries. The cross-cultural studies reviewed previously demonstrate the relative cultural fairness of the NEPSY. In addition, the NEPSY contains most types of tests necessary in a neuropsychological assessment, which is an advantage in countries where such instruments are lacking.

The study of normal development may continue. Possibly, factor-based summary scores may be envisioned. In the research on clinical groups one topic that awaits future exploration is typical broader patterns of impairments in different clinical groups. Another theme is changing patterns of impairments in the course of development as revealed by long-term follow-up of clinical groups.

Further, the NEPSY would also be suitable for clinical case studies as it may provide large test profiles. A possible line of research would be to analyze which specific deficits may be related to disorders of complex functions on a case level. This approach was characteristic of Luria's clinical approach (see, e.g., Luria, 1973; 1980). It is also characteristic of emerging traditions in cognitive developmental neuropsychology. Similar to Luria's approach, cognitive neuropsychological views as applied to developmental disorders regard complex functions as being composed of subparts that are mutually interdependent and biologically determined. Characteristic of case studies is that case studies are favored over group studies to disentangle the mechanisms of cognitive disorders (see e.g., Temple, 1997; Fodor, 1983). For case studies of children, it would be essential to use tests that are standardized on normal children to evaluate which performances are poor and which are adequate for a child at a certain age.

Altogether, case and group studies may serve the same purpose: to clarify which underlying deficits are related to observed impairments of complex functions. Research along these lines may ultimately produce a theory of different mechanisms leading to different types of disorders of language, reading, attention, and executive functions, in the way that was outlined in Table 11.4.

REFERENCES

American Psychological Association, American Educational Research Association, & National Council on Measurement in Education. (1985). *Standards for educational and psychological testing.* Washington, DC: Author.

Autti-Rämö. I., Autti, T., Korkman, M., Kettunen, S., Salonen, O., & Valanne, L. (2002). MRI findings of children with school problems who had been exposed prenatally to alcohol. *Developmental Medicine and Child Neurology, 44,* 98–106.

Barkley, R.A. (1997). Behavioral inhibition, sustained attention, and executive functions: Constructing a unifying theory of ADHD. *Psychological Bulletin, 121,* 65–94.

Benton, A.L., & Hamsher, K. deS. (1989). *Multilingual aphasia examination* (2nd ed.). Iowa City, IA: Aja Associates.

Benton, A.L., Hamsher, K. de S., Varney, N.R., & Spreen, O. (1983). *Contributions to neuropsychological assessment: A clinical manual.* New York: Oxford University Press.

Bradley, L., & Bryant, P. (1985). *Rhyme and reason in reading and spelling.* Ann Arbor: The University of Michigan Press.

Carmichael Olson, H., Sampson, P.D., Barr, H., Streissguth, A.P., & Bookstein, F.L. (1992). Prenatal exposure to alcohol and school problems in late childhood: A longitudinal prospective study. *Development and Psychopathology, 4,* 341–359.

Christensen, A.L. (1984). The Luria method of examination of the brain-impaired patient. In P.E. Logue, & J.M. Schear (Eds.), *Clinical neuropsychology—a multidisciplinary approach* (pp. 5–28). Springfield, IL: Charles C. Thomas.

Cohen, M.J. (1997). *Children's memory scale.* San Antonio, TX: The Psychological Corporation.

Conners, C.K. (1994). *Conners' continuous performance test computer program* (Version 3.0). Toronto, Canada: Multi-Health Systems.

Conry, J. (1990). Neuropsychological deficits in fetal alcohol syndrome and fetal alcohol effects. *Alcoholism: Clinical and Experimental Research, 14,* 650–655.

Cronbach, L.J. (1988). Five perspectives on validity argument. In H. Wainer & H.I. Braun (Eds.), *Test validity* (pp. 3–17). Hillsdale, NJ: Lawrence Erlbaum.

DeJong, P.F. (1998). Working memory deficits of reading disabled children. *Journal of Experimental Child Psychology, 70,* 75–96.

Delis, D.C., Kramer, J.H., Kaplan, E., & Ober, B.A. (1987). *The California verbal learning test.* San Antonio, TX: The Psychological Corporation.

Denckla, M.B. (1973). Development of speed in repetitive and successive finger-movements in normal children. *Developmental Medicine and Child Neurology, 15,* 635–645.

Denckla, M.B. (1985). Motor coordination in dyslexic children: Theoretical and clinical implications. In F.H. Duffy & N. Geschwind (Eds.), *Dyslexia: A neuroscientific approach to clinical evaluation* (pp. 187–195). Boston: Little, Brown.

Dixon, L.A.A., & Kelly, T.P. (2001). A comparison of the performance of preschool children from England and USA on the NEPSY: Developmental neuropsychological assessment. *Clinical Neuropsychological Assessment, 2,* 43–59.

Don, A., & Rourke, B.P. (1995). Fetal alcohol syndrome. In B.P. Rourke (Ed.), *Syndrome of nonverbal learning disabilities. neurodevelopmental manifestations* (pp. 372–406). New York: Guilford Press.

Dykman, R.A., & Ackerman, P.T. (1991). Attention deficit disorder and specific reading disability: Separate but often overlapping disorders. *Journal of Learning Disabilities, 24,* 96–103.

Fletcher-Flinn, C., Elmes, H., & Strugnell, D. (1997). Visual-perceptual and phonological factors in the acquisition of literacy among children with congenital developmental coordination disorder. *Developmental Medicine & Child Neurology, 39,* 158–166.

Fodor, J.A. (1983). *The modularity of mind.* Cambridge, MA: Bradford Books.

Gathercole, S.E., & Baddeley, A.D. (1993). Phonological working memory: A critical building block for reading development and vocabulary acquisition? *European Journal of Psychology of Education, 8,* 259–272.

Gilger, J.W., Pennington, B.F., & De Fries, J.C. (1992). A twin study of the etiology of comorbidity: Attention-deficit hyperactivity disorder and dyslexia. *Journal of the American Academy of Child and Adolescent Psychiatry, 31,* 343–8.

Gupta, A., & Garg, A. (1996). Visuo-perceptual and phonological processes in dyslexic children. *Journal of Personality and Clinical Studies, 12,* 67–73.

Herrgård, E., Luoma, L., Tuppurainen, K., Karjalainen, S., & Martikainen, A. (1993). Neurodevelopmental profile at five years of children born at ≤32 weeks gestation. *Developmental Medicine and Child Neurology, 35,* 1083–1096.

Keith, R.W. (1994). *Auditory continuous performance test.* San Antonio TX: The Psychological Corporation.

Kemp, S.L., Kirk, U., & Korkman, M. (2001). *Essentials of NEPSY assessment.* New York: John Wiley & Sons.

Klenberg, L., Korkman, M., & Lahti-Nuuttila, P. (2001). Differential development of attention and executive functions in 3- to 12-year-old Finnish children. *Developmental Neuropsychology, 20,* 407–428.

Kolk, A., Beilman, A., Tomberg, T., Napa, A., & Talvik, T. (2001). Neurocognitive development of children with congenital unilateral brain lesions and epilepsy. *Brain Development, 23,* 88–96.

Korkman, M. (1980). *NEPS. Lasten neuropsykologinen tutkimus.* Helsinki, Finland: Psykologien Kustannus Oy.

Korkman, M. (1988a). NEPSY—an adaptation of Luria's investigation for young children. *The Clinical Neuropsychologist, 2,* 375–9.

Korkman, M. (1988b). *NEPS-U. Lasten neuropsykologinen tutkimus. Uudistettu versio.* [NEPSY. neuropsychological assessment of children. Revised Edition]. Helsinki, Finland: Psykologien Kustannus Oy.

Korkman, M. (1990). *NEPSY. Neuropsykologisk undersökning: 4–7 år. Svensk version.* [NEPSY. neuropsychological assessment: 4–7 years. Swedish version]. Stockholm, Sweden: Psykologiförlaget.

Korkman, M. (1993). *NEPSY. Neuropsykologisk undersøgelse 4–7 år. Dansk vejledning* [NEPSY. neuropsychological assessment: 4–7 years. Danish manual]. Translated from Swedish by K. Holm, K. Frandsen, J. Jordal, & A. Trillingsgaard. Denmark: Dansk Psykologisk Forlag.

Korkman, M. (1995). A test-profile approach in analyzing cognitive disorders in children: Experiences of the NEPSY. In M.G. Tramontana, & S.R. Hooper (Eds.), *Advances in child neuropsychology, Vol 3* (pp. 84–116). New York: Springer-Verlag.

Korkman, M. (1999). Applying Luria's diagnostic principles in the neuropsychological assessment of children. *Neuropsychology Review, 9,* 89–105.

Korkman, M., Autti-Rämö, I., Koivulehto, H., & Granström, M.-L. (1998a). Neuropsychological effects at early school age of fetal alcohol exposure of varying duration. *Child Neuropsychology, 4,* 199–212.

Korkman, M., & Häkkinen-Rihu, P. (1994). A new classification of developmental language disorders (DLD). *Brain and Language, 47,* 96–116.

Korkman, M., Kemp, S.L., & Kirk, U. (2001a). Developmental assessment of neuropsychological function with the aid of the NEPSY. In A.S. Kaufman & N.L. Kaufman (Eds.), *Specific learning disabilities and difficulties in children and adolescents. Psychological assessment and evaluation* (pp. 347–386). New York: Cambridge University Press.

Korkman, M., Kemp, S.L., & Kirk, U. (2001b). Effects of age on neurocognitive measures of children ages 5 to 12: a cross-sectional study on 800 children from the United States. *Developmental Neuropsychology, 20,* 331–354.

Korkman, M., Kettunen, S., & Autti-Rämö, I. (in press). Neurocognitive impairments in early adolescence after prenatal alcohol exposure. *Child Neuropsychology.*

Korkman, M., Kirk, U., & Kemp, S.L. (1997). *NEPSY. Lasten neuropsykologinen tutkimus* (NEPSY. A developmental neuropsychological assessment. In Finnish). Helsinki, Finland: Psykologien Kustannus.

Korkman, M., Kirk, U., & Kemp, S.L. (1998). *NEPSY—A developmental neuropsychological assessment.* San Antonio, TX: The Psychological Corporation.

Korkman, M., Kirk, U., & Kemp, S.L. (2000). NEPSY. *A neuropsychological assessment 3.00 to 12.11 years manual for administration.* Stockholm, Sweden: Psykologiförlaget.

Korkman, M., Liikanen, A., & Fellman, V. (1996). Neuropsychological consequences of very low birth weight and asphyxia at term: Follow-up until school-age. *Journal of Clinical and Experimental Neuropsychology, 18* (2), 220–233.

Korkman, M., & Peltomaa, K. (1991). A pattern of test findings predicting attention problems at school. *Journal of Abnormal Child Psychology, 19* (4), 451–467.

Korkman, M., & Peltomaa, K. (1993). Preventive treatment of dyslexia by a preschool training program for children with language impairments. *Journal of Clinical Child Psychology, 22,* 277–287.

Korkman, M., & Pesonen, A.-E. (1994). A comparison of neuropsychological test profiles of children with attention deficit-hyperactivity disorder and/or learning disorder. *Journal of Learning Disabilities, 27,* 383–392.

Korkman, M., Renvaktar, A., & Sjöström, P. (2001). Verbal and comorbid impairments in Finnish children with specific reading disorder. *Clinical Neuropsychological Assessment, 2,* 43–59.

Korkman, M., & von Wendt, L. (1995). Evidence of altered dominance in children with congenital spastic hemiplegia. *Journal of the International Neuropsychological Society, 1,* 251–70.

Lamminranta, S., Åberg, L.E., Autti, T., Moren, R., Laine, T., Kaukoranta, J., & Santavuori, P. (2001). Neuropsychological test battery in the follow-up of patients with juvenile neuronal ceroid lipofuscinosis. *Journal of Intellectual Disabilities Research, 45,* 8–17.

Lovett, M.W., Steinbach, K.A., & Frijters, J.C. (2000). Remediating the core deficits of developmental reading disability: A double-deficit perspective. *Journal of Learning Disabilities, 33,* 334–358.

Luria, A.R. (1961a). Speech development and the formation of mental processes. In US Joint Publication Services (Eds.), *Psychological science in the USSR, Vol. 1.* Washington, DC: US Joint Publication Services.

Luria, A.R. (1961b). *The role of speech in the regulation of normal and abnormal behavior.* Oxford: Pergamon Press.

Luria, A.R. (1973). *The working brain: An introduction to neuropsychology* (translated by B. Haigh). London: Penguin.

Luria, A.R. (1980). *Higher cortical functions in man,* 2nd edition (translated by B. Haigh). New York: Basic Books.

Masutto, C., & Bravar, L. (1994). Neurolinguistic differentiation of children with subtypes of dyslexia. *Journal of Learning Disabilities, 27,* 259–270.

Mauer, D.M., & Kamhi, A.G. (1996). Factors that influence phoneme-grapheme correspondence learning. *Journal of Learning Disabilities, 29,* 520–527.

McKay, K.E., Halperin, J.M., Schwartz, S.T., & Sharma, V. (1994). Developmental analysis of three aspects of information processing: Sustained attention, selective attention, and response organization. *Developmental Neuropsychology, 10,* 121–132.

Messik, S. (1988). The once and future issues of validity: Assessing the meaning and consequences of measurement. In H. Wainer & H.I. Braun (Eds.), *Test validity* (pp. 33–45). Hillsdale, NJ: Lawrence Erlbaum.

Mulenga, K., Ahonen, T., & Aro, M. (2001). Performance of Zambian children on the NEPSY: A pilot study. *Developmental Neuropsychology, 20,* 375–383.

Olsén, P.M., Vainionpää, L.K., Pääkkö, L.E., Korkman, M., Pyhtinen, J., Järvelin, M.R. (1998). Psychological findings in preterm children related to neurologic status and MRI. *Journal of Pediatrics, 102,* 329–336

Psychological Corporation, The. (2000). *NEPSY scoring assistant.* San Antonio, TX: Author.

Purvis, K.L., & Tannock, R. (2000). Phonological processing, not inhibitory control, differentiates ADHD and reading disability. *Journal of the American Academy of Child and Adolescent Psychiatry, 39,* 485–494.

Qvist, E., Pihko, H., Fagerudd, P., Valanne, L., Lamminranta, S., Karikoski, J., Sainio, K., Rönnholm, K., Jalanko, H., & Holmberg, C. (2002). Neurodevelopmental outcome in high-risk patients after renal transplantation in early childhood. *Pediatric Transplantations, 6,* 53–62.

Regard, M., Strauss, E., & Knapp, P. (1982). Children's production on verbal and non-verbal fluency tasks. *Perceptual and Motor Skills, 55,* 839–844.

Robertson, C.M.T., & Finer, N.N. (1993). Long-term follow-up of term neonates with perinatal asphyxia. *Clinics in Perinatology, 20,* 483–497.

Satz, P., Strauss, E., Hunter, M., & Wada, J. (1994). Re-examination of the crowding hypothesis: Effects of age at onset. *Neuropsychology, 8,* 255–262.

Schuerholz, L.J., Harris, E.L., Baumgardner, T.L., Reiss, A.L., Freund, L.S., Church, R.P., Mohr, J., & Denckla, M.B. (1995). An analysis of two discrepancy-based models and a processing-deficit approach in identifying learning disabilities. *Journal of Learning Disabilities, 28,* 18–19.

Shallice, T. (1982). Specific impairments of planning. *Philosophical Transactions. The Royal Society of London B, 298,* 199–209.

Shaywitz, S.E. (1996). Dyslexia. *Scientific American, 275,* 98–104.

Stanford, L.D., & Hynd, G.W. (1994). Congruence of behavioral symptomatology in children with ADD/H, ADD/WO, and learning disabilities. *Journal of Learning Disabilities, 27,* 243–253.

Steese-Seda, D., Brown, W.S., & Caetano, C. (1995). Development of visuomotor coordination in school-aged children: The bimanual coordination test. *Developmental Neuropsychology, 11,* 181–199.

Temple, C.M. (1997). *Developmental cognitive neuropsychology.* Hove, UK: Lawrence Erlbaum.

Till, C., Koren, G., & Rovet, J.F. (2001). Prenatal exposure to organic solvents and child neurobehavioral performance. *Neurtoxicology and Teratology, 23,* 235–245.

Torgesen, J.K., Wagner, R.K., & Rashotte, C. (1994). Longitudinal studies of phonological processing and reading. *Journal of Learning Disabilities, 27,* 276–287.

Vakil, E., Blachstein, H., & Sheinman, M. (1998). Rey AVLT: Developmental norms for children and the sensitivity of different measures to age. *Child Neuropsychology, 4,* 161–177.

Vargha-Khadem, F., & Polkey, C.E. (1992). A review of cognitive outcome after hemidecortication in humans. *Advances in Experimental Biological Medicine, 325,* 137–51.

Waber, D.P., & Bernstein, J.H. (1995). Performance of learning-disabled and non-learning-disabled children on the Rey-Osterrieth complex figure: Validation of the developmental scoring system. *Developmental Neuropsychology, 11,* 237–252.

Wechsler, D. (1989). *Wechsler preschool and primary scale of intelligence—revised.* San Antonio, TX: The Psychological Corporation.

Wolf, M., & Obregón, M. (1992). Early naming deficits, developmental dyslexia, and a specific deficit hypothesis. *Brain and Language, 42,* 219–247.

PART TWO

NEUROPSYCHOLOGICAL ASSESSMENT OF COGNITIVE DOMAINS

CHAPTER 12

Language and Communication Assessment in Adults

GUILA GLOSSER AND PATRICIA M. FITZPATRICK

Language is an essential part of the neuropsychological assessment because of its importance for diagnosing specific neurobehavioral disorders that have particular neuroanatomical or neurophysiological implications. Language is important in the assessment of aphasic disorders that occur as a result of focal left-hemisphere dysfunction (Alexander & Benson, 1991), as well as in the assessment of nonaphasic language disorders that occur in various neurodegenerative dementias (Cummings & Benson, 1992), acute confusional states (Chedru & Geschwind, 1972), and certain syndromes associated with right-hemisphere dysfunction (Joanette, Goulet, & Hannequin, 1990). Assessing language impairment is also important because it can impact the performance of other neuropsychological tests of reasoning and memory and result in the modification of interpretations of such findings. Language impairment may affect patients' comprehension of verbal instructions, even on nonlinguistic tasks. Language impairment also limits the capacity to encode verbal information for memory and can disrupt a person's ability to demonstrate knowledge through verbal response. Language impairment may actually preclude the use of certain common neuropsy-

chological procedures that presuppose intact linguistic skills (e.g., Trail Making and Stroop Interference Tests; Spreen & Strauss, 1998). Finally, language ability is a critical component in the assessment of functional problems in interpersonal, social, and vocational adjustment.

THEORETICAL BACKGROUND

Two complimentary theoretical approaches can guide language assessment: the traditional or *syndromal approach* and the more recently developed *cognitive neuropsychological approach.*

The *syndromal approach* is primarily concerned with assessing language behaviors or symptoms as they relate to specific syndromes or neurological disorders. The syndromal approach is particularly suited to differential diagnosis and classification of groups of patients. It focuses on profiles of component language skills that together define different aphasic or nonaphasic neurological language disorders. This section details the language skills that are most essential for diagnosing a neurologically based language disorder. Table 12.1 shows how these skills map to the different neurolinguistic syndromes.

Acknowledgments: Our thanks to our teachers Harold Goodglass, Nancy Helm-Estabrooks, and Edith Kaplan.

TABLE 12.1   Language Behaviors Associated with Specific Syndromes or Disorders

	Broca's Aphasia	Wernicke's Aphasia	Conduction Aphasia	Transcortical Motor Aphasia	Transcortical Sensory Aphasia	Right Hemisphere Damage	Alzheimer's Disease
Fluent		✓	✓		✓	✓	✓
Nonfluent	✓			✓			
Impaired Prosody	✓					✓	
Agrammatism	✓						
Paragrammatism		✓	?				
Anomia	✓	✓	✓	✓	✓		✓
Impaired Repetition	✓	✓	✓				
Impaired Syntactic Comprehension	✓						
Impaired Lexical-Semantic Comprehension		✓			✓	?	✓
Alexia	✓	✓	◆	?	★		★
Agraphia	✓	✓	◆	✓	★		★

✓ Symptom is present.
★ Impaired reading comprehension and writing from meaning with preserved oral reading and spelling to dictation.
? Symptom is variable.
◆ Impaired oral reading and spelling with preserved reading comprehension.

Fluency as applied in the differential diagnosis of neuro-linguistic disorders refers to the length of coherent word runs that are produced most typically. Fluent language refers to utterances of six or more words, whereas nonfluent production almost never exceeds four uninterrupted words. The dimension of fluency is central to the diagnosis of aphasia patients as it is highly related to lesion location, articulatory agility, and grammatical ability (Benson, 1967; Goodglass, Quadfasel, & Timberlake, 1964).

Articulation refers to the motor realization of speech sounds and can become disrupted independent of linguistic structure. Dysarthria (articulatory distortion), apraxia (the loss of control of purposeful movements), and hypophonia (reduced voice volume) can occur in combination with disorders of language, but these symptoms represent a breakdown in nonlinguistic speech functions.

Prosody refers to the pitch, voice quality, rate, rhythm, and melodic intonation patterns of speech. Impairments in prosody may accompany linguistic disorders. Nonfluent aphasic disorders can be associated with disturbed prosody for propositional and grammatical aspects of language. Dysprosody may also be a consequence of problems in word finding or speech formulation. By contrast, focal damage to the right hemisphere can impair the comprehension, production, and repetition of affective prosody (Ross, 2000).

Grammar can be impaired in both fluent and nonfluent language disorders. At its most extreme, agrammatism refers to an inability to connect words syntactically and is a common finding in nonfluent aphasia. Agrammatic speech is non-

fluent and is limited to isolated words—usually nouns and, to a lesser extent, verbs—with loss of grammatical words and syntactic markers. Paragrammatism, on the other hand, refers to incorrect or inappropriate use of syntactic forms and is usually seen in the context of fluent speech disorders.

Word finding impairment (*anomia*) refers to reduced access to one's vocabulary and is a characteristic of virtually all aphasic and nonaphasic neurolinguistic disorders. Paraphasias, or substitutions of incorrect linguistic forms, can occur with word-finding impairments. Different types of paraphasias (e.g., *literal* or *phonemic, verbal* or *semantic,* and *neologistic*) are associated with different neurolinguistic disorders (Goodglass, 1993).

Repetition from a spoken model is a linguistic activity that can be disrupted or spared selectively in various neurolinguistic disorders. Different patterns may emerge for the repetition of words, nonwords, and sentences. The kinds of errors produced in repetition are significant for identifying different neurolinguistic syndromes (Caplan, 1992).

Auditory comprehension, like other linguistic skills, is multidetermined, and different types of comprehension impairment characterize different neurolinguistic disorders. Broadly speaking, a distinction can be made between comprehension impairments that are specific for lexically or semantically complex information and other cases where comprehension impairment is more specific to syntactically complex sentences (Goodglass, 1993). In recent years, research has highlighted ways in which comprehension can be selectively impaired for certain word types, such as body parts, verbs or nouns, and living versus nonliving things (Damasio & Tranel, 1993; Goodglass, & Budin, 1988; Warrington, & Shallice, 1984).

Reading impairments (alexias) are common in many different neurolinguistic syndromes. The pattern of reading impairments often mirrors the oral language disturbance. However, reading performance can reveal impairments in other cognitive processes. Characterization of a reading impairment requires, at minimum, distinguishing between oral reading ability and the capacity to comprehend written language. Reading disorders also may be distinguished by the different kinds of errors (e.g., grammatical errors, paraphasias or paralexias, and orthographic errors) that are produced and by differential impairment for reading various linguistic stimuli, including words with regular or unusual correspondence between the letters and sounds and pronounceable nonwords, or pseudowords (Glosser & Friedman, 1995).

Writing impairments (agraphia), like naming problems, are common symptoms of most injuries to the language regions of the left cerebral hemisphere. As with reading, the pattern of impaired writing differs among neurolinguistic disorders. Writing often parallels oral language and reading performance. Although writing may be impaired because of disturbances in different component language processes, writing can become impaired as a result of manual motor or visual-spatial disorders (Roeltgen, 1993).

The *cognitive neuropsychological approach* to language assessment is newer than the syndromal approach. The cognitive neuropsychological approach is concerned with identifying and understanding the particulars of the cognitive dysfunction underlying disturbed language behaviors. Using this approach, researchers analyze language symptoms or behaviors in terms of constituent information processing components. Such analysis yields detailed cognitive data that are particularly well suited to planning treatment (Behrmann & Byng, 1992).

The cognitive neuropsychological approach is guided by a model of normal language functions. A simplified cognitive model of *single word processing,* incorporating the central features of many current psycholinguistic theories, is presented in Figure 12.1. The following sections outline the essential components of this model.

Information processing begins with the perceptual analysis of inputs. This is accomplished through several modality and material-specific modules, including auditory analysis, phonemic analysis, and letter identification. These procedures analyze the physical characteristics of visual or auditory stimuli. Perceptual analysis leads to the assignment of a structural description or abstract representation of the stimulus (Marr, 1982). For written word stimuli, for example, this process entails coding the physical shapes of letters—which may be written in different fonts, sizes, and prints—into more abstract letter identities. For auditorally presented words, acoustic properties of the input are matched to linguistically driven phonetic features. For visual objects, perceptual analysis involves computing a detailed abstract representation of the component parts and the spatial relationships among the parts of familiar visual objects. Problems involving these perceptual components can result in modality or material-specific disorders, such as alexia without agraphia, or letter-by-letter reading (Patterson & Kay, 1982), and apperceptive visual agnosia (Farah, 1990).

After perceptual analysis, language processing proceeds to the conceptual system, a central processor, which is generally thought to consist of the amodal representations of the meanings of objects, events, facts, and words. At this point in processing, the lexicons are engaged. These consist of the stored memories of language-specific knowledge of word forms and meanings. The phonological lexicon is the repository of abstract representations of the structure of word sounds. Word spellings are represented in the orthographic lexicon. The semantic lexicon refers to procedures whereby word meanings are accessed from the conceptual system. Disturbance within the conceptual system can result in a global semantic impairment, such as the one that occurs with certain forms of dementia and is manifested as difficulty recognizing the meanings of visual objects and comprehending and producing word meanings (Hodges, Patterson, Oxbury, & Funnell, 1992). Conceptual deficits may occur in a modality specific manner (e.g., visual associative agnosia and auditory agnosia or word meaning deafness) whereby certain modalities of input fail to access conceptual representations. Conceptual deficits specific to certain word types (e.g., abstract words) or concepts (e.g., living things) may also occur when perceptual information fails to access particular categories of conceptual knowledge (Warrington et al., 1984). Disturbances involving the lexicons result in deficits of specific language processes. A cognitive disturbance involving the phonological lexicon may be manifested in problems reading or repeating pronounceable nonwords or pseudowords, or phonological alexia (Friedman, 1995). Disturbance involving the orthographic lexicon can result in another form of impaired reading (surface alexia) or, more commonly, impaired writing (lexical agraphia) of irregularly spelled words, such as *ache,* in which the word's spelling is not isomorphic with its sound (Beauvois, & Derousene, 1981; Patterson, Marshall, & Coltheart, 1985). A lexical semantic impairment results in parallel deficits comprehending or matching word forms to their meanings and assigning names to concepts or objects.

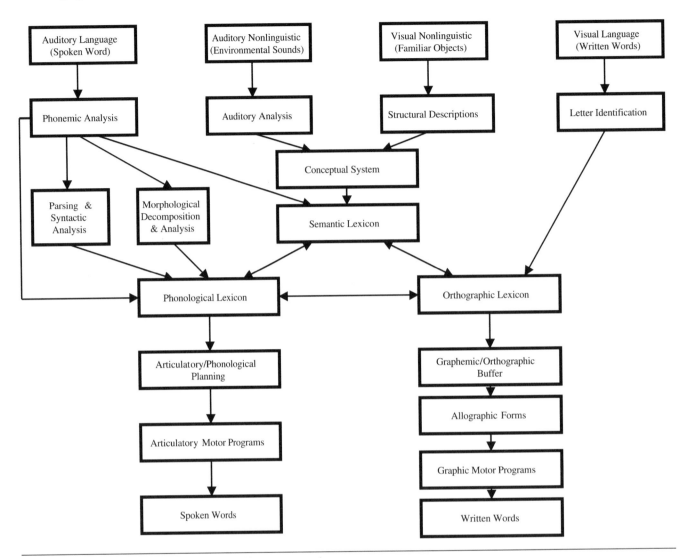

Figure 12.1 Cognitive model of normal single-word language processing.

In addition to whole word knowledge represented in the lexicons, many psycholinguistic models posit that lexical knowledge is represented in decomposed form. Separate from the representations of morphological word roots (e.g., pay), are representations of derivational (e.g., pay-*ment*) and inflectional syntactic (e.g., pay-*ed*) features of words. Various disorders can selectively affect processing of morphological forms. For example, agrammatism is classically associated with impaired production of morphological forms in sentences (Goodglass, 1993); whereas deep dyslexia involves impaired pronunciation of written words with certain syntactic characteristics (Coltheart, Patterson, & Marshall, 1987).

The processing of outputs from the phonological and orthographic lexicons proceeds on different paths for producing spoken or written words. For speaking, processing from the phonological lexicon continues on to articulatory-phonological

planning where the abstract representation of the word's phonological form is held in a buffer while it is translated into a detailed phonetic realization of the word's sound (Butterworth, 1992). Articulatory motor programs then prepare the motor commands for actual speech production. Disorders in articulatory phonological planning may result in articulate production of the wrong sound segment in a word form. This production is termed a literal or phonemic paraphasic error (Blumstein, 1998). Apraxia of speech, on the other hand, refers to distorted phonetic articulatory implementation of the correct sound (Buckingham, 1998).

Output from the orthographic lexicon undergoes further processing through several peripheral operations prior to writing. After it is retrieved from the lexicon, the orthographic or spelling code is maintained in a graphemic or orthographic buffer to allow selection of the corresponding physical or allographic forms of letters for writing or oral spelling. Graphemic motor programs specify the actual shapes of the letters for written output. An agraphia caused by a graphemic buffer deficit results in errors in written and oral spelling characterized by difficulties spelling longer words and violations of the phonemic structure of the target word (Hillis & Caramazza, 1989). By contrast, impairments in the more peripheral allographic and graphic motor processes of writing result in apraxic agraphia, which refers to a selective disturbance of writing in the context of spared oral spelling (Friedman & Alexander, 1989).

The psycholinguistic model previously described deals with the processing of single words. A schematic cognitive model of *normal sentence production,* taken from Garrett (1982; see also Bock & Levelt, 1994), appears in Figure 12.2. Sentence production within this model, as in most other conceptions, begins with a *message,* which is formulated within the conceptual system that is the repository of semantic knowledge. This message activates related word meanings, represented in the semantic lexicon, which are simultaneously coordinated into a predicate-argument structure in a *functional representation.* Next, the selected lexical semantic units activate their corresponding representations in the phonological lexicon at the same time that the word units are ordered in phonologically specified, syntactically organized, phrase-like structures at the *positional level.* The *phonetic level* further elaborates the phonological form of the sentence, including features such as phrasal stress. In the final stages of production, articulatory motor programs are implemented. This model of sentence production in its reverse order corresponds in a broad way to the procedures for sentence comprehension.

Various aphasic disorders have been mapped onto this model of sentence processing. For example, one type of agrammatism that involves problems in verb production has been associated with a disturbance in the coordination of functional-level relations (Saffran, Schwartz, & Marin, 1980). Other forms of agrammatism that involve loss or impoverishment of syntactic structure reflect a disturbance in the construction of positional-level sentence representations (Caplan, 1992). Finally, certain Broca's and Wernicke's aphasics show abnormalities in realizing intonational features that encode syntactic structure. These patients have impairment at the phonetic level of sentence representation (Danly & Shapiro, 1982; Danly, Cooper, & Shapiro, 1983).

Nonlinguistic Aspects of Communication The discussion thus far has focused on the cognitive mechanisms that are specifically devoted to language processing. However, some impairments on language tasks may actually be caused by

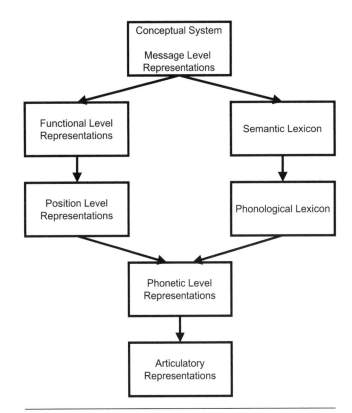

Figure 12.2   Cognitive model of normal sentence production.

disruption of nonlinguistic cognitive functions. For example, Grossman (1997) hypothesized that a working memory disturbance, part of a more general dysexecutive syndrome, underlies the sentence comprehension problems of patients with idiopathic Parkinson's disease. Some investigators have attributed the naming problem of patients diagnosed with probable Alzheimer's disease to a loss of general conceptual knowledge that spans verbal and nonverbal domains (Nebes, 1992). As another example, the aprosodias that occur with certain forms of right hemisphere damage, and are believed to stem from a problem in affective expression and comprehension, can also give the appearance of a linguistic problem.

Pragmatics is another important area that needs to be considered in the assessment of language and language disorders. Pragmatics deals with the social aspects of language. It refers to the ways in which language is used to perform communicative activities in different social situations and to the relationships between language behaviors and the social contexts in which these behaviors occur. Pragmatics involves the knowledge and application of regularities regarding what can be said to whom, where, and how. It entails more than just the correctness of the linguistic forms of communication and focuses also on the appropriateness and effectiveness of communications. Pragmatics subsumes issues such as how language is used differently within different social contexts or with different listeners; the degree to which speakers are successful in communicating their message irrespective of verbal accuracy; the performance of various speech acts (Searle, 1969); the production of connected ideas in organized suprasentential discourse; use of paralinguistic channels of gestural, intonational, and facial communications; and the ability to maintain and repair the flow of social communication exchanges. Pragmatic aspects of communication can dissociate from the linguistic aspects of communication in brain-damaged populations (Brownell, Gardner, Prather, & Martino, 1995; Foldi, 1987; Glosser, Weiner, & Kaplan, 1988; Glosser & Deser, 1990; Ulatowska, Freedman-Stern, Doyel, Macaluso-Hayes, & North, 1983), indicating a need to assess pragmatics as an additional component of the language evaluation.

ASSESSMENT METHODS

Spontaneous Speech analysis forms the starting point of any language assessment. Analysis of spontaneous speech provides important information regarding fluency, articulation, prosody, grammar, word finding, and pragmatics. By attending to the structure and manner of communications, not just the content, the clinician can begin to generate hypotheses regarding linguistic abilities and disabilities and formulate questions that can be answered through formal testing. An open-ended narrative, elicited by a prompt such as "tell me about your work," yields the broadest range of linguistic forms for analysis (Glosser et al., 1988). Ideally, however, the clinician should elicit different types of discourse. The most common types of elicited discourse are descriptive (e.g., picture description) and narrative (e.g., telling or retelling a familiar story, such as a fairy tale). Other types of discourse that can be used to assess language include procedural (e.g., relating how to perform a familiar task, such as making a cup of coffee), and conversational (managing the give and take in an interactive communication exchange).

Several formal methods quantify features of spontaneous speech. Two of the best-known methods come from standardized aphasia batteries: The Boston Diagnostic Aphasia Examination–Third Edition (BDAE-Third Edition; Goodglass, Kaplan, & Barresi, 2001) and the Shewan Spontaneous Language Analysis (Shewan, 1988). The BDAE-Third Edition provides guidelines for rating speech characteristics that include articulatory agility, phrase length, grammatical form, melodic line (prosody), paraphasias in running speech, and word finding. A global severity rating scale (0–5) summarizes the overall extent of the communicative impairment. Although the BDAE-Third Edition specifically addresses aphasia, this

rating scale of communicative ability also can be applied to other types of communication disorders. To assess functional communication and evaluate speech output patterns, the BDAE-Third Edition samples simple social responses, free conversation, picture description, and story retelling. The conversational and expository speech sample is audiotaped and transcribed. Discourse analysis involves segmentation into utterances (clauses, subclausal utterances, multiclausal utterances, and agrammatic deletions) and computation of a complexity index (the ratio of clauses to total utterances.) The Shewan Spontaneous Language Analysis uses 12 dimensions, including speech rate, sentence complexity, content units, and communication efficiency to rate the oral description of a picture. This rating method yields high interrater reliabilities between judges and has been shown to discriminate among patient groups. The ratings provide data that can be extremely useful for planning language treatment.

Content, as opposed to structure, in connected language samples can be analyzed by means of different criteria. The Yorkston and Beukelman (Yorkston & Beukelman, 1980) method involves counting the number of content units expressed in a description of the Cookie Theft picture from the BDAE (Goodglass & Kaplan, 1983). This quantitative method provides an index of the degree to which discourse is impoverished informationally. Another scoring system based on a verbal description of the Cookie Theft picture (Menn, Ramsberger, & Helm-Estabrooks, 1994) addresses three dimensions of narrative language production: (1) the amount of information or number of content units expressed, (2) the relative proportion of informative to noninformative words produced, and (3) the grammaticality of the narrative. Finally, the scoring system developed by Nicholas and Brookshire (Nicholas, & Brookshire, 1992) analyzes content in language samples using several different kinds of stimulus materials. This method tabulates the number of words produced and the number of correct information units to describe the presence, completeness, accuracy, and efficiency of the information transmitted in discourse.

Formal Language Testing, as guided by the theoretical approaches to language assessment described previously, consists of four basic types: language screening, tests based on the syndromal approach, functional communication and pragmatic skills assessment, and the cognitive neuropsychological approach.

Language screening tests are sensitive to milder forms of language impairment and are used to assess patients with no obvious or only subtle language disturbance. They focus on the functions most vulnerable to disruption in acquired neurolinguistic disorders (i.e., naming, complex comprehension, and written language). Language screening test results can serve to direct more detailed assessments after the presence of a language disorder has been established.

The Boston Naming Test (Kaplan et al., 1983) is a commonly used measure that is sensitive to milder forms of language impairment in healthy elderly (Nicholas, Obler, Albert, & Goodglass, 1985), patients with dementia (Hodges, Salmon, & Butters, 1991), and aphasic patients (Kohn & Goodglass, 1985). The test consists of 60 line drawings of common objects, graded in the word frequency of their names, that are presented for visual confrontation naming. Several shortened versions of the test that have acceptably high correlations with each other as well as with the full 60-item score have been developed (Frazen, Haut, Rankin, & Keefover, 1995; Mack, Freed, Williams, & Henderson, 1992; Williams, Mack, & Henderson, 1989). In addition to yielding a measure of the severity of lexical retrieval impairment, qualitative analyses of errors can identify sources of naming problems. For example, the production of an erroneous name that shares semantic properties with the target (e.g., naming a compass as a protractor") might suggest a semantic impairment. A problem in phonological processing might be inferred from errors that distort the phonological structure of the target word (e.g., naming an abacus as *abatracus*). Finally, the test can help identify nonlinguistic factors that sometimes contribute to naming problems, such as visual-perceptual defects that can be manifested in the production of names of objects that are visually related to the target (e.g., naming tongs as a casket) or perseverations of previously produced answers. The Boston Naming Test can yield rich and detailed information about lexical abilities and help to generate hypotheses for further language assessment, though extracting information beyond a simple measure of severity of word-finding impairment. This process requires a fairly sophisticated test administrator and clinician.

The Action Naming Test (Nicholas et al., 1985) was designed to be similar to the Boston Naming Test, but it elicits verb responses rather than nouns. In the test, 57 easily pictured actions (such as saluting) are presented for visual confrontation naming. The Action Naming Test can be an important adjunct in assessing patients with category-specific naming problems (Damasio et al., 1993; Glosser & Donofrio, 2001).

The Peabody Picture Vocabulary Test-III (PPVT-III; Dunn & Dunn, 1997) involves a word-to-picture matching format that is used to assess single word auditory comprehension. The test consists of two equivalent forms that have been standardized across a broad age range of 2½ to 90 years. Norms for English and Spanish versions of the test exist. A spoken word is presented to the patient, who matches it to one of four line drawings. Using criteria for establishing basal and ceiling levels clinicians can restrict testing to items within the

patient's individual ability level, minimizing both administration time and patient discomfort. The use of a pointing response minimizes the confounding between impairments in auditory comprehension and verbal expression that is common to some other language tests. Because of its simplicity, the PPVT-III can be used to ascertain lexical semantic capacities in patients with very low ability levels.

The Multilingual Aphasia Examination (MAE; Benton, Hamsher, Varney, & Spreen, 1994) consists of seven component subtests. Some of the subtests have multiple forms, making them useful for repeated testing. The test has been translated into other languages using functionally equivalent content. For some subtests norms have been collected from patients within a broad age range, from children to the very elderly (Ivnik, Malec, Smith, Tangelos, & Petersen, 1996). Several of the subtests of the MAE are used frequently to screen language functions. The Token Test contained in the MAE is a modification of a task that has been in clinical use since the 1960s (DeRenzi & Vignolo, 1962). The patient is presented with verbal commands of increasing length and syntactic complexity that direct the patient to manipulate different plastic shapes. This test of auditory sentence comprehension correlates highly with other measures of language comprehension and can be used with higher functioning aphasics, such as patients with closed head injuries and patients with confusional states, making it especially useful for testing individuals with more subtle language impairments (Spreen & Risser, 1998). The major disadvantage of the Token Test is that it relies on a limited set of stimulus materials, restricting the type of language knowledge that is sampled. Also, it cannot be administered to patients with color blindness. The MAE includes another commonly used test requiring Sentence Repetition of increasingly long stimuli. Qualitative analyses of errors can reveal lexical or syntactic difficulties and problems with auditory verbal working memory or span. A subtest of the MAE that has gained considerable popularity is the Controlled Oral Word Association task. This subtest takes less than five minutes to administer and requires the patient to produce as many words beginning with a specified letter as possible in one minute. The test is sensitive to language impairments as well as impairments in verbal executive control functions, which can be seen in patients with frontal lobe lesions, especially left frontal lobe lesions, as well as in dementia patients (Benton, 1968; Butters, Granholm, Salmon, Grant, & Wolfe, 1987). A caveat when interpreting the results of this test is that it presumes a relatively high level of literacy and writing fluency.

Written language skills can be screened using the Wide Range Achievement Test 3 (WRAT-3; Wilkinson, 1993), which assesses single-word oral reading and single-word spelling to dictation (in addition to written arithmetic) using graded word lists that are designed to be administered to individuals between the ages of 5 and 74. Two matched forms of the test can be administered individually or in combination, and the test can be scored quickly. This screening test measures overall oral reading and spelling ability. It is not particularly well suited for qualitative item analysis. Although frequently used in educational settings, this test has been criticized for its lack of construct and criterion validity (Impara & Plake, 1998). It is best used to identify those individuals who require further detailed evaluation of written language skills.

More detailed assessment of reading begins with analysis of phonological processing because problems in this domain have been shown to underlie many developmental and acquired reading disorders. Phonological processing of written words is evaluated most directly by tests involving the oral reading of pronounceable nonwords or pseudowords. Because pseudowords have no meaning or preexisting memory representation, their pronunciation can be assembled only by drawing on phonological knowledge of grapheme-to-phoneme (spelling-to-sound) associations. The only well-standardized measure that assesses pseudoword reading and is applicable to adults of all ages and ability levels is contained in the Woodcock-Johnson Psycho-Educational Battery (Woodcock & Johnson, 1990). Using the Word Attack subtest, testers present 30 items (e.g., zoop, paraphonity) for oral reading. Performance on this subtest can be compared with that on a subtest assessing oral reading of real words (Letter-Word Identification) using age and grade equivalent measures to determine the extent to which problems in phonological decoding may be selectively compromising reading performance. A problem in orthographic processing, as demonstrated by difficulties reading words with irregular spelling-to-sound correspondence, is believed to be the source of other common developmental and acquired reading disorders. Tests based on the cognitive neuropsychological approach, which are detailed in the following section, can be used to evaluate regularity effects in oral reading.

It is important to complement assessment of oral reading with an assessment of reading comprehension, as these two abilities frequently dissociate in neurologically impaired patients (Glosser et al., 1995). Unfortunately, most existing tests of reading comprehension present a number of problems when used in neurological populations. Some tests, such as the Peabody Individual Achievement Test—Revised (Markwardt, 1998) and the Gray Oral Reading Tests (Wiederholt & Bryant, 2001), place relatively high demands on episodic memory, which can confound interpretation of the results. The former test involves reading a sentence silently, and then, without referring to the sentence, choosing which one of four pictures

best illustrates the sentence. The latter test involves reading aloud passages of increasing length and complexity. Immediately after reading each passage, the patient must answer multiple choice questions involving concrete details and inferences about the passage without referring back to it. In addition to this memory confound, some have criticized the Gray Oral Reading Tests and similar approaches because the effort of oral reading can compromise some patients' attention to the meaning and comprehension of the written material. Other reading comprehension measures, such as the Passage Comprehension subtest of the Woodcock-Johnson Psycho-Educational Battery—Revised (Woodcock et al., 1990), limit memory demands, but they may be confounded by the fact that they require a verbal response, which may be problematic for patients with word-finding problems. This test involves silent reading of phrases and short passages followed by oral completion of a missing key word. Measures such as the Gates-MacGinitie Reading Tests–Third Edition (MacGinitie & MacGinitie, 1989) assess passage comprehension using silent reading followed by multiple choice responses. Although minimizing demands on memory and verbal production, these measures are constrained by time limits that are imposed on responses, which are always problematic with brain-injured patients. Finally, an important limitation of several of the aforementioned measures (MacGinitie et al., 1989; Markwardt, 1998; Wiederholt et al., 2001) is that, because they were developed chiefly to assess academic achievement among children, their norms only extend to 12th grade and they may not be appropriate for adults with higher educational levels.

For lower functioning aphasia patients, the Reading Comprehension Battery for Aphasia (LaPointe & Horner, 1998) assesses functional reading comprehension by means of a 10-item subtest that includes reading a recipe, a weather report, a letter, a phone book, and a prescription. Other subtests include sentence picture matching and inferential and factual paragraph comprehension using nonverbal pointing and recognition responses.

Like the assessment of reading comprehension, assessment of writing from meaning is fraught with problems. The ideal test for screening single word writing from meaning (e.g., written confrontation naming) has not been developed yet. Instead many clinicians use open-ended written narratives or written descriptions of pictures to assess writing abilities. Such samples provide qualitatively rich data regarding linguistic abilities (e.g., grammar and vocabulary), spelling, informational content, and discourse structure, as well as nonlinguistic factors such as visual-spatial organization and graphomotor adequacy. However, such writing samples can be difficult to score in a standardized fashion. In one such task, the Written Expression subtest of the Peabody Individual Achievement Test—Revised (Markwardt, 1998), the tester presents a picture and allows the patient 20 minutes to write a story description. The written sample is scored according to a holistic rating as well as a detailed analytic rating that focuses on content, organization, and mechanics. Like other open-ended narrative tasks, results of this subtest show only modest reliability and validity so they are not even included in the composite achievement score. The Writing Samples subtest of the Woodcock-Johnson Psycho-Educational Battery-Revised (Woodcock et al., 1990) offers a different means of assessing writing skill. The patient is required to write sentences in response to various instructions (e.g., "write a good sentence that tells what a snake looks like" or "write a good sentence using the words *despite her anger*"). Scoring focuses on factors such as inclusion of specific details or attributes, correct use of conceptually complex terms, accurate description of presented pictures, and adherence to a certain writing style. Punctuation, capitalization, spelling, and most usage errors are specifically excluded from consideration in scoring. The Writing Samples subtest has acceptable scoring reliability and seems to be best suited for assessing the higher level conceptual, inferential, and organizational aspects of writing.

Tests based on the syndromal approach are more appropriate for differential diagnosis of patients with obvious language impairments who often score at floor levels on screening measures. These more detailed language tests are lengthier and require more specialized knowledge and expertise to administer.

The Minnesota Test for Differential Diagnosis for Aphasia (MTDDA; Schuell, 1973) is a comprehensive examination that addresses five language modalities: auditory disturbances (9 subtests), visual and reading disturbances (9 subtests), speech and language disturbances (15 subtests), visuomotor and writing disturbances (10 subtests), and numerical relations and arithmetic processes (4 subtests). In addition to subtest scores, a clinical rating (0–6) and a diagnostic scale (0–4) are tabulated. Though it yields much data, the MTDDA does not classify aphasia into traditional diagnostic categories, thus limiting its clinical usefulness. Aphasia classification, according to the MTDDA, is based on the notion that a single unitary central disorder results in reduction of all language abilities but is modified by certain peripheral disorders. The MTDDA identifies five aphasic syndromes: simple aphasia, aphasia with visual involvement, aphasia with sensorimotor involvement, aphasia with scattered findings compatible with generalized brain damage, and irreversible aphasic syndrome. Two additional minor syndromes are defined: mild aphasia with persistent dysfluency (dysarthria) and aphasia

with intermittent auditory imperception. The test takes several hours to administer, though reliable short forms have been developed (Powell, Bailey, & Clark, 1980).

The Western Aphasia Battery (WAB; Kertesz, 1982) is a modification of the original version of the Boston Diagnostic Aphasia Examination (Goodglass & Kaplan, 1972). It uses similar content and materials, but unlike the BDAE, which relies on a qualitative analysis of the response profile to describe patients, the WAB uses language test scores to classify all patients into one of eight aphasia syndromes. The test has been criticized because it ignores individual differences and empirical data showing that not all patients fit neatly into one of the limited number of aphasia syndromes. The WAB groups tasks into those assessing oral language abilities (10 subtests involving spontaneous speech, auditory comprehension, repetition, and naming) and those assessing visual language (7 subtests involving reading, writing, praxis, and construction abilities). Spontaneous speech is rated with two 10-point scales: one for information content and one for fluency. The information content rating estimates functional communication (Kertesz, 1979). The fluency scale classifies patients into two dichotomous groups: nonfluent and fluent. The Raven's Colored Progressive Matrices (Raven, 1976) is included in the WAB as a measure of general cognitive capacity. Four summary scores can be calculated: Aphasia Quotient (AQ), Language Quotient (LQ), Performance Quotient (PQ), and Cortical Quotient (CQ). Although quantitatively rigorous, the WAB's major shortcoming is that it does not yield qualitative information that is useful for treatment planning.

The Porch Index of Communicative Ability (PICA; Porch, 1981) consists of 18 subtests that each use the same 10 common objects. Using PICA, testers assess three modalities: verbal, gestural, and graphic. A unique multidimensional score is generated for each response. This score can range from 1 point (no response) to 16 points for a complex response (accurate, responsive, complete, prompt, and efficient). Performance is summarized through mean scores or response levels for the verbal, gestural, and graphic modalities and an overall performance score. The PICA does not allow classification of aphasia and does not address the issue of functional communication, although it yields information in a unique format that can be useful for prognosis and measurement of recovery. Competence to administer the test requires a 40-hour training workshop.

The Aphasia Diagnostic Profile (ADP; Helm-Estabrooks, 1992) addresses classification and severity of aphasia, as well as issues regarding recovery and general social-emotional status of the patient. A major advantage of the ADP is that it can usually be completed within an hour. It has been designed for use with a wide range of neurogenic impairments in addition to aphasia. The ADP consists of nine subtests and a behavioral profile. The subtests include personal information, writing, reading, fluency, naming, auditory comprehension, repetition, elicited gestures, and singing. Based on subtest performance, five profiles can be evaluated: aphasia severity profile, error profile, classification profile, alternative communication profile, and behavioral profile.

The Boston Assessment of Severe Aphasia (BASA; Helm-Estabrooks, Ramsberger, Moyan, & Nicholas, 1989) was developed for patients with severe language impairments. It elicits nonpropositional speech through emotionally laden stimuli. The BASA includes a variety of tasks and modalities including social greetings and simple conversation, personally relevant yes/no question pairs, orientation to time and place, bucco-facial and limb praxis, singing, repetition, comprehension of number symbols, object naming, action picture items, comprehension of coin names, famous faces, emotional words, phrases and symbols, and visual-spatial items. Results of the test can be summarized in relation to auditory comprehension, praxis, oral-gestural expression, reading comprehension, gesture recognition, writing, and visual-spatial skills. The patient's responses are scored for response modality (verbal or gestural), communicative quality, perseveration, and presence of affect. This test provides information regarding functional communication strengths and weaknesses, which is helpful in planning language treatment.

Finally, the Arizona Battery for Communication Disorders of Dementia (ABCD; Bayles & Tomoeda, 1990) is a comprehensive assessment of cognitive-communicative functioning that enables testers to identify and quantify linguistic communication processes and provides information about verbal, episodic, and semantic memory, mental status, figure copying, drawing abilities, and story retelling. In contrast to most of the other measures described previously, which are intended for assessing patients who develop language disorders following an acute central nervous system insult such as a stroke or traumatic brain injury, the ABCD is designed to be especially sensitive to the language disturbances associated with different neurodegenerative dementia syndromes.

Functional communication and pragmatic skills are particularly important to assess in patients with more severe language dysfunction. Communication involves production of language and reception of language in an interactive social process. Functional communication refers to the way the patient communicates in everyday environments and includes nonverbal as well as verbal behaviors.

One type of functional assessment consists of multidimensional measurement of activities of daily living, which can also include communication as one of several activities. The Functional Independence Measure (FIM) is one such as-

sessment (State University of New York at Buffalo, 1993). FIM quantifies the overall severity of a disability, as well as functional impairment in six areas including self-care, sphincter control, mobility, locomotion, social cognition, and communication. The assessment is brief and involves two aspects of communication—functional expression and comprehension—that are rated globally on a seven-point scale ranging from total dependence on a helper to total independence. Brief global functional assessments are most useful in the rehabilitation or acute hospital settings, where they can be used for screening as a prelude to more detailed language assessment.

The second type of functional assessment consists of unidimensional measurements emphasizing speech and language. Functional communication can be assessed by formal tests in which the clinician observes the patient's behavior in the clinic or by rating scales and inventories that are completed, usually by caregivers, on the basis of behavior observed outside of the clinic.

An example of a formal test is the Communication Activities of Daily Living-Second Edition (CADL-2; Holland, Frattali, & Fromm, 1999). The CADL was designed to enable assessment of the functional communication skills of adults with neurogenic disorders. Testers assess verbal and nonverbal aspects of communication during role playing of familiar situations such as shopping or making a telephone call. Seven categories of communication are evaluated: social interactions; divergent communication; contextual communication; sequential relationships; nonverbal communication; reading, writing and using numbers; and humor/metaphor/absurdity. Responses are scored on a three-point scale (0 = wrong, 1 = adequate, 2 = correct), where a higher score reflects greater appropriateness and success of the communication, rather than correctness of the language. This is a psychometrically sound measure that correlates well with other measures of aphasia severity and also provides unique information about functional capacities.

The Functional Communication Profile (FCP; Sarno, 1969) describes assessment of functional capacity through observation of the patient's behavior in interaction with the clinician. Clinicians evaluate performances in five categories: movement, speaking, understanding, reading, and other (e.g., writing and calculations). Each item is rated on a nine-point scale, relative to estimated premorbid capacity. When used by a skilled and knowledgeable professional rater, this method provides sensitive measures of aphasia severity in everyday functioning and changes in behavior related to treatment or recovery.

The Pragmatic Protocol (Prutting & Kirchner, 1987) is another measure that relies on observation of natural communication in the clinic. Clinicians use 15 minutes of conversation between the patient and a familiar partner as the basis for rating 30 pragmatic parameters covering a wide range of speech acts and discourse abilities. Verbal, nonverbal, and paralinguistic behaviors are rated as appropriate, inappropriate, or not observed.

The Functional Assessment of Communication Skills (ASHA-FACS; Frattali, Thompson, Holland, Wohl, & Ferketic, 1995) provides tools to assess the use of language and other communicative skills in functional settings of daily life. A clinician generates a rating based on information provided by a knowledgeable caregiver. The ASHA-FACS uses the World Health Organization (WHO) framework that distinguishes among impairment (a loss or disruption in physical or psychological structure or function), disability (functional consequences of the impairment, e.g., communication problems in the context of daily life), and handicap (the social consequences of the disability, i.e., quality of life). The ASHA-FACS measures disability. It covers four domains: social communication, communication of basic needs, daily planning, and reading/writing/number concepts. The ASHA-FACS has qualitative and quantitative rating scales. A mean score in each domain is calculated and these scores make up the *Profile of Communication Independence.* A computerized version of the assessment is available.

The cognitive neuropsychological approach has led to the development of test batteries that provide detailed characterization of psycholinguistic aspects of a language disturbance and are intended primarily to direct rehabilitation planning. These tests are not designed to be administered in toto; rather the batteries provide a number of discrete tasks that can be used to explore component cognitive abilities and disabilities specific to an individual patient and can identify which language processes are operating at suboptimal levels.

The design of the Psycholinguistic Assessments of Language Processing in Aphasia (PALPA; Kay, Lesser, & Coltheart, 1992) was guided by an explicit psycholinguistic cognitive model. The test assesses specific language processing skills in patients already known to have aphasia or another neurolinguistic disorder. Sixty subtests fall within four broad sections: auditory processing, reading and spelling, picture and word semantics, and sentence comprehension. Each subtest is designed to assess the effects of one or two psycholinguistic variables on performance (e.g., word frequency and imageability). Clinicians can map the results onto the psycholinguistic model detailed by the PALPA authors by following the instructions for each subtest. These instructions identify the variables assessed and suggest additional variables and subtests that may be further explored depending on results of the subtest. The battery is to be used in a flexible

manner. No rigid guidelines as to the starting point of the assessment or the choice or order of administration of tasks are provided. The assessment is completely driven by hypotheses generated by the clinician. The advantages of the PALPA are that it yields very precise information to characterize the language abilities of an individual patient and provides important data for guiding language treatment. Despite its psycholinguistic rigor, however, this instrument lacks psychometric sophistication. Normative data are presented for only 32 non-brain-damaged individuals. The authors suggest that users of the test might need to collect their own norms. They admit that the performances of non-brain-damaged individuals and even most aphasia patients are at ceiling levels for a number of subtests, so actually discerning the more subtle effects of different psycholinguistic variables on performance can be difficult. Successful use of this battery presupposes a great deal of psycholinguistic knowledge on the part of the clinician. One further consideration in using the PALPA is that it was developed in the United Kingdom and a number of its tasks contain items not familiar to American speakers (e.g., *hosepipe* and *pram*). The Psycholinguistic Assessment of Language (Caplan, 1992) is another language measure derived from cognitive neuropsychological theory, still in experimental form. This assessment, which is similar to the PALPA, was developed in the United States and Canada.

The Boston Diagnostic Aphasia Examination-Third Edition (see p. 11) (BDAE-Third Edition; Goodglass et al., 2001) represents a unique procedure for language assessment that combines principles from each of the three approaches: psycholinguistic, cognitive neuropsychological, and syndromal. The BDAE-Third Edition is a comprehensive, multimodality evaluation designed to three purposes: (1) to diagnose and classify aphasia syndromes and lead to inferences regarding cerebral localization, underlying impaired linguistic processes and consequent compensatory strategies; (2) to measure a wide range of language performances in order to provide a baseline as well as a reliable measurement of change over time; and (3) to assess individual assets and liabilities within language domains to facilitate treatment plans. The BDAE-Third Edition provides comprehensive measures of conversational and expository speech, auditory comprehension, oral expression (including the Boston Naming Test), repetition, reading, and writing, as well as an appended apraxia assessment. A diagnostic summary is provided by means of a rating scale that profiles speech characteristics including articulatory agility, phrase length, grammatical form, melodic line (prosody), paraphasias in running speech, word-finding, repetition, and auditory comprehension. Scores on individual subtests are interpreted with respect to those of a heterogeneous sample of aphasic patients. A global severity rating scale

(0–5) is also included. In addition to its use for diagnosis, classification, and description of aphasia, the BDAE-Third Edition is expanded to provide measures for psycholinguistic and cognitive characterization of aphasic patients. In addition to traditional aphasia measures, the BDAE-Third Edition includes detailed measures of syntactic processing, assessment of discrete cognitive components of reading and writing, and an expanded analysis of discourse abilities. Like other language assessment tools driven by cognitive neuropsychological theory, the BDAE-Third Edition is not intended to be administered in its entirety to each patient. In addition to a standard form, a short form as well as extended testing subtests are available.

CONCLUSIONS

Language assessment has several goals. The first purpose of assessment is to determine the presence of language dysfunction. To do this, it is important to obtain an estimate of premorbid verbal capacities. Because language ability is closely related to education and intelligence, careful analysis of premorbid history is necessary for ascertaining whether current abilities are discrepant with estimated premorbid capacities. A second goal of assessment is to determine the type and severity of the language problem for differential diagnosis and classification. This requires analyzing the ways in which language is impaired as well as the evaluation of preserved areas of function. Another important goal of language assessment is to address prognostic issues and issues regarding language treatment and rehabilitation using the aforementioned data. Language assessment is often used to document progress or change in symptoms over time. Finally, determining the relationship of the language disturbance to other cognitive and behavioral deficits is critical. Language disorders occur as part of many different neurobehavioral syndromes. The presence of defective language performance should not be taken to indicate an aphasic disorder, as many nonaphasic language problems can occur as the result of various neurological syndromes. Assessment of language and language dysfunction, therefore, needs to be integrated with comprehensive evaluation of other cognitive and behavioral symptoms.

REFERENCES

Alexander, M.P., & Benson, D.F. (1991). The aphasias and related disturbances. In R.J. Joynt (Ed.), *Clinical neurology* (Vol. 1, pp. 1–58). Philadelphia: Lippincott.

Bayles, K.A., & Tomoeda, C.K. (1990). *Arizona Battery for Communication Disorders of Dementia.* Tuscon, AZ: Canyonlands Publishing.

Beauvois, M.F., & Derousene, J. (1981). Lexical or orthographic agraphia. *Brain, 104,* 21–49.

Behrmann, M., & Byng, S. (1992). A cognitive approach to the neurorehabilitation of acquired language disorders. In D.I. Margolin (Ed.), *Cognitive Neuropsychology in Clinical Practice* (pp. 327–350). New York: Oxford University Press.

Benson, D.F. (1967). Fluency in aphasia: Correlation with radioactive scan localization. *Cortex, 3,* 373–394.

Benton, A., Hamsher, K., Varney, N.R., & Spreen, O. (1994). *Multilingual aphasia examination.* San Antonio, TX: Psychological Corporation.

Benton, A.L. (1968). Differential behavioral effects in frontal lobe disease. *Neuropsychologia, 6,* 53–60.

Blumstein, S.E. (1998). Phonological aspects of aphasia. In M.T. Sarno (Ed.), *Acquired aphasia* (pp. 157–185). San Diego, CA: Academic Press.

Bock, K., & Levelt, W.J.M. (1994). Language production: Grammatical encoding. In M.A. Gernsbacher (Ed.), *Handbook of Psycholinguistics* (pp. 945–984). San Diego, CA: Academic Press.

Brownell, H.H., Gardner, H., Prather, P., & Martino, G. (1995). Language, communication, and the right hemisphere. In H.S. Kirshner (Ed.), *Handbook of neurological speech and language disorders* (pp. 325–349). New York: Marcel Dekker.

Buckingham, H.W. (1998). Explanations for the concept of apraxia of speech. In M.T. Taylor (Ed.), *Acquired aphasia* (pp. 269–307). San Diego, CA: Academic Press.

Butters, N., Granholm, E., Salmon, D.P., Grant, I., & Wolfe, J. (1987). Episodic and semantic memory: A comparison of amnesic and demented patients. *Journal of Clinical and Experimental Neuropsychology, 9,* 479–497.

Butterworth, B. (1992). Disorders of phonological encoding. *Cognition, 42,* 261–286.

Caplan, D. (1992). *Language: Structure, processing, and disorders.* Cambridge, MA: MIT Press.

Chedru, F., & Geschwind, N. (1972). Disorders of higher cortical functions in acute confusional states. *Cortex, 8,* 395–411.

Coltheart, M., Patterson, K.E., & Marshall, J.C. (1987). *Deep dyslexia.* London: Routledge & Kegan Paul.

Cummings, J.L., & Benson, D.F. (1992). *Dementia: A clinical approach.* Boston: Butterworth-Heinemann.

Damasio, A.R., & Tranel, D. (1993). Nouns and verbs are retrieved with differently distributed neural systems. *Proceedings of the National Academy of Sciences of the USA, 90,* 4957–4960.

Danly, M., Cooper, W., & Shapiro, B. (1983). Fundamental frequency, language processing, and linguistic structure in Wernicke's aphasia. *Brain and Language, 19,* 1–24.

Danly, M., & Shapiro, B. (1982). Speech prosody in Broca's aphasia. *Brain and Language, 16,* 171–190.

DeRenzi, E., & Vignolo, L.A. (1962). The token test: A sensitive test to detect receptive disturbances in aphasics. *Brain, 85,* 665–678.

Dunn, L.M., & Dunn, E.S. (1997). *Peabody picture vocabulary test—III.* Circle Pines, MN: American Guidance Service.

Farah, M. (1990). *Visual agnosia.* Cambridge, MA: MIT Press.

Foldi, N. (1987). Appreciation of pragmatic interpretations of indirect commands: Comparison of right and left hemisphere brain-damaged patients. *Brain & Language, 31,* 88–108.

Frattali, C., Thompson, C.K., Holland, A.L., Wohl, C.B., & Ferketic, M.M. (1995). *American speech-language-hearing association functional assessment of communication skills for adults.* Rockville, MD: ASHA.

Frazen, M.D., Haut, M.W., Rankin, E., & Keefover, R. (1995). Empirical comparison of alternate forms of the Boston naming test. *The Clinical Neuropsychologist, 9,* 225–229.

Friedman, R., & Alexander, M.P. (1989). Written spelling agraphia. *Brain and Language, 36,* 503–517.

Friedman, R.B. (1995). Two types of phonological alexia. *Cortex, 31,* 397–403.

Garrett, M.F. (1982). Production of speech: Observations from normal and pathological language use. In A.W. Ellis (Ed.), *Normality and pathology in cognitive functions* (pp. 19–76). New York: Academic Press.

Glosser, G., & Deser, T. (1990). Patterns of discourse production among neurological patients with fluent language disorders. *Brain and Language, 40,* 67–88.

Glosser, G., & Donofrio, N. (2001). Differences between nouns and verbs after anterior temporal lobectomy. *Neuropsychology, 15,* 39–47.

Glosser, G., & Friedman, R.B. (1995). A cognitive neuropsychological framework for assessing reading disorders. In R.L. Mapou & J. Spector (Eds.), *Neuropsychological assessment of cognitive function* (pp. 115–136). New York: Plenum.

Glosser, G., Weiner, M., & Kaplan, E. (1988). Variations in aphasic language behaviors. *Journal of Speech and Hearing Disorders, 53,* 115–124.

Goodglass, H. (1993). *Understanding aphasia.* San Diego, CA: Academic Press.

Goodglass, H., & Budin, C. (1988). Category and modality-specific dissociations in word comprehension and concurrent phonological dyslexia: A case study. *Neuropsychologia, 26,* 67–88.

Goodglass, H., & Kaplan, E. (1972). *The assessment of aphasia and related disorders.* Philadelphia: Lea & Febiger.

Goodglass, H., & Kaplan, E. (1983). *The assessment of aphasia and related disorders* (2nd ed.). Philadelphia: Lea and Febiger.

Goodglass, H., Kaplan, E., & Barresi, B. (2001). *Boston diagnostic aphasia examination* (3rd ed.). Philadelphia: Lippincott Williams & Wilkins.

Goodglass, H., Quadfasel, F., & Timberlake, W. (1964). Phrase length and the type and severity of aphasia. *Cortex, 1,* 133–153.

Grossman, M. (1999). Sentence processing in Parkinson's disease. *Brain and Cognition, 40,* 387–413.

Helm-Estabrooks, N. (1992). *Aphasia diagnostic profiles.* Austin, TX: Pro-Ed.

Helm-Estabrooks, N., Ramsberger, G., Moyan, A.L., & Nicholas, M. (1989). *Boston assessment of severe aphasia.* Chicago: Riverside Press.

Hillis, A.E., & Caramazza, A. (1989). The graphemic buffer and attentional mechanisms. *Brain and language, 36,* 208–235.

Hodges, J.R., Patterson, K., Oxbury, S., & Funnell, E. (1992). Semantic dementia: Progressive fluent aphasia with temporal lobe atrophy. *Brain, 115,* 1783–1806.

Hodges, J.R., Salmon, D.P., & Butters, N. (1991). The nature of the naming deficit in Alzheimer's and Huntington's disease. *Brain, 114,* 1547–1558.

Holland, A., Frattali, C., & Fromm, D. (1999). *Communication abilities in daily living (CADL-2)* (2nd ed.). Austin, TX: Pro-Ed.

Impara, J.C., & Plake, B.S. (1998). *The thirteenth mental measurements yearbook.* Lincoln, NE: Buros Institute of Mental Measurements.

Ivnik, R., Malec, J.F., Smith, G.E., Tangelos, E.G., & Petersen, R.C. (1996). Neuropsychological tests' norms above age 55. *The Clinical Neuropsychologist, 10,* 262–278.

Joanette, Y., Goulet, P., & Hannequin, D. (1990). *Right hemisphere and verbal communication.* New York: Springer-Verlag.

Kaplan, E., Goodglass, H., & Weintraub, S. (1983). *Boston naming test.* Philadelphia: Lea & Febiger.

Kay, J., Lesser, R., & Coltheart, M. (1992). *Psycholinguistic assessments of language processing in aphasia.* Hove, East Sussex: Lawrence Erlbaum Associates.

Kertesz, A. (1979). *Aphasia and associated disorders.* (1st ed.). New York: Grune and Stratton.

Kertesz, A. (1982). *Western aphasia battery.* New York: Grune & Stratton.

Kohn, S.E., & Goodglass, H. (1985). Picture naming in aphasia. *Brain and Language, 24,* 266–283.

LaPointe, L.L., & Horner, J. (1998). *Reading comprehension battery for aphasia* (2nd ed.). Austin, TX: Pro-Ed.

MacGinitie, W.H., & MacGinitie, R. K. (1989). *Gates-MacGinitie reading tests* (3rd ed.). Chicago, IL: The Riverside Publishing Co.

Mack, W.J., Freed, D.M., Williams, B.W., & Henderson, V.W. (1992). Boston naming test: Shortened versions for use in Alzheimer's disease. *Journal of Gerontology: Psychological Sciences, 47,* P154–P158.

Markwardt, F.C. (1998). *Peabody individual achievement test-revised.* Circle Pines, MN: American Guidance Service.

Marr, D. (1982). *Vision.* San Francisco: W.H. Freeman Company.

Menn, L., Ramsberger, G., & Helm-Estabrooks, N. (1994). A linguistic communication measure for aphasic narratives. *Aphasiology, 8,* 343–359.

Nebes, R.D. (1992). Cognitive dysfunction in Alzheimer's disease. In F.I.M. Craik & T.A. Salthouse (Eds.), *The handbook of aging and cognition* (pp. 373–446). Hillsdale, N.J.: Erlbaum Associates.

Nicholas, L.D., & Brookshire, R.H. (1992). A system for scoring main concepts in the discourse of non-brain-damaged and aphasic speakers. *Clinical Aphasiology, 21,* 87–99.

Nicholas, M., Obler, L., Albert, M., & Goodglass, H. (1985). Lexical retrieval in healthy aging. *Cortex, 21,* 595–606.

Patterson, K.E., & Kay, J. (1982). Letter-by-letter reading: Psychological description of a neurological syndrome. *Quarterly Journal of Experimental Psychology, 34A,* 411–441.

Patterson, K.E., Marshall, J.C., & Coltheart, M. (1985). *Surface dyslexia: Neuropsychological and cognitive studies of phonological reading.* London: Lawrence Erlbaum Associates.

Porch, B.E. (1981). *Porch index of communicative ability: Vol. 2 Administration, scoring, and interpretation* (3rd ed.). Palo Alto, CA: Consulting Psychologists Press.

Powell, G.E., Bailey, S., & Clark, E. (1980). A very short form of the Minnesota aphasia test. *British Journal of Social and Clinical Psychology, 19,* 189–194.

Prutting, C.A., & Kirchner, D.M. (1987). A clinical appraisal of the pragmatic aspects of language. *Journal of Speech and Hearing Disorders, 52,* 105–119.

Raven, J.C. (1976). *Manual for the Raven's Progressive Matrices.* London: H.K. Lewis.

Roeltgen, D.P. (1993). Agraphia. In K.M. Heilman & E. Valenstein (Eds.), *Clinical neuropsychology* (3rd ed., pp. 65–90). New York: Oxford University Press.

Ross, E.D. (2000). Affective prosody and the aprosodias. In M.M. Mesulam (Ed.), *Principles of behavioral and cognitive neurology* (2nd ed., pp. 316–331). New York: Oxford University Press.

Saffran, E.M., Schwartz, M.F., & Marin, O.S.M. (1980). Evidence from aphasia: Isolating the components of a production model. In *Language production* (Vol. 1). London: Academic Press.

Sarno, M.T. (1969). *Functional communication profile.* New York: Institute of Rehabilitation Medicine.

Schuell, H. (1973). *Differential diagnosis of aphasia with the Minnesota test.* (2nd ed.) Minneapolis, MN: University of Minnesota Press.

Searle, J. (1969). *Speech acts.* London: Cambridge University Press.

Shewan, C.M. (1988). The Shewan spontaneous language analysis (SSLA) system for aphasic adults: Description, reliability and validity. *Journal of Communication Disorders, 21,* 103–138.

Spreen, O., & Risser, A.H. (1998). Assessment of aphasia. In M.T. Sarno (Ed.), *Acquired aphasia* (3rd ed., pp. 71–156). San Diego, CA: Academic Press.

Spreen, O., & Strauss, E. (1998). *A Compendium of neuropsychological tests.* New York: Oxford University Press.

State University of New York at Buffalo (1993). *Guide for the uniform data set for medical rehabilitation (adult FIM).* Buffalo, NY: State University of New York at Buffalo.

Ulatowska, H.K., Freedman-Stern, R.F., Doyel, A.W., Macaluso-Hayes, S., & North, A.J. (1983). Production of narrative discourse in aphasia. *Brain & Language, 19,* 317–334.

Warrington, E.K., & Shallice, T. (1984). Category-specific semantic impairments. *Brain, 107,* 829–854.

Wiederholt, J.L., & Bryant, B.R. (2001). *Gray oral reading tests.* (4th ed.) Austin, TX: Pro-Ed.

Wilkinson, G.S. (1993). *WRAT3 administration manual.* Wilmington, DE: Wide Range, Inc.

Williams, B.W., Mack, W., & Henderson, V.W. (1989). Boston naming test in Alzheimer's disease. *Neuropsychologia, 27,* 1073–1079.

Woodcock, R.W., & Johnson, M.B. (1990). *Woodcock-Johnson psycho-educational battery-revised.* Chicago, IL: The Riverside Publishing Company.

Yorkston, K., & Beukelman, D. (1980). An analysis of connected speech samples of aphasic and normal speakers. *Journal of Speech and Hearing Disorders, 45,* 27–36.

CHAPTER 13

Language Assessment in Children

ELIZABETH KELLEY, GARLAND JONES, AND DEBORAH FEIN

Language is one of the central components of being human and is an aspect that separates us from the other primates with whom we share so much of our genetic structure. Language is an essential constituent of human cognition, culture, and day-to-day lives. Although language is such an intrinsic part of what it means to be human, many individuals experience great difficulties in acquiring language. The majority of children acquire the basic components of language with no formal instruction and are quite fluent in their native language before they enter school. For some children, however, learning language is not so simple.

The rates and ages at which typically developing children acquire language vary a great deal. Some children may say their first words at 10 months; other children may not utter a word until they are well into their second year of life. Some children begin speaking in two-word utterances, or *telegraphic speech,* shortly after they begin speaking; others do not begin to put words together for some time. This variation makes a "normative" study of language acquisition quite difficult. However, regular patterns of language development that are common to all children who develop in a typical manner occur. Typically developing children acquire all aspects of language—phonology and prosody, syntax and morphology, semantics, and pragmatics—in tandem, although these aspects may develop along different pathways (Berko-Gleason, 1993).

These patterns of language development allow clinicians to assess whether children are simply "late talkers" (Thal & Bates, 1988), or whether those who appear to be having difficulties are progressing along the "correct" path. Much of the research in the area of atypical language development

examines this question of whether language is deviant or merely delayed (Curtiss, Katz, & Tallal, 1992; Garcia O'Shea, Harel, & Fein, in press). To address this issue it is necessary to follow how children develop language over time and note the age of onset of a particular aspect of language, whether development of this aspect follows a typical developmental rate and course, and the level at which the child plateaus (Garcia O'Shea et al., in press). Do children with mental retardation develop language according to the same pattern as typically developing children, merely at a slower rate, or is something fundamentally different in the manner by which they acquire their language? Is Specific Language Impairment (SLI) in children simply a delay in the acquisition of language, or is the cause of these children's difficulties a basic underlying deficit in their ability to learn language? Are children with MR simply delayed in all aspects of their development, or do specific aspects of language cause them particular difficulty? Do children with autism experience communicative difficulties because of their difficulties in social relatedness, or is something inherently different about the way these children process language?

Another important issue to address in the study of atypical language development is whether the different aspects of language develop in tandem or asynchronously in these children (Berko-Gleason, 1993; Kelley et al., 2001). Do phonology and prosody, syntax and morphology, semantics, and pragmatics develop at a uniform rate, or do relative strengths occur in some areas and relative weaknesses in others? It is also important to determine whether language acquisition and nonlinguistic aspects of cognition are developing in tandem. Currently the diagnostic criteria for SLI requires that these children have nonverbal IQs that are within the normal range and verbal IQs that are at least one standard deviation below the norm (Aram, Morris, & Hall, 1993; Cole & Fey, 1996; Francis; Fletcher; Shaywitz, B.A.; Shaywitz, S.E.; & Rourke, 1996; Stark, Tallal, Kallman, & Mellits, 1983), although this criterion is controversial (McCauley, 2001). The majority of IQ tests are language-based; at the very least, the test instructions are given in a verbal format. Children with language impairment thus experience a "double jeopardy" (Warner & Nelson, 2000; p.149) in which they must perform higher on the nonverbal parts of the assessments, which are nonetheless presented in verbal form (for an excellent discussion of this issue, refer to Francis et al., 1996). Furthermore, the discrepancy between verbal and nonverbal IQ depends on the specific tests used (Cole, Mills, & Kelley, 1994), and discrepancy scores are more unreliable than the individual tests (Cole, Dale, & Mills, 1992). Children with low IQs can have all the other characteristics of language-disordered children (Bishop, 1997), and recommendations for intervention should be based on a need for intervention for these children to benefit from education, rather than on an artificial discrepancy criterion (Warner et al., 2000). It is also crucial to distinguish SLI, which is a developmental language disorder, from acquired language disorders that occur as a result of brain damage (Garcia O'Shea et al., in press).

The relationship between language and social development is also important. This relationship is crucial in ruling in or out such diagnoses as mental retardation and autism. Children whose social development is proceeding at the same delayed pace or at a slower pace than their language development are likely to receive a diagnosis on the Pervasive Development Disorder (PDD) spectrum (Fein et al., 1996). Language assessment must therefore be carried out in the context of a larger assessment that includes tests of hearing, social development and play, nonverbal communication, attention and nonverbal cognition, and family and cultural patterns of language and communication (Garcia O'Shea et al., in press). If articulation is an issue, an examination of the oro-motor cavity by a speech and language pathologist may be in order (Warner et al., 2000). Because verbal memory is usually impaired in children with language impairments (Rapin, 1996), both verbal and nonverbal memory should be assessed.

The purpose of such a language assessment is first to provide a diagnosis and level of functioning for the different aspects of language discussed later in this chapter. The findings of this assessment document the need for intervention, specify the areas most in need of intervention as well as areas of strength, and establish a baseline for documenting progress. Assessments may also address whether low achievement in language has a linguistic basis or rests in part on cultural, attentional, or cognitive factors. Repeated assessments help in determining long-term prognosis and the effectiveness of ongoing interventions.

In general, the younger the child, the poorer the psychometric properties of tests are, the less reliable and predictive the test results are, and the more situationally dependent the child's behavior is (Garcia O'Shea, et al., in press). Thus, it is important to observe, or at least gather information about, the child's communicative competence in multiple settings and with multiple partners, include parents in the evaluation, and rely on informant reports as well as observed behaviors. Even for the older child, where test scores are more reliable, it is necessary to compare test scores with actual communicative behavior with the examiner and with more familiar interaction partners. In addition to observation, parents and teachers should be interviewed about the child's communicative behavior with adults and peers. A history of delayed early language milestones supports the presence of SLI, MR, or one of the PDDs.

It is imperative that clinicians keep these questions in mind when assessing the language of developing children. An understanding of how typical language development proceeds is crucial in assessing a child's language difficulties (McCauley, 2001). This chapter addresses issues of typical and atypical language development from an assessment perspective. We begin the chapter by discussing prelinguistic forms of communication, which may be the only forms of communication that can be assessed in very young children or children with serious disability. The four major components of language are discussed: phonology and prosody; syntax and morphology; semantics; and pragmatics and discourse. For each of these aspects of language, we briefly discuss their development in typically developing children, some representative tests for assessing them, and the limitations of these tests.

In addition to tests that assess a single linguistic function, we briefly discuss a few batteries that are designed to comprehensively assess multiple functions. These assessment tools are beneficial in that their subtests are all normed on the same populations, allowing the comparison of subtests across different aspects of language. In the course of our discussion, we offer a brief description of particular subtests as they relate to specific aspects of language. These comprehensive language assessments include the Clinical Evaluation of Language-Fundamentals (CELF-3), which assesses receptive and expressive language abilities in the areas of word meanings, word and sentence structure, and recall of spoken language. The Clinical Evaluation of Language Fundamentals-Preschool (CELF-Preschool; Wiig, Secord, & Semel, 1992) assesses several aspects of receptive and expressive language and includes a screening test. The Test of Language Development-Primary, 3rd Edition, (TOLD-P:3; Newcomer & Hammill, 1997) focuses on expressive and receptive competencies in multiple linguistic areas. The Comprehensive Assessment of Spoken Language (CASL; Carrow-Woolfolk, 1999) is designed to measure multiple aspects of speech through a series of subtests that become progressively more complex. The Test of Early Language Development, 2nd Edition, (TELD-2; Hresko, Reid, & Hammill, 1991) assesses expressive and receptive language form and content. The Preschool Language Scale-3 (PLS-3; Zimmerman, Steiner, & Pond, 1992) provides total language, auditory comprehension, and expressive communication scores. We also refer to a few neuropsychological assessment instruments like the NEPSY (Korkman, Kirk, & Kemp, 1998) and The Boston Diagnostic Aphasia Exam (BDAE; Goodglass, Kaplan, & Barresi, 2001) with respect to their contributions to the assessment of specific language functions. This is not a complete listing of all language tests; for a more comprehensive listing, we refer you to Warner et al. (2000).

We conclude the chapter with a discussion of several important issues in the clinical assessment of language, including the difficulties clinicians experience in assessing language in clinical or minority populations; modifications that can be made to tests to better assess true capability; some alternatives to standardized testing; and the importance of conducting an in-depth assessment of the child.

PRELINGUISTIC COMMUNICATION

A clinician may be required to assess communicative competence in a child who is either too young or too impaired to speak (McCauley, 2001). How is it possible to assess communication without spoken language? One can assess several forms of communication that are precursors to language in infants (McCathren, Warren, & Yoder, 1996; Warner et al., 2000). Some behaviors used by the severely disabled that appear to be symptoms of their disorders may also represent efforts to communicate and should be taken into account when assessing a child's communicative abilities.

Babbling is one of the precursors to language that is thought to be essential to language development (McCathren et al., 1996; Sachs, 1993). By six months of age, most infants begin to form consonants and babble with consonant-vowel combinations. At approximately 10 months of age, babbling overlaps considerably with the onset of meaningful speech; infants at this stage begin to use a rich prosody in their babbling. To adults it may seem like infants are indeed using their own

language to speak. Infants try to communicate; they use eye contact, intonation, and gesture while delivering these babbles (Sachs, 1993). Babbling is often interpreted by parents as an intentional act on the part of the infant to communicate, and by having it treated as such, infants begin to learn the pragmatics of language as well as phonological aspects (Bremner, 1994; McCathren et al., 1996). Even deaf infants engage in babbling, although this babbling is not sustained when the infants are unable to receive feedback from hearing themselves (Oller & Eilers, 1988). Many retrospective reports of parents of children with autism suggest that children with autism may not progress normally through the stages of babbling; this may have a deleterious effect on their language acquisition (Prizant, 1996).

Another important prelinguistic communicative act is joint attention. Infants and their caregivers need to engage in shared gaze and turn-taking actions (Tomasello, 1999). By four months of age, typically developing children are engaging in *proto-conversations* with their caregivers (McCathren et al., 1996). A mother's smile at an infant seems to encourage the infant to smile in return. This leads to the mother making some sort of vocalization, which the infant replies to with her own vocalization. The term proto-conversation is used because these exchanges have the turn-taking nature of conversations (Sachs, 1993).

These exchanges develop into joint attention where the infant and caregiver share attention with each other and with an object in their environment. Joint attention and the intersubjectivity of caregiver and infant that it fosters play an important role in the acquisition of the semantics and pragmatics of language (Tomasello, 1999). The infant learns not only to follow an adult's line of gaze, but that when both are attending to an object and the adult makes a sound, this sound is the name of this object (Tomasello, 1999). Retrospective (and prospective) reports and studies with older children suggest that children with autism develop joint attention capabilities with their caregivers extremely late in development; this may be because of these children's aversion to eye gaze (Mundy & Stella, 2000), deficient Theory of Mind (Charman, 1997), or more general lack of social understanding (Leekam, Lopez, & Moore, 2000).

Pointing is another prelinguistic means of communication and type of joint attention. Infants use two types of points: those that are used to request objects, or proto-imperatives, and those that are used to comment upon an object of interest, or proto-declaratives (Bates, 1976). Pointing generally develops in typically developing children by about 10 months of age. By 12 months of age, children are able to point and shift their gaze between the object they are pointing at and the person with whom they are communicating (Sachs, 1993).

The ability to point appears to be differentially affected in special populations. Infants with autism display an almost complete lack of pointing; if they are able to point, it is generally only to request objects and almost never to comment upon them (Tager-Flusberg, 2001). Indeed, lack of pointing was recently found to be one of the clearest indicators leading to early diagnosis of children with pervasive developmental disorders (Robins, Fein, Barton, Green, & Janovicz, 2001). Children with Down syndrome, on the other hand, may be quite adept at sharing interest by proto-declarative pointing, yet may be impaired in using their pointing capabilities to request objects (Franco & Wishart, 1995).

Assessment of play is another means of evaluating preverbal children (Warner et al., 2000). Bates (Bates, Thal, & Janowsky, 1992), Beeghly (1998), and others have written about the relationship between the two symbolic systems of play and language. Although symbolic play development tends to be mildly delayed in children with SLI (Wainwright, Fein, & Waterhouse, 1991), these children do not show the severe delays or absences found in children with autism.

Clinicians who work with atypical populations need to be aware that these children may use unusual methods to attempt to communicate. Behaviors that may at first glance appear to be noncommunicative may in fact be behaviors that are intended to communicate or at least achieve a certain end. Echolalia, a form of speech in which children with autism or mental retardation repeat back what has just been spoken to them, used to be thought to be merely a symptom of these children's difficulties. It is now recognized by most researchers as an attempt at communication (Prizant, 1996). Prizant and his colleagues (Prizant, 1996) have demonstrated that many different types of echolalia with different communicative functions are spoken by these children. Children with autism seem to be aware of the need to communicate with others, yet appear unable to do so by conventional means (Lord & Paul, 1997; Prizant, 1996).

Other behaviors may also serve a communicative function for children who are unable to communicate with language. Behaviors such as taking a caregiver's hand to use as a tool, having temper tantrums, acting out, and hoarding food may be used by children without language to express their needs or their frustrations. Clinicians must keep these behaviors in mind when assessing communicative function. These negative behaviors significantly decrease when children learn to communicate their needs through speech (Kern-Koegel, 2000).

THE FOUR MAJOR COMPONENTS OF LANGUAGE

As mentioned earlier, there are four separate aspects of language that develop in tandem in typically developing chil-

dren. In certain populations, these aspects of language may develop asynchronously, providing the clinician with valuable clues as to the nature of the child's difficulties. These four aspects of language are phonology and prosody, morphology and syntax, semantics, and pragmatics and discourse.

Phonology and Prosody

The phonological aspect of a language includes all the sounds that are present in the words of that language and the rules for combining them. Prosody is included with phonology because prosody is the understanding and use of the intonation patterns of a language, which are part of the sound of a language. Phonemes are the smallest units of a language that can change the meaning of a word, for example, substituting the *h* in *hat* with *c* creates *cat,* a significant change in meaning of the word (Berko-Gleason, 1993).

By six months of age, infants are able to distinguish and categorize all the possible phonemes of the world's languages. At 10 months of age, infants prefer to listen to phonemic combinations that are present in their own language (Werker, 1989). By 12 months of age, infants have lost the capability to distinguish all possible phonemes and remain able to distinguish only the sounds of their native language. With intensive training, however, the amazing distinguishing capability of the young infant can be regained (Werker, 1989).

From an early age, typically developing children appear to understand at least the rudimentary basics of prosodic contrasts (Berko-Gleason, 1993). Before children begin to speak, they use prosody in their babbling, for example, correctly raising the intonation when requesting an object (Sachs, 1993). However, prosody entails more than simply raising intonation for a question and dropping intonation at the end of a sentence. Children must learn to understand contrastive stress, an element of prosody in which the information that is the most important facet of the sentence is stressed (e.g., John said Mary would *not* be coming, where the emphasis is on the fact that Mary will not be coming and not on Mary herself or the fact that John is talking about her). Children must also learn to pick up the pragmatics of intonation, for example, the difference in intonation between a sarcastic statement and one of straightforward humor (Caplan, 1999). Individuals on the autism spectrum tend to have particular difficulty with the comprehension and production of prosody (Shriberg, Paul, McSweeney, Klin, & Cohen, 2001).

Phonemes vary in the ease by which they are produced, and typically developing children generally acquire phonemes in about the same order. Although a detailed description of the classification of sounds in a language is beyond the scope of this chapter, clinicians should be aware of the major sound classes and the most common pronunciation difficulties that children experience (see Yavas, 1998, for an excellent review). Vowels do not tend to cause difficulties in pronunciation for young children, however, clearly enunciating particular consonants often does (Menn & Stoel-Gammon, 1993). The four major classes of consonant sounds are fricatives (e.g., *f* and *v*), stops (e.g., *p* and *b*), glides (e.g., *w* and *j*), and liquids (e.g., *l* and *r*). Fricatives and liquids tend to be more difficult for children to pronounce (Menn et al., 1993). Consonant clusters, or consonants that are grouped together, also cause a lot of difficulty; some consonant clusters may not be mastered until children reach the age of 8 or 9 (McLeod, van Doorn, & Reed, 2001).

Individual phonemes had been used as the unit of assessment; clinicians now recognize that this approach is fruitless and phonemes must be assessed within syllables or, better yet, within words or sentences (Stoel-Gammon, 1996). Phoneme production varies considerably within children and depends on a number of factors. First, children tend to produce phonemes more accurately if the phonemes are in the word-initial position (i.e., the first phoneme in the word). The length of the word has an effect: Longer words lead to more inaccurate phoneme production (Stoel-Gammon, 1996). Phonemes are generally pronounced more accurately in stressed syllables rather than in unstressed syllables. Finally, phonemes are more accurately pronounced in open-class (i.e., nouns, verbs, adverbs, and adjectives) rather than in closed-class words (i.e., articles, conjunctives, prepositions, and pronouns). Clinicians must consider these tendencies and give varying opportunities to produce phonemes to the child who is being assessed (Stoel-Gammon, 1996).

If a child appears to have phonological difficulties and, more generally, language delay, the clinician should first rule out difficulty in hearing. Many children with less-than-perfect hearing experience difficulties with phonological production and comprehension (Menn et al., 1993). Recurrent otitis media may also cause difficulties in discriminating and enunciating phonemes (Warner et al., 2000). Oral motor difficulties must also be ruled out is (Warner et al., 2000). Referral to a speech pathologist can rule out whether the child is experiencing enunciation difficulties because of immature or irregular alignment and development of teeth and hard and soft palates; abnormal muscle tone; or other difficulties with the formation of speech (Warner et al., 2000).

Phonological production and comprehension cause difficulties for several child clinical populations. In phonological disorders, phonological abilities are severely compromised or delayed (Yavas, 1998). Like many aspects of language, development of phonology, especially productive phonology,

has a wide range of competency among typically developing children so the clinician must be careful not to conclude a child has a disorder when the child is simply somewhat delayed but still within normal range (Menn et al., 1993). A good rule of thumb is that adults unfamiliar to a child should be able to understand that child by the age of three; if not, testing the child's phonological structure should be undertaken (Warner et al., 2000). Children with strictly phonological difficulties and no other language problems usually have a good prognosis (Menn et al., 1993). Problems in the phonological realm of language, however, are usually accompanied by deficits in other areas of language (McCauley, 2001).

Mentally retarded children, especially those with Down syndrome and Fragile X, often have difficulties with enunciation (McCauley, 2001). Children with SLI often have difficulty with phonemic production as well (McCauley, 2001). Children with autism who have expressive language generally fall within the normal range of phonological production; however, their comprehension and production of prosody is often compromised (Tager-Flusberg, 2001).

Only a few standardized tests assess phonology in children. The NEPSY (Korkman et al., 1998), a neuropsychological test battery designed to assess children between the ages of 3 and 12, includes three subtests that may be used to test phonology. The Phonological Processing subtest requires the child to identify words from segments and form auditory gestalts. A second task assesses phonological segmentation at the level of letter sounds and word segments. The child is asked to create new words by omitting a word segment or letter sound, or by substituting one phoneme for another. Repetition of Nonsense Words assesses phonological encoding and decoding of sound patterns, and articulation of complex nonwords. Children are asked to repeat nonsense words presented by audiotape. The Verbal Fluency subtest of the NEPSY assesses a child's ability to generate words according to semantic and phonemic categories. The phonemic category is specifically designed for children 7 to 12 years of age and requires them to produce as many words that begin with the letters *F* and *S* as possible in one-minute trials. In addition, the Oromotor Sequences subtest assesses rhythmic oromotor coordination difficulties.

The Goldman-Fristoe Test of Articulation (GFTA; Goldman & Fristoe, 1972, 1986) is a widely used test of phonological processing in children. The GFTA can be used to assess children as young as 2 years, and extends beyond age 16. The GFTA comprises three subtests that measure articulation of sounds-in-words, sounds-in-sentences, and stimulability. The GFTA also provides percentile ranks for the

Sounds-in-Words and Stimulability subtests, particularly helpful in distinguishing phonological deviance from delay.

The Photo Articulation Test, 3rd Edition, (PAT-3; Lippke, Dickey, Selmar, & Soder, 1997) is another tool used to assess preschoolers' phonological errors. The PAT-3 uses 72 color photographs to assess initial, medial, and final position articulation errors in children 3 to 9 years of age. The PAT-3 specifically examines blends, *L* sounds, and articulation of consonants at the beginning and end of words (see Table 13.1).

Testing of phonology is often accomplished by taking spontaneous samples of the child's speech and analyzing them for phonological problems. In some cases, children may avoid using words with phonemes that they are unable to produce. In these cases the clinician may use an elicitation method that requires the child to imitate what the clinician says or uses probes to elicit answers that require using the phoneme in question (Menn et al., 1993).

Two main standardized tests assess prosodic understanding, however, these tests were designed to assess adults. What little research has been done in this area with children has generally looked at the acoustics of the child's production, or the child's ability to understand contrastive stress (Shriberg et al., 2001). The clinician can assess the child's prosody on an informal basis to determine whether the child appears to have typical prosody. Children with autism often have monotonic prosody, whereas children with Williams syndrome often have a sing-song prosody (Karmiloff-Smith, 2001).

Morphology and Syntax

A morpheme is the smallest unit of meaning in a language; it cannot be broken into any smaller parts that have meaning unto themselves. Words can consist of one or more morphemes. Free morphemes are those that can stand alone—words such as *hit* or *cat*. Bound morphemes cannot stand alone; they must always be attached to free morphemes as a suffix or prefix (e.g., *ing, ed,* and *un*). Derivational morphemes are bound morphemes that can be used to change a word into another part of speech; for example, *ness* changes the adjective *sad* into the noun *sadness.* Other bound morphemes do not change a word's meaning but merely modify it to indicate such aspects as tense, person, number, case, and gender. English does not contain many of these inflections; other languages, such as Greek, Italian and French, are more inflected languages and contain many of these morphemes attached to their verbs.

The syntactic system of a language contains the rules for how to combine words into phrases and sentences and how to transform sentences into other forms, such as making a declarative sentence into a question. Much controversy exists in the field of language development as to whether children are born with some innate syntactic structure, or whether they acquire it over time as they acquire vocabulary. Typically developing children acquire morphology and syntax in a predictable manner, however. Children begin by learning the word order of their particular language and move on to simple morphology such as past tense endings. By the primary school years, children are able to understand complex embedded sentences (Tager-Flusberg, 1993).

Difficulties in producing and understanding the morphology and syntactic structure of language are one of the hallmarks of the child with SLI (Leonard, 1998). Although children never seem to break some basic grammatical rules (e.g., the particular word order of their language), children with SLI experience great difficulty in understanding the rules of morphology and syntax (Curtiss et al., 1992). A number of theories attempt to account for this difficulty; the majority of these theories fall into one of two camps. In the first camp are researchers who assert that children with SLI experience difficulty with the grammatical components of language because something is inherently wrong with the part of their brains that process language. These types of theories are in the nature of Chomsky and posit some sort of language module in the brain is impaired in children with SLI. The second type of theory is that these children are experiencing subtle processing difficulties that are not linguistic but more broadly cognitive in nature (Evans, 2001). Researchers who fall into this camp are examining other types of processing difficulties that children with SLI experience, such as difficulties processing rapidly presented auditory information (Stark et al., 1983). For a more thorough discussion of these issues, refer to Nelson (1998) and Leonard (1998).

Other clinical populations also seem to have particular difficulty with morphology and syntactic structure. Children with Down syndrome, for example, tend to have an understanding of grammar that lags far behind their comprehension of vocabulary (McCauley, 2001). Although it was thought for a long time that children with Williams syndrome had a relatively intact syntactic structure, recent studies have shown that is not necessarily the case (Karmiloff-Smith, 2001). It is unclear whether children with Fragile X have particular difficulty with the syntactic aspect of language; research results are mixed in this area (McCauley, 2001). As a group, children with autism appear to have relatively intact grammatical capabilities, although a subgroup of children with autism have agrammatic speech and display a linguistic profile similar to

TABLE 13.1   Representative Test of the Four Major Components of Language

Name	Age Range	Subtests	Function Assessed	Comments
Ages and Stages Questionnaire (ASQ): A Parent Completed, Child Monitoring System Bricker, D., Squires, J., Mounts, L., Potter, L., Nickel, R., & Farrell, J., 1997. Paul H. Brookes Baltimore, MD	4 months to 4 years		Attempts to identify children who have developmental delays or are at risk for developmental delays.	Allows parents and family members to become actively involved in assessment, intervention, and evaluation.
Assessing Prelinguistic and Early Linguistic Behaviors in Developmentally Young Children Olswang, L.B., Stoel-Gammon, C., Coggins, T.E., & Carpenter, R.L., 1987 University of Washington Press Seattle, WA	0 to 3 years	5 scales	Cognitive antecedents to word meaning, play, communication intention, language comprehension, and language production	Based on 3-year longitudinal study of prelinguistic and early linguistic behaviors of 37 typically developing children.
Assessment of Children's Language Comprehension (ACLC) Foster, R., Giddan, J., & Stark, J., 1983 Consulting Psychologists Press Palo Alto, CA	3 to 7 years		Vocabulary and comprehension	Establishes recognition of single-word vocabulary, then uses this vocabulary to assess comprehension of 2-, 3-, and 4-word phrases using picture-pointing task.
Assessment of Phonological Processes–Revised (APP–R) Hodson, B., 1986 Pro-Ed Austin, TX	3 to 12 years		Phonological processes	Can be administered and scored quickly; yields categorization of phonological processes useful for intervention planning.
Bankson Language Text–Second Edition (BLT–2) Bankson, N.M., 1990 Pro-Ed Austin, TX	3 to 8 years		Semantic knowledge, morphological/syntactic rules, and pragmatics	Yields standard scores and percentile ranks; standardized on 1,200 children in 19 states.
Bankson-Bernthal Test of Phonology (BBTOP) Bankson, N.W., Bernthal, J.E., 1990 Applied Symbolix Chicago, IL	3 to 9 years		Articulation and phonological processes	Expressive only.
Boehm-R-Boehm Test of Basic Concepts (BTBC) Ann E. Boehm, 1986 The Psychological Corporation San Antonio, TX	Kindergarten through 2nd grade	Space Quantity Time Miscellaneous	Measures basic conceptual knowledge: more/less, same/different, and identify problems.	Does not need to be individually administered. Allows for error analysis. Related highest to language development. Validity: different SES, race blind, MR, LD, deaf, SLI. Submitted to experts to eliminate ethnic stereotyping. Stratified sampling. Preschool edition is available.
Boehm Test of Basic Concepts–Preschool Version (BTBC–Preschool) Ann E. Boehm, 1986 The Psychological Corporation San Antonio, TX	3–5 years and older children with special needs	26 familiar concepts	Conceptual knowledge	Must be tested individually and give all items; allows testing of comprehension of basic relational concepts. Pretested on 214 urban children, 50% black, 25% white, 25% Hispanic. Standard sample of 433 children with stratified sampling of race, region, and SES. Provides standard errors of measurement and is correlated with PPVT.

(continued)

TABLE 13.1   *(Continued)*

Name	Age Range	Subtests	Function Assessed	Comments
Bracken Basic Concept Scale–Revised (BBCS–R) Bracken, B.A., 1998 The Psychological Corporation San Antonio, TX	Preschool and primary age	Items that require either short verbal responses or pointing.	Designed to be used with children with receptive language difficulties	Yields standard scores with a mean of 10 and standard deviation of 3, percentile ranks, and *z*-scores based on national norms.
Clinical Assessment of Language Comprehension Miller, J.F., & Paul, R., 1995 Paul H. Brookes Publishing Company Baltimore, MD	8 months to 10 years	Informal assessment. Type of response includes pointing, object manipulation, conversation, and behavioral compliance.	Designed for use with very young children or children who are difficult to test	Designed to supplement formal measures. Includes score sheets for use with procedures.
Clinical Evaluation of Language Fundamentals–Third Edition (CELF–3) Semel, E., Wiig, E., & Secord, W., 1995 The Psychological Corporation San Antonio, TX CELF-Preschool Wiig, E.H., Secord, W., & Semel, E., 1992 The Psychological Corporation San Antonio, TX	6 years to 8 years, 11 months, and 9 years to 21 years, 11 months 3 years to 6 years, 11 months	Concepts and directions Sentence structure Word classes Semantic relationship Listening to paragraphs Word structure Recalling sentences Formulated sentences Sentence assembly Word association Rapid automatic naming 6 diagnostic subtests	Receptive: Identifies shapes correlated to orally presented directions, and recognition of concepts and logical operations. Points to pictures corresponding to sentences, comprehending syntax. Selects 2, 3, or 4 words that go together best, understanding associative relationships. Picks pictures that represent semantic relationships in sentences. Answers questions about paragraphs, requiring comprehension of factual or general information. Expressive: Complex sentences, assesses use of morpheme rules. Imitates sentences of increasing level of complexity, assessing immediate verbal memory. Formulates complex sentences using words given by examiner. Assembles syntactic structures into correct sentences. Rapidly produce members of a given category. Names familiar colors and shapes as rapidly as possible. Three expressive and three receptive.	Adequate sample sizes, standardized on ethnic and geographical populations, internal consistency moderate to high, test-retest with good sample variable composite scores. Factor analysis yields one general factor, validated by ability to classify language disorders, correlated with VIQ of WISC-III. CELF-Preschool assesses receptive and expressive language abilities in the areas of word meanings, word and sentence structure, and recall of spoken language. CELF-Screening Test provides criterion scores. Subtests are core at each age level.
Communication and Symbolic Behavior Scales (CSBS–Norm-referenced edition) Wetherby, A.M., & Prizant, B.M., 1991 Applied Symbolix Chicago, IL	9 months to 2 years	Caregiver questionnaire, direct sampling of verbal and nonverbal communicative behaviors, and observation of relatively unstructured play activities	Communication skills and symbolic behavior. 16 communication scales (subdivided into 4 areas) and 4 symbolic behavior rating scales (subdivided into 2 areas)	Scoring is based on a rating of 1 to 5 for each of 20 separate scales.

TABLE 13.1   *(Continued)*

Name	Age Range	Subtests	Function Assessed	Comments
Comprehensive Assessment of Spoken Language (CASL) Carrow-Woolfolk, E., 1999 AGS Circle Pines, MN	3 years to 21 years	Comprehension of basic concepts	Auditory comprehension of words that refer to basic perceptual and conceptual relations	
		Antonyms	Word knowledge, retrieval, and oral expression in a linguistically decontextualized environment	
		Synonyms	Knowledge of the meaning of spoken words in a linguistically decontextualized environment	
		Sentence completion	Word knowledge, retrieval, and oral expression in a linguistic context	
		Idiomatic language	Knowledge, retrieval, oral expression of idioms	
		Syntax construction	Oral expression of words, phrases, and sentences using a variety of morphosyntactic rules	
		Paragraph comprehension of syntax	Auditory comprehension of syntax in spoken narratives	
		Grammatical morphemes	Metalinguistic knowledge and use of the form and meaning of grammatical morphemes	
		Sentence comprehension of syntax	Auditory recognition of whether sentence pairs with different surface structures have the same or different meaning	
		Grammaticality judgment	Judgment of and ability to correct the grammar of sentences	
		Nonliteral language	Understanding of the meaning of spoken messages independent of the literal interpretation of the surface structure	
		Meaning from context	Derivation of the meaning of words from their oral linguistic context	
		Inference	Use of previously acquired world knowledge to derive meaning from inferences in spoken language	
		Ambiguous sentences	Auditory comprehension of words, phrases, and sentences that have more than one meaning	
		Pragmatic judgment	Knowledge and use of pragmatic language rules and judgment of their appropriate application	
Comprehensive Receptive and Expressive Vocabulary Test (CREVT) Wallace, G., & Hammill, D.D., 1994 Pro-Ed Austin, TX	4 to 18 years		Receptive and expressive oral vocabulary strengths and weaknesses	Scores are correlated with scores from the TOLD:P-2, PPVT-R, EOWPVT-R, and CELF. Designed to identify students significantly below their peers in oral abilities.

(continued)

TABLE 13.1 *(Continued)*

Name	Age Range	Subtests	Function Assessed	Comments
Denver Developmental Screening Test (DDST) Frankenburg, W.K., Dodds, J.B., & Fandal, A.W., 1969 (Second revision, 1990, now called Denver II) University of Colorado Medical Center Denver, CO	0 to 6 years		Designed to screen children from the general population in 4 areas, including language, who may need further evaluation	Standardized on 1,036 Denver children. Items can be identified as to what percent of the normative sample passed them.
Developmental Indicators for the Assessment of Learning–Revised (DIAL–R) Mardell-Czudnowski, C., & Goldenberg, D.S., 1990 AGS Circle Pines, MN	2 to 6 years		3 developmental skill areas: motor, concepts, and language	A screening assessment that can be completed in 20 to 30 minutes. Includes statistical data from norming groups: 1990 census, minority, and Caucasian. Cutoff scores are provided for comparison to test results at $+1$, $+1.5$, or $+2$SD.
Early Language Milestone Scale, Second Edition (ELM Scale–2) Coplan, J., 1993 Pro-Ed Austin, TX	0 to 36 months		Auditory expressive, auditory receptive, and visual skills	Ability to score as pass/fail or with a point system. Provides percentile and standard score equivalents. Administered in 10 minutes or less to older children with developmental delay in this range.
Expressive One-Word Picture Vocabulary Test–Revised (EOWPVT–R) Morrison F. Gardner, 1990 Academic Therapy

Upper extension, 1993 Academic Therapy | 2 to 12 years

12 to 16 years | | Expressive vocabulary | Several questions with ability to group by concepts. Standard sample of 1,118 children. Tested for item, content, criterion validity. Standardized on different races. Basal and ceiling. Provides standard errors of measurement. Designed to obtain an estimate of verbal intelligence. Appears to well serve purpose of measuring expressive vocabulary.

Companion to ROWPVT (compare expressive and receptive). English and Spanish versions. |
| Goldman-Fristoe Test of Articulation (GFTA) Goldman, R., & Fristoe, M., 1972, 1986 AGS Circle Pines, MN | 2 to 16+ years | Sounds-in-words Sounds-in-sentences Stimulability | Expressive: articulation | Percentile ranks for sounds-in-words and stimulability subtests. |
| Grammatical Analysis of Elicited Language (GAEL) Moog, J.S., & Geers, A.E., 1980 Central Institute for the Deaf St. Louis, MO | 8 to 12 years for hearing-impaired children

3 to 6 years for children with unimpaired hearing | Manipulable toys | Meaningful elements of spoken and signed English | Assessment of 16 grammatical structures is core feature. |

TABLE 13.1   *(Continued)*

Name	Age Range	Subtests	Function Assessed	Comments
Kaufman Survey of Early Academic and Language Skillls (K-SEALS) Kaufman, A.S., & Kaufman, N.L., 1993 AGS Circle Pines, MN	3 years to 6 years, 11 months		Expressive and receptive language skills, preacademic skills, and articulation	Nationally normed.
MacArthur Communicative Development Inventories (CDI) Fenson, L., Dale, P.S., Resnick, J.S., Thal, D., Bates, E., Hartung, J.P., Pethick, S., & Reilly, J.S., 1993 Singular Publishing Group San Diego, CA	1 to 3 years	Parental checklist, vocabulary checklist	First signs of understanding, comprehension of early phrases, and starting to talk. Vocabulary checklist assesses understanding and saying. The Words and Sentences CDI investigates sentences and grammar, including morphological endings and varied expressions of two-word meanings.	Involves parents in assessment. Older children at early stages may also be assessed. Early gestures, play, pretending, and imitating behaviors are also assessed.
NEPSY Korkman, M., Kirk, U., & Kemp, S., 1998 The Psychological Corporation San Antonio, TX	3 to 12 years 3 to 9 years for the Finnish version and 4 to 7 years for the Swedish version	Body part naming Phonological processing Speeded naming Comprehension of instructions Repetition of nonsense words Verbal fluency Oromotor sequences	Naming Identifying and creating words Accessing and producing familiar words rapidly Processing and responding to verbal instructions of increasing syntactic complexity Phonological encoding and decoding, and articulation Generating words according to semantic and phonemic categories Rhythmic oromotor coordination	Standardization sample of 1,000 cases: 100 children in each of 10 age groups ranging from 3 through 12 years. Stratification along age, gender, race/ethnicity, geographic region, and parent education based on 1995 U.S. census data. Assesses 5 functional domains: Attention/Executive functions, Language, Sensorimotor functions, Visuospatial processing, and Memory and Learning. Subtests designed to be used in various combinations. All subtests begin at age 3 except speeded naming, repetition of nonsense words (age 5), and verbal fluency (age 7). Provides standard scores, percentile ranks, performance profiles, and quantitative and qualitative interpretations.
Oral and Written Language Scales (OWLS) Carrow-Woolfolk, E., 1995 AGS Circle Pines, MN	3 years to 21 years, 11 months	Listening comprehension Oral expression	Measures variety of receptive functions, nouns, verbs, prepositions, adjectives, combinations, syntax, and inferences. Labels, prepositions, syntax, and pragmatics	Raw scores, standard scores, mental age equivalents. Validated against other language test. Applicable for different populations. Easier and quicker than multiple subtests, but only separates receptive and expressive aspects. High internal consistency and test-retest.
Peabody Picture Vocabulary Test–R (PPVT–R) Dunn, L.M., Dunn, L.M., 1981 AGS Circle Pines, MN PPVT-III Dunn, L.M., Dunn, L.M., & Williams, K.T., 1997	2 years, 6 months to 40 years 2 to 85 + years		Measures receptive hearing vocabulary for standard American English.	Administered in 10 to 20 minutes. Normed on a national sample of 4,200 children aged 2½ to 18 years and 828 adults aged 19 to 40 years. Standardized on one form. Developmental norms and grade referenced scores are available. No oral or written responses are required, and the pictures are free of fine detail.

(continued)

TABLE 13.1   *(Continued)*

Name	Age Range	Subtests	Function Assessed	Comments
Photo Articulation Test–Third Edition (PAT–3) Lippke, B.A., Dickey, S.E., Selmar, J.W., & Soder, A.L., 1997. Pro-Ed Austin, TX	3 to 9 years	72 color photographs	Expressive: initial, medial, and final position articulation errors	Expressive only. Specifically examines blends, "L" sounds, and articulation of consonants at the beginning and end of words.
Preschool Language Scale–Third Edition (PLS–3) Zimmerman, I.L., Steiner, V.G., & Pond, R.E., 1992 The Psychological Corporation San Antonio, TX	0 to 7 years		Receptive and expressive language ability. Focuses on language precursors, semantics, structure, and integrative thinking skills.	Easy and quick to administer; provides total language, auditory comprehension, and expressive communication standard scores, percentile ranks, and language-age equivalents. A Spanish-language version has norms based on Spanish-speaking children in the United States.
Receptive One-Word Picture Vocabulary Test (ROWPVT) Morrison F. Gardner, 1985 Academic Therapy	2 to 11 years		Receptive vocabulary only	Companion to EOWPVT (compare expressive and receptive). Basal and ceiling. Standard sample of 1,128 kids in San Francisco public, private, and parochial schools, and clinics. (Kids were also given EOWPVT, WPPSI or WISC.) English and Spanish versions.
ROWPVT–Upper Extension Rick Brownell, 1987 Academic Therapy	12 years to 15 years, 11 months			
Smit-Hand Articulation and Phonology Evaluation (SHAPE) Smit, A.B., & Hand, L., 1997 Western Psychological Services Los Angeles, CA	3 to 9 years	Photo cards of common objects	Production of initial and final consonants and initial two- and three-consonant blends; grouped by semantic categories	Nationally normed.
Spanish Structured Photographic Expressive Language Test (Spanish SPELT–Preschool) (Spanish SPELT-II) Werner, E.O., & Kresheck, J.D., 1989 Janelle Publications Sandwich, IL	3 to 6 years 4 to 10 years	Snapshots	Spanish morphological and syntactic forms	15 minutes to administer. Developmental guidelines for Spanish morphology and syntax are provided. Issues regarding assessing children with limited English proficiency are addressed.
Structured Photographic Expressive Language Test (SPELT-Preschool) (SPELT-II) Werner, E.O., & Kresheck, J.D., 1983 Janelle Publications Sandwich, IL	3 to 6 years 4 to 10 years	Snapshots	Morphological and syntactic forms	15 minutes to administer. Guidelines for analyzing speech productions of Black English are provided.
Test of Auditory Comprehension of Language–Revised (TACL–R) Carrow-Woolfolk, E., 1985 Pro-Ed Austin, TX	3 to 10 years	3 areas: word classes and relations, grammatical morphemes, and elaborated sentences	Auditory comprehension	Provides standard scores, percentile ranks, and age equivalents. A computerized scoring system is available. Also used to distinguish individuals with receptive language disorders.
Test of Awareness of Language Segments (TALS) Sawyer, D.J., 1987 Pro-Ed Austin, TX	4 to 7 years	Sentences-to-words, words-to-syllables, and words-to-sounds	A screening instrument for readiness for beginning reading programs and for type of introductory reading approach that may be easier for a particular child	Cutoff scores facilitate making inferences regarding language abilities.

TABLE 13.1   *(Continued)*

Name	Age Range	Subtests	Function Assessed	Comments
Test of Early Language Development, Second Edition (TELD–2) Hresko, W.P., Reid, D.K., & Hammill, D.D., 1991 Pro-Ed Austin, TX	2 to 8 years		Expressive and receptive language, syntax and semantics	Expanded diagnostic profile, extended age range, and alternative forms are included.
Test of Language Competence– Expanded Edition Wiig, E. & Secord, W., 1989 The Psychological Corporation San Antonio, TX	Level 1: 5 years to 9 years, 11 months Level 2: 9 years to 18 years, 11 months	Ambiguous sentences Listening comprehension: making inferences Oral expression Figurative language	Picking two meanings for ambiguous sentences or phrases Pick two appropriate choices for interpreting events inferred from two events. Creating an appropriate utterance given words and social contexts Interpretation of metaphors	Subtests paired with educational objectives. Standardized on 1,800 normal-language individuals aged 9 to 19 years and 2,000 normal language children aged 5 to 9 years balanced geographically and ethnically. Valid against the TOAL and clinically diagnosed LLD, CELF-R, TOLD-2, and PPVT-R. Subtests moderately intercorrelated. Factor solution indicates one factor. Moderate-high internal consistency and test-retest. Better for younger children.
Test of Language Development– Primary, Third Edition (TOLD–P-3) Newcomer, P.L., Hammill, D.D., 1997 Pro-Ed Austin, TX	4 years to 8 years, 11 months		Expressive and receptive language skills	Determines specific strengths and weaknesses in major linguistic domains.
Test of Language Development–I (TOLD–I) Newcomer, P.L., Hammill, D.D., 1985 Pro-Ed Austin, TX	8 years, 6 months to 12 years, 11 months	Sentence combining Characteristics Word ordering Generals Grammatic comprehension	Receptive and expressive ability Receptive ability Expressive ability Expressive ability Receptive ability	Normed on 871 children from 13 states, mostly from cities. 88% white and 57% white collar. Each subtest encompasses a linguistic system (listening or speaking) and a linguistic feature (semantic or syntactic). No grade equivalents. Not intended as a measure of achievement.
Test of Pragmatic Language Phelps-Terasaki, D., & Phelps-Gunn, T., 1992 Pro-Ed Austin, TX	5 to 12 years	No subtests 44 items	One score tapping use of setting, audience, topic, purpose, visual-gestural cues, and abstractions (e.g., metaphors)	Raw scores, standard scores, test age statistics for variety of demographics. Good sample size, internal consistency moderately high for most ages, no retest reported. Validated against teacher ratings, other language tests (small samples). All subjects get all items.
The Token Test for Children Di Simoni, 1978 Teaching Resources	3 years to 12 years, 6 months.	5 subtests that are progressively more complex: Touch the red circle, touch the squares slowly and the circles quickly.	Receptive: ability to follow oral directions, understand basic language concepts, and integrate verbal information	Standardized on 1304 kids. No special populations. No comment on ethnic populations. Not standardized on 3- or 12 + -year-olds, and 12 years is ceiling.
Transdisciplinary Play-Based Assessment-Revised (TPBA) Linder, T.W., 1993 Paul H. Brookes Publishing Company Baltimore, MD	6 months to 6 years	Informal assessment scales used in scoring a 60- to 90-minute videotaped play interaction with facilitator, parent, and peer.	Social-emotional, cognitive, language and communication, and sensorimotor skills	Multiple professional scorers. No standardized scores. Designed to assess developmental level, learning style, interaction patterns, and other relevant behaviors. Aimed at intervention planning.

that seen in SLI (Kelley et al., 2002; Kjelgaard & Tager-Flusberg, 2001).

In comparison with phonology and prosody, a relatively high number of standardized tests examine morphology and basic syntax. The Preschool Language Scale-3 (PLS-3; Zimmerman, Steiner, & Pond, 1992) is designed to assess children from birth to 6 years, 11 months of age. The PLS-3 yields scores in auditory comprehension and expressive communication, including aspects of syntactic structure, though it does not provide a separate score for syntax. The Clinical Evaluation of Language Fundamentals-Preschool (CELF-Preschool; Wiig, Secord, & Semel, 1992) assesses performance in communication skills in children aged 3 years to 6 years, 11 months. The use of morpheme rules is assessed by the Word Structure subtest. Syntax is assessed with the Sentence Structure subtest, in which the child points to pictures that correspond to sentences. The Test of Early Language Development, 2nd Edition (TELD-2; Hresko et al., 1991) is designed to assess the early development of spoken language in the areas of syntax and semantics in children aged 2 years to 7 years, 11 months. The Test of Language Development-Primary, 3rd Edition (TOLD-P:3; Newcomer & Hammill, 1997) is used to assess language skills of children aged 4 years to 8 years, 11 months, and the TOLD-I (Newcomer & Hammill, 1985) is designed to assess children aged 8 years, 6 months to 12 years, 11 months. The TOLD-I assesses syntax and morphology with its subtests: Sentence Combining (combining two simple sentences into one complex one), Word Ordering (reordering words to form complete, correct sentences), and Grammatic Comprehension (recognizing grammatically incorrect sentences). The Test for Auditory Comprehension of Language-Revised (TACL-R; Carrow-Woolfolk, 1985) is organized into three sections (word classes and relations, grammatical morphemes, and elaborated sentences) designed to measure auditory comprehension of language in children aged 3 to 10 years and to help identify individuals with receptive language disorders. The Comprehensive Assessment of Spoken Language (CASL; Carrow-Woolfolk, 1999) focuses on the assessment of language knowledge and performance in individuals aged 3 to 21 years. The CASL includes subtests that measure expression of words, phrases, and sentences using a series of morphosyntactic rules (Syntax Construction), comprehension and production of grammatical morphemes (Grammatical Morphemes), and auditory comprehension of syntax in spoken narratives (Paragraph Comprehension of Syntax).

Unfortunately, these tests do not examine the more complex aspects of syntax but instead focus on the child's understanding of morphology and basic sentence structure. Syntactic transformations such as embedded clauses, do-support, and verb argument structure are not adequately addressed by standardized tests (Kelley et al., 2001). Criterion-referenced tests such as the Mean Length of Utterance (MLU) or the Index for Productive Syntax (IPSyn), which measures the complexity of syntactic structure (Scarborough, Rescorla, Tager-Flusberg, Fowler, & Sudhalter, 1991), are increasingly popular in the assessment literature (McCauley, 2001). The MLU is generally a good indicator of the child's language level in the early stages of language development (Berko-Gleason, 1993). The IPSyn addresses more complex syntactical structures, such as embedded clauses and sentence complements (Scarborough et al., 1991).

Semantics

Semantic acquisition refers to the acquisition of vocabulary and the meanings associated with words. Word meanings are difficult to learn; the child has to learn that words have referents out in the world, belong to different syntactic categories, and are organized hierarchically. Very young children may use a word without having full understanding of all of its layers of meaning. Children progress from a very simple understanding of vocabulary to metalinguistic awareness, which involves understanding the nature of words and the meanings contained within them.

Children with language difficulties generally do not have as much difficulty with the acquisition of vocabulary as they may have with other aspects of the language system such as phonology and syntax. For example, because children with SLI are generally good at vocabulary but poor at grammar, a test that merely assesses vocabulary will underestimate the degree of impairment in the child (Evans, 2001; Miller, 1996; Rice & Watkins, 1996). Some studies have shown that children with autism do not have a complete understanding of many of the words that they use (Prizant, 1996). Children with autism may test higher in their expressive vocabulary than their receptive vocabulary. This unusual circumstance must be considered when assessing these children (Fein et al., 1996). Children with Fragile X and Fetal Alcohol Syndrome may also appear to be better at language production than comprehension, at least in comparison with typically developing children, whose comprehension far surpasses their production in the early stages of language learning.

Many standardized tests examine receptive and expressive vocabulary. The Preschool Language Scale (PLS-3) measures the receptive and expressive vocabulary of children between birth and 6 years, 11 months of age. The Peabody Picture Vocabulary Test-Third Edition (PPVT-III; Dunn & Dunn, 1997) is designed to measure receptive vocabulary in individuals aged 2 years to adulthood. The Expressive One-Word

Picture Vocabulary Test-Revised (EOWPVT-R; Gardner, 1990) and the Receptive One-Word Picture Vocabulary Test (ROWPVT; Gardner, 1985) are widely used tests of expressive and receptive vocabulary in children aged 2 years to 12 years, and 2 years to 11 years, respectively. These tests include English and Spanish versions, and upper extensions that can be used to test adolescents. The EOWPVT-R (Gardner, 1990) extends to test children as old as 16 years of age, and the ROWPVT (Brownell, 1987) tests those as old as 15 years, 11 months of age. The Boston Naming Test (BNT; Kaplan, Goodglass, & Weintraub, 1983), included in the revised Boston Diagnostic Aphasia Examination (BDAE; Goodglass et al., 2001), assesses naming-to-visual presentation, a sensitive and universally used measure for aphasia. Moreover, the BNT allows the clinician to analyze the form of the errors, which are related to particular aspects of expressive language impairment.

The MacArthur Communicative Development Inventories (CDI; Fenson et al., 1993) attempt a comprehensive assessment of vocabulary and comprehension in children 1 to 3 years of age. The Infant version of the CDI uses a parental checklist to assess a child's comprehension of early phrases, a vocabulary checklist to assess understanding and saying, and behaviors like play, pretending, and imitating. The Toddler version of the CDI assesses sentences and grammar, including morphological endings and varied expressions of two-word meanings, and can be used to assess the early stages of language development.

These tests often do not examine whether the child has a true understanding of the vocabulary words as an adult does (Kelley et al., 2001). They do not test whether the child understands that *cat* is a noun and *run* is a verb. Standardized tests are not designed to examine if the child understands that an ostrich is a bird and a whale is a mammal, even though they do not look like the prototypical birds or mammals (Miller & Paul, 1995). These tests are unable to uncover whether the child understands that in the sentence "The dog ran to the _____," the blank can be filled with just about any noun. Standardized tests fall short of testing the child's true understanding of this aspect of language. Miller and Paul (1995) suggest that during the assessment the child be given objects to play with and asked to perform actions with these objects; unusual requests (e.g., "hug the shoe") should be made to ensure the child is not simply doing what is normally done with these objects.

Pragmatics and Discourse

The study of pragmatics examines the way in which individuals express themselves appropriately in various social situa-

tions. Pragmatics involves four main aspects: quantity, quality, relevance, and manner (Berko-Gleason, 1993). Children must learn to give enough information to their conversational partners, but not too much; this is the aspect of quantity. Quality refers to the fact that children are expected to tell the truth (more or less) in their utterances. The aspect of relevance refers to children's ability to reply to their partner in an appropriate manner, commenting on the topic at hand and not speaking of some irrelevant topic. Manner refers to the expectation that the child speak in turn, take into consideration the social and cognitive status of their conversational partner, and present their words in an understandable way. Pragmatics involves the use of speech to achieve one's communicative ends (Berko-Gleason, 1993).

The study of discourse involves exploring the child's ability to string words into sentences, sentences into paragraphs, and paragraphs into narratives (McCabe, 1996). It also relates to communicative competence, addressing such aspects as how well children express themselves in a conversation, how well they express themselves while telling a story, and how well they answer open-ended questions. The ability to communicate with different types of speech acts is also relevant to language assessment. Several categories of speech acts have been proposed, including directives, or trying to get listeners to do something; questions, or requesting information; commenting, or making general comments about a given topic or situation; commissives, or committing to a future course of action; expressives, or expressing one's feelings; declarations, or bringing about a new situation; and representatives, or asserting one's beliefs about the truth of a proposition (Searle, 1969). Research has found, for example, that children with autism have difficulty with particular types of speech acts, such as questioning and commenting (Tager-Flusberg, 2001). In such children, protesting and requesting generally precede more truly social speech acts, such as commenting, spontaneous labeling, and asking and answering questions.

Pragmatics and discourse abilities are affected in the majority of children who experience difficulties with language. Children who fall on the autistic spectrum have notorious difficulties with the pragmatic and discourse aspects of language, probably caused in part by their lack of social relatedness. For many children with autism, their earliest failures on tests such as the Vineland Adaptive Behavior Scales and the Preschool Language Scale, for example, are caused by their inability to use language to spontaneously relate experiences and their difficulties with answering open-ended questions (Van Meter, Fein, Morris, Waterhouse, & Allen, 1997). Although children with mental retardation and children with SLI do not experience the extreme difficulties with pragmatics and discourse that children with autism do, most research examining this question demonstrates that these clinical populations have less communicative competence than their vocabularies would suggest (McCabe, 1996).

Two standardized tests are commonly used to assess pragmatic competence in children. The CASL includes a subtest (Pragmatic Judgment) that assesses knowledge and use of pragmatic language rules (i.e., how to express oneself in particular social situations) and judgment of their appropriate application. The subtest tests individuals 3 to 21 years of age. The Test of Pragmatic Language (Phelps-Terasaki & Phelps-Gunn, 1992) has 44 items and yields one score that assesses abilities including use of setting, audience, visual-gestural cues, and abstractions (e.g., metaphors) in children aged 5 to 12 years. The Communication Domain of the Vineland Adaptive Behavior Scales (Sparrow, Balla, & Cicchetti, 1984) includes some pragmatic items such as ability to relate experiences, effectively deliver a message, and answer questions.

Perhaps because so many children experience pragmatic difficulties, several criterion-referenced tests have been designed to assess these communicative problems. These tests include assessments of children's understanding of humor, understanding of irony, and ability to adjust their speech depending on whom it is directed to (St. James & Tager-Flusberg, 1994; Surian, Baron-Cohen, & Van der Lely, 1996; Tager-Flusberg, 2000). However, none of these tests have been norm-referenced. The field would certainly benefit from more tests designed to test pragmatic competence in a more rigorous manner.

Discourse cannot readily be examined by the use of norm-referenced tests. The analysis of discourse is widely regarded by researchers as a vital component of the assessment process, yet clinicians seldom use this method (Togher, 2001). Computer programs that analyze the transcripts of spontaneous speech samples are available (MacWhinney, 2000), however, these programs are too time-consuming for most clinicians. This does not mean that discourse samples are of no use to clinicians. Obtaining a sample of speech of the child interacting with her mother, for example, will likely be quite informative for the clinician even if it is analyzed at an informal level; understanding the child's functional use of language is better addressed in this manner than by standardized tests (Evans, 2001). If the spontaneous speech sample is obtained in interaction with the clinician, it is very important that the child has a good rapport with the clinician; if the child is uncomfortable in any way, the sample may underestimate the child's capabilities (Warner et al., 2000).

Spontaneous speech samples are excellent for determining the focus of treatment (Fey, 1986). Fey (1986) describes four main patterns of a child's interactions with others. The child who is balanced in assertive and responsive utterances develops typically and is known as an *active conversationalist.* Children with autism often speak regardless of whether they are being listened to and have problems responding to the utterances of others; Fey (1986) terms these children *verbal noncommunicators.* Those children who speak only when they are spoken to are *passive conversationalists,* and those who are capable of speech but barely speak at all are *inactive communicators* (Fey, 1986). Thus, one can focus on whether the child has more difficulty with assertions or responses (Fey, 1986). The analysis of discourse samples may also be used to investigate aspects of speech such as problems with utterance formation, unusually slow or fast rate of speech, referencing problems, false starts, stuttering, simple or repetitive syntax, overly simple vocabulary, word-finding difficulties, and unusual prosody (Miller, 1996). Word-finding difficulties, especially in the older child, can be observed by circumlocution, self-cueing, use of only high-frequency words, or use of words like *thing* in place of the desired word.

Clinicians should keep several very important issues in mind when discourse analysis is undertaken. Children may learn speech in unanalyzed chunks, so-called "frozen phrases" (Leonard & Eyer, 1996). Because of this tendency, it is necessary to assess whether semantic or grammatical forms occur in varied types of utterances. Leonard and Eyer suggest that spontaneous speech samples need to contain at least five separate instances of a particular grammatical form before one can say with certainty that the child possesses the form. Similarly, absence of a form does not mean that the child is not in possession of that form, merely that the form was not elicited in the speech sample (Leonard et al., 1996). It is also suggested to, if possible, obtain speech samples with the child interacting with several conversational partners. For example, children may differ in their ability to communicate with peers (Togher, 2001).

Several researchers have examined the ability for children with various disorders to tell stories from a wordless picture book. McCabe (1996) argues that this means of assessment is too difficult; even typically developing children seldom engage in such acts. She suggests that children should be asked to relate personal narratives—this is also generally more enjoyable for the children (McCabe, 1996). When assessing discourse, especially narrative, it is important to keep in mind that different cultures have different approaches to storytelling (Hester, 1996; McCabe, 1996). The clinician also needs to be aware of phonemic, semantic, and syntactic differences that occur across cultures (McCauley, 2001). Differences among languages mean that SLI manifests in different ways across cultures (Leonard et al., 1996).

Additional Clinical Issues

As is discussed throughout this chapter, each of the clinical populations likely to experience language difficulties has its own profile of strengths and weaknesses. Children with SLI tend to have relative strengths in semantics and relative weaknesses in the other three aspects of language, although pragmatics is often not as severely affected as phonology and grammar (Curtiss et al., 1992; Leonard et al., 1996). A subgroup of children, however, appears to suffer from such severe pragmatic difficulties that these children may be mistaken for children with autism (Bishop, 2000; Kjelgaard et al., 2001). Clinicians should keep in mind that the name Specific Language Impairment refers to the fact that these children experience difficulties with language that cannot be attributed to mental retardation or other developmental or physical disabilities. Thus, other diagnoses, such as autism or mental retardation, must be ruled out before making a diagnosis of SLI (Leonard et al., 1996). For more detail on Specific Language Impairment, we refer you to reference works by Leonard (1998), Miller and Paul (1995), Nelson (1998), and Paul (1992).

Mental retardation has different etiologies. These differing etiologies lead to differing language profiles. Children with Down syndrome tend to have relatively strong pragmatic capabilities (probably because of their social nature) and relatively advanced receptive vocabularies, at least with regard to their mental age. Down syndrome children often experience great difficulties with phonology, however, and their syntax is poor in comparison to their vocabularies (McCauley, 2001). Children with Fragile X are generally better at expressive language than receptive language, and they are relatively poor at the pragmatic aspect of language; their language profile is very similar to that of children with autism (McCauley, 2001). The language capabilities of children with Fetal Alcohol Syndrome (FAS) are relatively spared—that is, their verbal and performance IQs are generally comparable. Some children with FAS experience particular difficulties in the pragmatic realm, however, and research has found that their expressive language skills exceed their receptive language abilities (McCauley, 2001).

Children who fall on the autistic spectrum also tend to have a particular language profile. These children tend to have relatively intact phonological and syntactic capabilities, at least if they have language capability; a significant minority of children with autism have no functional verbal communication (Fein et al., 1996; Kjelgaard et al., 2001). Their expressive vocabulary tends to be higher than their receptive vocabulary, perhaps because of their preponderant use of echolalia (Prizant, 1996). This may be an artifact of testing

procedures; that is, simply making a verbal response to a picture may be reflective of simple associative learning procedures, whereas receptive language tasks tap into the ability to hold several items in memory and make decisions about them. Pragmatic capabilities in children with autism are severely restricted, however, and some evidence suggests that their understanding of the semantics of language may not be as sophisticated as it appears to be at first glance (Kelley et al., 2001; Kjelgaard et al., 2001). A recent examination of children with a history of autism (these children have lost their diagnosis) who are largely recovered documented residual semantic and pragmatic difficulties, as well as syntactic difficulties in a subset of these children (Kelley et al., 2002).

Language outcomes in children who have sustained a traumatic brain injury (TBI) vary with age, locus, and severity of injury (Bates, 1999). If the TBI occurs in later childhood, verbal deficits are often milder than deficits in attention, memory, and executive functions, but can include deficits in oral fluency, comprehension, and reading (Ewing-Cobbs, Fletcher, & Levin, 1986). Kolb and Wishaw (1996) suggest that the best outcome occurs when the injury is sustained between the ages of 1 and 5. Mild to moderate TBI in preschoolers results in lower verbal IQ than performance IQ; expressive language appears to be more impaired than receptive language (Ewing-Cobbs et al., 1997); and later difficulties occur with reading decoding and comprehension (Barnes, Dennis, & Wilkinson, 1999). Language outcome after TBI, however, is a complex and unresolved issue with no clear-cut relationship between injury and prognosis (Aram, 1999; Bates, 1999).

A number of issues must be taken into account when attempting to assess clinical populations. Children with disabilities are generally more difficult to test than typically developing children for a number of reasons. Clinical populations of children often experience great difficulty in paying attention for extended periods and remaining on task (Scherer, 2001). Children with autism in particular may display a complete lack of motivation to comply with instructions or complete the task. While typically developing children and children from other clinical populations wish to please the experimenter, children with autism may not experience this intrinsic social motivation but may do relatively well with liberal use of preferred reinforcers (Garretson, Fein, & Waterhouse, 1990). Motivation can affect performance in dramatic ways (McCauley, 2001). Often mentally retarded children experience motor difficulties that may be an issue if, as in many standardized tests, the children are required to point to the stimuli that they choose or verbally express a word (McCauley, 2001).

The clinician should be alert to a common pattern in which the child displays disproportionate attentional problems on language tests. This may signal language impairment, secondary to SLI or PDD. It is possible, however, that the manipulatives and pictures used in many performance subtests, as well as the highly structured nature of these tests, prevent inattentive behavior on these tests in a child who truly has Attention Deficit Hyperactivity Disorder (ADHD). The clinician should also remember that language and reading difficulties frequently coexist with ADHD (Tannock, 2000).

Assessing language in hearing-impaired children is problematic. In children with mild to moderate hearing loss, the assessment may be accomplished with standardized measures by reducing background noise, speaking loudly and clearly, and providing an unobstructed view of the speaker's mouth (Garcia O'Shea et al., in press). In deaf children, the assessment must be conducted using the child's usual mode of communication (e.g., American Sign Language; ASL). These issues are discussed in some detail by Mullen (1999).

In addition, most language tests are not normed for visually impaired children and depend to a greater or lesser degree on visual stimuli. Children with visual impairment often achieve fundamental language milestones within a normal age range, with differences in concepts and word choices attributable to differences in visual and social experiences (Landau & Gleitman, 1985). Moore (1999) reviews the criterion-referenced tests and spontaneous language samples that can be used to assess these children, and some tests (e.g., Receptive Expressive Language Assessment for the Visually Impaired; Anderson & Smith, 1979) have been normed on these children.

Although most standardized tests include a rigorously structured method of administration, modifications may be needed when assessing children with language difficulties. These modifications may include giving an uncooperative child tangible reinforcers for staying on task; breaking up the testing time into smaller and more manageable periods; using auditory or visual cues to more effectively direct attention to the task; allowing the child with motor difficulties an alternative response mode; offering multiple-choice responses; enlarging test materials; offering objects to manipulate in place of pictorial stimuli; and removing response time restrictions to allow children who simply process information at a slower rate to have more time (Garretson et al., 1990; Kaplan, Fein, Kramer, Delis, & Morris, 1999; McCauley, 2001; Morse, 1988; Wainwright et al., 1991). It should be stressed, however, that modifying a standardized test does not allow the results to be interpreted in terms of the norm-referenced scores (McCauley, 2001; Morse, 1988). In addition, all modifica-

tions made to a test must be described within the child's assessment report (McCauley, 2001).

If a child performs poorly on a modified test, there is still no guarantee that performance on the test reflects the child's true capabilities. Poor motivation or attention, or unfamiliarity with the implicit demands of the testing situation or examiner may cause the child difficulty (Garretson et al., 1990; Morse, 1988). This may be alleviated by having someone familiar to the child present in the assessment or even help administer the assessment (Morse, 1988). It is also important to be certain that the child listens well to the instructions; the clinician may want to have the child repeat the instructions back to ensure the child understands them (Morse, 1988). Some children with disorders (e.g., autism or ADHD) may have difficulty with the behavioral restrictions required by the standardized testing situation (Scherer, 2001). In these cases, it is wise to minimize distractions as much as possible, give the children plenty of breaks, and provide strong social reinforcement for staying on task (Garcia O'Shea et al., in press). On the other hand, testing may overestimate the everyday abilities of the child with ADHD as the testing situation is generally more structured and less distracting than the environment in which the child normally has to function (Garcia O'Shea et al., in press).

Clinicians should keep other issues in mind when primarily using standardized tests to assess a child's language capabilities. The main benefit of standardized tests is that they have been tested for reliability and validity, and thus provide better means of judging where children stand on a particular test in relation to their peers (McCauley, 2001). However, standardized tests have a relatively poor ability to predict outcomes in individual children (Pena, 1996). This limited predictive validity occurs because standardized tests are not addressing the full range of the child's linguistic ability. This is similar to the problems occurring with small sample sizes in experiments where not enough information is obtained to get a full picture (McCauley, 2001). Although standardized tests generally provide a great deal of structure that may be beneficial to children with language impairment, they do not get at the reasoning behind the children's answers (Gutierrez-Clellan, 1996). Also, as discussed previously, many aspects of language, such as prosody, metalinguistic skills, complex syntax, and narrative and discourse capability, are not well addressed by standardized tests (Miller, 1996). Cultural bias, discussed in the following section, is also an issue. Although much effort has been put into making standardized tests less culturally biased in recent years, the fact remains that children whose first language is not English or who speak particular dialects in the home environment continue to perform more poorly than White middle-to-upper class children (Gutierrez-Clellen, 1996).

Like standardized tests, criterion-referenced tasks have advantages and disadvantages. Because criterion-referenced tests are designed to assess one particular aspect of language in depth, they may illuminate a particular child's difficulties more clearly than standardized tests (McCauley, 2001). The disadvantage to these tests, however, is that they have no point of comparison. Most of these tests were not developed with clinical assessment in mind, but as a means of investigating typically developing children's language development. Although some tasks have been used to test a number of different clinical populations of children, such as the Wug test of productive morphology (Berko, 1958), the majority of them have not. The assessment community has only recently shown interest in criterion-referenced tests. Thus, these tests have not yet been normed on larger samples (McCauley, 2001).

So what is a clinician to do? The fact remains, children with language impairment need to receive a diagnosis and be assessed for strengths and weaknesses for them to receive services to help them improve (Garcia O'Shea et al., in press; McCauley, 2001). No test is perfect, however, and researchers have long argued for converging evidence in the field. Which tests are used carry important implications for what information is to be gained (McCauley, 2001). This means that each child should be assessed as completely as possible within the available time and resources. Standardized tests are very useful for initial screening purposes, but for a true picture of a child's linguistic capability, criterion-referenced tests and spontaneous speech should be examined (Warner et al., 2000). Clinicians need to familiarize themselves with the tests discussed in this chapter so they are able to determine the best tests to use with each individual client. It is also important to continue to test children over time, both to determine their progress in treatment and to obtain converging evidence for each child (Warner et al., 2000).

Communicative disorders have a larger impact on the child than merely their difficulty with language. Problems with communication lead to an increased risk of emotional, behavioral, social, and academic difficulties (McCauley, 2001). Although initially pragmatic capabilities may be within the normal range, most children with any type of language disorder have difficulty with any domain that requires verbal skills, increasingly including the social domain (Rice et al., 1996; Scherer, 2001).

Early intervention is a primary concern; language difficulties in 3-year-old children often persist into the school years and interfere with all aspects of academic progress

(Thal & Katich, 1996). Although standardized language tests should be interpreted with caution for children aged 3 years or younger (Rice et al., 1996) and less than one-half of "late-talkers" go on to develop a clinical diagnosis of language disorder, the impact of language disorder on all aspects of a child's functioning warrants an inclusive approach with regard to intervention (McCauley, 2001).

Current Limitations of Child Language Assessment

One of the most glaring limitations of the current method of assessing children's language ability is the continued reliance on purely standardized testing. Cultural issues are increasingly important as students from ethnic minorities become the majority of students enrolled in large city school systems (Li, Walton, & Nuttall, 1998). Although struggling to make standardized tests less culturally biased, researchers remain insensitive to cultural diversity (Gutierrez-Clellan, 1996; Rice et al., 1996). Clinicians interpreting the results of many standardized tests are unable to discriminate children with true language impairment from children who are having difficulty merely because English is their second language (Gutierrez-Clellan, 1996).

Tests of bilingual children tend to underestimate their vocabulary skills as the two language vocabularies are not taken into account (Li et al., 1998). Federal law makes it mandatory for children to be assessed in their native language (McCauley, 2001). If an interpreter needs to be used, it is important to train the interpreter in proper linguistic assessment procedures (Li et al., 1998). When possible, it is highly recommended that clinicians use tests that have been standardized on children within the language in question as well as use a tester who is fluent in the child's first language. A host of problems in interpreting scores occur when an English test is translated within the assessment situation (Harris, Echemendia, Ardila, & Rosselli, 2001).

Standardized tests are not the only assessments that culturally discriminate. Far too often cultural issues are not taken into account when naturalistic speech samples are examined (Hester, 1996). Children's speech is affected by many factors, including the presence of the experimenter; whether the speech is collected in the office, school or home; and the demographics of the speaker and listener (McCabe, 1996; McCauley, 2001). In examining naturalistic speech samples, a clinician is attempting to assess the child's acquisition of the language and dialect to which the child has been exposed, not of the language and dialect of the dominant culture. The clinician must be familiar with the language or dialect that is being examined and not score word choices or syntactic forms present in that language or dialect as errors. Children should be made to feel as comfortable as possible to obtain an accurate sample of their capability (McCabe, 1996). This can be facilitated with a comfortable testing environment, the taking of extra time to build rapport, and the liberal use of snacks and reinforcers (Garretson et al., 1990).

Several methods can minimize the cultural bias inherent in the assessment situation. Although it may be very difficult to completely eliminate cultural bias, it can certainly be alleviated to some degree (Gutierrez-Clellen, 1996). An analysis of code-switching behavior can be undertaken; that is, assessing whether the child is adept at switching to the appropriate language for the appropriate conversational partner (Gutierrez-Clellen, 1996). A growing number of authors suggest that so-called dynamic assessment might be used to overcome cultural biases (Li et al., 1998; Pena, 1996; Warner et al., 2000). Dynamic assessment addresses not what children already know, but how easy it is for them to learn. A baseline assessment is taken, teaching or intervention is given, and then the children are tested again. Not only does this method assess a child's ability to learn, it allows the clinician to determine the best methods for teaching the child (Li et al., 1998). As Pena (1996) states, "Dynamic assessment yields predictive *and* prescriptive information" (p. 283). But again, these methods have not yet been standardized and must be interpreted with caution. (If you are interested in reading further about cultural issues in assessment, we suggest Anderson & Goldberg, 1991; Barrera, 1993; Barrera; 1996; Garcia O'Shea et al., in press; Gopaul-McNicol & Thomas-Presswood, 1998; Hester, 1996; Nuttall, Romero, & Kalesnick, 1999; Stockman & Vaughn-Cooke, 1986; Terrell & Terrell, 1983; Warner et al., 2000).

Although many clinicians may be reluctant to use parental report, doing so may greatly contribute to the assessment process in some instances. Parents are generally much better at reporting specific abilities rather than overall achievement (Garcia O'Shea et al., in press). Three factors greatly increase the accuracy of parental reports: (1) when the parents are asked to comment only on current behaviors; (2) when the parents are asked to report on linguistic forms that their child is currently learning; and (3) when the parents are asked to recognize (generally in checklist form) rather than recall their child's linguistic capabilities (Dale, 1996).

The most common form of parental reports are the MacCarthur Communicative Development Inventories (Fenson et al., 2000). These checklists have been translated into many languages. One means of addressing the cultural biases in testing children for whom English is their second language is to assess them in both languages. The clinician must bear in mind, however, that a minimum level of skill is required for the parent to fill out these reports—at least a high school education is necessary for accurate reporting (Dale, 1996).

Rapport with the child's family is a crucial aspect of the assessment and treatment procedures. Every effort should be made to keep the parents informed and engaged in the process (Warner et al., 2000). Parents may become quite distressed when their child is given a formal diagnosis, and the clinician needs to be sensitive to this. It is very important to gain the trust of the child's family, especially if the clinician is not of the same culture or socioeconomic background (Harris et al., 2001). Parents must also be encouraged to provide a "facilitative environment for good communicative development" (Warner et al., p. 173).

Perhaps most important, at least from a clinician's perspective, is the need for more research that integrates assessment with treatment suggestions (Tallal, Merzenich, Miller, & Jenkins, 1998). It is crucial to remember that the general purpose of the assessment process is to create an individualized treatment program for the child (Garcia O'Shea et al., in press; Warner et al., 2000).

Clinicians may be reluctant to label a child, particularly a young child, with a particular disorder. Some researchers advocate a "watch and see" approach toward children who appear to be delayed in their language development (Paul, 1996). These researchers are concerned that the child will be stigmatized and the child's parents and teachers will reduce their expectations of the child. Unfortunately, however, it is necessary for a child to receive a diagnosis to receive intervention. The clinician must take care to clearly describe the nature of the disorder, explain the treatment strategies to parents and teachers, and stress a positive prognosis whenever realistically possible.

REFERENCES

Anderson, P.P., & Goldberg, P.G. (1991). *Cultural competence in screening and assessment.* Minneapolis, MN: Pacer Center.

Aram, D.M. (1999). Neuroplasticity: Evidence from unilateral brain lesions in children. In S.H. Broman & J.M. Fletcher (Eds.), *The changing nervous system: Neurobehavioral consequences of early brain disorders* (pp. 254–273). New York: Oxford University Press.

Aram, D.M., Morris, R., & Hall, N.E. (1993). Clinical and research congruence in identifying children with specific language impairment. *Journal of Speech and Hearing Research, 36,* 580–591.

Bankson, N.M. (1990). *Bankson language test* (2nd ed.). Austin, TX: Pro-Ed.

Bankson, N.M., & Bernthal, J.E. (1990). *Bankson-Bernthal test of phonology.* Chicago: Applied Symbolix.

Barnes, M.A., Dennis, M., & Wilkinson, M. (1999). Reading after closed head injury in childhood: Effects on accuracy, fluency, and comprehension. *Developmental Neuropsychology, 15,* 1–24.

Barrera, I. (1993). Effective and appropriate instruction for all children: The challenge of cultural linguistic diversity and young children with special needs. *Topics in Early Childhood Special Education, 13,* 461–487.

Barrera, I. (1996). Thoughts on the assessment of young children whose sociocultural background is unfamiliar to the assessor. In S.J. Meisels, & E. Fenichel (Eds.), *New visions for the developmental assessment of infants and young children* (pp. 69–84). Washington, DC: Zero to Three: National Center for Infants, Toddlers, and Families.

Bates, E. (1976). *Language in context: Studies in the acquisition of pragmatics.* New York: Academic Press.

Bates, E. (1992). Early language development and its neural correlates. In S.J. Segalowitz, & I. Rapin (Eds.), *Handbook of Neuropsychology* (Vol. 7, pp. 69–110). New York: Elsevier Science Publishers.

Bates, E. (1999). Plasticity: localization and language development. In S.H. Broman, & J.M. Fletcher (Eds.), *The changing nervous system: Neurobehavioral consequences of early brain disorders* (pp. 254–273). New York: Oxford University Press.

Bates, E., Thal, D., & Janowsky, J.S. (1992). Early language development and its neural correlates. In I. Rapin & S. Segalowitz (Eds.), *Handbook of Neuropsychology* (Vol. 6, pp. 69–110). Amsterdam, Netherlands: Elsevier Science Publishers.

Beeghly, M. (1998). Emergence of symbolic play: Perspectives from typical and atypical development. In J.A. Burack, R.M. Hodapp, & M. Robert (Eds.), *Handbook of mental retardation and development* (pp. 240–289). New York: Cambridge University Press.

Berko, J. (1958). The child's learning of English morphology. *Word, 14,* 150–177.

Berko-Gleason, J. (1993). *The development of language.* New York: Macmillan Publishing Co.

Bishop, D. (1997). *Uncommon understanding: Development and disorders of language comprehension in children.* Hove, England: Psychology Press.

Bishop, D.V.M. (2000). Pragmatic language impairment: A correlate of SLI, a distinct subgroup, or part of the autistic continuum? In D.V.M. Bishop, & L.B. Leonard (Eds.), *Speech and language impairments in children: Causes, characteristics, interventions, and outcomes* (pp. 99–113). Philadelphia: Psychology Press.

Boehm, A.E. (1986). *Boehm test of basic concepts.* San Antonio, TX: The Psychological Corporation.

Boehm, A.E. (1986). *Boehm test of basic concepts-Preschool version.* San Antonio, TX: The Psychological Corporation.

Bracken, B.A. (1998). *Bracken basic concept scale-Revised.* San Antonio, TX: The Psychological Corporation.

Bremner, J.G. (1994). *Infancy.* Cambridge, MA: Blackwell Publishers.

Bricker, D., Squires, J., Mounts, L., Potter, L., Nickel, R., & Farrell, J. (1997). *Ages and stages questionnaire (ASQ): A parent-completed child monitoring system.* Baltimore: Paul H. Brookes Publishing Co.

Brownell, R. (1987). *Receptive one-word picture vocabulary test-upper extension.* Academic Therapy. Novato, Ca: Academic Therapy Press.

Carrow-Woolfolk, E. (1985). *Test of auditory comprehension of language-Revised.* Austin, TX: Pro-Ed.

Carrow-Woolfolk, E. (1995). *Oral and written language scales.* Circle Pines, MN: American Guidance Services.

Carrow-Woolfolk, E. (1999). *Comprehensive assessment of spoken language.* Circle Pines, MN: American Guidance Services.

Charman, T. (1997). The relationship between joint attention and pretend play in autism. *Development and Psychopathology, 9,* 1–16.

Cole, K.N., Dale, P.S., & Mills, P.E. (1992). Stability of the intelligence quotient-language quotient relation: Is discrepancy modeling based on a myth? *American Journal on Mental Retardation, 97,* 131–143.

Cole, K.N., Dale, P.S., & Thal, D.J. (1996). *Assessment of communication and language.* Baltimore: Paul Brookes Publishing Co.

Cole, K.N., & Fey, M.E. (1996). Cognitive referencing in language assessment. In K.N. Cole, P.S. Dale, & D.J. Thal (Eds.), *Assessment of Communication and Language* (pp. 143–160). Baltimore, MD: Paul Brooks Publishing.

Cole, K.N., Mills, P.E., & Kelley, D. (1994). Agreement of assessment profiles used in cognitive referencing. *Language, Speech, and Hearing Services in the Schools, 25,* 25–31.

Coplan, J. (1993). *Early language milestone scale* (2nd ed.). Austin, TX: Pro-Ed.

Curtiss, S., Katz, W., & Tallal, P. (1992). Delay versus deviance in the language acquisition of language-delayed children. *Journal of Speech and Hearing Research, 35,* 373–383.

Dale, P.S. (1996). Parent report assessment of language and communication. In K.N. Cole, P.S. Dale, & D.J. Thal (Eds.), *Assessment of communication and language* (pp. 161–182). Baltimore: Paul Brookes Publishing Co.

DiSimoni, (1978). *The token test for children.* Golden, CO: Teaching Resources.

Dunn, L.M., & Dunn, L.M. (1997). *Peabody picture vocabulary test-Revised.* Circle Pines, MN: American Guidance Services.

Evans, J.L. (2001). An emergent account of language impairments in children with SLI: Implications for assessment and intervention. *Journal of Communication Disorders, 34,* 39–54.

Ewing-Cobbs, L., Fletcher, J.M., & Levin, H.S. (1986). Neurobehavioral sequelae following head injury in children: Educational implications. *Journal of Head Trauma Rehabilitation, 1,* 57–65.

Ewing-Cobbs, L., Fletcher, J.M., Levin, H.S., Francis, D.J., Davidson, K., & Miner, M.E. (1997). Longitudinal neuropsychological outcome in infants and preschoolers with traumatic brain injury. *Journal of the International Neuropsychological Society, 3,* 581–591.

Fein, D., Dunn, M., Allen, D.A., Aram, D.M., Hall, N., Morris, R., & Wilson, B.C. (1996). Language and neuropsychological findings. In I. Rapin (Ed.), *Preschool children with inadequate communication* (pp. 123–154). London: MacKeith Press.

Fenson, L., Dale, P.S., Resnick, J.S., Thal, D., Bates, E., Hartung, J.P., Pethick, S., & Reilly, J.S. (1993). *MacArthur communicative development inventories.* San Diego, CA: Singular Publishing Group.

Fenson, L., Pethick, S., Renna, C., Cox, J.L., Dale, P.S., & Reznick, J.S. (2000). Short-form versions of the MacCarthur communicative development inventories. *Applied Psycholinguistics, 21,* 95–115.

Fey, M. (1986). *Language intervention with young children.* San Diego, CA: College-Hill.

Foster, R., Giddan, J., & Stark, J. (1983). *Assessment of children's language comprehension.* Palo Alto, CA: Consulting Psychologists Press.

Francis, D.J., Fletcher, J.M., Shaywitz, B.A., Shaywitz, S.E., & Rourke, B.P. (1996). Defining learning and language disabilities: Conceptual and psychometric issues with the use of IQ tests. *Language, Speech, and Hearing Services in the Schools, 27,* 132–143.

Franco, F., & Wishart, J.G. (1995). Use of pointing and other gestures by young children with Down syndrome. *American Journal on Mental Retardation, 100(2),* 160–182.

Frankenburg, W.K., Dodds, J.B., & Fandal, A.W. (1969). *Denver developmental screening test.* Denver, CO: University of Colorado Medical Center.

Garcia O'Shea, A., Harel, B., & Fein, D. (in press). Neuropsychological assessment of the preschool child. In I. Rapin & S.J. Segalowitz (Vol. Eds.) *Handbook of Neuropsychology, 2nd ed.* (Vol. 8, Part 1 *Child Neuropsychology,* Part 1). New York: Elsevier Science Publishers.

Gardner, M.F. (1985). *Receptive one-word picture vocabulary test.* Novato, CA: Academic Therapy Press.

Gardner, M.F. (1990). *Expressive one-word picture vocabulary test-Revised.* Novato, CA: Academic Therapy Press.

Garretson, H.B., Fein, D., & Waterhouse, L. (1990). Sustained attention in children with autism. *Journal of Autism and Developmental Disorders, 20,* 101–114.

Goldman, R., & Fristoe, M. (1986). *Goldman-Fristoe test of articulation.* Circle Pines, MN: American Guidance Services.

Gopaul-McNicol, S., & Thomas-Presswood, T. (1998). *Working with linguistically and culturally different children: Innovative clinical and educational approaches.* Needham Heights, MA: Allyn & Bacon, Inc.

Gutierrez-Clellan, V.F. (1996). Language diversity: Implications for assessment. In K.N. Cole, P.S. Dale, & D.J. Thal (Eds.), *Assessment of communication and language* (pp. 29–56). Baltimore: Paul Brookes Publishing Co.

Hall, D.M.B. (1992). Early screening and intervention. In P. Fletcher, & D.M.B. Hall (Eds.), *Specific speech and language disorders in children: Correlates, characteristics, and outcomes.* San Diego, CA: Singular Publishing Group.

Harris, J.G., Echemendia, R., Ardila, A., & Rosselli, M. (2001). Cross-cultural cognitive and neuropsychological assessment. In

J.J.W. Andrews, D.H. Saklofske, & H.L. Janzen (Eds.), *Handbook of psychoeducational assessment: Ability, achievement, and behavior in children* (pp. 391–414). San Diego, CA: Academic Press.

Hester, E.J. (1996). Narratives of young African American children. In A.G. Kamhi, K.E. Pollock, & J.L. Harris (Eds.), *Communication development and disorders in African American children: Research, assessment, and intervention* (pp. 227–245). Baltimore: Paul H. Brookes Publishing Co.

Hodson, B. (1986). *Assessment of phonological processes-Revised.* Austin, TX: Pro-Ed.

Hresko, W.P., Reid, D.K., & Hammill, D.D. (1991). *Test of early language development* (3rd ed.). Austin, TX: Pro-Ed.

Kaplan, E., Fein, D., Kramer, J., Delis, D., & Morris, R. (1999). *The WISC-III as a process instrument.* San Antonio, TX: The Psychological Corporation.

Kaplan, E., Goodglass, H., & Weintraub, S. (1983). *The Boston Naming Test.* Philadelphia, PA: Lea and Febiger Publishers.

Karmiloff-Smith, A. (2001, April). *Genotype/phenotype relations: Why a cognitive developmental perspective is essential.* Invited Master Lecture given at the Society for Research in Child Development, Minneapolis, MN.

Kaufman, A.S., & Kaufman, N.L. (1993). *Kaufman survey of early academic and language skills.* Circle Pines, MN: American Guidance Services.

Kelley, E., Janovicz, A., Mayeux, L., Omdoll, J., Vear, D., Fein, D., & Naigles, L. (2001, June). *Grammatical and semantic productivity in high-functioning children with autism.* Poster session presented at the 22nd annual symposium on Research in Child Language Disorders, Madison, WI.

Kelley, E., Janovicz, A., Mayeux, L., Paul, J., Vear, D., Fein, D., & Naigles, L. (2002, February). *An examination of the language capabilities of children with a history of autism.* Poster session presented at the 30th annual meeting of the International Neuropsychological Society, Toronto, Ontario, Canada.

Kern-Koegel, L. (2000). Interventions to facilitate communication in autism. *Journal of Autism and Developmental Disorders, 30,* 383–391.

Kjelgaard, M.M., & Tager-Flusberg, H. (2001). An investigation of language impairment in autism: Implications for genetic subgroups. *Language and Cognitive Processes, 16,* 287–308.

Kolb, B., & Wishaw, Q. (1996). *Fundamentals of Human Neuropsychology* (4th ed.). New York: W.H. Freeman Press.

Korkman, M., Kirk, U., & Kemp, S. (1998). *NEPSY.* San Antonio, TX: The Psychological Corporation.

Landau, B., & Gleitman, L.R. (1985). *Language and experience: Evidence from the blind child.* Cambridge, MA: Harvard University Press.

Leekam, S.R., Lopez, B., & Moore, C. (2000). Attention and joint attention in preschool children with autism. *Developmental Psychology, 36,* 261–273.

Leonard, L.B. (1998). *Children with specific language impairment.* Cambridge, MA: MIT Press.

Leonard, L.B., & Eyer, J.A. (1996). Linguistic theory and the assessment of grammar. In C.N. Cole, P.S. Dale, & D.J. Thal (Eds.), *Assessment of communication and language* (pp. 97–120). Baltimore: Paul Brookes Publishing Co.

Li, C., Walton, J.R., & Nuttall, E.V. (1998). Preschool evaluation of culturally and linguistically diverse children. In E.V. Nuttall, & I. Romero (Eds.), *Assessing and screening preschoolers: Psychological and educational dimensions* (pp. 296–317). Needham Heights, MA: Allyn & Bacon.

Linder, T.W. (1993). *Transdisciplinary play-based assessment-revised (TPBA).* Baltimore: Paul H. Brookes Publishing Co.

Lippke, B.A., Dickey, S.E., Selmar, J.W., & Soder, A.L. (1997). *Photo-articulation test* (3rd ed.). San Antonio, TX: The Psychological Corporation.

Lord, C., & Paul, R. (1997). Language and communication in autism. In D.J. Cohen, & F.R. Volkmar (Eds.), *Handbook of autism and developmental disorders* (pp. 195–225). New York: John Wiley & Sons, Inc.

MacWhinney, B. (2000). *The CHILDES project: Tools for analyzing talk: Vol. 1. Transcription format and programs.* Mahwah, NJ: Lawrence Erlbaum Incorporated.

Mardell-Czudnowki, C., & Goldenberg, D.S. (1990). *Developmental indicators for the assessment of learning-Revised.* Circle Pines, MN: American Guidance Service.

McCabe, A. (1996). Evaluating narrative discourse skills. In K.N. Cole, P.S. Dale, & D.J. Thal (Eds.), *Assessment of communication and language* (pp. 121–141). Baltimore: Paul Brookes Publishing Co.

McCathren, R.B., Warren, S.F., & Yoder, P.J. (1996). Prelinguistic predictors of later language development. In K.N. Cole, P.S. Dale, & D.J. Thal (Eds.), *Assessment of communication and language* (pp. 57–75). Baltimore: Paul Brookes Publishing Co.

McCauley, R.J. (2001). *Assessment of language disorders in children.* Mahwah, NJ: Lawrence Erlbaum Publishers.

McLeod, S., van Doorn, J., & Reed, V.A. (2001). Normal acquisition of consonant clusters. *American Journal of Speech-Language Pathology, 10,* 99–110.

Menn, L., & Stoel-Gammon, C. (1993). Phonological development: Learning sounds and sound patterns. In J. Berko-Gleason (Ed.), *The development of language* (pp. 65–115). New York: Macmillan Publishing Co.

Miller, J.F. (1996). Progress in assessing, describing, and defining child language disorder. In C.N. Cole, P.S. Dale, & D.J. Thal (Eds.), *Assessment of communication and language* (pp. 309–324). Baltimore: Paul Brookes Publishing Co.

Miller, J.F., & Paul, R. (1995). *The clinical assessment of language comprehension.* Baltimore: Paul Brookes Publishing Co.

Moog, J.S., & Geers, A.E. (1980). *Grammatical analysis of elicited language.* St. Louis, MO: Central Institute for the Deaf.

Moore, M. (1999). Assessing the preschool child with visual impairment. In E.V. Nuttall, I. Romero, & J. Kalesnik (Eds.), *Assessing and screening preschoolers: Psychological and educational dimensions* (pp. 360–380). Needham Heights, MA: Allyn and Bacon.

Morse, J.L. (1988). Assessment procedures for people with mental retardation: The dilemma and suggested adaptive procedures. In S.N. Calculator, & J.L. Bedrosian (Eds.), *Communication, assessment, and intervention for adults with mental retardation* (pp. 109–138). Boston: Little, Brown, and Company.

Mullen, Y. (1999). Assessment of the preschool child with a hearing loss. In E.V. Nuttall, I. Romero, & J. Kalesnick (Eds.), *Assessing and screening preschoolers: Psychological and educational dimensions* (2nd ed.). Needham Heights, MA: Allyn & Bacon, Inc.

Mundy, P., & Stella, J. (2000). Joint attention, social orienting, and nonverbal communication in autism. In A.M. Wetherby, & B.M. Prizant (Eds.), *Autism spectrum disorders: A transactional developmental perspective* (pp. 55–77). Baltimore: Paul H. Brookes Publishing Co.

Nelson, N. (1998). *Childhood language disorders in context: Infancy through adolescence.* Needham Heights, MA: Allyn and Bacon.

Neville, H.J., Coffey, S.A., Holcomb, P.J., & Tallal, P. (1993). The neurobiology of sensory and language processing in language-impaired children. *Journal of Cognitive Neuroscience, 5,* 235–253.

Newcomer, P.L., & Hammill, D.D. (1985). *Test of language development.* Austin, TX: Pro-Ed.

Newcomer, P.L., & Hammill, D.D. (1997). *Test of language development-Primary* (3rd ed.). Austin, TX: Pro-Ed.

Nuttall, E.V., Romero, I., & Kalesnick, J. (1999). *Assessing and screening preschoolers: Psychological and educational dimensions* (2nd ed.). Needham Heights, MA: Allyn & Bacon, Inc.

Oller, D.K., & Eilers, R.E. (1988). The role of audition in infant babbling. *Child Development, 59,* 441–449.

Olswang, L.B., Stoel-Gammon, C., Coggins, T.E., & Carpenter, R.L. (1987). *Assessing prelinguistic and early linguistic behaviors in developmentally young children.* Seattle, WA: University of Washington Press.

Paul, R. (1992). Language and speech disorders. In S.R. Hooper, G.W. Hynd, & R.E. Mattison. (Eds.), *Developmental disorders: Diagnostic criteria and clinical assessment* (pp. 209–238). Hillsdale, NJ: Lawrence Erlbaum Associates, Inc.

Paul, R. (1996). Clinical implications of the natural history of slow expressive language development. *American Journal of Speech-Language Pathology, 5,* 5–21.

Pena, E.D. (1996). Dynamic assessment: The model and its language applications. In C.N. Cole, P.S. Dale, & D.J. Thal (Eds.), *Assessment of communication and language* (pp. 281–303). Baltimore: Paul Brookes Publishing Co.

Phelps-Terasaki, D., & Phelps-Gunn, T. (1992). *Test of pragmatic language.* Austin, TX: Pro-Ed.

Prizant, B.M. (1996). Brief report: Communication, language, social, and emotional development. *Journal of Autism and Developmental Disorders, 26,* 173–179.

Rapin, I. (1996). *Preschool children with inadequate communication: Developmental language disorder, autism, low IQ.* London: Mac Keith Press.

Rice, M.L. & Watkins, R.V. (1996). "Show me X." New views of an old assessment technique. In K.N. Cole, P.S. Dale, & D.J. Thal (Eds.), *Assessment of communication and language* (pp. 183–206). Baltimore: Paul Brookes Publishing Co.

Robins, D., Fein, D., Barton, M., Green, J., & Janovicz, A. (2001, November). *The modified checklist for autism in toddlers (M-CHAT): Longitudinal data suggests successful screening at two years.* Paper presented at the First Annual International Meeting for Autism Research, San Diego, CA.

Sachs, J. (1993). The emergence of intentional communication. In J. Berko-Gleason (Ed.), *The development of language* (pp. 40–64). New York: Macmillan Publishing Co.

Sawyer, D.J. (1987). *Test of awareness of language segments.* Austin, TX: Pro-Ed.

Scarborough, H.S., Rescorla, L., Tager-Flusberg, H., Fowler, A.E., & Sudhalter, V. (1991). The relation of utterance length to grammatical complexity in normal and language-disordered groups. *Applied Psycholinguistics, 12,* 23–45.

Scherer. N.J. (2001). Communicative disorders. In H.B. Vance & A.J. Pumariega (Eds.), *Clinical assessment of child and adolescent behavior* (pp. 170–187). New York: John Wiley & Sons, Inc.

Searle, J.R. (1969). *Speech acts: An essay in the philosophy of language.* New York: Cambridge University Press.

Semel, E., Wiig, E., & Secord, W. (1995). *Clinical evaluation of language fundamentals* (3rd ed.). San Antonio, TX: The Psychological Corporation.

Shriberg, L.D., Paul, R., McSweeney, J.L., Klin, A., & Cohen, D.J. (2001). Speech and prosody characteristics of adolescents and adults with high-functioning autism and Asperger syndrome. *Journal of Speech, Language, and Hearing Research, 44,* 1097–1115.

Sparrow, S.S., Balla, D.A., & Cicchetti, D.V. (1984). *Vineland adaptive behavior scales.* Circle Pines, MN: American Guidance Service.

St. James, P.J., & Tager-Flusberg, H. (1994). An observational study of humor in autism and Down syndrome. *Journal of Autism and Developmental Disorders, 24,* 603–617.

Stark, R.E., Tallal, P., Kallman, C., & Mellits, E.D. (1983). Cognitive abilities of language-delayed children. *The Journal of Psychology, 114,* 9–19.

Stockman, I.J., & Vaughn-Cooke, F.B. (1986). Implications of semantic category research for the language assessment of nonstandard speakers. *Topics in Language Disorders, 6,* 15–25.

Stoel-Gammon, C. (1996). Phonological assessment using a hierarchical framework. In C.N. Cole, P.S. Dale, & D.J. Thal (Eds.), *Assessment of communication and language* (pp. 77–95). Baltimore: Paul Brookes Publishing Co.

Surian, L., Baron-Cohen, S., & Van der Lely, H. (1996). Are children with autism deaf to Gricean maxims? *Cognitive Neuropsychiatry, 1,* 55–71.

Tager-Flusberg, H. (1993). Putting words together: Morphology and syntax in the preschool years. In J. Berko-Gleason (Ed.), *The development of language* (pp. 151–193). New York: MacMillan Publishing Co.

Tager-Flusberg, H. (2000). The challenge of studying language development in children with autism. In L. Menn & N.B. Ratner (Eds.), *Methods for studying language production* (pp. 313–322). Mahwah, NJ: Lawrence Erlbaum Associates.

Tager-Flusberg, H. (2001). Understanding the language and communicative impairments in autism. *International Review of Research in Mental Retardation, 23,* 185–205.

Tallal, P., Merzenich, M., Miller, S., & Jenkins, S.W. (1998). Language learning impairment: Integrating research and remediation. *Scandinavian Journal of Psychology, 39,* 197–199.

Tannock, R. (2000). Language, reading, and motor control problems in ADHD: A potential behavioral phenotype. In L.L. Greenhill (Ed.), *Learning disabilities: Implications for psychiatric treatment* (pp. 129–167). Washington, DC: American Psychiatric Press, Inc.

Terrell, S.L., & Terrell, F. (1983). Distinguishing linguistic differences from disorders: The past, present, and future of nonbiased assessment. *Topics in Language Disorders, 3,* 1–7.

Thal, D.J., & Bates, E. (1988). Language and gesture in late talkers. *Journal of Speech and Hearing Research, 31,* 115–123.

Thal, D.J. & Katich, J. (1996). Predicaments in early identification of Specific Language Impairment. In K.N. Cole, P.S. Dale, & D.J. Thal (Eds.), *Assessment of communication and language* (pp. 1–28). Baltimore: Paul Brookes Publishing Co.

Togher, L. (2001). Discourse sampling in the 21st century. *Journal of Communication Disorders, 34,* 131–150.

Tomasello, M. (1999). *The cultural origins of human cognition.* Cambridge, MA: Harvard University Press.

VanMeter, L., Fein, D., Morris, R., Waterhouse, L., & Allen, D. (1997). Delay versus deviance in autistic social behavior. *Journal of Autism and Developmental Disorders, 27,* 557–569.

Wainwright, L., Fein, D., & Waterhouse, L. (1991). Neuropsychological assessment of children with developmental disabilities. In N. Amir, I. Rapin, & D. Branski (Eds.), *Pediatric neurology: Behavior and cognition of the child with brain dysfunction.* Basel, Switzerland: S. Kargen Publishing.

Wallace, G., & Hammill, D.D. (1994). *Comprehensive receptive and expressive vocabulary test.* Austin, TX: Pro-Ed.

Warner, C., & Nelson, N.W. (2000). Assessment of communication, language, and speech: Questions of "What to do next?" In B.A. Bracken (Ed.), *The psychoeducational assessment of preschool children* (pp. 145–185). Needham Heights, MA: Allyn & Bacon.

Werker, J. (1989). Becoming a native listener. *American Scientist, 77,* 54–59.

Werner, E.O., & Kresheck, J.D. (1983). *Structured photographic expressive language test.* Sandwich, IL: Janelle Publications.

Werner, E.O., & Kresheck, J.D. (1989). *Spanish structured photographic expressive language test.* Sandwich, IL: Janelle Publications.

Wetherby, A.M., & Prizant, B.M. (1991). *Communication and symbolic behavior scales.* Chicago: Applied Symbolix.

Wiig, E., & Secord, W. (1989). *Test of language competence-expanded edition.* San Antonio, TX: The Psychological Corporation.

Wiig, E.H., Secord, W., & Semel, E. (1992). *Clinical evaluation of language fundamentals-Preschool.* San Antonio, TX: The Psychological Corporation.

Yavas, M. (1998). *Phonology: Development and disorders.* San Diego, CA: Singular Publishing Group.

Zimmerman, I.L., Steiner, V.G., & Pond, R.E. (1992). *Preschool language scale* (3rd ed.). San Antonio, TX: The Psychological Corporation.

CHAPTER 14

Memory and Learning in Adults

JOHN DELUCA AND NANCY D. CHIARAVALLOTI

> They have learned nothing, and forgotten nothing.
> —Charles Maurice De Talleyrand-Perigord, 1796

The clinical assessment of learning and memory has been a major focus of clinical psychology since the early twentieth century, and it remains the key feature of most neuropsychological and educational evaluations. Although significant advances have been made in the understanding of the cognitive and cerebral aspects of learning and memory during the twentieth century, modern clinical assessment has lagged far behind such advances.

The present chapter presents a basic understanding of modern clinical assessment of learning and memory in adults. We begin with a general historical perspective on views of memory, which provides a framework for understanding the current state of affairs in learning and memory assessment. This is followed by a discussion of the different approaches to the conceptual understanding of learning and memory (e.g., process versus systems approach), as well as touching upon the key brain structures responsible for aspects of memory. The heart of the chapter is found in the section on the clinical assessment of memory, which addresses issues in modern clinical assessment, including the role of learning, the recall versus recognition dissociation, the role of pre-assessment activities, how the integrity of other cognitive functions affects the accuracy of memory assessment, and a short discussion on cultural and legal/ethical issues in memory assessment. Finally, a discussion of future directions and recommendations for improving the quality of memory assessment is presented.

GENERAL HISTORICAL PERSPECTIVE

Historically, human memory has been thought of as part of the intellectual faculties and by the mid-1800s, was associated with the frontal lobes (see Markowitsch, 2000). By the turn of the century, an amnestic syndrome, primarily associated with Korsakoff's syndrome, became widely accepted. As a result, memory dysfunction became associated with damage to diencephalic structures (i.e., thalamic nuclei and mammillary bodies). By the 1950s and 1960s, through work with amnesic patients like HM, mesial temporal structures also became a primary focus of understanding the cerebral substrates of human memory. Interestingly, coming full circle, more recent conceptualizations of learning and memory once again have returned to the important role played by the frontal lobes.

The formal *scientific* study of learning and memory did not begin until the late 1800s, with the work of Ebbinghaus, who established several cognitive principles of memory, many of which are still valid today. This initial work led to a plethora of scientific investigations in experimental or cognitive psychology. Unfortunately, the experimental and clinical literature on learning and memory soon branched into independent lines of investigation with cross talk being the exception rather than the rule.

The clinical assessment of memory has taken a path that has largely neglected the experimental study of learning and memory in psychology. The formal clinical assessment of memory can be traced back to at least 1917 when David Wechsler used an unpublished version of Verbal Paired Associates (Wechsler, 1917) to assess verbal memory in patients with Korsakoff's syndrome. However, it was not until 1945 that the Wechsler Memory Scale was published, which was designed to provide a "rapid, simple, and practical memory examination" (Wechsler, 1945 p. 87). Since this initial publication, the field of clinical memory assessment has seen tremendous growth in the conduct of clinical and experimental research, resulting in the numerous assessment tools for memory functioning that are available today.

Memory scales or batteries have historically been developed with little regard for the vast cognitive psychology and cognitive neuroscience literature, often resulting in an assessment that seemed clinically meaningful (face valid), but was typically not well grounded theoretically (construct validity). In addition, such batteries often failed to reflect abilities in everyday life (ecological validity). For instance, the initial Wechsler Memory Scale (1945) conceptualized human memory as a unitary construct. That is, a Memory Quotient or MQ score was obtained by collapsing across scores of verbal and visual memory, even including scores on measures of orientation. There was no focus on the role of learning in this assessment. Although the development of a memory test battery was a landmark event in psychology, it was abundantly criticized. Areas of weakness within the battery included a limited standardization sample (Prigatano, 1978), few reliability statistics, a weak factor structure, and a high reliance on verbal memory, with only one test of visual memory. Although the WMS revision (WMS-R; Wechsler, 1987) published in 1987 made significant improvements to the test battery, weaknesses still remained including a limited normative sample, a lack of face validity, a continued overemphasis on verbal memory (Loring, 1989) and a factor structure failing to support the differentiation between verbal and visual memory. Finally, the WMS-R was developed with little regard for the large body of research evidence on memory and learning that had accumulated between the publication of the original WMS and the 1987 revision. Specifically, the WMS-R remained focused on immediate memory with no distinction between acquisition, retention, and retrieval. With the most recent revision in 1997, the WMS-III (Wechsler, 1997) has attempted to address many of these prior criticisms. Major advances of the WMS-III include a large standardization sample, improved face validity, particularly evident in the visual memory subtests, and an expansion of the subtests measuring visual memory functions. However, although efforts were made to improve the ability of the test battery to assess important constructs, such as acquisition, the clinical assessment of such empirically derived constructs of learning and memory continues to lag behind the knowledge gained through research.

LEARNING, MEMORY, AND THE BRAIN

Today, it is well understood that memory is not a unitary construct. This, however, is in contrast to the way memory is often viewed clinically, particularly by nonpsychologist health-care professionals (How is the patient's memory?). Memory is a complex and multidimensional construct with dissociable subsystems, or processes. For instance, the recollection of events that occurred during childhood (e.g., name of your elementary school) operate differently from those that are newly acquired. Furthermore, learning new facts (memorizing a phone number) utilizes a different memory subsystem than the acquisition of new motor skills (learning to ride a bike or to read). Importantly, some, but not all of these subsystems are particularly sensitive to disruption following trauma or other acquired brain insult such as a stroke. As such, an understanding of how the brain represents and processes information is essential in the clinical assessment of learning and memory.

It must be recognized at the outset that there cannot be any "memory" without "learning". *Learning* can be defined as "the process of acquiring new information", whereas the term *memory* refers to "the persistence of learning in a state that can be revealed at a later time" (Squire, 1987 p. 3). As such, memory (i.e., recall and recognition) cannot be adequately assessed unless the to-be-remembered information has been acquired through learning.

To help explain the complicated construct we commonly refer to as "memory," two general approaches have been utilized: the systems approach and the process approach. While some debate the benefits of a systems versus process approach to the study of learning and memory, these approaches are likely more complimentary than incompatible (Schacter, Wagner, & Buckner, 2000).

A systems approach to memory functioning examines memory in terms of a number of interrelated but dissociable systems (see Figure 14.1). Each system is somewhat independent, in that different brain structures and resources may be utilized for each system to function. Therefore, an injury may result in damage to one system, while leaving the others largely intact. The major distinction in human memory is the dichotomy between the procedural memory system, for example knowing how, and the declarative memory system, for example, knowing that, (Tulving, 2000).

Procedural, or nondeclarative, memory refers to the acquisition of motor and cognitive skills or routines. Such skills or routines are characterized by gradual and incremental learning and are maintained without conscious effort. Examples of procedural memory include learning to ride a bike, read, or drive a car. The distinction between procedural and

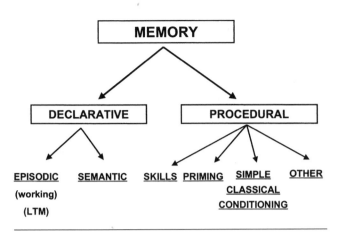

Figure 14.1   The structure of the memory system.

declarative memory is based on the fact that amnesic patients (with severe declarative memory impairment) can be taught to acquire new perceptual, cognitive and motor skills (for example, learning to play a melody on the piano) as well as healthy individuals, despite an inability to explicitly recall the experiences that lead to learning.

The major subdivisions of procedural memory are illustrated in Figure 14.1. Procedural memory is thought to be hippocampal independent, with the basal ganglia and the cerebellum thought to be the major brain structures involved (Cohen & Eichenbaum, 1993). As such, clinical populations, such as patients with Huntington's disease, with damage to these regions have demonstrated impairment in the acquisition of tasks sensitive to procedural memory (Mayes, 2000).

Declarative memory refers to the conscious recollection of facts and events, which are acquired through learning. Therefore, the declarative memory system can be viewed as knowing *that* something was learned (e.g., skill) and the procedural memory system as knowing *how* to perform (without conscious reflection) the learned skill (Baur, Tobias, & Valenstien, 1993). In contrast to procedural memory, the declarative memory system is sensitive to acquired brain damage. This memory system in the brain consists of a complex interaction between mesial temporal (especially hippocampus), diencephalic (primarily anterior structures), basal forebrain, and frontal lobe structures.

The declarative memory system can be divided into the episodic and semantic memory systems. Episodic memory refers to the learning and recollection of facts, such as state capitals, and of personally experienced events, episodes, or time frames, such as recalling the name of your second grade teacher or what you had for dinner the night before. In contrast, semantic memory refers to the acquisition of general knowledge, such as the meaning of words. Neuropsychological studies with amnesic patients have generally shown intact

retention of verbal intellectual, linguistic, and semantic skills (i.e., intact semantic memory). In contrast, these amnesics show profound deficits in the ability to recall specific details and episodes of learned information (e.g., impaired episodic memory). For instance, an amnesic may not be able to recall a list of 10 words presented 5 minutes earlier but will display no difficulty describing the meaning of each of these words.

In addition to the multidimensional, modular "systems" approach, learning and memory can be viewed in an information-processing framework (Tulving, 2000). Within this framework, memory can be conceptualized in terms of stages or processes. Modern conceptualizations of this notion stem from the work of Atkinson and Shiffrin (1968), which is an update of William James's notion of primary and secondary memory. Essentially, the information-processing approach to learning and memory refers to how information is initially encoded, processed in short-term buffer, consolidated and stored into long-term memory and later retrieved from long term storage (see Figure 14.2).

For information to move from temporary to long-term storage in the brain, the information must pass through several stages. Information from the environment enters via sensory registers and is initially stored and processed in a short-term, temporary buffer called working memory (Baddely,

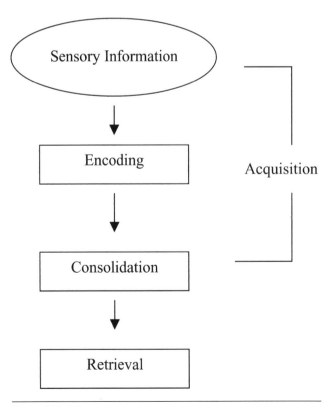

Figure 14.2   The memory process.

2000). Working memory refers to the temporary storage and active maintenance and manipulation of internal representations for on-line use, such as keeping a phone number in mind, or performing simple arithmetic (Baddeley, 2000). Working memory is therefore thought of as a key step in the encoding of information and the transfer of this information into episodic memory (Johnson, 1992). It is fairly well established that structures in the prefrontal cortex and the parietal lobes are critical in storage and manipulation within working memory (Fletcher & Henson, 2001). Importantly, the cognitive functions occurring at this early stage in information processing directly impact later memory processing (DeLuca, Schultheis, Madigan, Christodoulou, & Averill, 2000). As such, the clinical assessment of working memory, discussed in the next section, is a key component to the overall evaluation of learning and memory.

Encoding refers to the process of acquiring information, which takes place within the working memory stage of declarative memory. While information is rehearsed in working memory, memory traces are developed. These memory traces are the products of *encoding*. Encoding is not an all or none phenomenon however. The strength of encoding can be either deep or shallow, or can be fragmented, in that only parts of a learning stimulus can be encoded (e.g., context) leaving other elements with little or no encoding. After information is encoded, if deemed sufficiently important, it can then be transferred from this short-term, temporary store to more enduring (or long-term) storage. This process is referred to as *consolidation*, or *elaboration* (Squire, Cohen, & Nadel, 1983). Numerous structures have been implicated in the consolidation of declarative information, including the hippocampus and surrounding regions, diencephalic structures, basal forebrain, and the cingulate gyrus (for more detailed information, see Markowitsch, 2000). Memory *acquisition* refers to the initial sensing, encoding, and consolidation of new information. That is, *acquisition* refers to the combined processes of initial encoding and subsequent consolidation of learned material in long-term storage (see Figure 14.2). Finally, when needed, the information must be available for use. *Retrieval* refers to the process of accessing previously encoded information from long-term storage for use (Squire et al., 1983).

The brain systems involved in memory retrieval remain controversial. Even the most modern imaging studies have not yet been able to identify adequately the structures responsible for the process of retrieval. This is largely due to the fact that retrieval tasks often simultaneously involve re-encoding of the information retrieved (Markowitsch, 2000). Tulving and colleagues (1994) present a left hemisphere prefrontal pattern of activation for the encoding of episodic memory, with a right hemisphere prefrontal pattern of acti-

vation for retrieval from episodic memory, called the Hemispheric Encoding/Retrieval Asymmetry (HERA) model. However, additional regions may be involved with distinct types of information. For example, temporal-polar regions may be involved when autobiographical memories are being retrieved (Fink, Markowitsch, Reinkemeier, Kessler, & Heiss, 1996; Markowitsch, 1997).

Clearly, learning and memory are complex and multi-dimensional. However, the transfer of knowledge obtained through research needs to be applied to the clinical assessment of persons with impairments in learning and memory. This is described in the next section.

THE CLINICAL ASSESSMENT OF MEMORY

Given the complexity of memory in terms of multiple processes and subsystems, it should not be surprising that the clinical assessment of memory abilities is also quite complex. The clinical assessment of learning and memory is not simply the administration of psychometric tests. Assessment is multifaceted, consisting of several levels of evaluation, including the referral question, record review, the clinical interview (examining behavioral observations), and psychometric testing. See Lezak (1995) for more in depth information regarding issues related to referral, record review, and interviewing.

Pretesting Assessment

Clinically, learning and memory assessment begins with the referral question. Too often, referral questions are vague and of little help in precisely identifying the need for an in-depth evaluation of a person's learning and memory abilities. Questions such as "document memory problems," "rule out dementia," or examine "functional versus organic factors" offer little insight into the true nature of the referral. Spending time with the referral source to pinpoint the exact nature of the question(s) to be addressed fosters a more focused and clinically meaningful assessment and is in the best interest of the patient. A thorough review of records should constitute the initial step in every assessment. In fact, a thorough record review is often the first step in the hypothesis testing approach to assessment. These records (e.g., MRI results, neurology consultation notes, litigation information), in addition to the referral question and the clinician's knowledge of the condition in question (e.g., dementia, multiple sclerosis), form the basis for the development of initial hypotheses to be addressed during the interview and psychometric evaluation.

Within the interview, the psychologist has the opportunity to refine the initial hypotheses and actually do some fundamental assessments. For instance, it is well known that even amnesic and severely demented patients can recall remote memories from the distant past. For instance, the actual inability (or markedly reduced ability) to recall information from childhood is unlikely to follow from most acquired or developmental insults to the brain. Additionally, as described previously, it is well established that following most neurological insults that affect memory, procedural memory remains intact. So for instance, complaints of forgetting how to play a musical instrument in a relatively accomplished performer may raise concerns regarding the "motivation" or veracity of the individual's memory complaints. Based on the referral question and/or the review of the records, such responses may suggest "nonorganic" factors in the individual's complaints of impaired memory, such as a factitious disorder, dissociative amnesia (previously referred to as psychogenic amnesia), or malingering. Therefore, such patient reports may lead the clinician to administer specific measures of symptom validity during the assessment and be particularly sensitive to red flags in tasks administered for other purposes. This issue is discussed in more detail at a later point in this chapter. However, the choice of psychometric instruments used for the evaluation can be significantly influenced by information obtained during the clinical interview.

The interview also provides the clinician with the opportunity to integrate personal historical issues with the current clinical profile. Specifically, a comprehensive clinical interview gathers a complete patient history, including topics such as alcohol use/abuse, drug use/abuse, and diagnosed or suspected learning disabilities. This information can then be integrated with the results of the psychometric assessment to provide a comprehensive picture of the patient and provide the most optimal treatment recommendations.

Quantitative Psychometric Assessment

Typically, the assessment of adult learning and memory is performed in an attempt to identify observed or suspected impairments in functioning. As such, the psychometric approach to testing learning and memory is based on the extraction of a sample of behavior (e.g., learning and remembering a list of words), subsequently determining whether a person is impaired on that sample of behavior, compared to a normative group. The traditional definition of clinical memory impairment is memory performance below expected levels, given the patient's age, education, and estimated premorbid intelligence. This inference can then be used to determine whether the patient indeed has a deficit in learning and/or memory. The actual testing of behavior is just one part of the larger assessment of learning and memory.

The quantitative testing of learning and memory usually consists of employing a test instrument that has been standardized in terms of administration, and evaluated in terms of psychometric properties, such as reliability and validity. Table 14.1 provides a list of some of the more popular instruments used for this purpose. (For a thorough discussion, see Lezak, 1995.) Memory testing can involve administering a test that is specialized for a specific function (e.g., verbal memory) or administering a larger battery of memory tests that are designed to be more inclusive (e.g., verbal and visual memory, immediate and delayed recall). It should be recognized that virtually all tests of "memory" that have been developed and are popularly used are in fact tests of episodic memory. The typical neuropsychological or educational evaluation of memory is often limited to episodic memory assessment. This is perhaps due to the fact that episodic memory is the system most vulnerable to brain damage or dysfunction.

One of the most fundamental tenets of assessment is that memory (i.e., recall and recognition) cannot be assessed adequately without the information being initially learned or acquired. This has major implications for the clinical assessment of memory. Unfortunately, current clinical tools generally do not assess learning per se (or do so poorly), consequently confounding how to interpret recall and recognition. In recognizing this flaw, in their 1977 review of clinical memory assessment, Erickson and Scott strongly recommended: "Patients should have stimuli repeated until they learn the task to criterion. After a given amount of time has passed, they should be retested for retention" (pp. 1144–1145). More recently, Hart (1994) argued that only paradigms that "attempt to minimize the confounding effects of deficient encoding by matching samples on initial learning" can be used to disentangle the complex issues of acquisition, storage, and retrieval (Hart, 1994, p. 331). Unfortunately, such

TABLE 14.1 Common Neuropsychological Tests of Memory Ability

Verbal Memory
Rey Auditory Verbal Learning Test
California Verbal Learning Test
Hopkins Verbal Learning Test
Selective Reminding Procedure

Nonverbal Memory
Rey Osterrieth
Benton Visual Retention Test
Brief Visuospatial Memory Test
Warrington Facial Recognition Test
Biber Figural Learning Test

Test Batteries
Wechsler Memory Scale–III
Memory Assessment Scales

calls for improving assessment methods have gone largely unheeded, even today. Table 14.2 lists common memory assessment measures and the degree to which they assess learning.

The following illustrates the importance of assessing both learning and memory in the clinical assessment. It is well established that persons with traumatic brain injury (TBI) and multiple sclerosis (MS) have significant problems on tests of

TABLE 14.2   Common Neuropsychological Tests of Memory Functioning, Strengths, and Weaknesses

Name	Form	Adequacy of Assessing Learning	Strengths	Weaknesses
California Verbal Learning Test (CVLT)–II	List learning test	Good	• Multiple trials • Many indices available • Good difficulty level • Good norms • 16 items are in 4 categories allowing assessment of organization	• Fixed number of learning trials
Rey Auditory Verbal Learning Test (RAVLT)	List learning test	Not adequate	• Multiple trials	
Bushke Selective Reminding Test (SRT)	List learning test	Not adequate	• Multiple trials • Many alternate forms	• Many versions, making decision of which to use difficult
Hopkins Verbal Learning Test– Revised	List learning test	Not adequate	• Multiple trials • Simple words are easier for those with lower education • Many alternate forms • 12 items are in 4 categories allowing assessment of organization	• Many higher-functioning patients ceiling out • Only 3 learning trials
Rey Osterrieth Complex Figure	Figure copy	Not adequate	• Figure is complex, allowing assessment of complex figural memory • Allows assessment of organizational ability	• No learning trials
Brief Visual Spatial Memory Test	Figural list learning	Not adequate	• Multiple trials • Nonverbal list learning task is fairly rare but useful	• Only 3 learning trials • Stimuli can be verbalized fairly easily
Biber Figural Learning Test	Figural list learning	Not adequate	• Multiple trials • Nonverbal list learning task is fairly rare, but useful • Many learning items in each trial, making the task more difficult	• Fixed number of learning trials • Certain stimuli can be verbalized fairly easily
Wechsler Memory Scale–Revised	Battery of subtests	Not adequate	• Multiple types of memory assessed, both verbal and nonverbal	• Nonverbal tasks are easily verbalized and limited in difficulty
Wechsler Memory Scale–III	Battery of subtests	Not adequate, but better than the revised edition	• Multiple types of memory assessed, both verbal and nonverbal • Includes facial memory and memory for everyday scenes	• Few measures of learning for a very extensive battery • Time consuming to administer
Memory Assessment Scales	Battery of subtests	Not adequate	• Multiple types of memory assessed, both verbal and nonverbal	• Few measures of learning for a very extensive battery • Subtests are limited in difficulty level
Warrington Recognition Memory Test	Facial memory and word memory	Not adequate	• Includes verbal and nonverbal stimuli	• Only uses a recognition format

memory (Beatty et al., 1996; Brassington & Marsh, 1998; Crosson, Novack, Trenerry, & Craig, 1988; Haut & Shutty, 1992; Levin et al., 1990; Millis & Ricker, 1994; Rao, Leo, Bernardin, & Unverzagt, 1991). These tests typically consist of one-trial learning assessments (e.g., paragraph recall) or list-learning tasks with a fixed number of "learning" trials (e.g., 5 trials to learn 16 words). Following the initial presentation(s), recall and/or recognition is then assessed, and performance is compared to healthy controls. The difficulty with using these paradigms is that it is unclear whether the TBI or MS samples have actually "learned" the information to the same degree as the healthy control subjects. This lack of knowledge about degree of learning is obvious with the single-trial presentation. However, even in the five-trial list-learning paradigm, the clinical groups typically learn less information across trials, and recall and recognition are often interpreted without regard to this decreased acquisition of information. The lack of knowledge of the integrity of the individual's learning capacity makes it virtually impossible to understand the cause of any observed difficulties in memory (e.g., recall) performance (i.e., impaired learning of information, forgetting or compromised retrieval from long-term storage, or both). That is, without controlling for the amount of information initially learned, inferences about retrieval problems cannot be adequately made.

DeLuca and colleagues embarked on a series of studies to address this limitation in clinical assessment. In one study (DeLuca et al., 2000) persons with TBI were equated with healthy controls on the amount of information initially learned. This was accomplished by training the TBI and healthy subjects to the same learning criterion (i.e., criterion-based learning) rather than administering a fixed number of learning trials. Specifically, to-be-learned material was presented repeatedly until a preset learning criterion was reached. Once equated on acquisition, recall and recognition could be assessed. Using this paradigm, an understanding of the nature of impaired learning and memory (i.e., acquisition versus retrieval) could be achieved. If the TBI group differed in recall performance from healthy controls after being equated for acquisition, this would support the notion of retrieval failure, that is, an inability to retrieve information from long-term storage. In contrast, if the TBI subjects required more learning trials to be equated to healthy controls on acquisition, but did not differ from healthy controls in recall and recognition performance, this would suggest difficulties in the learning of material from the environment. This latter hypothesis was indeed supported (Figure 14.3). Despite taking more trials to learn the material, TBI subjects who met the learning criterion showed no difficulties in subsequent recall and recognition performance. These data argue that persons with TBI

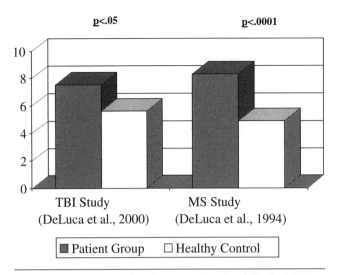

Figure 14.3 On a task designed to measure learning ability, both TBI and MS participants demonstrate learning deficits. Both groups took significantly more trials to reach the learning criterion than healthy controls, but once the information was acquired, they demonstrated recall and recognition abilities comparable to those of a healthy control group. (Adapted from DeLuca et al., 1994; DeLuca et al., 2000)

suffer from significant problems in the acquisition of new information. After they adequately learned the information, recall and recognition abilities did not differ from that of healthy individuals. Interestingly, these same results have been replicated by others (e.g., Vanderploeg, Crowell, & Curtiss, 2001) and have also been shown in persons with MS, as shown in Figure 14.3 (DeLuca, Barbieri-Berger, & Johnson, 1994; DeLuca, Gaudino, Diamond, Christodoulou, & Engel, 1998; Demaree, Gaudino, DeLuca, & Ricker, 2000).

What do studies such as these say about the clinical assessment of learning and memory in the individual? Today, it is no longer sufficient to simply indicate that a person suffers from a memory problem. Rather, the clinical assessment should be designed to determine where in the memory process (i.e., encoding, consolidation, retrieval) a patient is exhibiting difficulty. This is not a trivial matter, in that the treatment of a patient with difficulties in acquisition can be vastly different than the treatment of a patient who has difficulties in the retrieval of information from long-term storage (Cicerone et al., 2000).

Unfortunately, as mentioned earlier, current clinical tools are not designed to assess learning ability adequately, consequently they confound the ability to make a fine-grained analysis of the nature of the observed impairment. For instance, the Logical Memory subtest of the Wechsler Memory Scales (Wechsler, 1987, 1997) is perhaps the most popular clinical assessment instrument for verbal memory. This test has the examiner read a short story to the patients, which they are then asked to recall immediately following presentation and 30 minutes later. Based on these results, the clinician draws conclusions regarding the individual's memory functioning. However, because there is no way to know whether the patient had indeed acquired the information prior to recall (e.g., difficulties in attending, did not learn all of the items presented due to slowed processing speed) the clinician cannot conclude anything other than poor performance. In their review of clinical memory assessment, Erickson and Scott wrote: ". . . Basing one's inferences about learning and memory on . . . material that has been presented one time seems a poor way of assessing memory. It confounds acquisition and retention . . . only provides a cursory look at the process of acquisition" (p. 1144). The most recent version of the Wechsler Memory Scale (WMS-III; Wechsler, 1997) provides a slight improvement in that two learning trials are allowed for one of the two Logical Memory narratives, and a recognition assessment was added. However, despite these improvements, a clear differential between impaired learning versus impaired retrieval remains complex and difficult to ascertain with certainty.

Attempts have been made to incorporate principles from cognitive psychology and neuroscience into clinical assessment. However, these attempts have often been rudimentary. For example, using the Selective Reminding Tests (SRT), Bushke and Fuld (1974) attempted to advance the ability to differentiate between the various processes involved in memory functioning, specifically retention, storage, and retrieval, through their usage of a selective reminding procedure. Specifically, the examiner reads to the examinee a list of words (10 or 12) that are either semantically related (e.g., clothing) or unrelated (depending on the version of the test). Following the initial presentation of the list, the examinee is immediately required to recall as many items as he or she can remember. On all subsequent trials, the patient is reminded only of items he or she has missed on the previous trial and then asked to recall all of the items on the list again. This procedure has been used by various researchers and clinicians with lists of varying lengths and semantic associations (Hannay & Levin, 1985; Gentili, Nichelli, & Schoenhuber, 1989; Masur, Fuld, Blau, Thal, Levin, & Aronson, 1989; Masur, Fuld, Blau, Crystal, & Aronson, 1990; McLean, Temkin, Dikmen, & Wyler, 1983). The SRT is usually administered for a set number of trials (i.e., 6 or 12), although some discontinue administration after a learning criterion is achieved.

The most important contribution of the SRT was the creation of a scoring system that purportedly differentiates between concepts such as retention, storage and retrieval. A total of 11 scores can be obtained through the selective reminding procedure, although few clinicians compute every

score. These include Long Term Retrieval (LTR), Long Term Storage (LTS), and Consistent Long Term Retrieval (CLTR), which were designed to measures learning. The major problem with the SRT is its dubious construct validity. For instance, a word is assumed to enter permanent long-term storage (LTS) if the patient recalls the word on two consecutive trials. It is then assumed that failure to recall this word on subsequent trials must reflect retrieval failure. There are at least two problems with the LTS assumption. First, it is just an assumption. There is no evidence that the words a patient recalls on two consecutive occasions have entered long-term storage. In fact, Loring and Papanicolaou (1987) suggest that the operational definitions of measures of storage and retrieval on the SRT have little to do with these actual constructs. Second, Loring and Papanicolaou state that it is equally plausible that LTS quantifies "memory traces [that] have been stored in a weak or degraded form, and that, through the process of repetitions . . . the word is encoded more deeply and efficiently . . ." (p. 349). As such, constructs such as LTS and CLTR (words recalled consistently throughout learning) may actually be a reflection of the "depth of encoding" rather than a measure of retrieval from long-term storage (DeLuca, Gaudino, Diamond, Christodoulou, & Engel, 1998). This lack of construct validity in the SRT makes it exceedingly difficult to truly differentiate the nature of impaired learning and memory as originally promised.

Perhaps the best test available that allows for differentiation between learning and retrieval is the California Verbal Learning Test (CVLT; Delis, Kramer, Kaplan, & Ober, 1987). Borrowing constructs from cognitive psychology, the CVLT allows for the examination of the learning process through a variety of procedures. These include scores that quantify the rate of learning and examine recall consistency, as well as scores that quantify the learning strategy employed (i.e., serial versus semantic clustering), an additional factor that may reflect learning efficiency. Unfortunately, despite the availability of such advances for assessing an individual's learning and memory abilities, these scores are often not computed or interpreted by the clinician in the clinical memory assessment, thereby limiting the ability to differentiate problems of acquisition versus retrieval in a given patient. The CVLT also continues to make available the traditional measures of recall and recognition, such as examining free recall in contrast to cued recall, or recognition in contrast to recall.

Perhaps the greatest limitation in the CVLT is not its development, but its utilization by clinicians. Specifically, many clinicians continue to rely on the recall versus recognition contrast in their clinical assessments to draw conclusions regarding retrieval abilities. However, the essential flaw in this assessment design is that impaired delayed recall can have two potential sources. First, impaired recall can be due to the inability to retrieve information, or a *retrieval failure*. However, as suggested by Lezak, and others (DeLuca, Barbieri-Berger, & Johnson, 1994; DeLuca et al., 1998) deficient recall could also be attributed to impaired learning. Traditionally, it has been thought that intact recognition is indicative of intact learning. However, is impaired recall in the presence of intact recognition related to poor retrieval, as traditionally thought, or could there be an alternative explanation for this pattern of results?

This issue has triggered much debate among psychologists. For example, the originators of the CVLT (Delis et al., 1987) suggest that a high Recognition Discriminability standard score in the presence of a low Long Delay Free Recall standard score *may* indicate retrieval failure on the CVLT. While this indeed may be true, retrieval failure has since become a standard interpretation of such a dissociation in performance. Wilde and colleagues (1995) tested this dissociation, concluding that their results do not support the use of a recognition-recall dissociation as a marker for retrieval deficits in closed-head injury, a conclusion that sparked a great deal of debate (Feurst, 1997; Veiel, 1997; Wilde, Boake, & Sherer, 1997). However, independently, other authors have questioned the validity of concluding a retrieval deficit from a recall—recognition dissociation as well (Crosson, Novack, Trennery, & Craig, 1989). Yet clinicians continue to draw this conclusion fairly consistently.

By concluding that initial learning is intact due to the presence of adequate recognition abilities, clinicians may be making a number of erroneous assumptions. First, the clinician is assuming that recall and recognition procedures are matched for difficulty. This is clearly not the case; free recall is clearly more difficult on the CVLT. It is well recognized that better recognition versus recall performance can also be associated with a "weak" memory trace secondary to poor encoding (Baur et al., 1993). Recognition may provide just enough of a cue for the individual to recognize the stimulus, but its strength may not be sufficient for effective recall. Second, it is often assumed that learning is an all-or-none phenomenon: Either you learn the information, or you don't. This simplistic notion is not supported by the vast cognitive psychology literature on learning and memory. Cognitive psychologists frequently talk about the depth or quality of encoding or "levels of processing" (Brown & Craik, 2000). These terms refer to the strength of the memory trace, and cognitive psychologists have discussed various methods for strengthening that memory trace, such as repetition (e.g., Slamecka & McElree, 1983), generation (e.g., Slamecka & Graf, 1978), or spacing (e.g., Challis, 1993).

Based on this literature, it must be recognized that a simple recall versus recognition analysis of clinical data is insufficient to disentangle whether impaired performance is due to deficient acquisition or retrieval failure. Much work has been done to examine the relationship between the strength of encoding new information and a person's ability to retrieve that information (Thornton, Raz, & Tucker, 2002), indicating that an assessment of learning is *essential* in evaluating memory abilities. The weakness in current clinical assessment of memory functioning lies in the fact that clinicians assume adequate acquisition, without assessing it.

Thus far, we have discussed in much detail, the assessment of new learning and memory. However, it is important to reemphasize that the clinical examination of learning and memory is *not* simply the administration of tests that measure memory. A major theme throughout this chapter is that there are numerous cognitive (and noncognitive) factors that affect the ability to acquire and subsequently recall or recognize material. As such, these other factors must also be assessed to provide an understanding as to why an individual may perform poorly on tests of learning and memory. The next section discusses many of these factors.

Other Factors Affecting Learning

The assessment of learning and memory cannot be accomplished effectively by simply employing tests of memory alone. Several other factors (cognitive and noncognitive) can influence the integrity of the process of learning and remembering information. These factors include (but are not limited to) working memory, information processing speed, executive abilities, and effort.

Working Memory

As mentioned previously, working memory can be considered the first step in the encoding of information into episodic memory (Johnson, 1992). It has been argued for many years that limitations in working memory can be responsible for difficulties in learning new information (Kyllonen & Christal, 1987, 1990). As such, impairments in working memory can lead to decreased learning efficiency and subsequently, impaired recall and recognition in long-term memory.

The term *working memory* commonly refers to the cognitive process that enables individuals to maintain and manipulate a limited amount of information over a brief period of time (Baddeley, 1986, 1992). The term *working memory* replaces (or updates) the term *short-term memory* in that working memory represents an active form of information processing; whereas short-term memory represented more of a passive cognitive system. Working memory is a critical component for a variety of cognitive skills, such as problem solving, planning, and active listening (Jonides, 1995). In addition, working memory plays a key role in many everyday activities that are essential for occupational (e.g., engaging in a telephone conversation while taking notes) and scholastic (e.g., mental arithmetic) functioning. Individuals with significant working-memory deficits have great difficulty recording features from a changing environment and keeping them in mind to guide behavior (Smith, Jonides, & Koeppe, 1996). In addition, everyday activities, such as writing and reading comprehension, may be affected by impairments in working memory (Engle, 1996). As such, the clinical assessment of working memory and how it relates to the acquisition of information is a crucial part of the overall evaluation of episodic memory.

The intricate relationship between working memory functioning and long-term memory has also been demonstrated in numerous studies utilizing functional neuroimaging techniques. In their comprehensive review of neuroimaging studies examining frontal cortical activation involved in learning, Fletcher and Henson (2001) draw attention to the close relationship between working memory and long-term memory. They indicate that dorsolateral frontal cortex, ventrolateral frontal cortex, and anterior frontal cortex are all intricately involved in working memory and long-term memory, theorizing that frontal cortical activations during long-term memory tasks actually reflect control processes aiding in and optimizing memory encoding and retrieval. This position highlights the importance of working-memory processes in encoding, with working memory holding the potential to maximize the encoding process, thus impacting later retrieval.

A great deal of research has been conducted in the field of working memory, using various populations including animals, healthy human beings, and individuals with neurological illness. As a result of such a large body of literature, there are multiple theories describing the concept and processes involved in working memory. One of the most popular and well-referenced theories of working memory is that of Baddeley (1992). In this model, working memory is comprised of three components (see Figure 14.4). The first two components are referred to as "slave" systems: the phonological loop and the visuospatial sketchpad (Figure 14.4). These slave systems are responsible for the temporary maintenance or storage of information, as well as the rehearsal of this information. Each slave system processes a different type of information. The phonological loop stores auditory information; whereas the visual-spatial sketchpad is responsible for visual-spatial storage and maintenance. The third component of working memory, as described by Baddeley, is that of the central executive system (CES). The CES is thought to be responsible for the selection, initiation, and termination of processing routines within working memory. The CES is a limited-capacity system for the temporary manipulation of

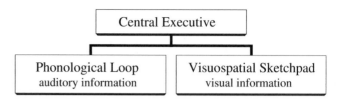

Figure 14.4 Schematic illustrating the relationship between the phonological and visuospatial slave systems and the central executive. (Adapted from Baddeley, 1992.)

complex information. The CES uses the stored information in the slave systems to perform complex cognitive manipulations of this material. The CES is used for a variety of purposes, including tasks involving planning or decision making; troubleshooting in situations in which the automatic processes appear to be running into difficulty; novel situations; technically difficult situations; and situations where strong habitual responses or temptations are involved.

Clearly, the evaluation of working memory is an integral part of the assessment of learning and memory. However, in spite of the significant advances in cognitive psychology and functional neuroimaging that enhance the understanding of human working memory, few of these advances have made their way into clinical memory assessment.

In modern clinical assessment, working memory is conceptualized as a unitary construct. This contrasts with the well-developed theoretical conceptualizations of the multifaceted components of working memory, and the neuroimaging studies validating this mulifactorial model described previously. For instance, the WAIS-III and WMS-III provide working memory index scores, which collapse across the CES and slave systems. Unfortunately, such a singular factor score diminishes the ability to differentiate between impairment between the CES and slave systems. This can lead to diagnostic errors in the assessment of working memory and its components. For instance, the Working Memory Index for the WAIS-III (Wechsler, 1997) consists of three tests: Arithmetic, Digit Span, and Letter-Number Sequence (LNS), a new alpha-numeric task that has a substantial load on the CES. Recent work in persons with TBI has shown that the Working Memory Index could be within normal limits in persons with moderate-severe TBI. However, a close examination of the specific scores that make up the Working Memory Index reveals that the CES may be significantly compromised in persons with TBI with intact slave system functioning (Donders, Tulsky, & Zhu, 2001; Martin, Donders, & Thompson, 2000). In this study, Arithmetic and Digit Span did not differ between TBI and healthy controls; whereas significant group differences were observed on LNS (targeting CES).

This study illustrates how, in the clinical evaluation, a more fine-grained analysis can be performed within the Working Memory Index. The following example further illustrates this point. The Working Memory Index for the WMS-III consists of Spatial Span (a visual analog of Digit Span) and LNS. (Both the WAIS-III and WMS-III use LNS in calculating separate Working Memory indices.) Spatial Span forward is a measure of rehearsal within the visual-spatial sketchpad. Spatial Span backward increases the CES load slightly from forward span, while LNS requires substantial CES involvement. Intact Spatial Span forward, with borderline backward span and compromised LNS, would suggest that the visual-spatial sketchpad is intact, but the patient is having significant difficulties in the CES, or manipulation component of WM. This observed dissociation, based on the existing theories of working memory and the working memory literature, may aid in the clinician's ability to identify the specific cognitive deficit and make recommendations toward its remediation.

Another major problem in the assessment of working memory in psychology is that tests developed purportedly to assess working memory are not construct-specific. That is, tests of working memory are also contaminated by other cognitive constructs. For example, the Paced Auditory Serial Addition Test (PASAT; Gronwall, 1977) is a common standardized test purported to measure working memory. It has proven to be sensitive in identifying cognitive problems in various clinical populations (e.g., DeLuca et al., 1993; Levander & Sonesson, 1998; Maddocks & Saling, 1996). Unfortunately, the PASAT is also influenced by several other cognitive factors, such as attention and speed of information processing. Clinicians must use such tests wisely to factor out the impaired versus intact cognitive factors responsible for any particular deficit. An example of such a technique is provided in the next section on processing speed.

As is evident from the preceding discussion, the integrity of working memory functions has a significant impact on long-term episodic memory. Adequate attention to the effects of working memory performance is critical to the understanding of long-term episodic memory ability.

Information Processing Speed

Information processing speed represents a key cognitive construct in humans. Processing speed has been recognized as the cognitive factor most associated with variance in IQ (Deary & Stough, 1996), is extremely vulnerable to cerebral dysfunction (Demaree, DeLuca, Gaudino, & Diamond, 1999; Litvan, Grafman, Vendrell, & Martinez, 1988; Madigan, DeLuca, Diamond, Tramontano, & Averill, 2000; Schmitter-

Edgecomb & Rogers, 1997), and is a key element in normal aging (Salthouse, 1996, 2000).

The speed by which information is processed by the brain can significantly influence whether (or in what form) information is learned, which in turn, influences whether such information can be subsequently retrieved. For example, Salthouse (1994) suggests that age-related decline in information processing speed leads to decreased efficiency of encoding in memory systems, which results in a "fragile representation" of information in long-term memory. Furthermore, in persons with MS for instance, speed of processing is correlated with the number of learning trials it takes to achieve a learning criterion (DeLuca et al., 1994; Gaudino, Chiaravalloti, DeLuca, & Diamond, 2001).

Because of the relationship between processing speed and the acquisition of information, an analysis of processing speed must be part of the clinical assessment of learning and memory. Unfortunately, clinical tests of pure "processing speed" do not exist. Therefore, multiple instruments should be used so that related cognitive constructs can be factored out in an attempt to isolate speed of processing deficits. For instance, the Paced Auditory Serial Addition Test (PASAT) is a neuropsychological instrument that some have referred to as a test of information processing speed and has been shown to be sensitive to brain dysfunction (Levander et al., 1998; Litvan et al., 1988; Maddocks et al., 1996). However, in addition to speed, the PASAT also measures other constructs, such as attention/concentration (Gronwall & Wrightson, 1981) and divided attention (Kessels, Keyser, Verhagen, & van Luijtelaar, 1998). Consider the sample clinical profile in Table 14.3. The impaired PASAT, coupled with an impairment on the Processing Speed Index in the presence of an intact Working Memory Index on the WAIS-III, provides evidence of selective impairment in processing speed. These data suggest that the compromised verbal memory performance on the Logical Memory subtest of the WMS-III may be at least partially influenced by the processing speed deficit. If so, a hypothesis to consider in the clinical assessment of memory is the possibility that impaired memory performance is due

TABLE 14.3 Clinical Vignette of Processing Speed and Learning and Memory

WAIS-III		
Verbal Comprehension Index	101	Average
Perceptual Organization Index	103	Average
Working Memory Index	99	Average
Processing Speed Index	82	Impaired
PASAT	80	Impaired
Logical Memory	85	Impaired

Note. Test scores are in scaled scores with a mean of 100 and SD of 15.

to difficulties in the acquisition of information, secondary to impaired processing speed.

The cognitive psychology literature (Salthouse, 1996) offers two distinct mechanisms for why speed of processing affects the ability to learn and subsequently retrieve information from long-term storage. The first is the *limited time mechanism,* which states, "relevant cognitive operations are executed too slowly to be successfully completed in the available time" (p. 404). That is, acquisition of information is reduced, because necessary operations may not be completed if the processing is slow (e.g., not enough time to perform later operations). The second is the *simultaneity mechanism,* which refers to the idea that slowed processing reduces the amount of information that can be processed simultaneously with other critical operations. For example, "higher level" problem solving effectiveness may be compromised when "lower level" operations may be too slow (Salthouse, 1996).

Clearly, information processing speed is a key factor that must be assessed and integrated into the overall assessment of learning and memory.

Executive Functions and Frontal Lobe Factors

Executive functions refer to the ability to engage in independent, purposive, and goal-directed behavior. These functions are conceptualized as having four components: volition, planning, purposive action, and effective performance (Lezak, 1995). Executive functions are thought to be related to the integrity of frontal lobe structures, as implicated by clinical observations of individuals sustaining frontal lobe trauma (Lezak, 1995) and neuroimaging techniques (Fletcher & Henson, 2001). A number of studies point to a significant relationship between the integrity of executive functions and memory performance. For example, in a population with Parkinson's disease, Ringe, Frol, Saine, and Cullum (1999) found that organization and executive functioning independently accounted for a significant proportion of the variance in memory scores, noted in verbal memory, as measured by the CVLT, and nonverbal memory, as measured by the Rey-Osterrieth Complex Figure. It should be recognized however, that the construct of executive processes is complex and multidimensional and that not all aspects of executive functions are necessarily associated with learning and memory (e.g., Tremont, Halpert, Javorsky, & Stern, 2000).

One key element of executive functioning is organizational skills. The ability to organize information can significantly influence the acquisition and subsequent recall and recognition of material, a fact that is demonstrated most effectively in individuals with frontal lobe damage. Patients with focal frontal lobe damage are impaired in using orga-

nizational strategies to aid learning, as well as in the use of organized search strategies for retrieving information from long-term storage (Gershberg & Shimamura, 1995; Hirst & Volpe, 1988; Stuss et al., 1994). Such difficulties, particularly in the acquisition of information have been observed in a number of patient populations including those with Alzheimer's disease and frontotemporal dementia (Glosser, Gallo, Clark, & Grossman, 2002); amnesics (Diamond, DeLuca, & Kelley, 1997), stroke, (Lange, Waked, Kirshblum, & DeLuca, 2000), and TBI (DeLuca et al., 2000; Goldstein, Levin, & Boake, 1989). In addition, performance of such patients has been shown to be significantly enhanced when organizational strategies are provided at the time of learning (e.g., Diamond et al., 1997).

The clinical assessment of learning and memory must, therefore, take into account the potential influence of executive dysfunction on tests of learning and memory. Figure 14.5 depicts the improvements in memory performance in stroke patients when using an organizational strategy during learning. These data show that stroke subjects who employed an organized approach to copying this figure displayed better recall performance than those subjects who showed poor organizational skills (Lange et al., 2000). Clinically, the examination can show whether a patient utilizes an organized or unorganized approach in copying the Rey-Osterrieth Complex Figure. Clinicians can then note whether this approach has influenced recall performance (Lange et al., 2000; Lezak, 1995). If the copy portion of the test is clearly disorganized, recall scores may have been influenced by poor planning and organization. It is up to the clinician to select test instruments to try to disentangle the relative role of executive dysfunction on acquisition and remembering.

Another executive function that influences learning and memory is a person's ability to remember when and where he or she acquired new information, commonly referred to as *source memory.* Patients with frontal lobe lesions may perform fairly well on tests of recall or recognition of facts or items on a test (e.g., episodic memory such as list learning or paragraph recall). However, such patients are often impaired when recalling the origin (i.e., source) of that information (Glisky, Polster, & Routhieaux, 1995; Janowsky, Shimamura, & Squire, 1989). Traditional neuropsychological tests do not assess problems in source memory. As such, an assessment of source memory must currently be left up to the knowledge and skills of the clinician.

Evaluating Effort

Diminished effort can also significantly influence performance on tests of learning and memory. Symptom validity testing is

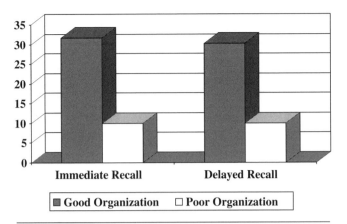

Figure 14.5 The use of an organizational strategy has been shown to improve recall ability on the Rey Osterrieth Complex Figure following stroke, even following a 20-minute delay period. A higher score indicates better memory performance. (Adapted from Lange et al., 2000.)

an important component of a memory assessment, because poor effort can result in poor memory test performance, often resembling a memory deficit. Poor memory performance due to diminished effort (or frank malingering) is often observed in the forensic arena where secondary gains (e.g., financial) can provide significant motivation to perform less than adequately. In addition, the feigning of symptoms, such as cognitive deficits, can be a marker for some psychiatric syndromes, such as factitious disorder. Therefore tests designed to measure symptom validity are necessary components in a neuropsychological assessment.

Individuals who are malingering commonly complain of poor memory and as such, numerous mechanisms for objectively evaluating "effort" have been developed (Brandt, 1988; Etcoff & Kampfer, 1996; Iverson,& Binder, 2000; Millis & Putnam, 1996; Nies & Sweet, 1994; Rogers, Harrell, & Liff, 1993). In general, there are two approaches to consider within the psychometric portion of the evaluation (see the section on pretesting assessment for techniques used during the clinical interview). First, within a typical evaluation, clinicians can look for a discrepancy in test scores that is not ordinarily observed in persons with brain dysfunction. Perhaps the best red flag for reduced effort is recognition memory performance that is worse than free recall (Lezak, 1995). As discussed previously, the typical learning and memory instrument usually employs a simple and easy two-alternative, forced-choice recognition memory format. On average, a patient should achieve at least a score of 50% correct by chance alone. The clinician can look for other things as well, including an abnormally minimal digit span forward in the presence of intact

language and attention or good performance on a more difficult memory test (Lezak, 1995).

Alternatively, a number of objective tests have been developed specifically for the examination of effort-related variables, particularly memory. These tests have been designed to be quite simplistic in nature, such that they would be considered "too easy to fail" (Lezak, 1995). Examples include Dot Counting: Grouped and Ungrouped Dots (Rey, 1941), which require the examinee to count dots on individually presented cards as quickly as possible. The speed with which the examinee counts the grouped dots is then contrasted with the speed with which the examinee counts the ungrouped dots, the former of which should be faster. If this is not the case, the examinee's effort is suspect. Rey also presents an additional symptom validity test (Rey 15-Item Memory) in which 15 items are exposed to the examinee for 10 seconds for memorization. The examinee is then asked to draw as many items as possible. The task is extremely simple in that the items can be grouped into five groups rather quickly (capital letters, numbers, lower case letters, shapes, roman numerals), with only the first three representative items from each groups included (ABC, 123, abc, etc.).

A third example of symptom validity testing includes psychometric tests specifically developed to assess memory malingering. Many of these employ a forced-choice format, where a stimulus is presented (e.g., picture or number) followed by a two-choice recognition task, with one item being the original stimulus. The subject is asked to identify the original stimulus. Tests such as the Portland Digit Recognition Test (Binder, 1993) and the Test of Memory Malingering (TOMM; Tombaugh, 1997) have shown that memory impaired groups (e.g., dementia, amnesics, TBI) perform well on such easy tests (e.g., over 90% correct on the TOMM). Thus, impaired performance would suggest poor effort or malingering.

The problem with the use of such tests alone is that they do not prove malingering or poor effort. They only provide evidence for reduced performance. Information from other sources, such as the clinical interview, history, records, and so on must be combined and incorporated to reach a meaningful conclusion.

TESTING SPECIAL POPULATIONS

Very often, individuals referred for a neuropsychological evaluation have special needs or unique backgrounds that cannot be overlooked in the conduct of evaluations. This section focuses on special considerations in assessing learning and memory in populations such as these.

Assessing Individuals with Disabilities

Numerous factors affect the process of learning and remembering information. Therefore, a valid assessment of learning and memory must ensure that information is presented to the examinee so that the information is available to the memory systems. Under normal circumstances, this is not problematic. Specifically, in a healthy, nondisabled individual, information can typically be presented in any modality (e.g., visually, auditorily) and remain available for encoding and transfer into long-term memory without degradation or misrepresentation of the original stimulus. However, when testing individuals with disabilities, special attention needs to be directed toward consideration of the integrity of the stimulus being processed and stored. Accommodations are frequently made in the testing of disabled individuals for this purpose, and such methods often increase the probability of a valid assessment. Unfortunately, test manufacturers provide few guidelines regarding the limitations of accommodations or the appropriateness of particular accommodations for particular populations. Therefore, training and clinical judgment both play a vital role in such decisions.

Messick (1995) discusses the provision of accommodations as necessary to increase the validity of assessment and offers a decision-making framework to help guide clinicians in this regard. Messick focused on the source of invalidity to aid decisions regarding the provision of accommodations. Specifically, two forms of invalidity are presented: construct under-representation and construct-irrelevant variance. Construct under-representation refers to an assessment procedure in which the construct of interest is not adequately assessed. This can be problematic in individuals with disabilities or individuals without disabilities. For example, an assessment of memory functioning should examine all aspects of memory, including verbal and visual-spatial material. If only verbal memory is assessed, the construct of memory is under-represented (see Braden, 1999). Alternatively, construct irrelevant variance refers to the situation in which the assessment technique applied is impacted by skills not central to the construct of interest. For example, a clinician interested in measuring verbal memory functions in a deaf client could not read a list of words to the client, as in the standard administration of word list learning tests. This procedure would introduce construct irrelevant variance associated with hearing ability. Rather, an accommodation must be made for this particular client, in which, the words can be presented on index cards for instance. The goal is for accommodations to be made for disabled individuals to reduce construct irrelevant variance, while maximizing construct representation (Braden, 1999). However, the maximization of construct representation as in the given example raises additional issues,

such as standardization and the utilization of normative data as a point of comparison.

In this regard, Caplan and Schechter (1996) provide the distinction between *testing* and *evaluation.* As its name implies, *testing* is described as a mechanical enterprise, rigid in nature. Alternatively, an *evaluation* is described as more of an art applied to an individual, involving testing, creativity, expertise, flexibility, and ingenuity in striving to understand a given patient. Cognitive, emotional, or physical limitations may, in fact, limit the validity of certain tests, thus weakening the clinician's ability to gather meaningful information. Importantly, the provision of accommodations in assessment procedures is no longer optional. Professional ethics highlight the need for effective assessment of clients with disabilities (American Psychological Association, 1992). Furthermore, increased legislation concerning such techniques has made the provision of accommodations in assessment procedures and settings mandatory (i.e., Title VI of the Civil Rights Act of 1964, Title IX of the Education Amendments of 1972, Section 504 of the Rehabilitation Act of 1973, and Title II of the Americans with Disabilities Act of 1990; Office of Civil Rights, 2000). Unfortunately, the way these accommodations affect the accurate assessment of constructs and thus the validity of the assessment procedure has not yet been well studied (Braden, 1999).

Construct representation is not the only challenge in the provision of accommodations in assessment. The appropriate mechanisms for scoring test performance also remains an issue given that the normative data is gathered on a normal sample without the provision of accommodations. So, in the visual presentation of a list-learning task, the examiner would likely score the test utilizing the same scoring criteria as if the task were presented in a standard oral fashion. But, does the visual presentation of the stimuli make the task easier, thus invalidating the norms? The improvement in assessment results for individuals with disabilities through such accommodations, while not improving those for individuals without disabilities, is called *differential boost.* This idea suggests that individuals with disabilities may benefit differentially from accommodations, potentially improving performance. However, can a clinician compare these scores to that of a normative sample that was not provided with such accommodations? This serious issue has spurred much research utilizing specific neuropsychological tests. Very often, through the use of specific, appropriate testing materials, clinicians circumvent the need for modifications to accommodate disabilities.

Specifically, many tests have been adapted to improve their ability to assess populations with special needs. In addition, normative studies have been performed on test administrations including the adaptation, essentially resulting in new normative data with the adapted version of the test. For example, individuals with MS often present with physical limitations restricting the speed with which they can use their upper extremities. Therefore, the written Trail Making Test, a common test of visual-motor attention and mental flexibility, would be confounded by motor deficits, limiting the clinician's ability to assess these cognitive capacities accurately. The modification of the Trail Making Test to an oral version precludes such a confound, and normative data has been gathered on this oral version of the task. Other examples of such adapted tests include the WAIS-R as a Neuropsycholgical Instrument (WAIS-R-NI; Kaplan, Fein, Morris, & Delis, 1991), Caltagirone, Gainotti, and Miceli's (1977) adaptation of the Colored Matrices for use with patients with unilateral neglect, and the multiple choice version of the Benton Visual Retention Test (Sivan, 1992). But, what do clinicians do when norms do not exist for a given modification? Clinicians continue to make numerous other necessary test adaptations, without the availability of suitable normative data.

In the absence of suitable adaptations and norms, modifications often remain necessary. Many authors have noted the necessity for modifications to test protocols. Sattler and Tozier (1970) noted that such strategies may be needed for standardized tests to be used appropriately with specific populations, also noting that little is known about the effects of modifications on test performance. In presenting numerous modifications for tests of children's abilities, Sattler (1982) further noted that such nonstandard administration will, "likely result in scores that differ from those obtained under standard administrative procedures."

The Impact of Language and Culture

Many of the issues mentioned in the discussion of accommodations for disabilities also directly apply to language-based differences. Specifically, when memory tests are developed, they are developed in a particular language, within the context of a specific culture. For example, the California Verbal Learning Test (Delis et al., 1987) was developed in English for use in the United States, keeping U.S. culture in mind. However, given the varied language representations in the United States alone, a clinician may desire a translation into other languages, such as Spanish. Although test administration is certainly possible through the use of a translator, the translation and subsequent presentation of a list of words, for example, to an individual of another culture of origin may alter the difficulty level of the test and/or the meaning of the stimuli. Taking the CVLT example, 4 of the 16 words on the original CVLT list are spices and herbs. These ingredients are often used in American culture and individuals exposed to

American cuisine are often somewhat familiar with them. However, cuisine preferences in a family of Chinese, Indian, or even Spanish culture tends to be quite distinct, marked by the usage of different spices and herbs and potentially limited exposure to those used in mainstream American culture. This basic cultural difference, even within families living in the United States, causes the test to be more difficult for individuals coming from homes emphasizing an alternative culture due to differences in word exposure and knowledge of the meaning of the stimuli. As in the preceding discussion of individuals with disability, the result is construct-irrelevant variance (semantic knowledge and exposure) and construct under-representation (memory abilities). The validity of the assessment in persons with diverse cultural backgrounds, or who were raised in foreign countries (even many years ago) may significantly impact performance on tests of learning and memory.

However, standard 2.04(c) of the ethical principles by the American Psychological Association requires that the psychologist take patient factors, such as "gender, age, race, ethnicity, . . . disability, language or socioeconomic status" into account and adjust for them in their administration and interpretation of performance (American Psychological Association, 1992). How to best carry out this standard remains hotly debated. In America, for example, a translation is not always deemed necessary to accomplish this goal, due to the fact that most patients are proficient in English, regardless of their cultural background. However, given the cultural and ethnic diversity in the United States, American neuropsychologists are frequently called upon to perform an evaluation on individuals for whom English is a second language. Although many neuropsychologists would proceed with such an evaluation without particular concern, some have argued that performing an evaluation on an individual with a different language or culture than the examiner's is unethical (Artiola i Fortuny & Mullaney, 1997). The opposing argument is that the alternative is simply unrealistic; the American culture is too diverse to match the language, culture, and experience of every given patient to an appropriate psychologist (Harris, Echemendia, Ardila, & Rosselli, 2001). Often locating an ethnically matched neuropsychologist is not feasible, in which case it is incumbent upon the neuropsychologist to obtain the training, consultation, and/or supervision necessary to work effectively with a given patient.

LEGAL-ETHICAL

Neuropsychologists performing assessments of memory and new learning are often working with individuals with disabilities, such as neurological illness or injury, psychiatric illness, or developmental disorders. As such, many of the ethical issues encountered deal with the need for accommodations for patients with disabilities or diverse backgrounds and have already been discussed previously. However, several ethical issues put forth in the Ethical Principles for Psychologists (American Psychological Association, 1992) are often seen in the realm of assessment and may present legal challenges for the clinician involved.

The American Psychological Association devotes an entire segment of the Ethical code to the areas of evaluation, assessment, and intervention. Many of the issues presented therein are directly applicable to memory assessment, but may be overlooked by clinicians. For example, guideline 2.02 addresses the importance of competence and appropriate use of assessments, calling to light the need for training and supervision with new instruments or techniques, as well as selecting the appropriate measures to address the referral question. As stated earlier, the referral question may be vague, in which case a clarification of the referral question may be necessary to facilitate appropriate test selection. A complete discussion of the potential ethical issues in memory assessment is beyond the scope of this chapter. However, clinicians should be aware that it is their ethical responsibility to remain knowledgeable of the current literature and practice in accordance with the most current practice standard. Much of that current literature has been provided through discussions in the current chapter.

FUTURE DIRECTIONS AND RECOMMENDATIONS

Over fifty years of focused neuropsychological and cognitive neuroscience, research has significantly improved our understanding of how learning and memory is accomplished in the brain and how brain damage results in significant memory disturbances. It is clear that the clinical assessment of learning and memory has lagged far behind this level of scientific understanding. What is needed is not the occasional updating of old test protocols, designed and developed decades earlier. Rather, a new generation of test instruments is needed based on new scientific knowledge regarding the way the brain accomplishes learning and memory.

Several specific recommendations can be made. First, episodic memory must be considered as a process. Although in some assessment situations discovering whether a patient has a memory problem can be the primary referral question, the assessment should also include where in the *process* (i.e., encoding, consolidation, retrieval) the patient is experiencing difficulty. This information can then be used in designing

more effective treatment interventions aimed toward improving functional ability.

Second, in adequately assessing the nature of impaired learning and memory, it is necessary to demonstrate that the preliminary steps in this process are intact prior to concluding that the later steps are deficient. For example, a clinician cannot conclude that an individual has a deficit in memory if he or she shows deficits in attention or executive functions. The more appropriate conclusion may be that the integrity of the memory system is compromised, potentially due to the impact of poor attention or executive skills. Third, learning and memory cannot be assessed simply by the administration of tests of memory alone. As we have illustrated, various other cognitive constructs can significantly influence whether information is adequately acquired, hence affecting the ability to retrieve this information from long-term storage successfully. The clinical assessment of learning and memory must do the detective work to decipher which factors may be responsible for impaired learning and memory performance.

Finally, traditional psychological assessment has focused on a norm-based approach to the understanding of cognitive constructs and deficits in these cognitive constructs (Anastasi, 1988). Another fruitful approach would be the increased utilization of a criterion-based assessment of learning and memory. Tests designed to measure the ability to achieve a learning criterion (e.g., number of trials to acquire information) can be particularly effective in the assessment of learning difficulties. Unfortunately, few if any current test instruments provide such assessment opportunities. A combination of criterion-based assessment (for example, repeating the word list until the criterion of all words correct on two trials is reached) with a normative-based assessment (such as comparing the trials it takes an individual to reach the criterion to that of an age and education matched normative sample) may be particularly fruitful.

Memory tests need to be grounded in theory and research with the ability to assess all components of the memory process. It is only through a broad, comprehensive approach to memory assessment that neuropsychologists can obtain valid, clinically meaningful conclusions and recommendations for their patients.

REFERENCES

American Psychological Association (1990). Ethical principles of psychologists. *American Psychologist, 45,* 390–395.

Anastasi, A. (1988). *Psychological testing (6th ed).* New York: MacMillan.

Artiola i Fortuny, L., & Mullaney, H.A. (1997). Neuropsychology with Spanish speakers: Language use and proficiency issues for test development. *Journal of Clinical and Experimental Neuropsychology, 19*(4), 615–622.

Atkinson, R.C., & Shiffrin, R.M. (1968). Human memory: A proposed system and its control processes. In K.W. Spence & J.T. Spence (Eds.), *The psychology of learning and motivation: Advances in research and theory.* New York: Academic Press.

Baddeley, A. (1986). *Working memory.* Oxford: Oxford University Press.

Baddeley, A. (1992). Working memory. *Science, 255,* 556–559.

Baddeley, A. (2000) Short-term and working memory. In E. Tulving & F.I.M. Craik (Eds.), *The Oxford handbook of memory* (pp. 77–92). New York: Oxford University Press.

Baur, R.M., Tobias, B., & Valenstien, E. (1993). Amnestic disorders. In K.M. Heilman & E. Valenstein (Eds.), *Clinical neuropsychology.* New York: Oxford University Press.

Beatty, W.W., Wilbanks, S.L., Blanco, C.R., Hames, K.A., Tivis, R., & Paul, R.H. (1996). Memory disturbance in multiple sclerosis: Reconsideration of patterns of performance on the selective reminding test. *Journal of Clinical & Experimental Neuropsychology, 18:* 56–62.

Benton, A., Hamsher, K., & Stone, F. (1983). *Visual retention test: Multiple choice form I.* Iowa City: Department of Neurology, University Hospitals, University of Iowa.

Binder, L.M. (1993). Assessment of malingering after mild head trauma with the Portland Digit Recognition Test. *Journal of Clinical and Experimental Neuropsychology, 15,* 170–182.

Braden, J.P. (1999). Accommodations in testing: Methods to ensure validity. *Assessment Focus, 8*(1), pp. 1–3. San Antonio, TX: The Psychological Corp. (Available at http://www.psychcorp.com /pdf/assessspr99.pdf*).*

Brandt, J. (1988). Malingered amnesia. In R. Rogers (Ed.), *Clinical assessment of malingering and deception.* New York: Guilford.

Brassington, J.C., & Marsh, N.V. (1988). Neuropsychological aspects of multiple sclerosis. [Review] [184 refs]. *Neuropsychology Review, 8,* 43–77.

Brown, S.C., & Craik, F.I.M. (2000). Encoding and retrieval of information. In E. Tulving & F.I.M. Craik (Eds.), *The Oxford handbook of memory* (p. 37). New York, Oxford University Press.

Buschke, H., & Fuld, P.A. (1974). Evaluating storage, retention, and retrieval in disordered memory and learning. *Neurology, 24,* 1019–1025.

Caltagirone, C., Gainotti, G., & Miceli, G. (1977). Una nuova versone delle matrici colorate elaborate specificamente per i pazienti con lesioni emesferiche focali. [A new version of the Colored Matrices developed specifically for patients with focal hemispheric lesions]. *Minerva Psichiatrica, 18,* 9–16.

Caplan, B., & Schecthter, J. (1996). The role of nonstandard neuropsychological assessment in rehabilitation: History, rationale, and examples. In L.A. Cushamn & M.J. Scherer (Eds.), *Psychological assessment in medical rehabilitation.* Washington, DC: American Psychological Association.

Challis, B.H. (1993). Spacing effect on cued-memory tests depend upon level of processing. *Journal of Experimental Psychology, Learning, Memory, and Cognition, 19, 2,* 389–396.

Cicerone, K.D., Dahlberg, C., Kalmar, K., Langenbahn, D.M., Malec, J.J., Bergquist, T.F., Felicetti, T., Giacino, J.T., Harley, J.P., Harrington, D.E., Herzog, J., Kneipp, P., Laatsch, L., & Morse, P.A. (2000). Evidence-based cognitive rehabilitation: Recommendations for clinical practice. *Archives of Physical Medicine and Rehabilitation, 81,* 1596–1615.

Cohen, N.J., & Eichenbaum, H. (1994). *Memory, amnesia, and the hippocampal system.* Cambridge: The MIT Press.

Crosson, B., Novack, T.A., Trenerry, M.R., & Craig, P.L. (1988). California verbal learning test (CVLT) performance in severely head-injured and neurologically normal adult males. *Journal of Clinical and Experimental Neuropsychology, 10,* 754–768.

Crosson, B., Novack, T.A., Trenerry, M.R., & Craig, P.L. (1989). Differentiation of verbal memory deficits in blunt head injury using the recognition trial of the California Verbal Learning Test: An exploratory study. *The Clinical Neuropsychologist, 3,* 29–44.

Deary, I.J., & Stough, C. (1996). Intelligence and inspection time: Achievements, prospects and problems. *American Psychologist, 51,* 599–608.

Delis, D.C., Kramer, J.H., Kaplan, E., & Ober, B.A. (1987). California verbal learning test. San Antonio, TX: The Psychological Corporation.

DeLuca, J., Barbieri-Berger, S., & Johnson, S.K. (1994). The nature of memory impairments in multiple sclerosis: Acquisition versus retrieval. *Journal of Clinical & Experimental Neuropsychology, 16,* 183–9.

DeLuca, J., Gaudino, E.A., Diamond, B.J., Christodoulou, C., & Engel, R.A. (1998). Acquisition and storage deficits in multiple sclerosis. *Journal of Clinical & Experimental Neuropsychology, 20,* 376–90.

DeLuca, J., Johnson, S.K., & Natelson, B.H. (1993). Information processing efficiency in chronic fatigue syndrome and multiple sclerosis. *Archives of Neurology, 50,* 301–304.

DeLuca, J., Schultheis, M.T., Madigan, N.K., Christodoulou, C., & Averill, A. (2000). Acquisition versus retrieval deficits in traumatic brain injury: Implications for memory rehabilitation. *Archives of Physical Medicine and Rehabilitation, 81*(10), 1327–1333.

Demaree, H.A., DeLuca, J., Gaudino, E.A., & Diamond, B.J. (1999). Speed of information processing as a key deficit in multiple sclerosis: Implications for rehabilitation. *Journal of Neurology, Neurosurgery, and Psychiatry, 67,* 661–663.

Demaree, H.A., Gaudino, E.A., DeLuca, J., & Ricker, J.H. (2000). Learning impairment is associated with recall ability in multiple sclerosis. *Journal of Clinical and Experimental Neuropsychology, 22,* 865–873.

Diamond, B.J., DeLuca, J., Kelley, S.M. (1997). Memory and executive functions in amnesic and non-amnesic patients with aneurysms of the anterior communicating artery. *Brain, 120,* 1015–1025.

Donders, J., Tulsky, D.S., & Zhu, J. (2001). Criterion validity of new WAIS-III subtest scores after traumatic brain injury. *Journal of the International Neuropsychological Society, 7,* 892–898.

Echemendía, R., Ardila, A., & Rosselli, M. (2001). Cross-cultural cognitive and neuropsychological assessment. In J.W. Andrews, H. Janzen, & D. Saklofske (Eds.), *Ability, achievement, and behavioral assessment.* San Diego, CA: Academic Press.

Engle, R.W. (1996). Working memory and retrieval: An inhibition-resource approach. J.T.E. Richardson (Ed.), *Working memory and human cognition* (pp. 1130–1149). New York: Oxford University Press.

Erickson, R.C., & Scott, M.L. (1977). Clinical memory testing: A review. *Psychological Bulletin,* 84: 1130–1149.

Etcoff, L.M., & Kampfer, K.M. (1996). Practical guidelines in the use of symptom validity and other psychological tests to measure malingering and symptom exaggeration in traumatic brain injury cases. *Neuropsychology Review, 6,* 171–201.

Fink, G.R., Markowitsch, H.J., Reinkemeier, M., Kessler, J., & Heiss, W.D. (1996). A PET study of autobiographical memory recognition. *Journal of Neuroscience, 16,* 4275–4282.

Fletcher, P.C., & Henson, R.N.A. (2001). Frontal lobes and human memory: Insights from functional neuroimaging. *Brain, 124,* 849–881.

Fuerst, D.R. (1997). Some critical remarks regarding Veiel's comment on Wilde, et al. (1995). *Journal of Clinical and Experimental Neuropsychology, 19*(1), 149–152.

Gaudino, E.A., Chiaravalloti, N.D., DeLuca, J., & Diamond, B.J. (2001). A comparison of memory performance in relapse-remitting, primary-progressive and secondary progressive multiple sclerosis. *Neuropsychiatry, Neuropsychology, and Behavioral Neurology, 14,* 32–44.

Gentilini, N., Nichelli, P., & Schoenhuber, R. (1989). Assessment of attention in mild head injury. In H.S. Levin, H.M. Elsenberg, & A.L. Benton (Eds.), *Mild head injury.* New York: University Press.

Gershberg, F.B., & Shimamura, A.P. (1995). Impaired use of organizational strategies in free recall following frontal lobe damage. *Neuropsychologia, 13,* 1305–1333.

Glisky, E.L., Polster, M.R., & Routhieaux, B.C. (1995). Double dissociation between item and source memory. *Neuropsychology, 9,* 229–235.

Glosser, G., Gallo, J.L., Clark, C.M & Grossman, M. (2002). Memory encoding and retrieval in frontotemporal dementia and alzheimer's disease. *Neuropsychology, 16,* 190–196.

Goldstein, F.C., Levin, H.S., & Boake, C. (1989). Conceptual encoding following severe closed head injury. *Cortex, 25,* 541–554.

Gronwall, D., & Wrightson, P. (1981). Memory and information processing capacity after closed head injury. *Journal of Neurology, Neurosurgery, & Psychiatry, 44*(10), 889–895.

Gronwall, D.M.A. (1977). Paced auditory serial addition task: A measure of recovery from concussion. *Perceptual Motor Skills, 44,* 367–373.

Hannay, H.J., & Levin, H.S. (1985). Selective reminding test: An examination of the equivalence of four forms. *Journal of Clinical and Experimental Neuropsychology, 7,* 251–263.

Harris, J.G., Echemendía, R., Ardila, A., & Rosselli, M. (2001). Cross-cultural cognitive and neuropsychological assessment. In J.W. Andrews, H. Janzen, & D. Saklofske (Eds.), Ability, achievement, and behavioral assessment. San Diego, CA: Academic Press.

Hart R.P. (1994). Forgetting in traumatic brain-injured patients with persistent memory impairment. *Neuropscholology, 8,* 325–332.

Haut, M.W., & Shutty, M.S. (1992). Patterns of verbal learning after closed head injury. *Neuropsychology, 6*(1), 51–58.

Hirst, W., & Volpe, B.T. (1988). Memory strategies and brain damage. *Brain and Cognition, 8,* 379–408.

Iverson, G.L., & Binder, L.M. (2000). Detecting exaggeration and malingering in neuropsychological assessment. *Journal of Head Trauma Rehabilitation, 15,* 829–858.

Janowsky, J.S., Shimamura, A.P., & Squire, L.R. (1989). Source memory impairment in patients with frontal lesions. *Neuropsychologia, 27,* 1043–1056.

Johnson, M.K. (1992). MEM: Mechanisms of recollection. *Journal of Cognitive Neuroscience, 4*(3), 268–280.

Jonides J. (1995). Working memory and thinking. In E.E. Smith & D.N. Osheron (Eds.), *Invitation to cognitive science: thinking* (pp. 215–265). (Second ed.). Cambridge, MA: MIT Press.

Kaplan, E., Fein, D., Morris, R., & Delis, D.C. (1991). *WAIS-R as a neuropsychological instrument: WAIS-R-NI manual.* New York: The Psychological Corporation.

Kessels, R.P., Keyser, A., Verhagen, W.I., & van Luijtelaar, E.L. (1998). The whiplash syndrome: A psychophysiological and neuropsychological study towards attention. *Acta Neurologica Scandinavica, 97*(3), 188–193.

Kyllonen, P.C., & Christal, R.E. (1990). Reasoning ability is (little more than) working-memory capacity. *Intelligence, 14,* 389–433.

Lange, G., Waked, W., Kirshblum, S., & DeLuca, J. (2000). Organizational strategy influence on visual memory performance following stroke: Cortical/subcortical and left/right hemisphere contrasts. *Archives of Physical Medicine and Rehabilitation, 81,* 89–94.

Levander, M.B., & Sonesson, B.G. (1998). Are there any mild interhemispheric effects after moderately severe closed head injury? *Brain Injury, 12*(2), 165–173.

Levin, H.S., Gary, H.E., Jr., Eisenberg, H.M., Ruff, R.M., Barth, J.T., Kreutzer, J., High, W.M., Portman, S., Foulkes, M.A., Jane,

J.A., Marmarou, A., & Marshall, L.F. (1990). Neurobehavioral outcome 1 year after severe head injury. *Journal of Neurosurgery, 73*, 669–709.

Lezak, M. (1995). *Neuropsychological assessment, 3rd edition.* New York: Oxford University Press.

Li, S-C., Lindenberger, U., & Sikstrom, S. (2001). Aging cognition: From neuromodulation to representation. *Trends in Cognitive Sciences, 5*, 479–486.

Litvan, I., Grafman, J., Vendrell, P., & Martinez, J.M. (1988). Slowed information processing in multiple sclerosis. *Archives of Neurology, 45*, 281–285.

Loring, D.W. (1989). The Wechsler memory scale-revised, or the Wechsler memory scale-revisited. *The Clinical Neuropsychologist, 3*, 59–69.

Loring, D.W., & Papanicolaou, A.W. (1987). Memory assessment in neuropsychology: Theoretical consideration and practical utility. *Journal of Clinical and Experimental Neuropsychology, 9*, 340–358.

Maddocks, D., & Saling, M. (1996). Neuropsychological deficits following concussion. *Brain Injury, 10*(2), 99–103.

Madigan, N.K., DeLuca, J., Diamond, B.J., Tramontano, G., & Averill, A. (2000). Speed of information processing in traumatic brain injury: Modality-specific factors. *Journal of Head Trauma and Rehabilitation, 15*(3), 943–956.

Markowitsch, H.J. (1997). The functional neuroanatomy of episodic memory retrieval. *Trends in Neurosciences, 20*, 557–558.

Markowitsch, H.J. (2000). Neuroanatomy of memory. In E. Tulving & F.I.M. Craik (Eds.), *The Oxford handbook of memory* (pp. 465–484). New York: Oxford University Press.

Martin, T.A., Donders, J., & Thompson, E. (2000). Potential of problems with new measures of psychometric intelligence after traumatic brain injury. *Rehabilitation Psychology, 45*, 402–408.

Masur, D.M., Fuld, P.A., Blau, A.D., Crystal, H., & Aronson, M.K. (1990). Predicting development of dementia in the elderly with the selective reminding test. *Journal of Clinical and Experimental Neuropsychology, 12*, 529–538.

Masur, D.M., Fuld, P.A., Blau, A.D., Thal, L.J., Levin, H.S., & Aronson, M.K. (1989). Distinguishing normal and demented elderly with the selective reminding test. *Journal of Clinical and Experimental Neuropsychology, 11*, 615–630.

Mayes, A.R. (2000). Selective memory disorders. In E. Tulving & F.I.M. Craik (Eds.), *The Oxford handbook of memory* (pp. 427–440). New York: Oxford University Press.

McGaugh, J.L., Cahill, L., & Roozendaal, B. (1996). Involvement of the amygdala in memory storage: Interaction with other brain systems. *Proceedings of the National Academy of Sciences of the USA, 93*, 13508–13514.

McLean, A., Jr., Temkin, N.R., Dikmen, S., & Wyler, A.R. (1983). The behavioral sequelae of head injury. *Journal of Clinical Neuropsychology, 5*, 361–376.

Messick, S. (1995). Validity of psychological assessment: Validation of inferences from person's responses and performances as scientific inquiry into score meaning. *American Psychologist, 50*(9), 741–749.

Millis, S.R., & Putnam, S.H. (1996). Detection of malingering in postconcussive syndrome. In M. Rizzo & D. Tranel (Eds.), *Head injury and postconcussive syndrome* (pp. 481–198). New York: Churchill Livingstone.

Millis, S.R., & Ricker, J.H. (1994). Verbal learning patterns in moderate and severe traumatic brain injury. *Journal of Clinical and Experimental Neuropsychology, 16*, 498–507.

Nies, K.J., & Sweet, J.J. (1994). Neuropsychological assessment and malingering: A critical review of past and present strategies. *Archives of Clinical Neuropsychology, 9*, 501–552.

Office of Civil Rights (2000). *The use of tests as part of high-stakes decision-making for students: A resource guide for educators and policy makers.* Washington, DC: U.S. Department of Education (author). (Available at http://www.ed.gov/offices/OCR/testing/index1.html).

Prigatano, G.P. (1978) Wechsler memory scale: A selective review of the literature. *Journal of Clinical Psychology, 34*, 816–832.

The Psychological Corporation (1997). *WAIS-III, WMS-III technical manual.* San Antonio, TX: The Psychological Corporation.

Rao, S.M., Leo, G.J., Bernardin, L., & Unverzagt, F. (1991). Cognitive dysfunction in multiple sclerosis: Frequency, patterns, and prediction. *Neurology, 41*, 685–691.

Rey, A. (1941). Psychological examination of traumatic encephalopathy. *Archives de Psychologie, 28*, 286–340; sections translated by J. Corwin & F.W. Bylsma. *The Clinical Neuropsychologist* (1993), 4–9.

Ringe, W.K., Frol, A.B., Saine, K.C., & Cullum, M.C. (1999). Organization and its relationship with other measures of executive functioning and memory. *Archives of Clinical Neuropsychology, 14*, 142.

Rogers, R., Harrell, E.H., & Liff, C.D. (1993). Feigning neuropsychological impairment: A critical review of methodological and clinical considerations. *Clinical Psychology Review, 13*, 255–274.

Salthouse, T.A. (1994). Aging associations: influence of speed on adult age differences in associative learning. *Journal of Experimental Psychology: Learning, Memory, & Cognition, 20*(6), 1486–1503.

Salthouse, T.A. (1996). The processing speed theory of adult age differences in cognition. *Psychological Review, 103*, 403–428.

Salthouse, T.A. (2000). Aging and measures of processing speed. *Biological Psychology, 54*, 35–54.

Sarter, M., & Markowitsch, H.J (1985). The amygdala's role in human mneumonic processing. *Cortex, 21*, 7–24.

Sattler, J. (1982). *Assessment of children's intelligence and special abilities (2nd Ed.).* Boston, MA: Allyn & Bacon.

Sattler, J., & Tozier, L. (1970). A review of intelligence test modifications used with cerebral palsied and other handicapped groups. *The Journal of Special Education, 4*, 391–398.

Schacter, D.L., Wagner, A.D., & Buckner, R.L. (2000). Memory systems of 1999. In E. Tulving & F.I.M. Craik (Eds.), *The Oxford handbook of memory* (pp. 627–643). New York, Oxford University Press.

Schmitter-Edgecomb, M., & Rogers, W.A. (1997). Automatic process development following severe closed head injury. *Neuropsychology, 11,* 296–308.

Sivan, A.B. (1992). The Benton Visual Retention Test. 5th ed. San Antonio, TX: The Psychological Corporation.

Slamecka, N.J., & Graf, P. (1978). The generation effect: delineation of a phenomenon. *Journal of Experimental Psychology: Human Learning and Memory, 4,* 592–604.

Slamecka, N.J., & McElree, B. (1983). Normal forgetting of verbal lists as a function of their degree of learning. *Journal of Experimental Psychology, 9,* 384–97.

Smith E.E., Jonides J., & Koeppe, R.A. (1996). Dissociating verbal and spatial working memory using PET. *Cerebral Cortex, 6,* 11–20.

Stuss, D.T., Alexander, M.P., Palumbo, C.L., Buckle, L., Sayer, L., & Pogue, J.M. (1994). Organizational strategies of patients with unilateral or bilateral frontal lobe injury in word list learning tasks. *Neuropsychology, 8,* 355–373.

Squire, L.R. (1987). *Memory and brain.* New York: Oxford University Press.

Squire, L.R., Cohen, N.J., & Nadel, L. (1983). The medial temporal region and memory consolidation: A new hypothesis. In H. Weingartner & E. Parker (Eds.), *Memory consolidation* (pp. 185–210). Hillsdale, NJ: Erlbaum.

Squire, L.R., Knowlton, B., & Musen, G. (1993). The structure and organization of memory. *Annual Review of Psychology, 44,* 453–495.

Thompson, R.F., & Kim, J.J. (1996). Memory systems in the brain and localization of memory. *Proceedings of the National Academy of Sciences of the USA, 93,* 13428–13444.

Thornton, A.E., Raz, N., & Tucker, K.A. (2002). Memory in multiple sclerosis: Contextual encoding deficits. *Journal of the International Neuropsychological Society, 8,* 395–409.

Tombaugh, T.N. (1997). The Test of memory malingering (TOMM): Normative data from cognitively intact and cognitively impaired individuals. *Psychological Assessment, 9,* 260–268.

Tremont, G., Halpert, S., Javorsky, D.J., & Stern, R.A. (2000). Differential impact of executive dysfunction on verbal list learning and story recall. *The Clinical Neuropsychologist, 14*(3), 295–302.

Tulving, E. (2000). Concepts of memory. In E. Tulving & F.I.M. Craik (Eds.), *The Oxford handbook of memory* (p. 37). New York: Oxford University Press.

Tulving, E., Kapur, S., Craik, F.I.M., Moscovitch, M., & Houle, S. (1994). Hemispheric encoding/retrieval asymmetry in episodic memory: Positron emission tomography findings. *Proceedings of the National Academy of Sciences of the USA, 91,* 2016–2020.

Wechsler, D. (1917). Retention defect in korsakoff psychosis. *Psychiatric Bulletin of the New York State Hospitals, 2,* 403–451.

Wechsler, D. (1945). A standardized memory scale for clinical use. *The Journal of Psychology, 19,* 87–95.

Wechsler, D. (1987). *Wechsler memory scale—revised manual.* New York: The Psychological Corporation.

Wechsler, D. (1997). *Wechsler memory scale–3rd edition.* San Antonio, TX: The Psychological Corporation.

Wilde, M.C., Boake, C., & Sherer, M. (1995). Do recognition-free recall discrepancies detect retrieval deficits in closed head injury? An exploratory analysis with the California verbal learning test. *Journal of Clinical and Experimental Neuropsychology, 17*(6), 849–855.

Wilde, M.C., Boake, C., & Sherer, M. (1997). Do recognition-free recall discrepancies detect retrieval deficits? A response to Veiel. *Journal of Clinical and Experimental Neuropsychology, 19*(1), 153–155.

Vanderploeg, R.D., Crowell, T.A., & Curtiss, G. (2001). Verbal learning and memory deficits in traumatic brain injury: Encoding, consolidation and retrieval. *Journal of Clinical and Experimental Neuropsychology, 23,* 185–195.

Veiel, H.O.F. (1997). CVLT recognition-recall discrepancies and retrieval deficits. A comment on Wilde et al. (1995). *Journal of Clinical and Experimental Neuropsychology, 19*(1), 141–143.

CHAPTER 15

Comprehensive Assessment of Child and Adolescent Memory: The Wide Range Assessment of Memory and Learning, the Test of Memory and Learning, and the California Verbal Learning Test—Children's Version

MICHAEL J. MILLER, JO ANN PETRIE, ERIN D. BIGLER, AND WAYNE V. ADAMS

Memory, across all of its heuristic divisions, is the conduit that makes higher cognitive functioning possible. For example, aspects of executive abilities are dependent on working memory, expressive language requires retrieval of words from memory stores, certain spatial abilities may be contingent on cognitive maps, and sophisticated processes such as

judgment may require the retrieval of context-specific memories. Although in some cases memory is affected and other cognitive abilities remain intact, the functional ramifications of the memory disturbance alone may be considerable. Such was the case with H.M., a 27-year-old man who underwent a bilateral resection of the medial temporal lobe for intractable epilepsy. Despite H.M.'s preserved intelligence, he was unable to care for himself because of a severe anterograde amnesia, which prevented the formation of new memories. Although he could carry on an intelligent conversation, H.M.

This chapter is based on a previous work by Bigler and Adams (2001) and is printed with the permission of Cambridge University Press.

TABLE 15.1   Most Frequent Childhood Disorders in Which Memory and Learning Are Likely to Be Compromised

ADHD	*In utero* toxic exposure (e.g., cocaine, alcohol, etc.)	Neurofibromatosis
Autism and other developmental disorders	Juvenile Huntington's disease	Prader-Willi syndrome
Cancer (especially brain tumors, lung cancer, parathyroid tumors, leukemia, and lymphoma)	Juvenile Parkinsonism	Rett's syndrome
Cerebral palsy	Kidney disease/transplant	Schizophrenia
Down syndrome	Learning disability	Seizure disorders
Endocrine disorders	Lesch-Nyhan disease	Tourette's syndrome
Extremely low birth weight	Major depressive disorder	Toxic exposure (e.g., lead, mercury, carbon monoxide)
Fragile X syndrome	Meningitis	Traumatic brain injury
Hydrocephalus	Mental retardation	Turner's syndrome
Hypoxic-ischemic injury	Myotonic dystrophy	XXY syndrome
Inborn errors of metabolism (e.g., PKU, galactosemia)	Neurodevelopmental abnormalities affecting brain development (e.g., anencephaly, microcephaly, callosal dysgenesis)	XYY syndrome

had to be reminded to shave, had to read magazines over and over, was only vaguely aware (years after the fact) that his father had died, and was capable of doing only vocational work designed for persons with mental retardation. H.M. appeared to be perpetually disoriented, as he could not remember events that had recently transpired. His comment, "Every day is alone in itself, whatever enjoyment I've had, and whatever sorrow I've had," (p. 359, Kolb & Whishaw, 1996), underscores that his experience from moment to moment was encapsulated, with no connection to the past or present. Memory may, therefore, provide a context for the self. As Mesulam, (2000) recently wrote, "Memory is the glue that holds together our thoughts, impressions, and experiences—without it, past and future would lose their meaning and self awareness would be lost as well" (p. 257). These observations suggest that memory is at the core of what makes us uniquely human. The case of H.M. is important, not only because of what it teaches about the profound implications of circumscribed memory disturbance, but also because of its central role in delineating the functions of the medial temporal lobe structures in memory processes as discussed in later sections.

In light of the broad neural distribution of cortical and subcortical brain regions associated with memory and the diverse cognitive, behavioral, and emotional processes dependent on these substrates, it is not surprising that many neurological and neuropsychiatric disorders disrupt memory and associated functions (Baron, Fennell, & Voeller, 1995; Cullum, Kuck, & Ruff, 1990; Cytowic, 1996; Gillberg, 1995; Knight, 1992; Lezak, 1995; Mapou & Spector, 1995; Reeves & Wedding, 1994). Indeed, memory assessment is critical because of its relevance in evaluating the overall functional

and physiological integrity of the brain (Cowan, 1997; Parkin, 1993). In fact, in cases of traumatic brain injury (TBI), memory disturbances are the most common patient complaints (Cronwall, Wrightson, & Waddell, 1990; Golden, Zillmer, & Spiers, 1992; Reeves et al., 1994). Because of the prevalence of TBI in children (Goldstein & Levin, 1990), assessment of memory disorder in children who have experienced TBI has become a particular focus for pediatric neuropsychologists and other clinicians involved in the assessment of children. In addition, memory deficits, which often accompany learning disorders, are among the most common referrals for children requiring psychological assessment (Bull & Johnston, 1997; de Jong, 1998; Lorsbach, Wilson, & Reimer, 1996; Nation, Adams, Bowyer-Crain, & Snowling, 1999; Swanson, Ashbacker, & Lee, 1996). In the rehabilitation setting, memory disorders are also the most common therapeutic focus in cognitive rehabilitation (Prigatano, 1990). Given that the probability of positive outcomes for individuals with memory impairment is dependent on the identification of highly specific deficits that can be determined only through comprehensive assessment, it is surprising that inclusive memory batteries have not been available for children until recently. Table 15.1 presents the most common childhood disorders in which memory and learning are affected.

Although formal memory batteries for children are a relatively recent phenomenon, it appears that assessment of memory in children and adolescents was considered to be of some importance, because the earliest of modern intelligence tests (for example, the 1907 Binet and the early Wechsler scales) incorporated brief assessments of immediate recall. Evidence of early attention to the import of memory assessment can also be found in one subtest of the McCarthy Scales of Children's Abilities (McCarthy, 1972) and in the more detailed four-subtest Visual–Aural Digit Span Test (Koppitz, 1977). Although 80% of a sample of clinicians interviewed in 1987 cited memory as a core component of cognitive assessment (Snyderman & Rothman, 1987), the major child neuropsychology texts of the 1970s and 1980s (see Bakker, Fisk, & Strang, 1985; Hynd & Obrzut, 1981) made little reference to memory assessment. Not until the 1990s was this gap between theory and practice addressed (e.g., Gillberg, 1995). The increasing focus on assessment of memory is now also evident in the major works of child neuropsychology (Pennington, 1991; Rourke, 1991; Tramontana & Hooper, 1988).

The Wide Range Assessment of Memory and Learning (WRAML; Sheslow & Adams, 1990) represented the first effort to develop an inclusive memory battery for children and adolescents. The Test of Memory and Learning (TOMAL; Reynolds & Bigler, 1994b) and the California Verbal Learning Test–Children's Version (CVLT–C, Delis, Kramer, Kaplan, & Ober, 1994) are additional batteries specifically designed for the assessment of childhood memory. All three batteries are reviewed in this chapter following a discussion of the basic neurobiology of memory.

A PRIMER ON THE NEUROBIOLOGY OF MEMORY

Although a comprehensive review of the neurobiology of memory is beyond the scope of this chapter, a brief discussion of the neural substrates of memory systems is provided as a critical foundation for discussing the assessment of memory. For more in-depth discussion of this topic, excellent reviews are provided by Bauer, Tobias, and Valenstein (1993), Cohen (1993), Diamond (1990),and Scheibel (1990). The current primer is cursory because of space limitations. Given the importance of this background for clinical assessment, we hope that readers will seek a further grounding in the basic neurobiology of memory.

For memories to be formed, an individual must experience a single sensation or multiple sensations in combination. These sensations can emanate from the environment or can be produced internally. The manner in which sensory processing occurs lays the foundation for the modality (i.e., auditory, verbal, olfactory, gustatory, or somatosensory) in which learning occurs. A recent memory that is common to virtually all Americans may illustrate this point. For example, most Americans first learned of the events of September 11, 2001, through horrific images viewed on television, over the Internet, or in newspapers, which showed a commercial aircraft plowing

through the North Tower of the World Trade Center, followed by a second aircraft 10 minutes later that banked left and crashed into the South Tower. Others may have first heard of the tragedy on the radio or been told the news by another person. People working near the World Trade Center may recall the smell of the burning steel in the towers; others who were very close to "Ground Zero" may recall the taste of the clouds of smoke that filled the streets; still others may recall their awareness of their physical reaction (e.g., racing heart, goose bumps, feeling faint, etc.). Regardless of the modality in which an event is processed, memories are formed and often recalled via the sensory channel(s) in which they were experienced. Although memories can be formed and retrieved within each of these modalities, the visual and auditory senses are dominant in most individuals. Assessment of memory has therefore focused on these modalities, although a greater emphasis has been placed on verbal processing. As will be discussed in detail later in this chapter, the verbal-visual distinction provides an important heuristic for the clinician, as the left hemisphere is more oriented toward language-based memory and the right toward visual-spatial memory (Bigler & Clement, 1997).

Regardless of the sensory modality, several critical brain structures—including the hippocampus, amygdala, fornix, mammillary bodies, diverse thalamic nuclei, and distributed regions of the neocortex—are involved in the development of memories (see Figure 15.1). Briefly, from the sensory stimulus, neural impulses travel from the sensory organs, primary cortex, and association neocortex (attention/working memory) to the hippocampus via pathways that course through the medial-inferior aspect of the temporal lobe en route to the hippocampus. The hippocampus and associated limbic structures represent a way station of sorts, in which a stimulus is either attended to for further processing or ignored. After the stimulus is experienced as relevant, further processing (including binding) occurs in the medial temporal lobe structures. Binding is the process wherein associations are formed between a new relevant stimulus and previously processed information. Following damage to the hippocampus or its efferent projections (i.e., the fornix, mammillary bodies, and anterior thalamus), short-term or working memory may remain intact, and the patient may be able to recall a brief stimulus, such as a list of two or three words or numbers. However, for retention of information beyond immediate or short-term memory (greater than several seconds), additional processing subsumed by hippocampal and associated limbic structures must occur. Following processing of information in the hippocampal circuit, long-term storage occurs in the distributed neural networks of the cerebral cortex, where memories receive the most extensive processing and are the least

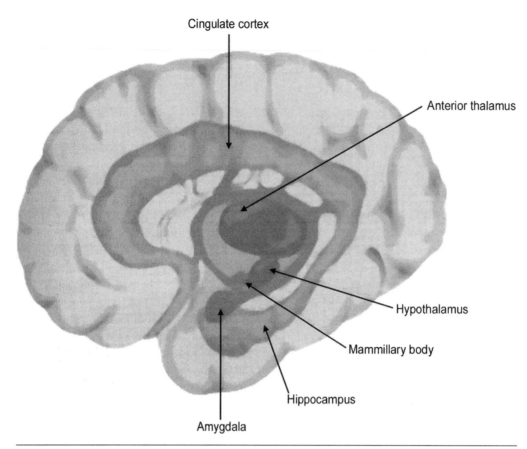

Figure 15.1   Schematic diagram of the brain highlighting the limbic system, particularly the hippocampus. The hippocampus is located in the temporal lobe and is critical in the process of memory function. From M.T. Banich, (1997). Houghton-Mifflin. Reprinted by permission.

vulnerable to injury. In fact, the recall of well-established memories tends to be one of the most robust of neural functions; whereas sustained attention, concentration, and the formation of new memories, tend to be the most fragile.[1]

The World Trade Center example is also useful in illustrating the emotional processing that is critical to memory. In addition to the previously mentioned limbic circuit involved in memory processes, a second limbic circuit exists that includes the amygdala and related structures. This circuit is responsible for processing emotional material and "coloring" memories with feeling. Why would it be important that memories are given an emotional hue? In short, the emotion associated with a memory brings greater richness and dimensionality to the experience recalled from memory. If we return to the example of the World Trade Center disaster, it is likely that the very mention of "September 11" or "9/11" evokes strong emotions tied to memories of the tragedy. Previous to these events "September 11" for most persons was a neutral stimulus that bore no particular meaning. However, in light of the horrific events the world experienced on September 11, 2001, the mere mention of the month and day may for

many people be inextricably bound to the emotions associated with these events. Indeed, strong emotions associated with memories cause people to pay attention and may therefore contribute to their survival. Americans (and citizens of other countries) have developed a new awareness of terrorism and are consequently more likely to react to suspicious behavior. On an individual basis, many people have debated as to when (or even whether) they will resume their lives as they were before September 11, 2001. Thus, a previously meaningless date is now fraught with meaning that has caused billions of people to reconsider their very existence. Although this example is extreme, the binding of emotion to memory is an ongoing part of consciousness that, when disrupted, may manifest itself clinically as an inability to recognize facial expressions indicating fear or threat (Phelps et al., 2001), as well as verbal and nonverbal memory deficits (Buchanan, Denburg, Tranel, & Adolph, 2001).

Two additional concepts that have important implications for the assessment of memory disorders deserve brief discussion. First, as mentioned earlier, lateralization of brain function (Stark & McGregor, 1997) provides a useful heuristic for the clinician. That is, in most individuals, the left hemisphere of the brain is more dedicated to language-based functions and the right hemisphere to visual-spatial processes. Lateralization of functions, therefore, provides useful generalizations for assessing differences in memory processes, based on whether the information is language-based or visual-spatial in nature. Therefore, damage to the left hemisphere (particularly the left temporal lobe) may result in verbal memory deficits; whereas visual-spatial abilities are likely to be spared. The converse is true with damage to the right hemisphere (particularly the right temporal lobe), which is more involved in visual-spatial aspects of memory.

Finally, it is important to recognize that learning and memory are dependent on attention. Making distinctions between attention and memory processes has proven to be one of the most difficult challenges for neuropsychologists. Although the reticular activating system and diffuse thalamic projecting systems have been recognized as essential to arousal, there is no specific neuroanatomical mapping of the construct of attention. From the neuropsychological perspective, "attention" is probably a nonlocalized neural process with major contributions from frontal and temporal lobe regions. However, it is also well known that damage to diverse regions of the cerebral cortex has the potential to cause attentional deficits. Thus, at the most basic level, attention may be considered a function of the integrated brain—a function that is vulnerable when the integrity of the brain as a whole is threatened. The clinician must become adept at distinguishing attentional deficits from impairment in memory functions during the early stages of information processing (e.g., attention vs. encoding). Presently there are "attention" components of memory batteries as well as independent measures of attention, but due to the inherent difficulty in distinguishing between attentional deficits and memory-processing deficits, these measures are far from perfect. The assessment of attention in relation to memory thus requires the integration of formal assessment, careful observation, and data collected from the patient and his or her family.

WIDE RANGE ASSESSMENT OF MEMORY AND LEARNING

Structure

The Wide-Range Assessment of Memory and Learning (WRAML; Sheslow et al., 1990) was the first inclusive memory battery for children and adolescents. Prior to the WRAMLs inception, clinicians interested in assessing child and adolescent memory had to rely upon measures from various independent sources, because no cohesive memory battery, designed specifically for children, existed. The norms associated with these tests of memory varied in quality and were often based on different samples of children, thus limiting their usefulness. These shortcomings were addressed with introduction of the WRAML, which provided clinicians and researchers with a comprehensive sampling of memory tasks based on a common normative group, permitting meaningful, intertask comparisons.

The WRAML is normed for children 5 through 17 years of age. Administration ranges from 45 to 60 minutes, depending on the child's age and response rate as well as the experience of the examiner. An Examiner Record form and an Examinee Response form are utilized in the standard administration.

Figure 15.2 illustrates the structure and hierarchical organization of the WRAML. Combined performance in the Verbal Memory, Visual Memory, and Learning domains determine the composite General Memory Index. The first two domains evaluate verbal and visual modalities, the principal information-processing modalities of memory for children and adolescents, and the third WRAML domain assesses memory acquired across consecutive learning opportunities. These opportunities occur across trials involving visual, verbal, and dual modality (visual with verbal) modality tasks, and allow for the assessment of learning gradients.

The Verbal Memory and Visual Memory domains are organized according to a similar rationale. As subtests from each domain progress, the information to be immediately recalled is increased. Tasks within these domains vary from rote memory tasks, with little meaningful content, to tasks with significantly greater meaning. Thus, the examiner has the opportunity to observe a child's immediate memory ability across varied modalities and degrees of meaningfulness. "Meaning" refers both to the complexity of the task and the relevance to everyday functioning. This concept will become clearer as we discuss the individual subtests in the following sections.

Each of the WRAML's three domains is composed of three subtests. Each subtest produces a scaled score (M = 10, SD = 3), and each domain produces a standard score (M = 100, SD = 15). The scaled scores of all nine subtests are combined to produce the General Memory Index (M = 100, SD = 15). These familiar metrics are intuitive for the examiner and allow for comparison with the results of other cognitive measures, such as intelligence and achievement tests.

In addition to the nine primary subtests composing the three major domains, "optional" Delayed Recall components are associated with each of the learning across trials subtests.

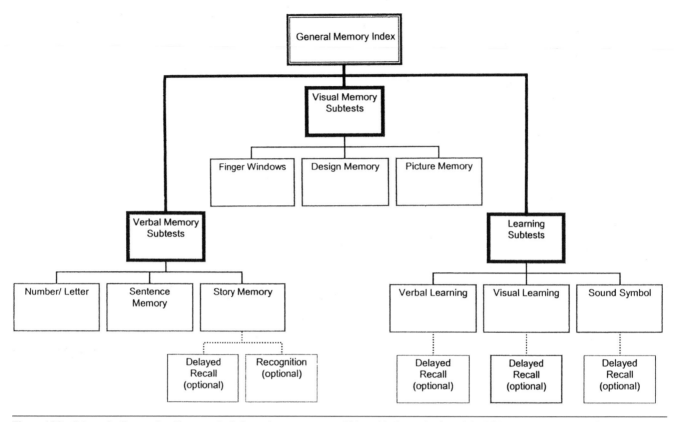

Figure 15.2   Schematic diagram that illustrates the index, subtest structure, and hierarchical organization of the Wide Range Assessment of Memory and Learning (WRAML).

One of the Verbal Memory subtests (Story Memory) also provides a Delayed Recall and a Recognition option.

Description, Rationale, and Clinical Applications of Subtests

Table 15.2 provides a description of the subtests within each domain. The rationale for each subtest is discussed in the following sections, along with clinical uses and interpretations of testing patterns.

Verbal Memory Scale

The subtests that encompass the Verbal Memory scale provide an opportunity for the examiner to assess the child's capabilities on rote auditory memory tasks and to contrast this performance with tasks placing greater language demands on the child. This comparison allows the examiner to generate hypotheses about whether the child utilizes language as an aid or whether it is a hindrance in remembering. The three subtests (i.e., Number/Letter, Sentence Memory, and Story Memory) can be conceptualized as placing increasing de-

mands on language processing. This allows the clinician to assess language deficits, which may confound memory assessment within the Verbal Memory domain. The three subtests constituting the Verbal Memory scale are as follows.

Number/Letter. The format of the Number/Letter subtest may be familiar to most clinicians; however, only a "forward" trial of recall is required in this subtest. This distinction was made because evidence suggests that backward recall taps a different cognitive skill than forward recall does (Lezak, 1995).

Sentence Memory. The units of information presented for recall on the Sentence Memory Task are more sophisticated than those in the Number/Letter subtest because of the "mental glue" that language affords (Howes, Bigler, Burlingame, & Lawson, 2003). In clinical terms, because this task requires the ability to remember one or two sentences, this task is believed to tap the kind of memory skills that may carry functional significance for a child (e.g., following oral directions at home or at school).

Story Memory. Two stories that differ in developmental level of interest and linguistic complexity are read to the child. Using two stories permits better sampling than using a

TABLE 15.2   Description of Subtests Associated with Each WRAML Domain

Domain	Subtest Name	Subtest Description
Verbal Memory		
	Number/Letter	The child is asked to repeat a series of numbers and letters verbally presented one per second. The subtest begins with an item two units in length (e.g., "1-A") and proceeds until the discontinue rule is satisfied.
	Sentence Memory	The child is asked to repeat meaningful sentences. Starting with a three-word sentence, the child attempts to repeat progressively longer sentences, until the discontinue rule is satisfied.
	Story Memory	The child is read and then asked to retell a one- to two-paragraph story. A second story is then read and again the child is asked to retell the story. The examiner records both exact and "gist" recalled information for scoring.
Visual Memory		
	Finger Windows	The child indicates his or her memory of a rote visual pattern by sequentially placing a finger into "windows," or holes, in a plastic card, attempting to reproduce a sequence demonstrated by the examiner. Starting with a sequence of two holes, the child continues until the discontinue rule is satisfied.
	Design Memory	A card with geometric shapes is shown to the child for 5 seconds. Following a 10-second delay, the child is asked to draw what was seen. A blank card with spatial demarcations is provided for the child's drawing. Four different cards are presented in this fashion.
	Picture Memory	The child is shown a meaningful scene with people and objects for 10 seconds. The child is then asked to look at a second, similar scene. Memory of the original picture is indicated by the child's marking elements that have been altered or added in the second picture. This procedure is repeated with three additional cards.
Learning		
	Verbal Learning	The child is read a list of common, single-syllable words and is provided a free recall opportunity. Three additional learning trials are administered in a similar fashion. A delayed recall trial is available following an interference task.
	Visual Learning	After initially seeing all locations, the child is asked to indicate the specific location of 12 or 14 (depending on age) visual stimuli nested within a 4 × 4 array. Correction of errors occurs. Three additional learning trials follow. A delayed recall trial is also available.
	Sound Symbol	The child is presented a paired-associate task requiring him/her to recall which sound is associated with which abstract and unfamiliar symbol-shape. Four separate learning trials are administered, and a delayed recall trial is also available.

single story. It is then reasonable to assume that a greater than chance difference between the child's recall of the first and second stories suggests lower verbal intellectual ability, a language disorder, or an inefficient or inconsistent ability to attend to oral information.

Similarly, a child who retells a story in an erratic sequence may have sequencing or organizational problems. By comparing sequencing in Number/Letter and Sentence Memory with that in Story Memory, the clinician can begin to distinguish between sequencing, organizational, and language deficits. Because of the importance of memory in classroom and social functioning, the clinician may wish to examine whether a child performing poorly on Story Memory recognizes the material but fails to produce it in a free recall format.

The Recognition option for the Story Memory subtest affords this opportunity by presenting 15 questions related to the harder story, using a multiple-choice format to help determine whether the child is experiencing a deficit in retention or retrieval.

Comparison of performance on the Sentence Memory and Story Memory subtests can also be of utility in making predictions about a child's functioning. For example, if performance on Sentence Memory is relatively poor, the child may experience difficulties understanding directions. In contrast, relatively better performance on Story Memory would support the hypothesis that the child may be able to understand the "essence" of the orally delivered directions (or lecture), despite difficulties in remembering rote details.

Visual Memory Scale

Similar to the Verbal Memory subtests, the Visual Memory subtests vary from rote memory to more complex memory demands. The three Visual Memory subtests are as follows:

Finger Windows. The Finger Windows subtest is analogous to the Number/Letter subtest within the Verbal Memory Domain, as discrete and relatively nonmeaningful units of information are presented at a rate of one per second, and immediate recall is required. This task taps the ability to retain a visual trace in a sequence.

Design Memory. This subtest introduces a greater degree of meaningfulness than Finger Windows, as the child is instructed to copy a display of common shapes (e.g., circles, dots, straight lines, rectangles, and triangles). A 5-second exposure to the shape is followed by a 10-second delay before the child begins drawing. For a youngster who may struggle to reproduce such shapes because of perceptual-motor difficulties, an optional copy task is first administered, so that the child's reproduction of each shape becomes the criterion for scoring in the recall phase. The design is scored on the inclusion and placement of design components. Poor placement may indicate spatial memory deficits; whereas shape omission may indicate impaired memory for visual detail. The relatively brief five-second exposure allowed for each stimulus card is intended to minimize the use of verbal strategies to aid in completion of the task. Everyday tasks, such as copying from a classroom chalkboard, or remembering visual details of a room after leaving, were included to maximize ecological validity.

Picture Memory. Building upon the Design Memory subtest (which includes rote and configural memory tasks), the Picture Memory subtest adds increased meaning, as each of four stimulus pictures depicts a scene that most children will find familiar. Children possessing "photographic" memory abilities may excel on this subtest, because task expectations demand storage of a visually presented scene to be compared with memory from a similar scene in which 20%–40% of the visual details have been altered in some manner.

Clinically, it should be noted that children with attention deficit hyperactivity disorder (ADHD) score as well as or better than nonreferred children on the Picture Memory subtest because of a confound in the scoring procedure (Adams, Hyde, & deLancey, 1995). The subtest's directions indicate that the examiner is to instruct the child to identify perceived changes in each scene with a marker, "marking the things you are sure of." The examiner is instructed to discourage guessing (but not to penalize guessing), and to give credit only for correct responses in the scoring. Because of their impulsivity, children with ADHD may mark some correct

details by chance, resulting in a spuriously inflated score. We have observed that children with ADHD between the ages of five and eight typically make three incorrect selections per picture, compared to one incorrect selection per picture made by their age-matched counterparts in the standardization sample. It is noteworthy that although the errors-per-picture ratio drops from 3:1 to 2:1 for the older children with ADHD, the effect remains statistically significant.

Learning Scale

The three learning subtests are as follows:

Verbal Learning. The Verbal Learning subtest was adapted from Rey (1958) to assess learning across trials. In this procedure the child is read a list of 13 or 16 (depending on the child's age) common words, immediately followed by instructions to recall as many words as possible. The procedure is then repeated three times. The procedure in the WRAML differs in two ways. First, in contrast to Rey's (1958) procedure, four rather than five learning trials are administered on the WRAML; prestandardization data demonstrated, similar to Rey's (1958) findings, that a fifth trial contributes little additional information. Second, an interference trial following the final list recall trial is not included on the WRAML, as learning in everyday life is usually not followed by an almost identical activity serving as interference. Thus, to reduce the time of administration and the potential frustration that some children may experience, the Story Memory subtest follows the Verbal Learning subtest, and serves as the interference task. Approximately five minutes later, a delay trial of the Verbal Learning task is administered.

On occasion, children produce words not on the list during recall tasks. Such errors, termed "intrusion errors," occurred once or twice over the four trials among the standardization sample, especially with younger children. However, children with ADHD often average four to five intrusion errors over the four trials (Adams, Robins, Sheslow, & Hyde, 2001). Some believe that the nature of the intrusion error may be relevant. For instance, semantic errors (e.g., responding with eye instead of ear) may suggest expressive language difficulties; whereas phonetic errors (e.g., responding with bake instead of lake) may suggest phonological or auditory processing difficulties.

Visual Learning. Analogous to its verbal counterpart, the Visual Learning task asks the child to learn a set number of stimuli presented across four trials. Visual designs are presented in a specific position on a "game" board, and the child is asked to recall the spatial location related to each design. Immediate feedback for item correctness is provided to promote learning. As with the Verbal Learning subtest, a delayed recall trial may be administered following the Sound Symbol subtest, which may, in turn, serve as an "interference" task.

Sound Symbol. The phonological and visual symbolic requirements of the cross-modal Sound Symbol task approach the demands of early reading mastery. The child is asked to remember a sound that goes with a printed "nonsense" symbol. In a paired-associate format, shapes are presented, and the child is asked to produce the corresponding sound across four sound/shape learning trials. A delayed recall trial is also available.

Although it has not been established empirically, substantial anecdotal evidence suggests that children who produce responses that resemble few of the sounds associated within the subtest (typically on the third and fourth trials), may experience considerable difficulty learning phonics in their early elementary school years. Should this assertion be empirically demonstrated, one form of a reading disorder might be conceptualized as a selective memory disorder that effects processes involved in remembering units of sound associated with symbols.

Short Form

A Short Form version of the WRAML was developed to serve as a "memory screen" to aid the examiner in determining whether a more in-depth assessment is indicated. Preliminary research identified four subtests that are varied in content but highly correlated with the General Memory Index (r = .84). The four subtests constituting the Short Form—Picture Memory, Design Memory, Verbal Learning, and Story Memory—are consequently ordered first in the WRAML. Thus, the Short Form samples aspects of visual and verbal memory, along with verbal learning, while maintaining a reasonable portion of the utility of the General Memory Index. The Screening Form requires approximately 10–15 minutes to administer. The psychometric integrity of the norms associated with the Screening Form is commensurate with that of the full WRAML, because the complete standardization sample was utilized to derive the norms. In practice, the General Memory Index, estimated from the Short Form version, averages about four points higher than the General Memory Index generated from the entire battery (Kennedy & Guilmette, 1997).

Standardization

The WRAML was standardized on a population-proportionate sample stratified by age, gender, ethnicity, socioeconomic status, geographic region, and community size. The sample consisted of 2,363 children ranging in age from 5 to 17 years.

Details of the standardization procedure and stratification data are provided in the test manual (Sheslow et al., 1990).

Reliability

The WRAML subtests and composite indexes show high internal consistency reliability, as indicated by the following statistics. Item separation statistics ranged from .99 to 1.0; whereas person separation statistics ranged from .70 to .94. Coefficient alphas ranged from .78 to .90 for the nine individual subtests, and median coefficient alphas for the Verbal Memory Index, the Visual Memory Index, and the Learning Index were .93, .90, and .91 respectively. The General Memory Index coefficient alpha was .96.

A test-retest study was conducted with a subgroup of the standardization sample (N = 153). Because memory and learning tasks are vulnerable to practice effects, an analysis of the incremental effect of re-administration was performed. On average, a one-point increase in scores on the Verbal Memory and Visual Memory subtests, and a two-point increase in scores on the learning subtests were observed. Across a three- to six-month interval, no correlation existed between the number of days elapsed and the initial incremental increase in score within the time interval assessed. That is, the slight incremental increase in WRAML subtest performance appears to be consistently maintained over a three- to six-month post-test interval.

Validity

In light of the considerable and varied demands of memory in the school setting, memory ability is expected to relate to academic achievement. Moreover, as children progress in school, verbal memory would be expected to be more predictive than visual memory of academic achievement. Tables 15.3 and 15.4 illustrate that this is indeed the case as WRAML indexes are correlated with measures of reading, spelling, and arithmetic. Similarly, verbal memory appears to play only a minimal role for children in early elementary school, but vi-

TABLE 15.3   Correlations of WRAML Index Scores and Wide Range Achievement Test Revised (WRAT–R) Subtests Ages 6 Years, 0 Months–8 Years, 11 Months

	Verbal Memory Index	Visual Memory Index	Learning Index	General Memory Index
Reading	.18	.26*	.40*	.35*
Spelling	.22	.32*	.42*	.39*
Arithmetic	.24	.46*	.40*	.46*

*p < .05.

TABLE 15.4   Correlations of WRAML Index Scores and WRAT–R Subtests Ages 16 Years, 0 Months–17 Years, 11 Months

	Verbal Memory Index	Visual Memory Index	Learning Index	General Memory Index
Reading	.41*	.14	.05	.23
Spelling	.40*	.09	.24	.30
Arithmetic	.34*	.26	.34*	.38*

*$p < .05$.

sual memory and especially learning over trials plays a more dominant role in scholastic achievement. In high school the pattern appears to reverse, suggesting that these differences may be associated with content demands. For example, learning to identify letters, numbers, and words visually and learning to write are major tasks in the first and second grades. Conversely, traditional high school curricula (e.g., history, science, literature, and mathematics courses) require greater verbal memory demands relative to those of visual memory and rote learning across trials.

Factor Structure

Three-factor principal components analyses were conducted on the nine WRAML subtests using the complete standardization sample of 2,363 children and adolescents. Separate factors were derived from two age groups of children, determined by the test's age division. (There were negligible differences in administration between the two age groups.). The results are reported in Tables 15.5 and 15.6.

As observed in the tables, the Visual factor for younger children was composed of Picture Memory, Design Memory, and Finger Windows. This outcome was expected. However, Visual Learning, also loaded on this same factor. Further counterintuitive findings included the clustering of Sentence Memory and Number/Letter with the Verbal factor, but not Story Memory. Verbal Learning and Sound Symbol loaded according to theoretical expectations (i.e., on the Learning factor), but as previously mentioned, Visual Learning did not load on the same predicted factor.

A similar pattern was evident within the older sample (see Table 15.6), again casting doubt on the validity of the Learning construct. Several investigators have reported similar factor analytic results with the WRAML using nonreferred and clinical samples (Aylward, Gioia, Verhulst, & Bell, 1995; Burton, Donders, & Mittenberg, 1996; Burton, Mittenberg, Gold, & Drabman, 1999; Dewey, Kaplan, & Crawford, 1997; Gioia, 1998; Phelps, 1995). Gioia (1998) suggested, based upon some of the inconsistent factor analytic results of the WRAML Index scores, that the subtest scores may be a more

TABLE 15.5   Results of Principal Components Analysis with Varimax Rotation of WRAML Subtests (Completed on Children 5 Years, 0 Months–8 Years, 11 Months of Age)

	Factor		
	Visual	Verbal	Learning
Picture Memory	**.569**	−.148	.320
Design Memory	**.669**	.078	.259
Finger Windows	**.655**	.382	−.160
Story Memory	.285	.222	.585
Sentence Memory	.159	**.800**	.320
Number/Letter	.082	**.859**	.113
Verbal Learning	.311	.111	**.615**
Visual Learning	.605	.158	.157
Sound Symbol	−.004	.125	**.749**

Note. Boldface connotes the subtest loaded on the predicted factor.

TABLE 15.6   Results of Principal Components Analysis with Varimax Rotation of WRAML Subtests (Completed on Children 5 Years, 0 Months–8 Years, 11 Months of Age)

	Factor		
	Visual	Verbal	Learning
Picture Memory	**.674**	.012	.221
Design Memory	**.720**	.023	.277
Finger Windows	**.584**	.585	−.145
Story Memory	.216	.196	.695
Sentence Memory	.017	**.749**	.441
Number/Letter	.005	**.837**	.215
Verbal Learning	.239	.091	**.648**
Visual Learning	.583	.076	.401
Sound Symbol	.214	.240	**.638**

Note. Boldface connotes the subtest loaded on the predicted factor.

appropriate level of analysis. Others have asserted that this recommendation is somewhat extreme as only two of nine subtests (Story Memory and Visual Learning) loaded inconsistently. It should be kept in mind that the Learning factor clearly consists of visual and verbal memory components, contributing nonorthogonality to the analyses.

Another manner in which to approach these inconsistencies is to retain the Visual factor, rename the Learning factor "Verbal," and substitute "Attention" for the original Verbal factor designation. The results of this relatively minor alteration are illustrated in Tables 15.7 and 15.8. This conceptual organization continues to group the highly intercorrelated subtests of Sentence Memory and Number/Letter together, but as measures of attention/concentration rather than of verbal memory. Clinically, this is relevant to the research reported later in this section, which suggests that children with attention problems consistently perform poorly on these two subtests as well as Finger Windows. With regard to older children, Finger Windows loads on the renamed Attention factor and the Visual factor almost equally, suggesting that both visual memory skills and attention are required to suc-

TABLE 15.7 Alternative Interpretation of the Principal Components Analysis of WRAML Subtests (Completed on Children 9 Years, 0 Months–17 Years, 11 Months of Age)

	Factor		
	Visual	Attention	Verbal
Picture Memory	**.569**	−.148	.320
Design Memory	**.669**	.078	.259
Finger Windows	**.655**	.382	−.160
Story Memory	.285	.222	**.585**
Sentence Memory	.159	**.800**	.320
Number/Letter	.082	**.859**	.113
Verbal Learning	.311	.111	**.615**
Visual Learning	**.605**	.158	.157
Sound Symbol	−.004	.125	**.749**

Note. Boldface connotes the subtest loaded on the predicted factor.

TABLE 15.8 Alternative Interpretation of the Principal Components Analysis of WRAML Subtests (Completed on Children 9 Years, 0 Months–17 Years, 11 Months of Age)

	Factor		
	Visual	Attention	Verbal
Picture Memory	**.674**	.012	.221
Design Memory	**.720**	.023	.277
Finger Windows	**.584**	**.585**	−.145
Story Memory	.216	.196	**.695**
Sentence Memory	.017	**.749**	.441
Number/Letter	.005	**.837**	.215
Verbal Learning	.239	.091	**.648**
Visual Learning	**.583**	.076	.401
Sound Symbol	.214	.240	**.638**

Note. Boldface connotes the subtest loaded on the predicted factor.

ceed on this subtest. This reorganization would then leave Verbal and Visual factors but add the Attention factor. Such a reconceptualization avoids the apparent shared variance of the Learning subtests and provides a conceptual organization for all WRAML subtests within the new empirically derived factors.

WRAML Performance in Children with Reading Disability and ADHD

Adams et al. (2001) administered the WRAML to children with common referral diagnoses including Reading Disability (RD) and ADHD. In total, four groups were examined including an RD group, an ADHD group, an RD/ADHD group, and a nonclinical comparison group. Children with RD were those who had Wechsler Intelligence Scale for Children–Third Edition (WISC–III; Wechsler, 1991) Full Scale IQs greater than or equal to 85, reading achievement scores at least 15 points below their Verbal IQs, and arithmetic achievement scores that were not statistically different from their Full Scale IQs. The second group consisted of children

diagnosed with ADHD. Each child was diagnosed through a hospital-based ADHD clinic, and most scored at least 2 standard deviations above average on a standard attention rating scale at home and at school. To be included, children in the ADHD group also had to have Full Scale IQs greater than or equal to 85, with reading, spelling, and math achievements that were not statistically different from their Full Scale IQs. The third group met criteria for both clinical conditions. The mean age of children in each group was approximately 10 years; no subject had a history of neurological disorder (e.g., seizures, head injury, etc.) or significant comorbid psychiatric diagnoses. Finally, the nonclinical comparison group was culled from the standardization sample, which allowed matching by age, gender, geographic region, urban/rural, and socioeconomic status.

Each child was administered the WRAML. A discriminant function analysis was completed on the WRAMLs nine subtest scores. The results showed that WRAML scores discriminated between groups (Wilks' Lambda = .560, X^2 = 115.2, df (27), $p < .001$). The two significant functions, in succession, accounted for 73.5% and 26.5% of the between group variability.

The group centroids in the upper part of Table 15.9 reveal that the first function best distinguished the clinical groups (i.e., those with ADHD, RD, and ADHD/RD) from the nonreferred cohort. The second function best differentiated children with RD from those with ADHD and those who were not referred. The pattern of correlations indicates that the first function is defined by appreciable contributions from the Number/Letter, Sound Symbol, Sentence Memory, and Finger Windows subtests. Data from the group centroid com-

TABLE 15.9 Canonical Discriminant Functions Using WRAML Subtest Performance

	Canonical Loadings	
	Function I	Function II
Number/Letter	.75	−.08
Sound Symbol	.60	.31
Sentence Memory	.51	.33
Finger Windows	.50	−.09
Verbal Learning	.22	.64

	Canonical Discriminant Functions (Group Centroids)	
Group	Function I	Function II
ADHD	−.5935	.3655
RD	−.6407	−.4762
Nonreferred	.6785	.0087
RD/ADHD	−.8462	.4191

Note. WRAML = Wide Range Assessment of Memory and Learning; ADHD = attention deficit hyperactivity disorder; RD = reading disorder.

parisons, as well as from the discriminant-function variable correlations, suggest that the construct of rote, short-term memory best distinguishes children with ADHD and RD from those without documented symptomatology. Support for this assertion comes from a recent study (Howes, Bigler, Lawson, & Burlingame, 1999), which also showed that subjects with RD performed the poorest on TOMAL subtests requiring rote oral recall (reciting digits or letters forward, as well as backwards).

The Verbal Learning subtest represents the second function, which distinguished the RD group from the other three groups. A univariate analysis of this subtest showed that the RD scaled score group mean (M = 8.8) was statistically lower than that of the other groups, with the RD/ADHD group mean (M = 9.3) only trending toward significance (p < .10), compared to the ADHD (M = 10.5) and nonreferred (M = 10.4) group means.

We can conclude from these results that children with average intelligence, who perform poorly on Number/Letter, Sound Symbol, Sentence Memory, and Finger Windows (but perform reasonably well on the remaining WRAML subtests) are likely to have some kind of psychopathology. In such children, low Verbal Learning scores increase the probability that the diagnosis is RD. It should be noted that children with dual diagnoses (RD and ADHD) could not be adequately distinguished from those children with a single diagnoses.

From a methodological standpoint, the diagnostic diversity in this study was critical. For example, if only children with ADHD (or only children with RD) had been compared to the nonreferred sample, it might have been falsely concluded that lower scores on Number/Letter, Sound Symbol, Sentence Memory, and Finger Windows represent a "cluster" useful in diagnosing ADHD (or RD). Initial findings from a study of depressed children also demonstrate lower scores on the "pathology" cluster composed of the four WRAML subtests (Whitney, 1996). Including diverse diagnostic groups may therefore be especially important in cognitive investigations to reduce the potential that erroneous conclusions will be drawn about findings appearing to be specific to a given clinical population.

Clinical Applications of the WRAML: TBI and Other Central Nervous System Disorders

A recent investigation (Duis et al., 1998) demonstrated that children who had experienced moderate or severe TBI proved to have residual deficits on all WRAML subtests following a period of rehabilitation and recovery. Table 15.10 included WRAML subtest means and standard deviations for groups with ADHD, RD, and TBI. The WRAML subtest scores of

TABLE 15.10   WRAML Subtest Means and Standard Deviations (in Parentheses) for Children with ADHD, RD, and TBI (Adapted from Duis et al., in press)

Subtests	Groups			
	ADHD	RD	TBI	Nonreferred
Number/Letter	7.3 (2.5)	7.8 (2.5)	7.1 (2.8)	10.1 (2.4)
Sound Symbol	8.5 (3.1)	7.6 (2.1)	7.6 (3.0)	10.3 (2.9)
Sentence Memory	9.1 (2.8)	8.1 (2.9)	7.1 (3.4)	10.6 (3.2)
Finger Windows	8.3 (2.5)	8.7 (3.0)	7.5 (3.2)	10.1 (2.6)
Verbal Learning	10.5 (2.9)	8.8 (2.9)	8.2 (3.1)	10.5 (2.9)
Story Memory	10.1 (2.7)	9.7 (2.8)	7.2 (3.7)	10.1 (2.6)
Design Memory	7.9 (3.1)	9.5 (2.8)	7.2 (3.5)	9.8 (2.9)
Picture Memory	10.1 (2.6)	9.8 (2.3)	8.7 (3.4)	10.1 (3.0)
Visual Learning	9.4 (3.1)	9.7 (3.0)	8.5 (3.1)	10.1 (3.2)

Note. WRAML = Wide Range Assessment of Memory and Learning; ADHD = attention deficit hyperactivity disorder; RD = reading disorder; TBI = traumatic brain injury.

the children with TBI were approximately one standard deviation below average and the scores of the children with RD and ADHD were approximately 0.5 standard deviations below average. Farmer et al. (1999) reported similar degrees of memory impairment in children who had experienced severe TBI. Research utilizing the WRAML Screening form shows significant negative correlations with length of coma. This finding rivals similar negative correlations reported with the WISC Performance IQ and length of coma (Woodward & Donders, 1998). Moreover, children who incurred severe TBI exhibited significantly lower Screening form indexes than did children with mild or moderate injuries, suggesting that the WRAML Screening form may be useful in delineating memory impairments associated with varying degrees of TBI severity.

In contrast to the WRAML subtest pattern demonstrated by children with ADHD, RD, or TBI, children with seizure disorders performed at a slightly higher level as a group than children with TBI did. However, these patients also showed greater subtest variability than the ADHD, RD, or TBI injured children (Williams & Haut, 1995). Child survivors of lymphoblastic leukemia who were treated with intrathecal chemotherapy exhibited mild but consistent residual deficits on most WRAML Visual Memory and Verbal Memory subtests, as well as the Visual Learning subtest. These results correspond to lower IQ scores in the same sample of children, compared to healthy, matched controls (Hill, Ciesielski, Sethre-Hofstad, Duncan, & Lorenzi, 1997).

Case Study: Burt

    Age: 13 years, 09 months

    Sex: M

    Education: K + 7

Medications: none

Date of Injury: 07/02/01

Date of Evaluation: 05/16/02

Background and Presenting Problem

Burt was referred by his pediatrician, school personnel, and his parents to better understand why Burt experienced a discouraging academic year. Prior to the current school year, Burt "was an A student," and his report card reflected mostly As and several academic commendations. However, since beginning junior high school, Burt's grades dropped to Bs and Cs for the first term, and even lower for the spring semester. Burt's parents at first thought the academic struggles were due to "entering adolescence" and not studying, because Burt was spending too much time with his friends. Upon further reflection during our interview, the parents indicated that Burt has always been very involved socially and tended to any homework assignments in school or on the bus ride home. "Things came easy to him" and Burt was able to maintain high grades with a relatively minimal investment of time. His parents also reflected that during the initial part of the fall semester, Burt insisted that he was working longer on his school work and was trying hard to improve his grades. However, his grades did not improve but got worse. His parents wondered whether Burt really had been trying harder but eventually gave up because he continued to experience difficulty. Upon questioning, his parents agreed that Burt continued to comply with chore requests and household rules throughout the past year.

The interview also uncovered a bicycle accident Burt sustained the previous summer. He apparently swerved to avoid a small child also riding a bike and in so doing ran into a street sign. According to medical records, Burt apparently lost consciousness but was awake, although "woozy," when the Rescue Squad arrived; they assigned a Glasgow Coma Scale of 12. He was taken by ambulance to a local hospital where no neck or spinal injuries were found; a GCS of 15 was also assigned. An ER magnetic resonance imaging (MRI) study was read as unremarkable; however upon discharge three days later, a second MRI scan indicated "possible contusion in aspects of both frontal lobes." Nonetheless, Burt returned home and after about a week assumed a fairly normal routine for the remainder of the summer. His parents said that Burt tired more rapidly than usual and seemed less attentive to long-term tasks, such as reading or working on woodworking projects, both of which were hobbies he enjoyed. Because of questions surrounding Burt's decline in school performance following a moderate closed head injury, a neuropsychological evaluation was completed.

Behavioral Observations

Burt was met in the waiting area and welcomed the examiner with a number of well-developed social skills. He accompanied the examiner to the testing room, engaging in socially appropriate conversation, which included impressive vocabulary. Throughout our time together Burt was cooperative and motivated. He seemed interested in solving the mystery concerning the struggles that had newly characterized his meeting academic demands. His stamina, expressive language, persistence, frustration tolerance, and the other skills often observed during testing seemed well within normal limits compared to age mates (see Table 15.11). At the conclusion of the three and a half hour evaluation, Burt seemed genuinely interested in the findings and how they might be used to help out in the coming school year.

Conclusions and Recommendations

The results in Table 15.11 indicate that Burt's intellectual ability is well above average, near the 99th percentile when compared to teens his age. Correspondingly, basic academic skills are also strong. These scores are consistent with Burt's academic history; that is, they predict a student who would find traditional school work easy and with minimal investment, excel at it. However, some findings seem related to the head injury he sustained during the summer, which may explain his academic struggles. Although Burt has solid visual and verbal memory for tasks requiring short-term memory using rote and meaningful stimuli, it is noticeably different when the quantity of what must be learned requires incremental learning. Therefore, with a list-learning task, Burt appears less able to encode as much information as his agemates at the initial trial. As importantly, what he stores from each learning trial remains somewhat below average. Therefore, at the end of four learning episodes, Burt mastered the amount most average age mates achieve. Given the learning curve demonstrated, Burt would likely need a trial or two more to reach mastery of the material. It seems that Burt retains what he learns as well as his age mates do. Similar learning curves were found for visual and a visual-verbal rote association task. Like the WRAML Learning subtest scores, the WCST results, while adequate for a young man this age, are much less impressive than one would expect for an individual with a 133 Verbal IQ. The struggles Burt is experiencing in school seem to be related to his apparent inability to process and store large quantities of new information upon initial exposure, which was probably his style before the head injury. Instead, with additional learning trials, Burt shows improvement, but the rate of learning across trials is about

TABLE 15.11   WRAML Case Study

Wechsler Intelligence Scale for Children–III

Full Scale IQ	133
VIQ	128
PIQ	132
VCI	131
POI	135
FDI	109
PSI	n/a

Subtest	Scaled Score
Information	14
Similarities	17
Arithmetic	12
Vocabulary	15
Comprehension	16
Digit Span	12
Picture Completion	15
Coding	11
Picture Arrangement	14
Block Design	18
Object Assembly	16

Wide Range Achievement Test

Reading	126
Spelling	119
Arithmetic	130

Wide Range Assessment of Memory and Learning

Verbal Memory		126
	Number/Letter	12
	Sentence Memory	14
	Story Memory	16
Visual Memory		114
	Finger Windows	10
	Design Memory	14
	Picture Memory	12
Learning		97
	Verbal Learning	09 (4, 6, 10, 12 11)
	Visual Learning	11 (4, 5, 10, 12 12)
	Sound-Symbol Learning	09 (2, 4, 7, 7 07)
Delay Task		
	Story Memory	WNL
	Verbal Learning	WNL
	Visual Learning	WNL
	Sound-Symbol	WNL

Wisconsin Card Sorting Test (Computerized Version)

Categories Completed	6
Total Trials	105
Total Correct	69
% Errors	34
% Perseverative Errors	18
Failure to Maintain Set	0
Learning to Learn	−1.75

Note. VIQ = Verbal IQ; PIQ = Performance IQ; VCI = Verbal Comprehension Index; POI = Perceptual Organization Index; FDI = Freedom from Distractibility Index; PSI = Processing Speed Index; n/a = not applicable; WNL = within normal limits.

average, rather than well above average as would be expected from Burt's Full Scale IQ.

We recommend that Burt work with a tutor experienced in working with teens. First, he will need to be informed that at least for the time being, he must change his approach to school work; the system he once used successfully will no longer help him earn the grades he wants. Instead, the tutor and he will collaborate to develop a more effective system. Burt and the tutor need to devise an efficient review system so Burt can learn the amount of information found in many of his text-book assignments. Because Burt does improve with each learning trial, the system developed needs to provide additional review in as efficient a fashion as possible. After he learns the material he will likely retain it well enough to perform at the level to which he aspires. Working collaboratively with Burt should allow him to feel less victimized as he works to compensate for some of the unfortunate effects of his head injury. He retains many impressive cognitive and social strengths, which should help him during this remediation process. Applying these strengths should prove beneficial as the suggestions mentioned previously and others are implemented and perfected, so that the upcoming school year will be one in which Burt will realize more success. We planned to consult with Burt and the tutor as they identified specific everyday academic skill areas that prove problematic. Data from the current evaluation, plus results from additional evaluation, should be helpful in this evolving educational intervention process.

TEST OF MEMORY AND LEARNING

Structure

The Test of Memory and Learning (TOMAL; Reynolds & Bigler, 1994a, b) is a comprehensive battery of 14 tasks, assessing learning and memory for children and adolescents ranging in age from 5 years 0 months to 19 years 11 months (see Table 15.12). Ten primary subtests are divided into the Verbal Memory and Nonverbal Memory domains, which can be combined to form a Composite Memory Index. The Delayed Recall Index is composed of repeat recall trials of the first four subtests.

As previously noted, the pattern of overall memory functioning for a particular individual may be singular and variable; in such cases, content approaches to memory may be limited. Therefore the TOMAL provides alternative groupings of the subtests into five supplementary indexes: Sequential Recall, Free Recall, Associative Recall, Learning, and Attention and Concentration. Renowned neuropsychologists

TABLE 15.12 Core and Supplementary Subtests and Indexes Available for the TOMAL

	M	SD
Core Subtests		
Verbal Memory		
Memory for Stories	10	3
Word Selective Reminding	10	3
Object Recall	10	3
Digits Forward	10	3
Paired Recall	10	3
Nonverbal Memory		
Facial Memory	10	3
Visual Selective Reminding	10	3
Abstract Visual Memory	10	3
Visual Sequential Memory	10	3
Memory for Location	10	3
Supplementary Subtests		
Verbal		
Letters Forward	10	3
Digits Backward	10	3
Letters Backward	10	3
Nonverbal		
Manual imitation	10	3
Summary Scores		
Core Indexes		
Verbal Memory Index	100	15
Nonverbal Memory Index	100	15
Composite Memory Index	100	15
Delayed Recall Index	100	15
Supplementary Indexes (Expert Derived)		
Sequential Recall Index	100	15
Free Recall Index	100	15
Associative Recall Index	100	15
Learning Index	100	15
Attention Concentration Index	100	15
Factor Scores (Empirically Derived)		
Complex Memory Index	100	15
Sequential Recall Index	100	15
Backwards Recall Index	100	15
Spatial Memory Index	100	15

Note. M = mean; SD = standard deviation.

who were asked to arrange the 14 TOMAL subtests into categories with face validity (Reynolds & Bigler, 1994a) organized the supplementary indexes. In addition, four empirically derived factor indexes representing Complex Memory, Sequential Recall, Backward Recall, and Spatial Memory were provided to give greater flexibility to the clinician (Reynolds & Bigler, 1996).

Table 15.12 lists each of the subtests/indices and their respective standardized means and standard deviations. Each TOMAL subtest is scaled according to the often-used metric with a mean value of 10 and a standard deviation of 3. Each index is similarly scaled to the common mean of 100 and

standard deviation of 15. Scaling was accomplished through the rolling weighted averages method described in detail by Reynolds and Bigler (1994a).

Subtests of the TOMAL

The 10 core subtests, the 4 supplementary subtests, and the delayed recall trials of the TOMAL take approximately 60 minutes for the experienced examiner to administer. The subtests are named and briefly described in Table 15.13.

The administration of the TOMAL subtests is varied, so that verbal, visual, and motor modalities, and combinations of these modalities are sampled from alternating presentation and response formats. Learning and acquisition curves are made possible by multiple "trials to a criterion," which are included on several tasks. For example, multiple trials are included on the Word and Visual Selective Reminding subtests to allow for a "depth of processing" analysis (Kaplan, 1996). In the selective reminding format (in which examinees are reminded of omitted words), if items that were correctly recalled are not recalled on subsequent trials, it may be inferred that there is a deficit in transfer of information from immediate/working memory to long-term storage. At the end of selected subtests, cuing is allowed so that depth of processing can be further explored. For instance, differences between cued recall and free recall may be associated with certain neurological disorders, and therefore may serve as a diagnostic aid.

Traditional memory tasks (e.g., Memory for Stories) that are associated with academic learning are also included. In addition, memory tasks more common to experimental neuropsychology that have high (e.g., Facial Memory) and low (e.g., Visual Selective Reminding) ecological validity are included in the TOMAL. Similarly, subtests vary in meaningfulness. For example, Memory for Stories is high in meaning compared to Abstract Visual Memory, which requires abstract visual processing (i.e., analysis of complex geometric forms).

The TOMAL's comprehensive review of multiple memory functions allows for a relatively fine-grained and inclusive assessment of potential memory deficits. It cannot be emphasized enough that "memory" is a complex construct, and that the most effective batteries will be those that assess a wide range of well-defined functions that are clinically relevant and ecologically valid. The TOMAL succeeds on these grounds because of its breadth, and the opportunity for detailed analysis of diverse memory processes within the information-processing paradigm.

TABLE 15.13   Description of TOMAL Subtests

Core

Memory for Stories	A verbal subtest requiring recall of a short story read to the examinee. Provides a measure of meaningful and semantic recall and is also related to sequential recall in some instances.
Facial Memory	A nonverbal subtest requiring recognition and identification from a set of distractors: black-and-white photos of various ages, males and females, and various ethnic backgrounds. Assesses nonverbal meaningful memory in a practical fashion and has been extensively researched. Sequencing of responses is unimportant.
Word Selective Reminding	A verbal free-recall task in which the examinee learns a word list and repeats it only to be reminded of words left out in each case: tests learning and immediate recall functions in verbal memory. Trials continue until mastery is achieved or until eight trials have been attempted. Sequence of recall is unimportant.
Visual Selective Reminding	A nonverbal analogue to Word Selective Reminding where examinees point to specified dots on a card, following a demonstration of the examiner, and are reminded only of items recalled incorrectly. As with WSR, trials continue until mastery is achieved or until eight trials have been attempted.
Object Recall	The examiner presents a series of pictures, names them, has the examinee recall them, and repeats this process across four trials. Verbal and nonverbal stimuli are thus paired, and recall is entirely verbal, creating a situation found to interfere with recall for many children with learning disabilities but to be neutral or facilitative for children without disabilities.
Abstract Visual Memory	A nonverbal task that assesses immediate recall for meaningless figures when order is unimportant. The examinee is presented with a standard stimulus and required to recognize the standard from any of six distractors.
Digits Forward	A standard verbal number recall task; it measures low-level rote recall of a sequence of numbers.
Visual Sequential Memory	A nonverbal task requiring recall of the sequence of a series of meaningless geometric designs. The designs are shown in a standard order, followed by a presentation in a different order, and the examinee is required to indicate the order in which they originally appeared.
Paired Recall	A verbal paired-associate learning task is provided by the examiner. Easy and hard pairs, and measures of immediate associative recall and learning are provided.
Memory for Location	A nonverbal task that assesses spatial memory. The examinee is presented with a set of large dots distributed on a page and asked to recall the locations of the dots in order.

Supplementary Subtests

Manual Imitation	A psychomotor, visually based assessment of sequential memory in which the examinee is required to reproduce a set of ordered hand movements in the same sequence as presented by the examiner.
Letters Forward	A language-related analogue to the Digits Forward task, using letters as the stimuli in place of numbers.
Digits Backward	This is the same basic task as Digits Forward, except the examinee recalls the numbers in reverse order.
Letters Backward	A language-related analogue to the Digits Backward task, using letters as the stimuli instead of numbers.

Note. TOMAL = Test of Memory and Learning.

Standardization

The TOMAL was standardized on a population-proportionate sample of children throughout the United States stratified by age, gender, ethnicity, socioeconomic status, region of residence, and community size). Standardization and norming were conducted for children and adolescents ages 5 to 20.

Reynolds and Bigler (1994a) provide details of the standardization and specific statistics on the sample.

Reliability

The TOMAL subtests and summary indexes exhibit excellent internal consistency reliability. Reynolds and Bigler (1994a) report coefficient alpha reliability estimates that often exceed .90 for individual subtests and .95 for composite scores. Stability coefficients are typically in the .80 range.

Validity

The TOMAL scores show correlations of approximately .50 with standard measures of intelligence and achievement—indicating that the TOMAL shares variance with intelligence and achievement measures, but also that it taps unique constructs (Reynolds et al., 1994a). The specificity of the TOMAL in relation to intellectual measures is bolstered by the observation that measures of intelligence characteristically exhibit intersubtest correlations of approximately .75 to .85. This is true to a lesser extent with the achievement measures, which typically show subtest correlations of approximately .55 to .65. Similarly, select subtests (i.e., word selective reminding) correlate positively with the previously accepted standard test of verbal memory, the Rey-Auditory Verbal Learning Test (RAVLT; Rey, 1964). Likewise, for adolescents (16–20 years), the Memory for Stories subtest correlates highly with a similar subtest from the well-established Wechsler Memory Scale–Revised (see Reynolds & Bigler, 1997; Wechsler, 1987).

The nonverbal sections of the TOMAL are relatively orthogonal to existing nonverbal memory tests (see Reynolds et al., 1997). In contrast to other tests of visual and nonverbal memory, which do not attempt to prevent verbally mediated strategies for encoding and recalling of to be remembered stimuli, the TOMAL, by virtue of its design, reduces the opportunities for such attempts and thus may be a "purer" measure of visual/nonverbal memory. Thus examiners using visual and verbal tasks on traditional memory batteries should expect larger scatter across tests than on verbal memory measures.

Factor Structure

Detailed analyses of the factor structure and indexes of the TOMAL, based on a normative sample of 1,342 children, have been extensively reviewed by Reynolds and Bigler (1996; 1997). In a method of principal factors analysis with varimax and promax rotations, the correlation matrix for all 14 TOMAL subtests was examined. Factors were extracted and found to be consistent across children/adolescents ages 5–8, 9–12, and 13–18 years of age. It is noteworthy that the analyses discussed in this section are based on normal, nonreferred children, and that the factor analyses will not demonstrate the same consistency in clinic-referred subjects,

particularly children with central nervous system dysfunction (see review material by Kamphaus & Reynolds, 1987).

The two-factor solutions for the TOMAL did not support the verbal-nonverbal dichotomy. The factor structure of the TOMAL is clearly more multifaceted than is represented by the verbal-nonverbal groupings. Nevertheless, Reynolds and Bigler (1994b) preserved the verbal-nonverbal construct because of its clinical utility. A general factor was evident, similar in concept to the intelligence factor g, but weaker in magnitude. Nonetheless, this factor supports the use of a composite score, such as the composite memory index with nonclinical populations. Exploratory factor analyses were also conducted; exhibiting a four-factor solution, which appeared to best characterize the clinical organization of the TOMAL, as outlined in the following list (Reynolds et al., 1997):

1. Complex Memory = Memory for Stories + Word Selective Reminding + Object Recall + Paired Recall + Visual Selective Reminding + Facial Memory.
2. Sequential Recall = Digits Forward + Letters Forward + Visual Sequential Memory + Manual Imitation.
3. Backward Recall = Digits Backward + Letters Backward.
4. Spatial Memory = Abstract Visual Memory + Memory for Location.

The first and most robust factor derived from the promax solution appeared to be a general factor, reflective of overall memory skills subsuming multiple modalities and memory processes. The second factor seemed to represent sequential recall and attention processes. The third factor was composed of Digits Backward and Letters Backward, suggesting that backward and forward memory span tasks should be separately scaled. Backward digit recall is known to be a more highly g-loaded task than forward digit recall and places more information processing demands on the examinee (e.g., see Jensen & Figueroa, 1975). The fourth factor was comprised of Abstract Visual Memory and Memory for Location, which appeared to represent a nonverbal factor. This factor appeared to capture spatial memory more strongly than other tasks. The four-factor varimax solution resulted in similar findings.

At one-year age intervals, internal consistency reliability data for the four TOMAL factor indexes were above .90, with the exception of the spatial Memory Index at 5 years of age (reliability coefficient = .85). It is noteworthy that the values of the other three factors fell between .94 and .99 with median values of .95 for the Complex Memory Factor Index, and .94 for the Spatial Memory Index. The reliability coefficients of the empirically derived factor indexes are therefore comparable to those of the TOMAL Core Indexes and Supplementary Indexes described in the TOMAL manual (Reynolds et al., 1994a).

The strong psychometrics of the four-factor indexes support constructs representing useful tools that the clinician can use to better understand individual cases. The TOMAL factor structure suggests that the aspects of memory assessed in this instrument may be more process driven than content driven. Although the verbal-nonverbal memory distinction is clinically useful, particularly for patients with TBI or with hemispherically distinct lesions, process appears to be more relevant than content or presentation modality in healthy individuals.

Subtest Specificities

Variance specific to each subtest can be derived from factor analysis and represents the proportion of variance for a particular subtest that is specific to the subtest and is not shared with other factors. That is, a particular subtest may inform the clinician about aspects of an examinee's performance that are independent of those revealed by other subtests. A specificity value of 0.25 has been considered appropriate to support interpretation of an individual subtest score (e.g., see Kaufman, 1979). The values reported by Reynolds and Bigler (1994a; 1994b; 1996) represent rather respectable specificity compared to measures of intelligence and achievement, which often show more highly interrelated subtests. Indeed, each of the TOMAL subtests shows specificity values > 0.40, and each specificity value exceeds the error variance of the subtest. Such sound psychometrics allow the clinician to be confident with respect to interpretation of component subtests. Direction in generating such hypotheses from clinical observation is included in the TOMAL manual (Reynolds et al., 1994a), as well as through automated software designed for the TOMAL (Stanton, Reynolds, & Bigler, 1995).

Cross-Ethnic Stability of Factor Indexes

Normative data for the TOMAL were standardized on an ethnically diverse population. This is a particular strength of the TOMAL, as little research has been conducted with regard to neuropsychological measures and the cultural test bias hypothesis, particularly by comparison with the large body of such research on intelligence tests (e.g., see Reynolds, 1995). Preliminary analyses suggest consistency of the factor structures of the TOMAL across race for African American and European American subjects (see Mayfield & Reynolds, 1997; Reynolds et al., 1994a; 1996). These findings, although preliminary, suggest that the African Americans and Caucasians perceive the stimuli of the TOMAL in a highly com-

parable manner. Although changes in interpretation as a function of race do not appear to be warranted based on current results, further research is needed to validate this finding and explore comparisons between other ethnicities.

Forward Versus Backward Recall of Digits

As mentioned earlier in this chapter, assessment of recall of digits in the forward and reverse directions has been a staple in cognitive assessment. It has also been the tradition on many tests to sum the number of digits recalled in the forward direction with those recalled in the reverse direction to form a total score of "digit span." As previous research has suggested that digits forward and digits backward tasks demand different, although overlapping abilities (Ramsey & Reynolds, 1995; Reynolds et al., 1997), the TOMAL normed each of these subtests separately. It appears that forward digit span has strong attentional and sequential components, and that backward digit span appears to have spatial and/or integrative elements that are not prominent in forward digit span. Current evidence and clinical observation suggest that a digits forward task carries fewer cognitive demands and may be more verbally oriented, requiring sequential memory abilities. In contrast, a digits backward task appears to tap more complex processes, requiring cognitive manipulations that are not necessary with a digits forward task. For instance, backward recall may also require visual-spatial imaging processes (for some individuals); this may be true even when ostensibly verbal material (e.g., letters) rather than digits, are being recalled. Because of these distinctions between forward and backward recall and the clinical implications for differences in performance, the tasks are presented and interpreted separately on the TOMAL.

Delayed Recall

Delayed recall has been another mainstay in the area of memory assessment. On the TOMAL, the examinee is asked to recall stimuli from the first four subtests administered (two verbal, two nonverbal) 30 minutes after testing has begun. In essence, the Delayed Recall Index serves as a measure of forgetting. Most examinees score within about 10 points of their Composite Memory Index on the Delayed Recall Index. The TOMAL manual contains values for evaluating differences between Delayed Recall Index and Composite Memory Index. The TOMAL's computer scoring program also provides an analysis of index comparisons.

A Delayed Recall Index score significantly lower than the Composite Memory Index is often an indication of a memory disturbance with an organic basis, although several neuropsychiatric disorders with varied etiology can produce memory deficits (e.g., Grossman, Kaufman, Mednitsky, Scharff, & Dennis, 1994). The Delayed Recall Index provides the clinician with a useful tool to explore hypotheses about processing depth, forgetting, and motivation, among other things.

Interpretation

Kaufman's (1994; 1979) top-down interpretive strategy that requires a systematic integration of history and other test data is reviewed in the TOMAL manual. In addition, Reynolds and Bigler (1994a), provide further considerations for interpretation including data on within-test variability and the relationship between the TOMAL and intellectual and achievement measures.

An example of the clinical usefulness of the TOMAL is demonstrated in Table 15.14, which shows the performance of children with varying severities of TBI (Lajiness-O'Neill, 1996).

In the following study, memory disturbance increased as a function of severity.

Case Study: John

Age: 16

Sex: M

Grade: 10

TABLE 15.14 Means and Standard Deviations by Group for TOMAL Indices, WRAT–III and PPVT Scaled Scores, and FSIQ Score

	Control	Mild	Moderate	Severe
TOMAL				
VMI	102 (8)*	95 (12)*	96 (12)*	86 (16)*[a,b,c]
NMI	104 (11)*	97 (11)	92 (19)*[a]	89 (14)*[a]
CMI	103 (8)*	96 (10)*	94 (15)*[a]	87 (14)*[a,b]
DRI	104 (7)*	99 (7)*	96 (9)*[a]	92 (13)*[a,b]
WRAT–III				
ASS	103 (12)*	94 (13)	94 (17)	93 (21)*[a]
RSS	104 (11)*	98 (11)	87 (14)*[a]	92 (18)*[a]
SSS	103 (12)*	96 (22)	88 (16)*[a]	91 (15)*[a]
PPVT–R	106 (12)*	99 (14)	98 (21)	94 (18)*[a]
FSIQ	105 (12)*	99 (13)	95 (15)	94 (18)*[a]

Note. TOMAL = Test of Memory and Learning; VMI = Verbal Memory Index; NMI = Nonverbal Memory Index; CMI = Composite Memory Index; DRI = Delayed Recall Index; WRAT–III = Wide Range Achievement Test–III; ASS = Arithmetic Scale Score; RSS = Reading Scaled Score; SSS = Spelling Scaled Score; PPVT–R = Peabody Picture Vocabulary Test–Revised; FSIQ = Wechsler Full-Scale IQ.
[a]Reliably different from control group.
[b]Reliably different from mild brain injury group.
[c]Reliably different from moderate brain injury group.
*$p < .05$ as examined by post-hoc Tukey's HSD procedure.

Date of Injury: 09/03/95

Data of Evaluation: 05/31/00

Reason for Referral

John was referred for follow-up neuropsychological assessment five years after he experienced a gunshot wound to the head, which caused extensive damage to the right side of the brain (see Figure 15.3). He was in a coma following the injury and experienced post-traumatic amnesia for approximately one month. With the exception of a possible seizure at the age of 3, John's general medical history was unremarkable. Although, his parents believe that John appears to be reasonably adjusted emotionally, they have concerns about his ability to learn as well as his future vocational adjustment. At the time of the assessment, John's grades ranged widely and included a D in mathematics, and an A in biology.

Summary of Findings

John's performance on the WISC–III suggests below average abilities on tasks that require visual-spatial, motor, holistic processing, and sequencing abilities (PIQ = 84). Despite relative visual-spatial weaknesses, John's verbal abilities are in the average range (VIQ = 105). John's scaled scores on a screening measure of academic achievement, the Wide Range Achievement Test–Third edition (WRAT–III) were 101, 107, and 95 for reading, spelling, and math, respectively. These scores are roughly commensurate with John's intellectual ability, although it is clear that from John's current scholastic performance that he struggles with mathematics. Self-report measures of depression, anxiety, and other psychiatric symptoms were within normal limits.

John's scores on The Visual Motor Integration Test, the Tactual Performance Test, the Benton Visual Retention Test and the Rey-Osterrieth Complex Figure test were in the impaired range and consistent with right hemisphere dysfunction.

Memory

John's performance on the Verbal Memory Index (scaled score = 86) and Nonverbal Memory Index (scaled score = 81) of the TOMAL was similar (see Table 15.15). These scores are approximately one standard deviation below the mean of his peers. However, there was considerable interscale scatter within the Verbal and Nonverbal domains, with scaled scores ranging from 4–13 and 5–11, respectively. In the Verbal domain, John showed relative strengths for Memory for Stories ($p = .01$) and Paired Recall ($p = .01$), and a relative weakness for Object Recall ($p = .01$) and Digits

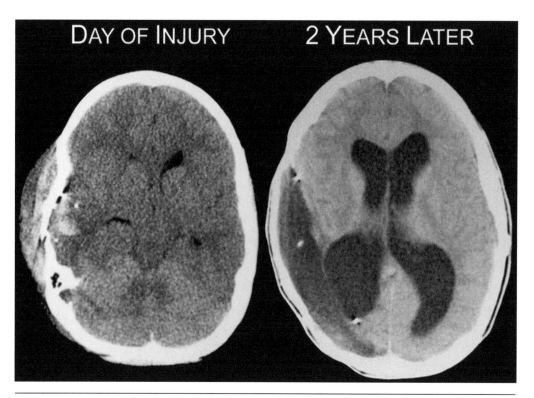

Figure 15.3 The computerized tomogram (CT) scan on the left is from the day of injury when this adolescent male was accidentally shot in the head by a .22 caliber bullet. The scan is presented in radiologic perspective where left is viewed on the reader's right. Accordingly, the abnormalities identified in the scan on the day of injury are on the right side of the brain, where there is extensive hemorrhaging (white areas) as well as brain swelling (effacement of the lateral ventricles). The follow-up scan clearly demonstrates generalized ventricular dilation, a large area of fluid collection over the right hemisphere and some bullet fragments. As shown in the TOMAL results, this patient demonstrated generalized memory deficits, but greater impairment with nonverbal memory tasks. The imaging abnormalities depicted in the follow-up scan show generalized cerebral damage, greater in the right hemisphere, which would be consistent with the neuropsychological and memory results.

Forward ($p = .05$). In the Nonverbal domain, John exhibited a relative strength for Memory for Location and relative weaknesses on Facial Memory and Abstract Visual Memory. Although no clear pattern of subtest performance emerged, his above average score on Memory for Stories suggests that John can remember meaningful auditory stimuli that are presented in sequence. This test is noted for its "ecological validity," because remembering details as well as the overall gist of a conversation, instructions, and so on are relevant and adaptive to everyday functioning. Similarly, John's relatively high score on paired associates suggests strong associative learning abilities. With respect to John's weaknesses, it is noteworthy that several of these subtests rely heavily on attentional processes (see the following discussion of attention).

The clustering of several of John's memory index scores around his Attention/Concentration Index score suggests that attention and concentration may be rate-limiting factors, with respect to John's overall memory functioning. John's Delayed Recall Index score suggests that his consolidation and

retrieval processes from long-term memory stores are consistent with his overall memory performance. On the TOMAL and CVLT–C, John demonstrated a flat learning curve suggestive of proactive interference, which suggests that previously learned material may be interfering with acquisition and retrieval of new memories. Finally, his scaled score on the Associative Learning Index compared to his other index scores was remarkably high (scaled score = 112).

Conclusions and Recommendations

Taken together, the results suggest that John has significant memory impairment that may be in part mediated by attention/concentration deficits. The findings further suggest that John may learn best when instructions are given orally, associative learning strategies are utilized, subjects with similar content are separated, and potential distractions are limited. It is recommended that John tape record classroom lectures so that he can devote his full attention to the lecture and later refer

TABLE 15.15   TOMAL Case Study

Wechsler Intelligence Scale for Children–III

VIQ = 105
PIQ = 84

Information	10
Similarities	9
Arithmetic	12
Vocabulary	11
Comprehension	12
Digit Span	11
Picture Completion	9
Coding	6
Picture Arrangement	7
Block Design	10
Object Assembly	6

Wide Range Achievement Test

Reading	101
Spelling	107
Arithmetic	95

Test of Memory and Learning

Index Scores	SS	%
Verbal Memory Index	86	18
Nonverbal Memory Index	81	10
Composite Memory Index	83	13
Delayed Recall Index	85	16
Attention/Con. Index	86	18
Sequential Recall Index	92	30
Free Recall Index	75	5
Associative Recall Index	112	79
Learning Index	80	8

Note. VIQ = Verbal IQ; PIQ = Performance IQ.

to his recordings during study sessions. One-on-one tutoring is also recommended to compensate for attentional deficits. A change in seating position (e.g., to the front row) may also help John better attend to classroom lectures. Observation of John's classroom may be helpful in identifying distractions and other learning obstacles. Consistent positive reinforcement and vocational counseling may also be useful. Formal assessment of attention/concentration is recommended as well as further assessment of academic achievement (e.g., with the Woodcock-Johnson–R) to identify additional problem areas that may be contributing to John's current learning difficulties.

CALIFORNIA VERBAL LEARNING TEST–CHILDREN'S VERSION

Structure

The California Verbal Learning Test–Children's Version (CVLT–C, Delis et al., 1994) is a measure of auditory-verbal learning and recall that was adapted from its adult counterpart, the California Verbal Learning Test (CVLT; Delis, Kramer, Kaplan, & Kaplan, 1987). It also shares characteristics with the RAVLT (Rey, 1964) and the Verbal Learning subtest of the WRAML (Sheslow et al., 1990). The CVLT–C was designed for children ranging in age from 5 to 16 years. The primary task is designed with respect to everyday memory tasks and includes two lists of familiar and categorized words presented as "shopping lists." In particular, the child is read a list of 15 words and is then asked to recall as many words as possible in a free recall format. Four additional recall trials are then administered to evaluate learning across trials. Although strategies are not given to the child, the words are such that they can be sorted into three semantic categories including clothes, fruits, and toys, with an equal number of words in each category.

Following this administration of the first list of words, the second "shopping list" is then read aloud to the child. The second list, which is also composed of 15 different words, can be sorted into the semantic groupings of furniture, fruits, and desserts. After a learning/recall trial with the second list, the child is instructed to recall the first shopping list. The child is then given the three categories in which the words of the first list may be grouped. With this strategy offered, recall for each category is repeated.

A 20-minute delay period is then introduced during which other nonverbal testing may be completed. After 20 minutes, the child is again administered a free-recall trial of the first list, followed by a cued recall trial. Finally, the child is asked to listen to a list of words that include items from both learning lists as well as distractor words. The child is then asked to identify those words from the first shopping list. The entire procedure requires approximately 30 minutes to complete, not including the 20-minute delay.

Great care was taken in selecting the items for the CVLT–C. For instance, words chosen for the shopping lists were selected based on their frequency in the English language, as well as by how often they were reported by children. To avoid the potential confound in which children would simply respond with the most common words in a given category rather than a word from the list, the three most commonly used words for each category were excluded.

Standardization

The CVLT–C standardization was stratified by age, gender, ethnicity, geographic region, and parental education, based on the 1988 U.S. Census. Details of the standardization procedures, including sampling statistics, can be found in the CVLT–C manual (Delis et al., 1994).

Reliability

Reliability estimates for the CVLT–C are reported as measures of internal consistency, as well as test-retest reliability. Across the five trials for the first shopping list, the average internal consistency correlations ranged from .84 to .91, with a mean of .88. Reliability across categories yielded an average internal consistency coefficient of .72 for all age groups. Test-retest measures were obtained across average test-retest intervals of 28 days. Recall performance on the second CVLT–C administration increased by 5, 6, and 9 words for the 8-, 12-, and 16-year-old age groups, respectively. Reliability coefficients based on the first and second administration scores ranged from .31 to .90, which the test authors considered acceptable, based on the auditory verbal memory nature of the CVLT–C.

Clinical Utility of the CVLT–C

The CVLT–C is relatively brief, simple to administer, and provides useful information for the clinician. For instance, perseverations and intrusions are recorded, allowing inferences about inhibition as well as expressive and phonological language impairment. Various process scores can also be calculated to provide an empirical basis for more qualitative analyses of memory. These process scores answer questions, such as does the child tend to learn things in categories or randomly? Does the child benefit from greater intervals between presentations of stimuli? Answers to such questions may carry implications for treatment recommendations. For example, in a case of the child who shows difficulty with learning tasks that are presented too close together, it may be recommended that academic subjects with similar content should be separated throughout the child's day/week to avoid interference effects from previously learned material. A software program for the CVLT–C is available that provides computation and multilevel interpretive analyses.

COMMENTS

This chapter briefly reviewed the neurobiology of memory, child neurological and neuropsychiatric disorders that impact memory functioning, and the history of assessment of memory in pediatric populations. Within this context, the psychometrics, structure, and clinical utility of three batteries commonly used to assess memory in children and adolescents were discussed in detail. This review illustrates that although each battery assesses overlapping constructs, clearly the tests discussed also tap unique aspects of memory functioning. For example, the WRAML divides its verbal memory tasks into

a hierarchy that varies as a function of increasing language processing demands, the TOMAL is noted for its breadth of assessment including several unique indexes (e.g., Sequential Recall Index, Associative Recall Index, Complex Memory Index, and Attention Concentration Index), and the CVLT–C provides information about encoding strategies. Because of these distinctive qualities, the neuropsychologist must be well versed in the properties of each battery as well as contextual variables that may guide the choice of a battery or combination of tests. For instance, a particular test may be more sensitive to deficits in a defined population or, based on the judgment of the assessor, more ecologically valid than another given the context of a specific patient and the demands of his or her environment. Although it is understandable that neuropsychologists often use preferred tests of memory, a flexible approach utilizing the strengths of the available batteries may be the most useful. This chapter is a starting point to understanding the use of popular methods of child memory assessment, but clinicians must also stay abreast with the growing literature, which provides a richer empirical grounding for the application of current assessment tools to diverse clinical populations. Future research directions include investigations of tasks that may better discriminate between memory and attentional processes as well as a general focus on developing measures with the most ecological validity.

NOTE

1. The scientific debate over memory terminology (Fuster, 1995) will not be discussed in this chapter. We acknowledge differences between immediate and short-term memory and for simplicity of presentation have maintained this older taxonomy rather than the more recent declarative (or explicit), nondeclarative (or implicit or procedural) and the term "working memory." Other memory terms, such as episodic and semantic memory, are not discussed, because the older classification of memory is in step with the way the general clinician approaches the pragmatic conceptualization of memory assessment. For instance, when providing feedback to parents, teachers, and school counselors, the use of terms that extend beyond immediate, short-term, and long-term, may become confusing.

REFERENCES

Adams, W.V., Hyde, C.L., & deLancey, E.R. (1995). *Use of the Wide range assessment of memory and learning in diagnosing ADHD in children.* Paper presented at the Child Health Psychology Conference, Gainesville, FL.

Adams, W.V., Robins, P.R., Sheslow, D.V., & Hyde, C.L. (2001). *Performance children with ADHD and/or reading disabilities on the wide range assessment of memory and learning.*

Aylward, G.P., Gioia, G., Verhulst, S.J., & Bell, S. (1995). Factor structure of the wide range assessment of memory and learning in a clinical population. *Assessment, 13,* 132–142.

Bachevalier, J. (1994). Medial temporal lobe structures and autism: A review of clinical and experimental findings. *Neuropsychologia, 32*(6), 627–648.

Bakker, D.J., Fisk, J.L., & Strang, J.D. (1985). *Child neuropsychology.* New York: Guilford Press.

Baron, I.S., Fennell, E.B., & Voeller, K.K.S. (1995). *Pediatric neuropsychology in the medical setting.* London: University Press.

Bauer, R.M., Tobias, B.A., & Valenstein, E. (1993). Amnestic disorders. In E. Valenstein (Ed.), *Clinical neuropsychology* (pp. 523–602). New York: Oxford University Press.

Bigler, E.D., & Clement, P. (1997). *Diagnostic clinical neuropsychology* (3rd ed.). Austin, TX: University of Texas Press.

Buchanan, T.W., Denburg, N.L., Tranel, D., & Adolph, R. (2001). Verbal and nonverbal emotional memory following unilateral amygdala damage. *Learning and Memory, 8*(6), 326–335.

Bull, R., & Johnston, R.S. (1997). Children's arithmetical difficulties: Contributions from processing speed, item identification, and short-term memory. *Journal of Experimental Child Psychology, 65,* 1–24.

Burton, D.B., Donders, J., & Mittenberg, W. (1996). A structural equation analysis of the wide range assessment of memory and learning in the standardization sample. *Child Neuropsychology, 2,* 39–47.

Burton, D.B., Mittenberg, W., Gold, S., & Drabman, R. (1999). A structural equation analysis of the wide range assessment of memory and learning in a clinical sample. *Child Neuropsychology, 5,* 34–40.

Cohen, R.A. (1993). *The neuropsychology of attention.* New York: Plenum Press.

Cowan, N. (1997). *The development of memory in childhood.* Hove, U.K.: Psychology Press.

Cronwall, D., Wrightson, P., & Waddell, P. (1990). *Head injury: T facts.* London: Oxford University Press.

Cullum, M., Kuck, J., & Ruff, R.M. (1990). Neuropsychological assessment of traumatic brain injury in adults. In E.D. Bigler (Ed.), *Traumatic brain injury* (pp. 129–163). Austin, TX: PRO-ED.

Cytowic, R.E. (1996). *The neurological side of neuropsychology.* Cambridge, MA: MIT Press.

de Jong, P.F. (1998). Working memory deficits of reading disabled children. *Journal of Experimental Child Psychology, 70,* 75–96.

Delis, D.C., Kramer, J.H., Kaplan, E., & Ober, B.A. (1994). *California verbal learning test–children's version.* San Antonio, TX: The Psychological Corporation.

Delis, D.C., Kramer, J.H., Kaplan, J.H., & Kaplan, E. (1987). *California verbal learning test.* San Antonio, TX: The Psychological Corporation.

Dewey, D., Kaplan, B.J., & Crawford, S.G. (1997). Factor structure of the WRAML in children with ADHD or reading disabilities: Further evidence of an attention/concentration factor. *Developmental Neuropsychology, 13,* 501–506.

Diamond, M.C. (1990). Morphological cortical changes as a consequence of learning and experience. In A. Wechsler (Ed.), *Neurobiology of higher cognitive function.* New York: Guilford Press.

Duis, S.S., Summers, M., Sheslow, D.V., Adams, W.V., Robins, P.R., deLancey, E.R., Luerssen, T., & Reed, J. (1998). Differential performances on the wide range assessment of memory and learning of children diagnosed with either reading disorder, attention-deficit/hyperactivity disorder, or traumatic brain injury. *Dissertation Abstracts International: The Sciences & Engineering, 58* (7B), 3919.

Farmer, J.E., Haut, J.S., Williams, J., Kapila, C., Johnstone, B., & Kirk, K.S. (1999). Comprehensive assessment of memory functioning following traumatic brain injury in children. *Developmental Neuropsychology, 15,* 269–289.

Fuster, J.M. (1995). *Memory in the cerebral cortex: An empirical approach to neural networks in the human and nonhuman primate.* Cambridge: MIT Press.

Gillberg, C. (1995). *Clinical child neuropsychiatry.* London: Cambridge University Press.

Gioia, G.A. (1998). Re-examining the factor structure of the wide range assessment of memory and learning: Implications for clinical interpretation. *Assessment, 5,* 127–139.

Golden, C.J., Zillmer, E., & Spiers, M. (1992). *Neuropsychological assessment and intervention.* Springfield, IL: Thomas.

Goldstein, F.C., & Levin, H.S. (1990). Epidemiology of traumatic brain injury: Incidence, clinical characteristics, and risk factors. In E.D. Bigler (Ed.), *Traumatic brain injury* (pp. 51–67). Austin, TX: Pro-ed.

Grossman, I., Kaufman, A.S., Mednitsky, S., Scharff, L., & Dennis, B. (1994). Neurocognitive abilities for a clinically depressed sample versus a matched control group of normal individuals. *Psychiatry Research, 51,* 231–244.

Hill, D.E., Ciesielski, K.T., Sethre-Hofstad, L., Duncan, M.H., & Lorenzi, M. (1997). Visual and verbal short-term memory deficits in childhood leukemia survivors after intrathecal chemotherapy. *Journal of Pediatric Psychology, 22,* 861–870.

Howes, N.L., Bigler, E.D., Burlingame, G.M., & Lawson, J.S. (2003). Memory performance of children with dyslexia: A comparative analysis of theoretical perspectives. *Journal of Learning Disabilities, in press.*

Howes, N.L., Bigler, E.D., Lawson, J.S., & Burlingame, G.M. (1999). Reading disability subtypes and the test of memory and learning. *Archives of Clinical Neuropsychology, 14*(3), 317–339.

Hynd, G., & Obrzut, J. (1981). *Neuropsychological assessment of the school-aged child: Issues and procedures.* New York: Grune & Stratton.

Jensen, A.R., & Figueroa, R. (1975). Forward and backward digit span interaction with race and IQ: Predictions from Jensen's theory. *Journal of Educational Psychology, 67,* 882–893.

Kamphaus, R.W., & Reynolds, C.R. (1987). *Clinical and research application of the K-ABC.* Circle Pines, MN: American Guidance Service.

Kaplan, E. (1996). *Discussant.* Paper presented at the Symposium presented at the annual meeting of the National Association of School Psychologists, Atlanta.

Kaufman, A.S. (1979). *Intelligent testing with the WISC–R.* New York: Wiley.

Kennedy, M.L., & Guilmette, T.J. (1997). The relationship between the WRAML memory screening and general memory indices in a clinical population. *Assessment, 4,* 69–72.

Knight, R.G. (1992). *The neuropsychology of degenerative brain diseases.* Hillsdale, NJ: Erlbaum.

Kolb, B., & Whishaw, I.Q. (1996). *Fundamentals of human neuropsychology* (4th ed.). New York: W.H. Freeman.

Koppitz, E.M. (1977). *The visual aural digit span test.* New York: Grune & Stratton.

Lajiness-O'Neill, R. (1996). *Age at injury as predictor of memory performance in children with traumatic brain injury.* Unpublished Doctoral Dissertation, Brigham Young University, Provo, UT.

Lezak, M.D. (1995). *Neuropsychological assessment* (Third ed.). New York: Oxford University Press.

Lorsbach, T.C., Wilson, S., & Reimer, J.F. (1996). Memory for relevant and irrelevant information: Evidence for deficient inhibitory processes in language/learning disabled children. *Contemporary Educational Psychology, 21,* 447–466.

Mapou, R.L., & Spector, J. (Eds.). (1995). *Clinical neuropsychological assessment.* New York: Plenum Press.

Mayfield, J.W., & Reynolds, C.R. (1997). Black-white differences in memory test performance among children and adolescents. *Archives of Clinical Neuropsychology, 12* (2), 111–122.

McCarthy, D. (1972). *McCarthy scales of children's abilities.* San Antonio, TX: The Psychological Corporation.

Mesulam, M.M. (2000). *Principles of behavioral and cognitive neurology* (2nd ed.). New York: Oxford University Press.

Nation, K., Adams, J.W., Bowyer-Crain, A., & Snowling, M.J. (1999). Working memory deficits in poor comprehenders reflect underlying language impairments. *Journal of Experimental Child Psychology, 73,* 139–158.

Parkin, A.J. (1993). *Memory: Phenomena, experiment and theory.* Oxford: Blackwell.

Pennington, B.F. (1991). *Diagnosing learning disorders: A neuropsychological framework.* New York: Guilford Press.

Phelps, E.A., O'Connor, K.J., Gatenby, J.C., Grillon, C., Gore, J.C., & Davis, M. (2001). Activation of the human amygdala to a cognitive representation of fear. *Nature Neuroscience, 4,* 437–441.

Phelps, L. (1995). Exploratory factor analysis of the WRAML with academically at-risk students. *Journal of Psychoeducational Assessment, 13,* 384–390.

Prigatano, G.P. (1990). Recovery and cognitive retraining after cognitive brain injury. In E.D. Bigler (Ed.), *Traumatic brain injury* (pp. 273–295). Austin, TX: PRO-ED.

Ramsey, M.C., & Reynolds, C.R. (1995). Separate digit tests: A brief history, a literature review, and a reexamination of the factor structure of the Test of Memory and Learning (TOMAL). *Neuropsychology Review, 5,* 151–171.

Reeves, D., & Wedding, D. (1994). *The clinical assessment of memory.* Berlin: Springer, Verlag.

Rey, A. (1958). *L'examen clinique en psychologie.* Paris: Presses Universitaires de France.

Rey, A. (1964). *L'examen clinique en psychologie.* Paris: Presses Universitaires de France.

Reynolds, C.R. (1995). Test bias and the assessment of intelligence and personality. In M. Zeidner (Ed.), *International handbook of personality and intelligence* (pp. 545–573). New York: Plenum Press.

Reynolds, C.R., & Bigler, E.D. (1994a). *Manual for the test of memory and learning.* Austin, TX: PRO-ED.

Reynolds, C.R., & Bigler, E.D. (1994b). *Test of memory and learning.* Austin, TX: PRO-ED.

Reynolds, C.R., & Bigler, E.D. (1996). Factor structure, factor indexes, and other useful statistics for interpretation of the Test of Memory and Learning (TOMAL). *Archives of Clinical Neuropsychology, 11* (1), 29–43.

Reynolds, C.R., & Bigler, E.D. (1997). Clinical neuropsychological assessment of child and adolescent memory with the test of memory and learning. In E. Fletcher-Janzen (Ed.), *Handbook of clinical child neuropsychology* (2 ed., pp. 296–319). New York: Plenum Press.

Rourke, B.P. (1991). *Neuropsychological validation of learning disability subtypes.* New York: Guilford Press.

Scheibel, A.B. (1990). Dendritic correlates of higher cognitive function. In A. Wechsler (Ed.), *Neurobiology of higher cognitive function.* New York: Guilford Press.

Sheslow, D., & Adams, W. (1990). *Wide range assessment of memory and learning.* Wilmington, DE: Jastak Associates.

Snyderman, M., & Rothman, S. (1987). Survey of expert opinion on intelligence and aptitude testing. *American Psychologist, 42,* 137–144.

Stanton, H.C., Reynolds, C.R., & Bigler, E.D. (1995). *PRO-SCORE: Computer scoring system for the test of memory and learning.* Austin, TX: PRO-ED.

Stark, R.E., & McGregor, K.K. (1997). Follow-up study of a right- and left-hemispherectomized child: Implications for localization and impairment of language in children. *Brain and Language, 60,* 222–242.

Swanson, H.L., Ashbacker, M.H., & Lee, C. (1996). Learning-disabled readers' working memory as a function of processing demands. *Journal of Experimental Child Psychology, 61,* 242–275.

Tramontana, M.G., & Hooper, S.R. (1988). *Assessment issues in child neuropsychology.* New York: Plenum Press.

Wechsler, D. (1987). *Wechsler memory scale–revised.* San Antonio: The Psychological Corporation.

Wechsler, D. (1991). *Wechsler intelligence scale for children–third edition (WISC-III).* San Antonio: The Psychological Corporation.

Whitney, S.J. (1996). The performance of children who are depressed on the wide range assessment of memory and learning. New Brunswick, NJ: Rutgers University.

Williams, J., & Haut, J.S. (1995). Differential performances on the WRAML in children and adolescents diagnosed with epilepsy, head injury, and substance abuse. *Developmental Neuropsychology, 11*(2), 201–213.

Woodward, H., & Donders, J. (1998). The performance of children with traumatic head injury on the Wide Range Assessment of Memory and Learning—Screening. *Applied Neuropsychology, 5,* 113–119.

CHAPTER 16

The Attention Battery for Adults:
A Systematic Approach to Assessment

CONNIE C. DUNCAN AND ALLAN F. MIRSKY

The analysis and assessment of normal and disordered attention has been the focus of our research over the past decades (e.g., Duncan, Kosmidis, & Mirsky, 2003; Fedio & Mirsky, 1969; Jones, Duncan, Brouwers, & Mirsky, 1991; Jones, Duncan, Mirsky, Post, & Theodore, 1994; Lansdell & Mirsky, 1964; Levav, Mirsky, Cruz, & Cruz, 1995; Levav et al., 2002; Mirsky, 1987, 1992, 1995; Mirsky, Anthony, Duncan, Ahearn, & Kellam, 1991; Mirsky, Fantie, & Tatman, 1995a; Mirsky et al., 1992; Mirsky, Primac, Ajmone Marsan, Rosvold, & Stevens, 1960; Mirsky, Ingraham, & Kugelmass, 1995b; Mirsky, Pascualvaca, Duncan, & French, 1999; Mirsky, Yardley, Jones, Walsh, & Kendler, 1995c; Rosvold, Mirsky, Sarason, Bransome, & Beck, 1956). In the course of these investigations, it became apparent that disturbances of attention are a prominent symptom of a number of clinical disorders, such as epilepsy, schizophrenia, and closed head injury. Our goal has been to develop an overarching scheme that would encompass these and other disorders of attention and

lead to a better understanding of the pathophysiological bases of these disturbances.

In our studies, we have utilized a set of measures that appear to be effective in identifying specific impairments of attention. These methods comprise an "Attention Battery for Adults," © Duncan & Mirsky, 2002, which helped us to conceptualize five independent components, or "elements," of attention. These elements appear to be supported by, and to correspond approximately to, a set of brain structures underlying attention (Mirsky, 1987; Mirsky et al., 1991, 1995a, 1999). Our neuropsychologically based model of the elements of attention (Mirsky, 1987; Mirsky et al., 1991) has been used to assess attention in the laboratory and the clinic and has been cited often in the research literature. The model has also led to a preliminary nosology of disorders of attention (Mirsky & Duncan, 2001).

In this chapter, we review the tests of the Attention Battery for Adults, the elements of attention, and the nosology of attentional disorders. We present normative data for the Attention Battery for Adults as well as for additional tests that supplement the standard battery. We review selected research findings that illustrate attention impairments in neuropsychi-

---

Acknowledgment: The authors thank Adrienne Elliott, M.A., for her
assistance in preparing the tables and figures.

atric disorders. The chapter concludes with a description of several case studies that highlight the importance of a thorough assessment of attention in a neuropsychological evaluation and illustrate the relationships between specific types of injury to the brain and the ensuing effects on attention.

ATTENTION BATTERY FOR ADULTS: DESCRIPTION OF MEASURES

Table 16.1 presents a summary of the eight standard neuropsychological tests comprising the Attention Battery for Adults. The tests were selected initially because they are thought to tap different aspects of attention (Mirsky, 1987). The battery was administered to a large sample of adults representing a wide spectrum of clinical disorders as well as healthy adult volunteers (Mirsky et al., 1991). The participants represented a broad range of performance on the tests of the battery; this heterogeneity helped to ensure the nec-

essary variance in test scores that would otherwise have been lacking due to the rather limited range of IQs, educational levels, and attentional capacities that characterize healthy volunteers.

ELEMENTS OF ATTENTION

The 13 attention test scores derived from the 8 tests were subjected to principal components analysis and a Varimax rotation. The component loadings from this analysis are presented in Table 16.2. Each test was assigned to a component, or "element," of attention based on the principal components analysis. The highest component loadings within a column were used to interpret the identity of the component. The four components that were identified initially accounted for 80% of the variance in the test scores. In addition, we speculated on the identity of the putative supporting brain structure or structures for each of the elements. The assignment of distinct

TABLE 16.1   Tests of the Attention Battery

Test	Score(s) Used
Stroop Color-Word Interference Test[a] (Stroop, 1935)	Mean number of correct responses in word, color, and color-word trials
Letter Cancellation Test[b] (Talland, 1965)	Mean number of correct cancellations in six sets of trials
Trail Making Test (Reitan & Davison, 1974; Reitan & Wolfson, 1985)	Scores (in sec) on Parts A and B
Digit Symbol Substitution[c] (Wechsler, 1981)	Number correct
Arithmetic[c] (Wechsler, 1981)	Number correct
Digit Span[c] (Wechsler, 1981)	Number correct
Continuous Performance Test (Rosvold, Mirsky, Sarason, Bransome, & Beck, 1956)	Mean percentage of correct responses, visual X and AX tasks
	Mean reaction time, visual X and AX tasks
	Mean number of commission errors, visual X and AX tasks
Wisconsin Card Sorting Test (Grant & Berg, 1948; Heaton, 1981)	Number of categories
	Number of correct responses
	Number of errors achieved in reaching six categories or 128 sorts, whichever is first

Note. From Analysis of the elements of attention: A neuropsychological approach by A.F. Mirsky, B.J. Anthony, C.C. Duncan, M.B. Ahearn, and S.G. Kellam, 1991, *Neuropsychology Review, 2,* p. 114. Copyright 1991 by Plenum Publishing. Adapted with permission.
[a]The number of correct responses for each trial (word, color, color-word) are converted to scaled scores, according to normative data provided by Golden (1978), and then averaged.
[b]The participant has two trials of each of three cancellation tasks: cross out capital letters in a page of random letters; cross out letters preceding and following a double space in a page of random letters; cross out both capital letters *and* letters preceding and following a double space.
[c]Subtests of the Wechsler Adult Intelligence Scale–Revised (1981); scores are scaled for the age of the subject.

TABLE 16.2 Rotated Component Loadings

	Component 1	Component 2	Component 3	Component 4
Digit Span	.22	.19	.02	*.80*
Arithmetic	.17	.13	.28	*.72*
Digit Symbol Substitution	*.82*[a]	.07	.12	.26
Stroop test	*.69*	.24	.27	.29
Letter Cancellation Test	*.81*	.17	.22	.18
Trail Making, Part A	*.70*	.21	.43	−.06
Trail Making, Part B	*.63*	.34	.45	.14
CPT % correct responses	.32	.25	*.86*	.11
CPT % commission errors	.33	.27	*.83*	.11
CPT reaction time	.18	−.10	*.81*	.16
WCST # categories	.22	*.89*	.16	.08
WCST % correct	.17	*.94*	.09	.17
WCST # errors	.17	*.95*	.09	.18
Variance explained (%)	24.1	23.3	21.0	11.5
Proposed identity of factor	Perceptual-motor speed	Flexibility	Vigilance	Numerical-mnemonic
Element of attention	Focus-execute	Shift	Sustain	Encode

Note. From Analysis of the elements of attention: A neuropsychological approach by A.F. Mirsky, B.J. Anthony, C.C. Duncan, M.B. Ahearn, and S.G. Kellam, 1991, *Neuropsychology Review, 2,* p. 117. Copyright 1991 by Plenum Publishing. Adapted with permission.

[a]The highest component loadings within a column (shown in bold italics) were used to interpret the identity of the component.

cerebral structures in support of the different attentional elements is meant to be a relative specialization rather than an absolute one, as the attentional system is to some extent equipotential. Thus, healthy components of the system may partially compensate for the dysfunction of injured components.

The results of the principal components analysis revealed distinct components of attentional performance that form the basis of the multi-element model. The first component comprises loadings from four tests of focusing and perceptual-motor speed, namely, the Digit Symbol Substitution, Stroop, Letter Cancellation, and Trail Making tests. This component appears to represent a visual-perceptual ability to scan stimulus material for predetermined targets, and an ability to make verbal (Stroop) or skilled manual (Digit Symbol, Letter Cancellation, Trail Making) responses. Hence, the designation *focus-execute* for this component is an effort to encompass both aspects of the performance required by these tasks. We have proposed that structures within the inferior parietal lobule and superior temporal gyrus, and parts of the corpus striatum, support this aspect of attentive behavior (Battig, Rosvold, & Mishkin, 1960; Heilman, Watson, Valenstein, & Damasio, 1983; Hermann & Wyler, 1988; Mirsky et al., 1991; Pandya & Yeterian, 1985).

The second component to emerge has loadings from the measures on a single test—the Wisconsin Card Sorting Test—and has been labeled *shift*. It appears to reflect the abstract ability to shift in an adaptive and flexible manner from attending to one aspect or feature of stimuli to another aspect. The dorsolateral prefrontal cortex and anterior cingulate

gyrus are thought to support this attentional function (Bakay Pragay, Mirsky, & Nakamura, 1987; Milner, 1963).

The third component, designated *sustain,* has high loadings on the performance measures derived from the visual Continuous Performance Test (CPT). Both the X and AX versions of this test, which vary in level of task demands, require visual sustained attention and yield measures of performance accuracy, impulsive errors, and reaction time. The sustain element represents the capacity to maintain an attentional focus—a vigilant attitude—for an appreciable period of time. Our research (Bakay Pragay, Mirsky, Fullerton, Oshima, & Arnold, 1975; Bakay Pragay, Mirsky, Ray, Turner, & Mirsky, 1978; Mirsky, Bakay Pragay, & Harris, 1977; Mirsky & Oshima, 1973; Mirsky & van Buren, 1965; Ray, Mirsky, & Bakay Pragay, 1982), as well as that of others (e.g., Aston-Jones, Rajkowski, & Cohen, 1999; Yingling & Skinner, 1975) promotes the view that structures within the brainstem reticular formation and parts of the midline thalamus are key elements supporting this component of attentive behavior.

The visual sustained attention tests (CPT-X and CPT-AX), on which the initial principal components analysis was based, comprise letter stimuli presented in quasi-random order at the rate of one/sec. Subjects are instructed to press for the letter *X* in the X task, and for X only if it follows the letter *A* in the AX task. Allowable response time for a correct response is 700 msec from stimulus onset. In both tasks, the probability of a target is .20, and 76 targets (X trials or AX sequences) are presented. Subjects receive sufficient practice to ensure that they understand the task requirements.

The fourth component of attention, labeled *encode,* loads on two tests involved in manipulation of numbers: Digit Span and Arithmetic. This attentional element appears to reflect the capacity to hold stimulus information in memory briefly, to allow performance of a mental operation on the information. Our usage of encode is equivalent to the term *working memory.* Based on behavioral and electrophysiological studies (Adey, 1969; Blakemore, Iversen, & Zangwill, 1972; Mishkin, 1978; Scoville & Milner, 1957), we have proposed that the encode component is supported by brain structures in and around the anterior hippocampus, temporal cortex, and amygdala.

Not present in the table are data relating to a fifth element of attention, *stabilize.* The stabilize element is thought to reflect the consistency or stability of response speed over trials in a task of sustained attention. This element emerges when the *variance* of reaction time to correctly detected targets on the CPT is entered into the principal components analysis (Mirsky et al., 1995a; Tatman, 1992). Our assumption is that this element is supported in part by the same cerebral structures that support the sustain element, most likely the frontal-brainstem axis (Goldberg, Bilder, Hughes, Antin, & Mattis, 1989); however, the precise assignment remains to be determined.

CHARACTERISTICS OF AN ATTENTION BATTERY FOR ADULTS

We thus view attention as a process involving five (or more) independent elements. The results of a number of other investigations, stimulated in part by a preliminary description of the model (Mirsky, 1987), have provided varying degrees of confirmation of our findings. Since the analysis of attentional elements was first published, the component structure of the Attention Battery for Adults has been replicated by a number of other investigators (Kelly, 2000; Kendler et al., 1991; Kremen, Seidman, Faraone, Pepple, & Tsuang, 1992; Pogge, Stokes, & Harvey, 1994; Steinhauer et al., 1991; Tatman, 1992).

We submit that the preferred means of assessing attention involves the use of a variety of tests, with the following characteristics: (a) They measure different aspects or components of attention, thus recognizing that attention is not a unitary brain process, but comprises highly articulated functions; (b) the validity and reliability of the tests have been established; (c) the tests assess independent elements of attention, as supported by statistical analysis of their component structure; (d) normative data for each test are available, preferably based on groups of different ages and educational and socio-economic (and/or cultural) backgrounds; and (e) data exist for persons with diverse neuropsychiatric diagnoses.

SUPPLEMENTS TO THE ATTENTION BATTERY FOR ADULTS

One of the considerations in the use of CPT, both in research studies and in clinical practice, concerns possible ceiling effects on performance. The X and AX versions of the CPT are frequently performed without error by healthy participants as well as those in some clinical populations. In order to make the tasks more challenging, that is, to "raise the ceiling," a number of modifications of the original task have been implemented. These are described in the following sections. It should be noted that the first systematic efforts to increase the difficulty level of the CPT were reported by Stammeyer (1961) and by Wohlberg and Kornetsky (1973). In these investigations, either visual distracters (simultaneous photic stimulation) or auditory distracters (noise delivered to the participant via earphones) were used. Patients with active (Stammeyer, 1961) or remitted (Wohlberg & Kornetsky, 1973) schizophrenia were significantly more likely to be impaired by distraction than healthy controls or patients with neurotic disorders, even when the groups were matched on performance on a standard version of the CPT. These results suggest that manipulations of the difficulty level of the task might reveal deficits that simpler tasks would miss. This is discussed in the section "Degraded Stimulus CPTs."

Auditory CPTs

Research published subsequent to our original proposal for the Attention Battery for Adults has revealed the value of measuring sustained attention in the auditory and the visual modality. We observed that patients with absence epilepsy were distinguished reliably from patients with other types of epilepsy and healthy volunteers by their performance on an auditory version of the CPT (Duncan, 1988; Mirsky, 1992). Our studies of patients with schizophrenia also showed that probands and their first-degree relatives are more impaired on auditory than visual tests of sustained attention (Mirsky et al., 1992, 1995c). Similar results, for example, greater deficits on auditory than visual tests of sustained attention, were reported recently in fetal alcohol-affected adults (Connor, Streissguth, Sampson, Bookstein, & Barr, 1999). Thus, the accumulating evidence supports the assessment of sustained attention in the visual and auditory modalities.

The auditory CPT tasks used in the Attention Battery for Adults comprise either pure tones or spoken letters. In the

CPT-X Tones task, the stimuli are 640, 1000, or 1600 Hz, with the high-pitched, 1600-Hz tone designated as the target. In the Letters version of the auditory CPT-X, the stimuli comprise spoken letters of the alphabet, and the target is the letter *O*. The "AX" equivalent of the Letters CPT requires responding to "O" only if it follows the letter *L*. As in the visual CPT, stimuli in the auditory tasks are presented at a rate of one/sec, with targets occurring with a probability of .20. Task durations for the auditory CPT tasks are identical to comparable versions of the visual CPT.

The reason for the apparently greater vulnerability of the auditory than the visual attention system in some disorders is unknown. What is known, however, is that some of the auditory relay nuclei in the brainstem (i.e., inferior colliculus, superior olivary complex) are especially sensitive to the effects of neonatal asphyxia and can be damaged permanently by a prolonged or difficult labor and delivery (Myers, 1969, 1971). In addition, chronic ear infections during childhood may damage auditory structures and compromise the ability to process auditory information. Recent studies indicate that over 25% of preschool children in the United States suffer from otitis media, and that over one million children have hearing losses ranging from mild to moderate or greater (Lanphear, Byrd, Auinger, & Hall, 1997; Lee, Gomez-Marin, & Lee, 1996). These considerations lend support to the notion that the brain systems supporting auditory and visual attention may possess distinct vulnerabilities, and that the auditory "attention system" may be the more vulnerable of the two.

Degraded Stimulus CPTs

A number of papers have reported the use of a degraded stimulus version of the CPT. In this task, the perceptibility of the stimulus material is reduced by using frosted glass to obscure the stimulus display or by decreasing the density of pixels in a computer-generated display of the stimuli (Nuechterlein, Parasuraman, & Qiyuan, 1983; Mirsky, 1996; Mirsky et al., 1995c). The rationale for using a Degraded Stimulus CPT is that it requires more effort than standard versions. Whereas compensatory mechanisms might mask deficits in attention on a less demanding task, such mechanisms might falter under more challenging conditions. Increasing task demands by reducing the perceptibility of the stimuli could thereby unmask impairments in sustained attention. Some reports suggest that the Degraded Stimulus CPT may be more sensitive to attention disturbances in schizophrenia than other versions (e.g., Mirsky, 1996; Mirsky et al., 1995c).

The "degrading" in the auditory CPT is accomplished by presenting the letter stimuli against a background of noise, thereby decreasing the perceptibility of the spoken letters (Gabbay & Duncan, 1999). Healthy adults are moderately less accurate on the degraded than on the nondegraded versions of the CPT.

NOTES ON APPLICATIONS OF THE ATTENTION BATTERY FOR ADULTS

In the sections that follow, we present normative data for several versions of the CPT, both visual and auditory, as well as a method of assessing or "titrating" the level of effort at which sustained attention may falter. This modular approach differs from most commercially available versions of the CPT, which assess attentional capacity on the basis of a single, long task.

Normative Data

In Table 16.3, we present normative data from a group of 180 healthy adults ranging in age from 16 to 94 years of age. Demographic data are presented along with measures derived from the tests of the Attention Battery for Adults. In addition, normative data for five versions of the CPT, including three auditory tasks that supplement the original battery, are provided in Table 16.4. Shown are CPT data for a group of 111 healthy adult men between the ages of 20 and 35 (Gabbay et al., 1999).

Titrating Impairment in Sustained Attention in the Attention Battery for Adults: A Modular Approach

In clinical applications, we routinely administer several versions of the visual and auditory CPT. We begin with the visual X task, continue with the AX task; and, if the subject is still performing within normal limits, conclude our assessment of visual sustained attention with the Degraded Stimulus task. As can be inferred from the normative data in Table 16.3, the AX task is somewhat more difficult for healthy participants than the X task (lower accuracy). The visual Degraded CPT-X is the most difficult of the three visual tasks (Table 16.4).

When the visual tasks have been administered, auditory testing is commenced. We begin with the Tones task, follow it with the Letters task, and conclude with the Degraded Letters task. Healthy controls typically perform somewhat better on the Tones than the Letters CPT. The Degraded Letters task is the most difficult test of auditory sustained attention, yielding mean accuracy scores of approximately 88%.

TABLE 16.3 Attention Battery: Normative Data Stratified by Age

Age (years)	16–24	25–34	35–44	45–54	55–64	65–74	75–84	85–94
n	32	48	23	11	17	27	16	6
Education (years)								
Mean	14.7	15.9	16.6	15.7	15.6	16.3	15.6	13.0
SD	1.5	1.9	2.2	2.1	3.2	3.2	3.9	4.6
WAIS-R Full Scale IQ								
Mean	116.5	114.7	121.4	117.2	121.3	122.1	118.4	101.8
SD	12.5	10.4	10.7	14.0	15.9	13.7	15.0	12.5
Attention Battery Variables								
Digit Span								
Mean	12.2	11.8	12.0	12.3	12.6	11.8	12.0	9.0
SD	2.4	2.5	1.8	3.4	3.6	2.6	3.2	2.2
Arithmetic								
Mean	12.5	11.3	13.1	12.3	11.4	11.5	10.9	10.0
SD	2.7	2.0	2.3	1.4	3.7	2.9	2.8	2.1
Digit Symbol Substitution								
Mean	12.7	12.5	12.3	12.3	12.4	13.1	10.5	9.2
SD	2.3	2.6	2.2	2.9	2.7	3.1	1.9	1.7
Stroop test								
Mean	52.3	50.7	47.9	51.1	50.8	51.3	43.5	39.3
SD	6.3	7.4	7.2	5.9	6.4	8.0	7.5	5.1
Letter Cancellation Test								
Mean (6 trials)	81.3	80.0	72.8	69.6	62.1	54.9	42.7	32.2
SD	11.5	11.0	11.2	11.9	17.6	11.4	11.6	5.1
Trail Making, Part A								
Mean	24.2	27.3	26.8	28.0	31.3	42.7	46.1	62.2
SD	7.5	11.4	5.7	8.5	19.4	23.1	16.7	17.5
Trail Making, Part B								
Mean	48.9	53.6	54.3	61.3	74.2	114.9	120.4	168.8
SD	14.7	19.0	15.5	21.9	46.9	107.6	63.5	60.8
CPT-X % correct responses								
Mean	98.9	99.1	99.8	97.8	98.7	96.6	96.2	92.8
SD	1.3	1.6	0.4	3.0	2.8	6.1	4.5	8.4
CPT-AX % correct responses								
Mean	95.0	95.6	97.3	91.6	94.9	94.2	90.3	83.2
SD	5.8	4.7	4.1	17.9	6.1	6.8	9.3	14.0
CPT-X % commission errors								
Mean	0.37	0.36	0.20	0.24	0.29	0.26	0.26	0.44
SD	0.36	0.51	0.25	0.32	0.49	0.40	0.34	0.34
CPT-AX % commission errors								
Mean	1.05	0.81	0.37	0.17	0.26	0.46	0.49	1.11
SD	1.14	1.15	0.60	0.31	0.37	0.59	0.41	0.76
CPT-X reaction time								
Mean	426.3	428.6	386.3	450.0	390.8	420.7	440.0	453.3
SD	51.9	53.3	31.4	62.3	43.3	43.9	62.2	48.9
CPT-AX reaction time								
Mean	404.2	431.0	377.0	443.3	386.2	400.9	416.7	410.0
SD	80.1	64.9	51.8	85.8	65.0	47.9	55.8	79.4
WCST # categories								
Mean	5.6	5.9	5.6	5.8	5.1	5.0	4.3	3.2
SD	1.0	0.5	1.3	0.6	1.6	1.5	1.7	3.0
WCST # correct								
Mean	67.3	69.0	67.0	68.4	71.6	73.1	74.8	63.0
SD	6.8	7.4	9.3	2.8	11.1	10.4	9.8	23.4
WCST # errors								
Mean	18.4	14.8	19.3	19.5	32.7	31.7	40.6	59.0
SD	18.3	10.4	15.8	16.7	24.7	20.7	18.0	28.8

Note. From Assessment of attention across the lifespan by A.F. Mirsky, B.D. Fantie, and J.E. Tatman, 1995. In R.L. Mapou and J. Spector (Eds.), *Clinical neuropsychological assessment: A cognitive approach* (pp. 36–37). New York: Plenum Publishing. Copyright 1995 by Plenum Publishing. Adapted with permission.

TABLE 16.4 CPT: Normative Data

Task	Correct Responses (%)	Commission Errors (%)	Reaction Time (msec)
Visual			
CPT-X	99 (2.3)	0.2 (1.0)	374 (46)
CPT-X Degraded	86 (11.3)	2.1 (6.0)	506 (60)
Auditory			
CPT-X Tones	97 (6.0)	0.9 (5.4)	391 (56)
CPT-X Letters	94 (6.4)	0.9 (3.5)	482 (55)
CPT-X Degraded Letters	88 (10.6)	1.0 (3.3)	534 (51)

Note. N = 111 men, aged 18–35 (M = 27.6 yrs). The values represent means; values enclosed in parentheses represent *SD*s. The data are from Sustained attention and performance: Effects of sex, season, and menstrual cycle phase by F.H. Gabbay and C.C. Duncan, 1999, Report to the Department of the Army, U.S. Department of Defense. Adapted with permission.

A PROPOSED NOSOLOGY OF ATTENTION DISORDERS

Impairment of attention—in contrast to normal fluctuations— is a common symptom of neuropsychiatric disorder. As such, the various etiologies of impaired attention merit an attempt at systematic classification (Mirsky, 1995). The nosology of disorders of attention that we have proposed categorizes the possible etiologies of impaired attention (i.e., genetic, metabolic, environmental, etc.). Moreover, it describes the type of attentional impairment (to the extent that it has been characterized) for the various causes. Our ultimate goal is to create a framework for classifying all disorders of attention in relation to a model of the brain system supporting the elements of attention. A nosology of disorders of attention is also useful in emphasizing that the symptom of impaired attention may stem from a number of causes that comprise diverse etiologies.

Table 16.5 summarizes an initial proposal for a nosology of attention disorders (Mirsky et al., 2001). For each etiology—familial/genetic, metabolic, environmental, and "other" (including head injuries)—the specific attentional elements that have been found to be impaired in each disorder are noted. In many instances, the attention disorder may stem from more than one etiology, for example, genetic *and* en-

TABLE 16.5 Impaired Attentional Elements in Four Categories of Etiology

Etiology	Attentional Element				
	Encode	Focus/ Execute	Shift	Sustain	Stabilize
Familial/Genetic					
Absence, other IGE[a]	YES	?	YES	YES	YES
Schizophrenia[b]	YES	YES	YES	YES	YES
Autism[c]	?	?	YES	NO	?
Narcolepsy	YES/?	YES/?	YES/?	YES/?	YES/?
ADD, ADHD	?	YES	YES	YES	YES
Metabolic					
Phenylketonuria	?	?	?	YES	?
Uremia	?	YES	?	YES	?
Environmental					
Malnutrition	NO	YES	YES	NO	NO
Lead Intoxication	NO	NO	NO	YES	YES
Pregnancy/Birth Complications	?	?	?	?	?
Fetal Alcohol Syndrome/ Effect	?	YES	?	YES	YES
Neurocysticercosis/Other Parasitic Infections	YES	YES	YES	YES	NO
Lack of Intellectual Stimulation	?	?	YES	NO	NO
Other					
Head Injury	?	?	YES	YES	?
Brain Infections/Tumors	?	?	?	YES	?
Sleep/Breathing Disorders	?	?	?	YES	?
Eating Disorders	?	YES	?	NO	NO

Note. From A nosology of disorders of attention by A.F. Mirsky and C.C. Duncan, 2001. In J. Wasserstein, L.E. Wolf, & F.F. LeFever (Eds.), *Adult attention deficit disorder: Brain mechanisms and life outcomes* (p. 22). New York: Annals of the New York Academy of Sciences (Vol. 931). Copyright 2001 by New York Academy of Sciences. Adapted with permission.
[a]IGE = idiopathic generalized epilepsies.
[b]These data were derived from a sample of persons from a rural area of Ireland with limited education and therefore may not be representative of patients with higher levels of education.
[c]Participants with autism were classified as high-functioning.

vironmental. This is a preliminary classification, based primarily on research we have conducted or in which we have collaborated. Although preliminary, we believe that the proposed nosology has heuristic value.

THE ATTENTION BATTERY FOR ADULTS IN CLINICAL RESEARCH

The concept of an Attention Battery for Adults originated from a comparison of the cognitive capacities of patients with seizure disorders. In these studies (see the following section), it was apparent that disorders differing in etiology had unique attention profiles. Thus, the patients with focal disorders, which were presumed to be the result of cortical injury or disease, faltered in tasks that required encoding information or shifting attentional sets. These skills were relatively spared in patients with idiopathic (of unknown origin, presumably genetic), generalized seizures. In contrast, the latter group had difficulty in tasks requiring sustained attention. The fact that unique profiles of performance were associated with distinct etiologies provided a stimulus to evaluate attentional capacities in other clinical populations. The aim is to enhance our understanding of the disorders and support efforts to discover better therapies (Mirsky et al., 2001).

Attention Profiles in Seizure Disorders

We used the Attention Battery for Adults to assess the attentional capacities in individuals with different types of seizure disorders. The attentional profiles of individuals with absence seizures, complex partial seizures, and healthy controls were compared (Mirsky et al., 1991). Because the two groups of patients with seizure disorders have distinct types of cerebral pathology, we anticipated that their patterns of attentional deficit would differ as well. The pathology in the absence group is considered to involve subcortical structures in the midline thalamus-brainstem reticular formation axis (Gloor, 1988; Mirsky, Duncan, & Myslobodsky, 1986; Penfield & Jasper, 1954); whereas the pathology in the complex-partial group has been shown to involve frontotemporal cortical regions (Penfield et al., 1954).

Our results showed that in comparison to the other groups, the absence seizure group's performance was significantly worse on measures of sustained attention, whereas the complex partial seizure group was more impaired on tests of the focus-execute and shift elements of attention. These results, illustrated in Figure 16.1, provide support for our model of the elements of attention (Mirsky et al., 1991). Specifically, the performance of patients with absence seizures was most

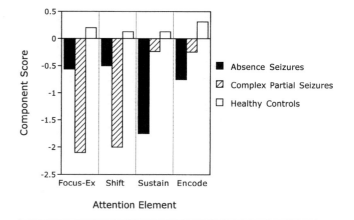

Figure 16.1 Mean component scores extracted by principal components analysis of scores on attention tests for patients with a generalized seizure disorder (absence), patients with a focal seizure disorder (complex partial), and healthy matched controls. From "Analysis of the Elements of Attention: A Neuropsychological Approach," by A.F. Mirsky, B.J. Anthony, C.C. Duncan, M.B. Ahearn, and S.G. Kellam, 1991, *Neuropsychology Review,* 2, p. 134. Copyright 1991 by Plenum Publishing. Adapted with permission.

impaired on the CPT, which is thought to depend on the integrity of the subcortical structures in the midline thalamus-brainstem reticular formation axis. In contrast, those with complex partial seizures showed maximal impairment on tasks thought to require integrity of frontotemporal cortical regions (i.e., Digit Symbol Substitution, Letter Cancellation, Trail Making, and Wisconsin Card Sorting tests).

Attention Profiles in Patients with Schizophrenia

We administered the Attention Battery for Adults to a sample of patients with a diagnosis of schizophrenia, their first-degree relatives, and a group of healthy controls. The results, displayed in Figure 16.2, indicate that the patients performed less well than the other two groups on all of the elements of attention. Moreover, the most significant differences among groups were found on the focus/execute and sustain elements (Mirsky, 1996). It is also noteworthy that the scores of the nondisordered relatives on the focus/execute, shift, and encode elements were between those of the probands and the healthy controls. This finding, of attention impairment in relatives of probands, has also been observed in other studies (e.g., Asarnow et al., 2002; Cornblatt, Obuchowski, Roberts, Pollack, & Erlenmeyer-Kimling, 1999; Hans et al., 1999; Mirsky et al., 1995b, 1995c). Impaired attention in nondisordered relatives is thought to be relevant to the familial transmission of the schizophrenic disorder. Moreover, the fact that the deficit in schizophrenia is seen in several attentional elements is consistent with the view that the pathophysiology

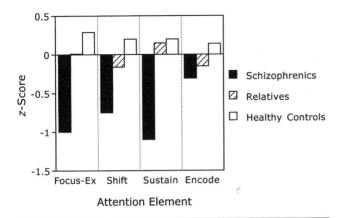

Figure 16.2   Mean *z*-scores on four elements of attention for patients with schizophrenia, their first-degree relatives, and healthy controls. From "Familial Factors in the Impairment of Attention in Schizophrenia: Data from Ireland, Israel, and the District of Columbia," by A.F. Mirsky, 1996. In S. Matthysse, D. Levy, J. Kagan, & D.F. Benes (Eds.), *Psychopathology: The evolving science of mental disorders* (p. 386). Cambridge, England: Cambridge University Press. Copyright 1996 by Cambridge University Press. Adapted with permission.

of schizophrenia may not be confined to a specific region of the brain, but may represent a more generalized disorder.

CASE STUDIES USING THE ATTENTION BATTERY FOR ADULTS

We present here four case studies, differing in diagnostic and clinical questions. The patients described were evaluated either as part of a research protocol (Case CW) or as referrals from treating physicians following motor vehicle accidents (Cases LP and NQ) or possible incipient dementia (Case OP). They were chosen to illustrate the utility of the Attention Battery for Adults in evaluating individuals, as opposed to comparing groups in research studies.

Case CW

The case of CW has been documented extensively (Valenstein, 1986; Mirsky, & Rosvold, 1990); however, the results of CW's neuropsychological evaluation provide a clear illustration of the specificity of attentional deficits. CW, the daughter of a wealthy businessman, was hospitalized for schizophrenia during her second year of study at an Ivy League medical school. After more than 10 years of unsuccessful psychiatric treatment, including lengthy hospitalizations at private sanataria, a prefrontal lobotomy was recommended. CW underwent the first of two surgeries in 1946, and seven months later, the second one, in which the incision in the prefrontal lobes was more posterior to the first. Within a short time, she

was able to leave the institution but required extensive rehabilitation and constant care thereafter.

At the age of 72, CW was evaluated at NIMH. She had a comprehensive series of tests, including a PET scan, a CT scan, and a neuropsychological assessment. Figure 16.3 presents two representative sections of her CT scan and those of a healthy control woman. The CT scan documents the extensive destruction of frontal lobe tissue following the two lobotomies.

CW's performance on the neuropsychological tests provides a striking example of the specificity of her attentional impairment. Her scores on the tests that assess the focus/execute, sustain, and encode elements of attention were in the expected or mildly impaired range at worst. In contrast, her performance on the Wisconsin Card Sorting Test, which measures the ability to shift attention, was severely impaired (0 categories; > 80 perseverative errors). This element of attention is thought to be supported by frontal lobe structures (e.g., Milner, 1963). Whereas it is likely that CW's perfor-

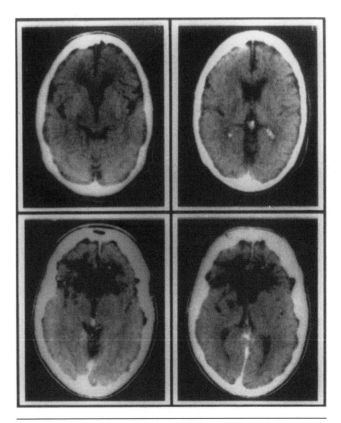

Figure 16.3   Two representative sections from a CT scan of a 73-year-old healthy female (top row) and CW (bottom row). CW's scan shows evidence of massive damage to the prefrontal areas and increased ventricular size. Evidence of the first (more anterior) and second (more posterior) prefrontal lobotomies can be seen in the more anterior and posterior darkened regions, which indicate tissue loss.

mance in all domains of attention was below expected premorbid levels, her ability to shift attention was markedly worse.

Case LP

This 38-year-old woman, a successful patent attorney with degrees in engineering and law, was injured in a motor vehicle collision. Following her injury, she reported a number of symptoms, including dizziness, nausea, memory problems, sleep disturbance, mild depression, and a "shorter temper." Although the dizziness and nausea resolved within six to seven months, the majority of her symptoms persist to some degree. Approximately two and a half years after her injury, she was referred for neuropsychological testing to evaluate the nature and severity of any residual brain dysfunction.

LP was administered a battery of neuropsychological tests, including the Attention Battery for Adults. On the tests comprising the encode, focus/execute, and shift elements of attention, LP scored within normal limits, with many of her scores in the above average to superior range. On measures of the ability to sustain attention, as assessed by visual and auditory versions of the CPT, LP's performance was mixed. With one exception, her scores on the visual X and AX tasks were within normal limits. The exception was in the accuracy of her performance on the AX task, which was mildly impaired. On auditory tasks, however, she performed much more poorly, showing moderate impairment on measures of the accuracy and speed of performance.

On the basis of these and other test data (Hopkins Verbal Learning Test; Spreen-Benton Sentence Repetition Test), it was concluded that LP exhibits significant impairment in the processing of auditory information—both in sustaining attention to auditory stimuli and in recalling information presented in the auditory modality.

LP's considerable strengths in many areas of intellectual functioning may have served to compensate, to some extent, for her impaired auditory processing capacities. However, given the demands of her highly complex occupation, the additional effort required to maintain concentration, and perform at an acceptable level, must produce considerable strain and fatigue. Recognition of her diminished capacity is evident in her remarks that she is no longer able to deal with complex technology. In view of this, it is not surprising that she experiences depression and frustration—the latter manifest as a "shorter temper."

In some instances, impaired attention of the type seen in LP following a closed head injury may be ameliorated with the use of stimulant medication. A dramatic example of such amelioration is seen in the following case study.

Case NQ

NQ is a 44-year-old supervisory employee at a large research hospital, who reported difficulties in concentration, memory, learning, and "focusing" consequent to an automobile accident four months earlier. She stated that her cognitive difficulties have caused significant problems at work. Her physician had prescribed a course of methylphenidate, which she said had been helpful in alleviating her symptoms.

NQ was referred for neuropsychological testing to assess the level of her cognitive functions. Her performance on the Attention Battery for Adults was generally unremarkable, and her performance on the CPT was superior. In an effort to ascertain whether the stimulant medication had improved her capacity for sustained attention, the CPT was readministered following withdrawal of methylphenidate. Two weeks separated the two tests; and at the time of the second test, she had been medication-free for several days.

Her scores on and off medication are presented in Table 16.6. NQ's performance on the CPT was dramatically affected by withdrawal of methylphenidate: there was a substantial reduction in the accuracy of her performance accompanied by marked slowing of her responses. Her scores on the CPT fell from the superior range to the moderately impaired range on visual tasks, to the severely impaired range on auditory tasks. It is apparent from her performance on these tests that the medication had disguised a significant deficit in sustained attention in general and in auditory sustained attention in particular. We recently showed that auditory processing is particularly compromised following closed head injury (Duncan et al., 2003).

Case OP

This 73-year-old male was referred by his psychiatrist because of increasing difficulties managing his extended family's finances and consequent concerns about incipient dementia. Highly educated, with a Ph.D. degree in history and a degree in law, he had retired after a successful career as a professor and an attorney. OP had been told by a neurologist that a recent MRI scan revealed that he had the "brain of a much older man"; however, he reported no obvious changes in concentration or memory.

In the neuropsychological evaluation, OP showed no impairment on tasks requiring the capacity to sustain attention in either the visual or auditory modalities. His performance, including measures of response latency, was in the expected range for 30- to 40-year olds. Similarly, there were no deficits in his capacities to encode or focus/execute: His scores on the tests in these domains of attention were uniformly in the

TABLE 16.6 NQ's Performance on Different Versions of the Visual and Auditory CPT On and Off Methylphenidate

Task	Correct Responses (%)			Late Responses (%)[a]			Reaction Time (msec)		
	On	Off	Δ[b]	On	Off	Δ	On	Off	Δ
Visual									
CPT-X	100	70	−30	0	24	+24	360	630	+270
CPT-AX	95	79	−16	1	13	+12	300	550	+250
CPT-X Degraded	98	44	−54	0	48	+48	470	690	+220
Auditory									
CPT-X Tones	97	59	−36	0	29	+29	340	710	+370
CPT-X Letters	96	44	−52	2	46	+44	480	660	+180

[a]Responses with latencies of 701–900 msec.
[b]Change in performance after medication was withdrawn.

average to superior range. His scores on the Trail Making Test were also better than expected. The sole exception to his excellent attention profile was on the Wisconsin Card Sorting Test: He was unable to shift from color to form as the sorting principle, as required by the test protocol. From his comments, it was apparent that he was trying to sort the cards on the basis of complicated strategies, rather than on the simpler basis of form.

In view of his excellent performance on most of the tests in the Attention Battery for Adults, as well as on tests of verbal and visual-spatial memory, it was concluded that there was no evidence of a generalized dementia. However, it could be argued that his impaired ability to shift concepts seen in the Wisconsin Card Sorting Test is an early sign of frontal lobe or other anterior cortical compromise. Such a conclusion would be consistent with the MRI finding reported to OP (presumed to be cerebral atrophy). The Wisconsin Card Sorting Test is age sensitive (see Table 16.3), and the mean number of categories achieved for healthy individuals in their early 70s is 5.0. Nevertheless, this highly specific deficit may suggest an early dementing process, which is difficult to detect using neuropsychological testing. OP's attention profile suggests that his superior cognitive skills may allow him to compensate for an incipient loss of function in most, but not all, attentional functions. Follow-up evaluations to monitor his progress were recommended.

CONCLUDING REMARKS

We have presented a number of considerations that argue for the systematic assessment of attention as an essential component of a neuropsychological evaluation. Our model assumes that attention is not a monolithic concept, but an integrated group of behaviors dependent on a brain system that incorporates brainstem, limbic, and cortical structures. Although attention is a complex hypothetical construct, its elements are dissociable. We have reviewed the neuropsychologically based elements of attention, derived from principal components analysis. Based on the several replications of the component structure and the numerous references to the "elements" of attention in the literature, the clinical validity and usefulness of the Attention Battery for Adults have been demonstrated. We believe the battery to be a robust assessment tool and an essential part of any neuropsychological evaluation. Moreover, the valid assessment of other cognitive processes, including language and memory, is dependent upon the prior demonstration of intact attentional processes.

We have proposed a method for the systematic assessment of attention in clinical and research settings and have presented normative data for the Attention Battery for Adults across the adult lifespan. We have also illustrated ways of augmenting the tests in the original battery and offered a sampling of illustrative case studies. The nosology of disorders of attention that we have outlined can serve to alert the clinician and researcher to the numerous etiologies that can lead to impairment of one or more of the elements of attention.

Clinicians who fail to assess attention properly may miss a critical feature of their patient's symptoms, and thereby deny the patient the opportunity for appropriate and effective treatment. The Attention Battery for Adults provides one approach to preventing this omission.

REFERENCES

Adey, W.R. (1969). Spectral analysis of EEG data from animals and man during alerting, orienting and discriminative responses. In C.R. Evans & T.B. Mulholland (Eds.), *Attention and neurophysiology: An international conference* (pp. 194–229). London: Butterworth.

Asarnow, R.F., Nuechterlein, K.H., Asamen, J., Fogelson, D., Subotnik, K.L., Zaucha, K., & Guthrie, D. (2002). Neurocognitive functioning and schizophrenia spectrum disorders can be independent expressions of familial liability for schizophrenia in community control children: The UCLA family study. *Schizophrenia Research, 54,* 111–120.

Aston-Jones, G., Rajkowski, J., & Cohen, J. (1999). Role of locus coeruleus in attention and behavioral flexibility. *Biological Psychiatry, 46,* 1309–1320.

Bakay Pragay, E., Mirsky, A.F., Fullerton, B.C., Oshima, H., & Arnold, S.W. (1975). Effect of electrical stimulation of the brain on visually controlled (attentive) behavior in the *Macaca mulatta. Experimental Neurology, 49,* 203–220.

Bakay Pragay, E., Mirsky, A.F., Ray, C.L., Turner, D.F., & Mirsky, C.V. (1978). Neuronal activity in the brain stem reticular formation during performance of a "go-no go" visual attention task in the monkey. *Experimental Neurology, 60,* 83–95.

Battig, K., Rosvold, H.E., & Mishkin, M. (1960). Comparison of the effects of frontal and caudate lesions on delayed response and alternation in monkeys. *Journal of Comparative and Physiological Psychology, 53,* 400–404.

Blakemore, C., Iversen, S.D., & Zangwill, O.L. (1972). Brain functions. *Annual Review of Psychology, 23,* 413–456.

Connor, P.D., Streissguth, A.P., Sampson, P.D., Bookstein, F.L., & Barr, H.J.M. (1999). Individual differences in auditory and visual attention among fetal alcohol-affected adults. *Alcoholism: Clinical and Experimental Research, 23,* 1395–1402.

Cornblatt, B., Obuchowski, M., Roberts, S., Pollack, S., & Erlenmeyer-Kimling, L. (1999). Cognitive and behavioral precursors of schizophrenia. *Development and Psychopathology, 11,* 487–508.

Duncan, C.C. (1988). Application of event-related brain potentials to the analysis of interictal attention in absence epilepsy. In M.S. Myslobodsky & A.F. Mirsky (Eds.), *Elements of petit mal epilepsy* (pp. 341–364). New York: Peter Lang.

Duncan, C.C., Kosmidis, M.K., & Mirsky, A.F. (2003). Event-related potential assessment of information processing after closed head injury. *Psychophysiology, 40,* 45–59.

Fedio, P., & Mirsky, A.F. (1969). Selective intellectual deficits in children with temporal lobe or centrencephalic epilepsy. *Neuropsychologia, 7,* 287–300.

Gabbay, F.G., & Duncan, C.C. (1999). Sustained attention and performance: Effects of sex, season, and menstrual cycle phase. Report to the Department of the Army, U.S. Department of Defense.

Gloor, P. (1988). Neurophysiological mechanism of generalized spike and wave discharge and its implication for understanding absence seizures. In M.S. Myslobodsky & A.F. Mirsky (Eds.), *Elements of petit mal epilepsy* (pp. 159–209). New York: Peter Lang.

Goldberg, E., Bilder, R.M., Hughes, J.E.O., Antin, S.P., & Mattis, S. (1989). A reticulo-frontal disconnection syndrome. *Cortex, 25,* 687–695.

Golden, C.J. (1978). *Stroop Color and Word Test: A manual for clinical and experimental uses.* Chicago: Stoelting.

Grant, D.A., & Berg, E.A. (1948). A behavioral analysis of degree of reinforcement and ease of shifting two new responses in a Weigl-type card sorting problem. *Journal of Experimental Psychology, 38,* 404–411.

Hans, S.L., Marcus, J., Nuechterlein, K.H., Asarnow, R.F., Styr, B., & Auerbach, J.G. (1999). Neurobehavioral deficits at adolescence in children at risk for schizophrenia: The Jerusalem Development Study. *Archives of General Psychiatry, 56,* 741–748.

Heaton, R.K. (1981). The Wisconsin Card Sorting Test Manual. Odessa, FL: Psychological Assessment Resources.

Heilman, R.M., Watson, R.T., Valenstein, E., & Damasio, A.R. (1983). Localization of lesions in neglect. In A. Kertesz (Ed.), *Localization in neuropsychology* (pp. 319–331). New York: Academic Press.

Hermann, B.P., & Wyler, A.R. (1988). Neuropsychological outcome of anterior temporal lobectomy. *Journal of Epilepsy, 1,* 35–45.

Jones, B.P., Duncan, C.C., Brouwers, P., & Mirsky, A.F. (1991). Cognition in eating disorders. *Journal of Clinical and Experimental Neuropsychology, 13,* 711–728.

Jones, B.P., Duncan, C.C., Mirsky, A.F., Post, R.M., & Theodore, W.H. (1994). Neuropsychological profiles in bipolar affective disorder and complex partial seizure disorder. *Neuropsychology, 8,* 55–64.

Kelly, T.P. (2000). The clinical neuropsychology of attention in school-aged children. *Child Neuropsychology, 6,* 24–36.

Kendler, K.S., Ochs, A.L., Gorman, A.M., Hewitt, J.K., Ross, D.E., & Mirsky, A.F. (1991). The structure of schizotypy: A pilot multitrait twin study. *Psychiatry Research, 36,* 19–36,

Kremen, W.S., Seidman, L.J., Faraone, S.V., Pepple, J.R., & Tsuang, M.T. (1992). Attention/information-processing factors in psychotic disorders: Replication and extension of recent neuropsychological findings. *Journal of Nervous and Mental Disease, 180,* 89–93.

Lanphear, B.P., Byrd, R.S., Auinger, P., & Hall, C.B. (1997). Increasing prevalence of recurrent otitis media among children in the United States. *Pediatrics, 99,* e1.

Lansdell, H., & Mirsky, A.F. (1964). Attention in focal and centrencephalic epilepsy. *Experimental Neurology, 9,* 463–469.

Lee, D.J., Gomez-Marin, O., & Lee, H.M. (1996). Prevalence of hearing loss: The Hispanic Health and Nutrition Examination Survey and the National Health And Nutrition Examination Survey II. *American Journal of Epidemiology, 144,* 442–449.

Levav, M., Mirsky, A.F., Cruz, M.E., & Cruz, I. (1995). Neurocysticercosis and performance on neuropsychological tests: A family study in Ecuador. *American Journal of Tropical Medical Hygiene, 53,* 552–557.

Levav, M., Mirsky, A.F., Herault, J., Xiong, L., Amir, N., & Andermann, E. (2002). Familial association of neuropsychological traits in patients with generalized and partial seizure disorders. *Journal of Clinical and Experimental Neuropsychology, 24,* 311–326.

Milner, B. (1963). Effects of different brain lesions on card sorting. *Archives of Neurology, 9,* 90–100.

Mirsky, A.F. (1987). Behavioral and psychophysiological markers of disordered attention. *Environmental Health Perspectives, 74,* 191–199.

Mirsky, A.F. (1992). Neuropsychological assessment of epilepsy. *New Issues in Neurosciences, 4,* 25–39.

Mirsky, A.F. (1995). Perils and pitfalls on the path to normal potential: The role of impaired attention. Homage to Herbert G. Birch. *Journal of Clinical and Experimental Neuropsychology, 17,* 481–498.

Mirsky, A.F. (1996). Familial factors in the impairment of attention in schizophrenia: Data From Ireland, Israel, and the District of Columbia. In S. Matthysse, D. Levy, J. Kagan, & D.F. Benes (Eds.), *Psychopathology: The evolving science of mental disorders* (pp. 364–406). Cambridge, England: Cambridge University Press.

Mirsky, A.F., Anthony, B.J., Duncan, C.C., Ahearn, M.B., & Kellam, S.G. (1991). Analysis of the elements of attention: A neuropsychological approach. *Neuropsychology Review, 2,* 109–145.

Mirsky, A.F., Bakay Pragay, E., & Harris, S. (1977). Evoked potential correlates of stimulation-induced impairment of attention in *Macaca mulatta. Experimental Neurology, 57,* 242–256.

Mirsky, A.F., & Duncan, C.C. (2001). A nosology of disorders of attention. In J. Wasserstein, L.E. Wolf, & F.F. LeFever (Eds.), *Adult attention deficit disorder: Brain mechanisms and life outcomes* (Vol. 931, pp. 17–32). New York: New York Academy of Sciences.

Mirsky, A.F., Duncan, C.C., & Myslobodsky, M.S. (1986). Petit mal epilepsy: A review and integration of recent information. *Journal of Clinical Neurophysiology, 3,* 179–208.

Mirsky, A.F., Fantie, B.D., & Tatman, J.E. (1995a). Assessment of attention across the lifespan. In R.L. Mapou & J. Spector (Eds.), *Clinical neuropsychological assessment: A cognitive approach* (pp. 17–48). New York: Plenum Press.

Mirsky, A.F., Ingraham, L.J., & Kugelmass, S. (1995b). Neuropsychological assessment of attention and its pathology in the Israeli cohort. *Schizophrenia Bulletin, 21,* 193–204.

Mirsky, A.F., Lochhead, S.J., Jones, B.P., Kugelmass, S., Walsh, D., & Kendler, K.S. (1992). On familial factors in the attentional deficit in schizophrenia: A review and report of two new subject samples. *Journal of Psychiatric Research, 26,* 383–403.

Mirsky, A.F., & Oshima, H.I. (1973). Effect of subcortical aluminum cream lesions on attentive behavior and the electroencephalogram in monkeys. *Experimental Neurology, 39,* 1–18.

Mirsky, A.F., Pascualvaca, D.M., Duncan, C.C., & French, L.M. (1999). A model of attention and its relation to ADHD. *Mental Retardation and Developmental Disabilities Research Review, 5,* 169–176.

Mirsky, A.F., Primac, D.W., Ajmone Marsan, C., Rosvold, H.E., & Stevens, J.A. (1960). A comparison of the psychological test performance of patients with focal and nonfocal epilepsy. *Experimental Neurology, 2,* 75–89.

Mirsky, A.F., & Rosvold, H.E. (1990). The case of Carolyn Wilson—A 38-year follow-up of a schizophrenic patient with two prefrontal lobotomies. In E. Goldberg (Ed.), *Contemporary neuropsychology and the legacy of Luria* (pp. 51–75). Hillsdale, NJ: Erlbaum.

Mirsky, A.F., & van Buren, J.M. (1965). On the nature of the "absence" in centrencephalic epilepsy: A study of some behavioral, electroencephalic and autonomic factors. *Electroencephalography and Clinical Neurophysiology, 18,* 334–348.

Mirsky, A.F., Yardley, S.L., Jones, B.P., Walsh, D., & Kendler, K.S. (1995c). Analysis of the attention deficit in schizophrenia: A study of patients and their relatives in Ireland. *Journal of Psychiatric Research, 29,* 23–42.

Mishkin, M. (1978). Memory in monkeys severely impaired by combined but not separate removal of the amygdala and hippocampus. *Nature, 273,* 297–298.

Myers, R.E. (1969). The clinical and pathological effects of asphyxiation in the fetal rhesus monkey. In K. Adamsons (Ed.), *Diagnosis and treatment of fetal disorders* (pp. 226–249). New York: Springer-Verlag.

Myers, R.E. (1971). Brain damage induced by umbilical cord compression at different gestational ages in monkeys. In E.I. Goldsmith & J. Moor-Jankowski (Eds.), *Second conference on experimental medicine and surgery in primates* (pp. 394–425). New York: S. Karger.

Nuechterlein, K.H., Parasuraman, R., & Qiyuan, J. (1983). Visual sustained attention: Image degradation produces rapid sensitivity decrement over time. S*cience, 220,* 327–329.

Pandya, D.N., & Yeterian, E.H. (1985). Architecture and connection of cortical association areas. In A. Peters & E.G. Jones (Eds.), *Cerebral cortex: Association and auditory cortices (Vol. 4)* (pp. 3–61). New York: Plenum.

Penfield, W., & Jasper, H. (1954). *Epilepsy and the functional anatomy of the human brain.* Boston: Little, Brown.

Pogge, D.L., Stokes, J.M., & Harvey, P.D. (1994). An empirical evaluation of the factorial structure of attention in adolescent psychiatric patients. *Journal of Clinical and Experimental Neuropsychology, 16,* 334–353.

Ray, C.L., Mirsky, A.F., & Bakay Pragay, E. (1982). Functional analysis of attention-related unit activity in the reticular formation of the monkey. *Experimental Neurology, 77,* 544–562.

Reitan, R.M., & Davison, L.A. (1974). *Clinical neuropsychology: Current status and applications.* Washington, DC: Winston and Sons.

Reitan, R.M., & Wolfson, D. (1985). *The Halstead-Reitan Neuropsychological Test Battery.* Tucson, AZ: Clinical Neuropsychology Press.

Rosvold, H.E., Mirsky, A.F., Sarason, I., Bransome, E.D., Jr., & Beck, L.H. (1956). A continuous performance test of brain damage. *Journal of Consulting Psychology, 20,* 343–350.

Scoville, W.B., & Milner, B. (1957). Loss of recent memory after bilateral hippocampal lesions. *Journal of Neurology, Neurosurgery and Psychiatry, 20,* 11–21.

Steinhauer, S.R., Zubin, J., Condray, R., Shaw, D.B., Peters, J.L., & van Kammen, D.P. (1991). Electrophysiological and behavioral signs of attentional disturbance in schizophrenics and their siblings. In C.A. Tamminga & C. Shultz (Eds.), *Advances in neuropsychiatry and psychopharmacology (Vol. 1): Schizophrenia research* (pp. 169–178). New York: Raven Press.

Stroop, J.R. (1935). Studies of verbal interference in serial verbal reactions. *Journal of Experimental Psychology, 18, 643–662.*

Talland, G.A. (1965). *Deranged memory.* New York: Academic Press.

Tatman, J.E. (1992). Elements of attention and concentration in normal aging adults: Locus of decline. Unpublished master's thesis, The American University, Washington, DC.

Valenstein, E. (1986). *Great and desperate cures.* New York: Basic Books.

Wechsler, D. (1981). Wechsler Adult Intelligence Scale (Rev. ed.). New York: Psychological Corporation.

Wohlberg, G.W., & Kornetsky, C. (1973). Sustained attention in remitted schizophrenics. *Archives of General Psychiatry, 28,* 533–537.

Yingling, C.D., & Skinner, J.E. (1975). Regulation of unit activity in nucleus reticularis thalami by the mesencephalic reticular formation and the frontal granular cortex. *Electroencephalography and Clinical Neurophysiology, 39,* 635–642.

CHAPTER 17

The Attention Battery for Children*:
A Systematic Approach to Assessment

ALLAN F. MIRSKY AND CONNIE C. DUNCAN

INTRODUCTION

In our companion chapter, we reviewed the model of the elements of attention and presented a systematic approach to assessing attention in adults (Duncan & Mirsky, this volume). In this chapter, we present a modified version of the Attention Battery for Adults, for use in the evaluation of children, as well as data obtained from a large cohort of children that led to the development of the model (Mirsky, Anthony, Duncan, Ahearn, & Kellam, 1991). We review research findings on attention from several clinical investigations, including new data that suggest a complex but significant relationship between impaired attentional capacity and aggression in school children. The focus of the review is to highlight the effects of agents that may alter the development of attentional capacity, especially among children growing up in impoverished environments. We conclude the chapter with illustrative case histories in which the assessment of attention was a key element.

A MODEL OF ATTENTION

The essential tenets of our approach to the study of attention are that attention is a complex process or set of processes, which can be subdivided into a number of distinct functions, including encode, focus/execute, sustain, and shift. These functions are supported by different brain regions, which are specialized, but which nevertheless are organized into a system.

Encoding of stimuli, the ability to hold information in storage long enough to perform a cognitive operation on it, is dependent upon the amygdala and hippocampus (Adey, 1969; Blakemore, Iversen, & Zangwill, 1972; Mishkin, 1978). The function of focusing on environmental events, and screening out distracting stimuli, is shared by superior temporal and inferior parietal cortices as well as structures that comprise the corpus striatum (Heilman, Watson, Valenstein, & Damasio, 1983; Mesulam, 1987). The execution of responses requires the integrity of inferior parietal and corpus striatal regions (Battig, Rosvold, & Mishkin, 1960; Heilman et al., 1983; Mesulam, 1987).

Sustaining a focus of attention on environmental events (vigilance) is the major responsibility of rostral midbrain structures, including structures within the mesopontine retic-

---

*Attention Battery for Children (ABC) © Mirsky & Duncan, 2002.

ular formation and midline and reticular thalamic nuclei. The key role of these structures in support of sustained attention has been demonstrated in animal models (Aston-Jones, Rajkowski, Kubiak, & Alexinsky, 1994; Mirsky et al., 1991).

The capacity to shift from one salient aspect of the environment to another is supported by structures in the prefrontal lobes, as demonstrated by the research of Milner (1963) on patients with focal seizure disorders.

A fifth aspect of attention, stabilize/regulate, was added to the original list (Tatman, 1992). This attentional element reflects the consistency or stability of responses to designated task stimuli. The cerebral correlates of this attentional element are not well understood, but are thought to be related to frontal-brainstem reciprocal connections (Hetherington, Stuss, & Finlayson, 1996).

The assignment of functional specialization of components of attention to different brain regions is not meant to be absolute, and it is likely that some brain regions support more than one attentional function. Moreover, although we maintain that damage or dysfunction in one of these brain regions can lead to circumscribed or specific deficits in a particular attentional function, we also contend that the system is to some extent equipotential. Thus, under some circumstances, the system can assume the function that has been impaired as a result of injury.

THE ATTENTION BATTERY FOR CHILDREN

The tests of the Attention Battery for Children (or ABC, © Mirsky & Duncan, 2002) are modifications of the tests in the adult Attention Battery for Adults (Duncan & Mirsky, Chapter 16) and are listed in Table 17.1. Justification and support for selecting these tests is provided by the convergence of the results derived from the principal components analysis of the data from adults and children. The latter comprised a sample of 435 eight-year-olds (Mirsky et al., 1991). The same relationship between attentional elements and the tests that assess them emerged from the two analyses.

The focus/execute attentional element is measured by the Coding subtest of the Wechsler Intelligence Scale for Children-Revised (WISC-R, Wechsler, 1974) and the Digit Cancellation Test (Lifshitz, Kugelmass, & Karov, 1985). Similarly, the encode element is assessed by performance on the Arithmetic and Digit Span subtests of the WISC-R. As in the Attention Battery for Adults, the sustain element of attention is assessed with the Continuous Performance Test (CPT; Rosvold, Mirsky, Sarason, Bransome, & Beck, 1956); and the shift element with the Wisconsin Card Sorting Test (WCST; Grant & Berg, 1948).

TABLE 17.1 Tests of the Attention Battery for Children

Test	Score(s) Used
Digit Cancellation Test[a] (Lifshitz, Kugelmass, & Karov, 1985)	Completion time Omission errors
Coding[b] (Wechsler, 1974)	Number correct
Arithmetic[b] (Wechsler, 1974)	Number correct
Digit Span[b] (Wechsler, 1974)	Number correct
Continuous Performance Test (Rosvold, Mirsky, Sarason, Bransome, & Beck, 1956)	Percentage of correct responses, visual X task Reaction time, visual X task Percentage of commission errors, visual X task
Wisconsin Card Sorting Test (Grant & Berg, 1948; Heaton, 1981)	Number of categories Percentage of correct responses

Note. From Analysis of the elements of attention: A neuropsychological approach by A.F. Mirsky, B.J. Anthony, C.C. Duncan, M.B. Ahearn, and S.G. Kellam, 1991, *Neuropsychology Review, 2,* p. 119. Copyright 1991 by Plenum Publishing. Adapted with permission.
[a]This test was used in place of the Letter Cancellation Test (Talland, 1965), which was used in the Attention Battery for adults. In each of two trials, the child is required to cross out two specified digits.
[b]Subtests of the Wechsler Intelligence Scale for Children (WISC-R, Wechsler, 1974); scores are scaled for the age of the subject.

TABLE 17.2 Descriptive Variables and Scores on the Attention Battery for Children

Measure	M	SD
Descriptive variables		
Age (months)[a]	95.3	5.4
Peabody Picture Vocabulary Test[b]	87.4	16.7
Attention Battery for Children variables		
Digit Cancellation completion time	72.8	18.8
Digit Cancellation omission errors	3.4	2.9
Coding	10.9	3.3
Arithmetic	9.3	3.2
Digit Span	9.3	2.6
CPT % correct responses	80.3	14.4
CPT reaction time	610.0	55.0
CPT % commission errors	2.2	2.5
WCST # of categories	2.9	1.8
WCST % correct	48.9	14.6

Note. From Analysis of the elements of attention: A neuropsychological approach by A.F. Mirsky, B.J. Anthony, C.C. Duncan, M.B. Ahearn, and S.G. Kellam, 1991, *Neuropsychology Review, 2,* p. 120. Copyright 1991 by Plenum Publishing. Adapted with permission.
[a]Of the children, 380 were in the second grade and 53 in the first grade at the time of testing. There were 217 males, mean age = 95.5 (SD = 6.0) and 218 females, mean age = 95.2 (SD = 5.2).
[b]Dunn and Dunn, (1981). This test yields scores approximately equivalent to verbal IQ. The mean score for the males was 89.3 (SD = 17.2); for the females, it was 85.5 (SD = 16.1).

TABLE 17.3 Rotated Component Loadings

	Component 1	Component 2	Component 3	Component 4
Digit Cancellation completion time	−.12	−.07	.14	***.80***
Digit Cancellation omission errors	−.27	−.16	.18	***−.57***
Coding	.06	.38	−.11	***−.58***
Arithmetic	.22	***.74***	−.16	.01
Digit Span	.03	***.75***	−.04	−.12
CPT % correct responses	−.03	−.19	***.85***	.01
CPT reaction time	−.14	.27	***.65***	.35
CPT % commission errors	.01	−.35	***.5***	−.13
WCST # categories	***.95***[a]	.11	−.06	.01
WCST % correct	***.95***	.10	−.03	−.01
Variance explained (%)	19.7	15.3	15.1	14.5
Proposed identity of component	Flexibility	Numerical-mnemonic	Vigilance	Perceptual-motor speed
Element of attention	Shift	Encode	Sustain	Focus-execute

Note. From Analysis of the elements of attention: A neuropsychological approach by A.F. Mirsky, B.J. Anthony, C.C. Duncan, M.B. Ahearn, and S.G. Kellam, 1991, *Neuropsychology Review, 2,* p. 120. Copyright 1991 by Plenum Publishing. Adapted with permission.
[a]The highest component loadings within a column (shown in bold italics) were used to interpret the identity of the component.

The attention test parameters used for adults were modified for children; these modified parameters were used in the investigation summarized in Tables 17.2 and 17.3. The values of the parameters depend on the age of the child. In children younger than 11 years, the duration of visual stimuli in the CPT is lengthened from 200 to 500 msec, and the interstimulus interval is increased from 1000 to 1500 msec. However, task duration is shortened to a maximum of five to seven minutes. For children under the age of six, familiar items (e.g., chair, butterfly, ice cream cone) rather than letters are used as stimuli. As a number of the tests in the battery are derived from the WISC-R (i.e., Arithmetic, Digit Span, Coding; Wechsler, 1974), we use the scoring norms provided by the appropriate manuals. For the Digit Cancellation Test, we use the norms from our own sample of eight-year-olds.

Norms for inner-city children on the ABC have been published (Rebok et al., 1996). Portions of the ABC were administered to 216 children when they were 8, 10, and 13 years of age. The test battery comprised several versions of the CPT, the Digit Cancellation Test, the Coding, Arithmetic, and Digit Span subtests of the WISC-R, and the WCST. Norms for the latter test have also been published by Chelune and Baer (1986), although their sample may have had a higher average IQ than our inner-city population.

Rebok et al.'s (1996) data suggest that accuracy on the visual versions of the CPT reach adult levels by age 11 and by age 13 on the auditory tones CPT. The data further suggest that reaction time may not yet have reached adult levels by age 13. A similar trajectory for the growth of attentional skills was reported by Kelly (2000), based on an investigation of a group of English school children.

DISORDERED ATTENTION: A SYMPTOM WITH MULTIPLE ETIOLOGIES

Environmental conditions associated with poverty (ignorance, malnutrition, and infection) are persistent problems in underdeveloped countries (Cravioto, DeLicardie, & Birch, 1966; Mirsky, 1995). These conditions also affect the poor in the United States. These problems, inevitably, have resulted in impaired cognitive development for millions, if not billions, of the world's people. Whereas some of these problems are not associated solely with poverty (i.e., maternal drinking and substance abuse, pregnancy/birth complications), there is a greater likelihood that the poor will be afflicted.

The effects of maternal drinking on later cognitive development have been carefully documented by Streissguth et al. (1994). The deleterious effects of maternal cocaine abuse on attention have been reported by Bandstra's group (Bandstra, Morrow, Anthony, Accornero, & Fried, 2001). Among the impairments observed in those who suffer from fetal alcohol syndrome, or fetal alcohol effect, are deficits in sustained attention, especially in the auditory modality (Connor, Streissguth, Sampson, Bookstein, & Barr, 1999). The results of the British studies done in the 1970s demonstrated the catastrophic effects of poverty on pregnancy and birth complications—as reflected in fetal deaths and nonlethal mental defects (presumably including impaired attention)—in the offspring of unwed, teenage (and usually impoverished) mothers (Chamberlin, Chamberlin, Howlett, & Claireaux, 1975, 1978).

In collaboration with public health workers in Ecuador, we studied the effects of malnutrition and parasitic infection on the residents of a small mountain village north of Quito.

The results documented the effects of these conditions on attention (Cruz et al., 1993; Levav, Cruz, & Mirsky, 1995a; Levav, Mirsky, Cruz, & Cruz, 1995b; Levav, Mirsky, Schantz, Castro, & Cruz, 1995c). Whereas all parasitic infections act to sap energy needed for learning and development of cognition, the most virulent parasite may be the larva of the pork tapeworm or *Taenia solium*. This organism infests the brain and produces a condition known as neurocysticercosis, which is a leading cause of cognitive decline as well as seizures (Levav et al., 1995b).

In addition to neurocysticercosis, the larvae of the nematode *Toxocara*, found in feces of domestic cats, dogs, and mice, as well as cockroaches, are known to infect humans and to be associated with a variety of childhood disorders, including some that involve the eye, lungs, liver, and brain (Marmor et al., 1987; Nicoletti et al., 2002; Ruttinger & Hadidi, 1991; Varga, Auer, & Zach, 1998).

The results of these investigations, as well as those to be presented in the next several sections, offer strong support for the view that deleterious environmental conditions associated with poverty result in reduced attentional capacity in children. Whereas the etiology of attention-deficit/hyperactivity disorder (ADHD) is at least partly genetic (Mirsky & Duncan, 2001), attention is also vulnerable to poverty-associated factors. Table 17.4 summarizes these factors. The reduced attentional capacity is presumably due to the effects of these environmental agents on the developing brain, including, but not restricted to, what we refer to in the following section as the "vulnerable brainstem" (Mirsky & Duncan, in press).

TABLE 17.4   Deleterious Environmental Effects Associated with Poverty That Act to Reduce Attentional Capacity

Environmental Effect	Representative Reference(s)
Malnutrition	Levav et al., 1995a, 1995c
Lead intoxication	Needleman et al., 1995; Mirsky et al., 2001
Pregnancy/Birth complications	Chamberlin et al., 1975, 1978; Myers 1967; 1969; 1971; Mirsky et al., 1979
Fetal alcohol syndrome/effect	Streissguth et al., 1994; Connor et al., 1999
Fetal cocaine syndrome	Bandstra et al., 2001
Neurocysticercosis, toxocariasis, other parasitic infections	Levav et al., 1995b; Cruz et al., 1993; Marmor et al., 1987
Lack of intellectual stimulation	Bahrudin and Luster, 1998; Mirsky, 1995

Note. From Perils and pitfalls on the path to normal potential: The role of impaired attention—Homage to Herbert G. Birch by A.F. Mirsky, 1995, *Journal of Clinical and Experimental Neuropsychology, 17,* p. 493. Copyright 1995 by Swets and Zeitlinger. And from A nosology of disorders of attention by A.F. Mirsky and C.C. Duncan, 2001, in *Adult attention deficit disorder: Brain mechanisms and life outcomes,* vol. 931, (p. 22), edited by J. Wasserstein, L.E. Wolf, and F.F. LeFever, 2001, New York: Annals of the New York Academy of Sciences. Adapted with permission.

THE VULNERABLE BRAINSTEM HYPOTHESIS

We propose that many of the environmental conditions listed in Table 17.4 share common neurodevelopmental effects. Specifically, each is thought to compromise brainstem structures necessary for the most basic of attentional functions, the capacity to sustain attention (Aston-Jones, Rajkowski, & Cohen, 1999; Bakay Pragay, Mirsky, Ray, Turner, & Mirsky, 1978; Mirsky et al., 1991; Usher, Cohen, Servan-Schreiber, Rajowski, & Aston-Jones, 1999). This elemental attentional capacity is well developed in reptiles, whose cerebral development does not extend beyond the brainstem (MacLean, 1990).

From Myers' experimental asphyxia studies in monkeys, it is well known that acute total asphyxia and prolonged partial asphyxia (corresponding to types of difficult labor and delivery in humans) are accompanied by damage to brainstem structures (Mirsky et al., 1979; Myers, 1967, 1969, 1971). The damaged structures include the inferior colliculus, the superior olivary complex (both of which are auditory relay nuclei), and other regions of the mesencephalon. This research presents a model for understanding the effects of perinatal brain damage in humans, damage that compromises the integrity of the brainstem component of the attention system.

We noted previously, based in part on British studies of perinatal mortality, that perinatal damage to the brain is prevalent in the offspring of poor, young women, due to the lack of adequate prenatal care and obstetrical services (Chamberlin et al., 1975, 1978). We conclude that perinatal damage, as well as other poverty-associated factors, including malnutrition, lead intoxication, maternal drinking and substance abuse during pregnancy, and parasitic infections, can all contribute to reduced attentional capacity in poor children via damage to brainstem structures.

The category of environmental etiologies would not be complete without reference to lack of intellectual stimulation. An impoverished intellectual environment is clearly not restricted to impoverished populations. The fact remains, however, that in many studies of factors associated with impaired cognitive development, maternal education emerges as a factor with a significant positive correlation with children's achievement (Baharudin & Luster, 1998). We observed in our studies in Ecuador that children with higher levels of education had less cognitive impairment following parasitic infection of the brain than those with lower levels of education (Levav et al., 1995b). The suggestion is that levels of education, in probands and mothers of probands, may be related to the severity of the attentional disorder. Poorly educated mothers, especially in single-parent families, may provide less than optimum environments for developing and nurturing cognitive skills. Such skills may protect against, or mitigate, the development of disordered attention in vulnerable children.

The message in this review of conditions associated with poverty is therefore that there are a variety of factors associated with growing up in an impoverished environment that may lead to disordered attention. Specifically, it has been demonstrated that many, if not all, of these factors degrade the capacity for sustained attention in children. This information should be borne in mind when considering the etiologies of disordered attention, and the effects on school performance, in children from impoverished environments.

CLINICAL RESEARCH STUDIES OF ATTENTION IN CHILDREN

The first clinical research study involving a measure of sustained attention (CPT) in children was published in 1956 (Rosvold et al., 1956). In that study, a group of brain-injured children from several clinics in and around the city of New Haven, Connecticut, were compared with a group of non-brain-injured controls. Despite matching them with the controls on measures of overall intellectual ability, the results revealed a significant inferiority of the brain-injured group on the CPT. Shortly after publication of this finding, there was recognition among child development researchers that the function of sustained attention was a significant aspect of cognitive capacities in children. Numerous scientific studies employing the method have been published. Because the CPT appeared especially useful in the diagnosis and evaluation of treatment of ADHD, a number of commercial versions of the test were published, aimed at the burgeoning market for assessing and evaluating children (and adults) with this disorder. A recent survey employing the Web of Science/Institute of Scientific Information Web site indicates that the original 1956 paper has been cited in literature well over 1,000 times. The following section details some recent research on attention in children in the context of ADHD, lead intoxication, seizure disorders, aggression, maternal substance abuse, a predictor of school readiness, and a predictor of later psychopathology.

Attention-Deficit/Hyperactivity Disorder

There have been numerous studies demonstrating the sensitivity of the CPT to deficits of attention in children. In the study reported here, the ABC was administered to a group of inner-city children who had been referred to a family clinic for diagnosis and treatment recommendations for ADHD and related disorders.

The diagnoses of the children were based on structured clinical interviews with one or both parents, observations of the child during a standard activity session, and teacher and parent ratings (Erickson, 1997). Participants comprised 119 children (94 boys) referred to the clinic and 25 healthy controls (10 boys) from the same socioeconomic milieu as the referred children. The mean age in years of the groups was 7.9 (ADHD) and 9.0 (controls). As this difference in age was statistically significant, all test score comparisons were corrected by covariance analysis. Full Scale IQ for the two groups did not differ significantly (ADHD = 91; controls = 96). However, the groups differed significantly in the expected direction on the Arithmetic, Reading, and Spelling components of the Wide Range Achievement Test (Jastak & Wilkinson, 1984).

The results of the evaluation using the ABC suggest that the children diagnosed with ADHD were impaired in at least four, and possibly five, elements of attention, as compared with non-ADHD controls: Whereas differences on the tests of the encode element of attention (Digit Span, Arithmetic) were in the expected direction, neither difference was statistically significant. However, the capacity to focus on a task in the presence of distraction, and to execute brisk, efficient responses (Digit Cancellation Test, Coding) were significantly impaired. Additional deficits that appeared in the ADHD group were the ability to shift attention flexibly (WCST), the ability to sustain attention in the visual and auditory modalities (CPT), and the capacity to maintain a stable response rhythm in the auditory modality (CPT). Scores on these tests for both groups are presented in Table 17.5.

Although our results suggest that responses tended to be faster in the ADHD group than in the controls, the responses also tended to be impulsive and poorly regulated. This is seen in the trend towards more errors of commission and in the significant difference in responses to partial information (responses to the letter A in the AX task [A-not X errors in Table 17.5]).

Another question that arises in the consideration of our ADHD sample concerns the possible contribution of learning disorders to the observed attentional deficits. We do not have, at this time, a definitive answer to that question. However, additional analyses were performed on a subset of children derived from the total sample. Three groups of children were compared: those diagnosed as ADHD $(n = 24)$ using the criteria defined earlier, those diagnosed as both ADHD and learning disordered (ADHD + LD, $n = 20$), and healthy controls $(n = 20)$. Learning disorder was defined as 15 scaled score points or more below Full Scale IQ on one or more of the subtests (Reading, Arithmetic, or Spelling) of the Wide Range Achievement Test, and an absolute score below 85. The three groups did not differ significantly in age (overall

TABLE 17.5   Mean Performance Scores of the ADHD and Healthy Control Groups on Tests Measuring the Five Elements of Attention

Test	Score	ADHD	Control	p-value
Focus/Execute element				
Digit Cancellation time (sec)		83.5	65.1	.03
Coding number correct[a]		9.0	11.0	.02
Encode element				
Digit Span	# correct[a]	9.1	9.3	.07
Arithmetic	# correct[a]	8.0	9.3	.80
Shift element				
WCST	# of categories	3.7	5.2	.0001
WCST	% correct	31.1	19.0	.03
Sustain Element				
Visual				
CPT-AX	% Correct responses	67	78	.05
CPT-AX	% Commission errors[b]	8.2	4.5	.06
CPT-AX	# A–not X errors[c]	6.2	2.9	.01
CPT-AX	RT[d]	480	510	.28
Auditory				
CPT-AX	% Correct responses	67	80	.01
CPT-AX	% Commission errors[b]	8.0	4.0	.07
CPT-AX	# A–not X errors[c]	3.3	1.6	.03
CPT-AX	RT[d]	710	730	.46
Stabilize Element				
Visual				
CPT-AX	RT variance	218	190	.14
Auditory				
CPT-AX	RT variance	321	273	.03

Note. From A model of attention and its relation to ADHD by A.F. Mirsky, D.M. Pascualvaca, C.C. Duncan, and L.M. French, 1999, *Mental Retardation and Developmental Disabilities, 5,* p. 173. Copyright 1999 by Wiley-Liss. Adapted with permission.

[a]Scaled score.

[b]Commission errors refer to responses to nontarget stimuli.

[c]In the CPT-AX, responses are required to the letter X only if it followed immediately after the letter A.
"A–not X" refers to anticipatory, erroneous responses to the letter A, a subset of commission errors.

[d]RT = reaction time (msec).

mean = 8.8 years) or in Verbal, Performance, or Full Scale IQ measures (mean scores ranged from 92–100).

In general, the ADHD and ADHD+LD groups performed similarly. The sole exception was in performance on the visual version of the CPT-AX: Measures of CPT-AX performance differentiated the "pure" ADHD group from the ADHD+LD and the controls. These data are presented in Table 17.6.

Our results indicate that children with a diagnosis of ADHD alone are more impaired on sustained attention than those with the dual diagnosis of ADHD and learning disorder. This finding is somewhat counter-intuitive and merits further study. However, the impaired attentional elements in the ADHD population are not generally attributable to learning disorders per se. A tentative conclusion, assuming that this finding is replicated, is that ADHD+LD does not merely represent a dual diagnosis, but instead represents a disorder distinct from either ADHD or learning disorder. A more complete description of the results of this investigation is contained in Erickson (1997).

Lead Intoxication

As part of a prevention-intervention research project, a battery of neuropsychological tests was administered to an epidemiological sample of 8 year olds, comprising 435 boys and girls (Kellam, Ialongo, Rebok, Mayer, & Dolan, 1992; Kellam et al., 1991). Subsequent samples (at ages 10 and 14) of the original cohort was comprised of 200–300 children. Forty-two of the original participants were reevaluated at age 19. In addition to a neuropsychological test battery, blood lead and bone lead were assayed, the latter by means of a K X-ray technique. We analyzed the neuropsychological and lead level data obtained when the participants were age 19 and

TABLE 17.6 Scores on the Visual CPT-AX for Three Subgroups of Children

Score	ADHD	ADHD + LD	Control	p-value
% Correct responses	68	80	88	.001
% Commission errors[a]	6	4	1	.003

Note. From A model of attention and its relation to ADHD by A.F. Mirsky, D.M. Pascualvaca, C.C. Duncan, and L.M. French, 1999, *Mental Retardation and Developmental Disabilities, 5,* p. 174. Copyright 1999 by Wiley-Liss. Adapted with permission.

[a]Responses to nontargets.

took a retrospective look at the relationship between lead levels at 19 years of age and the neuropsychological test data obtained at 10 years of age (Mirsky, Kellam, Pascualvaca, Petras, & Todd, 2001).

The ABC was administered to the children at age 10. At age 19, the neuropsychological test battery included the Digit Symbol Substitution, Arithmetic, and Digit Span subtests of the Wechsler Adult Intelligence Scale-Revised (WAIS-R; Wechsler, 1981), the visual CPT-AX, the auditory CPT-X Tones, the Logical Memory subtest of the Wechsler Memory Scale-Revised (WMS-R; Wechsler, 1987), the Purdue Pegboard Test (Purdue Research Foundation, no date), and the Rey-Osterrieth Complex Figure (Corwin, & Bylsma, 1993).

There were no significant correlations between blood lead levels and neuropsychological test scores. However, statistically significant correlations, ranging from .31 to .41, were found between bone lead levels and neuropsychological test scores at age 19. These were found almost exclusively in measures of visual sustained attention, as derived from the CPT. Significant correlations (ranging from .28 to .86) were also found between visual CPT scores at age 10 and bone lead at age 19.

Impairment in executive functions, and in particular, sustained attention (as assessed by the CPT), is associated with increased aggressiveness in grade school children (Sun et al., 2001) and later academic failure (Kellam et al., 1991, 1992). Lead burden may contribute to the impairment in sustained attention that leads to academic failure and subsequent antisocial behavior in inner-city children. These findings are consonant with the extensive research on the effects of lead on cognitive functions and life-course conducted by Needleman, Reiss, and Tobin (1995).

Childhood Seizure Disorders

Prior research on patients with idiopathic generalized epilepsy of the absence type has indicated that they have a specific pattern of attentional deficit that does not appear in patients with focal seizure disorders (Duncan, 1988; Lansdell & Mirsky, 1964; Levav et al., 2002; Mirsky, Primac, Ajmone Marsan, Rosvold, & Stevens, 1960; Mirsky & Duncan, 1990).

In an earlier study, Fedio and Mirsky (1969) reported a comparison of the cognitive capacities of three groups of children with seizure disorders, comprising those with absence seizures, right-temporal lobe foci, and left-temporal lobe foci. A group of healthy control children was also studied. Although the ABC was not conceived at that time, some of the tests used would seem to assess the same or similar attention elements. The results (Figure 17.1) indicate that the pattern of deficits was specific to the type of seizure disorder. Patients with absence seizures were impaired in comparison with the other groups on the test of sustained attention (the visual CPT-AX). In contrast, the group with left-temporal foci was most impaired on a verbal learning task (related to the encode element), and the group with right-temporal foci was most impaired on a visual-spatial task, the Rey-Osterrieth Complex Figure, related in part to the focus/execute element (Corwin et al., 1993).

These results, which have been confirmed in other studies of patients with seizure disorders, emphasize the relative specificity of the deficit in sustained attention seen in children with generalized seizures of the absence type. This deficit is presumably related to the locus of the pathophysiological process in this disorder, postulated to involve the "centrencephalon," a cortical-reticular formation (brainstem) circuit (Gloor, 1988; Penfield & Jasper, 1954).

Childhood Aggression

In a group of inner-city school children, we examined the association between performance on tests tapping the elements of attention and ratings of aggressive behavior in the classroom (Sun et al., 2000). A cohort of 435 children was tested on the ABC at age 8, and a subsample was retested at age 10. Aggressive behavior was measured yearly from age 8 through age 13 using the Teacher Observation of Classroom Adaptation-Revised (TOCA-R), Authority Acceptance Scale.

After controlling for effects of gender, ethnicity, and other covariates, performance on tests measuring two elements of attention were found to be significantly related to measures of aggression: encode, as assessed with Digit Span (Figure 17.2), and sustain, as assessed with the CPT (Figure 17.3), were both found to correlate inversely with aggression scores. That is, poorer performance on the encode and sustain aspects of attention were associated with higher levels of aggression. Moreover, the perseverative error score on the test of the shift element (WCST, Figure 17.4) showed a significant positive correlation with aggressive behavior at age 10 (grades 4 and 5), but not at age 8 (not shown).

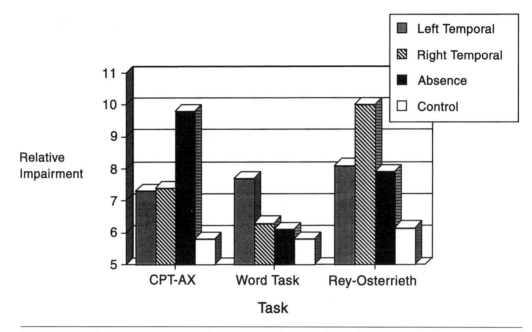

Figure 17.1   Performance of three groups of children with seizure disorders (left temporal lobe focus, right temporal lobe focus, generalized [absence] seizures) and matched healthy controls on three types of cognitive tasks. The CPT-AX is a test of visual sustained attention; the measure shown is the percentage of omission errors, divided by 5. The Word Task is a test of verbal learning; the measure used is the number of trials to learn a list of 10 words. The Rey-Osterrieth Complex Figure is a visual-spatial task; the measure is the number of figural elements missed on the recall trial, divided by 4. The CPT and Rey-Osterrieth measures were divided to equate the metrics and thereby facilitate comparison of scores across tasks. Note that the absence group performed most poorly on the test of sustained attention, the left temporal group most poorly on the verbal encoding task, and the right temporal group most poorly on the visual-spatial task. Each difference among groups was significant at $p < .05$. The data are from Selective intellectual deficits in children with temporal lobe or centrencephalic epilepsy by P. Fedio and A.F. Mirsky, 1969, *Neuropsychologia, 7,* pp. 294–295. Adapted with permission.

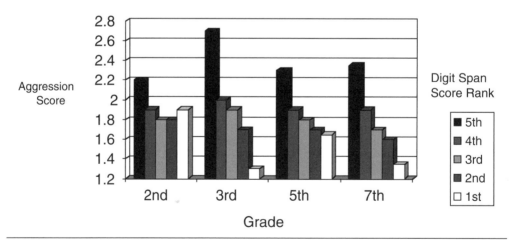

Figure 17.2   Teachers' ratings of aggression as a function of performance on the Digit Span subtest of the WISC-R, a measure of the encode element of attention. Children were ranked according to their scores on Digit Span: "1st" refers to the group with the highest scores (best performance) on Digit Span, "2nd" to the group with the second highest scores, etc. The children with the lowest scores on Digit Span ("5th") were found to be consistently most aggressive, by teachers' ratings of classroom behavior. The significant association between Digit Span scores and aggression ratings is evident from second through seventh grade. The data are from Aspects of executive function and the development of aggressive behavior by H.F. Sun, N. Ialongo, G.W. Rebok, A.Y. Tien, S.G. Kellam, and A.F. Mirsky, 2001. Adapted with permission.

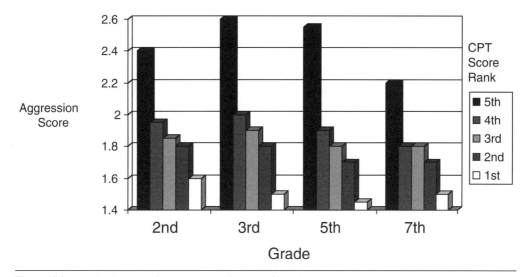

Figure 17.3 Teachers' ratings of aggression as a function of impulsive errors on the visual X task of the Continuous Performance Test (CPT), a measure of the capacity to sustain attention. Children were ranked according to their performance on the CPT: "1st" refers to the group with the fewest commission errors on the CPT, "2nd" to the group with the second fewest errors, etc. The children with the most impulsive errors on the CPT ("5th") were consistently found to be the most aggressive in every grade from second through seventh. The data are from Aspects of executive function and the development of aggressive behavior by H.F. Sun, N. Ialongo, G.W. Rebok, A.Y. Tien, S.G. Kellam, and A.F. Mirsky, 2001. Adapted with permission.

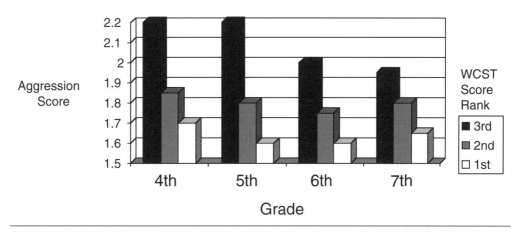

Figure 17.4 Teachers' ratings of aggression as a function of performance on the Wisconsin Card Sorting Test (WCST), a measure of the shift element of attention. Children were divided into three groups based on their performance on the WCST: "3rd refers to the group with the most perseverative errors on the WCST; "1st" to the group with the fewest errors; and "2nd" to the group with the intermediate number of errors. The children with the most errors of perseveration on the WCST were observed to be the most aggressive in every grade from fourth through seventh. The data are from Aspects of executive function and the development of aggressive behavior by H.F. Sun, N. Ialongo, G.W. Rebok, A.Y. Tien, S.G. Kellam, and A.F. Mirsky, 2001. Adapted with permission.

These results suggest a significant but complex association between measures of attentional functioning and the course of aggressive behavior during the elementary and middle school years. They also suggest that poor attentional functioning may be a marker for aggressive, acting-out behaviors in school children. A similar association between impulsive errors on the CPT and "externalizing" behavior was reported

recently and is presented in the section on sustained attention as a predictor of school readiness.

Maternal Substance Abuse: Effects on Offspring

An extensive body of research deals with the effects of maternal ingestion of alcohol or cocaine during pregnancy on the offspring. Streissguth and coworkers have conducted a long-term follow-up study that began with a daily log of alcohol use during pregnancy by a large cohort of mothers. The children of these mothers (the "Seattle 500") have been assessed repeatedly with numerous neuropsychological tests, from early childhood. The results have indicated that children whose mothers engaged in "binge" drinking (six or more drinks on one occasion) show persistent deficits in sustained attention. These deficits were observed in early childhood and were still evident at age 14 (Streissguth et al., 1994). The impairment may not reach the level found in fetal alcohol syndrome or fetal alcohol effect, but is measurable nevertheless, and can impact school performance.

With respect to cocaine abuse, Bandstra conducted extensive neuropsychological investigations of a large cohort of children exposed in utero to cocaine (Bandstra et al., 2001). The results indicate that sustained attention, as measured by visual CPT tasks, is impaired in these children. They concluded that cocaine exposure is linked to long-lasting disruption of the brain systems subserving arousal and attention.

Sustained Attention in Preschool Children: A Predictor of School Readiness?

A multicenter longitudinal study was conducted to explore the role of sustained attention as a possible mediator between family environment and school readiness. It forms part of an investigation designed to discover how variations in childcare are related to children's development (NICHD Early Child Care Research Network, in press).

The data in this study were obtained from a diverse sample of 1,002 children and their families, including information on child attention and school readiness when children were 54 months old. The family environment was assessed throughout the children's first years of life; an association between family environment and children' ability to sustain attention and inhibit impulsive responding was found. The former was indexed by errors of omission on the CPT, and the latter by errors of commission on the CPT. Omission and commission errors on the CPT predicted academic and social skills important for school success. Moreover, children's attention was shown to be a mechanism through which family environment relates to school readiness. Thus, sustained attention and impulsivity provided a link between family environment and cognitive, achievement, and language outcomes. For social outcomes, sustained attention mediated social competence, and impulsivity mediated externalizing behavior.

To our knowledge, the NICHD study is the first to use the CPT with a sample of preschool-age children who had not been identified as having deficits in attention. The CPT was shown to be valuable in assessing individual differences in attention in this population. Moreover, a child's ability to regulate attention, as measured by the CPT, is predictable from the nature of the home and the characteristics of the mother.

These findings have theoretical and empirical implications in relation to the mediators of parental influences on child outcome, individual differences in attention in the preschool period, and interventions to improve attention. Further research may ultimately allow parents and child-care providers to better prepare children for school.

Attention Measures as Predictors of Later Psychopathology

There have been numerous investigations of the attentional disturbance in patients with schizophrenia, including studies of their first-degree relatives (e.g., Mirsky, Kugelmass, Ingraham, Frenkel, & Nathan, 1995). These investigations have shown that relatives may share, to some extent, the deficits in attention (especially sustained attention, as assessed with the CPT) observed in the patients themselves.

In the past few decades, this research has focused on the children of patients with schizophrenia, in an effort to learn whether attention deficits in childhood would predict later development of disorder. Two long-term investigations will be mentioned in this context, the New York High Risk Project (Cornblatt, Obuchowski, Roberts, Pollack, & Erlenmeyer-Kimling, 1999), and the NIMH-Israeli High Risk Project (Mirsky et al., 1995). In both of these investigations, the offspring of patients with schizophrenia (mothers exclusively in the New York project) were followed for as long as 25 years. The investigations entailed repeated assessments of cognitive functions, including sustained attention. The results indicate that measures of attention are predictive of later development of disorder. The New York High Risk Project reported extensively on the use of the Identical Pairs version of the CPT, a task that requires a response when two subsequent stimuli are identical.

One result from the NIMH-Israeli High Risk Project is presented in Figure 17.5. Under conditions of distraction, scores at age 11 on the Digit Cancellation Test (which taps the focus/execute element of attention) predicted the development of a schizophrenia spectrum disorder 15 years later. This is one of the results that suggest that the underlying pathophysiology in schizophrenia can be assessed years before it is manifest in overt symptoms of the disorder. This finding led to a discussion of the possible benefits of neuroleptic treatment of children who are at high genetic risk for schizophrenia (Stone, Faraone, & Tsuang, in press).

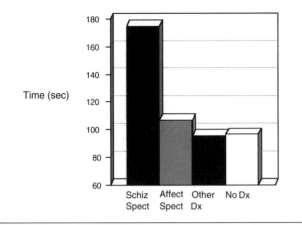

Figure 17.5 Performance on the Digit Cancellation Test, administered under conditions of distraction. Data were collected when children were, on the average, 11 years of age. The diagnoses (schizophrenia spectrum disorder, affective spectrum disorder, other diagnosis, no diagnosis) were ascertained when the participants were, on the average, 25 years of age. The data indicate that for this genetically high-risk group, scores on this test of the focus-execute element of attention predicted later development of a schizophrenia spectrum disorder. The data are from "The Israeli High-Risk Study" by A.F. Mirsky, 1988. In *Relatives at Risk for Mental Disorder* (p. 290), edited by D.L. Dunner, E.S. Gershon, and J.E. Barrett, 1988, New York: Raven Press. Adapted with permission.

CASE STUDIES USING THE ATTENTION BATTERY FOR CHILDREN

We present case studies of three children, one eight-and-a-half-year-old (DS) and two teenagers (FH and KT), who were referred for evaluation of problems of learning, attention, and school performance. In these cases, the data provided by the assessment of attention played a key role in the evaluation of the child's academic difficulties. In the first case, that of DS, the major issue concerned whether or not her global impairment could be attributed primarily to early lead intoxication. Although DS and KT differed widely in overall competence, the same agent, that is neonatal asphyxia, was implicated in the etiology of their attention impairments.

Case DS

DS, age 8-and-a-half, was referred for evaluation because of retarded development, including problems related to learning and attention. She had failing grades, had to repeat the second grade, and was being treated with methylphenidate for ADHD, with modest success.

DS's birth history was notable for meconium staining and for having had the umbilical cord wrapped twice around her neck at delivery. She was reportedly cyanotic at birth, with APGAR scores of 4 at one minute and 8 after five minutes. She had a history of repeated ear infections and ear tubes to facilitate drainage. Elevated blood lead levels had been found, which had been treated with chelation therapy. DS's developmental history was characterized by delays in the acquisition of language and motor skills.

DS was initially pleasant and cooperative during the examination; however, as the day wore on, and her dose of methylphenidate was overdue, she became restless and inattentive. Because her motivation and attention were erratic, the results obtained may provide only a minimal estimate of her current skills.

With one exception, DS showed moderate to severe deficits on tests assessing all elements of attention. The exception was her above-expected performance on the Coding test of the ABC, a measure of the focus-execute attentional element. Encoding, as measured by the Arithmetic and Digit Span tests, was impaired. DS appeared unable to grasp the shift-attentional element embodied in the sorting principle of the WCST, and achieved no categories. On the CPT, which measures the sustain element of attention, DS's scores showed low accuracy, with numerous impulsive errors, and long and variable response times on visual tasks. Despite extensive coaching, she was unable to perform auditory tests of sustained attention.

DS's performance on the ABC is consistent with a pervasive and severe attention-deficit disorder, possibly coupled with more basic impairments in auditory processing. She exhibited deficits, as compared to her peers, in almost all measured areas of attention and memory, as well as in visual-perceptual skills. Our observations during the testing session and the teacher's report suggest that the methylphenidate medication may be helping to normalize her attention.

The origin of her widespread deficits in basic academic skills, as well as her marked attentional problems, may be due to a variety of causes. In addition to the effects of lead exposure, other factors need to be considered. Experimental animal research and the human clinical literature have shown that partial asphyxiation at birth may injure brainstem auditory nuclei, as well as limbic and cortical structures. These brain structures are involved in the cognitive processes of attention and memory, as well as in motor development. The delay in DS's developmental milestones may thus be related to early asphyxic brain injury. Another factor underlying her impaired auditory information processing may be her chronic ear infections, which may have compromised structures involved in auditory processing.

Interventions on DS's behalf should continue, including classroom instruction and tutoring to address her learning problems, continued treatment with stimulant medication to ameliorate her deficits in attention, and counseling to address the problems with self-esteem, depression, and adjustment that frequently accompany impaired attention and classroom failure.

Case FH

FH, a 14-year-old student at a private school, was referred by his parents. FH's academic history was marked by consistent reports of disorganization, difficulty in completing assignments on time, and course grades below his measured potential. His teachers had noted that he sometimes failed to listen to instructions and disrupted the class. His academic record showed superior performance in a number of domains interspersed among a smaller number of average or below average performances; a pattern mirrored in standardized test measures at school. FH's developmental and medical history was unremarkable, although he reported that he was extremely anxious in social situations.

Testing was conducted on two occasions. In the first session, baseline measures were obtained. In the second session, testing was aimed at assessing the effects of a stimulant medication, methylphenidate, which he had begun taking. Neither FH nor his family reported noticeable changes since the initiation of the medication: Indeed, FH said that he felt no subjective change; however, reports from school had been more positive. On both occasions, he was pleasant and cooperative, albeit tense and anxious. Whereas FH approached the tasks in a serious way, his manner of responding was impulsive.

On measures comprising the encode, focus/execute, and shift elements of attention, as well as overall IQ scores, FH scored in the above average to superior range. Signs of impulsivity were noted on the Trail Making Test (Reitan & Davison, 1974; Reitan & Wolfson, 1985) and the Arithmetic subtest.

The capacity to sustain attention was assessed with the CPT. In the first session, FH was good at detecting targets but made impulsive, anticipatory errors of commission. Following administration of methylphenidate, his performance on the CPT showed modest improvement, primarily because of fewer errors. Following administration of medication, he also showed significant improvement on the Letter Cancellation Test (Talland, 1965), with better accuracy and fewer omission errors. Research has shown that practice effects on the CPT and Letter Cancellation Test are negligible, so that improvement could reasonably be attributed to the effects of the medication. Scores on the CPT and the Letter Cancellation Test obtained before and after initiation of methylphenidate are presented in Table 17.7.

FH's pattern of performance on the tests is consistent with that obtained in previous evaluations. The diagnosis of ADHD is somewhat difficult to verify, because FH's superior abilities

in many domains may mask his problems. Nevertheless, his test performance was characterized by impulsivity as well as impaired sustained attention—both hallmarks of the disorder. Moreover, it appears that the recently introduced methylphenidate had had significant beneficial effects on his performance. Whereas the medication had not eliminated the deficit in attention, it appears to have produced modest benefits. Further improvement might be expected over time and/or with adjustment of the dosage.

FH's difficulties, however, did not appear to be limited to attention. He exhibited significant anxiety, which was likely having an adverse affect on his academic performance and his social functioning. Reviews of the literature estimate that the overlap of ADHD and anxiety disorders ranges between 10% and 40%, suggesting that, on average, about 25% of children with ADHD are likely to receive such a dual diagnosis (Biederman, Faraone, Keenan, Steingard, & Tsuang, 1991). Moreover, the comorbidity of anxiety and ADHD is associated with reduced responsiveness to stimulant medication (Jensen, Martin, & Cantwell, 1997). Such a factor might account for FH's modest response to the stimulant medication. Whereas the methylphenidate had reportedly not exacerbated his anxiety, its effects should be monitored carefully. Alternative medications for ADHD, such as tricyclics or clonidine, could also be considered.

Case KT

KT, 15 years old, recently completed the eighth grade. KT's mother, who accompanied him to the evaluation, was concerned over her son's erratic grades in school, despite standardized test scores at or above grade level and several years of private tutoring. In addition, both KT's parents and teachers have remarked on his difficulties in following directions and in the processing of auditory information.

KT had previously undergone extensive psychoeducational testing. The most recent evaluation indicated that his IQ scores, as evaluated with the WISC-III, were generally in the average to high-average range. In contrast, scores obtained on the Woodcock-Johnson exhibited considerable variability: Measures of visual processing were in the 89th to 99th percentile; whereas measures of written language, including spelling, punctuation, and the ability to evaluate material from dictation, fell below the 20th percentile. A speech and language evaluation showed that there were relative weaknesses in interpreting information necessary to complete academic tasks accurately, especially with respect to written language. Among other recommendations in the previous evaluation was the suggestion that KT's attentional capacities be evaluated.

TABLE 17.7   FH's Performance on the CPT and Letter Cancellation Test Before and After Administration of Methylphenidate

Test	Omission Errors		Commission Errors		Correct Responses[a]	
	Pre	Post	Pre	Post	Pre	Post
Visual CPT-X	0	0	6	2	100	100
Visual CPT-AX	0	1	10	6	100	99
Visual CPT-X Degraded	16	3	26	23	79	96
Auditory CPT-X Tones	4	0	7	3	95	100
Letter Cancellation Test[b]	13	2	2	1	71	81

[a]Percentage correct on the CPT; number correct on the Letter Cancellation Test.
[b]Talland (1965). Used in lieu of the Digit Cancellation Test for participants ≥ 13 years of age.

The medical history of the patient, as reported by his mother, is significant for birth by "emergency" caesarean section. There was a surgical attempt to correct strabismus at age 5, which was reportedly unsuccessful. In addition, there is a history of high fevers at ages 5 and 6, accompanied by delusions. His developmental milestones were said to be normal, except for difficulty in learning to read, which had improved with academic tutoring. KT's health was reported to be good, although he was said to fatigue easily and sleep poorly. According to his mother, he does not use drugs or alcohol, and takes no medication.

KT was generally pleasant and cooperative during the examination. He had a tendency to approach tasks with some bravado, and appeared to challenge the examiners in a mildly provocative way. At times, when he perceived that he was performing poorly, he would attribute this to the equipment or to other external causes. He mentioned having had only about six hours of sleep the previous night, and yawned frequently during the evaluation. Nevertheless, his effort appeared genuine and substantial.

On measures of attention, KT showed considerable variability. Scores on some tests assessing attentional elements fell above expectation, while other scores were notably deficient. With respect to the encoding element, as measured by performance on the Arithmetic test, KT scored below normal (a scaled score of 6). This was not remarkably different from his earlier score on a similar test. During the task, he appeared notably restless and inattentive. He asked that many questions be repeated; despite the repetition, his computations entailed incorrect numbers with the correct or almost correct arithmetical process.

With respect to tests measuring the focus/execute attentional element, KT showed a number of deficiencies. On the Letter Cancellation Test, a timed test comprising three parts—each with distinct and different instructions—KT performed within normal limits overall. However, he had to be stopped near the start of the second part because he was using the test instructions that applied to the first part. When asked about

it, he said that he had simply forgotten. On the third part of the Letter Cancellation Test, he asked a question in the middle of the task. When told to focus on the task itself, he replied that asking the examiner a question and having it responded to would not slow him down. On another test assessing the focus/execute element, the Trail Making Test, KT performed slowly overall, retracing his lines at times and making one sequencing error.

On the measures of sustained visual attention provided by the CPT, KT showed generally good accuracy and few errors; this was the case even when task demands were increased. In contrast, he had poor accuracy on auditory tasks, with slow and variable response times.

KT scored at the 30th percentile for immediate recall and at the 11th percentile after a 30-minute delay on the Logical Memory subtest of the Wechsler Memory Scale-Revised (Wechsler, 1987). Of special note was his tendency either to report the auditory information incorrectly, or to confabulate details that he remembered only vaguely.

The test results indicate a mild to moderate impairment on attentional elements reflecting encoding, focusing/executing, and sustaining attention in the auditory modality. KT's below-expectation scores on a verbal memory task apparently reflect deficient encoding and poor sustained auditory attention.

These test results are consistent with the results of previous examinations and suggest that many of the deficits that KT manifests may be related to impaired processing of auditory information. It is not clear, however, whether this deficit is at the sensory level or reflects impairment in the higher processing of auditory input. There may have been fetal compromise associated with the somewhat traumatic caesarean delivery. It is well known from the experimental work of Myers (1969, 1971) that acute or even partial asphyxia at birth, if prolonged, may target auditory structures that have a high oxygen demand. Damage to these structures could result in subtle auditory processing deficits. An audiometric examination, and perhaps brainstem auditory evoked response testing, may help to rule out the presence of a subtle sensory loss. Whatever the etiology of KT's auditory processing deficit, it may be the basis of his attentional deficits. Such impairment may also be responsible for KT's tendency to confabulate information or invent details that he may not have heard accurately. This could also account for his apparent failure to follow directions.

SUMMARY AND CONCLUSIONS

We have presented a neuropsychological, test-based model for assessing attention in children. The model posits distinct aspects or elements of attention, which are assessed by different neuropsychological tests; there is evidence that each element may be supported by a distinct cerebral region. The basic elements of the model have been supported by its replication in a number of studies; its usefulness is attested by its application in a number of contexts. We have emphasized the importance of systematic and formal evaluation of attentional capacities in assessing children and illustrated the salience of the assessment of the elements of attention in several research studies. These have included investigations of ADHD in inner-city children, the relationship between attention and aggression in school children, the effects of exposure to lead, alcohol, and cocaine, and the use of attention measures as predictors of adjustment and psychopathology.

Finally, we have described three clinical cases in which attention assessment was a key aspect of the evaluation. Assessment of attentional capacities in children is more than just desirable; it is essential for understanding a child's academic and social difficulties and for the adoption of the appropriate remedial efforts.

REFERENCES

Adey, W.R. (1969). Spectral analysis of EEG data from animals and man during alerting, orienting and discriminative responses. In C.R. Evans & T.B. Mulholland (Eds.), *Attention and neurophysiology: An international conference* (pp. 194–229). London: Butterworth.

Aston-Jones, G., Rajkowski, J., & Cohen, J. (1999). Role of locus coeruleus in attention and behavioral flexibility. *Biological Psychiatry, 46,* 1309–1320.

Aston-Jones, G., Rajkowski, J., Kubiak, P., & Alexinsky, T. (1994). Locus-coeruleus neurons in monkey are selectively activated by attended cues in a vigilance task. *Journal of Neuroscience, 14,* 4467–4480.

Baharudin, R., & Luster, T. (1998). Factors related to the quality of the home environment and children's achievement. *Journal of Family Issues, 19,* 375–403.

Bakay Pragay E., Mirsky A.F., Ray C.L., Turner D.F., Mirsky C.V. (1978). Neuronal activity in the brain stem reticular formation during performance of a "go–no go" visual attention task in the monkey. *Experimental Neurology, 60,* 83–95.

Bandstra, E.S., Morrow, C.E., Anthony, J.C., Accornero, V.H., & Fried, P.A. (2001). Longitudinal investigation of task persistence and sustained attention in children with prenatal cocaine exposure. *Neurotoxicology and Teratology, 23,* 545–559.

Battig, K., Rosvold, H.E., & Mishkin, M. (1960). Comparison of the effects of frontal and caudate lesions in the monkey. *Experimental Neurology, 60,* 83–95.

Biederman, J., Faraone, S.V., Keenan, K., Steingard, R., & Tsuang, M.T. (1991). Familial association between attention-deficit disorder and anxiety disorders. *American Journal of Psychiatry, 148,* 251–256.

Blakemore, C., Iversen, S.D., & Zangwill, O.L. (1972). Brain functions. *Annual Review of Psychology, 23,* 413–456.

Chamberlin, R., Chamberlin, G., Howlett, B., & Claireaux, A. (1975). *British births 1970, Vol. I: The first week of life.* London: Heineman Medical Books.

Chamberlin, R., Chamberlin, G., Howlett, B., & Claireaux, A. (1978). *British births 1970, Vol. II: Obstetrical care.* London: Heineman Medical Books.

Chelune, G.J., & Baer, R.A. (1986). Developmental norms for the Wisconsin Card Sorting Test. *Journal of Clinical and Experimental Neuropsychology, 8,* 219–228.

Connor, P.D., Streissguth, A.P., Sampson, P.D., Bookstein, F.L., & Barr, H.J.M. (1999). Individual differences in auditory and visual attention among fetal alcohol-affected adults. *Alcoholism: Clinical and Experimental Research, 23,* 1395–1402.

Cornblatt, B., Obuchowski, M., Roberts, S., Pollack, S., Erlenmeyer-Kimling, L. (1999). Cognitive and behavioral precursors of schizophrenia. *Development and Psychopathology, 11,* 487–508.

Corwin, J., & Bylsma, F.W. (1993). Translations of excerpts from André Rey's Psychological examination of traumatic encephalopathy and P.A. Osterrieth's The Complex Figure Copy Test. *The Clinical Neuropsychologist, 7,* 3–15.

Cravioto, J., DeLicardie, E.R., & Birch, H.G. (1966). Nutrition, growth and neurointegrative development: an experimental and ecologic study. *Pediatrics, 38,* 319–320.

Cruz, M.E., Levav, M., Ramirez, I., Cruz, I., Mirsky, A., Bartko, J., Castro, S., & Izurieta, G. (1993). Niveles de nutricion y rendimiento en pruebas neuropsicologicas en niños escolares de una comunidad rural andina. In *Parasitos cerebral e intestinal problemas de salud publica.* Quito, Ecuador: Academia Ecuatoriana de Neurociencias.

Duncan, C.C. (1988). Application of event-related brain potentials to the analysis of interictal attention in absence epilepsy. In M.S. Myslobodsky & A.F. Mirsky (Eds.), *Elements of petit mal epilepsy* (pp. 341–364). New York: Peter Lang.

Duncan, C.C., & Mirsky, A.F. (2003). The attention battery for adults: A systematic approach to assessment. In M. Hersen, G. Goldstein, & S.R. Beers (Eds.), *The handbook of psychological assessment, Vol. 1: Intellectual and neuropsychological assessment* (pp. 582–610). New York: Wiley.

Dunn, L.M., & Dunn, L.M. (1981). Peabody Picture Vocabulary Test-Revised. Circle Pines, MN: American Guidance Service.

Erickson K. (1997). Attentional performance in children with attention-deficit/hyperactivity disorder with or without comorbid learning disabilities on neuropsychological tests. Unpublished master's thesis, The American University, Washington, DC.

Fedio, P., & Mirsky, A.F. (1969). Selective intellectual deficits in children with temporal lobe or centrencephalic epilepsy. *Neuropsychologia, 7,* 287–300.

Gloor, P. (1988). Neurophysiological mechanism of generalized spike and wave discharge and its implication for understanding absence seizures. In M.S. Myslobodsky & A.F. Mirsky (Eds.), *Elements of petit mal epilepsy* (pp. 159–209). New York: Peter Lang.

Grant, D.A., & Berg, E.A. (1948). A behavioral analysis of degree of reinforcement and ease of shifting two new responses in a Weigl-type card sorting problem. *Journal of Experimental Psychology, 38,* 404–411.

Heaton, R.K. (1981). *A Manual for the Card Sorting Test.* Odessa, FL: Psychological Assessment Resources.

Heilman, R.M., Watson, R.T., Valenstein, E., & Damasio, A.R. (1983). Localization of lesions in neglect. In A. Kertesz, (Ed.), *Localization in neuropsychology* (pp. 319–331). New York: Academic Press.

Hetherington, C.R., Stuss, D.T., & Finlayson, M.A.J. (1996). Reaction time and variability 5 and 10 years after traumatic brain injury. *Brain Injury, 10,* 473–486.

Jastak, S. & Wilkinson, G.S. (1984). WRAT-R: Wide Range Achievement Test Administration Manual. Los Angeles: Western Psychological Services.

Jensen, P.S., Martin, D., Cantwell, D.P. (1997). Comorbidity in ADHD: Implications for research, practice, and DSM-V. *Journal of the American Academy of Child and Adolescent Psychiatry, 36,* 1065–1079.

Kellam, S.G., Ialongo, N., Rebok, G.W., Mayer, L.S., & Dolan, L. (1992). *The course and malleability of aggressive behavior from early first grade into middle school: Results of a developmental epidemiologically-based preventive trial in Baltimore.* Paper presented at the NIMH/MacArthur Workshop: Developmental Perspectives on Conduct Disorder, Washington, DC.

Kellam, S.G., Werthamer-Larsson, L., Dolan, L.J., Brown, C.H., Mayer, L.S., Rebok, G.W., Anthony, J.C., Laudolff, J., Edelsohn, G., & Wheeler, L. (1991). Developmental epidemiologically based preventive trials: Base-line modeling of early target behaviors and depressive symptoms. *American Journal of Community Psychology, 19,* 563–584.

Kelly, T.P. (2000). The clinical neuropsychology of attention in school-aged children. *Child Neuropsychology, 6,* 24–36.

Lansdell, H., Mirsky, A.F. (1964). Attention in focal and centrencephalic epilepsy. *Experimental Neurology, 9,* 463–469.

Levav, M., Cruz, M.E., & Mirsky, A.F. (1995a). EEG abnormalities, malnutrition, parasitism and goiter: A study of children in Ecuador. *Acta Paediatrica, 84,* 197–202.

Levav, M., Mirsky, A.F., Cruz, M.E., & Cruz, I. (1995b). Neurocysticercosis and performance on neuropsychological tests: A family study in Ecuador. *American Journal of Tropical Medicine and Hygiene, 53,* 552–557.

Levav, M., Mirsky, A.F., Herault, J., Xiong, L., Amir, N., & Andermann, E. (2002). Familial association of neuropsychological traits in patients with generalized and partial seizure disorders. *Journal of Clinical and Experimental Neuropsychology, 24,* 311–326.

Levav, M., Mirsky, A.F., Schantz, P.M., Castro, S., & Cruz, M.E. (1995c). Parasitic infestation in malnourished school children: effects on behavior and EEG. *Parasitology, 110,* 103–111.

Lifshitz, M., Kugelmass, S., & Karov, M. (1985). Perceptual-motor and memory performance of high-risk children. *Schizophrenia Bulletin, 11,* 74–84.

MacLean, P.D. (1990). *The triune brain in evolution: Role in paleocerebral functions.* New York: Plenum Press.

Marmor, M., Glickman, L., Shofer, F., Amdurer, L., Rosenberg, C., Cornblatt, B., & Friedman, S. (1987). Toxocara-canis infection of children: Epidemiologic and neuropsychological findings. *American Journal of Public Health, 77,* 554–559.

Mesulam, M.M. (1987). Attention, confusional states and neglect. In M.M. Mesulam (Ed.), *Principles of behavioral neurology* (pp. 125–168). Philadelphia: F.A. Davis.

Milner, B. (1963). Effects of different brain lesions on card sorting. *Archives of Neurology, 9,* 90–100.

Mirsky, A.F. (1988). The Israeli high-risk study. In D.L. Dunner, E.S. Gershon, & J.E. Barrett, (Eds.), *Relatives at risk for mental disorder* (pp. 279–297). New York: Raven Press.

Mirsky, A.F. (1995). Perils and pitfalls on the path to normal potential: The role of impaired attention. Homage to Herbert G. Birch. *Journal of Clinical and Experimental Neuropsychology, 17,* 481–498.

Mirsky A.F., Anthony B.J., Duncan C.C., Ahearn M.B., & Kellam, S.G. (1991). Analysis of the elements of attention: A neuropsychological approach. *Neuropsychology Review, 2,* 109–145.

Mirsky, A.F. & Duncan, C.C. (1990). Behavioral and electrophysiological studies of absence epilepsy. In N. Avoli, P. Gloor, G. Kostopoulos, & R. Naquet (Eds.), *Generalized epilepsy: Cellular, molecular, and pharmacological approaches* (pp. 254–269). New York: Plenum.

Mirsky, A.F., & Duncan, C.C. (2001). A nosology of disorders of attention. In J. Wasserstein, L.E. Wolf, & F.F. LeFever (Eds.), *Adult attention deficit disorder: Brain mechanisms and life outcomes* (pp. 17–32). New York: New York Academy of Sciences (Vol. 931).

Mirsky, A.F. & Duncan, C.C. (in press). Lessons from high-risk studies: A neuropsychological perspective on vulnerability to schizophrenia. In W.S. Stone, S.V. Faraone, & M.T. Tsuang, (Eds.) *Early clinical intervention and prevention of schizophrenia.* Totowa, NJ: Humana Press.

Mirsky, A.F., Kellam, S.G., Pascualvaca, D., Petras H., & Todd, A.C. (2001). Bone lead level and sustained attention—A longitudinal study. *The Clinical Neuropsychologist, 15,* 265.

Mirsky, A.F., Kugelmass, S., Ingraham, L.J., Frenkel, E., & Nathan, M. (1995). Overview and summary: Twenty-five year followup of high-risk children. *Schizophrenia Bulletin, 21,* 227–239.

Mirsky, A.F., Orren, M.M., Stanton, L., Fullerton, B., Harris, S., & Myers, R.E. (1979). Auditory evoked potentials and auditory behavior following prenatal and perinatal asphyxia in rhesus monkeys. *Developmental Psychobiology, 12,* 369–379.

Mirsky, A.F., Primac, D.W., Ajmone Marsan, C., Rosvold, H.E., & Stevens, J.A. (1960). A comparison of the psychological test performance of patients with focal and nonfocal epilepsy. *Experimental Neurology, 2,* 75–89.

Mishkin, M. (1978). Memory in monkeys severely impaired by combined but not separate removal of the amygdala and hippocampus. *Nature, 273,* 297–298.

Myers, R.E. (1967). *Models of asphyxia brain damage in the newborn monkey.* Paper presented at 2nd Pan American Congress of Neurology. San Juan, Puerto Rico.

Myers, R.E. (1969). The clinical and pathological effects of asphyxiation in the fetal rhesus monkey. In K. Adamsons (Ed.), *Diagnosis and treatment of fetal disorders* (pp. 226–249). New York: Springer-Verlag.

Myers, R.E. (1971). Brain damage induced by umbilical cord compression at different gestational ages in monkeys. In E.I. Goldsmith & J. Moor-Jankowski (Eds.), *Second conference on experimental medicine and surgery in primates* (pp. 394–425). New York: S. Karger.

NICHD Early Child Care Research Network (2002, in press). Do Children's Attention Processes Mediate the Link between Family Predictors and School Readiness? *Developmental Psychology.*

Needleman, H.L., Reiss, J.A., & Tobin, M.J. (1995). Bone lead levels and delinquent behavior. *Journal of the American Medical Association, 275,* 363–369.

Nicoletti, A., Bartoloni, A., Reggio, A., Bartalesi, F., Roselli, M., Sofia, V., Chavez, J.R., Barahona, H.G., Paradisi, F., Cancrini, G., Tsang, V.C.W., & Hall, A.J. (2002). Epilepsy, cysticercosis, and toxocariasis—A population-based case-control study in rural Bolivia. *Neurology, 58,* 1256–1261.

Penfield, W., & Jasper, H. (Eds.) (1954). *Epilepsy and the functional anatomy of the human brain.* Boston: Little, Brown.

Purdue Research Foundation (no date). Purdue Pegboard Test. Purdue Research Foundation: Lafayette, IN: Lafayette Instrument Co.

Rebok, G.W., Smith, C.B., Pascualvaca, D.M., Mirsky, A.F., Anthony, B.J., & Kellam, S.G. (1996). Developmental changes in attentional performance in urban children from eight to thirteen years. *Child Neuropsychology, 2,* 1–19.

Reitan, R.M. & Davison, L.A. (Eds.) (1974). *Clinical neuropsychology: Current status and applications.* Washington, DC: Winston & Sons.

Reitan, R.M., & Wolfson, D. (1985). The Halstead-Reitan Neuropsychological Test Battery. Tucson, AZ: Clinical Neuropsychology Press.

Rosvold, H.E., Mirsky, A.F., Sarason, I., Bransome, E.D., Jr., & Beck, L.H. (1956). A continuous performance test of brain damage. *Journal of Consulting Psychology, 20,* 343–350.

Ruttinger, P., & Hadidi, H. (1991). MRI in cerebral toxocaral disease. *Journal of Neurology, Neurosurgery and Psychiatry, 54,* 361–362.

Stammeyer, E.C. (1961) *The effects of distraction on performance in schizophrenic, psychoneurotic, and normal individuals.* Unpublished doctoral dissertation, Catholic University of America, Washington, DC.

Stone, W.S., Faraone, S.V., & Tsuang, M.T. (Eds.) (in press). *Early clinical intervention and prevention of schizophrenia.* Totowa, NJ: Humana Press.

Streissguth, A.P., Sampson, P.D., Olson, H.C., Bookstein, F.L., Barr, H.M., Scott, M., Feldman, J., & Mirsky, A.F. (1994). Maternal drinking during pregnancy: Attention and short-term memory in 14-year-old offspring—A longitudinal study. *Alcoholism: Clinical and Experimental Research, 18,* 202–218.

Sun, H.F., Ialongo, N., Rebok, G.W., Tien, A.Y., Kellam, S.G., & Mirsky, A.F. (2001, August). *Aspects of executive function and the development of aggressive behavior.* Poster session presented at the annual meeting of the American Psychological Association, San Francisco, CA.

Talland, G.A. (1965). *Deranged memory.* New York: Academic Press.

Tatman, J.E. (1992). Elements of attention and concentration in normal aging adults: Locus of decline. Unpublished master's thesis. The American University, Washington, DC.

Usher, M., Cohen, J.D., Servan-Schreiber, D., Rajowski, J., & Aston-Jones, G. (1999). The role of coeruleus in the regulation of cognitive performance. *Science, 283,* 549–554.

Varga, E.M., Auer, H., & Zach, M. (1998). Toxocariasis in a five year old boy manifesting as bronchial asthma and behavioural abnormality. *Klinische Padiatrie, 210,* 128–131.

Wasserstein, J., Wolf, L.E., & Lefever, F.F. (2001). *Adult attention deficit disorder: Brain mechanisms and life outcome.* Vol. 931. New York: New York Academy of Sciences.

Wechsler, D. (1974). Wechsler Intelligence Scale for Children-Revised. New York: The Psychological Corporation.

Wechsler, D. (1981). WAIS-R manual. New York: The Psychological Corporation.

Wechsler, D. (1987). Wechsler Memory Scale-Revised manual. San Antonio, TX: The Psychological Corporation.

Wechsler, D. (1991). Wechsler Intelligence Scale for Children (3rd ed). San Antonio, TX: The Psychological Corporation.

Wohlberg, G.W., & Kornetsky, C. (1973). Sustained attention in remitted schizophrenics. *Archives of General Psychiatry, 28,* 533–537.

CHAPTER 18

Abstract Reasoning and Problem Solving in Adults

GERALD GOLDSTEIN

THEORETICAL FRAMEWORK

Abstract reasoning is no doubt the most advanced of the cognitive abilities. Whereas animals may be capable of problem solving, only humans can abstract. Thus, abstraction and problem solving are not synonymous, and problems can be solved without abstraction. However, formation of an abstract concept is often the most elegant way of solving a problem. The word *abstraction* connotes abstracting some unifying idea or principle on the basis of observation of diverse material. It is therefore an activity that is removed from direct sensory experience and constitutes a representation of such experience. The term *abstraction* is often contrasted to *concreteness,* the latter term indicating cognitive activity associated with direct experience, and without such representation. Concreteness is direct interaction with the "real world" without additional processing.

The "Abstract Attitude"

The relationship between brain function and abstract reasoning was probably first discussed during the late nineteenth century by the neurologists Henry Head and Hughlings Jackson. However, this relationship had its first full theoretical development in the work of Kurt Goldstein and Martin Scheerer and is best articulated in their 1941 monograph on abstract and concrete behavior (Goldstein & Scheerer, 1941). They characterized the abstract attitude with eight points.

1. To detach our ego from the outer world or from inner experiences.
2. To assume a mental set.
3. To account for acts to oneself; to verbalize the account.
4. To shift reflectively from one aspect of the situation to another.
5. To hold in mind simultaneously various aspects.
6. To grasp the essential of a given whole; to break up a given whole into parts, to isolate and synthesize them.
7. To abstract common properties reflectively; to form hierarchic concepts.
8. To plan ahead ideationally; to assume an attitude towards the "mere possible" and to think or perform symbolically.

Based on these points, tests of abstraction and problem solving abilities can be said to have the following task characteristics.

1. Learning to identify a relevant attribute or multiple attributes to solve a problem or make an accurate generalization.
2. Learning a rule or set of rules that solve a problem.
3. Concept formation, or spontaneous generation of hypotheses that relate disparate material.
4. Inductive reasoning through spontaneous formation of hypotheses that rule out alternative possibilities for a solution, and that finally lead to a correct solution.

5. Having an "attitude toward the possible" or forming and manipulating a mental representation of an object that is not physically present.

6. Spontaneous generation of plans that lead to ultimate solution of a problem.

7. The ability to shift, or change hypotheses or plans when the current one or the prepotent response is not productive.

The large variety of cognitive and neuropsychological tests available make it possible to identify procedures that provide assessments of all of these tasks. With respect to neuropsychology, patients with various forms of brain damage or disease lose all or some of these characteristics, as do some patients with psychiatric disorders, notably schizophrenia. Some of Goldstein and Scheerer's points are made in existential terms; whereas others are phrased in terms of abilities or attitudes. Goldstein and Scheerer use the term *attitude* to characterize abstract and concrete behavior, but they use it in an unconventional sense. To them, it is a phenomenological concept having to do with whether one views the outer world or inner experience in an abstract or concrete way. Thus, to Goldstein and Scheerer, the abstract attitude is a core aspect of the personality, and unlike contemporary neuropsychology, they did not treat it merely as one cognitive domain among others. Thus, one can remember, use language, exercise spatial abilities, solve problems, deploy attention, or perceive inner states or the outer world abstractly or concretely. The abstract attitude, or its absence, pervades all the cognitive domains and the modalities. Thus, tests of abstract ability are not viewed as part of a profile of numerous abilities, but are meant to document or illustrate the points made previously about the nature of the abstract attitude, and about behavior when the abstract attitude is impaired or absent.

Tests of abstract reasoning require to a greater or lesser degree the ability to maintain a mental set, to shift reflectively, to hold in mind simultaneously various aspects of a task (now known as dual processing), to abstract common properties, and to grasp essentials. Most scholars in the field would agree that these tests may be treated quantitatively, and would not agree with the relatively extreme view taken by Goldstein and Scheerer regarding numerical scoring. However, contemporary neuropsychology does not eschew the use of qualitative observation, and efforts are being made to make such observations objective, reliable, and perhaps quantifiable.

We have emphasized the distinction within abstract reasoning between those tasks in which the test-taker has to generate concepts and those in which an established concept has to be identified through experiencing a series of positive and negative instances. Whereas self-initiated concept for-

mation, attribute identification, and rule learning may all require the abstract attitude, they nevertheless appear to be separable cognitive abilities that may have differing clinical and adaptive implications. Absence of the abstract attitude, and consequent concreteness, may prevent solution of even the simplest conceptual tasks, but the capability of abstract reasoning can exist at numerous levels. Ability to identify relevant and irrelevant perceptual attributes and the ability to learn rules does not guarantee intact ability to generate conceptual strategies in "open-field" novel problem-solving situations (Minshew, Meyer, & Goldstein, 2002).

The importance of flexibility was also stressed, because attainment of a perfectly correct concept may not be adaptive when environmental circumstances necessitate a change. The Wisconsin Card Sorting Test stresses this latter consideration. The symptom of fixed perseverative rigidity is perhaps the end-point of this failure to reconceptualize under changing circumstances.

The Qualitative versus Quantitative Debate

Two statements, one made by Kurt Goldstein and the other by Martin Scheerer, reflect a philosophical view of the abstract attitude that is of great theoretical significance, but not without controversy. K. Goldstein (1951) said, "Even in its simplest form, however, abstraction is separate in principle from concrete behavior. There is no gradual transition from the one to the other" (p. 60). Scheerer (1962) said, "The average adult can, and often does, perform at either the level of successive functions or the level of simultaneous functions. However, the young and brain injured are capable of performing only at the first level" (p. X2).

Thus, the theory is that abstraction does not lie on a continuum with concreteness, but exists at a level of behavior that is qualitatively distinct. Thus, if one loses the abstract attitude as a result of brain damage, one does not simply become impaired in a still present ability; the ability is lost entirely. Put more philosophically, the abstract attitude is an emergent property and not the sum of more basic, lower-level, cognitive abilities. As Boring (1950) summarized nicely, emergence is rooted in Gestalt psychology, and particularly the concept that many properties of wholes are emergent, or inhere in no single part. The Gestalt psychologists repeatedly asserted that the whole is more than, or different from, the sum of its parts. With regard to abstraction, the process is viewed as an emergent entity, and not the sum of more elementary cognitive processes, such as association. Reitan (1958; 1959) took issue with this view, showing that brain-damaged patients improved their performance on Series VI of the Category Test relative to Series V. Both series involve the same principle. Furthermore, correlation matrices based upon neuropsychological tests taken by brain-damaged and control subjects revealed the same organization of abilities in both groups. Therefore, Reitan concluded that abstraction existed on a continuum of deviation from normal. The issue was of particular importance, because measurement of abstraction ability in the clinic or laboratory would be compromised if it were an all-or-none phenomenon, and it would be difficult to justify use of quantitative tests of abstract reasoning, such as the Category or Wisconsin Card Sorting Tests.

Subsequent consideration and study led us to conclude that both arguments were flawed. As Simmel and Counts (1957) have shown, there are ways of obtaining many correct answers on the Category Test without learning the principle, and it might not be correct to say that the brain-damaged subjects in the Reitan (1959) study improved in abstraction. Furthermore, some of the subjects in the Reitan study did not improve on Series VI. In an attempt to help resolve this matter, Goldstein, Neuringer, and Olson (1968) administered a concept-identification task that was resistant to solution by means other than learning the principle. They found that many brain-damaged subjects showed no evidence of learning even a simple task, but that some brain-damaged patients were able to learn both a simple and a more complex task. Therefore, they concluded that some brain-damaged patients did have apparently complete absence of abstraction ability; whereas others demonstrated clear learning ability, reflecting a quantitative deficit. Therefore, the Goldstein-Scheerer theory appeared to be overgeneralized, but on the other hand, there appear to be some brain-damaged patients who have a qualitative loss and who cannot assume the abstract attitude even in simple situations. Clinical or diagnostic distinctions between these groups were not identified in the Goldstein et al. (1968) study, but in a follow-up, Neuringer, Goldstein, and Jannes (1973) found that qualitative deficits appeared with greater frequency among older than among younger subjects. Age itself was not viewed as the explanation for the difference, but may have been associated with a number of factors including type of neurological disorder and age-associated changes in cognitive function. Many years later, this same distinction between qualitative and quantitative impairment reemerged in the case of schizophrenic patients. It was found in several studies that some schizophrenic patients performed quite normally on the Wisconsin Card Sorting Test; whereas others demonstrated severe impairment (Braff et al., 1990; Goldstein & Shemansky, 1995; Goldstein, Beers, & Shemansky, 1996). Correspondingly, several studies reported success in teaching schizophrenic patients to improve on the Wisconsin Card Sorting Test (Bellack, Mueser, Morrison, Tierney, & Podell, 1990; Goldman, Axelrod, & Tompkins,

1992; Green, Satz, Ganzell, & Vaclav, 1992; Summerfelt et al., 1991). Another study could find no such improvement despite substantial effort to obtain it (Goldberg, Weinberger, Berman, Pliskin, & Podd, 1987). Again, there appears to be variability with regard to existence of qualitative or quantitative impairment.

Current evidence indicates that it is an acceptable practice to measure abstraction ability with psychometric procedures, as most clinicians now do, but substantial, perhaps crucial, clinical information can be obtained through characterization of concreteness. On Block Design, does the patient use only one-color sides, or become fixed on sensory cohesion between similarly colored half sides and stick to it, although it may not lead to progress in reproducing the design? On the Stick Test, does the patient successfully reproduce items that can be named, but fail items that cannot be understood as concrete "things"? Efforts have been made to "score" these observations, but the common practice remains that of obtaining only the conventional scores involving number of errors and performance time.

Test Description

Within neuropsychological assessment, there are specialized tests of abstract reasoning as well as tests generally classed as assessing other abilities that can be interpreted from the standpoint of abstract and concrete behavior through qualitative observation. Although abstract reasoning may be involved in all these procedures, the specialized tests provide a direct assessment of the individual's ability to learn or form an abstract concept. Some of these procedures are paper and pencil tests that use language directly as the test medium. The most commonly used tests of this type are analogies and proverbs tests. The Raven Progressive Matrices Test (1982) contains analogy items that use pictorial material, but factor analytic studies have shown that the test has a strong verbal component, apparently because many of the pictures of objects are nameable (Lezak, 1995). Proverbs tests, such as the one developed by Gorham (1956), test the ability to form verbal abstractions in either a free-response or multiple-choice form. Some items from the Comprehension subtest of the various Wechsler intelligence scales are proverbs that require a free verbal response. Interpretation of a proverb, such as "One swallow doesn't make a summer" requires the forming of an abstract generalization from a metaphor.

The tests used most commonly in neuropsychological assessment are performance tests, which should not be characterized as nonverbal tests for various reasons, but which use nonverbal media, such as colored blocks, or geometric forms. The major reason for not characterizing these tests as nonverbal is that although the media used are generally not linguistic symbols, the test solution process may place heavy reliance on language. We will refer to them as performance tests, for want of a better term.

The most commonly used of these performance tests are sorting tasks. Many years ago Egon Weigl (1927) invented the prototype of these tasks that are still referred to as Weigl type sorting tests. The first tests developed were of the free-sorting type in which a variety of objects are placed on a table, and the subject is asked to group the objects through such instructions as "Sort those figures which you think belong together," or "Put those together which you think can be grouped together." After the first sorting, the subject is asked to put the objects together in another way. The sorting tests first made generally available in a published form were those described in a monograph on abstract and concrete behavior written by Kurt Goldstein and Martin Scheerer (1941). This monograph contains what is essentially a test manual for a series of procedures now known as the Goldstein-Scheerer tests. In the Goldstein-Scheerer series, there is one relatively simple sorting task: The Weigl-Goldstein-Scheerer Color Form Sorting Test, and two more complex tasks: the Gelb-Goldstein Color Sorting Test and the Gelb, Goldstein, Weigl and Scheerer Object Sorting Test. The test method, however, is the same in all cases; the materials are set out, the subject is asked to sort them and then to resort them. These tests assess the general capacities to form an abstraction or concept as the basis for the initial sorting and also evaluate cognitive flexibility, or the capacity to shift concepts. The administration of the Color Sorting Test is somewhat different from the other sorting tests. The test material consists of many skeins of wool (Holmgren Wools) that vary in hue and brightness. The subject is asked to select a skein of her or his preference, and to pick out the other skeins that can be grouped with it (e.g., different shades of green). When this procedure is completed, the examiner picks out a skein of a different hue and asks the subject to pick out the other skeins that go with it. This procedure is followed by triple matching. Three skeins at a time are placed before the subject varying in hue and brightness. The left and center skeins have the same hue but different brightnesses, and the right skein has the same brightness as the center skein, but differs in hue. The examiner points to the left and right skein and asks about where the center one belongs. The shift relates to whether the subject can sort according to hue and brightness. Shifting from hue to brightness is difficult for some normal people, and prompting about the idea of brightness is permissible, the point being whether the subject accepts the shift, and the idea of common brightness.

These free categorization tests provide abundant opportunity for qualitative assessment and variations of the procedure to elicit various features of concreteness. However, they differ from the concept identification procedures to be described later in this chapter in the sense that they are true measures of concept *formation*. That is, the subject is provided with an array of diverse material out of which the abstraction has to be formed. The concept has to be self-initiated, and the subject makes up the rule that provides the basis for grouping. The rule may be simple (e.g., color or shape) or quite complex as in the brightness or hue concept involved in the Color Sorting Test. Nevertheless, the subject is required to initiate his or her own categorization, or fail to do so.

The Goldstein-Scheerer tests are no longer commonly used, but their theoretical descendants are in common use. The most widely used ones are the Halstead Category Test (Halstead, 1947) and the Wisconsin Card Sorting Test (Grant & Berg, 1948; Heaton et al., 1993). Halstead (1947) was aware of Kurt Goldstein's theory of the abstract attitude, and it is historically important to note that the Wisconsin Card Sorting Test was first described as "a Weigl-type card sorting problem." In these tests that followed the Weigl-type sorting tests and the Goldstein-Scheerer tests, there was what turned out to be an important change. The concepts in these tests are not formed by the subject, but are inherent in the test materials themselves. The subject's task had changed from forming concepts to identifying concepts formed by the testmaker. Investigators in this area have therefore made a distinction between concept formation, which can be assessed with free sorting tests, and concept identification, which is what is involved in the Category and Card Sorting procedures. In a series of experimental studies by Bourne and collaborators, the process of concept identification was intensively studied, mainly in normal individuals, to provide a detailed understanding of its relevant parameters, such as complexity and the role of informative feedback (Bourne, 1966). In a sense, the difference between a concept formation and a concept identification procedure is analogous to the difference between a projective and an objective test. In the former, the subject can exercise free self-expression; whereas the latter requires adherence to a particular structure.

Perrine (1993) has made the important distinction in concept identification tests between attribute identification and rule learning. The Wisconsin Card Sorting Test stresses attribute identification. The correct answer is the stimulus attribute of form, color, or number. In the case of the Category Test, the correct principle is a rule, regardless of the attributes of the stimuli. For example, the correct answer is the odd object in an array. Interestingly, Perrine reported only 30% shared variance between the two procedures.

Brief descriptions of these two tests are as follows. The Halstead Category Test is administered through the use of an apparatus that displays the test stimuli and provides information to the subject regarding whether a response is correct. The subject looks at a screen below which are four numbered keys. The instructions are to look at the patterns on the screen and press the key that represents the right answer. If the correct key is pressed, the subject hears a pleasant chime. If the answer is incorrect, a rasping buzzer follows the response. The subject is told that he or she will be guessing at first, but when the concept or principle that unites the stimuli is learned, he or she will always get the chime. The test consists of seven subtests. The first of them is really a familiarization trial, and the second is a simple counting task. The remaining subtests require identification or learning of a concept, such as oddity or spatial location. The most commonly used score for this test is total errors, but error scores can be obtained for each subtest and are sometimes useful clinically. For example, some of the concepts are spatial in nature and some are numerical, each of which may have different implications for brain function.

The Wisconsin Card Sorting Test in its original version consists of a deck of cards with colored geometric forms printed on them. The cards vary with regard to forms, colors, and number of forms. Four of the cards are laid out as models, and the subject is given the deck. The general instruction is to place each card below the correct model card. After each placement, the examiner tells the subject whether the correct response was made. The task is to learn to sort the cards by form, color, or number based on the pattern of right and wrong answers. When ten consecutive correct responses are made, the examiner, unbeknown to the subject, changes the concept. For example, if color was the correct response, the correct concept may be changed to form. The test continues until the subject correctly solves the six categories tested, or the supply of 128 cards is exhausted. Numerous scores are derived from this test, the most commonly used ones being the number of the six categories achieved, total errors, and perseverative errors measuring persistence in sorting by a particular attribute after the relevant concept has been changed.

Some tests incorporate aspects of concept formation and concept identification. The Hanfmann-Kasanin Concept Formation Test (1937), also known as the Vygotsky Test, and a recent modification called the Modified Vygotsky Concept Formation Test (MVCFT; Wang, 1983) represent tasks of that type. The Hanfman-Kasanin is a challenging procedure in which the subject is asked to perform a number of sorts, much like the Color Form Sorting Test. However, there is a correct answer that the subject must learn through making sorts and obtaining information from the examiner concerning the correctness of the solution. The task is challenging because the concept is not a directly perceivable attribute, but is a second

order principle that has to be derived from the characteristics of multiple attributes. The MVCFT modifies the original procedure. It consists of 22 different blocks varying in color, size, shape, and height. In the first part (convergent thinking), the examiner selects a target block and asks the participant to identify all other blocks that would belong with it, telling participants whether each response is right or wrong. Participants are given correcting cues following each incorrect attempt. The procedure is repeated for four sets of blocks. A successful solution requires simultaneous consideration of the width and height of the blocks. Thus, the participant must combine abstract principles to determine the rule. When each complete set has been identified, the participant is then asked to state the sorting rule and then move on to the next set. Scores are based on the number of errors. After completion of this procedure, the examiner asks the participant to reclassify the blocks according to as many rules or ways as he/she can think of, one at a time (divergent thinking). After each classification, the examiner randomly mixes the blocks and asks for a new way of grouping. When the participant exhausts his/her means of classification, points are awarded for total number of logical principles. This test contains concept formation and concept identification elements.

The Twenty Questions task (Minshew, Siegel, Goldstein, & Weldy, 1994) also has a correct answer, but the subject has to self-initiate sorting strategies to arrive at that answer. The procedure is much like the Twenty Questions parlor game in which a target object must be named based on questions than can be answered only yes or no. The strategy for narrowing the possibilities and arriving at the right answer has to be formed by the player.

Another way of studying abstraction is through the examination of generalization. When the same response is made to a continuum of stimuli, the phenomenon is referred to as stimulus generalization. At a conceptual level, stimulus generalization allows for classification, such that all objects with the same invariant characteristics may be classed into specific categories. Thus, a table is still a table regardless of wide variations in size, color, shape, and other characteristics. When tasks are of a conceptual nature, stimulus generalization is referred to as equivalence range (Gardner & Schoen, 1962). Equivalence range problems assess an individual's tolerance for variability in stimulus characteristics within some category. In the case of the Color Sorting Test, for example, the equivalence range is the amount of variation in brightness accepted to categorize a skein as being of a common hue. Generalization procedures have been used mainly in research investigations. In a study by Olson, Goldstein, Neuringer, and Shelly (1969), the task involved presenting geometric figures, half of which were permutations of a circle and the other half of which were permutations of a diamond. The permutations reduced the figures in width in the direction of a common shape. Subjects were shown the figures one at a time and asked to indicate whether it was a circle, a diamond, or neither. The measure of equivalence range was correctly classified figures. A modified version of the Color Sorting Test was also administered. The literature suggested that brain-damaged individuals have narrow equivalence ranges, and that was what was found for both the color sorting and visual forms tasks. Thus, it would appear that abstraction of common properties by brain-damaged individuals has a narrow focus, probably limited to specific, concrete, stimulus properties.

Another aspect of abstract reasoning relates to what K. Goldstein and Scheerer (1941) referred to as an "attitude toward the possible." It consists of the ability to form a central representation of an object that is not perceptually present. They used the Block Design Test (Kohs Blocks) for evaluating this aspect of abstract and concrete behavior, because it is necessary to form a changing representation of the individual blocks in space to match the model. As the model presented in their version of the test becomes more like the desired production with the blocks, by making it larger or drawing in lines between the blocks, the task becomes more concrete and simpler for patients. Another form of abstract reasoning is challenged when a problem must be solved through logical inference. Situations requiring such processes generally require forming a plan or developing a strategy that ultimately leads to a solution. When lost in a forest, what is the best way of finding the way out? When shopping, what's the best way of completing errands in minimal time? In trying to reach a solution to a problem, what inductive methods are best for reaching the solution in the fewest steps? Psychological testing models for these abilities include searching strategy tests, the recently developed multiple errands tests (McCue et al., 1995), and game procedures in which a correct identification must be made with the fewest possible number of steps. The twenty-questions game task, in which the test-taker must identify an object contained in a large array of objects by asking as few questions as possible would be an example of a strategy task. (Minshew et al., 1994). The Tower of Hanoi or London problem is another strategy formation task. It is a puzzle in which rings are placed on pegs and the participant has to move the rings, one at a time, from one peg to another and put them in the same arrangement using the fewest possible moves (Shallice, 1982). The number of moves and time to solution are typically used as scores.

Recently, we have seen the development of more practical strategy tasks in which the participant is given a task to perform and must form a strategy to do it in an optimally effec-

tive and successful way. The Multiple Errands Test and the Modified Six Elements Test from the Behavioural Assessment of the Dysexecutive Syndrome tests (Wilson, Alderman, Burgess, Emslie, & Evans, 1996) are examples of such procedures. In both of them, the participant is assigned practical tasks and is scored for efficiency and success with which these tasks are performed. For example, on the Modified Six Elements subtest, the subject is rated for how he or she divides time among three assigned tasks.

Psychometric Characteristics

Perhaps the key methodological psychometric problem involving tests of abstraction has to do with construct validity. The issue becomes particularly important when a procedure has the appearance of being a measure of abstraction when, in fact, that need not be the case. The theoretical issue is that many tasks may be approached, and many problems may be solved, abstractly or concretely. Tests of abstraction with good construct validity are those that contain problems that can only be solved by abstract reasoning. Alternatively, tests and observational procedures that permit determination of the way in which the problem is being solved may also be useful tests of abstraction. We provide the following examples.

Scheerer, Rothman, and K. Goldstein (1945) described a boy who was an idiot savant. One remarkable thing the boy could do, despite his substantial mental retardation, was solve verbal analogy problems. However, further analysis of his performance suggested that he might not have been using actual analogical reasoning (i.e., abstraction) to solve these problems, but simple word association, clearly a lower functional level of behavior. Thus, observation of test performance permitted an evaluation of whether the abstract attitude was functioning. Subsequently, G. Goldstein (1962) and Willner (1971), in collaboration with Martin Scheerer, developed a new analogy test procedure that was resistant to solution by word association. They took verbal analogy problems, removed the first two words, and asked subjects to solve the problem with the third word only. Thus, in free choice format, the item "hot is to cold as up is to _____" was changed to "up _____", and the subject was asked to respond with the word that she or he thought was the right answer without having seen, no less solved, the analogy. In this research, they discovered that many analogy items could be solved in this manner at statistically significant levels. Willner went on to develop a new analogies test, called the Conceptual Level Analogy Test (CLAT; Willner, 1971), that was developed on the basis of excluding items that could be solved by word association at beyond chance levels. A children's version of this test was developed by G. Goldstein (1962). The point of this research is that correct answers to analogies problems can be obtained by two processes at different functional levels.

A second example is a study of the Halstead Category Test (Halstead, 1947) done by Simmel and Counts (1957). The Category Test is widely accepted as a challenging measure of abstraction ability, but these investigators make the following comment about that belief: "Our own data have consistently refused to bear out the above assumptions. We have found many correct responses given by subjects who had clearly not grasped the principle to be applied; we have also observed numerous incorrect answers of subjects who had apparently demonstrated their knowledge of the relevant principle by long errorless runs of immediately preceding items" (pp. 7–8). In a detailed and meticulous analysis of this test, Simmel and Counts showed that sometimes correct and sometimes incorrect responses to the test may be determined by perceptual characteristics of the stimuli, application to a new set of items of a previously learned principle, mental sets, and response tendencies learned during the course of the individual's lifetime. Based on their analyses, they concluded that a good score on the Category Test does not necessarily mean the attainment of principles, and conversely, errors may be made through misapplication of the correct principles. We would only note that although one may not have to identify the correct principles to do well on the Category Test, it, nevertheless, is probably the most effective way of doing well. These two examples are intended to illustrate that the construct validity of tests purported to assess abstraction ability may be weak, and that performance levels on these tests may be associated with other, usually lower, functional level abilities that do not require abstraction.

Two major methodological approaches can be used to determine whether abstract reasoning is being used to solve a problem. One of them, and perhaps the most desirable one, is to construct tests that are resistant to solution by other processes. That was the method Willner and Goldstein used in the case of their analogies tests. Simmel and Counts give some suggestions as to how such tests should be constructed. First, the coincidence of an initially preferred and the correct response should be avoided. Essentially that is what was done in the case of the CLAT, because correct responses were never common associations to the third word of the analogy. The correct response should involve weaker response tendencies. Simmel and Counts also suggest that the test should be long enough to allow for eventual rejection of initially preferred responses in favor of responding in a way that is consistent with the correct principle. Another effective method would appear to be the procedure used in the Wisconsin Card Sorting Test (Grant et al., 1948), in which the principle is changed unbeknownst to the test-taker. Thus, the first cate-

gory may be readily achieved on the basis of a preferred response tendency, but it is difficult to see how such tendencies would lead to solution after the first shift of the principle. Still another way of determining whether abstract reasoning is being used is to use principles that are not direct stimulus properties, such as color or shape. Higher order abstractions involving combinations of stimulus properties or relationships among stimuli may be used for this purpose. For example, Goldstein used the concept of causality in his verbal analogy item "Wind is to Sailboat as Gasoline is to (1) car (2) fuel (3) tank (4) oil (5) station." It is also useful in multiple choice analogies tests to include at least one associative foil, or incorrect answer that is a common association with the third word. For example, in the item "Slow is to Fast as Bicycle is to (1) Wheels (2) Airplane (3) Wagon (4) Ride (5) Play," "Wheels" or "Ride" are probably more common associates of bicycle than is the correct answer "Airplane."

The second major method of assessing abstraction ability is performance analysis, or systematic observation of how the individual takes the test (Scheerer, 1946). This systematic observation is guided by theoretically and clinically derived methods of analysis. Although performance analysis, sometimes described as analysis of process (Werner, 1937), typically involves observation of test behavior, it can also be applied to behavior in everyday life. Goldstein and Scheerer (1941) provide numerous anecdotal examples of concreteness in everyday life, such as a patient who was requested to bring someone a comb, but could not do so without combing her own hair. This example would illustrate forced responsiveness, or being stimulus bound, an aspect of concrete behavior.

Performance analysis is a method of determining whether some given problem-solving task is approached abstractly or concretely. A good example is the analysis provided by Goldstein and Scheerer (1941) of the Goldstein-Scheerer Cube Test (Block Design). Essentially, this analysis begins with the assumption that the models printed in the booklets for the Cube Test are representations of the pattern to be completed by the subject that is two rather than three dimensional, reduced in size, and without dividing lines. Subjects can approach the task abstractly by sharing that assumption, or concretely by a matching or copying procedure in which they try to match the impression of the design through manipulating the blocks until a match is achieved. Thus, a correct solution may be "happened upon," but is not reached by conceptual processes. Goldstein and Scheerer provide numerous examples of errors made by patients when they approach the task concretely. There might be concrete dependence upon size, seen when the subject bases the construction on the actual size of the model. The patient may have a preference for a triangle in its usual orientation with the base at the bottom, and thus may be unable to reproduce a model that contains an inverted triangle. These errors, and numerous others reflect an inability to break the pattern up imaginatively into squares. For each square, the corresponding block side must be found and the design becomes constructed by single block sides. A crucial point involves the imposing of an imaginal network upon the design, and holding in mind the square units contained in this network while matching them with the turned-up block sides. The extent of abnormal concreteness is evaluated by reducing the abstract challenge of the task. Models that are the same size as the construction to be completed, or in reduced size but with the lines drawn in are presented to the subject. Finally, the examiner reproduces the design with blocks, and the subject is asked to use that reproduction as a model.

The trend through the entire series of Goldstein-Scheerer tests is consistent with the previous example. The point of the tests is that of providing a number of problem-solving situations that provide the examiner an opportunity to observe whether the task is being approached abstractly or concretely. For example, the Stick Test is a simple procedure in which subjects are asked to reproduce stick patterns from memory immediately after they are presented. Normally, individuals learn to comprehend geometric directions in space, even when the object has no particular meaningful content. Thus, we can imagine a line tilted at a 45 degree angle. When such a line is displayed and removed, we readily reproduce it at the correct angle. However, an individual who has lost this abstract ability to appreciate directions in space may fail to make a correct reproduction. The interesting point is that when such an individual is shown a more complex figure with substantive content, performance may be normal. Thus, a patient may successfully reproduce a 9-stick stimulus assembled into a "house," but may fail to reproduce a single stick at the correct angle. This example illustrates not only a point about concreteness, but also suggests that abstract content and complexity are not always synonymous. The house was perceptually more complex than the single stick, but was associated with a normal response; whereas the single stick was not. Thus, increasing complexity of a task does not necessarily increase its difficulty from the standpoint of abstraction.

Range of Applicability and Limitations

Tests of abstraction and problem solving ability are commonly used in neuropsychological assessment of children and adults. However, limits of applicability exist at each end of the continuum of cognitive function. Severely impaired or disorganized patients typically cannot cooperate for these procedures. At the other extreme, because these tests were designed for assessment of brain-damaged patients, they do not have the complexity or difficulty level of tests developed for normal individuals. Therefore, unlike the intelligence tests that are often used as part of a neuropsychological assessment, these tests are not really useful for assessment of level of ability within the normal range. Furthermore, they are particularly susceptible to practice effects. Therefore retesting is difficult to interpret particularly among individuals who initially do reasonably well on these tests. For example, once a near normal or normal performance on the Wisconsin Card Sorting Test is obtained, retesting is compromised, because the individual already knows the right answers and may remember that the examiner changed the relevant concept after a series of correct responses.

Cross-Cultural Considerations and Accommodations for Persons with Disabilities

These tests would appear to be reasonably culture fair, because they do not rely heavily on language or knowledge of some specific environment or culture. The stimuli used, usually geometric forms, do not include artifacts associated with some particular culture. Obviously, instructions written in English would have to be interpreted for patients who do not speak English. The major sociocultural limitation would therefore relate mainly to general considerations concerning the meaning and acceptability of testing in different cultures (see Nell, Chapter 23 in this book).

These tests were designed for individuals with reasonably intact vision, hearing, and motor abilities. Typically, ad hoc accommodations are made for various disabilities where possible. There are two major issues with regard to accommodation: testing of patients with severe sensory or motor handicaps of the upper extremities and of patients who are not ambulatory. In general, the former matter is dealt with on an ad hoc basis. There are no formal versions of the Category Test or the Wisconsin Card Sorting Test for the blind or the deaf. However, the Wisconsin Card Sorting Test can be administered at bedside, and this can be accomplished for the Category Test as well if one wishes to use the booklet version of this test, or a version that can be administered with a lap top computer. In the case of individuals who are severely visually impaired, the traditional methodology has been to substitute auditory modality tests. In the case of abstract reasoning, proverbs or analogies tests may be used. Using tests based upon tactile perception is another useful strategy. The Halstead Tactual Performance Test may be administered to an individual who is blind and provides a good assessment of problem-solving ability. For patients with profound hearing loss, spoken instructions may be presented visually or any technology that provides sufficient amplification may be used. The absence of standard neuropsychological tests for individuals with severe sensory deficits is a limitation of the field that is in need of correction.

For patients with impaired mobility, the use of laptop computers and related software has greatly expanded the capability of bedside testing and testing of patients in their homes. Such technologies as headsticks, voice activation, and application of robotics should become increasingly viable methods of accommodating individuals with physical handicaps, or who are too ill to travel to an assessment laboratory.

Legal and Ethical Considerations

Neuropsychological assessment has become a well-established component of forensic psychology. Indeed, there is now a journal, *Forensic Neuropsychology,* that is entirely devoted to this area. There are no specific legal considerations for abstract reasoning and problem solving aside from those associated with forensic neuropsychology in general, but several issues may be raised that may be particularly pertinent to this area. First, when choosing tests of abstract reasoning and problem solving for legal purposes, as in the case of essentially all tests used, it is best to choose quantitative, well-standardized procedures that produce objective scores, and for which there is an adequate literature regarding the medical condition of the client. The Category and Wisconsin Card Sorting Tests are the most popular of these instruments. It is also important to be prepared to provide credentials attesting to qualifications to use those tests.

Perhaps most importantly, the psychologist should be able to explain the consequences of different levels of abstraction deficit observed in test performance for functional activities of daily living. In the case of abstraction and problem solving, the functional limitations produced by performance on the relevant tests are quite clear. Perhaps good guidelines are provided by Goldstein and Scheerer's (1941) description of the abstract attitude discussed previously. Matters of concern generally involve ability to plan, to solve new problems, to learn from experience in a way that allows for forming generalizations, and the ability to imagine events not present in the immediate environment. Questions may be raised as to whether these deficits produce severe disability such that they compromise the abilities to work, continue with education, or function independently in the community.

Particularly in litigation regarding injury or medical malpractice, the neuropsychologist is often questioned about the authenticity of test results, and the matter of malingering is raised. It is obviously easy to appear disabled on the standard abstraction and problem-solving tests by intentionally pressing the wrong key or sorting into the wrong category. Where this consideration is an issue, the use of one of the many available malingering tests is suggested. The psychologist declaring that it is not his or her opinion that the client was malingering may not be sufficient. Also, because the abstract reasoning and problem-solving tests measure complex behavior, the question may be raised as to whether the test results are based upon emotional considerations, such as anxiety or depression, rather than on injury or disease. To be prepared to answer this line of questioning, the neuropsychologist may wish to do at least a brief personality assessment for determining whether an emotional condition is present. We have evaluated patients in which it was our opinion that test performance was, in fact, largely determined by emotional considerations. Thus, the question is a reasonable one to raise, and testers should be prepared with an adequate assessment.

The major professional and ethical considerations associated with neuropsychological assessment have to do with qualifications and the use of technicians in testing. With regard to qualifications, the use of tests of abstract reasoning and problem solving within the context of employing these tests to assist in diagnosing brain disorders and inferring brain-behavior relationships requires special training and experience in clinical neuropsychology and the neurosciences. Application of these tests to psychiatric patients necessitates additional training and experience in psychopathology in a psychiatric or clinical psychological setting.

The use of technicians in neuropsychological assessment remains a controversial area. Some clinicians prefer to do all of the testing; whereas others rely entirely on technicians for test administration and scoring. With regard to the specific matter of tests of abstract reasoning and problem solving, it would appear to be reasonable to suggest that the older sorting tests that do not have formal scoring systems and that rely on qualitative observations should be given by experienced clinicians. However, the Category and Wisconsin Card Sorting Tests are partly or completely automated and have objective scoring systems. There seems no reason for not having technicians give these tests, as is now a common practice in the field.

Computerization

Computer versions of the Halstead Category Test and the Wisconsin Card Sorting Test are commercially available. For example, Psychological Assessment Resources provides computerized versions of the Category Test and the Wisconsin Card Sorting Test. The available computer packages administer the tests using a desktop computer and score them. However, their use is controversial and is not acceptable to some authorities in the field. With regard to the Category Test, the controversial issue concerns the matter of whether it is the same test as the one developed in Halstead's laboratory. The major issue appears to concern the buzzer and chime signals. In Halstead's (1947) description he said, "For each item selection of the correct key by the subject automatically sounds a chime, while selection of any wrong key sounds a buzzer, tuned to simulate the sound of a 'raspberry' or 'Bronx cheer'" (p. 58). Apparently he intended the buzzer to be aversive. The available computer versions do not reproduce these sounds with the same level of intensity, and the buzzer does not really have an aversive quality. The problem with the Wisconsin Card Sorting Test is that computer administration may alter performance, at least in some populations. In an important study, Ozonoff (1995) has shown that computer administration of the Wisconsin Card Sorting Test to individuals with autism attenuated performance deficits found on standard administration. The appeal of computer administration is substantial, but its increased acceptability would appear to await technological advances and in some cases the obtaining of new normative information and clinical validation for computerized versions.

Current Research Status

Impairment of abstraction ability, or features of abnormal concreteness, can occur in a broad variety of brain disorders and in a variety of types of psychopathology, notably schizophrenia, alcoholism, and several of the developmental disorders. Earlier in the history of the field of neuropsychology, there appears to have been a consensus that abstraction ability was localized in the frontal lobes, and consequently, that neuropsychological tests of abstract reasoning are particularly sensitive to frontal lobe dysfunction. Although it is not being suggested that the frontal lobes have nothing to do with abstraction, substantial evidence does not support specific localization. Impairment of abstract reasoning is found among patients with generalized brain damage and is often apparent when there is focal brain damage outside of the frontal lobes. There is impressive evidence from lesion (Milner, 1963) and imaging studies (Goldberg et al., 1987) that there is an association between performance on the Wisconsin Card Sorting Test and dysfunction of the dorsolateral surface of the frontal lobe. However, that finding may pertain to the specific symptoms of working memory deficits (Barcelo, Sanz, Molina, & Rubia, 1997) and perseverative rigidity, or incapacity to shift sets, and not to abstraction per se. Patients with a variety of disorders that do not involve the dorsolateral surface of

the frontal lobes also do poorly on the Wisconsin Card Sorting test, but abnormal concreteness may be manifested in different error patterns than are found in patients with focal frontal lobe lesions. Although the specific pathways have not been identified, abstraction is probably best thought of as being mediated by a widespread network involving numerous cortical, and perhaps subcortical, structures. This view of the frontal lobes and abstraction is supported in a review paper by Reitan and Wolfson (1994), which includes a detailed analysis of the research associated with the frontal lobes and tests of abstraction. Reitan concludes his review by stating in reference to the field of clinical neuropsychology, "It appears that such an approach would also lead investigators to recognize that other cerebral areas share essentially all of the higher level cognitive functions of the frontal lobes" (p. 192). If this is the case, clinicians should exercise caution in characterizing tests involving abstraction, such as the Wisconsin Card Sorting Test or the Trail Making Test as specific indicators of frontal lobe dysfunction.

Perhaps a more productive line of inquiry would involve study of particular disorders that exhibit interesting patterns of impaired abstract reasoning that could potentially clarify the nature of the underlying neurobiological substratum. We will therefore turn our attention to two such disorders that have received extensive investigation in recent times: schizophrenia and autism. The research involving the use of abstraction and problem-solving tests is so extensive that it is not possible to provide a comprehensive overview. We would emphasize that there are large amounts of work in such areas as brain trauma, degenerative diseases of the elderly, vascular disease, and the demyelinating diseases. However, a review of the areas of schizophrenia and autism should provide information about how research is done with abstraction and problem-solving tests, and what the scientific status of those tests are with regard to the psychological constructs they are based upon and their brain-behavior relationships.

Abstract Reasoning in Schizophrenia

Several generations of research are concerned with thought disorder in schizophrenia, much of it related to the schizophrenic patient's incapacity to reason conceptually. At least at a quantitative level, schizophrenic patients were characterized as performing like brain-damaged patients on sorting tests and related measures of abstract reasoning (Goldstein, 1978). However, in many ways, their concreteness was reported as being different from that found in patients with structural brain damage. It has been described as more physiognomic, personalized, paleological, or bizarre than the more primitive and simplified thinking of the brain-damaged patient. The equivalence range of schizophrenics may be overly broad rather than overly narrow. Thus, when asked how a dog and a lion are alike, the brain-damaged patient may say, "They both have tails." The schizophrenic may say, "They both exist in the universe." Thus, schizophrenics have been reported to overgeneralize or overinclude rather than undergeneralize (Payne, 1961). In recent years, great emphasis has been placed on perseverative rigidity in the thinking of schizophrenics, based largely on their tendency to produce a large number of perseverative errors or responses on the Wisconsin Card Sorting Test. Studies utilizing cerebral blood flow and PET demonstrated that unlike normals, schizophrenic patients failed to activate the dorsolateral surface of the frontal lobes when they took that test (Weinberger, Berman, & Zec, 1986). However, it has been suggested that schizophrenics do not entirely lose the abstract attitude, as do the seriously brain-damaged patients, but they fail to use it under conditions of high anxiety (K. Goldstein, 1959). Normal individuals under conditions of severe stress may also behave concretely. This behavior may be sustained in the schizophrenic because of the chronic high anxiety level associated with the disorder. Recent findings of structural brain abnormalities in schizophrenics tended to discourage the idea that concreteness in schizophrenia is entirely associated with anxiety, but the question remains as to the availability of abstract behavior. One way of evaluating this matter is to determine whether there is an improvement in abstract reasoning as a result of training or medication.

As indicated previously, several reports concern attempts to teach schizophrenic patients to improve their performance on the Wisconsin Card Sorting Test, with mixed results. Shemansky and Goldstein (1996) have applied Reitan's method of comparing performance on Series V and VI of the Category Test to schizophrenic, brain-damaged, and control subjects, finding that the improvement by the schizophrenic subjects was comparable to that of the controls, with both groups improving significantly more than the brain-damaged group. Perry, Potterat and Braff (2001) have shown that Wisconsin Card Sorting Test performance of patients with schizophrenia improves when patients are asked to verbalize the reason why they placed the card where they did after each sort. Cuesta and Zarzuela (2001) have reported that the cognitive functioning of patients with schizophrenia, including performance on the Wisconsin Card Sorting Test, improves with administration of several of the new "atypical" antipsychotic medications.

Based on the more recent literature, it would appear that impairment of abstraction ability in schizophrenia is a heterogeneous phenomenon. Some schizophrenic patients show no clear impairment of abstraction on the Wisconsin Card Sorting and Category Tests; whereas others show severe impairment. The conflicting literature on the effects of training also suggests heterogeneity, because some studies showed that training was effective and others did not. The basis for this heterogeneity is not well understood, but is not a simple matter of variation in age, education, medication status, or chronicity with regard to length of illness or of hospitalization (Goldstein, 1990). Most of the evidence suggests that the impairment is quantitative and does not reflect a complete loss of the abstract attitude. Nevertheless, the consensus appears to be that the deficit is primarily produced by impairment of brain function and is not directly associated with anxiety. One widely held view is that the nature of the concreteness is fixed, perseverative rigidity because of the high number of perseverative errors and responses often made by schizophrenics on the Wisconsin Card Sorting Test. It has been suggested that this impairment is associated with a more fundamental deficit in working memory (Kimberg & Farah, 1993), but Stratta et al. (1997) did a study indicating that the dysfunction on the Wisconsin Card Sorting Test found in schizophrenia is not attributable to impaired working memory. Much of the literature (Perry & Braff, 1998; Pantelis et al., 1999; Everett, Lavoie, Gagnon, & Gosselin, 2001) attributes the deficit to perseveration and inability to shift sets.

The denseness of concrete thinking in schizophrenia may actually be severity dependent. In a cluster analytic study, we identified a subgroup of patients that, on the average, completed only 1 out of 6 categories on the Wisconsin Card Sorting Test and made an average of 110 errors on the Category Test. Other subgroups achieved greater numbers of card sorting categories and made substantially fewer errors on the Category Test. We speculated that the former subgroup consisted largely of individuals with very poor outcome or "Kraepelinian" schizophrenia (Keefe, et al., 1987). Their inability to make even one card sorting conceptual shift and their performance at essentially a chance level on the Category Test suggest that they have a qualitative impairment of the abstract attitude. The other patients either did not have measurable impairment of abstract reasoning, or differed only quantitatively from normal. Wiedl, Wienobst, Schottke, Green, and Nuechterlein (2001) showed that patients with schizophrenia who obtained high scores on the Wisconsin Card Sorting Test obtained higher levels of discriminative sensitivity (d') on a continuous performance task, a measure of attention; patients who could not improve on card sorting with special training had significantly poorer d' scores. In summary, the clinician should expect to find diverse results when assessing abstraction ability in schizophrenic patients, reflecting the heterogeneity of the disorder. The basis for that heterogeneity, and whether it reflects actual subtypes, a continuum of severity, or a combination of the two remains a matter for future research.

Abstract Reasoning in Autism

Autism is a developmental disorder marked by inability to make affective social contact, a restricted range of interest, and delay in language development. In the more severe cases, there may be total lack of language and mental retardation. It is not possible to assess abstract reasoning abilities in this group, and so our discussion will be limited to so-called high-functioning autism, generally defined in terms of meeting all diagnostic criteria, and having a Verbal and Full Scale IQ score of 70 or greater (Schopler & Mesibov, 1992). In these cases, communicative language is present, and the individual is testable. There is an extensive literature on cognitive ability in high-functioning autism, but here we will restrict our discussion to abstraction ability. Studies using the Wisconsin Card Sorting Test have produced mixed results, with some reports of normal (Minshew, Goldstein, Muenz, & Payton, 1992) and some of abnormal findings (Rumsey & Hamburger, 1988). The most likely explanation for the discrepancies are differences in general intelligence (IQ) levels among the samples used in the various studies. Autism, although a single disorder, may vary extensively in severity. Rutter and Schopler (1987) initially proposed that IQ is a reasonable index of severity of autism, and that view has been widely accepted. The major point we wish to make, however, relates to those individuals with autism who perform normally on the Wisconsin Card Sorting Test. Minshew et al., (1992), reported that their individually age and IQ testing matched carefully diagnosed autistic older children and young adults, and controls did not differ from each other on the perseverative errors score from the Wisconsin Card Sorting Test, the total errors score from the Category Test, or time to complete Part B of the Trail Making Test. Thus, relative to controls, they did not differ from matched controls on the commonly used neuropsychological tests of abstraction ability. However, they were also administered the Goldstein-Scheerer Object Sorting Test. On this test, they were able to do an initial sorting comparable to the controls, but unlike the controls, when asked to find another basis for sorting the objects, they were unable to do so. Thus, autistic subjects who produced normal performance on the Wisconsin Card Sorting Test, the Category Test, and Part B of the Trail Making Test, were unable to shift concepts on a sorting procedure, producing a highly significant difference from controls on this measure. In a subsequent study, this group of investigators used the twenty-questions procedure described previously and found that the autistic group was impaired relative to controls on

this task (Minshew et al., 1994). Rather than logically approaching the task by asking questions that reduced the number of possible correct answers, they tended to guess, or to ask questions that did not lead to a solution. In other words, they did not self-initiate a productive strategy. Taking these results together, and recalling our distinction among concept formation, attribute identification, and rule-learning aspects of abstraction, it appears that individuals with high-functioning autism are not impaired with regard to identifying relevant attributes, or learning preestablished rules, but are substantially impaired in concept-formation ability. Thus, they do well on the more recently developed concept identification tests, but poorly on the classic Weigl-type sorting tests. Minshew, Meyer, and Goldstein (2002) demonstrated the dissociation between concept formation and identification in individuals with autism through use of a factor analysis. Tests of concept formation loaded on a different factor from tests of concept identification in autism, but not in normal control, subjects. Because autism is now thought to be produced by an as yet not fully understood abnormality of brain development, the implication is that this distinction among types of abstraction may have neurobiological significance, because we have a disorder in which they can be dissociated. More specifically, the cognitive processes involved in self-initiating a schema for problem solving may be quite different from those concerned with learning to separate relevant from irrelevant aspects of the environment, or from learning pre-existing rules on the basis of repeated experience. Because this is a chapter about abstraction and not about autism, we will not pursue this matter further, except to indicate that there is evidence that the difficulty individuals with autism have with organizing schemata or strategies is found in a number of areas of cognitive function including memory and language comprehension (Ameli, Courcheone, Lincoln, Kaufman, & Grillon, 1988; Minshew, & Goldstein, 1993; Minshew, Goldstein, & Siegel, 1995).

Clinical Applications

In the case of adults, the use of tests of abstract reasoning are mainly applicable to neurological and psychiatric patients. In the past, these tests were used extensively to detect the presence of brain damage, evaluate its severity, and provide evidence of localization when applicable. Although this tradition continues, numerous new applications have emerged over the course of time, both in neurology and psychiatry. Furthermore, neuropsychological assessment has expanded into general medicine, because there is now overwhelming evidence that several general medical disorders, such as pulmonary disease and diabetes, have important consequences for cognitive function (Tarter, Butters, & Beers, 2001). Additionally, neuropsychological assessment is frequently used in educational and vocational rehabilitation settings for assessment of adults with learning disabilities, attention-deficit hyperactivity disorders, and related conditions.

Assessment of abstract-reasoning and problem-solving abilities stands as a crucial component of neuropsychological assessment, and this area should always be evaluated as part of a comprehensive assessment. It is rarely, if ever, irrelevant. Abstraction and problem-solving deficits are noted in essentially all forms of brain injury and disease with the relatively rare exception of mild conditions. These deficits are also commonly found in patients with serious mental illness, and when such patients are referred for neuropsychological assessment, abstraction and problem-solving abilities should be evaluated. The role of such procedures as the Wisconsin Card Sorting Test with regard to localization of brain function, particularly with regard to the frontal lobes, has turned out to be a complex matter. The consensus is that these tests are quite complex, and association with a particular locus in the frontal lobes is not associated with test performance as a whole, but with some component of test performance. For example, the implications for localization from the Wisconsin Card Sorting Test may depend upon whether the patient makes excessive perseverative errors generally associated with a disability in set shifting, loses set following a number of correct responses, or makes a large number of both perseverative and nonperseverative or random errors. The involvement of working memory with regard to producing impaired performance is also thought to be of substantial importance (Hartman, Bolton, & Fehnel, 2001). With regard to localization within the frontal lobes, there appear to be very different behavioral consequences depending upon whether the dorsolateral or ventromedial aspects of the prefrontal cortex is involved, and within the ventromedial area, whether the left or right hemisphere is involved (Tranel, 2002).

Future Developments

Here we will discuss three areas of potential future development. The first of them simply involves more advanced computerization of the existing tests so that they capture more of the intent of the test authors who formulated the underlying theory of the test and designed the procedure to best implement that theory. An example would be the problem of improving the reinforcing value of the buzzer and chime stimuli for the computerized Category Test.

The second area is the development of new tests. Some view the Category and Wisconsin Card Sorting Tests as old-fashioned, not because they are old, but because they do not

provide assessment methods based upon the current experimental literature. In general, these tests are viewed as too complex to form relationships with relevant systems in the brain. Rather than trying to divide the existing tests into separate components, it is probably better to develop new tests that evaluate each of these components separately and less equivocally. Experimental literature reports on many new tests that will doubtlessly become available as standardized, published tests in the near future. Some of these tests based on the newer literature, such as the CANTAB (Robbins et al., 1994) are already available, but not in widespread clinical use.

A third development will doubtlessly be the construction of tests that can be used on-line during neuroimaging procedures, such as functional MRI. In many settings, patients can be tested while such procedures are taking place, but the standard tests in their conventional forms generally can not be used. People working in the area have been forced to improvise, but hopefully we will soon have available a large number of published tests designed to be used for on-line testing.

SUMMARY

Neuropsychological assessment of abstract reasoning may be accomplished with specialized tests of conceptual ability, or with a variety of tasks that may be accomplished abstractly or concretely. The former tasks are generally quantitative procedures; whereas the latter method typically involves qualitative observation. In assessment of abstraction ability, it is important to ascertain that the patient passes or fails the task because of a deficit in abstract reasoning ability. Some tasks appear to measure that ability, but may actually be accomplished through a variety of other methods. Impairment of abstraction ability in brain-damaged patients may be a qualitative loss of the abstract attitude, or a quantitative impairment of level of ability. Furthermore, there are varying levels of abstraction. We have characterized two of these levels as concept formation and concept identification. Concept formation refers to those tasks in which the subject must self-initiate concepts; concept identification describes the situation in which the subject must learn an established concept. Within concept identification, learning may involve identifying relevant attributes or learning rules that organize diverse stimuli. Abstraction ability is not represented in any particular locus in the brain and may be impaired by generalized brain damage or by focal brain lesions throughout the cerebral hemispheres. We have suggested that analysis of the differing patterns of impairment of abstract reasoning in schizophrenia and autism can contribute to the further delineation of the neurobiology of this uniquely human ability.

REFERENCES

Ameli, R., Courchesne, E., Lincoln, A., Kaufman, A.S., & Grillon, C. (1988). Visual memory processes in high-functioning individuals with autism. *Journal of Autism and Developmental Disorders, 18,* 601–615.

Barcelo, F., Sanz, M., Molina, V., & Rubia, F.J. (1997). The Wisconsin Card Sorting Test and the assessment of frontal function: A validation study with event-related potentials. *Neuropsychologia, 35,* 399–408.

Bellack, A.S., Mueser, K.T., Morrison, R.L., Tierney, A., & Podell, K. (1990). Remediation of cognitive deficits in schizophrenia. *American Journal of Psychiatry, 147,* 1650–1655.

Boring, E.G. (1950). *A history of experimental psychology* (2nd ed.). New York: Appleton-Century-Crofts.

Bourne. L.E. Jr. (1966). *Human conceptual behavior.* Boston: Allyn & Bacon.

Braff, D.L., Heaton, R.K., Kuck, J., Cullum, M., Moranville, J., Grant, I., & Zisook, S. (1990). The generalized pattern of neuropsychological deficits in outpatients with chronic schizophrenia with heterogeneous Wisconsin Card Sorting Test results. *Archives of General Psychiatry, 48,* 891–898.

Cuesta, M.J., Peralta, V., & Zarzuela, A. (2001). Effects of Olanzapine and other antipsychotics on cognitive function in chronic schizophrenia: A longitudinal study. *Schizophrenia Research, 48,* 17–28.

Everett, J., Lavoie, K., Gagnon, J.F. & Gosselin, N. (2001). Performance of patients with schizophrenia on the Wisconsin Card Sorting Test (WCST). *Journal of Psychiatry and Neuroscience, 26,* 123–130.

Gardner, R.W. & Schoen, R.A. (1962). Differentiation of abstraction in concept formation. *Psychological Monographs, 76,* No. 41 (While No. 560).

Goldberg, T.E., Weinberger, D.R., Berman, K.F., Pliskin, N.H., & Podd, M.H. (1987). Further evidence for dementia of the prefrontal type in schizophrenia? *Archives of General Psychiatry, 44,* 1008–1014.

Goldman, R.S., Axelrod, B.N., & Tompkins, L.M. (1992). Effect of instructional cues on schizophrenic patients' performance on the Wisconsin Card Sorting Test. *American Journal of Psychiatry, 149,* 1718–1722.

Goldstein, G. (1962). *Developmental studies in analogical reasoning.* Unpublished doctoral dissertation, University of Kansas, Lawrence.

Goldstein, G. (1978). Cognitive and perceptual differences between schizophrenics and organics. *Schizophrenia Bulletin, 4,* 160–185.

Goldstein, G. (1990). Neuropsychological heterogeneity in schizophrenia: A consideration of abstraction and problem solving abilities. *Archives of Clinical Neuropsychology, 5,* 251–264.

Goldstein, G., Beers, S.R., & Shemansky, W.J. (1996). Neuropsychological differences between schizophrenic patients with heterogeneous Wisconsin Card Sorting Test Performance. *Schizophrenia Research, 21,* 13–18.

Goldstein, G., Neuringer, C., & Olson, J.L. (1968). Impairment of abstract reasoning in the brain damaged: Qualitative or quantitative? *Cortex, 4,* 372–388.

Goldstein, G., & Shemansky, W.J. (1995). Influences on cognitive heterogeneity in schizophrenia. *Schizophrenia Research, 18,* 59–69.

Goldstein, K. (1959). The organismic approach. In S. Arieti (Ed.), *American handbook of psychiatry* (Vol. 2) (pp. 1333–1347). New York: Basic Books.

Goldstein, K. & Scheerer, M. (1941). Abstract and concrete behavior: An experimental study with special tests. *Psychological Monographs, 53,* (2, Whole No. 239).

Gorham, D.R. (1956). A Proverbs Test for clinical and experimental use. *Psychological Reports 2,* 1–12.

Grant, D.A., & Berg, E.A. (1948). A behavioral analysis of the degree of reinforcement and ease of shifting to new responses in a Weigl-type card sorting problem. *Journal of Experimental Psychology, 38,* 404–411.

Green, M.F., Satz, P., Ganzell, S., & Vaclav, J.F. (1992). Wisconsin Card Sorting Test performance in schizophrenia: Remediation of a stubborn deficit. *American Journal of Psychiatry, 149,* 62–67.

Halstead, W.C. (1947). *Brain and intelligence.* Chicago: University of Chicago Press, 1947.

Hanfmann, E., & Kasanin, J. (1937). A method for the study of concept formation. *Journal of Psychology, 3,* 521–540.

Hartman, M., Bolton, E., & Fehnel, S.E. (2001). Accounting for age differences on the Wisconsin Card Sorting Test: Decreased working memory, not inflexibility. *Psychology and Aging, 16,* 385–399.

Heaton, R.K., Chelune, C.J., Talley, J.L., Kay, G.G., & Curtiss, G. (1993). *Wisconsin Card Sorting Test manual, revised and expanded.* Odessa, FL: Psychological Assessment Resources.

Keefe, R.S.E., Mohs, R.C., Losonczy, M.F., Davidson, M., Silberman, J.M., Kendler, K.S., Horvath, T.B., Nora, N., & Davis, K.L. (1987). Characteristics of very poor outcome schizophrenia. *American Journal of Psychiatry, 144,* 889–895.

Kimberg, D.Y., & Farah, M.J. (1993). A unified account of cognitive impairments following frontal lobe damage: The role of working memory in complex, organized behavior. *Journal of Experimental Psychology: General, 122,* 411–428.

Lezak, M.D. (1995). *Neuropsychological assessment* (3rd ed.). New York: Oxford University Press.

McCue, M. (1995). Ecologically valid assessment of problem: The American Multiple Errands Test (Abstract). *Journal of the International Neuropsychological Society, 1,* 149.

Milner, B. (1963). Effects of different brain lesions on card sorting. *Archives of Neurology, 9,* 90–100.

Minshew, N.J., & Goldstein, G. (1993). Is autism an amnesic disorder? Evidence from the California verbal learning test. *Neuropsychology, 7,* 209–216.

Minshew, N.J., Goldstein, G., Muenz, L.R., & Payton, J.B. (1992). Neuropsychological functioning in non-mentally retarded autistic individuals. *Journal of Clinical and Experimental Neuropsychology, 14,* 740–761.

Minshew, N.J., Goldstein, G., & Siegel, D.J. (1995). Speech and language in high functioning autistic individuals. *Neuropsychology, 9,* 255–261.

Minshew, N.J., Meyer, J., & Goldstein, G. (2002). Abstract reasoning in autism: A dissociation between concept formation and concept identification. *Neuropsychology, 16,* 327–334.

Minshew, N.J., Siegel, D.J., Goldstein, G., & Weldy, S. (1994). Verbal problem solving in high functioning autistic individuals. *Archives of Clinical Neuropsychology, 9,* 31–40.

Neuringer, C., Goldstein, G., & Jannes, D.T. (1973). The relationship between age and qualitative or quantitative impairment of abstract reasoning in the brain damaged. *The Journal of Genetic Psychology, 123,* 195–200.

Olson, J.L., Goldstein, G., Neuringer, C. & Shelly, C.H. (1969). Relation between equivalence range and concept formation ability in brain-damaged patients. *Perceptual and Motor Skills, 28,* 743–749.

Ozonoff, S. (1995). Reliability and validity of the Wisconsin Card Sorting Test in studies of autism. *Neuropsychology, 9,* 491–500.

Pantelis, C., Barber, F.Z., Barnes, T.R., Nelson, H.E., Owen, A.M., & Robbins, T.W. (1999). Comparison of set-shifting ability in patients with chronic schizophrenia and frontal lobe damage. *Schizophrenia Research, 37,* 251–270.

Payne, R.W. (1961). Cognitive abnormalities. In H.J. Eysenck (Ed.), *Handbook of abnormal psychology:* An experimental approach (pp. 193–261). New York: Basic Books.

Perrine, K. (1993). Differential aspects of conceptual processing in the Category Test and Wisconsin Card Sorting Test. *Journal of Clinical and Experimental Psychology, 15,* 461–473.

Perry, W. & Braff, D.L. (1998). A multimethod approach to assessing perseverations in schizophrenia patients. *Schizophrenia Research, 33,* 69–77.

Perry, W., Potterat, E.G., & Braff, D.L. (2001). Self-monitoring enhances Wisconsin Card Sorting Test performance in patients with schizophrenia: Performance is improved by simply asking patients to verbalize their sorting strategy. *Journal of the International Neuropsychological Society, 7,* 344–352.

Raven, J.C. (1982). *Revised manual for Raven's Progressive Matrices and Vocabulary Scale.* Windsor, U.K.: NFER Nelson.

Reitan, R.M. (1958). Qualitative versus quantitative mental changes following brain damage. *Journal of Psychology, 46,* 339–346.

Reitan, R.M. (1959). Impairment of abstraction ability in brain damage: quantitative versus qualitative changes. *Journal of Psychology, 48,* 97–102.

Reitan, R.M. & Wolfson, D. (1994). A selective and critical review of neuropsychological deficits and the frontal lobes. *Neuropsychology Review, 4,* 161–198.

Robbins, T.W., James, M., Owen, A.M., Sahakian, B.J., McInnes, L., & Rabbitt, P. (1994). Cambridge neuropsychological test automated battery (CANTAB): A factor analytic study of a large sample of normal elderly volunteers. (1994). *Dementia, 5,* 266–281.

Rumsey, J.M., & Hamburger, S.D. (1988). Neuropsychological findings in high-functioning men with infantile autism, residual state. *Journal of Clinical and Experimental Neuropsychology, 10,* 201–221.

Russell, E.W., Neuringer, C., & Goldstein, G. (1970). *Assessment of brain damage: A neuropsychological key approach.* New York: Wiley-Interscience.

Rutter, M., & Schopler, E. (1987). Autism and pervasive developmental disorders: Concepts and diagnostic issues. *Journal of Autism and Developmental Disorders, 17,* 159–186.

Scheerer, M. (1946). Problems of performance analysis in the study of personality. *Annals of the New York Academy of Science, 46,* 653–678.

Scheerer, M. (1962). *Seminar in abnormal psychology.* Unpublished manuscript.

Scheerer, M., Rothman, E., & Goldstein, K. (1945). A case of "idiot savant:" An experimental study of personality organization. *Psychological Monographs, 58,* (Whole No. 269).

Schopler, E., & Mesibov, G.B. (Eds.). (1992). *High-functioning individuals with autism.* New York: Plenum Press.

Shallice, T. (1982). Specific impairments of planning. *Philosophical Transactions of the Royal Society of London, 298,* 199–209.

Shemansky, W.J., & Goldstein, G. (1996, November). Evidence for conceptual learning in schizophrenic patients. Poster presented at the annual meeting of the Reitan Society, New Orleans, LA.

Simmel, M.L. & Counts, S. (1957). Some stale response determinants of perception, thinking, and learning: A study based on the analysis of a single test. *Genetic Psychology Monographs, 56,* 3–157.

Stratta, P., Daneluzzo, E., Prosperini, P., Bustini, M., Mattei, P., & Rossi, A. (1997). Is Wisconsin Card Sorting Test performance related to "working memory" capacity? *Schizophrenia Research, 27,* 11–19.

Summerfelt, A.T., Alphs, L.D., Wagman, A.M.I., Funderburk, F.R., Hierholzer, R.M., & Strauss, M.E. (1991). Reduction of perseverative errors in patients with schizophrenia using monetary feedback. *Journal of Abnormal Psychology, 100,* 613–616.

Tarter, R.E., Butters, M., & Beers, S.R. (Eds.) (2001). *Medical neuropsychology.* New York: Plenum Publishing Corp.

Tranel, D. (2002). Asymmetric functional roles of the right and left sectors of the ventromedial prefrontal cortices in social conduct, decision-making and emotional processing. Paper presented at the 30th Annual Meeting, International Neuropsychological Society, Toronto.

Wang, P.L. (1983). *Modified Vygotsky Concept Formation Test: Instruction manual.* Wood Dale, IL: Stoelting.

Weigl, E. (1927). Zur psychologie sogenannter abstraktionsprozess. *Zeitschrift für psychologie, 103,* 1–45.

Weinberger, D.R., Berman, K., & Zec, R. (1986). Physiological dysfunction of dorsolateral prefrontal cortex in schizophrenia: I. Regional cerebral blood flow evidence. *Archives of General Psychiatry, 43,* 114–125.

Werner, H. (1937). Process and achievement. *Harvard Educational Review, 7,* 353–368.

Wiedl, K.H., Wienobst, J., Schottke, H.H., Green, M.F., Nuechterlein, K.H. (2001). Attentional characteristics of schizophrenia patients differing in learning proficiency on the Wisconsin card sorting test. *Schizophrenia Bulletin, 27,* 687–695.

Willner, A.E. (1971). *Conceptual Level Analogy Test.* New York: Author.

Wilson, B.A., Alderman, N., Burgess, P.W., Emslie, H., & Evans, J.J. (1996). *Behavioural assessment of dysexecutive syndrome.* Bury St. Edmunds, England (1996).

CHAPTER 19

Sensory-Perceptual and Motor Function

GERALD GOLDSTEIN AND RICHARD D. SANDERS

THEORETICAL FRAMEWORK

The neuropsychological assessment of sensory-perceptual and motor functions comes closer than any other aspect of neuropsychological assessment to the physical examination done by neurologists. This area of function is shared by the two disciplines, and, in fact, there have been formal studies demonstrating the overlap between the neurological examination and neuropsychological testing (Arango, Bartko, Gold, & Buchanan, 1999; Jenkyn, Walsh, Culver, & Reeves, 1977; Stern et al., 1991). Nevertheless, there are some important differences in perspective and in specific areas of detailed expertise. Unlike other neuropsychological functions, such as memory and language, sensory-perceptual and motor dysfunction can be caused by problems outside of the brain. Within the nervous system, it can be caused by pathology involving the peripheral nerves or the spinal cord. Sensory and perceptual deficits can be caused by disease or injury to the sensory organs themselves—the eyes, ears, and skin. Motor disorders can be caused by illnesses affecting muscles and joints. Neuropsychologists do not have expertise or competence to assess or treat disorders of this type, but must be aware of the nature of these disorders so as not to misinterpret neuropsychological test results. Paralysis of an arm because of a spinal cord injury should not be mistaken for paralysis from a stroke involving an area of the brain. A hearing loss should not be misinterpreted as a language comprehension disorder. Slowness on the Finger Tapping Test described later in this chapter can be caused by damage to the motor control

areas of the brain, but it can also be caused by arthritis of the hands. Thus, the neuropsychologist who performs sensory-perceptual and motor testing works in a conceptual framework that has a medical/neurological aspect incorporating an understanding of the role of the body as a whole in contributing to functioning.

As a way of conceptualizing this matter, we propose that the various domains of neuropsychological functioning operate in a hierarchy of increasingly complex levels. There is first the basic sensory-motor level that heavily involves the end-organs, peripheral nerves, and spinal cord. This level manages input-output functions of the nervous system and includes such areas as basic visual acuity, reflexes, thresholds, and simple visual, auditory, tactile, and motor skills. The physical neurological examination focuses primarily on this level. The next level involves attention and is assessed with perceptual and motor tasks that require some differential response to the environment. A stimulus needs to be detected as present or absent, or a motor response must be associated with some discriminative stimulus. Some neuropsychological tests require selective attention, such as cancellation tasks, and some require geographic attention in which the test-taker must focus on a particular portion of the environment. Testing for visual neglect is a clear example of this, because the test-taker has to attend to the right, left, or both halves of visual space. Attention tasks are in a borderland between neurological and neuropsychological assessment. For example, neurologists and neuropsychologists commonly give neglect tests. There is also a level of complexity at which perceptual and motor performance is associated with some meaningful activity, such as pantomime, or executing a motor performance in accordance with verbal instructions (e.g., "Show me your right hand.") The highest level is complex behavior in which perceptual or motor performance is directed toward problem solving. Tasks of the Block Design type, or finding hidden figures in a complex array are examples of these kinds of procedures.

Within this framework there is an elaborate and detailed body of knowledge within each of the modalities involved in sensory-perceptual and motor function. That is, there is an extensive neuropsychology of vision, hearing, touch, and movement. Associated with these basic science entities, a neuropathology literature covers disorders of vision, hearing, touch, and movement. In general, clinical neuropsychologists are interested in "central" disturbances of these modalities that are produced by brain dysfunction.

We will briefly outline these areas. Visual field disorders (blindness in portions of the visual field that are not caused by eye damage or disease) can be related to lesions in specific brain regions. Monocular visual loss results from injury to the eye or to the optic nerve. Bitemporal hemianopia (loss of the outer fields bilaterally) reflects injury to the optic chiasm, often from pituitary tumor. Unilateral homonymous hemianopia (loss of peripheral vision only on one side of the visual field) reflects injury to the contralateral occipital striate cortex when incomplete, but if complete can only be localized to posterior cortical or subcortical areas. A unilateral homonymous quadrantanopia (loss of approximately one fourth of the visual field) can reflect a deep temporal lobe lesion if the superior quadrant is affected, or parietal lobe if the inferior quadrant is affected. Homonymous altitudinal hemianopia (loss of the upper or lower half of the visual field) can result from bilateral occipital lobe lesions. Visual agnosia, in which visual acuity is normal but the individual cannot recognize objects, includes such probably overlapping concepts as simultagnosia (inability to synthesize the elements of a complex visual stimulus) and prosopagnosia (inability to recognize familiar faces). This group of deficits is attributed to lesions of the extra-striate occipital or occipital-temporal areas of cortex. Visual neglect occurs when hemianopia is not present, but the client does not attend to one hemifield of visual space. This represents a milder form of hemianopia, or dysfunction of the right parietal cortex.

There are parallel phenomena in hearing. Auditory agnosia, which involves reasonably normal auditory acuity but an inability to identify sounds (words or nonverbal sounds), reflects a temporal lobe lesion. Auditory discrimination, or the ability to distinguish among sounds, has major implications for language comprehension, and many tests measure it. Au-

ditory neglect can also occur, and there are numerous other tests of auditory attention.

In the case of touch, there are measures of tactile neglect. Conventional symmetric double simultaneous stimulation of the skin reveals mild sensory deficits, unidentified through testing with single tactile stimuli. The Face-Hand Test is an asymmetric variant on double-simultaneous stimulation, in which the hand or a cheek is lightly touched singly or simultaneously. Performance is abnormal when the examinee persistently reports feeling only one stimulus (usually the face) when simultaneous stimulation is applied. This may reflect generalized or parietal disease. Tactile agnosia, often assessed with fingertip number writing (agraphesthesia) and tactile recognition (astereognosis) involve dysfunction of the parietal lobe. Finger agnosia, an inability to identify one's own fingers, is a complex phenomenon that may represent a disturbance of the body image or a sensory defect. Benton (1959) indicated that its specific interpretation depends upon the procedures used to measure the phenomenon. For example, some assessments include identifying the fingers of the client and of the examiner. It is also important to note whether the phenomenon involves one or both hands. If both hands are involved, the possibility of a body image disturbance becomes more likely.

The neuropsychological assessment of the motor system is primarily involved with skilled movement and evaluates speed, dexterity, and accuracy. Motor dysfunction is involved in a wide variety of brain disorders, sometimes in combination with other areas of disability and sometimes as relatively specific movement disorders. Motor dysfunction may also be restricted to one side of the body, in which case it usually indicates contralateral brain dysfunction. Bilateral motor dysfunction is found in a number of movement disorders, the most common ones being Parkinson's disease (and various other Parkinsonian syndromes), Huntington's disease (and the very similar neuroleptic-induced tardive dyskinesia), and multiple sclerosis. Each of these disorders has different kinds of motor dysfunction. There is the resting tremor and rigidity found in Parkinsonism, the choreiform "dancing" movements of Huntingtonism, and the tremor and weakness of the individual with multiple sclerosis. These disturbances reflect dysfunction of the forebrain basal ganglia. They are often apparent on casual observation, or may be identified by the neurological examination. Neuropsychological assessment may provide a more refined description of the dysfunction with regard to speed, dexterity, and accuracy and generally produces quantitative information that may be valuable for assessing current level and course, and for assessing the effects of treatment.

TABLE 19.1 Motor and Sensory Tests in Some Neuropsychological Batteries and Neurologic Scales

	HRNB	LNNB	PANESS	NES
Station and Gait				
Stressed gait			X	
Tandem gait			X	X
Hopping			X	
Romberg			X	X
Motor				
Grip strength	X			
Fist opening-closing		X		
Fist-ring				X
Fist-edge-palm				X
Alternating drawn figures		X		
Simultaneous asymmetric movements		X		X
Rapid alternating movements				X
Finger-thumb opposition		X		X
Rhythm tap reproduction		X	X	X
Foot tapping			X	
Finger tapping	X		X	
Finger-foot synchronization			X	
Motor persistence			X	
Synkinesis				X
Finger-nose			X	X
Heel-shin			X	
Praxis based on position sense		X		
Praxis based on vision		X		
Praxis based on verbal instruction		X		X
Conditional responses (inc. go-no go)		X		
Mirror movement				X
Tremor				X
Adventitious movements			X	X
Tap production		X		X
Grooved pegboard	X			
Tactual performance test	X			
Drawing and writing		X	X	
Speech production	X	X		
Extraocular Movements				
Visual tracking			X	
Convergence				X
Gaze persistence				X
Sensory—Perceptual				
Visual sensitivity and extinction	X			
Visual object identification		X		
Visual pattern completion		X		
Reading		X		
Spatial orientation		X		
Complex spatial processing		X		
Auditory sensitivity and extinction	X			
Auditory signal counting		X		
Auditory rhythm matching	X		X	
Audiovisual integration				X
Pitch discrimination		X		
Pitch reproduction (humming)		X		
Speech syllable perception	X	X		
Speech reproduction		X		
Stereognosis/tactile form recognition	X	X	X	X

TABLE 19.1 *(Continued)*

	HRNB	LNNB	PANESS	NES
Sensory—Perceptual (continued)				
Graphesthesia	X	X	X	X
Tactile sensitivity and extinction	X	X	X	X
Sharp-dull discrimination		X		
Hard-soft tactile discrimination		X		
Two-point discrimination		X	X	
Tactile direction sensitivity		X		
Right-left orientation		X		X
Finger agnosia	X	X		

HRNB = Halstead-Reitan Neuropsychological Battery (Reitan & Wolfson, 1993); LNNB = Luria-Nebraska Neuropsychological Battery (Golden et al., 1980); PANESS = Physical and Neurological Examination for Soft Signs (Guy, 1976); NES = Neurological Evaluation Scale (Buchanan & Heinrichs, 1989)

Test Description

The tests to be reviewed in this chapter cover the procedures used by neuropsychologists to evaluate the senses and voluntary movement. Tasks in both domains vary in terms of their complexity and correspondingly vary in cognitive demands and in the number of different abilities required. Sensorimotor tests used in neuropsychology tend to be higher in complexity than comparable tests used in other disciplines. Within a given category, this chapter presents tests in order of increasing complexity.

Sensorimotor testing overlaps with assessments used in neurology, psychiatry, ophthalmology, optometry, audiology, physiatry (rehabilitation medicine), occupational, and physical therapy. Neuropsychologists do not do full neurological examinations, nor do they do standardized vision and hearing tests, nor the detailed motor function tests done in other disciplines. However, neuropsychological assessment typically involves the use of tests in these areas. Table 19.1 includes pertinent content from two prominent neuropsychological batteries, and two prominent neurological examination schedules. Although there is considerable overlap (particularly with the neurological "soft signs"), there are differences in history (Goldstein, 1986; Randolph, 2002), emphasis and focus from these other disciplines that will become clear as we proceed with a description of the tests.

Sensory and Perceptual Tests

Of the five senses (vision, hearing, touch, smell, and taste), neuropsychological testing has emphasized vision, hearing, and touch. Tests of smell are of interest primarily to researchers, and neuropsychologists rarely evaluate taste. Also, some tests intentionally require the use of more than one sensory modality (e.g., audiovisual integration; Buchanan & Heinrichs, 1989), and some test the interference of one modality with perception using another (e.g., face-noise test; Guy, 1976).

Vision

Visual acuity is of interest in neuropsychology only because undetected or uncorrected deficits may invalidate the assessment. Like the neurologist and ophthalmologist, the neuropsychologist is often interested in the status of the visual fields, particularly when the fields have been limited by damage to the brain (as opposed to the eyes or optic nerve). Thus, neuropsychologists may map out the visual fields using an instrument called a perimeter or may do the examination by confrontation involving use of finger wiggles in peripheral vision. Blindness in a half (homonymous hemianopia) or quarter (homonymous quadrantanopia) of the visual fields is often produced by a stroke involving the posterior portion of the brain. Sometimes the right or left side of visual space is not blind, but is not attended to by the patient. This condition is known as visual neglect and is often tested by a confrontation method called the method of double simultaneous stimulation. Neglect is present when the patient detects the presence of a finger wiggle when only a single stimulus is presented with the examiners right or left hand, but will report only one wiggle when two are presented simultaneously. The field in which the wiggle is not detected is characterized as the neglected field. Neglect is generally found more often in the left than in the right visual field, indicating that the right cerebral hemisphere is more involved in producing this phenomenon than the left. Patients with neglect tend to ignore one side of visual space in everyday life.

Other neuropsychological tests of vision assess capacity to perceive forms in situations that make such perception difficult. For example, an object may be presented in an unusual orientation, or a number of overlapping objects may be presented, and the task is to identify each of them. There are ambiguous and hidden figures tests in which objects are disguised or presented in conditions of illumination that make perception more difficult. Figures may be presented in an incomplete form, but enough information is present to detect what they are. Sometimes an object is presented in the absence of its usual context. For example, many studies have been done of perception of a luminous rod in a completely dark room, with the task being that of setting the rod to vertical.

Visual agnosia is a rare condition, in which the patient loses the capacity to identify objects. Visual acuity is intact, but these individuals are functionally blind, because they cannot recognize form and apparently see only patches of color.

Generally, when presented with colored objects, they can identify the color, but not the object. There are no standard tests for visual agnosia, but the condition becomes apparent by asking the patient to identify simple objects.

Many tests of vision perhaps belong more in the experimental psychology laboratory than the neuropsychology clinic, but some of them have been shown to be clinically relevant. In past years, there has been extensive study of flicker fusion as a neuropsychological test. This procedure determines the frequency threshold at which a flickering light appears to blend into a continuous light. Thresholds have been found to vary among different patient groups and in different parts of the retina in normal individuals. Visual perceptual adaptation has also been studied in patient groups. Adaptation is the process by which movements are coordinated with visual stimuli, an important behavior involved in pointing, reaching, and related activities. It is evaluated by having the individual wear displacing prisms and recording performance during relearning to point accurately to targets.

Hearing

Hearing acuity deficits interfere with neuropsychological assessment, but are not of primary interest. Neglect may occur in hearing as well as in vision. When sounds are presented to the ears singly, the patient may be able to identify which ear it was presented to, but the patient with neglect reports hearing only the sound presented to one ear when both ears are actually stimulated. Unlike visual neglect, auditory neglect is not known to be more common in the left as compared with the right ear. Perhaps the most well-known and widely studied neuropsychological procedure involving hearing is dichotic listening (Kimura, 1967). In the dichotic listening experiment, auditory stimuli, usually two different words, letter pairs, or digits are presented through earphones to each ear simultaneously. The patient is asked to report what is heard without regard to ear or in a specified ear. The normal response in right-handed, and most left-handed, individuals is typically consistent with what is called the "right ear advantage." That is, the word chosen is the one delivered to the right ear. Other indications are that if both words are reported, the word delivered to the right ear is reported first. If errors are made, more of them involve words presented to the left ear. The reason for this phenomenon is that in most individuals the part of the brain that identifies words is in the left hemisphere. Therefore there is a direct route from the right ear to that area. In the case of the left ear, the word most go to the right hemisphere and cross over the corpus callosum to the left hemisphere, where it is interpreted. This process is lengthier, more complex, and less efficient. Numerous studies of dichotic listening have been done with patients in whom the right ear advantage is compromised, because of damage to the left hemisphere or for other reasons.

The auditory equivalent of visual agnosia is called auditory agnosia. It is quite rare and when the impairment is only for speech, it is called pure word deafness. In rare cases, the patient may have normal auditory acuity, but cannot recognize nonverbal sounds. In the case of pure word deafness, the distinction between a perceptual and a linguistic disorder is unclear. When speech sounds are presented, the patient essentially hears noise that has no meaning. In general, agnosia has been defined as perception without meaning. More sophisticated neuropsychological assessment that goes beyond the use of standard clinical tests may measure sound localization, or the ability to identify the point in space from which a sound comes. In all of these cases, it is important to rule out hearing loss or deafness that involves the auditory system, but not the brain. Also, many auditory tests assess linguistic, attentional, or problem-solving abilities and not auditory perception in itself. Clinicians need to take precautions to be assured that impairment on these tests is not the result of hearing loss.

Touch

Tests of simple tactile acuity, most often using hairs to stimulate the skin around the hands and feet, are often conducted by internists, physical therapists, and neurologists. There are a great many tests of higher-order tactile perception. We will summarize the tests contained in the two most widely used standard neuropsychological batteries: the Halstead-Reitan Battery (Reitan & Wolfson, 1993) and the Luria-Nebraska Battery (Golden, Hammeke, & Purisch 1980). Each of these procedures contains sections for examination of tactile function. The Halstead-Reitan has a sensory-perceptual subbattery, and the Luria-Nebraska has a Tactile Functions scale.

Comparable to the phenomena of visual and auditory neglect or suppression is tactile neglect. In the Halstead-Reitan procedure, it is assessed with the method of double simultaneous stimulation. Over a series of trials, light touch is given to the right hands and cheeks, varying randomly between single and double simultaneous stimulation. On double simultaneous stimulation, all hand-cheek combinations are tested (e.g., right hand-left cheek). Reporting of a single stimulus when a double stimulus is administered is counted as suppression. Total number of right hand, left hand, right cheek, and left cheek suppressions are the scores

Finger agnosia is a condition in which the individual does not have the ability to recognize the fingers of his or her hands. In some cases, this is a tactile perceptual disorder;

whereas in others, it is a partial disturbance of the body image. In the Halstead-Reitan method of assessing this condition, the patient is given a numbering system for the fingers and, with eyes closed, is asked to provide the number assigned to the finger. Twenty trials are given for each hand. The score is the number of errors for each hand.

In tactile agnosia or astereognosis, loss is only for three-dimensional objects. When the stimulus material consists of words or objects written on the hands, impairment is called agraphesthesia. In all cases, there is an impairment of the ability to recognize objects by touch. Testing involves having the subject identify stimuli applied to the hands with eyes closed. The Halstead-Reitan procedure contains two tests; Finger-tip Number Writing and Tactile Form Recognition. In the case of Finger-tip Number Writing, with eyes closed, the patient is asked to identify numbers written with a pencil on the fingertips. Each finger of each hand is tested over a series of twenty trials for each hand. The score is the number of errors for each hand. In Tactile Form Recognition, the patient puts her or his hand behind a blind and plastic shapes are placed in it. The patient must then identify the shapes by pointing to the matching shape mounted on a board. Response time and errors are recorded for each trial.

The Luria-Nebraska neuropsychological battery contains a Tactile Functions scale that provides a series of brief items assessing a variety of sensory tests that are often given in lengthier versions. It therefore provides a quick screening that covers several procedures, some of which are often used in the physical neurological examination. The client is blindfolded for the entire procedure, which consists of 21 brief items. The first two items measure touch location. The clinician lightly touches the client's right and left hands and arms with the eraser end of a pencil. The client has to say where he or she was touched. The next set of items measures the ability to discriminate between sharp and dull or hard and soft stimulation. A third set of items measures two-point discrimination. It is administered with a compass, with one or two points applied to the palm of the right or left hand. The client is asked how many points they felt. The next item pair measures motion sense and involves having the client judge whether the blunt end of the compass is moved up or down on the client's arm. The next set of four items assesses tactile recognition through identification by touch of three objects and numbers written on the wrists. The next two items examine position sense by having the client place his or her arm in the same position as the other arm is placed by the examiner. The final set of items evaluates how accurately and quickly the client can identify three-dimensional objects, such as a paper clip, by touch.

The major difference between the Halstead-Reitan and the Luria-Nebraska procedures is that the Halstead-Reitan provides a detailed assessment of higher tactile functions, including form recognition, tactile neglect, and finger discrimination. The Luria-Nebraska Tactile Functions Scale, with more extensive coverage of sensory systems, includes many tests characteristic of the neurological examination. An important distinction between this and a clinical neurological examination is that the latter employs a more flexible "process" approach while seeking to localize and characterize specific neuropathology.

Motor Tests

With regard to movement, neuropsychological testing involves only deliberate movements generated in response to the tests' requirements. Among these, basic functions such as gait, balance and reflexes are rarely tested. The emphasis is on skilled movements of the hands, such as dexterity, coordination, speed, and on the ability to perform skilled activities, such as writing, drawing, or producing constructions.

There are numerous neuropsychological tests of motor function, but we will only describe the ones most commonly used in clinical settings. As in the case of the perceptual tests, some of them are parts of more comprehensive batteries; whereas others are independent assessment procedures. We limit our discussion here to tests of motor skills only and do not include tests of visual-motor or perceptual-motor coordination, such as the Bender-Gestalt Test or the Rey-Osterrieth Figure. These tests involve motor activity and several other abilities as well and require separate discussion. Basically, the parameters of motor function of interest to the neuropsychologist are speed, accuracy, and dexterity. The emphasis is mainly on skilled movement of the hands, and strength is sometimes considered.

The most basic motor tests commonly administered are grip strength and finger tapping. Grip strength is measured with a hand dynamometer, a commercially available device designed specifically for that purpose. Grip strength is assessed by neuropsychologists as a part of the lateral dominance examination. Right-handed people typically have stronger right hands than left hands, and the reverse is true for left-handed people. Clinical neuropsychologists do not usually evaluate the strength of muscle groups other than those involved in grip. Basic speed is generally assessed by a finger tapping test. The most commonly used one is the Halstead Finger Tapping Test, a part of the Halstead-Reitan Battery. The apparatus used is a typewriter key mounted on a mechanical counter. The client is asked to tap as rapidly as possible with the index finger for a series of 10 second trials.

The number of taps, averaged over at least 5 trials with each hand, provides a quantitative measure of motor speed. This test is well normed with normative data available by gender and age group (Heaton, Grant, & Matthews, 1991). It is one of the few neuropsychological tests in which there is a gender difference, with males tapping somewhat faster than females.

Dexterity is most commonly evaluated with pegboard tasks. The Purdue Pegboard was originally developed for industrial applications but is often used as a neuropsychological test. It involves placing pegs into a column of holes in a board. The Klove Matthew Grooved Pegboard Test was designed specifically for neuropsychological applications. It differs mainly from the Purdue Pegboard in that the dexterity task is made more difficult by shaping the pegs like keys and setting the holes at varying angles, so that the peg must be twisted into the right position to get into the hole.

The assessment of accuracy is made complex by the fact that motor accuracy tasks have strong associations with other domains and modalities. For example, there are cancellation tasks in which the client is presented with an array of stimuli and is asked to cancel out a given target. Here accuracy can be evaluated, because the test-taker can omit targets or cancel nontarget items. There are a variety of reaction-time or continuous-performance tasks in which the test-taker has to follow a given instruction, such as "Press the key only when the letter X follows the letter A." Reaction time, a motor response, is commonly used as an index of speed of information processing. Neurological and neuropsychological batteries may include tasks requiring that the client copy a pattern of taps; errors can reflect difficulty correctly perceiving the pattern of taps, as well as difficulty with motor control. These tests all involve motor function, but do not provide information exclusively about the motor system. Although unilateral slowness on a pegboard task often gives clear evidence of unilateral dysfunction of brain motor systems, slow reaction time on a continuous performance task may not have particular implications for the motor system.

A series of brief motor tests, largely developed by Luria, is designed to evaluate specific motor functions of the frontal lobes. Some of them are incorporated into the Motor Functions Scale of the Luria-Nebraska Battery. In general, they have to do with the programming and regulation of motor behavior. Perhaps the most well known of these items are the conditional reaction or "Go-No Go" tests: "If I say red, squeeze your hand; if I say green, do nothing." Sometimes a reversal is required: "If I knock once, you knock twice; if I knock twice, you knock once." Other related tests involve imitating movement sequences (alternating fist-palm, fist-edge-palm, etc.), and performing skilled movement activities to verbal commands (e.g., "Draw a circle beneath a triangle.")

Another related test, the alternating fist-palm or Ozeretski test, requires simultaneous but different movements of the two hands.

A specific neurological disorder that produces an impairment of purposeful, skilled movement is called apraxia. The individual with apraxia may not be paralyzed or impaired in coordination or strength, but nevertheless cannot execute skilled, learned movements or movement sequences. There are numerous types of apraxia, but the basic tests used to diagnose it are clinical in nature, involving having the client imitate movements or perform movements to verbal command. Apraxia may be quite specific, sometimes involving only specific activities, such as dressing or making purposeful mouth or eye movements. Apraxia may become apparent during the course of any extensive neuropsychological assessment, but is particularly probed in the Luria-Nebraska Battery (Table 19.1). Some of the aphasia tests have apraxia sections.

Psychometric Characteristics

Validity

The aim of most neuropsychological validity studies is to demonstrate a test's sensitivity to one or more brain conditions. Thus, most validity studies involve comparisons between samples of patients with brain damage and normal control subjects. Typically these comparisons are made utilizing demographically matched groups. If the test under investigation classifies a sufficiently high percentage of cases correctly, the test receives support as a valid index of brain dysfunction. A major methodological issue revolves around the nature of the neurological criterion. Some investigators have strongly preferred neurosurgical data, because the brain can be directly observed during surgery and the site and pathology of the lesion can be definitively identified. With the development of neuroimaging methods, neurosurgical evidence has become less crucial. Neuroimaging data are the most commonly used criteria in contemporary validity studies.

Establishment of validity goes far beyond presence or absence of brain damage and may involve the specific location of the damage or the disease entity itself. The question may involve, for example, whether some test or test combination is specifically sensitive to frontal lobe damage. Alternatively, the question may involve whether a particular test or test profile can detect multiple sclerosis. Controversies have arisen regarding differences in validity levels among various neuropsychological test batteries. There have been numerous studies comparing the predictive accuracies of the Luria-Nebraska as compared with the Halstead-Reitan neuropsy-

chological batteries. The validities of the sensory-perceptual and motor function tests described here were generally established within the context of an entire battery, and there have been few validity studies of the individual tests. Many studies involving the Finger Tapping Test have provided a great deal of normative information (Heaton et al., 1991). However, the test does not in itself provide specific information about any specific neurological disorder. Reduced tapping speed is seen in a variety of conditions; some not involving brain dysfunction, and ultimate interpretation has to be based upon the context provided by other tests administered (Volkow et al., 1998). The same is true for the Grooved Pegboard Test. The sensory-perceptual tests individually considered do not have many validation studies, but are included in validation studies of larger batteries. However, substantial research has been done involving finger agnosia (Benton, 1959) and neglect (Mesulam, 1985), and a great deal is known about brain function associated with these conditions. Russell, Neuringer, and Goldstein (1970) utilized the Halstead-Reitan Battery sensory-perceptual tests in their "neuropsychological keys," and they did make a contribution to correct classification into various groups, notably in discrimination among patients with left hemisphere, right hemisphere, and diffuse brain damage.

In general, validity studies of neuropsychological tests involve concurrent validity using some neurological variable as the criterion. There have been very few studies of predictive validity using sensory and motor tasks (Bohannon, 2001). However, neuropsychological assessment has been used in many outcome studies involving a numerous disorders, including child head injury, vascular surgery, stroke, and epilepsy. There has been extensive study of construct validity, generally accomplished through the use of factor analysis. More recent work has applied confirmatory factor analysis (Allen, Goldstein, & Mariano, 1999). Although sensory-perceptual and motor tests are often used in these studies, they are generally not separated out for more specific studies.

Reliability

Reliability has not been an area of great interest in clinical neuropsychological assessment. The main reason appears to be that the test-retest method is often not applicable to neurological patients. Often, these patients do not have stable disorders, and when an appropriate time for retesting occurs, the patient may have changed dramatically. Some neuropsychological tests of problem solving have correct answers or solutions that clients learn. After those answers are known, the test is spoiled for a second administration, because the client already knows the answers or solutions. Neuropsychological tests typically do not contain large lists of items that are needed to use the split-half method of determining reliability. The few reliability studies that have been done utilizing patients with stable conditions such as chronic schizophrenia indicated that test-retest reliability coefficients were quite high for many commonly used tests (Goldstein & Watson, 1989). There is an interest in what has been described as "clinical reliability" that evaluates a test's sensitivity to changes in patient status. The question here is whether test scores get better or worse in correspondence to changes in the patient's condition. Tests that have this capacity may be very useful in documenting recovery or deterioration in a degenerative disorder.

Norms

In recent years, a large amount of normative information has appeared in print. The need for such information is that the results of many neuropsychological tests are influenced by age, education, and sometimes gender. We therefore have published age, education, and gender norms for many of the most commonly used tests. The use of demographically corrected scores for age in particular is not without controversy. The critics of this practice say that these corrections are based upon correlations between test scores and age as found in normal individuals. However, after brain damage occurs, that association no longer exists, because the damage essentially obliterates the normal association between aging and cognitive function. Defenders of the use of corrected scores often give the case of assessment of elderly individuals. When trying to rule out a diagnosis of dementia, it is important to know how normal individuals of the same age as the patient score on the test. In any event, age, education, and gender norms for a wide variety of tests are available for those who wish to use them.

RANGE OF APPLICABILITY AND LIMITATIONS

Sensory-perceptual and motor tests are rarely given separately, but are incorporated into comprehensive neuropsychological assessments. Typically they are interpreted within the context of other tests. Because of the simple nature of these tasks and the test instructions, they may be administered to children and adults over a wide age range, and to individuals with extensive cognitive dysfunction. As indicated, sensory-perceptual and motor tests are sensitive to changes throughout the body, and performances in impaired ranges do not necessarily point to brain dysfunction. The sensory-perceptual tests involving vision and hearing may be done poorly because of

end-organ dysfunction, as in the case of visual or hearing impairments. People with peripheral nerve disorders may perform poorly on tests of tactile function. End-organ dysfunction may greatly limit the capability of detecting sensory-perceptual and motor deficits that are in fact produced by brain damage.

LEGAL AND ETHICAL CONSIDERATIONS

No legal and ethical considerations specifically involve the use of sensory-perceptual and motor tests. Some general guidelines are that these tests should be administered and scored by licensed neuropsychologists or adequately trained technicians. Only neuropsychologists should interpret results. In the case of tests that utilize apparatus, such as Finger Tapping, improvising such apparatuses should be discouraged, and they should be purchased from reliable sources with good quality control, and that provide full assurance that the device is properly configured and calibrated. Only in this way can available norms be applied.

COMPUTERIZATION

Although many neuropsychological tests have been computerized, applications of computerized sensory-perceptual and motor tests in neuropsychology have been modest. Computerized neuropsychological batteries, such as Cambridge Neuropsychological Test Automated Batteries (CANTAB; Lowe & Rabbitt, 1998) touch lightly on motor abilities. More detailed motor assessments exist (Gyntelberg et al., 1990), but are not applied in neuropsychological settings. Visual, tactile, and auditory acuity, depth perception, and visual fields are commonly tested by medical specialists using automated equipment, but rarely by neuropsychologists. The major problem appears to be that assembling and using the necessary apparatus for an automated survey of sensory motor systems would not be feasible. However, tasks involving visual or auditory stimuli and key-stroke responses, such as the Continuous Performance Test and Go-No Go, are readily adapted to the computer. Response measures include reaction time (speed), accuracy, and variability. However, a majority of sensory and motor variables cannot yet be conveniently ascertained through computerized testing.

CURRENT RESEARCH STATUS

Three areas in which sensory-perceptual and motor tests have been studied extensively (separate from their role in comprehensive neuropsychological test batteries) are neglect, tactile perception, and finger agnosia. Most of the neglect studies have concentrated on visual neglect. There are two conceptualizations of neglect, one proposed by Heilman, Watson, and Valenstein, (1993) and the other by Marsel-Mesulam (1985). Heilman and colleagues have gathered a great deal of evidence to support the view that neglect is associated with dysfunction of arousal or attention rather than sensory impairment. He introduced the concept of hemispace as something different from the visual hemifield. Hemispace is the field of attention that controls use of the hands in that space, regardless of which hand is used. His theory is that neglect is hemispatial, and that it is more common in right than in left hemisphere lesions because attentional cells found in the parietal lobe have more bilateral receptive fields than the left hemisphere has. Marsel-Mesulam has developed a neural network theory, also emphasizing attention. The brain structures involved are the posterior parietal cortex, the frontal cortex, and the cingulate cortex. Unilateral neglect may occur when there is damage to any of these structures. Left-sided neglect is more common and severe than right-sided neglect, because the right hemisphere is responsible for directed attention to both sides of space; whereas the left hemisphere controls only the right hemispace. These theoretical considerations are based on an extensive literature involving normal subjects, patients with unilateral lesions, and animal modeling.

The study of tactile perception goes back to nineteenth century neurology, but the recent literature concerning tactile perception tests stress their ability to compare the two sides of the body. Asymmetric scores between the right and left side are often indicative of unilateral brain damage. However, in tests that assess tactile form recognition (stereognosis) or skin writing (graphesthesia), right hemisphere brain damage may produce impairment in both hands, whereas left hemisphere damage affects only the right hand (Boll, 1981). Lezak (1995) indicates that tactile perceptual asymmetries may be more sensitive to unilateral brain damage than are measures of other functions.

Neurologists and neuropsychologists have studied finger agnosia for many years. Some time ago, Arthur Benton (1959) wrote a full book devoted to the topic and has developed a test for its assessment. The term finger agnosia was introduced by Gerstmann (1924), who characterized it as a disturbance of the body image. It later became part of a syndrome, called the Gerstmann Syndrome that included right-left disorientation, agraphia, and acalculia. One form of the disorder involves the fingers of both hands and those of the examiner, but in some patients only one hand is involved, and not the fingers of the examiner. The Gerstman syndrome did not hold up well as a genuine syndrome (Benton, 1959), and the dis-

order is not generally viewed as a disturbance of the body image. The distinction between unilateral and bilateral finger agnosia is important. According to Benton, bilateral impairment is associated with aphasia and general mental impairment; unilateral impairment is often found in the contralateral hand of patients with unilateral brain damage. Interestingly, there is an impressive literature indicating that the performance of kindergarten children on finger localization tests is a strong predictor of subsequent reading achievement.

Several functional imaging studies have used simple motor tasks, such as the finger-thumb test, to activate motor systems (e.g., Allison, Meador, Loring, Figueroa, & Wright, 2000). Several functional imaging studies have used response selection tests, such as Continuous Performance Tests and the Go-No Go variants, to activate relevant frontal and subfrontal systems, but these do not focus on motor systems.

CLINICAL APPLICATIONS

In clinical neuropsychological practice, sensory-perceptual and motor tests are rarely if ever administered independently, but are used as a part of a more comprehensive battery. These tests are included in batteries for numerous purposes. Assessment of tactile, auditory, and visual neglect is often of great importance in making a diagnosis and for counseling with the patient and those associated with the patient about this disabling disorder. Remediation methods are available for neglect. Tests of motor function are also important for diagnosis, but have major implications for adaptive functioning. Weakness, slowness, or impaired dexterity may affect the patient's ability to use equipment, and drive a car safely, as well as impact mobility in general. Numerous brain disorders impair not only cognitive function, but cognitive function combined with physical abilities. Stroke would be an example in which there may be impairment of language or other cognitive abilities and paralysis of one side of the body. The sensory-perceptual tests in particular are good indicators of unilateral brain damage. Neuropsychological testing generally compares the two sides of the body, and asymmetric findings are often diagnostic of damage to the contralateral hemisphere. In more subtle conditions, the sensory-perceptual tests may lateralize when other tests do not. Bilaterally contracted visual fields, as opposed to unilateral neglect, may be an early indicator of multiple sclerosis.

Motor tests are often useful in characterizing the movement disorders found in several diseases that specifically involve the motor system. Parkinson's disease, multiple sclerosis, amyotrophic lateral sclerosis, and Huntington's disease are predominantly motor disorders. The characteristics of these movement disorders differ from each other, and those distinctions can be documented by administering neuropsychological motor tests. Tapping speed is often reduced in diseases involving white matter in the brain, such as cerebral vascular disease and multiple sclerosis. Patients with Parkinson's disease or multiple sclerosis typically perform poorly on pegboard tasks. The motor programming tests developed by Luria are often of great importance for the assessment of frontal lobe function. Tests of the go-no-go type, or imitation of complex motor sequences are currently used by many clinicians. The Luria-Nebraska battery contains many items of that type.

Sometimes the neuropsychologist may use sensory-perceptual tests to identify specific syndromes. As indicated previously, finger agnosia is one of these disorders, but there are also the agnosias in which there is a failure of recognition. In the area of tactile function there is a rarely occurring disorder called astereognosis in which the patient cannot recognize three-dimensional objects by touch. The diagnosis of astereognosis requires a detailed examination because the patient may know what the object is but cannot name it because of aphasia. It is important to find out whether the patient can name the object when it is presented visually. The condition can also exist in cases of peripheral nerve damage to the sensory nerves that supply the hands. In this case, the patient has lost sense of touch, but does not have a cognitive object recognition deficit. Visual or auditory agnosias are evaluated by similarly detailed examination of visual and hearing abilities aimed at ruling out various conditions that may produce recognition disorders but are not agnosias. In visual agnosia, for example, the presence of at least adequate visual acuity must be demonstrated along with the failure of object recognition. For example, colors may be identifiable but not shapes. In children, motor tests are often used to make assessments of developmental coordination disorders.

FUTURE DEVELOPMENTS

Although much of neuropsychological assessment can now be easily accomplished using automated procedures, the obstacles to developing a convenient automated battery for sensory-perceptual and motor tests are formidable. The major advance in this area appears to have been in tests involving reaction time. However, the widespread use of computer assessment of strength, speed, and dexterity must await the further development of peripheral devices for input and output. At present such devices are not available for clinical application. Very speculatively, advances in robotic technologies may help advance developments in this field.

SUMMARY

Neuropsychological tests of sensory-perceptual and motor functions are typically administered as parts of more extensive batteries, providing evaluations of tactile, auditory, visual, and motor function. The most widely used of these tests are components of the Halstead-Reitan or Luria-Nebraska batteries. These tests are administered to detect impairment of vision, touch, hearing, or movement associated with brain dysfunction. They are of particular value in lateralization of brain lesions accomplished by comparing the two sides of the body or the visual fields. They assess several behaviors associated with various forms of brain dysfunction, including neglect, finger agnosia, tactile agnosias, and various forms of movement disorder involving slowness, weakness, and impaired coordination. Many neuropsychologists use motor programming tests devised by Luria that are particularly sensitive to frontal lobe function.

REFERENCES

Allen, D.N., Goldstein, G., & Mariano, E. (1999). Is the Halstead category test a multidimensional instrument? *Journal of Clinical and Experimental Neuropsychology, 21,* 237–244.

Allison J.D., Meador K.J., Loring, D.W., Figueroa, R.E., & Wright, J.C. (2000). Functional MRI cerebral activation and deactivation during finger movement. *Neurology, 54,* 135–142.

Arango C., Bartko J.J., Gold, J.M., & Buchanan, R.W. (1999). Prediction of neuropsychological performance by neurological signs in schizophrenia. *American Journal of Psychiatry, 156,* 1349–1357.

Benton, A.L. (1959). *Right-left discrimination and finger localization.* New York: Hoeber-Harper.

Bohannon R.W. (2001). Dynamometer measurements of hand-grip strength predict multiple outcomes. *Perceptual and Motor Skills, 93,* 323–328.

Boll, T.J. (1981). The Halstead-Reitan neuropsychology battery. In S.B. Filskov & T.J. Boll (Eds.), *Handbook of clinical neuropsychology,* (pp. 577–607). New York: Wiley-Interscience.

Buchanan R.W., & Heinrichs, D.W. (1989). The neurological evaluation scale (NES): A structured instrument for the assessment of neurological signs in schizophrenia. *Psychiatry Research 27,* 335–350.

Gerstmann, J. (1924). Fingeragnosie: eine umschriebene störung der orientierung am eigenen körper. *Wiener Klinische Wochenschrift, 37,* 1010–1012.

Golden C.J., Hammeke, T., & Purisch A. (1980). *The Luria-Nebraska battery manual.* Los Angeles: Western Psychological Services.

Goldstein, G. (1986). An overview of similarities and differences between the Halstead-Reitan and Luria-Nebraska neuropsychological batteries. T. Incagnoli, G. Goldstein, & C.J. Golden (Eds.), *Clinical application of neuropsychological test batteries* (pp. 235–275). New York: Plenum.

Goldstein, G., & Watson, J.R. (1989). Test-retest reliability of the Halstead-Reitan battery and the WAIS in a neuropsychiatric population. *The Clinical Neuropsychologist, 3,* 265–273.

Guy, W. (Ed.) (1976). *ECDEU assessment manual for psychopharmacology.* Rockville, MD: NIMH.

Gyntelberg, F., Flarup, M., Mikkelsen, S., Palm, T., Ryom, C., & Saudicani, P. (1990). Computerized coordination ability testing. *Acta Neurologica Scandinavica, 82* 39–42.

Heaton, R.K., Grant, I., & Matthews, C.G. (1991). *Comprehensive norms for an expanded Halstead-Reitan battery.* Odessa FL: Psychological Assessment Resources.

Heilman, K.M., Watson, R.T., & Valenstein, E. (1993). Neglect and related disorders. In K.M. Heilman & E. Valenstein (Eds.), *Clinical Neuropsychology* (3rd ed.), (pp. 279–336). New York: Oxford University Press.

Jenkyn, L.R., Walsh, D.B., Culver, C.M., & Reeves, A.G. (1977). Clinical signs of diffuse cerebral dysfunction. *Journal of Neurology, Neurosurgery and Psychiatry, 40,* 956–966.

Kimura, D. (1967). Functional asymmetry of the brain in dichotic listening. *Cortex, 3,* 163–178.

Lezak, M.D. (1995). *Neuropsychological assessment* (3rd ed.). New York: Oxford University Press.

Lowe C., & Rabbitt, P. (1998). Test/re-test reliability of the CANTAB and ISPOCD neuropsychological batteries: theoretical and practical issues. *Neuropsychologia, 36,* 915–923.

Mesulam, M.-M. (1985). Attention, confusional states, and neglect. In M-Marsel Mesulam (Ed.), *Principles of behavioral neurology* (pp. 125–168). Philadelphia: F.A. Davis.

Randolph, C. (2002). Neuropsychological testing: Evolution and emerging trends. *CNS Spectrums, 7,* 307–312, 2002.

Reitan, R.M., & Wolfson, D. (1993). *The Halstead-Reitan neuropsychological test battery T and clinical interpretation.* Tucson: Neuropsychology Press.

Russell, E.W., Neuringer, C., & Goldstein, G. (1970). Assessment of brain damage: A neuropsychological key approach. New York: Wiley-Interscience.

Stern, Y., Marder, K., Bell, K., Chen, J., Dooneief, G., Goldstien, S., Mindry, D., Richards, M., Sano, M., & Williams, J. (1991). Multidisciplinary baseline assessment of homosexual men with and without human immunodeficiency virus II. Neurologic and neuropsychological findings. *Archives of General Psychiatry, 48,* 131–138.

Volkow, N.D., Gur, R.C., Wang, G.J., Fowler, J.S., Moberg, P.J., Ding, Y.S., Hitzemann, R., Smith, G., & Logan, J. (1998). Association between decline in brain dopamine activity with age and cognitive and motor impairment in healthy individuals. *American Journal of Psychiatry, 155,* 344–349.

PART THREE

PROFESSIONAL ISSUES

CHAPTER 20

The Cultural in Cross-Cultural Neuropsychology

ANTONIO E. PUENTE AND ANNA V. AGRANOVICH

Although brain-behavior relations in a cultural context have been of interest to psychologists for a long time, there is still a lack of research in this complex area (Ardila, 1995; Fletcher-Janzen, Strickland, & Reynolds, 2000; Puente & Perez-Garcia, 2000a, 2000b). The question of how mental processes are shaped by sociocultural forms investigated by Vygotsky and Luria in the 1930s still presents a challenge for neuropsychologists in the twenty-first century because it is still unknown how current models of brain-behavior interaction fit in different cultural contexts. We could say that Ebbinghaus' statement about psychology as a scientific discipline may as well be applied to cross-cultural neuropsychological research: It has a long past, and a short history.

Are humans all the same in terms of cerebral organization of memory, cognition, and perception, or does culture affect the patterns of higher cortical functions? Is the way in which people perceive and solve problems determined by interaction of their genetic endowment and the culture in which they mature, or is the mind universal? These are the questions to which there are still no clear answers. To borrow from Nell (2000): "If mind, like brain, is one, and therefore unitary in all humans, then neuropsychological assessment founded on human universals will work equally well in London, New York, or the subsistence farming villages of South Africa and Brazil. If mind is many, however, . . . then identical tests may make geniuses of average people in one culture and imbeciles of equally average people in another" (p. 13).

Another important question is the subject of contemporary neuropsychology per se. Indeed, is what is measured by clinical neuropsychological instruments what neuropsychologists believe? Does brain dysfunction affect the performance on a given task, or could it be a lack of patient's familiarity with the cultural norms and attitudes that are being measured? If we, so to speak, set a brain apart to measure (neuropsychologically) its functioning without cultural context in which the mind has developed, what will we really assess? And what would be the ecological validity of the results? As noted by Massimini and Delle Fave (2000), biology, culture, and individuals are three interacting systems; hence, one of them should not be studied without considering the others.

CULTURE AS A VARIABLE IN NEUROPSYCHOLOGY

The role of culture in neuropsychology has traditionally been ignored, if not misunderstood. We believe that culture may play a much broader role than possibly age and education in shaping neuropsychological function.

Definitions

Culture is a broad concept that is not so easy to define. The study of culture as a unique phenomenon can be traced back to Greek historian and philosopher Herodotus (Cole, 1997), and by now several definitions of culture are in use (e.g., Herskovits, 1948; Triandis, Vassiliou, Vassiliou, Tanaka, & Shanmugam, 1972). Generally, culture refers to a body of customary beliefs and social norms that are shared by a particular group of people (Wong, Strickland, Fletcher-Janzen, Ardila, & Reynolds, 2000). It is important to discriminate between physical culture (tools, buildings, works of art, etc.) and subjective culture, that is, social norms, roles, beliefs, and values (Triandis et al., 1972), as the individual can be assimilated into the physical culture but carry on subjective culture, which is different from the individual's cultural environment.

Culture presents an independent variable of interest to neuropsychology (Wong et al., 2000). As emphasized in a number of publications discussed in this chapter, it is important to keep culture in mind while conducting neuropsychological investigations involving culturally dissimilar individuals to avoid potential problems and misleading conclusions.

The Origins of Cross-Cultural Neuropsychology

The application of culture to neuropsychology has both a long past and a short history, especially in North America. This section addresses such origins with a particular focus on Russian neuropsychology.

Cultural-Historical Psychology

Among the first attempts to bring cultural issues into scientific psychology and neuropsychology was the theory of cultural-historical psychology, which is associated with the Russian psychological school, and in this regard, with the prominent scholars Lev Vygotsky and Aleksandr Luria. Vygotsky's main argument was that mind is the product of the material conditions of culture (Vygotsky, 1987, 1996). Grounded on Marxian concept of a historically determined human psychology, his fundamental hypothesis was that the higher mental functions are socially formed and culturally transmitted.

Vygotsky's theory (1978) has three major postulates. First, evolution resulted in the capability of human beings to change their environment. Second, as a consequence, human beings have learned to operate with their own consciousness. This led to development of voluntary forms of actions, and in turn, to the emergence of higher mental functions. He emphasized that development of control over the environment and over one's own behavior are parallel processes deeply interrelated with each other. Additionally, these two processes are tool-mediated, that is, while mechanical tools are applied to operate with the nature, psychological tools—symbols—are used to operate with one's behavior. The third part of Vygotsky's concept is what he referred to as "interiorization," that is the reorganization of external psychological tools (e.g., symbols, words said out loud) into internal concepts and images. Thus, higher psychological functions are based on the usage of inner, usually verbal sources that were originally acquired in communication with others.

Vygotsky wrote that the origin of higher psychological functions is located "not in the hidden properties of nervous tissue, but outside the organism of the individual person in objectively existing social history which is independent of the individual" (Luria, 1965, p. 338). These higher cortical functions are seen by Vygotsky as complex functional systems rather than isolated functions, and "are formed in history and changing in the process of ontogenetic development" (p. 389). Vygotsky pointed out that functional systems "characterized by a new integration and co-relation of their parts. The whole and its parts develop parallel to each other and together." Vygotsky named the first structures "elementary." He described them as "psychological wholes, conditioned chiefly by biological determinants." The latter structures, "which emerge in the process of cultural development, are called higher structures . . . <which> are constructed on the basis of the use of signs and tools; these new formations unite the direct and indirect means of adaptation" (Vygotsky, *Tool and Symbol*—cited in John-Steiner & Souberman, 1978, p. 124). Thus, higher psychological functions are voluntary, tool-mediated, and social in their origin. That is why it is necessary to study ontogenesis and especially the acquisition of psychological tools of the society in which we live to understand psychological functioning.

The belief of cultural-historical psychologists is that historical change in human thought arises in two interrelated ways. First is the shift from natural and unmediated to cultural and mediated thought. Second is development in the complexity and sophistication of mediational means that entails a corresponding development of thinking (Cole, 1997). This view was largely based on the ideas and data of late nineteenth and early twentieth century sociological and anthropological research associated with the works of Levy-Bruhl (1910) and Thurnwald (1922). Vygotsky and his collaborators argued for "heterogeneity of levels of cognitive functioning depending upon the kind of activity that people habitually engaged in" (Cole, 1997, p. 108).

Vygotsky proposed "the general law of cultural development." He wrote:

> Any function in children's cultural development appears twice, or on two planes. First it appears on the social plane and then on psychological plane. . . . Social relations among people genetically underlie all higher functions and their relationship" (1996).

He suggested that specific relationships between particular centers of the brain emerge during the process of development. That is why, damage to a certain "center" in early ages leads to system damage of the nearest higher "center," while the same damage in adults causes deficit to a lower "center."

Luria (1979) further elaborated on Vygotsky's conception. He suggested that the development of a new "functional organs" occurs through the formation of new functional systems. "The human cerebral cortex, thanks to this principle, becomes an organ of civilization in which are hidden boundless possibilities and does not require new morphological apparatuses every time history creates the need for a new function" (1967, p. 54). Generally, in cultural-historical psychological school, higher cognitive processes are defined as social in their origin, culturally mediated in structure, and voluntary directed (Luria, 1980), each term in this formulation being tightly interconnected with the others (Cole, 1997). Cole (1997) suggested that if the Russian approach to psychological theory were to prevail, "all psychology would treat culture, along with biology and social interaction, as central" (p. 107).

Although written about 70 years ago, Vygotsky's theories are still of great influence to those scientists who are involved in cross-cultural studies. Quoting from Nell (1999), "Vygotsky's work has become the theoretical base for many psychologists and neuropsychologists, who see human development as a continuing process of change and growth rather than the achievement of a predetermined plateau" (p. 46).

The Lurian Expedition to Uzbekistan

Another "root" of cross-cultural neuropsychology can be traced back to 1930s, when Luria conducted a set of studies in the former Soviet republics of Uzbekistan and Kirgizia (Luria, 1976). The purpose of the expedition was to determine whether introduction of modern culture and public education, which accompanied collectivization occurring in the

former Soviet Union at that time, affected performance on simple cognitive tasks in native Uzbek people compared to those who had no formal education and were not exposed to "western" sociocultural norms. Luria implied that in line with Vygotsky's theory of cortical development through the mediation of social experiences, people on different levels of modernization would perform differently on given cognitive tasks. The results of the experiments showed that illiterate ("unsophisticated," in Luria's terminology) subjects were unable to form categories according to abstract characteristics. Instead, they used situational thinking that was resistant to change, consistently rejected the theoretical task in favor of the practical one, and classified objects on the basis of their practical experience and concrete operations. Following is a famous example of how one of Luria's "unsophisticated" subjects solved the syllogism:

> In the Far North, where there is snow, all bears are white.
> New Land is in the Far North and there is always snow there.
> What color are the bears there?

The subject replied: "I don't know; I've seen a black bear. I've never seen any others. . . . I've never seen one and hence I can't say" (Luria, 1976, pp. 108–109).

When this work was terminated in 1932, Luria concluded that introduction of schooling and new models of socioeconomic life brought a qualitative shift to processes of perception, categorization, imagination, and self-analysis. In 1979, he wrote, "the processes of abstraction and generalization are not invariant at all stages of socioeconomic and cultural development. Rather, such processes are themselves products of the cultural environment" (p. 74). Unfortunately, the findings of this research remained mostly unpublished until the 1970s due to misinterpretation of the meaning of Luria's experiments by the Soviet officials. Still, Luria and his collaborators proved the main idea of the expedition regarding historical origin and tool-mediated nature of human psychological processes (Khomskaya, 1999).

Luria emphasized the importance of the environment in the development of functional systems and the importance of the roles different brain areas play in a given task. The more complex the behavior, the more variable its underlying functional system can be among different cultures; the more basic the behavior, the more likely the systems are universal (Luria, 1976). According to the Lurian scheme of neuropsychological assessment, functions are evaluated from a variety of perspectives to ensure that a deficit is consistently present regardless of the way it is evaluated. Lurian methods are not highly utilized in the United States, which most likely results from a strong psychometric tradition in North American psychology as well as from current standards of practice, which, as noted by Tupper (1999a), "emphasize generation of numbers for payment." Still, there are a number of applications of Lurian conceptualizations in current neuropsychological practice (e.g., Das-Naglieri Cognitive Assessment System, Kaufman Assessment Battery for Children, Luria-Nebraska Neuropsychological Battery, Luria's Neuropsychological Investigation, and NEPSY). There are also new test measures being developed with an attempt to operationalize Lurian methods for use in different countries (e.g., Goldberg, Podell, Bilder, & Jaeger, 2000). Tupper (1999b) noted that development and standardization of the new tests consistent with Lurian theoretical approach "is expanding the traditional scope of cognitive assessment beyond a purely psychometric perspective" (p. 60).

Cross-Cultural Research in Other Areas of Psychology

In many ways, cultural issues have had a greater impact in other areas of psychology. Cross-cultural theories make three major assumptions: The general notion is that social evolution is a process that increases differentiation and complexity of social life. Basic mental operations of people are universal; and there is an ultimate relation between culture and mind (Cole, 1997). Within cross-cultural theories, comparisons have been conducted in various areas of psychology (e.g., sensation and perception, intelligence, and memory). These studies have also contributed to development of cross-cultural neuropsychology. For instance, a classic study of visual perception (Segall, Campbell, & Herskovits, 1966) demonstrated cultural differences in susceptibility to certain visual phenomena, including the Müller-Lyer Illusion. The researchers claimed that perceptual differences were due to differences in exposure to certain characteristics of visual information that are common to the western world and not common to other cultures. Studies of cross-cultural differences in memory focused on the serial position effect (Cole & Scribner, 1974) suggested that primacy and recency effects might be tied to specific memory strategies that develop through formal education. Therefore, these effects are not observed in individuals (or subcultures) with no formal education.

Cross-cultural research using IQ-tests technology has not advanced psychology's search for the nature of intelligence (Cole, 1997). If anything, it has reinforced doubts about the appropriateness of cross-cultural testing using such instruments. Nell (2000) adds with certain sarcasm that existing American research on IQ is "conducted as if the United States were the whole world" (p. 52) without actually considering different cultures.

Several investigations in social, personality, and clinical psychology in cross-cultural context (see S. Goldstein, 2000,

for a review) have had impact on research focused on brain-culture relations.

Toward Culture-Fair Neuropsychology

If indeed culture affects neuropsychological function, as proposed in this chapter, the question arises as to whether neuropsychology can be culturally fair. Historically, this concept has been ignored until very recently.

The History of Cultural Bias in Neuropsychological Assessment

In the past, neuropsychology was based on a world view that implied that all people would manifest the same behavior to the same stimulus in the brain (Sperry, 1961, 1965). Such historical foundations have led to partial or incorrect understanding of cultural effects on human behavior that is reflected in current western, male, and Caucasian-oriented methods of neuropsychological assessment (Puente & Agranovich, 2002). Despite unprecedented growth of neuropsychology over the last 20 years (Puente & Marcotte, 2000), to this date, culturally competent research studies relative to brain-behavior relationship are scarce.

In 1976, Lezak summed up the guidelines for the neuropsychological examination in his suggestion "to adapt the examination to the patient's needs, abilities, and limitations rather than other way around" (p. 105). However, a quarter-of-a-century later, the needs of the population that differ from the majority culture still have not come to the focus of neuropsychology. Although researchers have admitted that the United States could provide "the most fertile research database" (Puente et al., 2000b) for cross-cultural investigations, until recently only a few publications have related to cross-cultural issues in neuropsychology. Some of the recently published handbooks of neuropsychology addressed such factors as handedness, demographic variables, psychopathological, and medical issues in neuropsychological assessment (Goldstein & Hersen, 1990; Goldstein & Incagnoli, 1997; Puente & McCaffrey, 1992), but cultural variables were by and large neglected. Puente and Perez-Garcia (2000b) reviewed the tables of contents and reference lists of major neuropsychological publications from 1980s and 1990s and concluded that culture-related issues had not been addressed by that date. As a further illustration, the first workshop involving cultural issues in neuropsychology was presented by Puente at the annual meeting of the National Academy of Neuropsychology in 1993. Therefore, it is likely that our understanding of the brain organization of cognitive abilities, and their disturbances in cases of brain pathology, is not only partial but, undoubtedly, culturally biased.

There have been attempts in the history of psychological testing to develop "culture-fair" measures (Anastasi, 1988). The initial assumption was that if verbal items were eliminated from the tests, the nonverbal measures would be equivalent in any culture. However, this assumption was proved wrong. The nonverbal tests may also be culturally biased (Ardila, 1995; Ardila & Moreno, 2001), as most of them require strategies and cognitive styles specific to certain (usually Western) cultures. Marked differences in the way individuals from different cultures perceive pictures have been reported in the literature (Miller, 1973). Furthermore, nonverbal tests often require specific strategies and cognitive styles based on characteristics of middle-class Western cultures (Cohen, 1969).

Reynolds and Brown (1984) put forward the following reasons for biased tests: inappropriate content, inappropriate standardization samples, examiner and language bias, inequitable social consequences, measurements of different constructs, and differential predictive validity.

Reynolds (2000) observed that different value systems among cultures might produce cognitively equivalent answers, which are scored as incorrect because of biased judgments, not differences in ability. Among other circumstances that cause cultural bias in neuropsychological tests is underrepresentation of ethnic minorities in standardization samples and in collection of norms. Psychologists who speak only standard English may intimidate people from other cultural groups. Such a language barrier may cause inequitable social consequences (e.g., being labeled as learning disabled) for minority group members. Qualitatively different minority and majority aptitude and personality are also listed among sources of bias (Puente et al., 2000b; Reynolds, 2000).

Current Trends

Within the last decade, interest in cross-cultural issues has substantially increased in North America (see Ardila, 1995, 2001; Ardila et al., 2001; Fletcher-Jansen et al., 2000; Greenfield, 1997; Puente et al., 2000a, 2000b). The diversity of the American population with increasing numbers of ethnic minority members, new waves of non-English-proficient immigrants, as well as multiple forensic cases that involve assessment of culturally diverse individuals have increased interest cross-cultural neuropsychology. Following are a few examples of cross-cultural differences, addressed in recently published research, that can be easily misinterpreted in neuropsychological assessment.

Time

In 1997, Perez-Arce and Puente addressed the importance of understanding the ecological validity of neuropsychological tests for Hispanics living in North America. They suggested that Hispanics use different problem-solving strategies than Anglo-Americans use. Slowed performance could mean prolonging the task of interest for a Hispanic; whereas an Anglo-American psychologist could interpret it as a sign of brain dysfunction. Although time is a critical variable in North American culture, this is not necessarily true for other cultures. Comparison of the research data on tapping tests collected in Russia (Kurgansky & Akhutina, 1998) with American norms suggest that average performance on timed North American standardized tests could be lower among Russians, because certain time-related skills are not relevant in their culture.

Attitude Toward Testing

Puente and Perez-Garcia (2000b) brought attention to the fact that, in some cultures, the client's fear of testing or lack of testing experience could prevent researchers from obtaining valid data. For example, Asian and Hispanic individuals not acculturated to North American standards may not permit a psychologist to examine their minds. Furthermore, in some cultures, personal communications with strangers are not acceptable (Ardila, 2001).

Values and Meanings

The same test items do not necessarily have the same meaning to members of different cultural groups even when these items are accurately and appropriately translated. For example, a question from WAIS-III "Why should people pay taxes?" may trigger different associations in a society where taxes are considered fairly expended compared to a society in which taxes are believed to be misused (Ardila, 2001). Western-world oriented items that discuss the protection of animals can also produce contradictory responses in hunting societies.

Modes of Knowing

It was observed in both classic and modern studies (Ardila et al., 2001; Luria, 1979) that the distinction between the process of knowing and the object of knowledge is not universal. Thus, for some cultures, a question that refers to a person's opinion about certain facts might be not comprehensible; and the respondent might say that the point is not what an individual thinks or considers, the point is how it is.

Patterns of Abilities

Cognitive abilities measured by neuropsychological tests represent culturally learned abilities and therefore, are affected by different environmental and cultural contexts (Ardila, 1995, 2001; Puente et al., 2000a). Thus, what is worth learning in Western culture does not necessarily make sense in the Far East, or in remote villages of Russia or South Africa. That is why there is a need for the theory and methods developed in a framework of cultural neuropsychology to recognize that "the best interests of minority and culturally different people can be served by recognizing culture-specific differences" (Nell, 2000, p. 12).

Within the focus of cross-cultural neuropsychology in the United States is the understanding of how an ethnic minority group compares and contrasts to the larger, majority group. It is assumed that the same principles apply to understanding any subculture within a larger group in any national or international setting (e.g., Amazon Indians in Brazil, small Asian subcultures within Russian Federation, or a Maori population in Australia). By and large, American research on the effect of culture on neuropsychological functioning has been focused on Hispanics (Ardila, 1995; Ardila, Roselli, & Puente, 1994; Puente et al., 2000a, 2000b; Puente & Salazar, 1998). In the context of changing demographics of American society this is easy to understand, because Hispanics are expected to reflect about 33 to 40 percent of the national population by the year of 2020 (see Puente et al., 2000a for review). Statistics have also shown that a large percentage of specific types of brain-injured individuals are from an ethnic minority (Puente, 1992). Among the very few tests that have been applied to diverse population are the Halstead-Reitan and Luria-Nebraska Neuropsychological batteries. However, even for such widely used tests, there have been few investigations of their cross-cultural application (Evans, Miller, Byrd, & Heaton, 2000; Puente et al., 2000b). Of all standardized tests, the Weschler Adult Intelligence Scale (WAIS) has received the most attention with regard to cultural adaptation (Puente et al., 2000b). Some norms have been collected for Canadian, Puerto-Rican, Spanish, and Russian versions. Among the other tests that are reported to be culture-reduced are Raven's Progressive Matrices, Peabody Picture Vocabulary Test, the Quick Test, the Army Beta (Nell, 2000; Puente et al., 2000b), and Color Trails Test (Maj, et al., 1993). Still, little evidence exists that these tests are culture free.

Research showed that cultural differences influence such variables as lateralization of language and spatial disturbances (see Ardila, 1995 for review) and have a profound effect on nonverbal behavior, language, and assumptions regarding causality (Marlowe, 2000). Problem-solving styles also differ from culture to culture, and the more they differ, the more variable the results of tests that demand the use of such processes are. Furthermore, culturally different individuals may approach problems with different functional systems (Golden & Thomas, 2000). Greenfield (1997) noted that values and meanings, models of knowing, and conventions of communication could be culture specific and as such are not easy to translate across cultures. She concluded that because tests are not universal instruments, the criterion of a particular meaning must be understood before it is "translated." Evans and collaborators (Evans et al., 2000) added that there is a need for normative data to be collected on neuropsychological measures across cultures. Similar problems were addressed in a study of cultural bias in the Boston Naming Test (Barker-Collo, 2001), which compared performance on the test in New Zealand and the United States. Because New Zealand subjects made significantly more mistakes in naming some of the items, the author concluded that an adaptation of the test to a particular culture would be necessary to receive valid results.

Ardila (2001) suggested that cultural values involved in the assessment procedure, which are common for western cultures could at the same time be absurd for members of different cultural groups. Examples of such values include but are not limited to the following: one-to-one relationship between two strangers: the examiner and examinee; assumed background authority of the examiner; expectation of performance occurs at the examinee's highest possible level; isolated testing environment; stereotyped mode of communication; the requirement to perform as fast as possible on timed tasks; differences in subjective issues, such as concept of private information; and the use of specific testing elements and strategies, often referred to as "games" or "exercises."

Language is another cultural variable that can significantly affect test performance. Although certain characteristics of language can be found across cultures (deep meaning of sentences, distinction between nouns and verbs), only a few words occur universally across languages. Furthermore, there are words in different languages that cannot be literally translated from one language to another. Frequently used words in one language can have very low frequency if translated to another language. Grammatical differences exist across languages (e.g., verb tenses). Language usage differs according to cultural background and is highly correlated with a person's educational level. As a result, formal language used in testing can present a challenge for a person with limited education, because not all people are exposed to this kind of language in their everyday lives.

Most of the currently applied neuropsychological instruments have been validated for different age groups and educational levels. Several studies underlined the critical importance of educational level in performance on neuropsychological tests (Ardila, 1995, 2001; Ardila et al., 2001; Ardila et al., 1994; Ardila, Roselli, & Ostrosky-Solis, 1992; Harris, Echemendia, Ardila, & Roselli, 2001; Roselli, Ardila, & Rosas, 1990). Thus, Roselli and Ardila (1993) showed that some tests are more sensitive to educational variables (e.g., verbal tests) than others (e.g., the Wisconsin Card Sorting Test; WCST). Educational attainments significantly correlate with intelligence scales (Matarazzo, 1972), verbal meaning tests (Cornelious & Caspi, 1987), performance on memory task in elderly individuals (Ardila & Roselli, 1989), and a variety of neuropsychological measures including tests of language, problem solving, motor skills, and calculation abilities (Roselli et al., 1990). Ardila, Roselli, and Rosas (1989) suggested that educational variables might affect not only handedness, but also a degree of hemispheric dominance and cognitive abilities in general. Illiterates show greater involvement of the right hemisphere in language functions than do well-educated subjects (Lecours et al., 1988).

Ardila (1995) suggested that cross-cultural neuropsychology needs to address the following key points: standardization of current neuropsychological tests in different cultural contexts; development of new neuropsychological instruments, appropriate for different cultural groups; analysis of educational factors and cultural variations in relation to test performance; analysis of cognitive disturbances in different cultural and educational contexts; a search for common basis in neuropsychological performance among human groups; and analysis of origins of cognitive activity. Puente and Perez-Garcia (2000b) added to this that study of culture and psychopathology from a neurocognitive perspective provides a much larger pool of data about the human condition than the previously used paradigms offers. They suggested, that such an approach "could potentially yield unique insights into individual differences and general theories of psychological function and dysfunction" (p. 528).

CULTURALLY SENSITIVE NEUROPSYCHOLOGY ACROSS THE CONTINENTS

Gilbert (1986; see Nell, 2000 for review) replicated the Lurian Uzbek study, discussed earlier, in rural Kwa Zulu in South Africa. The results of Gilbert's study paralleled those of Luria. Less educated subjects showed patterns of concrete, situational responses on categorization tasks when asked to group geometric forms. Also, similar to the findings of Luria in Uzbekistan and Gilbert in South Africa, the relationship between exposure to western cultural norms and cognitive performance was reported by Mirski (1995) in his San Pablo studies, and by Cole and his colleagues (Cole, 1988; Cole, Gay, & Glick, 1968; Cole & Means, 1981).

An interesting investigation of neuropsychological differences among AIDS patients was completed under auspices of the World Health Organization (WHO) in five countries of Europe, North America, South America, Asia, and Africa (Maj, et al., 1993). The researchers developed two new tests, the Color Trails Test (CTT) and World Health Association/ University of California at Los Angeles Auditory Learning Test (WHO/UCLA AVLT), and they compared performance on these tests as well as on widely used Trail Making Test and Rey Auditory Verbal Learning Test (RAVLT) in different cultural groups. Among other objectives, they investigated whether these new tests were less influenced by cultural factors than the standard tests were. The reported results suggested that the Trail Making Test and RAVLT present problems to non-Western test takers because of the words specific to American culture in the latter, and English alphabet in the former. The new tests showed lower variability of the scores between cultures as compared to traditionally used tests. Therefore, CTT and WHO/UCLA AVLT were suggested to be appropriate for cross-cultural application.

Nell (2000) illustrated the failure of universalism to account for test score differences across cultures and countries on examples of data received in 24 studies in 13 countries on 4 continents—the largest available international comparative database, which was accumulated for the WHO Neurobehavioral Core Test Battery (WHO–NCTB). This core test battery—a "standard marker tests within larger batteries to allow cross-cultural comparison between studies and countries" (p. 172)—included several subtests from the Weschler Adult Intelligence Test (WAIS–III) and the Weschler Memory Scale (WMS–III), as well as the Grooved Pegboard Test, the Santa Ana Pegboard, the Pursuit Aiming, the Simple Reaction Time, and the Benton Visual Retention tests. From the examples of these well-known tests, Nell described cross-cultural differences between Western and non-Western cultural groups. In line with North American data (Ardila, 1995; Ardila et al., 2001; Puente et al., 2000a, 2000b), South African studies proved that researchers could hardly expect that cultural differences in testing to be eliminated by so-called test adaptation (Nell, 2000). It is apparent that such a variable as culture-dependent skills (or lack of such) could lead to significant differences in test performance.

Similarly, Sheperd, and Leathem (1999) conducted a study with Maori groups in Australia and suggested that ethnic minority clients might be adversely affected by the assessment experience because of cultural differences in their expectations, perceptions of the testing environment, and performance on neuropsychological tests.

Among a few examples of cross-cultural research in South America is an evaluation of Auca Indians of the Ecuadorian basin conducted by Pontius (1989). He administered a four-colored Kohs Block Design test and found that deficits in block design particularly related to representations and construction of certain spatial relations and graphic representational skills. Also, in 1993, Pontius conducted another neuropsychological evaluation of members of a hunters-gatherers society of Indonesia. He showed that because a hunter-gatherer's survival depends on prompt assessment of the salient shape of prey and attackers, their basic cognitive processes (i.e., visual-spatial pattern matching, representation, and construction) differ from those of Western urban societies.

Ardila and Moreno (2001) administered a brief neuropsychological test battery (visual-constructive and visual-perceptual abilities, memory, ideomotor praxis, verbal fluency, spatial abilities, and concept formation) to Aruaco Indians from Colombia. They proposed that age and cultural relevance significantly affected performance on these tasks, and therefore, evaluation of a culturally different group using existing neuropsychological instruments, procedures, and norms, would result in conceptual errors in assessment. For example, because time restrictions do not make any sense in the Aruaco culture, performance on the tests was extremely slow according to Western standards. These findings once again suggested that culture-mediated differences in attitudes toward time could significantly affect performance on neuropsychological tests.

Additional cross-cultural research includes a recent publication of Campbell and Xue (2001), who studied differences in arithmetic performance between Canadian and Chinese students. They found that Chinese students outperformed their Canadian peers in given tasks. The authors showed that the differences in performance are not related to formal education but are dependent on extracurricular, culture-specific factors. They suggested that the wide-spread, extensive use of calculators in early education in the Western world might restrict the level of expertise achieved in working memory skills for arithmetic.

REQUIREMENTS FOR THE DEVELOPMENT, VALIDATION, AND INTERPRETATION OF CULTURE-FAIR NEUROPSYCHOLOGICAL INSTRUMENTS

Development of the instruments appropriate for different cultural contexts represents a challenge for neuropsychologists.

Whether it is necessary to develop entirely new tests to use across cultures or careful translation and culture-specific validation of existing tools could be sufficient remains an open question. It is important to keep in mind that cultural variables should be taken into account during each stage of neuropsychological evaluation, beginning with a review of records and concluding with interpretation of the results.

Reviewing Records

Puente and Perez-Garcia (2000a) suggested that when reviewing records, researchers should be aware of the fact that some variables that seem equivalent at first sight hold different meaning across the cultures. For example, 10 years of formal education in Russia results in a high school diploma; whereas in the United States it takes 12 years to complete the program, and in Germany high school programs are based on 13 years of attendance. And still the diplomas may be comparable. College degrees from some of European countries are equivalent to a Master's degree in the United States.

Interview

During the interview, the researcher should consider the native culture of the client, the value and significance of specific cultural concepts, model of knowledge, and model of communication (Greenfield, 1997). Prior testing history, level of education, and acculturation also need to be taken into account (Puente et al., 2000a). Performing the interview as a drama with as close a connection to roles played in the real world as possible is an important suggestion for assessing culturally dissimilar individuals (Nell, 2000).

Selecting Methods

Puente and Perez-Garcia (2000a) suggested that when selecting assessment methods, researchers should address the variable that needs to be measured, and then select the test that measures those variables; select measures that have been accurately translated according to cognitive rather than linguistic equivalence; when possible, use tests that have appropriate norms accompanied with specific instructions and protocols; select tests that reflect the language ability and culture of the patient; and if available, use ecologically valid tests of function. The content of the tests needs to be varied to accommodate different cultures (Ardila, 1995; Luria, 1980). For instance, a picture of a telephone should not be used for visual identification in a culture that has never seen the telephone; on the other hand, the picture of a telephone used in the original Lurian battery might be not recognized by young individuals in modern society, as that model is obsolete.

Golden and Thomas (2000) recommended that, when translating the tests to apply to different cultures, researchers should choose the items that are relatively simple, and include words with about the same frequency as in the original. Each item of the test must be reviewed for appropriate cultural content with regard to the intentions of the item. They emphasized that while arithmetic and memory scales translate reasonably well, intelligence scales present the major challenge in cross-cultural adaptation. Ardila and Moreno (2001) offered the following criteria for test selection: short and easy to administer; adapted to the living conditions of the cultural group that is being tested; and sampling a large range of cognitive abilities (i.e., language, memory, spatial, constructive, perceptual, praxis, and conceptual abilities).

Testing

Preferably, native and well-trained members of other cultures should be consulted when carrying out cross-cultural analysis (Ardila, 1995). Furthermore, for the language scales, including writing and reading, it is not always enough to translate accurately when applying the scales to another cultural group. It is more important to maintain the original intent (i.e., cognitive equivalence) of the item, than to word it exactly. Where the repetition of basic phonemes is necessary, items must be modified to include frequent sounds in a given language. In the case of using abstract items, there may be a need to alter the ideas to fit a certain culture (Golden et al., 2000). One of the most important considerations in an assessment is to place the client in his or her own biopsychological context and not the psychologist's context (Puente et al., 2000b). However, the literature suggests that this advice has seldom been followed thus far (Ardila, 1995; Nell, 2000).

Interpreting the Results

Interpretation of the results must be based on an awareness of how individuals from a particular cultural group approach and analyze specific tasks. Thus, such cultural variables as patterns of abilities (Puente et al., 2000b), cultural values, familiarity with testing procedure (Ardila, 2001), exposure to schooling, and language proficiency (Ardila, 1995; Greenfield, 1997) should be taken into consideration.

Norms

An issue of significant complexity is that of norms. Taking the case of Hispanics, one of the major concerns is that most tests, including those that have been adequately translated into Spanish, for example the Minnesota Multiphasic Person-

ality Inventory (MMPI), do not have appropriate norms. Then comes the issue of what would be considered appropriate norms. In the case of Hispanics, there are significant between-group differences among Mexicans, Cubans, and Puerto Ricans. Next, there is the issue of acculturation. Is a Cuban residing in the United States since 1960 equivalent to one who just arrived in this country? And, finally, and most perplexing is the issue of who the reference sample is. If an individual has been living in the United States for 40 years but does not speak Spanish, as is sometimes the case in Miami, Los Angeles, and so on, who do we compare that person to?

Developing New Measures

When developing tests to be used across cultures, the researcher has to know what is relevant, and what is being measured in a particular neuropsychological domain. For example, while spelling is a significant task in English, it is not as relevant in Spanish, and nonexistent in Chinese. The results of a tapping test in undeveloped countries could be much lower when compared to North American norms due to the lack of relevant experience in those countries (e.g., as computers are not widespread in the countries of the Third World, very little "tapping" occurs on a day-to-day basis). American people are used to timed tests from the beginning of elementary school and assume that faster is better. In Russia, however, there is different concept of time. The tests require quality and depth of processing. Therefore, people are not generally as concerned with the speed of performance. This pattern is also reflected in neuropsychological testing. Thus, Vasserman and colleagues (1997) suggested that the speed of testing should be individualized and one should not require a patient to accomplish a task fast—a far cry from North American approaches.

Overall, the following types of equivalence ought to be considered in test development to control for cultural bias (Helms, 1997):

1. Functional equivalence—the extent to which the test scores have the same meaning in different cultural groups and measure the same psychological constructs with equal accuracy within these groups.

2. Conceptual equivalence—whether the groups have the same level of familiarity with the test items and therefore assign the same meaning to them.

3. Linguistic equivalence—the extent to which the language used in the tests has equivalent meaning across cultural groups.

4. Psychometric equivalence—the extent to which tests measure the same thing at the same level across cultural groups.

5. Testing condition equivalence—the idea of testing and the procedures are equally familiar and accessible across groups.

6. Contextual equivalence—the evidence that the cognitive ability being assessed is comparable across environments.

7. Sampling equivalence—the samples of subjects representing cultural groups are comparable.

CONCLUSION

Existing neuropsychological assessment tools are far from universal. Cultural bias and the inappropriateness of the majority of standardized, Western-culture-oriented tests and norms for evaluation of cognitive functions in individuals from different cultural background, as well as lack of attention to a variety of cultural variables, can significantly affect the outcome of neuropsychological evaluation. That is why it is important to "keep culture in mind" (Cole, 1997) while conducting the research or providing clinical evaluations using a neuropsychological approach.

In contrast, when studying the relationship between culture and brain, it is important to remember that, "the job of science is to find the orderly relationships among phenomena, not differences" (Sidman, 1960, p. 15). Furthermore, the foundation of cross-cultural neuropsychology should be the investigation of the existence of neuropsychological g (Puente et al., 2000b). That is, if neuropsychologists are ever able to define the common factors or cognitive mechanisms that are shared by all members of human race, it would be possible to develop culture-free measures of cognitive performance that could provide clinically and scientifically reliable data about the functioning of the human brain, and as such would allow neuropsychologists to diagnose and treat disturbances of the nervous system regardless of an individual's cultural identity.

From the clinical perspective, studying neuropsychological phenomena in the cross-cultural context could not only provide better possibilities for assessment to clinicians in different cultures and subcultures, but it could also enhance the understanding of the relationship between the brain and cognition (Ardila, 1995; Nell, 2000).

Meanwhile, it is critical to focus research on the revision and expansion of existing neuropsychological methods and on the development of the norms for non-Western cultural groups to make the methods applicable to assessment of culturally diverse individuals. To do otherwise would relegate clinical neuropsychology to a Western phenomenon perpetuating the concept that psychology and its specialties are ve-

hicles of "intellectual imperialism" and not of value to all cultures of this world.

REFERENCES

Anastasi, A. (1988). *Psychological testing.* New York: Macmillan.

Ardila, A. (1995). Directions of research in cross-cultural neuropsychology. *Journal of Clinical and Experimental Neuropsychology, 17,* 143–150.

Ardila, A. (2001). The impact of culture on neuropsychological test performance. Course 13. Presented at 21st Annual Conference of National Academy of Neuropsychology. San Francisco, CA.

Ardila, A., & Moreno, S. (2001). Neuropsychological test performance in Aruaco Indians: An exploratory study. *Journal of International Neuropsychological Society, 7,* 4, 510–515.

Ardila, A. & Roselli, M. (1989). Neuropsychological characteristics of normal aging. *Developmental Neuropsychology, 5,* 307–320.

Ardila, A., Roselli, M., & Ostrosky-Solis, F. (1992). Socioeducational. In A.E. Puente & R.J. McCaffrey (Eds.), *Handbook of neuropsychological assessment* (pp. 181–192). NY: Plenum.

Ardila, A., Rosselli, M., & Puente, A.E. (1994). *Neuropsychological assessment of Spanish-speaker.* New York: Plenum Press.

Ardila, A., Roselli, M., & Rosas, P. (1989). Neuropsychological assessment in illiterates: Visuo-spatial and memory abilities. *Brain and Cognition, 11,* 147–166.

Barker-Collo, S.L. (2001). The 60-item Boston naming test: Cultural bias and possible adaptations for New Zealand. *Aphasiology, 15,* 1, 85–92.

Campbell, J.I.D., & Xue, Q. (2001). Cognitive arithmetic across cultures. *Journal of Experimental Psychology: General, 130,* 2, 299–315.

Cohen, R.A. (1969). Conceptual styles, culture conflict, and nonverbal tests. *American Anthropologist, 71,* 828–856.

Cole, M. (1988). Cross-cultural research in the sociohistorical tradition. *Human Development, 31,* 137–151.

Cole, M. (1997). *Cultural psychology: a once and future discipline.* Cambridge, MA: Belknap Press of Harvard University Press.

Cole, M., Gay, J., & Glick, J.A. (1968). A cross-cultural study of information processing. *International Journal of Psychology, 3,* 93–102.

Cole, M., & Means, B. (1981). *Comparative studies of how people think.* Cambridge, MA: Harvard University Press.

Cole, M., & Scribner, S. (1974). *Culture and thought: A psychological introduction.* New York: Wiley.

Cornelious, S.W., & Caspi, A. (1987). Everyday problem solving in adulthood and old age. *Psychology and Aging, 2,* 144–153.

Evans, J.D., Miller, S.W., Byrd, D.A., & Heaton, R.K. (2000). Cross-cultural applications of the Halstead-Reitan batteries. In E. Fletcher-Janzen, T.L. Strickland, & C.R. Reynolds (Eds.),

Handbook of cross-cultural neuropsychology (pp. 287–303). New York: Kluwer/Plenum.

Fletcher-Janzen, E., Strickland, T.L., & Reynolds, C.R. (2000). (Eds.) *Handbook of cross-cultural neuropsychology.* New York: Kluwer/Plenum.

Gilbert, A.J. (1986). *Psychology and social change in the third world: A cognitive perspective.* Unpublished doctoral dissertation. University of South Africa, Pretoria.

Goldberg, E., Podell, K., Bilder, R., & Jaeger, J. (2000). *The Executive Control Battery.* Australia: Psych Press.

Golden, C.J., & Thomas, R.B. (2000). Cross-cultural application of the Luria-Nebraska neuropsychological test battery and Lurian principles of syndrome analysis. In E. Fletcher-Janzen, T.L. Strickland, & C.R Reynolds (Eds.), *Handbook of cross-cultural neuropsychology* (pp. 305–315). New York: Kluwer/Plenum.

Goldstein, G. & Hersen, M. (Eds.) (1990). *Handbook of psychological assessment.* 2nd ed. New York: Pergamon Press.

Goldstein, G., & Incagnoli, T.M. (Eds.) (1997). *Contemporary approaches to neuropsychological assessment.* New York: Plenum Press.

Goldstein, S. (2000). *Cross-cultural explorations.* Activities in culture and psychology. Boston: Allyn & Bacon.

Greenfield, P.M. (1997). You can't take it with you. Why ability assessment don't cross cultures. *American Psychologist, 52,* 1115–1124.

Harris, J.G., Echemendia, R., Ardila, A., & Roselli, M. (2001). Cross-cultural cognitive and neuropsychological assessment. In J.J.W. Andrews & D.H. Saklofske (Eds.), *Handbook of psychoeducational assessment. Ability, achievement, and behavior in children* (pp. 391–414). San Diego, CA: Academic Press.

Helms, J.E. (1997). The triple quandary of race, culture, and social class in standardized cognitive ability testing. In D.P. Flanagan, J.L. Genshaft, & P.L. Harrison (Eds.), *Contemporary intellectual assessment* (pp. 517–532). New York: Guilford.

Herskovits, M.J. (1948). *Man and his works: The science of cultural anthropology.* New York: Knopf.

John-Steiner, V., & Souberman, E. (1978). Afterword. In L.S. Vygotsky. *Mind in society. The development of higher psychological processes* (pp. 121–133). Cambridge, MA: Harvard University Press.

Khomskaya, E.D. (1999). L.S. Vygotsky's role in Luria's work. In E.D. Khomskaya & T.V. Akhutina (Eds.), *Handbook of neuropsychology* (pp. 32–37). Moscow: Russian Psychological Society (In Russian).

Kurgansky, A.V., & Akhutina, T.V. (1998). Temporal parameters of rhythmic tapping in adult and children: Dependence on structural complexity. In E.D. Khomskaya & T.V. Akhutina (Eds.), *Proceedings of the First Luria Memorial International Conference* (pp. 166–177). Moscow: Russian Psychological Society (in Russian).

Lecours, A.R., Mehler, J., Parente, M.A., Caldeira, A., Cary, L., Castro, M.J., Carrond, V., Chagastelles, L., Dehaut, F., (1988). Illiteracy and brain damage. *Neuropsychologia, 26,* 575–589.

Levy-Bruhl, L. (1910/1966). *How natives think.* New York: Washington Square Press.

Lezak, M.D. (1976). *Neuropsychological assessment.* New York: Oxford University Press.

Luria, A.R. (1965). L.S. Vygotsky and the problem of localization of functions. *Neuropsychologia, 3,* 387–392.

Luria, A.R. (1976). *Cognitive development: Its cultural and social foundations.* Cambridge, MA: Harvard University Press.

Luria, A.R. (1979). *The making of mind: A personal account of Soviet psychology.* Cambridge, MA: Harvard University Press.

Luria, A.R. (1980). *Higher cortical functions in man.* 2nd Ed. New York: Basic Books.

Maj, M., DiElia, L., Satz, P., Jansen, R., Zauding, M., Uchiyama, C., Starace, F., Galderisi, S. & Chervinsky, D. (1993). Evaluation of two new neuropsychological tests designed to minimize cultural bias in the assessment of HIV-1 seropositive persons: A WHO study. *Archives of Clinical Neuropsychology, 8,* 123–135.

Marlowe, W.B. (2000). Multicultural perspectives on neuropsychological assessment of children and adolescents. In E. Fletcher-Janzen, T.L. Strickland, & C.R. Reynolds (Eds.), *Handbook of cross-cultural neuropsychology* (pp. 145–165). New York: Kluwer/Plenum.

Massimini, F., & Delle Fave, A. (2000). Individual development in a bio-cultural perspective. *American Psychologist, 55,* 2, 24–33.

Matarazzo, J.D. (1972). *Wechsler's measurement and appraisal of adult intelligence.* Baltimore: Williams & Wilkins.

Miller, R.J. (1973). Cross-cultural research in the perception of pictorial materials. *Psychological Bulletin, 80,* 135–150.

Nell, V. (1999). Luria in Uzbekistan: The vicissitudes of cross-cultural neuropsychology. *Neuropsychology Review, 9,* 1, 45–52.

Nell, V. (2000). *Cross-cultural neuropsychological assessment: Theory and practice.* Mahwah, NJ: Lawrence Elbaum Associates.

Perez-Arce, P., & Puente, A.E. (1997). Neuropsychological assessment of ethnic minorities. The case of assessing Hispanics living in North America. In R.J. Shordone & C.J. Long (Eds.), *Ecological validity of neuropsychological tests* (pp. 283–300). Delray Beach, FL: St. Lucie Press.

Pontius, A.A. (1989). Color and spatial error in block design in stone age Auca Indians: Ecological underuse of occipital-parietal system in men and frontal lobes in women. *Brain & Cognition, 10,* 54–75.

Pontius, A.A. (1993). Spatial representation, modified by ecology: From hunter-gatherers to city dwellers in Indonesia. *Journal of Cross-Cultural Psychology, 24,* 4, 399–413.

Puente, A.E. (1992). The status of clinical neuropsychology. *Archives of Clinical Neuropsychology, 7,* 297–312.

Puente, A.E., & Agranovich, A.V. (2002). Are neuropsychological tests measuring cultural knowledge? A review of V. Nell, Cross-cultural neuropsychological assessment: Theory and practice. *Applied Neuropsychology, 9,* 2, 121–124.

Puente, A.E., & Marcotte, A.C. (2000). A history of division 40 (clinical neuropsychology). In D.A. Dewsbury (Ed.), *Unification through division: Histories of the divisions of the American Psychological Association,* Vol. 5 (pp. 137–160). American Psychological Association, Washington, DC.

Puente, A.E., & McCaffrey, R.J. (Eds.) *Handbook of neuropsychological assessment.* New York: Plenum.

Puente, A.E., & Perez-Garcia, M. (2000a). Neuropsychological assessment of ethnic minorities: Clinical issues. In Cuellar, S. & Paniagua, F. (Eds.), *Handbook of Multicultural Mental Health* (pp. 419–435). New York: Academic Press.

Puente, A.E., & Perez-Garcia, M. (2000b). Psychological assessment of ethnic minorities. In G. Goldstein & M. Hersen (Eds.), *Handbook of psychological assessment,* 3rd ed. (pp. 527–552). New York: Pergamon.

Puente, A.E., & Salazar, G.D. (1998). Assessment of minority and culturally diverse children. In A. Prifitera & D. Saklofske (Eds.), *WISC-III: Clinical use and interpretation* (pp. 227–248). San Diego: Academic Press.

Reynolds, C.R., & Brown, R. (1984). *Bias in mental testing.* New York: Plenum.

Reynolds, C.R. (2000). Methods for detecting and evaluating cultural bias in neuropsychological tests. In E. Fletcher-Janzen, T.L. Strickland & C.R. Reynolds (Eds.), *Handbook of cross-cultural neuropsychology* (pp. 249–285). Dordrecht, Netherlands: Kluwer.

Roselli, M., & Ardila, A. (1993). Effects of age, gender and socioeconomical level on the Wisconsin Card Sorting Test. *The Clinical Neuropsychologist, 7,* 145–154.

Roselli, M., Ardila, A. & Rosas, M. (1990). Neuropsychological assessment in illiterates II: Language and praxis abilities. *Brain and Cognition, 12,* 281–296.

Segall, M.H., Campbell, D.T., & Herskovitz, M.J. (1966). *The influence of culture on visual perception.* Indianapolis: Bobbs-Merrill.

Sheperd, I., & Leathem, J. (1999). Factors affecting performance in cross-cultural neuropsychology: From a New Zealand bicultural perspective. *Journal of the International Neuropsychological Society, 5,* 1, 83–84.

Sidman, M. (1960). *Tactics of scientific research: Evaluating experimental data in psychology.* New York: Basic Books.

Sperry, R.W. (1961). Cerebral organization and behavior. *Science, 133,* 1749–1757.

Sperry, R.W. (1965). Mind, brain, and humanist values. In J.R. Platt (Ed.), *New views of the nature of man* (pp. 71–92). Chicago: University of Chicago Press.

Thrunwald, R. (1922). Psychology of primitive men. In I.G. Kafka (Ed.), *Handbook of cultural psychology. Vol.1.* Munich: Verlag von Ernst Reinhardt (in German).

Triandis, H.C., Vassiliou, V., Vassiliou, G., Tanaka, Y, & Shanmugam, A.V. (1972). *The analysis of subjective culture.* New York: Wiley.

Tupper, D.E. (1999a). Introduction: Aleksandr Luria's continuing influence on worldwide neuropsychology. *Neuropsychology Review, 9,* 1, 1–7.

Tupper, D.E. (1999b). Introduction: Neuropsychological assessment apres Luria. *Neuropsychology Review, 9,* 2, 57–61.

Vasserman, L.I., Dorofeeva, S.A., & Meyerson, Y.A. (1997). *Methods of neuropsychological diagnostics: Practical manual.* St. Petersburg, Russia: Stoipechat (in Russian).

Vygotsky, L.S. (1978). *Mind in society. The development of higher psychological processes.* M. Cole, V. John-Stainer, S. Scribner, & E. Souberman (Eds.). Cambridge, MA: Harvard University Press.

Vygotsky, L.S. (1996). The Problem of development of higher psychical functions. In M.G. Yaroshevsky (Ed.), *L.S. Vygotsky. Developmental psychology as a cultural phenomenon. Selected chapters.* Moscow: Institut Prakticheskoi Psychologii (In Russian).

Wong, T.M., Strickland, T.L., Fletcher-Janzen, E., Ardila, A., & Reynolds, C.R. (2000). Theoretical and practical issues in the neuropsychological assessment and treatment of culturally dissimilar patients. In E. Fletcher-Janzen, T.L. Strickland & C.R Reynolds (Eds.), *Handbook of cross-cultural neuropsychology* (pp. 3–18). New York: Kluwer/Plenum.

CHAPTER 21

Translation and Test Administration Techniques to Meet the Assessment Needs of Ethnic Minorities, Migrants, and Refugees

VICTOR NELL

This chapter reviews specialized techniques for assessing persons who are culturally distinct from the populations on which psychological and neuropsychological tests have been normed and for whom these norms are likely to be misleading. Some of these techniques are described by Nell (2000) and are summarized here; others described in this chapter arise from the changing cross-cultural landscape in the industrialized countries, which makes the need for valid cross-cultural assessment techniques increasingly acute.

THE CHANGING CROSS-CULTURAL LANDSCAPE

Constitutionally entrenched human rights provisions in many western European countries and the United States mandate entry for political refugees and asylum seekers. Norway, a traditionally homogenous country with a population of 4.5 million, has 43,967 refugees (i.e., one refugee for every 102 residents), representing a kaleidoscope of languages and cultures from the Russian Federation, Croatia, Somalia, Iraq, and 33 different countries in Africa. In 2001, 14,782 individuals sought asylum in Norway, and although only a small percentage of these applicants were granted asylum, they received social and psychological services during the screening

process.[1] In Germany, with 180,000 refugees, the ratio is one refugee for every 456 residents. At the end of 2001, the United States had 396,000 asylum applicants from China, India, Afghanistan, Burma, and Ethiopia in addition to central and South America; the refugee-to-resident ratio was 1 to 572.[2]

Whereas the focus of cross-cultural assessment has hitherto been on historically old and familiar populations such as the Bantu peoples of Southern Africa or the Hispanics and African Americans of the United States, the refugees and asylum seekers, who are very recent arrivals in the industrialized countries, present cross-cultural psychologists with new and difficult assessment problems. Because of the greater likelihood of detention and torture that may include beating, suffocation, and heavy falls, political refugees are at higher risk of brain injury than other populations; neuropsychological expertise is essential in their assessment.

UNCONSCIOUS ASSUMPTIONS

Special assessment techniques are essential when working with culturally different clients, those who are historically familiar and the new waves of refugees, because their scores on standard neuropsychological tests may categorize normal people as brain damaged or retarded, blocking their access to mainstream education or to employment. These artificially depressed scores may be accepted as correct because they play into unconscious assumptions about genetic differences and racial inferiority, which is even more damaging to these clients.

Regrettably, racism did not vanish from the world with the collapse of apartheid in South Africa, which was the last bastion of legally sanctioned racism in the world. Despite the lessons of the Holocaust, ugly racial flare-ups continue to occur between Europe's older communities and refugee populations, and provide the impetus for racist political movements.

Against this background, even the best-intentioned professionals, confronted by test scores in the defective range, may conclude that differences arise from inherent genetic factors. These assumptions are reinforced by the belief that many abilities are human universals that are invariant across cultures. Thus, the most respected and widely used text on neuropsychological assessment claims that "skills that almost all physically intact adults can perform are counting change, drawing a recognizable person, basic map reading, and using a hammer and saw or basic cooking utensils. Each of these skills . . . is sufficiently simple that its mastery or potential mastery is taken for granted. Anything less than an acceptable performance in an adult raises the suspicion of impairment" (Lezak, 1995, p. 99). On the contrary, map reading, counting change, and drawing a person are complex, culturally mediated skills that vary greatly from one culture to another.

It is equally harmful to neurologically compromised individuals if they are found to be normal because this blocks their access to compensation and rehabilitation. The South African experience has been that if western tests are renormed or adapted for culturally different populations, the norms are typically set too low, so that even persons with debilitating brain damage are falsely judged to be of average ability (Nell, 1997).

There is overwhelming evidence that scores on neuropsychological tests vary dramatically across cultures (Nell, 2000, chapter 2), and that these differences intrude even on "universal" skills such as Digit Span: "Theory does not support even in the most meaningless of tasks the assumption of stimulus equivalence" (Irvine & Berry, 1988, pp. 51–52).

A benchmark study (Manly et al., 1998) has for the first time quantified acculturation effects in relation to test scores, and showed that the extent of African-American acculturation to mainstream culture, which is the culture of those who devise and administer psychological tests, predicts neuropsychological test scores. If allowance is made for these acculturation effects, many of the score differences among intact

and impaired individuals are eliminated. These findings powerfully reinforce the view that genetic inferences cannot be drawn until all cultural influence has been accounted for (Nell, 2000).

The gateway to test-wiseness (elaborated later in this chapter) is functional literacy (Nell, 2000, pp. 3–6), which is taken for granted in the industrialized countries but hard-won in the rest of the world. Table 21.1 (from UNESCO, 1998) shows that in 1996, only 33.9% of scholars worldwide were enrolled in secondary school and 7.5% in tertiary education—hardly better than in 1980, when these figures were 31% and 6% respectively.

The following sections describe some of the techniques neuropsychologists can use to address and minimize cultural artifacts.

RESPECT AND FEAR

Psychologists need to be acutely aware that for marginal and disempowered groups, authority figures, especially professionals, are not only respected but also feared. Puente and Agranovich (Chapter 20) provide a concise review of the many ways in which cultural differences may depress test scores because of negative attitudes to the test situation, to the psychologist-examiner, and to culturally unfamiliar demands to work quickly and accurately—which, for bearers of many traditional cultures, is an oxymoron! (For further examples, see Nell, 2000, pp. 3–4.)

A fearful client is an underachieving client. In most settings, because of the legacy of colonialism, fears are exacerbated if the examiner is White and the client Black. Simple courtesy, a warm greeting, and a straightforward explanation of the purpose of the interview go a long way toward allaying a client's fears, but they cannot do so in contexts of real or perceived threat, as the South African story in Box 1.1 (which reflects universal fears) illustrates.

TABLE 21.1   Percentage of Scholars Enrolled at Various Levels of Education

Region/Year	Secondary School	Tertiary Education	Those with a Primary School Education or Less
World, 1980	31.7	6.6	61.7
World, 1996	33.9	7.5	58.6
Sub-Saharan Africa, 1996	19.9	2.0	78.1
Latin America and Caribbean	22.1	7.4	70.5
Least developed countries, 1980	16.4	1.3	82.3
Least developed countries, 1996	18.5	2.1	79.4

Box 1.1   The Psychometrist and the Trade Union

In 1997, with funding from the South African Clinical Neuropsychology Association, a team of psychometrists (see note 5) set out to answer a crucial question: are the very large test performance differences between Black and White South Africans (Nell, 2000, Tables 2.1–2.2) attributable only to level of education, as many cross-cultural researchers have suggested, or to other as yet unidentified cultural differences? The study groups were Black and White South Africans with fewer than 12 years of education who completed a core test battery, that included marker tests, from the World Health Organization Neurobehavioral Core Test Battery (WHO-NCTB; Nell & Maboea, 1997). The subjects were drawn from staff at the University of South Africa, the Department of Education, and the Government printer, all located in Pretoria, South Africa's administrative capital. The preliminary results are reported in Nell, 1999; no final results exist because of the extraordinary levels of resistance encountered among both subject groups, but especially among White subjects.

At the University of South Africa, the lead psychometrist, a powerful Black woman, met with the trade union executive and then addressed a mass meeting of workers to allay fears that team members were stooges of the university's personnel department and being used to decide who to retrench. In the end, workers believed the team, although considerable suspicion remained and had to be dealt with by the psychometrists on a one-to-one basis. With the White subjects, the team was almost totally unsuccessful, in part because of the stigma attached to being a White person without a grade 12 education and the fear that these tests would show these otherwise successful men to be incompetent. Of particular concern were the vigorous affirmative action policies that South Africa's first fully democratic government had set in place that led Whites in government service to fear compulsory retirement.

Migrants and refugees have tenuous legal status and the power of authority figures—border police, welfare workers, and psychologists—is enormous. At the stroke of a pen, these individuals can decree the loss of a job, separation from a child, or deportation back to a homeland the migrants or refugees have fled.

Under these circumstances, a neuropsychologist's clients do all they can to fake good or bad performances to evade the examiner's X-ray eyes and attain the outcome they desire. Sometimes, because of ignorance of the host country's policies, subjects fake in the wrong direction.[3]

THE HOME LANGUAGE IMPERATIVE

A golden rule of cross-cultural testing is always and only to test in the client's home language. Red warning lights should flash if a report states, for example, "The client's home language is Urdu [or Zulu or Arabic], but he was fluent in English [or Norwegian or German], and the services of a translator were not required." Because of the pervasive power of the dominant culture and the bearers of its language, migrant clients may find it difficult to resist the pressure to claim fluency in the culturally dominant language, even if their vocabulary is impoverished and their comprehension limited. Under these circumstances, their test scores are depressed by receptive and expressive language difficulties. Psychometrists should firmly tell clients that tests are always conducted in the client's home language.

Concept Accessibility

The single exception to this rule is made for clients who have had their high school or university education in the dominant language. For such individuals, some concepts may be exclusively (or more easily) accessible in their language of education, which may not be the same as their home language.

Even when using a client's home language, some dominant language terms may be appropriate. For example, the mechanical translator may literally translate "here is a jigsaw puzzle" into the native language, but in that culture jigsaw puzzles do not exist. The skilled translator says, "Ipi [here is a] jigsaw puzzle," skilfully mixing the vernacular and dominant languages to facilitate access to the concepts.

The Cinderella of the Health Sciences

Even graver problems arise if unskilled translators are used; this is especially true for neuropsychology, which deals in subtleties and abstracts. As Franz Fanon's moving descriptions in the Wretched of the Earth (1968) show, clinical translation remains the Cinderella of the health sciences and is often thrust onto poorly educated staff who have no psychological training and are unable to grasp the abstract subtleties that the examiner seeks. Under these circumstances, test scores are artifacts of translation quality.

The Translator as a Cultural Guide

If the neuropsychologist is able to recruit and train a person drawn from the target community as a translator and test administrator, a whole new range of assessment possibilities opens. The method I have followed is to advertise for a person who has a three- or four-year degree in psychology, is fluent in English but whose home language is that of the target group, and has had specialist training in test administration and scoring (in South Africa, such individuals are termed psychometrists[4]). This individual receives intensive training in the administration of the core test batteries (Nell, 2000). One spin-off benefit of training these indigenous technicians is the creation of employment opportunities with considerable upward mobility for individuals in the target community. This generates goodwill for the psychologist and psychological testing, and contributes to the rootedness of psychological services in the community.

A TWO-FOLD LIBERATION

Psychometrists trained in this way are able not only to earn a decent living, but to become "cultural guides" to their target community. They can explain to you, the neuropsychologist, what your clients hope for from assessment, and what they fear; how you can join with them in the diagnostic interview with warmth and acceptance, but without overstepping the limits of professional appropriateness; and what hidden stressors may be operating on the client and family. This redefinition of the role of your translator, who is now your guide into the world of your clients, is a two-fold liberation.

Behavioral Neuropsychology: Moving Beyond Testing

For the skilled psychologist, the liberation is in reinventing the intake interview as a major diagnostic tool. This breaks western neuropsychology's heavy reliance on tests and testing, which, as emphasized previously in this chapter, have limited diagnostic power. Neuropsychologists are first and foremost psychologists; what psychologists do best is describe behavior—as it was in the past, as it is now, and as it's likely to be in the future. It follows that neuropsychology and testing are not synonyms, and that the neuropsychologist's core skill is to perceive and understand behavior. It is in the lengthy interview that precedes the testing, in which the neuropsychologist moves effortlessly between past and present and between the client and the caregivers, that the fabric of the diagnosis and prognosis is established (Nell, 2000, chapters 6 and 8).

This is not to say that testing has no place in the cross-cultural setting. Because psychologists are a scarce resource in all countries, especially in marginal communities where services are typically underfunded, testing remains an important modality. Though the cross-cultural neuropsychologist can achieve an accurate diagnosis with a good diagnostic

interview and very little testing (Nell, 2000), this is a time-intensive method that typically lasts two or three hours. In this context, judicious testing administered by a skilled technician who is also a cultural guide can rapidly generate a large data pool at a relatively low training cost. Although no test norms for culturally different minority groups in the industrialized countries exist and test publishers have little incentive to embark on this expensive exercise, the data from a core test battery are interpretable (Nell, 2000, chapters 5 and 10), allowing the neuropsychologist to draw valid conclusions with regard to prognosis, treatment, and vocational opportunities, even though there is always an upper limit to the diagnostic value of tests outside their culture of origin.

Translation as a Diagnostic Instrument

For psychometrists, the previous redefinition is liberating because they are no longer mere adjuncts to the psychologist, but active facilitators of the assessment process. Even with skilled translation during the diagnostic interview, the client and caregivers are soon marginalized; the translator interacts with the neuropsychologist in a language the clients don't understand. To the clients, the neuropsychologist seems to have no interest in them, paying attention only when the translator speaks to him or her.

The remedy for this unfortunate state of affairs is to ensure that the client and the client's family remain the focus of the neuropsychologist's attention throughout the interview. The neuropsychologist should maintain eye contact, even during note-taking; listen attentively when the clients speak; and address questions directly to the client group rather than to the translator (Nell, 2000).

CONSTRUCT VALIDITY AND TEST-WISENESS

Why do scores on neuropsychological tests vary dramatically across cultures, and why are these differences invariably in the direction of poorer performances for subjects in the less industrialized countries? The two major contributors to this state of affairs are construct validity and test-wiseness.

Construct Validity

Construct validity is an abstract and elusive concept, but in the real world, it has a concrete and down-to-earth meaning that is neatly captured in the term *stimulus equivalence* (Irvine et al., 1988), cited previously in this chapter. Stimulus equivalence means just what it says—the stimulus in the test giver's mind must have an equivalent existence in the mind of the test taker. To test immediate attention span, the test giver asks a subject to repeat a series of digits; but if this task has a different meaning for the test taker, for example, that the ability to add the numbers or to associate colors with the numbers is being tested, then something other than the test taker's immediate attention span is tested. Stimulus equivalence is none other than construct validity, and the cross-cultural literature abounds with striking examples of construct invalidity (for examples, see Nell, 2000, pp. 88–90).

Test-Wiseness

The other stumbling block to test score equivalence is test-wiseness, which means knowing how to get the best possible score on a test by reconciling speed and accuracy (which are irreconcilable). Test-taking skills are so taken for granted in Western society that it is difficult to grasp the extent to which they are acquired abilities. Westerners learn that to take a test, they need to be keyed up and a little nervous so that when the test session begins, they sit still, concentrate intensely, and work as quickly as possible.

Test-wiseness is most powerfully acquired through the formal education system. This happens explicitly, by multiple experiences with IQ, aptitude, and streaming tests, and the obvious similarities between these and school examinations; and implicitly, because success on psychological tests draws on behaviors valued in the classroom, such as sitting still, paying attention for long periods, using pen and pencil dexterously, copying designs and solving problems, and working fast to keep up with the class and to finish examinations on time.

BRIDGING THE GAP

For the bearers of other cultures, these test-wiseness skills are unknown. The most effective way of bridging this gap is by giving non-testwise clients the opportunity to familiarize themselves with test demands but not with test items. In this respect, South African test developers have led the way, declaring, for example, that "the subject should have ample opportunity to learn to do the task involved in the test by preliminary exercises. . . . The test should also provide scope for the insights . . . and experience acquired in the course of testing to progressively improve performance" (Simon Biesheuwel, 1972, cited in Nell, 2000, p. 161; see also Crawford-Nutt, 1976).

Familiarization Opportunities

How can non-testwise subjects be given an opportunity to familiarize themselves with test demands without detracting

from the essence of the test, which is its novelty?[5] Serendipitously, the third revisions of the Wechsler adult and child intelligence tests (the WAIS–III and the WISC–III) incorporate reversal items in several of the subtests. In the WAIS–III, these reversal items are Picture Completion, Vocabulary, Similarities, Block Design, Arithmetic, Matrix Reasoning, Information, and Comprehension. Arithmetic, for example, begins with Item 5; if the client fails Item 5 or 6, the two basal items, the four reversal items are administered in reverse sequence, continuing until two successive items are answered correctly. By using the reversal items in normal rather than reverse sequence at the beginning of each of the subtests in which they appear, the examiner creates a gentle and non-threatening familiarization opportunity for non-testwise clients to understand test demands and prepare gradually for the more difficult items that come later. Because full credit is given for the reversal items, whether or not they are administered, the comparability of standard scores is not affected by this change in the administration procedure.

The dramatic results of even brief familiarization with test demands have been demonstrated by Amir (2002), who found that on the Benton Visual Retention Test, differences in favor of better-educated subjects in the United Arab Emirates were eliminated by brief practice. Although the scores of subjects with a higher educational level were almost the same between the test and retest, the performance of the less-educated subjects improved dramatically. Gender differences were also eliminated by practice.

* * *

If these readily accessible methods enhance client dignity, elevate the status of translation, promote the translator from lackey to cultural guide, and produce more valid assessment findings, the extra effort they require is well rewarded.

NOTES

1. Norwegian Directorate of Immigration, www.udi.no.

2. United States Council on Refugees, www.refugees.org.

3. Although the detection of malingering and its obverse fall outside the scope of this chapter, it is appropriate to note in my experience of working with culturally different clients, formal tests of malingering are less productive than clinical observation. Test administrators should assess whether clients' symptoms tally with their medical, political, and employment history? If they don't, faking must be suspected.

4. In the United States, specialist test administrators are often called technicians or "techs." In South Africa, a specialist category, psychometrist, is recognized in the regulations governing the profession of psychology. These psychometrists are persons with an honors degree in psychology (i.e., a 3-year major followed by a year

of more advanced study of psychology). They are then eligible for a six-month internship in which they are supervised in the administration and scoring of psychological tests, though they are debarred from interpreting test results. Individuals thus trained become registered psychometrists.

5. The topic of extended practice is dealt with at length in *Cross-cultural neuropsychological assessment: Theory and practice* (Nell, 2000, chs. 9 and 10), which does not sufficiently emphasize that extended practice is a research rather than a clinical modality. In clinical practice, in which standard scores are used to determine whether an individual client is neuropsychologically compromised, this method is inappropriate, except in the context of the reversal items in the new Wechsler tests.

REFERENCES

Amir, T. (2002). Benton visual retention test: reliability, gender, and the effect of extended practice on the performance of participants from the UAE. *A Bulletin of the Faculty of Arts, United Arab Emirates University: Humanities and Social Sciences, 61, 7–17.*

Crawford-Nutt, D.H. (1976). Black scores on Raven's standard progressive matrices: An artifact of method of test presentation. *Psychologia Africana, 16,* 201–206.

Irvine, S.H., & Berry, J.W. (1988). The abilities of mankind: A revaluation. In S.H. Irvine & J.W. Berry (Eds.), *Human abilities in cultural context* (pp. 3–59). Cambridge, MA: Cambridge University Press.

Lezak, M.D. (1995). *Neuropsychological assessment* (3rd ed.). New York: Oxford University Press.

Manly, J.J., Miller, S.W., Heaton R.K., Byrd, D., Reilly, J., Velasquez, R.J., Saccuzzo, D.P., Grant, I., & the HIV Neurobehavioural Research Center Group. (1998). The effects of African-American acculturation on neuropsychological test performance in normal and HIV-positive individuals. *Journal of the International Neuropsychological Society, 4,* 291–302.

Nell, V. (1997). Science and politics meet at last: The South African insurance industry and neuropsychological test norms. *South African Journal of Psychology, 27,* 43–49.

Nell, V., & Maboea, D. (1997). *Core battery of psychological and neuropsychological tests for persons with less than 12 years of education. Administration Procedure and spoken instructions in English, South Sotho, North Sotho, Zulu, & Afrikaans.* Health Psychology Unit Technical Reports, 97/4–97/8. Pretoria: University of South Africa.

Nell, V. (2000). *Cross-cultural neuropsychological assessment: Theory and practice.* Mahwah, NJ: Lawrence Erlbaum Associates.

UNESCO. (1998). Statistical yearbook. Paris: Author.

CHAPTER 22

Forensic Neuropsychology

JIM HOM AND JANICE NICI

Forensic neuropsychology is a subspecialty of clinical neuropsychology that applies neuropsychological principles and practices to matters that pertain to legal decision making. Practitioners of forensic neuropsychology are trained as clinical neuropsychologists and subsequently specialize in the forensic application of their knowledge and skills. These practitioners will thus typically be doctoral-level psychologists with advanced training in brain-behavior relationships. Clinical neuropsychologists are trained to assess, diagnose, and treat individuals with central nervous system disorders or disease using various methods and procedures that have been shown to validly reflect brain function.

The field of forensic neuropsychology is new and rapidly evolving. There are, at the present time, no formal training programs, licensure requirements, or professional organizations devoted specifically to forensic neuropsychology. There is no formal process for assigning the title of forensic neuropsychologist upon a practitioner. Rather, this title can be claimed, in most states, by a practitioner who is first qualified as a licensed psychologist and who possesses the additional training and experience necessary to meet the guidelines for qualifications as a neuropsychologist. One's training, background, and knowledge must meet, at the minimum, the requirements for licensure in one's state and the ethical guidelines for practice of the American Psychological Association (APA; 1992). The National Academy of Neuropsychology (NAN) has proposed a specific definition of a clinical neuropsychologist (refer to the appendix). The title of forensic neuropsychologist requires further training and experience in the legal arena, although to date, the nature and type of this education has not been specified. The field is distinct from the more established and recognized field of forensic psychology, which has an established board for certifying qualified practitioners, an established professional organization, published standards for practice, and several well-accepted publications for dissemination of information and research (Otto & Heilbrun, 2002). In contrast, research in the field of forensic neuropsychology is generally disseminated in various clinical neuropsychology publications. Relatively few textbooks cover the field, and only a single journal is devoted solely to the field, the *Journal of Forensic Neuropsychology* (Haworth Press).

Although new, the field of forensic neuropsychology has grown significantly during the past 20 years. Several surveys of practicing psychologists have been conducted, illustrating the growth of the field of forensic neuropsychology. In a survey of members of APA Division 40 (Clinical Neuropsychology) and NAN, Seretny, Dean, Gray, and Hartlage (1986) found that referrals to psychologists from attorneys were equal in rank with referrals from neurosurgeons, psychologists, general physicians, and rehabilitation specialists. The mean number of occasions that respondents gave testimony was almost five times a year. In a 1985 survey of psychologists providing neuropsychological services, Guilmette, Faust, Hart, and

Arkes (1990) found that 71% of psychologists who devote more than 30% of their activities to neuropsychology had neuropsychological expert witness experience. Moreover, more than a third of psychologists who devoted less than 10% of their professional activities to neuropsychology reported having neuropsychological expert witness experience. This suggests a demand for neuropsychological experts, extending even to those who devoted relatively little of their time to the field. In a 1989 survey, Putnam described the features of compensation for clinical neuropsychologists and classified forensic neuropsychology as a source of supplemental income. He found that 20% of respondents who earned supplemental income were engaged in forensic neuropsychology, exclusively or with another income-generating activity. Psychologists at all levels of income indicated forensic neuropsychology was one of the two most common sources of supplemental income, according to this survey. Putnam and DeLuca (1990), in a survey of APA Division 40 members, found that legal entities accounted for almost one-third of private practice referral sources. Putnam, DeLuca, and Anderson (1994) found that respondents who engaged in forensic work had higher incomes than those who did not. Legal-forensic activities occupied 8% of respondents' professional time. More than half of the respondents reported engaging in some legal work. Sweet and colleagues surveyed neuropsychologists in 1989, 1994, and 1999 and found an important increase in the time spent in forensic neuropsychology activities from 1994 to 1999 (Sweet & Moberg, 1990; Sweet, Moberg, & Suchy, 2000a, 2000b; Sweet, Moberg, & Westergaard, 1996). However, inspection of their data show that forensic neuropsychology activities occupied only six or fewer work hours per week across respondent categories. However, across the three surveys, only neurology and psychiatry were more important referral sources than attorneys. Further, Sweet et al. (2000a, 2000b) found that, among private practitioners, attorneys were the top referral source. Additional evidence for the growth of forensic neuropsychology is the increasing number of presentations on this topic at national meetings, as well as increasing numbers of peer-reviewed publications. Recently, a subspecialty in forensic neuropsychology was added to the American Board of Professional Neuropsychology (ABPN).

Forensic neuropsychology's growth is a direct result of the growth in the field of clinical neuropsychology, the field that provides its scientific underpinnings. During the past 40 years, clinical neuropsychology has established principles of brain-behavior relations and valid and reliable methodologies for measuring these relationships. These principles and methodologies allow clinical neuropsychologists to provide the trier of fact with specialized information for use in the legal decision-making process. This information includes results and conclusions from a systematic and objective assessment of an individual's brain-related function, allowing decisions about the patient's underlying neurological condition, and his/her neurocognitive abilities, deficits, treatment needs, future work capacity, and prognosis. Clinical neuropsychology can provide information regarding the cause of a brain injury, for example, as well as the location of brain injury, the extent of damage, rehabilitative potential, and impact on daily function. As such, the contribution of clinical neuropsychology is unique and has been found to be valuable to the trier of fact. The scope and potential of the field of clinical neuropsychology is well documented. Further information about the field and its practices can be found in other chapters of this volume and elsewhere (Filskov & Boll, 1981, 1986; Reitan & Davison, 1974; Wedding, Horton & Webster, 1986).

NEUROPSYCHOLOGICAL TESTIMONY

Neuropsychological testimony is well accepted in the courts. In a review of 200 appellate court cases in the 1980s, Richardson and Adams (1992) found that decisions in all jurisdictions upheld the right of a clinical neuropsychologist to testify about the presence of brain dysfunction. It is important to note that, while such testimony is allowed, the credibility of that testimony is always left to the trier of fact, as with any expert witness.

In contrast to the apparent unanimity regarding a neuropsychologist's ability to testify concerning the presence of brain dysfunction, the clinical neuropsychologist's ability to testify about the cause of brain dysfunction has been less accepted. However, Richardson and Adams (1992) found that 9 of 11 jurisdictions allowed neuropsychological testimony regarding causation. They summarized the challenges to such testimony, which have typically been raised on the grounds that psychologists are not medical doctors and that the causal determination of brain damage is a medical issue.

An early case that addressed the question of a neuropsychologist's ability to provide expert testimony regarding brain impairment was *Indianapolis Union Railway v. Walker* (1974). In this case, a passenger was injured in an auto collision with a train. A neuropsychologist, Dr. Ralph M. Reitan, provided testimony as to the presence, location, cause, and permanence of brain impairment. His ability to testify as an expert was challenged on appeal by the defendant because his testimony was not based on reasonable medical certainty. Specifically, the defendant's argument was that Dr. Reitan was not a licensed medical doctor and, therefore, he was not competent to testify as an expert concerning the physical neurological condition of the plaintiff. However, the appellate court concluded that the defendant's argument was without merit, and cited Dr. Reitan's education, training, knowledge, and experience as evidence of his expertise. Called "the first seminal case in [our] subspecialty" (Puente, 1997, p. 168), this case likely laid the foundation for the acceptance of clinical neuropsychological testimony in the courtroom. This decision helped to spur the development of the field of forensic neuropsychology.

Clinical neuropsychologists are trained in the study of brain-behavior relationships. They are interested in the effects of brain-related disorders on various functions, such as language, intelligence, sensorimotor abilities, memory, attention, and other cognitive and noncognitive processes. Clinical neuropsychologists assess patients to determine their level of functional capacity in these areas and the presence, nature, and severity of any deficits in these areas. Clinical neuropsychologists also provide various therapies to patients with neurocognitive deficits to help restore their former level of adaptive function and to help them compensate for functional deficits.

The training process that neuropsychologists go through involves obtaining a thorough grounding in the scientific method, including theory development, hypothesis testing, and probability theory. The scientific method requires that ideas (hypotheses) be systematically studied, with the results disseminated, so that findings can be replicated and validated, leading to refinement of the working theory or to its dismissal if results do not support it. This process is an ongoing and collaborative one, with the accumulation of validated and scientifically accepted information over time. In contrast, the legal method involves an attempt to resolve conflict through an adversarial approach in which each side is allowed to present its position and supporting information. Information is tested by direct examination and cross-examination, rather than by controlled scientific methods. The legal method results in a specific decision that is essentially absolute and final without the qualifications and probability statements typically used in the scientific approach (Newman, 1991).

The differences between these two methodologies are well captured by Supreme Court Justice Blackmun. He described the scientific process as one of "perpetual revision. Law, on the other hand, must resolve disputes finally and quickly" (Giuliano, Barth, Hawk, & Ryan, 1997, p. 11). As such, the neuropsychologist is typically called into the legal process to help in reaching a final decision, while using methods that rely on probability statements and confidence intervals. That is, while the court is attempting to reach a definite decision, the neuropsychologist's role is to provide information within the standards of the field. The neuropsychologist does not make the decision, but is often asked for strongly stated opinions, which may not fit within the scientific limits of the field.

Neuropsychologists are called into legal proceedings typically as expert witnesses. Their value to the court is in their "scientific, technical, or other specialized knowledge [that] will assist the trier of fact to understand the evidence or to determine a fact in issue" (Rule 702, Federal Rules of Evidence). As an expert witness, the clinical neuropsychologist is often asked to render an opinion about a patient's brain-related function as it relates to the claim at hand. As part of this opinion, the clinical neuropsychologist is also often asked about the cause, nature, and extent of any injury or dysfunction, as well as the possible impact of these impairments on such things as the patient's daily function and occupation. Moreover, the clinical neuropsychologist is often asked about the prognosis and permanence of these deficits, as well as the potential for improvement through treatments or therapies. The neuropsychologist's opinion is typically based on a clinical assessment of the patient. This assessment is based on the methods and procedures currently accepted within the field. These methods are expected to be appropriately grounded in scientific validity and reliability.

ADMISSIBILITY OF EVIDENCE

Although neuropsychologists evaluate their methods and results by scientific standards, these standards are not necessarily the ones that determine whether neuropsychological expert testimony will be allowed in court. For more than 70 years, the standard for admissibility of scientific testimony has been the *Frye* rule (*Frye v. United States,* 1923), which states that ". . . while courts will go a long way in admitting expert testimony deduced from a well-recognized scientific principle or discovery, the thing from which the deduction is made must be sufficiently established to have gained *general acceptance* in the particular field in which it belongs [emphasis added]." General acceptance of a method or technique was often determined by peer publication. If a method had such general acceptance, then testimony regarding it would be admissible in court. This rule precluded admission of any novel or innovative technique. For example, it was not sufficient for experts to vouch for the validity of their own techniques without evidence for support and acceptance from their field. While the *Frye* rule addresses the issue of a technique's recognition and acceptance in a field, it does not address the scientific validity of the technique. Thus, a technique or procedure could be admissible in court on the basis of its general acceptance, but could still lack scientific validity. Despite this apparent shortcoming, the *Frye* rule is still used in a number of jurisdictions.

In 1993, the United States Supreme Court set a new evidentiary standard for admissibility of scientific testimony (*Daubert v. Merrell Dow Pharmaceuticals,* 1993). In this decision, the Court asserted that Federal Rule of Evidence 702 is the standard for admissibility of expert testimony in Federal courts. Rule 702 states, "If scientific, technical, or other specialized knowledge will assist the trier of fact to understand the evidence or to determine a fact in issue, a witness qualified as an expert by knowledge, skills, experience, training, or education, may testify thereto in the form of an opinion or otherwise." This rule establishes a criterion of relevancy for expert testimony, establishes the terms according to which a witness could qualify as an expert, and regulates the subjects about which an expert may testify. Moreover, in the ruling, several factors were outlined that could be considered by judges in determining whether a technique meets this standard:

- Has the technique been tested?
- Has the technique been subjected to peer review and publication?
- What is the error rate in applying the technique?
- To what extent has the technique received general acceptance in the relevant scientific community?

Subsequent rulings elaborated on the application of the *Daubert* standards (*General Electric v. Joiner,* 1997; *Moore v. Ashland Chemical,* 1997; *Kumho Tire v. Carmichael,* 1999). The requirements of the *Daubert* ruling apply in all Federal courts and guide judges in their gatekeeping role of determining the admissibility of scientific testimony. The *Daubert* ruling places a responsibility on judges to evaluate the scientific merit of testimony, a task that may be well outside their realm of knowledge.

The acceptance of *Daubert* is not uniform across all U.S. jurisdictions. In one analysis, Reed (1999) found that 33 states were using "at least some version of the Daubert standard, while 17 states continue to use the 'older' *Frye* standard" (p. 49). He also noted the differences in interpretation across jurisdictions as to whether *Daubert* standards apply to only scientific testimony or also to the other types of testimony mentioned in Rule 702 (technical or specialized knowledge).

While it is important for neuropsychologists to be informed about these rulings and their implications, it remains for the judge to determine admissibility. Neuropsychological testimony has been admitted in some cases and excluded in others. In trying to employ the most scientifically validated procedures and techniques, neuropsychologists can take into account the *Daubert* questions. However, overconcern about admissibility issues is unwarranted; the clinician must ultimately provide an opinion based on sound scientific principles and current knowledge in the field.

ROLES OF NEUROPSYCHOLOGISTS IN LEGAL PROCEEDINGS

Clinical neuropsychologists may be called upon to assist in criminal and civil cases, although their services are used more often in civil than in criminal cases.

Criminal law involves the prosecutor and a defendant who has been accused of some misdeed. Decisions by the jury have to be established on the basis of certainty that is beyond a reasonable doubt. Civil action involves a plaintiff who is claiming some injury or requesting some redress of a wrong and a defendant who is claimed to be the cause of the injury or wrong. Decisions in these cases are to be based on the preponderance of evidence, that is, whether they are more likely than not.

According to McMahon and Satz (1981), neuropsychologists "have nothing to contribute to the liability phase of a proceeding—that is, did or did not a given event occur and/ or is a specific individual or entity at fault for the event" (p. 687). The neuropsychologist does play several roles in both criminal and civil arenas. In criminal cases, the neuropsychologist may be called upon to address a defendant's competency to stand trial, possible insanity, ability to form intent to commit the crime under consideration, or the presence of mitigating circumstances such as a brain-related impairment (Denney & Wynkoop, 2000; Glass, 1991; McMahon et al., 1981; Rehkopf & Fisher, 1997). In addition, Denney and Wynkoop (2000) address additional areas in which neuropsychologists may contribute in criminal settings, including addressing defendants' future dangerousness and competency to act as their own attorneys.

In civil proceedings, a neuropsychologist may contribute in issues of disability determination, competence determination, and personal injury (Glass, 1991; McMahon et al., 1981). Disability determinations can involve the worker's compensation system, private disability insurance, Social Security, or the educational system. Neuropsychological examinations can be employed to document the presence of disability, as well as its nature, extent, directions for treatment, and prospects for improvement. Determination of competence can relate to an individual's ability to manage one's own affairs or the need for guardianship. This relates to a person's ability to make financial decisions, dispose of personal property, and handle medical treatment decisions. Competence issues can also revolve around an individual's ability to function in a certain professional capacity. By far the greatest involvement by clinical neuropsychologists in the legal system involves personal injury cases. In these cases, a plaintiff claims to have suffered an injury and seeks compensation for redress. In personal injury cases in which a neuropsychological deficit is claimed, the neuropsychologist can be employed to document the presence, nature, extent, and permanence of the injury. Clinical neuropsychologists can be called upon to examine patients and testify in cases of head injury, toxic exposure, medical malpractice, electric shock, near-drowning, or other neurological injury.

NEUROPSYCHOLOGICAL METHODOLOGY

Regardless of the legal venue, the primary responsibility of the clinical neuropsychologist participating in forensic work is to provide information based on scientifically validated neuropsychological principles and clinical methodology that is pertinent to the Forensic Question at hand—for example, does the plaintiff suffer from significant cognitive deficit as a result of the mild head injury sustained in a motor vehicle accident? Or, in a criminal case, can the defendant's criminal behaviors be explained by brain damage he sustained as a teenager?

Commonly, in a forensic neuropsychological evaluation, a battery of tests is used to assess neurocognitive functions in order to answer these questions. Different neuropsychologists may construct their batteries from different selections of tests. Some batteries are composed according to the patient's presenting complaints and the referral question ("flexible battery"). These batteries may be amended or supplemented as the evaluation proceeds and additional information about the patient's function is gained (Lezak, 1995). Other neuropsychologists begin with a specific set of tests, seldom deviating from this selection, although often supplementing the basic battery ("fixed battery"). The most widely used of these fixed batteries is the Halstead-Reitan Neuropsychological Test Battery, a comprehensive battery that addresses a broad range of brain-related functions (Reitan & Wolfson, 1993). The results of the battery of tests often form the primary basis for the neuropsychological testimony in answering the Forensic Question.

The critical Forensic Question is not just whether the patient has dysfunction, but whether the dysfunction results from the event under consideration. For example, the neuropsychologist might be faced with the question of whether a patient's impaired score on Digit Span, low-average score on

the verbal section of the Wechsler Memory Scale, and poor performance on Digit Symbol are reflective of brain impairment in light of a low-average intelligence, high school education, and former employment as a sales manager. If so, does this brain-related impairment relate to the head injury, to a previously diagnosed hypertension and diabetes, or to a psychological reaction to the accident?

It is crucial for the neuropsychologist to select techniques and procedures that will best answer these questions. The clinical neuropsychologist must use a methodology that can provide brain-relevant information about the patient's current cognitive function and dysfunction and can address the cause of any dysfunction found. The neuropsychologist must employ a methodology that has been scientifically validated on brain-impaired individuals and can distinguish various brain conditions from each other as well as from normal variation. Specifically, this methodology must have demonstrated validity in determining presence of brain impairment, location of the cerebral damage, nature of the brain condition, as well as differentiating various neurological disorders and other conditions that can afflict the brain. Finally, the methodology must be able to determine whether any dysfunction found is the result of a neurological condition as opposed to non-neurological, psychological, or even factitious disorders.

To accomplish this, the forensic neuropsychologist must use a methodology that allows the conclusion that findings are specific to the brain-related condition under dispute. Differentiating these complex conditions requires validated test patterns and relationships. Such patterns and relationships can show, for example, whether impaired scores on one or more tests (indicating the patient's level of performance), in comparison with scores on other tests, is an indication of brain impairment or is an indication of normal variability (Reitan et al., 1993; Russell, 1998; Williams, 1997). Most important, these patterns and relationships must be able to independently differentiate brain impairment resulting from one neurological etiology from impairment caused by another (Reitan et al., 2000). As noted by Russell (1998), "The pattern analysis method is primarily concerned with the relationships between tests rather than with the individual scores or level of functioning on particular tests. This method compares tests with each other in order to discover a pattern that reveals information about a cognitive condition" (p. 367). A more thorough discussion of pattern analysis in neuropsychological evaluation is presented by Russell (1984, 1997). Inherently, this assessment approach requires the use of a similar set of tests that has been given to persons with confirmed brain impairment of various types. This analysis cannot be done by a purely normative approach or by a tally approach (adding up the number of impaired scores and comparing it to the number of normal scores). The use of these patterns and relationships provides information that can be used to answer the Forensic Question.

Although many tests have been developed to measure function, they range in usefulness, scope, and applicability. Most are standardized and have normative data to provide a comparison of the patient's performance to a reference group (Mitrushina, Boone, & D'Elia, 1999). The model of test development employed is one where the reference group is composed of normal, non-brain-damaged individuals. A great deal of attention is paid to the psychometric properties of these tests, as advocated by the APA rules regarding the standards of tests (1985; Anastasi, 1988). These tests provide clinicians an understanding of the variation of performance within the normative population. Often, these tests clearly indicate a person's standing in comparison with others of the same age, education, and gender with respect to the attribute measured. The information regarding a patient's relative strengths and weaknesses can be useful in treatment planning and rehabilitation.

Sole reliance on normed tests of function has significant limitations in answering the Forensic Questions previously stated. While this approach addresses the patient's function, it is unable to address the cause of any dysfunction found. This model of assessment uses the function of normal individuals as the basis for comparison, and thus, any conclusions are limited to statements regarding a patient's standing with respect to normal variation. Moreover, if the test norms include only normal individuals, it is problematic to conclude that low test scores (determined, by whatever means, to be low for the patient's premorbid abilities) are the result of brain damage; that is, one cannot conclude that identified weaknesses are the result of brain impairment if the test was developed using only those with normal brain function. Is the fifth percentile of normal subjects the point below which patients can be considered brain damaged? Is a score that is one or more standard deviations below the mean for normal subjects an indication of brain damage?

The presence of cognitive deficits does not necessarily imply brain injury. A valid conclusion regarding brain injury can be made only through the use of a methodology that has been thoroughly validated in its ability to identify neurocognitive performances related to various brain-behavior conditions. The mere selection of standardized, psychometrically sound tests to identify cognitive deficits does not ensure that the results are forensically, or even neuropsychologically, relevant. The astute forensic neuropsychologist (and the knowledgeable attorney) readily realizes that cognitive impairment may be caused by a host of factors. The forensic neuropsychologist must be able to demonstrate a causative

link between the cognitive impairments and the event at hand. Typically, in a forensic situation, the neuropsychologist is asked for an opinion that is predicated on scientific evidence and can be stated with a reasonable degree of neuropsychological certainty. A methodology is required that can independently predict the cause of any deficits found. Too often the mere co-occurrence of the motor vehicle accident (MVA) (for example) and the patient's complaints are used to establish the accident as the cause of the cognitive deficits. However, considering that the patient has experienced the trauma of an MVA and has a financial incentive to appear impaired, it is the responsibility of the forensic neuropsychologist to determine whether the deficits found are the result of brain impairment from this accident, as opposed to psychological trauma, physical (peripheral) injury, malingering, a preexisting condition, or some combination of these factors (Faust, Ziskin, & Hiers, 1991; Reitan et al., 1993; Williams, 1997).

For a forensic situation, the Halstead-Reitan Neuropsychological Test Battery (HRB; Reitan et al., 1993) is the most appropriate methodology. The HRB is a well-validated procedure that can answer the Forensic Question and meets the methodological requirements previously stated. After reviewing guidelines for psychological testing in the forensic context, Williams (1997) recommended the use of the HRB, stating, "No other battery is as well validated with such a variety of neurological and psychiatric disorders. This is invaluable in making differential diagnoses" (p. 60). Laing and Fisher (1997) state, "A standardized or fixed battery approach, which requires the same tests to be administered regardless of the patient's presenting problem, is recommended for use in the forensic context" (p. 126). They add, "The Halstead-Reitan Neuropsychological Battery (HRB) is the best example of this fixed approach to neuropsychological testing" (p. 126). They also state, "In summary, a flexible battery approach to neuropsychological evaluation is subject to the criticism that it does not satisfy the major criteria for reliability and validity" (p. 126). Further, Russell (1998) states, "The HRB is a set of tests designed for pattern analysis, not an uncoordinated group of tests. Patterns between tests cannot be observed when tests are continually changing" (p. 367).

The issue of the admissibility of evidence from the Halstead-Reitan Neuropsychological Test Battery was addressed in a 1994 case, *Chapple v. Ganger.* According to Reed (1996), this case was the first time the *Daubert* standard was applied to evidence from fixed versus flexible neuropsychological test batteries in federal court. In this case, three neuropsychological evaluations were conducted on a child injured in a motor vehicle accident. Two of the evaluations employed a flexible battery approach, and one employed a fixed battery approach. The conclusions from the first flexible battery were that the patient had suffered a mild traumatic brain injury from the accident, resulting in mild cognitive and mild behavioral problems. A second flexible battery was subsequently administered by a different professional. The conclusion from this battery was that the patient had "suffered moderate to severe traumatic brain injury with frontal involvement secondary to the automobile accident" (Reed, 1996, p. 319). This neuropsychologist also concluded that the patient "would be left with permanent residual problems with attention, memory, and executive functions." (Reed, 1996, p. 319). Subsequently, an HRB was administered and Dr. Ralph Reitan, the defense neuropsychologist, concluded that, "most of the test scores were in the normal range except for some minor deviations which could be attributed to mild brain dysfunction, but overall the scores were representative of the non-brain-damaged child population" (Reed, 1996, p. 319).

The Court's reasoning regarding the admissibility of expert testimony was outlined thusly: "For purposes of determining whether expert testimony is sufficiently grounded on valid scientific principles so as to be admissible, general acceptance . . . is [a] factor to be considered; however, it is not dispositive. The focus is on the 'methodology' of the experts, and not the conclusions that they generate. This does not mean, however, that a conclusion will be admissible merely because some part of the methodology is scientifically valid. The entire reasoning process must be valid. A credible link must be established between the reasoning and the conclusion. Once that is accomplished, the inquiry crosses the line from one of admissibility to one of the weight the trier of fact should accord to the conclusion" (*Chapple v. Granger,* 1994, 1481 at 1496).

After consideration of the proffered expert neuropsychological testimony that included discussion of the neuropsychological assessment approaches, the *Chapple* court decided, "The court accepts the test results as they indicate normal scores in most areas. As to those areas which show below normal scores, there is not sufficient scientific evidence to support the conclusion those scores are indicative of permanent organic brain damage in children" (*Chapple v. Granger,* 1994, 1481 at 1498). As Reed (1996) notes, "this decision . . . currently functions as sole legal precedent regarding the scientific admissibility of neuropsychological test battery results and related scientific expert witness medical testimony in the federal courts" (p. 321). He states, "within clinical neuropsychology, professionals who use the validated or fixed neuropsychological test batteries to obtain reliable and valid objective test results will generally find the *Daubert* standard an easy threshold to pass; however, professionals who use only flexible neuropsychological test batteries to obtain valid

and reliable objective test results will find the *Daubert* standard more imposing, if not impossible to pass" (p. 321).

To the extent that the *Chapple* case represents the course that courts will take in judging neuropsychological evidence, practitioners should be cautious in drawing conclusions regarding brain impairment if they use a methodology that does not meet the scientific criteria described previously.

HALSTEAD-REITAN NEUROPSYCHOLOGICAL TEST BATTERY

The HRB is the most extensively researched and validated neuropsychological battery in use. Detailed information on the HRB is included in another chapter in this volume as well as elsewhere (Reitan & Wolfson, 1986; 1993). Of particular interest to the forensic neuropsychologist is the extensive published research on the HRB. The approach in developing the HRB was to compare control subjects to patients with known cerebral damage or dysfunction (Reitan, 1955, 1959b; Reitan et al., 1974). The sensitivity of the HRB was compared with other widely used psychological tests, in particular the Wechsler intelligence scales (Reitan, 1959a). Additional research was done to determine the differential sensitivity of the tests to lateralized dysfunction, as well as to acute versus chronic cerebral lesions (Fitzhugh, Fitzhugh, & Reitan, 1961). Further, the effects of age and education were studied (Finlayson, Johnson, & Reitan, 1977; Reitan & Wolfson, 1995b). Research has also been done on particular conditions, such as aphasia (Doehring & Reitan, 1961; Heimberger & Reitan, 1961), emotional problems (Dikmen & Reitan, 1974, 1977), and sensorimotor deficits (Hom & Reitan, 1982). The sensitivity of the HRB to various neurological conditions including cerebrovascular disease, head injury, brain tumors, multiple sclerosis, Huntington's disease, Parkinson's disease, Alzheimer's disease, epilepsy, aging, drug abuse, and mental retardation has been established (Boll, Heaton, & Reitan, 1974; Dikmen, McLean, & Temkin, 1986; Dikmen & Reitan, 1976; Grant, Mohns, Miller, & Reitan, 1976; Hom, 1991, 1992; Hom & Reitan, 1984, 1990; Matthews & Reitan, 1961, 1962, 1963; Reitan, 1962, 1967, 1976; Reitan & Boll, 1971; Reitan & Fitzhugh, 1971; Reitan, Reed, & Dyken, 1971; Reitan & Wolfson, 1985, 1988a, 1988b, 1993, 2000; Ross & Reitan, 1955). Further, numerous examples are published regarding the clinical application of the HRB (Reitan et al., 1993). This extensive body of research assists the forensic neuropsychologist in answering the Forensic Question.

The accuracy of the HRB in clinical diagnosis has been well established. In 1964, Reitan conducted a study to determine the clinical accuracy of the HRB in a variety of neurological conditions. In this seminal study, he established that clinical diagnoses made through consideration of the HRB test results alone were accurate in determining the patients' neurological conditions. In this study, 112 patients who had definite medical diagnoses based on comprehensive medical and neurological evaluation, including history, were used. Using only the patients' HRB test data, Reitan was able to classify correctly the patients by diagnosis with the following success: intrinsic tumor, 12 of 16; extrinsic tumor, 8 of 16; cerebrovascular lesions, 28 of 32; traumatic head injury, 30 of 32; multiple sclerosis, 15 of 16. A comparable study, addressing such a range of neurological conditions and blind test interpretation, has not been completed on any other battery or approach in clinical neuropsychology.

In a subsequent study that further illustrates the strength of the HRB methodology, Finkelstein (1977) developed a decision tree interpretive system to classify patients with various neurological conditions as well as control subjects. Specifically, the interpretive system provided information regarding presence or absence of brain damage, lateralization of brain damage, nature of the cerebral lesion, and diagnosis of specific neurological condition. The neurological conditions employed in this study included metastatic carcinoma, slowly growing intrinsic tumor, rapidly growing intrinsic tumor, extrinsic tumor, vascular anomaly with bleeding, vascular anomaly without bleeding, cerebrovascular accident, Parkinson's disease, primary neuronal degeneration/generalized arteriosclerosis, multiple sclerosis, and head trauma. Using 144 patients with brain disease or damage and 36 controls, Finkelstein found that the interpretive system correctly determined the presence of brain damage in 95% of the cases (96% of brain-damaged and 92% of controls), correctly lateralized the damage in 75% of cases (67% of left hemisphere lesions, 86% of right hemisphere lesions, and 74% of diffuse lesions), correctly determined the nature of cerebral lesion in 83% of cases (83% for those with evidence for recent tissue destruction, 83% for those without such evidence), and correctly diagnosed a specific neurological condition in 69% of cases. Among the specific diagnoses, the interpretive system identified each one in more than 50% of the cases, with the exception of the vascular anomalies. The vascular anomalies were correctly classified only 38% of the time, with most of the misclassifications called head trauma. In contrast, CVAs and trauma were correctly identified most often (75% and 83%, respectively).

This interpretive system clearly shows the clinical utility of the HRB methodology and provides validated algorithmic formulations for differential neurological diagnosis based on a patient's neuropsychological test performances (Hom, 1983).

Moreover, the Reitan (1964) and Finkelstein (1977) studies demonstrate the power of the HRB methodology to provide independent information regarding a causative link between cognitive deficits and brain impairment, often the most critical aspect of the Forensic Question.

ILLUSTRATIVE CASES

To illustrate the issues discussed previously, we present several cases that are representative of typical cases seen in a forensic neuropsychology practice.

Case SK

SK was a 57-year-old man who sustained a closed head injury in an MVA. One year before testing he suffered a large laceration of his forehead requiring stitches, a loss of hearing in his left ear, and an injury to his left upper extremity. After the accident, he reported significant cognitive problems that affected his daily function including problems in memory, attention and concentration, problem solving, and flexibility of thought. He also reported problems in visual-spatial function, including getting lost and feeling disoriented. He denied problems with language. These cognitive problems affected his job performance. He indicated that he was having severe headaches, although these improved somewhat over time. He reported experiencing some personality changes including irritability and crying spells.

He reported that he was dazed and confused at the time of the accident. There is no clear indication that he lost consciousness, but he reported being amnestic for the event and for several days afterwards. An initial neurological evaluation was found to be normal, CT scan was normal, and he was discharged from the emergency room the day of the accident. He received physical therapy for his arm injury as well as treatment for his headaches. For several months, he was treated by a neurologist who prescribed medication for his headaches and anxiety. An MRI was normal. The neurologist's diagnosis was closed head injury with cognitive deficit. Throughout his treatment of SK, the neurologist noted problems of cognitive and psychological function.

SK's prior medical history is negative for head injury or loss of consciousness; he reported that he had been basically healthy all his life. He denied having any prior psychological problems.

The patient owns a financial consulting company and previously held other executive positions in financial institutions. He denied any prior job difficulties. He has a bachelor's degree in business. He reported being an average student.

The current evaluation was requested by the patient's attorney as part of litigation regarding the MVA. He was given a full neuropsychological examination, including the Halstead-Reitan Neuropsychological Test Battery for Adults (HRB), Wechsler Adult Intelligence Scale (WAIS), Wechsler Memory Scale-Russell Revision (1975), Wide Range Achievement Test-3rd Edition (WRAT-3), Cornell Index, Minnesota Multiphasic Personality Inventory (MMPI), Personality Assessment Inventory (PAI), Mini Mental State Examination (MMSE), and Clinical Interview. The results are presented in Figures 22.1–22.3.

The patient was generally cooperative during testing. No problems were encountered in testing. He appeared to put forth his best effort on all tasks, and the test results were considered a valid representation of his current neuropsychological functioning.

On the WAIS, the patient demonstrated average intelligence overall. In terms of his verbal intellectual abilities, no particular strengthens or weaknesses were noted. Although a very mild degree of variability was found among the patient's perceptual-motor abilities, no specific conclusions regarding brain-related loss of intellectual abilities can be made. In cases of head injury, intellectual measures often do not reflect impairment because of their relative insensitivity to changes in brain function (Hom et al., 1984, 1990; Reitan et al., 1974; Reitan et al., 1993).

On the WRAT-3, the patient's spelling and arithmetic performances are lower than would be expected, especially considering his educational level. However, a conclusion that these performances are related to brain-related dysfunction would be speculative because the WRAT-3 has not been established as a brain-sensitive measure.

In contrast to the intellectual and academic measures, tests with demonstrated validity to the biological integrity of the brain clearly show brain-related impairment. The patient earned a Halstead Impairment Index of 0.7, indicating 70% of the Halstead tests were within the brain-damaged range. On the General Neuropsychological Deficit Scale (GNDS; Reitan et al., 1988b), the patient earned a score of 47. This score indicates an overall clinical severity level within the moderate range of brain impairment. The sensitivity of the GNDS to cerebral impairment is well established (Reitan et al., 1988b, 2000; Rojas & Bennett, 1995).

Overall, SK displayed a variable pattern of neuropsychological results; some brain functions reflected moderate to severe impairment while others were quite intact. This variability in neuropsychological function is often found in cases of craniocerebral trauma (Reitan et al., 1986, 1988a, 1988b, 2000). The patient demonstrated significant impairment of abstract reasoning, logical analysis, and complex psycho-

motor problem-solving as reflected in his very poor performances on the Category Test and the Tactual Performance Test (TPT). In addition, he showed mild to moderate impairment of incidental learning for both simple and complex stimuli (TPT Memory and Localization), and of flexibility of thought for complex stimuli (Trail Making Test Part B). In contrast, his performances on the Seashore Rhythm Test and Speech Sounds Perception Test were quite good, indicating intact attention and concentration for slowly and rapidly presented auditory materials. Intact scores on these two measures often reflect the nature of the cerebral impairment (acute vs. chronic or slowly progressive vs. highly destructive lesion (Reitan et al., 1993). In this case, the scores suggest a more chronic neurological disorder. Flexibility of thought for simple stimuli was intact. Overall, the results suggest moderate generalized neuropsychological dysfunction with a degree of variability.

With regards to tests specific to the neuropsychological functioning of each cerebral hemisphere, the patient demonstrated a bilateral pattern of cognitive dysfunction. This is reflected by scores of 9 on the Right Neuropsychological Deficit Scale and 10 on the Left Neuropsychological Deficit Scale (Reitan et al., 1988b). Right-hemisphere neurocognitive dysfunction was demonstrated by mild impairment of both immediate recall of figural material and 30-minute delayed recall. His retention of this material after it was encoded was intact. His visual constructional abilities, as represented by his ability to copy and reproduce simple geometric designs on the Aphasia Screening Examination, were impaired (drawings of the cross and key). Left-hemisphere dysfunction was shown by mild impairment of immediate recall of verbal material and mild to moderate impairment of 30-minute delayed recall. His retention of this material after it was encoded was mildly to moderately impaired. He demonstrated dyscalculia on the Aphasia Screening Examination. In craniocerebral trauma there are often specific findings of cognitive impairment, reflective of damage to the integrity of each cerebral hemisphere, in addition to the generalized findings of brain impairment.

Examination of the patient's sensorimotor functions indicated bilateral deficits. In terms of the left hemisphere, SK demonstrated a slower than expected right-handed tapping speed, a number of right-sided auditory imperceptions during bilateral simultaneous stimulation, and significantly greater difficulty with right-hand fingertip number writing recognition. He also demonstrated several sensorimotor deficits indicative of right cerebral hemisphere dysfunction, including a significantly weaker than expected left-handed grip strength, a significantly poorer left-handed performance on the complex psychomotor problem-solving task, and slightly more

Case: SK   Age: 57   Education: 16   Gender: M   Handedness: R

Wechsler Adult Intelligence Scale

VIQ	102
PIQ	101
FSIQ	102

Verbal Subtests

Information	9
Comprehension	10
Arithmetic	9
Similarities	11
Digit Span	9
Vocabulary	10

Performance Subtests

Digit Symbol	7
Picture Completion	9
Block Design	7
Picture Arrangement	9
Object Assembly	6

Wide Range Achievement Test — 3

	Standard Score	Grade Equivalent
Reading	96	HS
Spelling	89	7
Arithmetic	88	6

Halstead-Reitan Neuropsychological Test Battery

Halstead Impairment Index   0.7

Category Test	77				
Tactual Performance Test					
Total Time	37.2	Dominant hand	7.9	Blocks in	10
Memory	4	Non-dominant hand	15.0	Blocks in	6
Localization	3	Both hands	14.3	Blocks in	10
Seashore Rhythm Test	30				
Speech-sounds Perception Test	6				

Finger Tapping Test	Dominant hand	42	Trail Making Test	Part A	36
	Non-dominant	45		Part B	118

	Right	Left
Strength of Grip (kg)	53.5	15.0
Bilateral Simultaneous Sensory Stimulation		
Tactile	0	0
Auditory	3	1
Visual	0	0

Visual Fields: Full

	Right	
Tactile Finger Recognition	1	2
Finger-Tip Number Writing	4	1
Tactile Form Recognition Test		
Time (sec)	11	8
Errors	0	0

Wechsler Memory Scale — Russell Revision

	Immediate	Delayed	% Retained
Verbal	mild	m-mod	47
Figural	mild	mild	88

Figure 22.1   Test results for SK.

Reitan-Indiana
Aphasia Screening Test
Form for Adults and Older Children

Name ___SK___

Age ___57___ Educ ___16___ Date _____

Examiner _____

Copy SQUARE	Repeat TRIANGLE
Name SQUARE	Repeat MASSACHUSETTS
Spell SQUARE	Repeat METHODIST EPISCOPAL
Copy CROSS	Write SQUARE
Name CROSS	Read SEVEN
Spell CROSS	Repeat SEVEN
Copy TRIANGLE	Repeat/Explain HE SHOUTED THE WARNING. **"try to keep somebody from harm, protect them"**
Name TRIANGLE	Write HE SHOUTED THE WARNING.
Spell TRIANGLE	Compute 85 − 27 = **"57" (self-corrected to) "58"**
Name BABY	Compute 17 × 3 = **"41"**
Write CLOCK	Name KEY
Name FORK	Demonstrate use of KEY
Read 7 SIX 2	Draw KEY
Read MGW	Read PLACE LEFT HAND TO RIGHT EAR.
Reading I	Place LEFT HAND TO RIGHT EAR
Reading II	Place LEFT HAND TO LEFT ELBOW

Figure 22.2 Aphasia Screening Test protocol for SK.

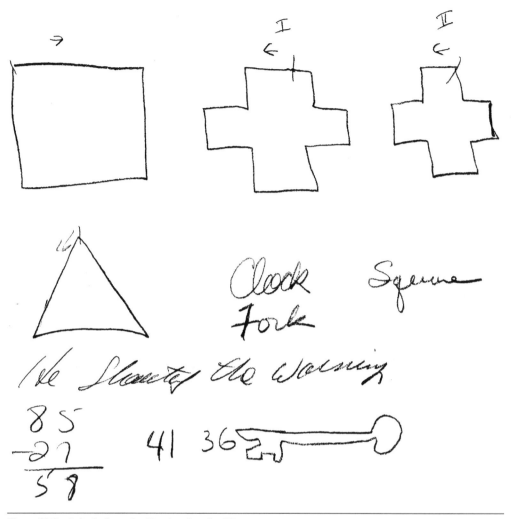

Figure 22.3   Aphasia Screening Test drawings for SK.

left-handed finger recognition errors than right-handed ones. However, it should be noted that these poor left-sided motor performances may be caused in part by the injury to his left upper extremity. In contrast, he had no tactile or visual imperceptions, his visual fields were full, and he made no errors on tactile form recognition. It should be noted that SK wears a hearing aid in his left ear. Sensorimotor findings are typically seen in craniocerebral trauma and provide important information regarding the neurological condition of the patient (Hom et al., 1982).

The tests of psychological function indicated significant difficulties in a number of areas of psychological function. The pattern of results is associated with individuals experiencing significant anxiety, tension, concerns about somatic function and health status, and depressive symptomatology. The psychological factors were likely contributing to his problems in function but would not be sufficient to explain his neuropsychological deficits.

Overall, these findings indicate moderate but variable impairment of both general and specific neuropsychological abilities. In addition, the results show a degree of sensorimotor deficit related to both the left and right cerebral hemispheres. The pattern of results is typical of residual neurocognitive deficits resulting from craniocerebral trauma. As is often the case in head injury, neuropsychological testing of this patient has revealed indications of impairment not shown on neurological examination. The neuropsychological findings clearly indicate that this patient has suffered brain damage from his head injury, in that the pattern of results is entirely consistent with that seen in patients with documented evidence of brain injury from head trauma (Dikmen et al., 1976; Dikmen, Reitan, & Temkin, 1983; Reitan et al., 2000). The forensic neuropsychologist can thus provide information regarding the patient's strengths and weaknesses, but also has a firm foundation for giving an opinion regarding the causative factor for these deficits.

Case MD

MD was a 44-year-old married female who was involved in a motor vehicle accident two years prior to testing in which she sustained multiple injuries of her head and shoulder. She apparently did not lose consciousness, in that she was able to provide a complete account of the event and its aftermath. She was taken to a local emergency room for evaluation and treatment and was discharged the same day. After the accident, she was treated for numerous physical problems including headaches, shoulder problems, pain, vision difficulties, dizziness, weakness, and reduced range of movement. Subsequent CT of the head and quantitative EEG were normal.

In addition to the physical symptoms, MD reports multiple cognitive problems that she attributes to the accident and injury to her head. These include problems with memory, attention and concentration, word finding, learning, and reading. She indicated that she no longer functions at her previous levels. For example, she reported bouncing many checks since the accident, forgetting to pay bills, and losing or misplacing items. She indicated that her abilities to perform as a college professor have been significantly compromised. She has been teaching six college courses per semester, and she has experienced significant problems doing her job. She indicated that she gets distracted, loses focus, has problems learning new material, and has difficulty reading and grading exams. In addition, she reports losing her train of thought while speaking, making paraphasic errors, being less fluent in speech, and having problems with writing. MD indicated that her cognitive symptoms have been basically stable since approximately three months after the accident. However, she reports that she is now more aware of them. She denies any significant recovery of her deficits.

MD denied any significant past medical history. She indicated that she had been basically healthy all her life. At the time of testing, she was experiencing significant headaches and had been treated for hypertension. She was also in psychotherapy with a psychiatrist for psychological problems associated with the accident. She reported problems with sleep and nightmares about the accident. Her medications included Paxil and Dexedrine. She denied any previous psychological or psychiatric treatment.

The patient was cooperative and appeared to work very hard during testing. At times she seemed befuddled and required frequent repetition of questions and test items. Further, she would frequently struggle and have difficulty with test materials. It was noted that she demonstrated some unusual responses and patterns of errors. However, no particular problems occurred in test administration. She was evaluated to provide a second opinion in connection with litigation concerning the accident.

The test battery administered was the same as for SK, and the results are presented in Figures 22.4–22.5.

As shown in these figures, she earned IQs in the average and high-average ranges. A notable difference between her Verbal and Performance IQs was demonstrated. Her Verbal IQ is lower than would be expected, considering her educational and professional background, and thus raises the question of possible loss of abilities in this area. A considerable degree of variability, ranging from impaired to superior, was noted among her subtest performances. In particular, her Digit Span and Digit Symbol scores outstandingly low, in comparison to the other subscale scores. While Digit Span has not been found to be neuropsychologically specific, Digit Symbol has been found to be sensitive to brain-related impairment. Thus, one can raise a question as to whether this poor score is a reflection of brain impairment.

The patient's academic abilities, as indicated by her scores on the WRAT–3, fell below expectation given her reported history of academic and professional attainment. However, to determine more accurately the degree of academic loss versus long-term function, her educational transcripts need to be examined. On tests that are more sensitive to the biological integrity of the brain, the patient earned a Halstead Impairment Index of 0.6. This indicates that 60% of the Halstead tests were within the brain-damaged range. On the General Neuropsychological Deficit Scale, the patient earned a score of 56. This score typically indicates an overall clinical severity level within the moderate range of brain impairment. In particular, MD demonstrated significant impairment in the areas of complex psychomotor problem-solving, incidental memory and learning, and simple and complex flexibility of thought. However, her performances were within normal limits for abstract reasoning and for auditory attention to rapidly-presented material. While variability in cognitive function is typical in head injury, as seen in SK (described in the previous section), the extent of this patient's variability is somewhat unexpected. In particular, her scores on the Category Test and Trail Making Test are discrepant from each other. Patients who perform this well on the Category Test do not have the level of difficulty she demonstrated on either Trails A or Trails B. Further, the extremely poor performance on Trails B is usually reflective of a very severe neurological condition, which is not consistent with her presenting history or neurological findings. Further, her very poor Trails B score is inconsistent with her very capable performance using both hands on the TPT.

With regards to the neuropsychological functioning specific to each cerebral hemisphere, the patient demonstrated a highly lateralized pattern of neuropsychological impairment that would typically suggest significant involvement of the

Case: MD   Age: 44   Education: 20   Gender: F   Handedness: R

Wechsler Adult Intelligence Scale - Revised

		Verbal Subtests		Performance Subtests	
VIQ	99	Information	13	Digit Symbol	5
PIQ	118	Comprehension	11	Picture Completion	9
FSIQ	108	Arithmetic	11	Block Design	11
		Similarities	9	Picture Arrangement	15
		Digit Span	3	Object Assembly	15
		Vocabulary	11		

Wide Range Achievement Test — 3

	Standard Score	Grade Equivalent
Reading	95	HS
Spelling	83	7
Arithmetic	109	Post HS

Halstead-Reitan Neuropsychological Test Battery

Halstead Impairment Index   0.6

Category Test	37				
Tactual Performance Test					
Total Time	17.9	Dominant hand	8.1	Blocks in	10
Memory	6	Non-dominant hand	7.0	Blocks in	10
Localization	2	Both hands	2.8	Blocks in	10
Seashore Rhythm Test	26				
Speech-sounds Perception Test	15				

Finger Tapping Test	Dominant hand	47	Trail Making Test	Part A	79
	Non-dominant	33		Part B	221

	Right	Left
Strength of Grip (kg)	38.8	17.0

Bilateral Simultaneous Sensory Stimulation		
Tactile	3	4
Auditory	1	0
Visual	0	0

Visual Fields: Rt Periph

	Right	Left
Tactile Finger Recognition	3	4
Finger-Tip Number Writing	0	7
Tactile Form Recognition Test		
Time (sec)	9	16
Errors	0	0

* No dysphasia

Wechsler Memory Scale — Russell Revision

	Immediate	Delayed	% Retained
Verbal	mod-sev	mod-sev	44
Figural	m-mod	mod-sev	46

Figure 22.4   Test results for MD.

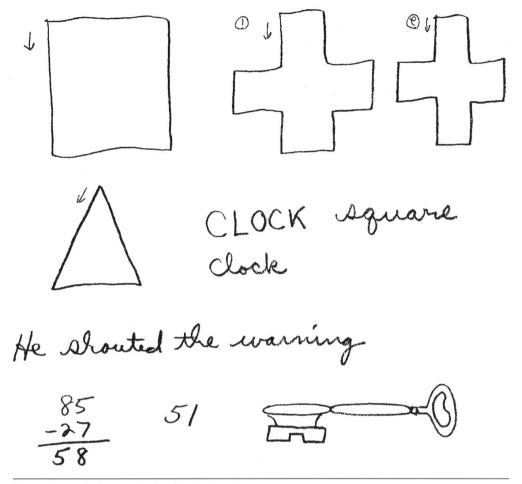

Figure 22.5   Aphasia Screening Test drawings for MD.

right cerebral hemisphere. This is reflected by scores of 16 on the Right Neuropsychological Deficit Scale and 3 on the Left Neuropsychological Deficit Scale. Inspection of the individual components that compose these scales indicates that the primary components contributing to the lateralized pattern are sensorimotor deficits. However, in addition to the sensorimotor deficits, problems in both verbal and figural memory were found. In contrast, she demonstrated no dysphasic symptoms and no problems in visual constructional abilities from the Aphasia Screening Examination.

Examination of the patient's sensorimotor functions indicated almost exclusively right cerebral hemisphere deficits. This included poor performances on left-handed tapping speed, grip strength, and complex psychomotor problem-solving. In addition, she had greater difficulty with her left side on tactile perception, finger recognition, fingertip number writing recognition, and tactile form recognition. She had some constriction of the visual field of her right eye.

In addition to the neuropsychological findings, the patient was found to have indications of significant psychological features. These included an unusual degree of concern regarding her physical functioning, as well as anxiety and panic attacks.

Preliminary review of the patient's neuropsychological results would seem to show a pattern of significant brain-related impairment. In particular, the pattern indicates variability in cognitive function, as was seen in SK, along with sensorimotor findings. Thus, a tentative conclusion of brain impairment from a head injury would seem appropriate. However, closer review of the findings shows numerous inconsistencies that raise questions about this conclusion. In fact, the pattern of results may not represent any neurological condition. For example, as noted above, the variability in higher cognitive function is much greater than is usually seen in patients with a neurological condition affecting brain function. That is, patients who perform as well as MD on the Category Test do not have the level of difficulty she had on a task as simple as Trails A. Other inconsistencies of this type are described previously in this chapter. Further, the patient showed no specific neuropsychological findings (no aphasia or constructional dyspraxia), which is unusual in light of the other, very significant findings. Finally, the sensorimotor results are highly lateralized, which is not typical in head injury, especially when there are no neurological findings. Thus, considering these results in light of known neuropsychological patterns in various neurological conditions raises questions as to whether the results reflect a valid neurological condition.

In this case, we had access to additional information regarding this patient's function; she had been evaluated about a year earlier by another neuropsychologist. Direct comparisons were made with this earlier testing and showed significant deterioration in function in several areas. Specifically, she exhibited notable declines on several verbal subtests of the WAIS–R, along with significant declines in the reading and spelling subtests of the WRAT–3. Sensorimotor findings were different on the two occasions. The earlier assessment showed sensorimotor functions to be bilateral. By the time of our evaluation, they were highly lateralized to the right hemisphere. In addition, impairment was seen in formerly intact sensorimotor functions. More important, she exhibited significant deterioration in overall abilities on the most sensitive brain-related measures, as indicated by a 10-point decline on the GNDS. Overall, this pattern of results is clearly inconsistent with expectation. In uncomplicated head injury, significant deterioration of neuropsychological abilities is not expected to occur two years post-injury.

Given the inconsistencies in the results of the second test battery and the unexpected changes from prior testing, the validity of the patient's test performances was suspect. The extent of the inconsistencies was further examined by computing the scores from Reitan and Wolfson's Dissimulation Index (1996, 1997b). The Dissimulation Index is computed from scores based on the consistency of specific responses on two testing occasions (Response Consistency Index; Reitan et al., 1995a), as well as the consistency of test scores on two testing occasions (Retest Consistency Index; Reitan et al., 1997a). MD's responses and test scores were found to be highly inconsistent, and both of her index scores were at the mean for the group of litigating head-injured patients.

In this case, the forensic neuropsychologist could provide the court important information beyond a simple recitation of the patient's strengths and weaknesses. With the methodology available, the forensic neuropsychologist can offer opinions regarding the causative link of the claimed deficits to the event under litigation. In this instance, it was concluded that the patient's results were not a valid reflection of brain impairment from her accident.

Case CC

CC was an 18-year-old single woman who presented with a history of cognitive problems related to exposure to mold and fungi. Apparently, about one year earlier, it was discovered that her home contained high levels of mold and fungi. As a result, she was forced to vacate her home and leave her possessions behind. She reported that she had not been feeling well for 2 to 2½ years. She indicated that she currently sleeps a lot, and has no energy, motivation, or interest. She reported that she does not do anything during the day except watch television, listen to the radio, or play with her pets. She reported problems with attention, concentration, and reading, and slowness in thought and action. She indicated that she is easily frustrated, lacks patience, and feels tired all the time.

On direct questioning regarding specific cognitive function, the patient denied any problems with memory, attention and concentration, problem-solving, reasoning, learning, flexibility of thought, language, or visual-spatial function. Further, she denied any specific sensorimotor deficits.

Her past medical history is unremarkable and noncontributory. CC reported that she has been basically healthy all her life, without any significant diseases or illnesses. However, she noted that she has had three episodes of bronchitis, which were treated with antibiotics. She takes no medications. She denied any loss of consciousness, head injury, seizure, or other neurological problem. She indicated no problem with her appetite, but indicated a problem with sleep, in that she never feels completely rested. She denied any tobacco, alcohol, or other substance use. She denied any history of psychological disorder or treatment.

In terms of educational history, the patient reported that she has been an "A" student with no particular academic weaknesses.

CC is currently involved in legal proceedings regarding the mold and fungi infestation of her home. She is claiming that her presenting problems in function are the direct result of her exposure to these agents. She was referred for a neuropsychological evaluation to determine her abilities and whether she has brain-related deficits. In this case, the evaluation was requested by the law firm working for the defense.

The test battery administered was similar to those previously discussed. The patient was quiet but cooperative throughout testing. She appeared to put forth her best effort on all tasks. No problems were noted during testing. All measures of validity were within expectation. Therefore, the following results can be considered a valid representation of her current neuropsychological functioning.

Test results are presented in Figures 22.6–22.7. As these results indicate, CC earned IQs that fell consistently at the

Case: CC   **Age:**   18   **Education:**   11   **Gender:**   F   **Handedness:**   L

Wechsler Adult Intelligence Scale

		Verbal Subtests			**Performance Subtests**	
VIQ	110	Information	11		Digit Symbol	13
PIQ	110	Comprehension	9		Picture Completion	10
FSIQ	110	Arithmetic	12		Block Design	14
		Similarities	11		Picture Arrangement	8
		Digit Span	14		Object Assembly	12
		Vocabulary	10			

Wide Range Achievement Test — 3

	Standard Score	Grade Equivalent
Reading	105	Post HS
Spelling	111	Post HS
Arithmetic	97	HS

Halstead-Reitan Neuropsychological Test Battery

Halstead Impairment Index   0.1

Category Test	23				
Tactual Performance Test					
Total Time	9.1	Dominant hand	4.3	Blocks in	10
Memory	8	Non-dominant hand	3.2	Blocks in	10
Localization	7	Both hands	1.6	Blocks in	10
Seashore Rhythm Test	29				
Speech-sounds Perception Test	3				

Finger Tapping Test	Dominant hand	40	**Trail Making Test** Part A	22
	Non-dominant	42	Part B	53

	Right	Left
Strength of Grip (kg)	40.8	36
Bilateral Simultaneous Sensory Stimulation		
Tactile	0	0
Auditory	0	0
Visual	0	1

Visual Fields: Full

	Right	Left
Tactile Finger Recognition	0	0
Finger-Tip Number Writing	1	1
Tactile Form Recognition Test		
Time (sec)	8	8
Errors	0	0

* No dysphasia

Wechsler Memory Scale — Russell Revision

	Immediate	Delayed	% Retained
Verbal	normal	normal	98
Figural	normal	normal	100

Figure 22.6   Test results for CC.

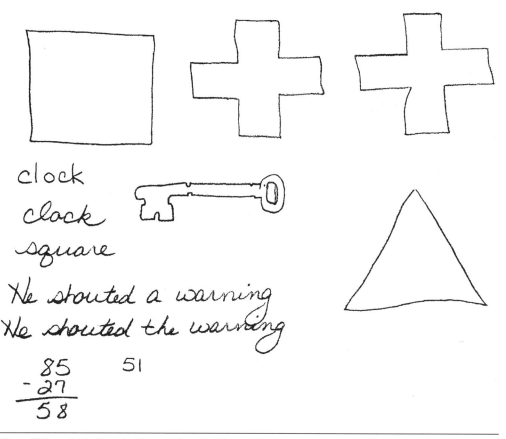

Figure 22.7 Aphasia Screening Test drawings for CC.

high end of the average range. No significant difference was evidenced between her verbal and performance scores. While some mild variability was evidenced within each intellectual domain, the results likely represent long-term intellectual function without evidence for any significant loss of abilities.

The patient's academic abilities were essentially consistent with her current verbal intelligence and in line with her reported education. Overall, the results suggest long-term academic skills without evidence for any significant losses.

On tests that are more sensitive to the biological integrity of the brain, the patient earned a Halstead Impairment Index of 0.1. This indicates normal brain function without evidence for brain impairment. On the General Neuropsychological Deficit Scale, an index of overall clinical severity, the patient earned a score of 14. This score also indicates normal brain functioning. Overall, the patient demonstrated good to excellent generalized neuropsychological function on all measures. She demonstrated excellent abilities for abstract reasoning and logical analysis, incidental memory, attention and concentration, and flexibility of thought. Complex psychomotor problem-solving was intact.

With regards to the neuropsychological functioning specific to each cerebral hemisphere, the patient demonstrated

intact function. She demonstrated excellent immediate recall and retention for verbal and figural material and 30-minute delayed recall and retention for this material. No specific aphasic errors were evidenced on an aphasia screening examination, and her visual constructive abilities were intact.

Examination of the patient's sensorimotor functions revealed essentially intact abilities. Mild deviations from expectation were noted on finger tapping and grip strength, likely related to her left hand dominance.

Evaluation of the patient's psychological function did not reveal significant problems, although she exhibited a tendency to deny common shortcomings.

Examination of this patient's neuropsychological functioning indicates normal generalized and specific neuropsychological functioning. Overall, the pattern of results is not suggestive of any significant neurocognitive impairments that would be associated with a neurological disorder.

Given these results, the forensic neuropsychologist would advise the court that the patient does not have neuropsychological deficits, thus obviating the issue of the contribution of mold and fungi to her problems.

As part of the litigation, the neuropsychologist was faced with the issue of test results from 6 months earlier, which apparently had shown significant cognitive impairments secondary to exposure to toxic molds. The neuropsychologist who conducted the prior examination reported that the patient had shown impairments in memory, learning, and aspects of executive function that she felt were not consistent with the patient's level of intellectual ability. She concluded that the patient's cognitive difficulties would be chronic and that no improvement would be anticipated.

The test battery given during the earlier assessment included the WAIS–3, Wechsler Memory Scale-3, the California Verbal Learning Test, a letter cancellation test, Trail Making Test, Booklet Category Test, Controlled Oral Word Fluency, Woodcock Johnson Test of Cognitive Abilities, Stroop Color Word Test, Paced Auditory Serial Addition Test, Grooved Pegboard, Conners Continuous Performance Test, and several questionnaires of symptoms, complaints, and psychological function. Although components of this battery are often used in clinical neuropsychological examinations, this battery has never been scientifically validated for its sensitivity to brain function. Moreover, no published studies address the patterns of results from this battery that might differentially diagnose brain-related conditions. At best, this selection of tests could provide information regarding the patient's cognitive strengths and weaknesses in comparison with her age peers. However, the relation of such results to any particular neurological condition is unknown, much less to the effects of mold and fungi.

In this case, the forensic neuropsychologist presented the court information about the patient's intact neuropsychological function, but also informed the court about the scientific shortcomings of the methodology employed in the prior examination. As in all cases, the admissibility and relevance of the information provided is ultimately the court's decision.

Case BH

This case is an example of the questions related to professional competency that arise, specifically, questions about the ability of an individual to carry out his duties safely. The patient was referred for evaluation by his primary care physician, who was concerned about BH's abilities to function in his long-time job as a pharmacist.

BH was a 66-year-old pharmacist who presented with a recent history of both cognitive and emotional difficulties. He reported that he has been unable to maintain a job as a pharmacist. He has recently been terminated from several positions because he was unable to learn the job requirements or was not proficient enough in the position. In addition to the problems maintaining a job, he is undergoing a divorce,

and this has been very traumatic for him. He admitted to being depressed and worried about his future.

Despite his problems maintaining a job, he denied any specific impairment of cognitive function. He reported that his functional capabilities are good. On specific questioning, he feels that he has no problems with memory, attention and concentration, problem solving, learning or information processing, flexibility of thought, language function, or visual-spatial abilities. He attributed his difficulties to his marital and emotional state.

The patient's past medical history is remarkable for sleep apnea and excessive daytime sleepiness. He was recently diagnosed with obstructive sleep apnea syndrome and has been treated with Continuous Positive Airway Pressure (CPAP) with improvement. In addition, the patient presented with a history of hypertension, hyperlipidemia, peripheral vascular disease, and coronary artery disease. EEG, Magnetic Resonance Angiography (MRA) studies of the head and neck, and MRI of the brain were all normal. He denied any loss of consciousness or head injuries. Medications included Zestril, Desyrel, niacin, and vitamins. He denied any significant psychiatric or psychological history.

The patient reported earning a degree in pharmacy from a state university. He indicated that he was an average student throughout his schooling. He owned and ran his own pharmacy for more than 25 years. He sold his business to a drugstore chain and worked there for about 6 months before being terminated. Since then, he has been terminated from several other pharmacies. At the time of this evaluation, he was working as a relief pharmacist for a grocery store chain.

The patient was cooperative with testing. He was often slow in responding and would provide lengthy answers. He had difficulty expressing himself, often talking around the point being made. On several occasions, he indicated that he was frustrated with his performance because he knew that he could do better. A second testing session was necessary to complete the evaluation. Nonetheless, he appeared to be putting forth his best effort. No specific problems in testing were noted. All validity testing was performed within expectation. Therefore, it is believed that the findings are a valid representation of the patient's current neuropsychological function.

The patient's test results are presented in Figures 22.8–22.10. As shown in Figure 22.8, the patient's intelligence scores fall in the average and high-average ranges. A significant difference is demonstrated between the verbal and perceptual-motor domains. Further, significant variability is demonstrated within the perceptual-motor intellectual area. Overall, the results suggest some loss of intellectual abilities. However, with the exception of one subscale score, his scores are average and low-average for his age. Thus, these findings

Case: BH   Age: 66   Education: 16   Gender: M   Handedness: R

Wechsler Adult Intelligence Scale

		Verbal Subtests		Performance Subtests	
VIQ	110	Information	12	Digit Symbol	8
PIQ	101	Comprehension	12	Picture Completion	9
FSIQ	106	Arithmetic	10	Block Design	7
		Similarities	12	Picture Arrangement	7
		Digit Span	10	Object Assembly	4
		Vocabulary	8		

Wide Range Achievement Test — 3

	Standard Score	Grade Equivalent
Reading	105	Post HS
Spelling	107	HS
Arithmetic	115	HS

Halstead-Reitan Neuropsychological Test Battery

Halstead Impairment Index   0.9

Category Test	79				
Tactual Performance Test					
Total Time	40.0	Dominant hand	15.0	Blocks in	6
Memory	2	Non-dominant hand	15.0	Blocks in	5
Localization	1	Both hands	10.0	Blocks in	10
Seashore Rhythm Test	23				
Speech-sounds Perception Test	6				

Finger Tapping Test	Dominant hand	39	Trail Making Test	Part A	50
	Non-dominant	45		Part B	99

	Right	Left
Strength of Grip (kg)	37.5	39.5
Bilateral Simultaneous Sensory Stimulation		
Tactile	0	0
Auditory	0	0
Visual	0	0

Visual Fields: Full

	Right	Left
Tactile Finger Recognition	6	5
Finger-Tip Number Writing	6	5
Tactile Form Recognition Test		
Time (sec)	39	8
Errors	1	1

* No dysphasia

Wechsler Memory Scale — Russell Revision

	Immediate	Delayed	% Retained
Verbal	mod-sev	mild	116
Figural	mild	m-mod	53

Figure 22.8   Test results for BH.

Figure 22.9   Aphasia Screening Test drawings for BH.

may be consistent with the influence of aging, rather than with brain impairment. The patient's academic abilities are generally average to high average, essentially consistent with his current verbal intelligence and reported education.

In contrast to the tests of intelligence and academic abilities, the tests that are more sensitive to the biological integrity of the brain clearly showed brain-related impairment. The patient earned a Halstead Impairment Index of 0.9, indicating that 90% of the Halstead tests were within the brain-damaged range. On the General Neuropsychological Deficit Scale, the patient earned a score of 51, which indicates moderate impairment of brain-related function.

In terms of general adaptive abilities, the patient demonstrated significant impairment in many areas of high cognitive function. Severe impairment was found for abstract reasoning and logical analysis, complex psychomotor problem-solving, and simple and complex incidental memory. Mild to moderate impairment was found for attention and concentration to rapidly presented auditory material, and simple and complex flexibility of thought. In contrast, attention and concentration to slowly presented auditory material was intact.

With regard to the neuropsychological functioning specific to each cerebral hemisphere, the patient earned a Left Neuropsychological Deficit Scale score of 9 and a Right

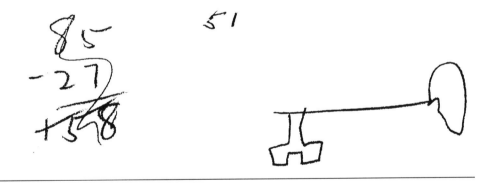

Figure 22.10 Aphasia Screening Test drawings for BH (continued).

Neuropsychological Deficit Scale score of 11. He demonstrated impairment of verbal and figural memory, although his retention of verbal information was essentially intact. No specific dysphasia was evidenced. His visual constructional abilities were impaired.

Examination of the patient's sensorimotor functions revealed numerous right-sided deficits suggesting left hemisphere involvement. These included slower and weaker than expected right-handed finger tapping speed, complex psychomotor problem-solving performance, and grip strength. In addition, he demonstrated more right-sided errors on finger recognition, fingertip number writing recognition, and tactile form recognition, although he had difficulties on both sides.

In contrast, tactile, auditory, and visual perception and visual fields were intact.

On psychological evaluation, his profile did not show significant psychopathology, but on interview he admitted to depression, anxiety, worry, and stress. Thus, it is likely that an underlying psychological factor is contributing to some of his problems in functioning. However, the neuropsychological findings cannot be solely accounted for by psychological factors.

Examination of this patient's neuropsychological functioning reveals moderate generalized and specific impairment of brain-related function. In addition, there were numerous right-sided sensorimotor findings, implicating the function of the left cerebral hemisphere. Although not specifically diagnostic, the pattern suggests a diffuse and generalized neurological disorder. In particular, the pattern of results is consistent with the results seen in several conditions including anoxic/metabolic disorders and cerebrovascular disorder. In contrast, the results are not particularly reflective of the pattern seen in a primary neuronal degenerative disorder such as Alzheimer's disease (Hom, 1992). Specifically, the discriminating feature for this pattern is the presence of numerous sensorimotor deficits that are not commonly found in Alzheimer's disease.

In this instance, the neuropsychologist provided the referring physician with detailed information about the patient's abilities, along with the recommendation that the patient should not continue in his practice as a pharmacist. His neurocognitive impairments would preclude adequate performance as a pharmacist. In addition, recommendations were offered to help the patient function to the best of his abilities in his present circumstances.

CONCLUDING REMARKS

Forensic neuropsychology is a rapidly developing field that has shown its potential for providing important and relevant information regarding brain-behavior relationships in legal situations. The forensic neuropsychologist provides the trier of fact with information about an individual's current neurocognitive function and dysfunction and, most importantly, with information regarding the cause of any dysfunction found. Forensic neuropsychologists' contributions to the legal field depend upon the appropriate application of scientifically validated methodology in efforts to answer the Forensic Questions that are posed. As discussed in this chapter, a body of research and clinical knowledge allows neuropsychologists to accomplish this (Reitan et al., 1997b). It is incumbent upon the forensic neuropsychologist to be well versed in these findings and techniques to fulfill their responsibilities. Future progress of the field depends upon their success in applying sound scientific methodology to questions from the legal arena.

APPENDIX: NAN DEFINITION OF A CLINICAL NEUROPSYCHOLOGIST

2001
Official Position of the
National Academy of Neuropsychology
Approved by the Board of Directors 05/05/2001

This 2001 definition expands upon and modifies the 1989 definition by Division 40 of the American Psychological Association, which was used as the foundation for this updated document.

A clinical neuropsychologist is a professional within the field of psychology with special expertise in the applied science of brain-behavior relationships. Clinical neuropsychologists use this knowledge in the assessment, diagnosis, treatment, and/or rehabilitation of patients across the lifespan with neurological, medical, neurodevelopmental and psychiatric conditions, as well as other cognitive and learning disorders. The clinical neuropsychologist uses psychological, neurological, cognitive, behavioral, and physiological principles, techniques and tests to evaluate patients' neurocognitive, behavioral, and emotional strengths and weaknesses and their relationship to normal and abnormal central nervous system functioning. The clinical neuropsychologist uses this information and information provided by other medical/healthcare providers to identify and diagnose neurobehavioral disorders, and plan and implement intervention strategies. The specialty of clinical neuropsychology is recognized by the American Psychological Association and the Canadian Psychological Association. Clinical neuropsychologists are independent practitioners (healthcare providers) of clinical neuropsychology and psychology.

The clinical neuropsychologist (minimal criteria) has:

1. A doctoral degree in psychology from an accredited university training program

2. An internship, or its equivalent, in a clinically relevant area of professional psychology

3. The equivalent of two (fulltime) years of experience and specialized training, at least one of which is at the postdoctoral level, in the study and practice of clinical neuropsychology and related neurosciences. These two years include supervision by a clinical neuropsychologist.[1]

4. A license in his or her state or province to practice psychology and/or clinical neuropsychology independently, or is employed as a neuropsychologist by an exempt agency.

---

[1] Individuals receiving training in clinical neuropsychology prior to this 2001 definition should be subject to the educational and experiential guidelines published by Division 40 of the American Psychological Association (APA, 1984; 1989). The 2001 definition should not be interpreted as negating the credentials of individuals whose education and experience predates the Division 40-APA definitions. Individuals meeting these prior criteria are and continue to be clinical neuropsychologists under this 2001 definition.

At present, board certification is not required for practice in clinical neuropsychology. Board certification (through formal credential verification, written and oral examination, and peer review) in the specialty of clinical neuropsychology is further evidence of the above advanced training, supervision, and applied fund of knowledge in clinical neuropsychology.

References

Report of the Division 40/INS Joint Task Force on Education, Accreditation, and Credentialing (1984). Division 40 Newsletter, Vol. 2, No. 2, pp. 3–8.

Definition of a Clinical Neuropsychologist, *The Clinical Neuropsychologist* 1989, Vol. 3, p. 22.

REFERENCES

American Psychological Association. (1992). Ethical principles of psychologists and code of conduct. *American Psychologist, 47,* 1597–1611.

American Psychological Association. (1985). *Standards for Educational and Psychological Testing.* Washington, DC: Author.

Anastasi, A. (1988). *Psychological Testing* (6th ed.). New York: Macmillan.

Boll, T.J., Heaton, R.K., & Reitan, R.M. (1974). Neuropsychological and emotional correlates of Huntington's chorea. *Journal of Nervous and Mental Disease, 158,* 61–69.

Chapple v. Ganger, 851 F. Supp. 1481 (E.D. Wa. 1994).

Daubert v. Merrell Dow Pharmaceuticals, 113 S. Ct. 2786, (1993).

Denney, R.L., & Wynkoop, T.F. (2000). Clinical neuropsychology in the criminal forensic setting. *Journal of Head Trauma Rehabilitation, 15*(2), 804–828.

Dikmen, S., McLean, A., & Temkin, N. (1986). Neuropsychological and psychosocial consequences of minor head injury. *Journal of Neurology, Neurosurgery, and Psychiatry, 49,* 1227–1232.

Dikmen, S., & Reitan, R.M. (1974). MMPI correlates of localized structural cerebral lesions. *Perceptual and Motor Skills, 39,* 831–840.

Dikmen, S., & Reitan, R.M. (1976). Psychological deficits and recovery of functions after head injury. *Transactions of the American Neurological Association, 101,* 72–77.

Dikmen, S., & Reitan, R.M. (1977). Emotional sequelae of head injury. *Annals of Neurology, 2,* 492–494.

Dikmen, S., Reitan, R.M., & Temkin, N.R. (1983). Neuropsychological recovery in head injury. *Archives of Neurology, 40,* 333–338.

Doehring, D.G., & Reitan, R.M. (1961). Certain language and non-language disorders in brain-damaged patients with homonymous visual field defects. *AMA Archives of Neurology and Psychiatry, 5,* 294–299.

Faust, D., Ziskin, J., & Hiers, J. (1991). *Brain damage claims: Coping with neuropsychological evidence: Vol. 1. The Scientific and Professional Literature.* Los Angeles: Law and Psychology Press.

Filskov, S.B., & Boll, T.J. (1981). *Handbook of clinical neuropsychology.* New York: Wiley.

Filskov, S.B., & Boll, T.J. (1986). *Handbook of clinical neuropsychology* (Vol. 2). New York: Wiley.

Finkelstein, J.N. (1977). BRAIN: A computer program for interpretation of the Halstead-Reitan neuropsychological test battery. *Dissertation Abstracts International. 37(10-B), 5349.*

Finlayson, M.A.J., Johnson, K.A., & Reitan, R.M. (1977). Relationship of level of education to neuropsychological measures in brain-damaged and non-brain-damaged adults. *Journal of Consulting and Clinical Psychology, 45,* 536–542.

Fitzhugh, K.B., Fitzhugh, L.C., & Reitan, R.M. (1961). Psychological deficits in relation to acuteness of brain dysfunction. *Journal of Consulting Psychology, 25,* 61–66.

Frye v. United States, 293 F. 1013 (D.C. Cir. 1923).

General Electric v. Joiner, 522 US 136 (1997).

General Electric v. Joiner, 117 S. Ct. 1243 (1997).

Giuliano, A.J., Barth, J.T., Hawk, G.L., & Ryan, T.V. (1997). The forensic neuropsychologist: Precedents, roles, and problems. In R.J. McCaffrey, A.D. Williams, J.M. Fisher, & L.C. Laing (Eds.), *The Practice of forensic neuropsychology: meeting challenges in the courtroom* (pp. 1–35). New York: Plenum.

Glass, L.S. (1991). Neuropsychology and the law: Structure and process. In H. O. Doerr & A. S. Carlin (Eds.), *Neuropsychology: Legal and scientific bases* (pp. 3–16). New York: Guilford Press.

Grant, I., Mohns, L., Miller, M., & Reitan, R.M. (1976). A neuropsychological study of polydrug users. *Archives of General Psychiatry, 33,* 973–978.

Guilmette, T.J., Faust, D., Hart, K., & Arkes, H.R. (1990). A national survey of psychologists who offer neuropsychological services. *Archives of Clinical Neuropsychology, 5,* 373–392.

Heimberger, R.F., & Reitan, R.M. (1961). Easily administered written test for lateralizing brain lesions. *Journal of Neurosurgery, 18,* 301–312.

Hom, J. (1983). A hand-scoring method for the Halstead-Reitan neuropsychological test battery for adults. In R.M. Reitan (Ed.), *A taxonomic procedure for neurological classification using neuropsychological data* (pp. 9–93). Tucson, AZ: Neuropsychology Press.

Hom, J. (1991). Contributions of the Halstead-Reitan battery in the neuropsychological investigation of stroke. In R.A. Bornstein & G. Brown (Eds.), *Neurobehavioral aspects of cerebrovascular disease* (pp. 165–181). New York: Oxford University Press.

Hom, J. (1992). General and specific cognitive dysfunctions in patients with Alzheimer's disease. *Archives of Clinical Neuropsychology, 7,* 121–133.

Hom, J. (1993). Brain tumors and dementia. In R.W. Parks, R.F. Zec, & R.S. Wilson (Eds.), *Neuropsychology of Alzheimer's dis-*

ease and other dementias (pp. 210–234). New York: Oxford University Press.

Hom, J., & Reitan, R.M. (1982). Effect of lateralized cerebral damage upon contralateral and ipsilateral sensorimotor performances. *Journal of Clinical Neuropsychology, 4,* 249–268.

Hom, J., & Reitan, R.M. (1984). Neuropsychological correlates of rapidly vs. slowly growing intrinsic cerebral neoplasms. *Journal of Clinical Neuropsychology, 6,* 309–324.

Hom, J., & Reitan, R.M. (1990). Generalized cognitive function in stroke. *Journal of Clinical and Experimental Neuropsychology, 12,* 644–654.

Indianapolis Union Railway v. Walker, Court of Appeals of Indiana, First District, 578–590. (1974).

Kumho Tire Co. v. Carmichael, 526 US 137 (1999).

Laing, L.C., & Fisher, J.M. (1997). Neuropsychology in civil proceedings. In R.J. McCaffrey, A.D. Williams, J.M. Fisher, & L.C. Laing (Eds.), *The practice of forensic neuropsychology: Meeting challenges in the courtroom* (pp. 117–133). New York: Plenum.

Lezak, M.D. (1995). *Neuropsychological assessment* (3rd ed.). New York: Oxford University Press.

Lubet, S. (1998). *Expert testimony: A guide for expert witnesses and the lawyers who examine them.* Notre Dame, IN: National Institute for Trial Advocacy.

Matthews, C.G., & Reitan, R.M. (1961). Comparison of abstraction ability in retardates and in patients with cerebral lesions. *Perceptual and Motor Skills, 13,* 327–333.

Matthews, C.G., & Reitan, R.M. (1962). Psychomotor abilities of retardates and patients with cerebral lesions. *American Journal of Mental Deficiency, 66,* 607–612.

Matthews, C.G., & Reitan, R.M. (1963). Relationship of differential abstraction ability levels to psychological test performances in mentally retarded subjects. *American Journal of Mental Deficiency, 68,* 235–244.

McMahon, E.A., & Satz, P. (1981). Clinical neuropsychology: Some forensic applications. In S.B. Filskov & T.J. Boll (Eds.), *Handbook of clinical neuropsychology* (pp. 686–701). New York: Wiley.

Mitrushina, M.N., Boone, K.B., & D'Elia, L.F. (1999). *Handbook of normative data for neuropsychological assessment.* New York: Oxford University Press.

Moore v. Ashland Chemical, 126 F. 3d 679 (5th Cir. 1997).

Newman, R. (1991). The role of the psychologist expert witness: Provider of perspective and input. *Neuropsychology Review, 2,* 241–249.

O'Connor, M., & Krauss, D. (2001). Legal update: New developments in Rule 702. *American Psychology Law Society News, 21,* 1–4, 18.

Otto, R.K., & Heilbrun, K. (2002). The practice of forensic psychology: A look toward the future in light of the past. *American Psychologist, 57,* 5–18.

Puente, A.E. (1997). Forensic clinical neuropsychology as a paradigm for clinical neuropsychological assessment: Basic and emerging issues. In R. J. McCaffrey, A.D. Williams, J.M. Fisher, & L.C. Laing (Eds.), *The practice of forensic neuropsychology: Meeting challenges in the courtroom* (pp. 165–175). New York: Plenum.

Putnam, S.H. (1989). The TCN salary survey: A salary survey of neuropsychologists. *The Clinical Neuropsychologist, 3,* 97–115.

Putnam, S.H., & Anderson, C. (1994). The second TCN salary survey: A survey of neuropsychologists Part I. *The Clinical Neuropsychologist, 8,* 3–37.

Putnam, S.H., & DeLuca, J.W. (1990). The TCN professional practice survey: Part I: General practices of neuropsychologists in primary employment and private practice settings. *The Clinical Neuropsychologist, 4,* 199–244.

Putnam, S.H., & DeLuca, J.W. (1991). The TCN professional practice survey: Part II: An analysis of the fees of neuropsychologists by practice demographics. *The Clinical Neuropsychologist, 5,* 103–124.

Putnam, S.H., DeLuca, J.W., & Anderson, C. (1994). The second TCN salary survey: A survey of neuropsychologists Part II. *The Clinical Neuropsychologist, 8,* 245–282.

Reed, J.E. (1996). Fixed vs. flexible neuropsychological test batteries under the *Daubert* standard for the admissibility of scientific evidence. *Behavioral Sciences and the Law, 14,* 315–322.

Reed, J. (1999). Current status of the admissibility of expert testimony after *Daubert* and *Joiner. Journal of Forensic Neuropsychology, 1* (1), 49–69.

Rehkopf, D.G., Jr., & Fisher, J.M. (1997). Neuropsychology in criminal proceedings. In R.J. McCaffrey, A.D. Williams, J.M. Fisher, & L.C. Laing (Eds.), *The practice of forensic neuropsychology: Meeting challenges in the courtroom* (pp. 135–151). New York: Plenum.

Reitan, R.M. (1955). Certain differential effects of left and right cerebral lesions in human adults. *Journal of Comparative and Physiological Psychology, 48,* 474–477.

Reitan, R.M. (1959a). The comparative effects of brain damage on the Halstead impairment index and the Wechsler-Bellevue scale. *Journal of Clinical Psychology, 15,* 281–285.

Reitan, R.M. (1959b). *The Effects of Brain Lesions on Adaptive Abilities in Human Beings.* Tucson, AZ: Reitan Neuropsychology Laboratories.

Reitan, R.M. (1962). The comparative psychological significance of aging in groups with and without organic brain damage. In C. Tibbitts & W. Donahue (Eds.), *Social and psychological aspects of aging* (pp. 880–887). New York: Columbia University Press.

Reitan, R.M. (1964). Psychological deficits resulting from cerebral lesions in man. In J.M. Warren & K. Aken (Eds.), *The frontal granular cortex and behavior* (pp. 295–312). New York: McGraw-Hill.

Reitan, R.M. (1967). Psychological assessment of deficits associated with brain lesions in subjects with normal and subnormal intelligence. In J.L. Khanna (Ed.), *Brain damage and mental retardation: A psychological evaluation.* Springfield, IL: Charles C. Thomas.

Reitan, R.M. (1976). Psychological testing of epileptic patients. In P.J. Vinken & G.W. Bruyn (Eds.), *Handbook of clinical neurology: The epilepsies* (Vols. 9, 10). New York: North Holland Publishing.

Reitan, R.M., & Boll, T.J. (1971). Intellectual and cognitive functions in Parkinson's disease. *Journal of Consulting and Clinical Psychology, 37,* 364–369.

Reitan, R.M., & Davison, L.A. (1974). *Clinical neuropsychology: Current status and applications.* New York: Wiley.

Reitan, R.M. & Fitzhugh, K.B. (1971). Behavioral deficits in groups with cerebral vascular lesions. *Journal of Consulting and Clinical Psychology, 37,* 215–223.

Reitan, R.M., Reed, J.C., & Dyken, M.L. (1971). Cognitive, psychomotor, and motor correlates of multiple sclerosis. *Journal of Nervous and Mental Disease, 153,* 218–224.

Reitan, R.M., & Wolfson, D. (1985). *Neuroanatomy and neuropathology: A clinical guide for neuropsychologists.* Tucson, AZ: Neuropsychology Press.

Reitan, R.M., & Wolfson, D. (1986). The Halstead-Reitan neuropsychological test battery. In D. Wedding, A.M. Horton, Jr., & J. Webster (Eds.), *The neuropsychology handbook* (pp. 134–160). New York: Springer.

Reitan, R.M., & Wolfson, D. (1988a). *Traumatic brain injury: Vol. 1: Pathophysiology and neuropsychological evaluation.* Tucson, AZ: Neuropsychology Press.

Reitan, R.M., & Wolfson, D. (1988b). *Traumatic brain injury: Vol. 2. Recovery and rehabilitation.* Tucson, AZ: Neuropsychology Press.

Reitan, R.M., & Wolfson, D. (1993). *The Halstead-Reitan neuropsychological test battery: Theory and clinical interpretation* (2nd ed.). Tucson, AZ: Neuropsychology Press.

Reitan, R.M., & Wolfson, D. (1995a). Consistency of responses on retesting among head-injured subjects in litigation versus head-injured subjects not in litigation. *Applied Neuropsychology, 2,* 67–71.

Reitan, R.M., & Wolfson, D. (1995b). Influence of age and education on neuropsychological test results. *The Clinical Neuropsychologist, 9,* 151–158.

Reitan, R.M., & Wolfson, D. (1996). The question of validity of neuropsychological test scores among head-injured litigants: Development of a Dissimulation Index. *Archives of Clinical Neuropsychology, 11,* 573–580.

Reitan, R.M., & Wolfson, D. (1997a). Consistency of neuropsychological test scores of head-injured subjects involved in litigation compared with head injured subjects not involved in litigation: Development of the Retest Consistency Index. *The Clinical Neuropsychologist, 11,* 69–76.

Reitan, R.M., & Wolfson, D. (1997b). *Detection of malingering and invalid test scores.* Tucson, AZ: Neuropsychology Press.

Reitan, R.M., & Wolfson, D. (2000). *Mild head injury: Intellectual, cognitive, and emotional consequences.* Tucson, AZ: Neuropsychology Press.

Richardson, R.E.L., & Adams, R.L. (1992). Neuropsychologists as expert witnesses: Issues of admissibility. *The Clinical Neuropsychologist, 6,* 295–308.

Rojas, D.C., & Bennett, T.L. (1995). Single versus composite score discriminative validity with the Halstead-Reitan Battery and the Stroop Test in mild head injury. *Archives of Clinical Neuropsychology, 2,* 101–110.

Ross, A.T., & Reitan, R.M. (1955). Intellectual and affective functions in multiple sclerosis: A quantitative study. *AMA Archives of Neurology and Psychiatry, 73,* 663–677.

Russell, E.W. (1984). Theory and developments of pattern analysis methods related to the Halstead-Reitan battery. In P.E. Logue & J.M. Shear (Eds.), *Clinical neuropsychology: A multidisciplinary approach* (pp. 50–98). Springfield, IL: Charles C. Thomas.

Russell, E.W. (1997). Developments in the psychometric foundations of neuropsychological assessment. In G. Goldstein & T.M. Incagnoli (Eds.), *Contemporary approaches to neuropsychological assessment* (pp. 15–65). New York: Plenum.

Russell, E.W. (1998). In defense of the Halstead-Reitan battery: A critique of Lezak's review. *Archives of Clinical Neuropsychology, 13,* 365–381.

Seretny, M.L., Dean, R.S., Gray, J.W., & Hartlage, L.C. (1986). The practice of clinical neuropsychology in the United States. *Archives of Clinical Neuropsychology, 1,* 5–12.

Sweet, J.J., & Moberg, P.J. (1990). A survey of practices and beliefs among ABPP and non-ABPP clinical neuropsychologists. *The Clinical Neuropsychologist, 4,* 101–120.

Sweet, J.J., Moberg, P.J., & Suchy, Y. (2000a). Ten-year follow-up survey of clinical neuropsychologists: Part I. practices and beliefs. *The Clinical Neuropsychologist, 14,* 18–37.

Sweet, J.J., Moberg, P.J., & Suchy, Y. (2000b). Ten-year follow-up survey of clinical neuropsychologists: Part II. private practice and economics. *The Clinical Neuropsychologist, 14,* 479–495.

Sweet, J.J., Moberg, P.J., & Westergaard, C.K. (1996). Five-year follow-up survey of practices and beliefs of clinical neuropsychologists. *The Clinical Neuropsychologist, 10,* 202–221.

Sweet, J.J., Westergaard, C.K., & Moberg, P.J. (1995). Managed care experiences of clinical neuropsychologists. *The Clinical Neuropsychologist, 9,* 214–218.

Wedding, D., Horton, A.M., Jr., & Webster, J. (1986). *The neuropsychology handbook.* New York: Springer.

Williams, A.D. (1997). Fixed versus flexible batteries. In R.J. McCaffrey, A.D. Williams, J.M. Fisher, & L.C. Laing (Eds.), *The practice of forensic neuropsychology: Meeting challenges in the courtroom* (pp. 57–70). New York: Plenum.

Author Index

Subject Index